W9-AQU-452

Publications
of the
State Department of Archives and History

THE PAPERS OF WILLIE PERSON MANGUM

1

Printed by
WINSTON PRINTING COMPANY
Winston-Salem, N. C., U. S. A.

THE PAPERS OF WILLIE PERSON MANGUM

Edited by
Henry Thomas Shanks

Volume Two
1833 - 1838

Raleigh
State Department of Archives and History
1952

CONTENTS

PREFACE

The second volume covers the years 1833-1838. The year 1838 has been arbitrarily selected for ending it; a more logical date would be 1836, when Mangum first retired from the Senate, or 1840, when he returned to that body after four years' retirement from public life. Unfortunately the material covering the years 1833-1836 or 1833-1840 would produce a volume either too short or too long. Therefore, since the third volume, now ready for the press, will be published during 1953, I am, as a mattter of convenience, ending this one with the year 1838.

The letters in this volume are more concerned with national politics than are those in the preceding one. In the period here covered, Mangum became a prominent figure in the fight against Jackson, especially in the contest over the removal of deposits from the United States Bank and in the development of the Whig Party. Accordingly, more of the letters are from leaders outside Mangum's own state; the majority are still from North Carolina.

Again I wish to express my particular gratitude to members of the Mangum family and to the staffs of the Department of Archives and History and the several libraries mentioned in the first volume for their continued coöperation and valuable assistance. An additional grant from the Research Fund of the Carnegie Foundation for the Advancement of Teaching and a leave of absence from Birmingham-Southern College have enabled me to complete this and the subsequent volumes. I am grateful to those responsible for the grant and for the leave. Also, I wish to thank Miss Jean Seymour for her patience and good spirit in typing the footnotes and letters and for retyping many marked copies as well as for rendering innumerable other small but essential services in preparing the manuscript for the press.

H. T. S.

Birmingham, Ala.
August 31, 1952

LIST OF ILLUSTRATIONS

A CALENDAR OF MANUSCRIPTS IN THE MANGUM PAPERS FOR THE PERIOD 1833-1838 OMITTED IN THIS VOLUME

1. March 20, 1833. Letter of Isaac S. Lyon, Boontin Fall, Monis County, New Jersey, to W. P. Mangum requesting a copy of Mangum's speech of February 7-8, 1832, on the tariff. Lyon stated that he could not obtain a copy in his local newspapers. MS in the Library of Congress.
2. September 19, 1833. Letter of J. L. Edwards to J. A. Craige, of Hawfield, Orange County, explaining the pensions of a Mr. Tate and a Mr. White. MS in the Library of Congress.
3. October 1 1833. Letter of Hugh L. White to W. P. Mangum asking Mangum to fill out information requested in an enclosed letter. The "enclosed letter" was not found. MS in the Library of Congress.
4. October 2, 1833. Affidavits of Ben Carroll in support of George Horner's claims for a military pension for service in the Revolutionary War. MS in the Library of Congress.
5. October 2, 1833. Letter of W. P. Mangum to W. S. Pratt enclosing "4" above. MS in the Library of Congress.
6. October 22, 1833. Brief letter of William Hill to W. P. Mangum explaining that Macajah Clark's claim for a pension was not valid. MS in the Library of Congress.
7. December 4, 1833. Brief note from R. H. Wilde to W. P. Mangum asking the latter to sign an enclosed paper. The "enclosed paper" was not found. MS in the Library of Congress.
8. December 26, 1833. Brief letter of C. Elliott of Engineering Department at Washington to W. P. Mangum informing the latter that the name of F. Sobieski Davis, of Wilmington, had been registered as a candidate for West Point. MS in the Library of Congress.
9. January 24, 1834. Letter of Elias Bryan to Thomas Hall about Hall's fox hounds which Bryan was keeping. MS in the Library of Congress.
10. February 22, 1834. Affidavits of Thomas Horner, of Orange County, for a military pension for service in the Revolutionary War. MS in the Library of Congress.
11. February 22, 1834. Affidavit of S. Hammond, District of Richland, South Carolina, in behalf of Isaac Marshall's petition for a pension for Revolutionary service. MS in the Library of Congress.
12. March 1, 1834. A letter of Isaac Marshall, of Iredell County, asking W. P. Mangum to assist him in having his pension for Revolutionary services increased. MS in the Library of Congress.
13. December 5, 1834. Augustine Harris, of Granville County, to................. (probably to Mangum) about the Revolutionary pension claims for Major Richard D. Cooke. He also includes sworn affidavits of Cooke's service. MS in the Library of Congress.
14. January 2, 1835. Letter of W. D. Carrington to W. P. Mangum, from Henderson County, Tennessee, asking Mangum's assistance to obtain

a pension for Nicholas Darnal, a neighbor of Carrington, for his service in "The Late War" with the Indians. MS in the Library of Congress.

15. January 19, 1835. Letter of Samuel King, of Iredell County, to W. P. Mangum asking his assistance in obtaining a pension for Villander Smith, the widow of William Ballenger, for the Revolutionary service of Ballenger. MS in the Library of Congress.
16. January 19, 1835. Letter of Ezekiel Brewer, of Clover Garden, N. C., to W. P. Mangum seeking his assistance in obtaining a pension for his Revolutionary service. MS in the Library of Congress.
17. No date, probably 1835. "A statement of my Services rendered in the revolutionary war." John Watson to W. P. Mangum. MS in the Library of Congress.
18. No date, probably 1835. Letter of George Work to H. L. White asking him to obtain from some North Carolina friend whether the name of Micajah Clark was on the Revolutionary Rolls of that state. MS in the Library of Congress.
19. February 11, 1836. Lewis Williams to........................ from Washington, D. C. It is a mailing list of people with their addresses in Surry, Wilkes, Iredell, and Ashe counties in the western part of the state. MS in the Library of Congress.
20. March 1, 1836. Letter of Isham Matthews, of Halifax County, to W. P. Mangum asking assistance in obtaining a pension for William Brinkley, who fought in the Revolution. MS in the Library of Congress.
21. April 27, 1836. Letter of Isaac Croom, from Mantua, to W. P. Mangum introducing Dr. R. Knox, of Kinston, who was planning to pass through Washington on his way to Massachusetts. MS in the Library of Congress.
22. June 11, 1836. Letter of James Webb to W. P. Mangum asking advice on obtaining a new certificate for William Crabtree to obtain a pension. MS in the Library of Congress.
23. November 28, 1838. Letter of P. Brittain, of Buncombe County, to W. P. Mangum and W. A. Graham requesting their assistance to obtain a pension for William Lafever for service in the Revolution. MS in the Library of Congress.

CHRONOLOGICAL LIST
of the
MANGUM PAPERS (1833-1838) INCLUDED IN THIS VOLUME

SYMBOLS USED TO DESIGNATE DEPOSITORS OF MANGUM PAPERS

(The location of papers from other collections is indicated by footnotes.)

WPM-D.	Willie P. Mangum Papers at Duke University, Durham, North Carolina.
WPM-LC.	Willie P. Mangum Papers in the Library of Congress, Washington, District of Columbia.
WPM-NC.	Willie P. Mangum Papers in the State Department of Archives and History, Raleigh, North Carolina.
WPM-UNC.	Willie P. Mangum Papers, Southern Collection, University of North Carolina, Chapel Hill North Carolina.

THE MANGUM PAPERS

1833

WPM-LC

Willie P. Mangum to Mrs. Charity A. Mangum

WASHINGTON CITY

Sunday Night 7th January 1833

My dear Love.

The day before yesterday, I received your letter and was very glad to hear that you and our children were all well.—The roads I learn, have become so very bad, that the arrival of letters and papers has become very irregular. I have continued to enjoy good health.—The winter has been so far, with the exception of five or six days, the mildest that I ever saw except the winter before Patty was born.—

I am still at Mrs. Arguelle's—but the mess has become so crowded that I would leave here, if I could get a situation that would be pleasing to me—But as the session will be short, and we shall not be here but about seven weeks—I may continue—I am very anxious to see you My Love, I visit but little, and have avoided Company much more than I did even last Winter.—

Hardeman Dukes[1] case has not been acted on yet—they take up the cases as they come to hand & several thousand are yet on hand—As soon as it can be done— I will send it on.—

Tell Sally and Patty, that they must be good children, and that they must learn their books—

Public Affairs are in a bad condition, and many fear that much evil will arise out [of] the present state of things—I yet hope, it may be avoided—

I have been in my room the whole day reading and looking into some questions.—

My time passes off with a good deal of melancholy. I have spent my time here unhappily—as I shall continue to spend it unhappily—I had much rather be at home—And if I could be there, & at perfect ease in my situation—I think I should never want to see much more of the world.

[1]See below, II, 41-42.

I have heard nothing from Walter,[2] since he was at the Gold Mines[3]—He sent me some money for E. G. Mangum[4]—I will either send a draft upon one of the banks for it, or send it in some other way—I don't like to send as much in a letter—

I enclose you $10.

Remember me often My Love, & Always think of me as your affectionate husband.

W. P. MANGUM

[Addressed:]

Mrs. Charity A. Mangum
Red Mountain
Red Mountain
No Carolina.

WPM-LC

Joseph H. Bryan[5] *to Willie P. Mangum*

OXFORD. Jany. 8. 1833.

Dear Sir

A young man of this place about fourteen years old by the name of Charles Kingsbury[6] is extremely anxious to get the appointment of Cadet and go to the School at West Point, he is poor but I do not know any young man in this part of the Country who in point of talents and information can be considered his equal—He is prepared to enter the school by undergoing the most rigid examination that they may think proper to subject him to, altho almost entirely self taught—I think you would not only be doing him service but it would be promoting the public interest by placing him in a situation where his Country may have an opportunity of availing themselves of his talent.

---

[2]W. P. Mangum's youngest brother.

[3]He refers to the gold mines in North Carolina. By 1833 gold mining had become an important business near Albemarle, Salisbury, and Charlotte. In all there were about 3,000 men engaged in gold mining in the state. F. M. Green, "Gold Mining: a Forgotten Industry in Ante-Bellum North Carolina," *North Carolina Historical Review*, XIV (1932), 1-19, 135-155.

[4]W. P. Mangum's first cousin.

[5]Joseph Hunger Bryan, a native of Bertie County, was a member of the state legislature in 1804, 1805, 1807-1809, and of Congress in 1815-1819. A trustee of the University of North Carolina from 1809 to 1817, he was sent to Tennessee in 1822 to help the University obtain claims to lands there. A member of the Spaight faction in 1830, he opposed Mangum's nomination for the Senate. In 1832 he was selected a delegate to the Democratic Baltimore Convention, but he sent Sandy Harris in his place. *Biog. Dir. of Cong.*, 752; see above, I, 585-586.

[6]In 1836 Charles P. Kingsbury, although born in New York, was appointed to the Military Academy from North Carolina. Graduating in 1840, he served with distinction in the Mexican War and in the American Civil War. He was superintendent of the Harper's Ferry Armory in 1861 when Jackson seized it for Virginia. Frequently he wrote articles for the *Southern Quarterly Review* and the *American Whig Review*. Cullum, *Biog. Reg. of Officers of U. S. Milt. Acad.*, II, 24-26.

If there should be a vacancy it would gratify me much to see him appointed he being a youth of uncommon promise, and extremely poor—persons in this condition of life Should have a preference over the rich and those who have powerful Connexions—The government after educating them, has claims of gratitude on them, that will always enable them to retain their services when desirable—

In the hope that your labours will terminate in restoring Harmony to the Country by the adjustment of the vexed questions which agitate and perplex the whole country

I am Dr Sir most respectfully

Yours ob serv[t].

JOS. H. BRYAN.

Hon. Willie P. Mangum.

[Addressed:]

Washington.

WPM-LC

Condy Raguet[7] to Willie P. Mangum

Philad. Jany. 10, 1833

Hon. Willie P. Mangum

Senator in Congress

Sir.

I received this day your letter of 7″ Inst. and feel highly flattered by the manner in which you have been pleased to express yourself in relation to my humble labours in a cause for the advancement of which, you have in common with many others of our distinguished citizens, displayed so patriotic a zeal. You probably do not know that I published in the Banner in October last, your speech[8] delivered at the last session of Congress; in relation to which I can sincerely say, that I, and the few of my friends here who retain any feeling for the old republican notions of liberty, read it with the greatest satisfaction, as an able, eloquent and manly production.

I have entered your name as a subscriber to "The Examiner," being *the second* only that I have received from Congress, amongst the members of which, the Banner had upwards of fifty *annual* subscribers. Whether it will ever go into operation, is

[7]Condy Raguet, who had edited the *Washington Banner* in 1822-1830, moved to Philadelphia in 1831 to edit the *Philadelphia Banner*. *Union List of Newspapers*, 86; Mary Westcott and Allene Ramage (Comp.), *A Checklist of United States Newspapers in the General Library of Duke University*, Part I, 41; *D.A.B.*, XV, 325-326.

[8]He refers to Mangum's speech on the tariff. See above, I, 478n.

extremely problematical. To sustain such a paper here, in a State where the doctrines of consolidation are held by nineteen men out of twenty, will be utterly impossible, and should the Southern people generally, not feel the importance of availing themselves, of what I devoutly believe to be, the last plank that will ever be offered them from the North, upon which they may escape from the wreck which has been made of State Rights by the President's Proclamation, it must be abandoned. There are but a few here, who are willing to risk any thing in support of the Republican doctrine of '98, and such a damp has been thrown upon their ardour, by the calculating spirit displayed in Virginia and North Carolina, which looks as if they loved Caesar more than Rome, that they have almost entirely given up the cause as lost. If the slave-holding States, which have a much deeper interest at stake than the others, are indifferent to the fact, whether we live under a government of limited or unlimited powers, they can hardly expect to avoid the calamity, which awaits them, just as certainly as the sun shines, that of having their *labourers* legislated away from them, as they have already had their *products*. Against such a scheme, if the current of consolidation be not at this moment stemmed, not a voice *dare be raised* at the North, ten years hence, and I need not say to you, that constitutional guarantees, would be as powerless as gossamer against a whirlwind.

In making these remarks, I beseech you, not to consider me as pleading my own cause. I have as little to fear from a government of unlimited powers, as any other humble citizen, and I am sure, that my peace of mind and pecuniary interest would best be promoted by withdrawing altogether from the political arena. I have no ambition to gratify, and therefore expect to reap no reward from engaging again in the violent conflicts of the day, except that glorious reward of an approving conscience resulting from the conviction, that when the liberties of my country were in danger, I lent her the feeble support which Providence had placed within my ability.

I am with much respect
Sir
You very obt. & Hble Sert
CONDY. RAGUET

[Addressed:]
Hon. Willie P. Mangum
Senate of The U. States
Washington.

WPM-LC

J. W. Gwinn[9] *to Willie P. Mangum*

Franklin, No Carolina Jany 10the 1833

My Dear Sir

I Receive yours of 22 Decr by this days mail I was much please to heare that it was beleaved that there was a redee[m]-ing action about to take place with Congress and that the[y] would reduce the tariff but times are likely to be serious hear bouth parties am deturmed upon resistance from all appearance The Union men are deturmind not to suffer the Nulifyers to put down the union men in South Carolina. times must change much heare if ever Mr Carson[10] is elected to Congress againe from this dicstrict it is understood that Mr Graham will be a Candidate and the warmest friends of Mr Carson heretofore will undoubtedly go for Graham without a mighty change in publick opinion. the proclimation of the president here has driven the Nulies from their strong holes Volunteers are plenty to be got here to enforce the doctrins laid down by the president in his proclimation the nuse is prevalient here that govenor Hamulton[11] is marching to Charlstown with an army of 2000 men and daily gethering Volunteers to drive the United States troops from the forte at Charlestown and publick opinion is much inflamed at sutch a treasonable attempt and a general bust of indignation is heard from allmost every mouth upon the subject and mutch of its vengence I am a fraid will fall upon the head of our representative for it is said hear without con[tra]-diction that he at Burk Court said (to wit) (I Samuel P. Carson) am a nulifyer[.] I have transmitted to you by this days mail 4 declaration for pension (to wit) John Henry Jacob Fulbright Luis Smith and Samuil Marshall. Henrys & Smith I have mutch at hart for I have evry reason to believe that them men

---

[9]James W. Gwinn represented Macon County in the state legislature in 1830-1831 and 1833-1837. *N. C. Manual,* 687-688.

[10]Samuel Price Carson, who was in Congress from 1825 to 1833, supported Calhoun's nullification doctrine. As a result he was defeated for reelection by James Graham. A. D. Smith, *Western North Carolina: Historical and Biographical,* Charlotte, 1890, 102-104.

[11]James Hamilton, governor of South Carolina.

was in the war for Smith was with my relations in the services please lay them before the department & inform me of their fait & tell the department to corrispond with me if any thing is lacking or if excepted also for I am authorised to do any thing in relation to them the Election of M. Vanburen has mutch gratifyd me as I was the first man who toock him upon in the back parte of the State but he is now the next man to General Jackson, and without a change will at the next Election git the vote of my Section for a presedency Morton [Martin] dont now how many warme friends he has in this parte of N Carolina we are good hear in about fifty miles of Mr Calhoun resadents for 4 fifth of an malitia rolles for Volunteers to coerce South Carolina into obedience to the laws of the United State for we have no notion of disunion[12] but aire deturmed old and young to take the feald in supporte of the intrest of ou Common Country excuse me for my trubling you with my political opinions and with the pensions for whom I have draw declaration I have time to send also to Mr Carson by request I am your obedient Servant

J. W. GWINN

Hon W P Mangum

[Addressed:] Franklin No Ca

Hon W P Mangum 11th Jany

Washington City

D C

[Endorsed:]

And.

23d Jan 1832

WPM-LC

J. P. Sneed[13] to Willie P. Mangum

Hillsborough Jany 14th 1833

Dear Sir

As I expect to start to Mississippi in April next and wish [to] fix my residence permanently in that State and am desirous of setling in the Choctaw purchase[14] you will please procure the necessary information to the following inquiries

---

[12]Gwinn was from the mountainous section of the state where Jackson's influence and the sentiment against nullification were very strong.

[13]See above, I, 18n.

[14]On May 28, 1830, in the treaty of Dancing Rabbit Creek, some Choctaw leaders ceded all their lands east of the Mississippi River and agreed to move within three years to Indian Territory. Many of the tribe opposed the treaty and claimed it was not made by the legal chieftains. As a result they petitioned the President and Congress and deposed the chiefs who had signed the treaty. The Federal authorities refused to recognize the new Indian rulers. Whites began moving into the region and the Indians began migrating to their new homes. By 1833 all but 7000 had left Mississippi. Foreman, *Indian Removal*, 28, 31, 95, 102-103.

When will the Choctaw lands be brought into market

May I safely settle on those lands with the expectation I may purchase them at a fair price when the government thinks proper to sell them

Are there any indian reservations among those lands and would I be safe in purchasing from them if there are such reservations

My negroes you know started with our friend Shaw[15] and I received a letter from him a few days past saying all were well and he was Just entering Fayette County in Tennessee

Any other information you may possess in relation to the mississippi lands you may think to my interest please communicate for the information of Shaw as well as myself

I expect to see your brother Walter in May next and suppose you will be making some inquiries for his benefit and our interests will be somewhat the same

Your ob[t] Servant

J P SNEED

[Addressed:]

Hon[l].

Willie P Mangum Free

Washington City.

[Postmarked:]

Hillsborough, N. C.

16 Jan 1833

WPM-LC

Nathaniel J. Palmer[16] to Willie P. Mangum

MILTON, N. C. Jan 16th 1833.

Dear Sir,

I have concluded to drop you a few lines to request your kind offices in behalf of this place and Hillsborough in procuring the establishment of a Stage route between the two places so as to give to the people in this section of the State a direct communication with the seat of Government and the towns of Newbern, Wilmington, Fayetteville &c. One of the largest mails which I send from my office goes on that route, and I have reason to believe that if it was made a stage route there would be a good deal of travelling on it Mr. Alexander Anderson the present Contractor of the route would undertake to carry a two horse stage or hack on the route on very low terms. If the thousand

---

[15]See above, I, 229n.

[16]See above, I, 414.

dollars per annum which has been given by the Department to Mr. Jeffreys[17] to carry the mail on his route three times a week, which is of little or no benefit to us, [torn] been given or expected on the Hillsborough route it would have been a great deal better for Milton. Please do your best for us, and whether you succeed or not you will place the people of Caswell & Orange under renewed obligations to you. Please write to me on the subject.

I wish you and Mr. [Bedford] Brown if you please to endeavour to procure for me the publication of the laws of Congress in my paper. It has an extensive circulation in the counties of Orange, Pearson, Caswell and Rockingham. I think therefore, that it would not be amiss for the government to bestow on me this little patronage. I have no news of importance to write you. Our Legislature as you will see at its recent session have chartered a bank[18] with a capital of two millions. The people [torn] are cheered with the prospect that the stock will be taken and that a Branch of the Bank will be located in their town. I am getting along tolerable well in my business, I have a very respectable subscription, but and as you will see a good deal of Advertising custom. The Post Office is likewise a source of some income. Please write to me as often as you have leisure, and give me the news, and also advise with me as to the course most proper for me to pursue in the present crisis. With sincere regard, yours &c

NATHANIEL J. PALMER.

Hon. Willie P. Mangum
Washington City, D. C.

P. S. I neglected to remark that a respectable petition was sent to the P. O. department last winter on the subject of the proposed stage route from this place.

Milton, N. C. N. J. PALMER.

January 17th.

[Addressed:]

Hon. Willie P. Mangum
(of the United States Senate)
Washington City
D. C.

---

[17]James W. Jeffreys. See above, I, 453-454.

[18]The state legislature chartered the Bank of North Carolina with a capitalization of $2,000,000, one-half of which was to be subscribed by the state and the other half by individuals. Afraid of state control, individuals refused to purchase the stock. As a result the bank was never organized. Next year it was changed to the Bank of the State of North Carolina with restrictions on state control so that capitalists would participate. Boyd, *Hist. of N. C.: Federal Period,* 135.

WPM-LC

William Montgomery to Willie P. Mangum

ALBRIGHTS N. C. January 18th 1833

My Dear Sir

I am again at Home, and Have not Heard a word from Congress only what the Raleigh papers Contain, and that is very little since I left Raleigh, I take no paper from Washington, I Hope the tariff Bill will pass, It Has created a great expectancy among the people and all seem to be satisfyed with the proposed reduction, But I fear the Senate Clay and Webster will die Hard, But I Hope you will beat them, the Mass of the people are greatly alarmed about the Southern Excitement, But It is Subsiding you will see that we passed a Bank Bill But I think it will only Be on paper I do not Believe that Individuals will take the Stock,

I understand that the general is calculating on a Ball, He Has not written me a line since He got to Washington. Nor Have I wrote to Him I Have made my arrangements not to [be] a candidate For any [ap]pointment out of My own County— Should [I be] a candidate For anything it will Be the [torn] Court Clerks office. My Friends wish [torn] -n for that and I am Inclined to Do [torn] -man is no doubt willing to run But all [torn] that His chance for success is dou[btful] I will write you more on this subject soon.

Pr[iest]ly[19] said to me the morning he left Raleigh that If I was not a candidate In the Senate, he would Be, Allison[20] is spoken of, I do not wish them to Come In Contact, But I Fear they May— Harrison parker Will Be a candidate In the Commons If priestly is not and Benny Hurdle[21] Boon[22] or Stockart[23] also, We are anctious to Have paper In our Town of some Respectability and there is a Wish that some printer would settle

[19]Priestley H. Mangum.
[20]Joseph Allison.
[21]Benny Hurdle was a Jackson supporter.
[22]John Boon.
[23]John Stockard.

there publish a paper that Could Have the Editorial Head Managed By an association of good politicians. Would this do or not, advise us, that is one Inducement My Friends Have to run me for Clerk that I Might at Head quarters, and should a paper Be published render my assistance and Be there to give publick opinion a proper Direction about Hillsborough where there is More poison than In any other place of its size in Christendum. We now Hope We Have the party there nearly or quite down and wish to press on, I wish you would advise us on these Matters Before Court as they may then Receive some action and wish to Start Right, Yours with the Highest Esteem, and Regards

W. MONTGOMERY

[Addressed:]
Honr^b. Wiley P. Mangum
Senator Congress of U. States
Washington City
D. C.

[Postmarked:]
Albright N. C
Janr 19th 1833

WPM-LC

James A. Craig to Willie P. Mangum

H[torn]ds 19th January 1833—

My dear Sir:

. . . .[24]

Pray what is to issue of the present unhappy controversy between the Federal Government and Georgia? I have been waiting with painful anxiety for weeks to hear from some of my friends in Congress, how this matter was about to settle down, but I have not had the first line from Washington City this winter. I hope therefore you will drop me line upon the receipt of this—

You have no doubt seen the act of the General assembly, vesting in the People the right of electing the Clerk of the County and Superior Courts—I expect to be a candidate for the office of C. C. Mr Taylor, Clancey Watts, & myself I expect will be the candidates—Rumor says that Dr. Montgomery will be, I do not think he will—If my friends should think me qualified to fill the

[24]The first paragraph of this letter concerns the Revolutionary claims of James A. Craig's father. This is omitted since it has little historical significance.

office I would thoughtfully accept it—What do you think of my being a candidate for it?

Yours truly
JAMES A. CRAIG

[Addressed:]
Hon Wi[torn]
pr Mail—
[Endorsed:]
Ans^{d}. 25 Jan 1833
opened by me
J. A. CRAIG

WPM-LC

Frederick Nash to Willie P. Mangum

Hillsboro the 23^{d}—Jan^{y}. [1833]

Dear Sir

You must not, from the tardiness of this answer, suppose me, either indifferent to the information, your letters are calculated to convey, or ungrateful, for the aid promised in the matter of my nephew— I should have written to you, immediately, on receiving yours, but was fearful you might, from such a prompt response, consider me, desirous to fasten upon you a correspondence, which it might not suit your convenience, to keep up— Under this consideration, I determined to wait awhile, untill something should turn up sufficiently extraordinary, to justify me, in again trespassing on you— Such an occurrence I consider Mr. Calhouns *maiden* speech in the Senate—it must have made some of you, venerable fathers—rub your eyes—"South Carolina loves the Union!![″]—"The Emperor" said Monsr. Turreau[25] ["]loves the Americans!![″]—But not a word more as to Mr. C —I know you & I differ *toto co[e]lo* as to this gentleman—I considering him as little less than arch angel fallen—you think him still a patriot—I speak of the principle in its enlarged sense—In your letter, you observe, that upon the subject of the South Carolina affairs, we differ irroncileably—However irreconcileable our differences upon that subject, may be, & on some others—I have no doubt it is an honest difference of opinion—& that each is equally ardent in the wish to perpetuate the Union In some respects, your position is calculated, to enable you to form the most correct opinion—in others to mislead you—Do not be offended at

[25]L. M. Turreau de Garambouville was French minister to Washington from 1804 to 1811.

the plainness of my speech—it is a friend who addresses you—I say, your position, is in some respects, calculated to mislead you—because it brings you into immediate contact with these hot & fiery spirits of the South—& you have a *natural* affinity with them—The judgement has no greater enemies to its clear & proper exercise than passion & sympathy—Now *I* am perfectly cool—cool as a cucumber—I look at this South Carolina business—with the calm & calculating eye of a husband & a father—When I look at the papers which brings us each mail fresh accounts of sanguinary battles which the *Seperate & Independent* States of South America are fighting—to see whether one bravo or another shall occupy the chair of State—When history tells me that the *Seperate & Independent* States of Europe—have for hundreds of years covered her bosom with the bones of her children—to settle some point of honor—to fix some disputed line of boundary—to gratify the passion of some kept mistress,—or to build a name for some conquering despot—And then turn my eyes to the happy, peaceful shores of our own, our happy land—how can I help cursing (God forgive me the feelings) the unprincipled demagogues—who would spoil this fair & happy scene—You will say perhapps that I permitt *my* feelings to runaway with my judgment—What is to protect this country from the interminable wars of Europe—the sanguinary & deadly contests of South America if the Federal Union is destroyed—are we not made of like materials with the people of those countries—imbued with the same passions & like vices—what is there to preserve us from their fate—Nothing but the immediate interposition of Divine Providence—& having impiously cast away his best & richest blessing—(I speak politically)—what right should we have to ask or expect his protection & blessing—I confess, Sir, freely for these South Carolina Nullifyers, I have neither charity nor pitty—I mean the leaders—I believe them to be unfaithful & unprincipled—Well, you will say, what is all this to me—nothing—only I was writing to you & you know, in the abundance of the heart, the mouth speaketh—I do however really pitty Calhoun in his present situation—He must feel his awful responsibility—& he must feel that he is sent to Congress to prop & sustain a fallen cause—

I thank you for the papers you sent me—The opinions expressed do not surprise me—there will be differences of opinions every where—Here however there is I believe but one opinion as to the Presidents Proclamation—that its principles are sound & its appearance well timed—if another opinion has been expressed I have not heard it—His late message I have not seen—but from the synopsis published in the Intelligencer, I think I shall still throw up my hat for old hickory—When you next see him tell him that one humble North-Carolinian, thanks him for the bold & noble stand he has taken in behalf of his country—no offence to those who think differently—I will close this epistle my dear Sir with the assurance that among y[r]. numerous friends there is not one who feels a deeper interest in you—

affectionately

F. NASH

[Addressed:]

Honorable

Willey P. Mangum

Washington—

City

Mail—

I have not asked you to answer this—I know your public duties are arduous and call for all your time—you will therefore answer it or not as you may think proper—Your silence however I promise you shall not avail you—in shaking me off—I shall write as the spirit moves me—

WPM-LC

Willie P. Mangum to Charity A. Mangum

WASHINGTON CITY

Saturday morning 26th. January 1833.

My dear Love.

I have been disappointed in hearing from you. I expected a letter yesterday, I hope I shall get one this morning—I have had [a] cold the past week—The winter is very warm, but we have had much wet for some days, in walking to the Capitol my feet have been often damp, and I have been a little unwell and I am still with some head ache—The weather seems now to be open & nearly fair.—I am very desirous, my Love, to see you & our dear children.—The time will not be very long, though I much dread travelling the first of March, if the roads in Virginia shall not get better—I hear they can hardly be travelled.—

Things here are in a very unpromising condition—and I fear nothing good will be done this session.—It is not improbable that Congress will be called together again in May or June, if we fail to settle the dangerous questions now before us.—I hope our school has commenced—I am very desirous that Sally should be at school.—

The mail boy is at my door—I must close & will write you perhaps to morrow—If this goes on with[out] being stopt, it will get to Red Mountain next Wednesday—

Kiss our dear children for me. & remember me often My Dear Love, as your affectionate husband

WILLIE P. MANGUM

WPM-LC

Edward J. Hale[26] *to Willie P. Mangum*

FAYETTEVILLE 30th January 1833

Dear Sir,

I am in the receipt of your much respected letter to me of the 15th inst, and beg you to accept my grateful acknowledgements for the manifestation it evinces of your friendship for me,—Will you please present my respects expressive of my thanks to Mr. Brown also for his feelings of similar kindness,—But

My dear Sir, in the present instance I am induced to address you upon a much more interesting subject *to us all* than the one to which my former communication related, and which I esteem to be momentous and paramount to all other considerations in this life.

The ides of a critical crisis is approaching, the attitude in which the Genl. Govt. and South Carolina have assumed in their Political relations to each other presents, to my view, a state of things, which if, not changed by a prudential course of action by the Genl. Govt., must terminate in the destruction of the Political institutions of this, once happy Republic, the effect of this controvercy already pervades the public mind and its unhappy consequences are becoming too apparent to render the result any longer a matter of doubtful speculation. The people begin to

[26]Edward Jones Hale was born in Chatham County in 1802. Left an orphan, he became the ward of Colonel Edward Jones, whose name he accepted. At an early age he worked under the guidance of Joseph Gales on the *Raleigh Register* and later on the *National Intelligencer*. He became a strong Whig and a friend of Webster, Clay, and Calhoun. In 1825 he bought the *Carolina Observer*, changed it to the *Fayetteville Observer*, and continued to edit it until 1865 when he moved to New York City, where he died in 1883. He was one of the strongest newspaper editors of the state. Ashe, *Biog. Hist. of N. C.*, VIII, 179-184.

think & see that matters are not every where right, and that the contest must necessarily be settled by the sword and you may rely upon it, the issue of the contest *will turne* upon the *legitimate question* or cause of the controvercy;—*The unconstitutionality of the Tariff Laws;* alias the protecting system, &c.

The right of Secession to the States can never be surrendered by the People of the South, it is that and by *that* alone we can prevent the influence of the Eastern & northern States in Congress, from being oppressively exercised against us, take that right from us and we shall be left without a protection against the exercise of any arbitrary power the Genl. Govt. may assume, it will then be necessary only for some *popular* President to pronounce to congress and the Judiciary that the Genl. Govt. is all Supreme and unlimited in its constitutional powers, and you will immediately find a host of implicit believers in the manufacturing States ready to prove by *constitutional technicalities* the truth of the absurdity. It is impossible therefore, with these facts before us that the public mind in the South can long remain divided upon *that* question, and it matters not whether the Contest be dicided by the *Sword* or whether it be a contest of opinions—the result will assuredly be the same.

We are aware that the opposing interest between the Eastern, Northern and Southern States is and ever will be a subject of much perplexity in regulating the genl. Policy of the Federal Govt. and as it is admited to be one of the fundamental truthes of Political Science, that *interest* is the strong cement which unite Societies, the difficulty of creating a standard of equal measure between the *two extremes* must *increase* in proportion as the opposing interest accumulates. The Eastern & northern States are destined to contain a greater population than the Southern, consequently they will retain the preponderance of Power in Congress and which *their interest will incline* them to exercise with *partiality to themselves,* and this is not all, the regulating of the concerns of a People who are manufacturing is attended with a much more complexed and expressive system of Policy than the plain & simple vocation of a Planter, the manufacturing interest is Necessarily brought in competition with the interest of *foreign* manufacturers & *foreign* Markets which Necessarily also involves the Govt. in the regulations of the commerce of *foreign* Markets. But the same difficulties do not, nor cannot occur in the commercial relations of the Southern

States who are *growers principally* of *raw Export articles,* such communities therefore whose productive capital consist in *raw export articles* stand in quite a different position in their *commercial relations* with foreign nations to those of manufacturing Societies, and which is evidently less expensive, less complexed and in a greater degre advances the wealth of the Nation.

As regards the Tariff, if by *impost,* we grant a *protection* to the manufacturer we assuredly thereby indirectly tax one class of citizens for the benefit of another, for if the Planter can raise an excess of *raw export* materials over and above the wants of the *home* manufacturer the *import thus laid* is evidently a drawback upon his (the farmers) *exports* which operates a Tax upon his purchases of Manufacturer articles, for he either pays the protecting duty say 40 P Ct. upon his *imports* or he must pay it upon the home manufactured articles.

Upon this representation of the subject, I am of the opinion that the Southern States will never become reconciled to the Protecting System.

Regarding the President Proclamation it can have no lasting effect towards allaying the public excitement, nay; there will be a reaction against it and which has commenced. Some of the principles it contains (are conceived by the more orthodox interpreters of the Federal Constitution) & which his last message sustains to be such as cannot be recognised by the Southern States, they strike at the root and foundation of the republican principles of the States; but yet I do not believe that the President was influenced by any feelings enemical to the republican cause; in his zeal and no doubt inspired with an *honest* desire to administer the Genl. Govt. in its *practical operations* strictly within the orb of its constitutional limits, he has been lead to overleap those essential sovereign state rights incident to its rightful action. I had hoped and expected untill I saw & read his last message that the *ultra* principles advanced & maintained in his Proclamation & Message would have been explained by the importance & *the Necessity* of the case as in other cases of great emmergency he has verified the old adage of "doing" that which might not be strictly orthodox "that good might come of it."

I regret to perceive that the principles of 98-99 are forgotten or misunderstood by so many of the present generation.—Those who defended the principles of those days and practically established them in 1800 are now off the stage, and I fear we shall be compeled to go over the work again. But the history of it may prove useful to the present generation as well as the means of perpetuating the liberties of this country to the future, but I must close this letter, it is already much longer than I intended it should be when I set down to address you, you will pardon the zeal with which I have written you and which it has not been in my power to repress. The subject to which this communication relates brings to my recollection the Political occurrences of my early life, in reviewing which they *revive* Principles that were *given* and *taught* to me by our *fathers, an enheretence* which the experience of 33 years of these practical blessings have rendered, to *me* at least, sacred and invaluable.

You will permit me however, Sir, to remark in conclusion that I have not written you with a design to influence you in any respect whatever. *I have no earthly motive than that of the good and welfar of our Common Country* & in the discharge of my duties promotive of the same I have confined the forgoing remarks to my own private views solely,—on reviewing what I have said, I find I have omited to make mention of the repeated *Expresses* that have passed through the Country from Washington to Charleston and at the rates of 18 to 20 miles the Hour, now, the fact is they have and will continue to have a bad effect upon the *Administration,* because it is not believed that the *People* of South Carolina *have* or *could be*

[The last part of the letter is missing].

WPM-LC

Willie P. Mangum to Charity A. Mangum

WASHINGTON CITY,

Saturday morning 2nd Feby 1833.

My dear Love.

I received yesterday your letter of the 24th. of January, & was much relieved, by it, as I had received none for a fortnight.—I felt great anxiety My Love, & was fearful, that something had happened, believing that you would not have omitted to write to me.—It gives me great uneasiness, when I fail to hear from you—For at last My dear, a letter from you comes to me as the best & dearest friend that I find in Washington.—Your last did not speak of any omission to write, & I suppose your letter must have miscarried.—I feel glad that the time is approaching when I may hope to see you & our dear children,—We are deeply engaged in the Senate, upon South Carolina affairs—I fear we shall make war upon her.—I am opposed to harsh measures, and shall make as strong a speech against it as I can.[27]—I had ex pected to take the floor, but shall not before Monday or Tuesday.

Pay Ellison [G. Mangum] for Mrs. Cozart,[28] the sum you mentioned.—

Give My Dear Children a Kiss for their Father, and tell them to be good & he will love them—

May God bless you My Dear Love, remember me often in affection & kindness. & always be sure that that [*sic*] you are dearer to me than any other or all other objects in this world.—I feel in my heart that in your kind & affectionate heart I have a treasure—& whatever may happen for good or for evil, I shall always look to it, with a more sincere feeling of gratitude than all other things can inspire.—

Farewell My Love
WILLIE P. MANGUM

The pensions of Hardeman Duke & Wm. Duke senr. have been granted[29]

W. P. M.

[Addressed:]
Mrs. Charity A. Mangum
Red Mountain
North Carolina.

WPM-LC

William Cain, Jr., to Willie P. Mangum

HILLSBOROUGH N. C. 2 Feby 1833.

My dear Sir.

Mr. James H. Ruffin[30] intends going out this Spring in March or before to Alabama and Mississippi and should he move out in the fall as I have no doubt he will I shall send my negroes by

[27]When the Force Bill was introduced, Mangum stated that it carried out too fully the old Federalist principles. On January 22 he tried to have the measure postponed. He worked against it but made no significant speech. *Register of Debates*, 22 Cong., 1 sess. 173-175, 236, 237; Pegg, "Whig Party in N. C.," 10-11.

[28]Probably Mangum's aunt, Mrs. Holly Cozart.

[29]See below, II, the order of Lewis Cass, Oct. 5, 1833.

[30]Son of Judge Thomas Ruffin, he moved to Alabama where he became a large planter in Marengo County. Hamilton, (ed.), *Papers of Ruffin*, II, 77-78, 111-112, 266, 319.

him, except some few that I shall keep at home—He is at this time very much in the notion of moving to the Choctaw Country in Mississippi, but his movements will depend much upon how he shall be pleased when he goes on—

I now beg information of you; from all quarters from which you can obtain it, touching the agricultural advantages of the South Western section of our Country and more particularly of the State of Mississippi, being determined to send my hands to that section

I wish, however, some intelligence as to matters about which, the most correct may be obtained by enquiries at the seat of Government. Is there likely to be a sale of public Lands in Mississippi this year or when? Has one a right to settle on public land at will, without interfering with prior occupants? Does he gain any advantage thereby in acquiring a pre-emption right? Is the health of the Country tolerably good and what parts of it are most so? What is the average value of land in the settled parts of the state? What is the average price of provisions, corn, Pork &c. and generally such information as may be of advantage to a man moving to that Country—What is the average hire of Negro Men & Women: The average price of Stock, mules, Horses, hogs & Sheep & Cattle—

I enclose you a ten Dollar note, which if good, you will please forward me ten Dollars United States money, it belongs to another person—

I have nothing new in Town, except there has been two or three Cases of Scarlet fever and one death Mrs. A. Camerons daughter is the only loss as yet. I have not been at my Fathers for some time but hear that he is as usual.

Hoping to hear from you soon, I subscribe myself,

Your friend & kindsman

WM. CAIN JR.

Hillsborough N. C.
2 Feby. 1833.

[Addressed:]
The Honble Willie P. Mangum
U. S. Senator
Washington City.

WPM-LC

Newton Cannon[31] *to Willie P. Mangum*

HARPETH TENNESSEE

Feby 5th 1833

Dear Sir

It is rumour[d] here that Judge McNairy[32] our present federal district Judge, either has or will very shortly resign, and that Alfred Balch[33] Esqr. one of the *Crawford* men here, will be recommended to the executive to fill the place. He is a good Lawyer, and his appointment would give as much satisfaction here, I think, as that of any other that will probably be recommended, and I would feel gratify[d]. If he could succeed, should you not think it out of the Line of duty he would feel quite gratify[d] in having your influence in his favour. He informs me he is not personally acquainted with you, therefore I have taken this Liberty

The Crawford men here have been much neglected thus far by the president. This ought not to continue for he owes his elevation in a great degree to them, at all events they ought not to be entirely proscrib[d] from his favour I am glad to see some prospect of the vapour of nullification blowing off, and I hope it will leave the political horizon more clear, and put the odious system of protection down.

Certainly there can be *no necessity now,* for as high duties as those we Laid in 1816, which was a revenue measure, to provide for the payment of the then Large national debt, as well as to meet the ordinary expences of government I would still Like to see expenses of our government reduc[d] greatly, in the depart-

---

[31]Newton Cannon, 1781-1841, was born in Guilford County, North Carolina, and moved with his parents to Tennessee when he was nine years old. In Tennessee he became a merchant and a wealthy planter in Williamson County. He was in the Tennessee legislature in 1811, 1812, and in Congress from 1813 to 1823. Elected as the first Whig governor in 1835, he served two terms. In 1839, after being defeated for reelection by James K. Polk, he retired from public life. *D. A. B.*, III, 477-478.

[32]John McNairy, a native of Guilford County, North Carolina, where he practiced law, went with Jackson to Tennessee, settled in Nashville and became Federal judge of the Territory of Tennessee. In 1797 Washington appointed him Federal District Judge of Tennessee, a post which he held until 1834 when he retired. He broke with Jackson in 1797 and remained in the opposition camp until his death in 1844. Levi Scott, "The Bench and Bar of Guilford County," in *Publications of the Guildford County Literary and Historical Annals,* I (1908), 48-49; Joshua W. Caldwell, *Sketches of the Bench and Bar of Tennessee,* Knoxville, 1898, 10-13.

[33]Alfred Balch, a prominent Nashville, Tennessee, attorney, served for a time as an attorney for the University of North Carolina in its claims for Tennessee lands. Later he turned against the University because the fees offered were too small. A close friend of Jackson and Van Buren, he was active in the affairs of the Democratic Party. Hoyt (ed.), *Papers of Murphey,* I, 303; Bassett (ed.), *Cor. of Jackson,* III, 266, 381n; IV, 27, 114, 230n, 302, 314-316.

ments, immediately under the eye of the executive, where all the auditors, accountants, & Clerks, that were deem[d] necessary to investigate, and settle the vast accounts growing out of the Late war, seem to have been retain[d] and continu[d] when not one fourth of the labour, is now to be perform[d] under a rigid system of industry and attention to business in those departments, I believe many very many might be dismiss[d]. and as to the Military academy it is too obnoxious to my notions of democracy to endure, though it seems to be the favourite of all the executives, excuse if you please the intrusion of these notions

The president has strengthen[d] his popularity here this session I think by his Messages to congress & Proclamation. He "backs water" on the Tariff elegantly We have no Local news, our political campaign has not yet open[d]. nor will it untill spring. Much pecuniary embarrassment pervades the middle and western part of our State, and considerable numbers intending to settle in the Lately acquir[d] Choctaw country, which is said to be & no doubt is a fine cotton country. Please to tender my respects to my old acquaintance your colleague Mr. Williams[34] and accept yourself my best wishes for [your] future prosperity, at a Liesure time I would be glad to hear from you, how matters are working in the city

With great respect & Esteem
Your obt. Servt.
N. CANNON

The Honble
Willie P. Mangum.

Harpeths Tenn
Feb 6th, 1833.

[Addressed:]
The Honble.
Willie P. Mangum
Senate Chamber
Washington City
D. C—

[34]Lewis Williams.

WPM-LC

P. H. Mangum to Willie P. Mangum

HILLSBORO' Feb: 12th 1833.

Dear Sir,

Our old friend John Ray,[35] requested me, a few days ago, to write you & request to know whether the communication heretofore made to you by Col. Wm. Horner,[36] in relation to the services of his Father, sets forth *a sufficiency* to entitle the old man to a pension—As I understand, the old man's declaration has not been made, but a sketch was sent to you, *as a feeler*, I suppose.—

Our people are usually well. No news worth mentioning. The Scarlet Fever is in Hillsboro'. Mrs. Cameron here has lost a daughter 8 years old, and one or two others in the family have had it, but are getting well. There has been no other case in Town. It is hoped it will not spread.—

We are anxiously waiting on the deliberations of congress. I think you have a war party & a peace party. I find my friend Brown has caught at the bait that I purposely threw, by way of amendment, into the resolution of instructions,[37] adopted by the Genl. Assembly, viz, "*peaceable*" 'adjustment'—which was at the time opposed by such as Eccles,[38] Pearson[39] & the rest of the Ultra-Federalists.—

I expect you may take a part in the discussion that has been going on in the Senate—and let me beseech you, to weigh well your *positions* & your language.—Your enemies & your friends look forward to that thing—one to assail, & the other to sustain.

Yrs P. H. MANGUM

[Addressed:]

The Hon:

Willie P. Mangum
(Senate)
Washington City
D. C.

Hillsboro N.C.
13th Feby 1833.

---

[35]John Ray was a prominent Whig of Orange County. *Hillsborough Recorder*, June 20, 1844.

[36]Col. William Horner was an attorney and justice of the peace of Orange County.

[37]On January 3-4, 1833, the House of Commons of the state legislature adopted resolutions against the tariff, but at the same time expressed its opposition to nullification. In the debate on the resolutions the fifth resolution mildly instructed the senators to procure an adjustment in the nullification fight. Priestley Mangum, member from Orange County, proposed that the word "peaceable" be inserted before "adjustment": *Journal of* [*N. C.*] *House of Commons*, 1832-1833, 224, 229.

[38]John D. Eccles, of Cumberland County.

[39]Richard M. Pearson, of Rowan County.

Willie P. Mangum to Gen. Samuel Smith[40]

WASHINGTON CITY the 9th. March 1833.

My dear Sir:

I send herewith the Resolution[41] of the General assembly of North Carolina, which His Excellency, The Governor of that State desired me to place in your hands, with the request that you will be so obliging as to convey them to the Representatives of the late venerable Charles Carroll of Carrollton—

You were so kind as to say to me, that you would promptly comply with this request, and I feel the less reluctance in giving you this trouble, as there is a peculiar appropriateness in selecting one of the most esteemed & venerable relicts of the Revolution as the organ of Conveying the universal sentiment of Condolence of one of the Sovereign States to the representatives of the venerable and illustrious deceased.—

Be pleased My dear Sir, to permit the expression of my most ardent wishes that your valuable life may be long extended, and accept the assurance of

My profound respect & esteem
WILLIE P. MANGUM

Gen. Samuel Smith
Baltimore

WPM-LC

Samuel Smith to Willie P. Mangum

BALTIMORE 12. March 1833

My dear Sir/

I had the pleasure to receive on yesterday, your friendly kind letter of the 9 Ins. and immey waited on Mrs- Caton[42] the Eldest daughter of the late Mr. Carroll, and delivered to her in person. the Act of the demi Sovereignty of that excellent *Safe State* "North Carolina," a State whose people has discountenanced the sophistry of Nullification, and only justifies *Secession* when there shall be a palpable violation of the Constitution. Such

[40]The original is in the Historical Society of Pennsylvania, Philadelphia, Pa. See above, I, 425n, for a brief sketch of General Samuel Smith.

[41]These were resolutions of sympathy to the relatives of Charles Carroll, who died in November, 1832. *N. C. Laws*, 1832-1833, 103.

[42]In 1787 Joseph Caton, an English merchant who entered business in Baltimore, married Mary Carroll, daughter of Charles Carroll. Mary Carroll was the second daughter of Carroll and was a favorite of George Washington during his administration. Kate Mason Rowland, *The Life of Charles Carroll of Carrollton, 1737-1832, with his Correspondence and Public Papers*, New York, 1898, II, 54, 106.

as all will acknowledg to be a direct, (not a constructive) departure from the plain meaning of the Constitution—

I said in Senate that the new tariff would be stronger by the new Congress—That sentiment, I am almost ready to dissent from, on full reflection I begin to believe that it will continue Eight years with little molestation. It will give strength to the Union by making the sovereign States subservient to and dependent on the General Government, and will go far to consolidate the whole into one nation. Now altho: I like a stronger government than you do, yet I think that a consolidated Republick, extensive as ours is—would not last long. Nothing can keep us together but the separate action of the States in their constructive sovereignty. If the present trial be not successful the world may bid farewell forever, to a governm[t]. by the people.

The new tariff will I verily believe increase the Revenue to Eight years. It will certainly for the present year yield the Surplus of Six millions as reported by the Sec[y]. of the Treasury. I think more, for the duties on Customs which we thought was made free of duty by it, will pay 25 P cent (the old duty prior to the act of 1832)—and So of Stuffs[?]. In fact the Bill was not understood. I told the Senate that I did not comprehend it. But to my point—What must be done with the Surplus of Six millions? There is no alternative—*a division among the States*. N. York will get a million. Penns[a]. $700.000 Virginia and the other States in proportion, and then all the States will be relieved from their home taxation. N. C. and Maryland pay little of taxes. they will have funds to carry on their internal improvements &c. &c.—The State legislature will find great relief from all the revenue being raised by Congress, and great pleasure in expending. The question then Occurs. Will Congress Ever (after having once tasted the increase) consent to the reduction of the Revenue? Of that you are just as good a judge as I am,—If they should, then the States will be placed in a situation of dependence, that will make them subservient to the general government, and make them more firm supporters of a government that pays all.—Whether that state of things will tend to consolidation. time only will show & you will percieve that my Opinion is that few if any modifications of the tariff will soon take place. that if continued for Eight years—It will strengthen the hands of government which may be for good or Evil according to the hands into which it may fall—Pardon this scrawl and Believe me—Ever

Your Sincere friend
S: SMITH

Honble
W. P. Mangum.

WPM-LC

Bedford Brown to Willie P. Mangum

CASWELL COUNTY, N. CAROLINA 16th March 1833.

My dear Sir.

Your letter of the 28th ult. was duly received, enclosing a check for fourteen dollars, in my favour, from Mr. Lowrie,[43] Secretary of the Senate, and likewise a Statement of my account for compensation. You inform me also, that you had receipted in your name, my account for compensation, so as to enable Mr. Lowrie to close his account. I thank you, for having done so, as Mr. Lowrie having been much engaged, in attending to his duties in the Senate, when I called to Settle with him, previous to my return home, it prevented our making a final settlement.

I found my family on my return home, all more or less indisposed with the Scarlet fever. Mrs. Brown had during the winter, enjoyed much better health than usual, but the afflicting bereavement which had befallen our family, together with an attack of Scarlet fever, had very greatly injured her health, though for some days past, it has been improving, and the rest of my family, have recovered their health.

I am much gratified, at the passage of Mr. Clay's bill to reduce the Tariff, and although the reduction, will not be as rapid, as *in justice*, it ought to have been, yet under the *peculiar circumstances* of our country, it goes as far, as the most Sanguine could at this time, have hoped for, and will be as it ought to be, regarded throughout the Southern country, and the moderate Tariff States, as a most fortunate termination, to a controversy, the consequences of which, were most deeply, to be deprecated.

I regretted to perceive, that the enforcing bill, had passed, though the passage of the bill, to reduce the Tariff, will render

[43]Walter Lowrie, a native of Scotland, came to the United States in 1791 and settled in Butler County, Pennsylvania. A school teacher, surveyor, and farmer, he served in the Pennsylvania legislature from 1811 to 1819. He represented his state in the national Senate from 1819 to 1825 when he became secretary of the Senate, a post which he held until 1836. He was a Democrat. *Biog. Dir. of Cong.*, 1242.

it inoperative and harmless, except as establishing a dangerous precedent.

You will please present me most respectfully to Mrs. Mangum.

I remain, My dear Sir,
Very truly yours,
B. BROWN.

Hon. W. P. Mangum.
[Addressed:]
Red Mountain,
Orange County, N. C.

Free B. Brown

[Postmarked:]
Brown's Store, N. C.
16 March

WPM-LC

D. L. Swain to Willie P. Mangum

RALEIGH, 19 March 1833.

My dear Sir,

I have just seen A. Jones Esq.[44] who informed me that a public entertainment dinner or [torn] may be will be offered to you from Citizens of Wake Forest [torn] of Wake Superior Court. It will be given at the house of Jesse Powel, Esq.[45] I have not been informed whether the invitation has yet been forwarded.

I hope you will not only find it convenient to attend, but that you will spend two or three days in Raleigh previous to the festival.—

I contemplate leaving this city for Buncombe Superior Court about the 15th. of April, and return via Charlotte about the 25th. of May. I am very anxious to see you in the interim,

Barringer is writing his circular and preparing for a vigorous campaign—

Yours very Truly,
D. L. SWAIN

Judge Mangum,
[Addressed:]
Honble. Willie P. Mangum,
Washington

---

[44]Probably Capt. Alfred Jones, who was a member of the Council of State from 1830 to 1834. *N. C. Manual*, 434-435.

[45]Jesse Powell was a large planter who lived near Wake Forest. He actively supported the Wake Forest Pleasant Grove Academy. He was prominent in Whig activities. *Hillsborough Recorder*, Apr. 1, 1841; Coon (ed.), *N. C. Schools and Academies*, 557; *Raleigh Register*, Jan. 4, 1828.

WPM-LC

Jo. Seawell Jones to Willie P. Mangum[46]

[March 27, 1833]

A Work will be published, during the ensuing Fall[47]
entitled,
A VINDICATION
of the character of the
State of North-Carolina,
from the
Aspersions of Mr. Jefferson
as contained
In his Letter to the late John Adams, published in the
4th volume of the Boston edition of his Works,
pp. 314-15.

By Jo. Seawell Jones,
of North-Carolina.

Subscriptions are solicited for the proposed work, returnable to Messrs. Turner & Hughes, of Raleigh, by the first of October; and the author embraces the opportunity to remark, that his work will comprise a History of the Revolution in North-Carolina, from the year 1771, to the fourth of July, 1776, as well as the other matters embraced in the title of the book. It will be published in one octavo volume, of about 270 pages. Price, $2.

March 27th, 1833.

---

[46]Jefferson's works, which were published in 1829, included a letter from Jefferson to Adams which stated that the Mecklenburg Declaration of May 20, 1775, was not genuine. This aroused North Carolinians. In 1830 a legislative committee appointed to report on the validity of the Declaration maintained that it was valid. Thereupon the legislature ordered the printing of two pamphlets in its defense. These were never published, but Joseph Seawell Jones, a nephew of Nathaniel Macon and one of the founders of the North Carolina Historical Society, published in 1834 the volume of which this is a prospectus. Four years later, 1838, in his *Memorials of North Carolina* he renewed the controversy by attacking Washington Irving, who had not accepted the North Carolina story. Jones was a caustic writer who constantly expressed the anti-Virginia feeling which was prevalent in North Carolina at the time. He was a well trained student who graduated from the state university in 1824 and in law from Harvard University in 1833. Although licensed to practice law, he never did. Johnson, *Ante-Bellum N. C.*, 818; Ashe, *Biog. Hist. of N. C.*, VI, 329-334; Joseph Seawell Jones, *A Defense of the Revolutionary History of the State of North Carolina from the Aspersions of Mr. Jefferson*, Raleigh, 1834; P. L. Ford (ed.), *Writings of Thomas Jefferson, XII*, 131.

[47]This is a printed prospectus.

Baltimore,[48] April 8th 1833—My Dear Sir I have been compeled to postpone the publication of my book until the fall—in consequence of the loss of a letter which I considered important—and shall spend the mean time in corrections and revision—Our friend Mr Parker—is I am glad to find a sound politician—Yours &c

JO. SEAWELL JONES

[Addressed:]
To
The Hon. Willie P. Mangum
Orange County
No— Carolina.

Willie P. Mangum to Henry Clay[49]

Sunday Morning .March 1833.

My dear Sir:

I regret extremely to inform you that I cannot hand you the $133 for Gov. Branch.

Knowing that it cannot be a matter of any moment to you, I regret it mainly on account of the delicacy of Gov B's feelings.—

I had disposed of my means here, more than three weeks ago, reserving as I supposed more than enough to meet my engagements here,—Last night I learned that I should be disappointed in receiving money, advanced to be returned under circumstances of the highest obligations.—I have staid two days to receive that money—I am finally disappointed—

Never having had any pecuniary transactions here, I prefer asking you a tempory indulgence, rather than ask another any sort of pecuniary favor.—I shall forward to you at Lexington immediately on my return home a draft for the amt.—not because I suppose, it matter of consequence to you but to relieve my friend Gov Branch of any feeling on this subject—

I shall leave here to day—

I am Dear Sir Mo. truly & sincerely
Yrs
WILLIE P. MANGUM

[Addressed to:]
The Hon. H. Clay
Washington

---

[48]At the bottom of the printed prospectus this paragraph was written in Jones' handwriting.

[49]The original of this letter is in the Henry Clay Papers, Library of Congress.

WPM-LC

Wm. S. Archer to Willie P. Mangum

ELK HALL VA, April 13,/33

My dear Mangum,

I have been designing to write to you for some time, but have been waiting to be enabled to speak with grounds of confidence as regards the results of our State Elections. I can wait no longer however, because I am about to set out in a few days for Mississippi.—

My own Election you know, I have always told you was hopeless, my District being the *Focus* of the most intense Jacksonism, aggravated by a peculiar hatred of Leigh, and yet more lately by having been the seat of the Jurisdiction, the supposed contempt of which, has awakened so much excitement. My friends would not allow me to retire on account of the discussions which there was no one else to conduct on our side. After the two first Elections however, in one of which I lost a majority and gained it in the other, as I was much disappointed in not getting majorities in both, I refused postively to go on. My vote would have been strong, but I could not have been elected.—

In the State I will not venture to predict the result. Our friend Pleasants[50] inclusive, think that we shall not lose and will probably gain. As yet there have been three changes each way, leaving no Equipoise

There can be no doubt I have the pleasure to inform you, that the State will go for White. The 10 counties of Fultons[51] District will of themselves be enough to turn the tide, and to these will be addressed many others which are Jackson violently. When the detested *Cabalism* of that name has passed away the character of the Country which it bears to the dust will re erect its head every where. Here we shall be able to regret even the bale-

---

[50]John H. Pleasants, 1797-1846, a native of Goochland County, Virginia, and a graduate of William and Mary, edited the *Virginian* before he established the *Richmond Whig* in 1824. For more than twenty years, as editor of the *Whig*, he carried tremendous influence in his state, the South, and the nation against Jackson and for Whig principles. In 1841 with Edward W. Johnston he had the Washington *Independent* established although he remained in control of the *Whig* until his death in 1846 as a result of a duel with Thomas Ritchie, Jr. *D. A. B.*, XV, 7-8.

[51]John H. Fulton, Congressman from the Abingdon district in 1833-1835.

ful spell, as regards the control for the Presidential Election.—

I see you have been put forward for Vice on our Ticket. I need not say with what pleasure I shall see your name selected for Instrumantality in the good work, and I hope & think that none other may promise a more effective Instrumentality. It shall take a good deal to persuade me that there is any better.

I gave you a letter of McLane expressing opinions on the Presidential Election. Be good enough to return it to me as soon as you get this.—

Yr fr[d]. Sincerly

WM. S. ARCHER.

WPM-LC

Printed Circular of Micajah T. Hawkins to his Constituents

TO THE FREEMEN OF GRANVILLE, FRANKLIN, NASH, & WARREN COUNTIES.

[June 27, 1833]

Fellow-Citizens:—

Having been your Representative in the last Congress of the United States, and being a candidate to serve you in the next; finding that my public conduct has been censured and misrepresented by some of those who are opposed to me, and the time for you to make a selection being near at hand; the District being large, and my situation such as to prevent me from seeing you all, and personally explaining myself, and refuting the misrepresentation, made against me, I have determined to adopt this mode of defending myself. I am conscious of having done what I thought your interest required of me. I laboured faithfully to discharge the duties my situation drew around me. It is however, for you, Fellow Citizens, and not for me to decide whether I am worthy again of your confidence; but I beg of you to give me a fair and impartial hearing before you decide; then should you prefer either of my competitors to me, I trust that I have Republicanism and generosity enough in my composition to submit to your decision as becomes a man professing my principles.

Mr. Gilliam[52] has made my vote on the Bill to enforce the collection of duties on imports, a theme of public discussion, and has denounced the Bill in the boldest language he could use—calling it a *Force Bill*, a *Bloody Bill*, and applying to it other epithets, intended to render it obnoxious to the public. He, in addressing the People, has said that I, on this subject was found voting with bad company, such as Daniel Webster, Clayton of Deleware, and Tristam Burgess, who are blue light Federalists. It is true those gentlemen did vote with me on this subject, but in refering to the Journals you will find it a rare case that we ever voted together before. The enforcing Bill was not introduced by either of those gentlemen or their party, it was recommended by the President and introduced by one of his warmest supporters. Now as Mr. Gilliam has denounced me for voting for it, I suppose he would have voted against it. Let us see who he would have voted with. He would have voted, with a few exceptions, with the strongest Nullifiers in this Government. Some of his friends have reviled and denounced me in writing and speaking, as servile and ignorant, as a traitor to my constituents, and unworthy of public confidence, because I voted for its passage. In fact every effort that the ingenuity of my enemies could suggest has been brought into requisition to deceive and mislead the people upon this important subject.

It is well known that South Carolina had declared that certain laws of the United States should not be enforced within her limits, and that to prevent their execution, armies were raised and every necessary military propataion [preparation] was made. The President was distinctly apprised of these facts, and knowing that he had taken an oath to see that the laws were faithfully executed, called upon Congress to grant him, as the chief Executive Officer of the United States, powers sufficient to have them enforced. In obedience to this call, after great care, consideration and argument, the Bill was framed and after a very able debate, passed the Senate by a vote of 32 to 1, [and the Hou]se of Representatives by a vote of 149 to 47. I [torn] Bill, for had I not, I think I would have admit-[ted] that a State has a right at any time and upon [torn] Nullify the laws of Congress. It has been [said] Gilliam, while addressing the people,

[52]Robert Ballard Gilliam of Oxford received his A.B. degree in 1823 and his A.M. in 1826 from the University of North Carolina. He was a member of the state convention in 1835, the state legislature in 1836-1841, 1846-1849, and 1862. A prominent attorney, he became a superior court judge, speaker of the state house of representatives, and a close friend of Mangum. Grant, *Alumni Hist. of U. N. C.*, 220; *N. C. Manual*, 470, 472, 474.

that the [torn] bill was altogether useless, as the bill reducing the Tariff had passed previous to the passage of this Bloody Bill, as he terms it. This I deny—The Tariff Bill was before the Senate when the enforcing bill was in the other House, and there were many Senators who would not vote to reduce the Tariff, unless the enforcing bill passed the House of Representatives first. The first and fifth sections of the Enforcing Bill which are mostly complained of by Mr. Gilliam, only give the President similar powers to those which were given to Gen. Washington and Mr. Jefferson, with a small exception, which is that of requiring cash duties and the removal of the Custom Houses, whenever any state shall Nullify the laws of Congress, and refuse to pay her proportion of the taxes.—There is not a feature in this bill that bears the stamp of tyranny. In no case is an officer authorised to use violence unless violence is first exerted to prevent the performance of his duty. No authority whatever is granted that will justify him in molesting the peaceable citizens of any state in the Union, or to infringe on the rights, or injure the property of any person. Yet Mr. Gilliam says that this Bill gives Gen. Jackson power which he would be willing to grant to no man that ever lived, not even to Gen. Washington, were he alive.—Now suppose there are some objections to the Bill, was it not better that I should have voted for the bill, when I saw it was the only way to disengage South Carolina from the difficulty in which she had involved herself with the Gen. Government, as the Senate would not have passed the Tariff Bill, unless the House of Representatives passed the enforcing bill.

My vote too, on the Pension Bill has been censured, and I have been arraigned for that vote, by Mr. Gilliam and Mr. Williams,[53] who has also raised his voice against it, after having said in an address to the people in Louisburg last fall, that he offered from no hostility to me; that he had always been my personal and political friend, & had he been in Congress, that he would have pursued the same course that I did.

The Pension Bill passed and became a law session before the last, and I never heard an objection to my vote against it, until it was raised by Mr. Gilliam at Nashville, during the last County court. I feel assured that you Fellow Citizens will approve of

[53]William P. Williams, of Franklin County. A graduate of the state university, he represented his county in the legislature in 1829-1832, 1838-1839, 1842-1843, and in the Constitutional Convention in 1835. He was a delegate to the Baltimore Democratic Convention in 1832 and voted for Van Buren for Vice President. Grant, *Alumni Hist. of U. N. C.*, 678; *N. C. Manual*, 609-610, 879.

my course as to this measure, when I state the reasons and principles upon which I acted. Often have I heard Representatives censured for wasting public money, never before have I known an instance where one was called to answer for *not squandering it.* Although the Pension Billl passed session before last, I heard of no objection to my course, until my opponents came out. Mr. Gilliam at Nashville, stated to the People that the *Pension Bill was a favorite measure with the President, and recommended by him to Congress,* and that I had voted against it. I then denied that the President ever recommended such a bill, which I now deny. Here are Gen. Jackson's own words from his first Message to Congress in 1829, relative to Pensioning the soldiers of the Revolution, to wit:

"I would also suggest a review of the Pension Law for the purpose of extending its benefits to every Revolutionary soldier, who aided in establishing our liberties, and who is unable to *maintain himself in comfort.*"

The above is what General Jackson recommended—It is the *favorite measure of which Mr. Gilliam spoke.* Now hear what I have to say in reply, and also, my answer to Mr. Williams, who has alleged that I voted against pensioning the *poor old soldiers of the Revolution,* who were unable to *feed and clothe themselves.* You see above what Gen. Jackson recommended. I did vote against the Bill in the shape in which it passed, I frankly admit, but it was because it was a high Tariff measure, and goes to Pension the richest men in this country, and furnishes a pretext for the imposition of high Tariff Duties; for it is known, that if the money in the Treasury could be squandered, that there would be more plausibility for the continuation of the Tariff, which is an indirect tax upon the People. The Northerners however, rejoiced at its passage, for it is a protection to their manufactures. But to show that I was disposed to go as far as necessity & gratitude required, I refer you to my votes, which are in the Journals of Congress. I voted for the motion of Mr. Craig, to Pension all not worth more than one thousand dollars. I voted to include the three months men, and I voted for the amendment of Mr. Blair, to include the Militia who fought at the battles of Kings Mountain and Guilford Court House.—Had the amendment to pension those worth under a thousand dollars prevailed, which would have been the substance of the Bill the President recommended, I would have voted for it.

If the Bill which passed had been such a favorite measure with the President, why did not the delegation from Tennessee, his personal and political friends vote for it—none from that state but Mr. T. D. Arnold, who is confessedly opposed to him, supported it, and but three members from this state voted for it. I never was opposed to pensioning those soldiers of the Revolution who are unable to maintain themselves in comfort; still, while perfectly willing to aid them, I could not think of taxing the laboring part of the People to make the rich richer; to pension such men as Gen. Wade Hampton, Col. Wm. Polk, Col. Phil. Hawkins[54] and Mr. Nath'l Macon, and thousands of others with princely estates. To tax the widows and children of the many brave men who fought and died to establish our liberties, would in my opinion be impolitic and unjust. It was not what the President recommended, nor what his friends desired. The Bill that passed is the first in this country that ever proposed to pension the rich. By its provisions the rich as well as the poor, will be living upon the bounty of the government. I could not consent that my constituent, who is not worth more than fifty or a hundred dollars should be taxed to support any man who is worth more than a thousand. This system is worse than a general tax on industry and property, for the relief of the indigent.

A poor rate is a tax imposed on the laboring & wealthy for the support of the poor who are destitute of the means of support; but this Pension Bill inverted the order of things, for the effect is to tax the poor for the support of those who are much wealthier than themselves. It was for the rights of even the poorest that I contended. Mr. Jefferson said, "take not from the mouth of labor the bread it has earned." Taxation, Fellow Citizens, is one of the greatest causes of poverty. I looked on the pension bill as an entire gratuity to the Revolutionary soldiers. I did not consider that the government owed them a debt. It is well known that every man was paid for his services; yet I was willing to lend a helping hand to the poor and needy, *but not the rich.*

As I have mentioned the names of Col. Phil. Hawkins, now no more, and Mr. Nathaniel Macon, I must do them the justice to state that I have been informed that they disapproved of the Bill, and never applied for a pension. Fellow citizens, there is

[54]He was a member of Tryon's staff at the battle of Alamance. He served as a member of the Provincial Congress in 1776, and the state legislature in 1787, 1789, 1803, 1805-1808, 1810, 1811, and 1817-1818. During the war he was a colonel. He died January 1833. Ashe, *Biog. Hist. of N. C.*, V, 139-143.

another charge it devolves on me to refute, with this I do not tax either Mr. Gilliam or Mr. Williams. It is that I cost the State five thousand dollars by sending papers, speeches, messages, &c. to the people of the District. I positively deny it. What I did forward to my constituents, I paid for with my own funds, except those with which as a member of the House I was furnished by its order, and they were transmitted through the medium of that conveyance government has provided. The franking privilege is giv[en to] members of Congress, in order that they may inform [their] constituents of the proceedings of Congress & that they m[ay] diffuse information free of expense, which many are unable to pay. With these remarks I conclude.

Very respectfully, your Fellow Citizen,
MICAJAH T. HAWKINS.

Warren County, June 27th. 1833.

Warrenton, N. C.

Reporter Press—

WPM-LC

W. Nichols, Jr.,[55] *to Willie P. Mangum*

FAYETTEVILLE July 16.th 1833—

Hon. W. P. Mangum
Dear Sir,

Since I had the pleasure of seeing you at Washington, I have been designated by the Executive of Georgia, Engineer to perform certain surveys authorized by the Legislature of that State, and to report to their next Session—

Being unknown in Georgia I take the liberty of requesting of you letters to Mr Wilde,[56] & Gov Troup,[57] gentlemen whose acquaintance I am desirous to make, and an introduction from yourself will be particularly gratifying to me—I take the liberty of making this from the flattering conviction that your favourable consideration will induce you readily to comply with it; and

[55]Possibly William Nichols, an architect, who designed several buildings in Edenton and the old state Capitol at Raleigh. Johnson, *Ante-Bellum N. C.*, 666; Battle, *Hist. of U. N. C.*, I, 282.

[56]Richard Henry Wilde, a native of Ireland, moved to Augusta, Georgia, in 1802 where he became a merchant, lawyer, and political figure. After serving as solicitor general of Richmond County, Georgia, and attorney general, he was elected to Congress in 1815. He served in 1815-1817, 1825, and 1827-1835. He traveled in Europe from 1835 to 1840. In 1843 he moved to New Orleans and served as professor of law at the University of Louisiana until his death in 1847. *Biog. Dir. of Cong.*, 1699.

[57]George M. Troup.

because my friends in Alabama being engaged in canvassing throughout the State, I could not apply to them with so much certainty of finding them at home, and in N. C. there is no other public individual, of my acquaintance whose friendly recommendation I would feel honoured in bearing.

As I intend visiting Columbia So. Ca. during the next session of their Legislature, a letter to Gov. Hayne[58] would confer on me additional obligation

Be pleased to direct your favour to Milledgeville as early as convenient to you—

With high respect
Your Obt Svt
W. NICHOLS JR—

[Addressed:]
To/
Hon. Willie P. Mangum
Red Mountain P: Office
Orange
N. Carolina.

WPM-LC

John Chavis to Willie P. Mangum

July 30th. 1833—

My dear Sir/

I think of you & your family daily & w^{d}. be glad to know of your welfare at all times, consequently not to see you nor to hear from you directly is a pain I am unwilling to bear any longer, therefore I have taken up my pen again—

I am glad to hear that you are exerting yourself in behalf of G. Barringer election, which causes me to hope that you are now willing to extend the charter of the United State Bank, nor do you blame him for voting for the enforcing bill For my part I have never blamed him for one vote he has given since he has been in Congress therefore I should be exceedingly sorry if he should not be elected, not only because I think him to be a faithful servant, but because of his pecuniary situation—

[58]Robert Y. Hayne.

I read with much satisfaction, the debate between Calhoun & Webster;[59] because from these I discovered that you had given me the true character. And although the former was radical on the wrong side of the question—yet the description Webster gave of his struggles was truly picturestic of the strength of his mind—

The contrast between Webster & Clay was one amongst the best things I ever read, & which corresponded also with the character you had given me of the two men—

I have long believed Clay to be a tryed & faithful patriot & I think his Tariff question proves it beyond a doubt & I do think that you must have a more favourable opinion of him than you had when I saw you last. & less opinion of G. Jackson (tho I approved of every letter of his proclamation) It was my firm belief that the Nullifiers had some hope of support from some other quarter than their own & I stated to some of my neighbours that I feared that these hopes were fixed upon G. J. that they thought that they had seen or discovered something in him that favoured their scheme, & you see that Calhoun came out boldly upon the subject, & it is plain to me that he would not have said what he did in the teeth of G. J. if it had not been so. And this was the foundation upon which those bitter daring & degrading Toast of the Nullifiers on the late 4th of July & which I was sorry to see—

The character given of Mr. John Randolph by some writers corresponds completely with the character you gave of him. He certainly was a man of an uncommon brilliancy of Talent, & had he been a uniform steady character, would have been one of the greatest statesmen that America could have boasted of — But pray what has taken place between you & Mr Harris[60] of Oxford, that you should have refused his hand & that he offered you a Pistol in presence of a number of gentlemen, & that you told him that you did not regard the bite of a seed tick nor a flee nor a chinch? I am sorry that you should be under the necessity of offending any of your neighbours or their children; because I would wish you could live in peace with all men. Not only for

[59]When Calhoun took his seat in the Senate in January 1833, he introduced some resolutions which embodied his nullification views. He then waited for three weeks for Webster to open the debate. Finally on February 15-16 he spoke and was followed by Webster, who attacked Calhoun's resolutions. This permitted Calhoun to call up his resolutions for debate. In his first speech he cautiously avoided explaining in much detail his constitutional views until after Webster had replied. Webster followed and according to his friends demolished Calhoun. Calhoun took careful notes on Webster's speech and a week later presented an argument that his friends felt was unanswerable. Webster made no serious reply. Charles M. Wiltse, *John C. Calhoun, Nullifier, 1829-1839*, Indianapolis, 1949, 188-195; William M. Meigs, *The Life of John Caldwell Calhoun*, New York, 1917, II, 10-18.

[60]See above, I, 585n.

you own sake but of that Mrs. Mangum & her children I have no doubt but you a just cause as you supposed for acting as you did, if it was so. I expect he had been dashing away at your political course—I myself was insulted a few days ago. a certain gen^{tn} came into my school house & told me to my face, that he believed that you were a Nullifier and I gave him a shot upon the spot, & sent him off hoping. You may blame me for that if you will, but when you are assailed I will speak right or wrong—no matter who it is too, & if I never see you again I am unshaken—

I am told that my son Priestly is likely to lose his election, & that it will be soly & alone, owing to his stuborn & unyielding disposition. Strange that he cannot or will not call to recollection that from the beginning of time to this moment, to be useful—, a man must be condesending, That the ignorance & prejudice of mankind must be met & overcome by genuine Phylosophy? That proud dignity & independency of character, as he calls it, appears to have swept all Idea of Philosophic experiments from his mind; & if he does not mind will instantly bring him to be a blank in election & his wife & children to suffer both in wealth & character This will be the evident consequence and I am sorry for it & I wish him to know what I say that after I am dead he may think of it and I wish he may do it before it is too late—

My wifes affliction has caused her to be a dead letter to the family ever since last Nov^{r} & I fear it will ever be the case—

I am now teaching a small school at home & it is all that I am able to do. & shall not be able to teach long for I am losing my hearing fast. Then what shall I do?

Give my love to Mrs Mangum & tell her I see her & her children daily & w^{d}. be glad to know what she has done with Sally. That if I could leave my family I would spend the next winter with her. If my wife dies before me I shall expect to come home there——

After the bustle of the election & the Courts are over I shall expect a letter from you to Rogers store

I am the same old two & sixpence
JOHN CHAVES

[Addressed:]
Hon. Willie P. Mangum Esqr
Red Mountain
Orange

WPM-LC

D. L. Barringer to Willie P. Mangum

RALEIGH 13th August 1833.

My dear Judge

Mr. Dilliard[61] is on his Horse at the door, and I cannot now do more than say a word to you. I have come well through a severe contest—versus a powerful combination—The vote in the contest is

	Barringer	McLean[62]
Orange	908	1518
Person	146	789
Wake	1443	129
	2497	2436

Let no man hereafter desire to encounter Bank vetoes & Jackson influence. Write me a word how you & yours are. I hear that Deberry[63] has Beaten Bethune,[64] & believe it—I should like to see you—and perhaps shall before long.

My best respects to Maj Jeff Horner[65] & your father & Mrs. M. ever yours

D. L. BARRINGER.

[Addressed:]
Hon
W. P. Mangum
Orange
Foward by)
)
M. Dillard Esq.)

[61]William Dillard was postmaster at Dillardville, Orange County. McIver, *N. C. Register*, 70.

[62]William L. McLean was a member of the state legislature in 1819-1823, 1827-1829, and 1831-1833. *N. C. Manual*, 526-527.

[63]Edmund Deberry, the owner of cotton and flour mills in Montgomery County, was a member of the legislature in 1806, 1811, 1813-1814, 1820-1821, and 1826-1828. He was in Congress in 1829-1831, 1833-1845 and 1849-1851. He became a Whig. *Biog. Dir. of Cong.*, 893.

[64]Lauchlin Bethune of Cumberland County was in the legislature in 1817, 1818, 1822-1825, 1827, and in Congress from 1831 to 1833. *Biog. Dir. of Cong.*, 697.

[65]Major Jefferson Horner, a neighbor and friend of Mangum, was a justice of the peace and later became a colonel of the local militia. *Hillsborough Recorder*, Sept. 10, 1834.

WPM-LC

Richd: H. Mosby[66] *to Willie P. Mangum*

MR LEATHER'S Septr 15th: 1833

Dear Sir

When I left Hillsboro on yesterday I neglected to mention to you; that I was desirous of obtaining further information from the 3d auditor—I am authorised by David Mebane[67] Esqr of this county to make the necessary inquiries of the Auditor relative to Col: Robert Mebane[68] who was first attached to the 7th: N. Ca. Regiment and afterwards to the 3d Reg: My object is to know if his pay Bounty Lands, & commutation pay, appear to have been settled— My want of health, (and at the time this subject was mentioned to me;) being ingaged in other inquiries I neglected to procure a written request from Mr Mebane to the auditor— You may rely on the fact that I am authorized to make the inquiry—I shall esteem it another link in the chain of obligation already incur'd by me, on this subject— if you will write the auditor saying that Mr Mebane is known to you; and that the inquiries; is made at his instance and request through me— and request the auditor to make to me an answer, stating the result of his inquiries; and the showing of the records of his office— and direct it to Woodsworth Stoore Granville cty N Ca—

I am well aware my dear sir that these applications so often repeated on my part are troublesome; but I trust when you reflect that information can only be had through you or some similar channel I shall stand disabused from importunity—in other words from my knowledge of *you* I feel less reluctance in making an appeal to your courtesy and urbanity than any other person of my acquaintance in this country—

I am really so much indisposed as scarcely to know what I have written in Haste I remain with sentiments of respect and Esteem You & C RICHD: H MOSBY

Write the auditor as soon as convenient—

[Addressed:] R H M

To the Hnble/ Orange County
Willie P. Mangum No Ca—

---

[66]Brother of John G. Mosby of Richmond, Virginia, he was an attorney who handled the pension cases of veterans living in Orange, Granville, and Warren counties. He owned a large plantation in Halifax County. *Johnson, Ante-Bellum N. C.*, 474-475.

[67]Youngest son of General Alexander Mebane and brother of James Mebane, he was a member of the state legislature from Orange County in 1805-1806 and 1808-1810. *N. C. Manual*, 739.

[68]Col. Robert Mebane was a colonel in the North Carolina Continental Line from 1776 to 1778. He saw action in Pennsylvania and South Carolina. He was captured at Charleston in 1780 and died in 1781. Ashe, *Biog. Hist. of N. C.*, VII, 329-330.

John Randolph of Roanoke. From the original water color which hung in Mangum's home, Walnut Hall, and which is now in possession of Mangum Weeks, Alexandria, Va.

WPM-LC

Affidavits in Support of Hardeman Duke's Application For a Pension[69]

STATE OF NORTH CAROLINA

ORANGE COUNTY

Oct 5, 1833

Be it known that before me Harrison Parker a Justice of the Peace in & for said County personally appeared Hardeman Duke & made oath in dur form of Law, that he is the identical Hardeman Duke named in the original certificate in his possession, of which (I certify) the following is a true copy:—

"War Department—Revolutionary claim. I certify that in conformity with the law of the United States of the 7th June 1832, Hardeman Duke of the State of North Carolina, who was a private in the army of the revolution, is entitled to receive Eighty dollars & — Cents per annum, during his natural life, commencing on the 4th of March 1831 & payable semiannually, on the 4th of March, & 4th of September, in every year.

Given at the War [O]ffice of the United States, this thirty first day of January, one thousand eight hundred & thirty three,—

LEW. CASS
Secretary of War

Examined &
Countersigned
J. L. Edwards

[69]Although most affidavits for pensions are omitted from this publication, these are included because of an earlier reference. See above, I, 486. In 1832, under Jackson's influence, Congress passed a bill to liberalize military pensions. Prior to this act, a veteran had to prove that he had been in the Continental army or navy to obtain a pension. In the act of 1832 any person who completed two years of service, whether in the state or Continental forces, would receive less a month but he would still receive a pension for life. Very few states kept accurate records. Consequently, the secretary of war accepted affidavits of persons of the community. In January 1833, a total of 24,260 in the country applied for pensions. Glasson, *Federal Military Pensions*, 81-83.

that he now resides in Orange county No. Carolina & has resided there during the whole of his life, being now seventy three or four years—

Sworn to & subscribed this 5th day of October 1833, before me.

Know all men by these presents, that I Hardeman Duke pensioner of the United States, do hereby constitute & appoint Thomas Horner of Orange County, North Carolina, my true & lawful attorney for me & in my name, to receive from the agent of the United States for paying pensions in Fayetteville the State of North Carolina my pension from the 4th day of March 1833 to the 4th day of September 1833.

Witness my hand & seal this 5th day of October, 1833.

(Seal)

Sealed & delivered
in presence of

STATE OF NORTH CAROLINA)
ORANGE COUNTY)

Be it known that on the 5th day of October 1833 before the subscriber, a Justice of the Peace in & for said County, personally appeared Hardeman Duke above named, and acknowledged the foregoing power of attorney to be his Act & Deed— In Testimony whereof I have hereunto set my hand, the day and year above mentioned—

STATE OF NORTH CAROLINA)
ORANGE COUNTY)

I John Taylor Clerk of the Court of Pleas & Quarter Sessions for Orange County & said State, Certify that Harrison Parker is a Justice of the Peace & Magistrate as above and that the foregoing signatures purporting to be his, are genuine.

In Testimony whereof I have hereunto affixed my seal of Office & subscribed my name this the day of October A.D. 1833.—

Clerk of the Court of Orange County.

WPM-LC

Will Gaston to Willie P. Mangum

NEWBERN October 26th 1833

Dear Sir,

At a large and numerous meeting of the citizens of the Town of Newbern and the County of Craven, of which meeting I had the honor to be Chairman, it was resolved that the Senators and representatives in Congress from this State should be respectfully and earnestly requested to urge on the completion of the operations at occacock with all practicable energy. In communicating to you this Resolution I take the liberty of adding that we have every reason to believe that those charged with the care of these operations have in the course of the present year, carried on the work (so far as the limited means in their power would permit) very efficiently and with great success. It must be admitted also that until the feasibility of the plan had been practically demonstrated, it was not to have been expected that a large expenditure would have been laid out on a doubtful project; and it is certainly true that until lately such different opinions prevailed as to the probable permanence of an artificial channel, and even as to its effect if permanent, in creating new impediments to navigation, that it was irrational to pronounce confidently whether the proposed scheme would or would not result in any great public good. But, *now,* Sir, I can venture to say that with all intelligent persons who have taken pains to examine and enquire, *these doubts are at an end.* A channel has been made over and through shoals of four and five feet more than eight feet deep, which has already superseded the use of all others for vessels from this section of the State. The sides of this Channel are solid and firm, and no difficulty is found in the way of rendering it equally deep with the waters above and below it. The opening of this channel instead of creating new impediments to navigation has by the more rapid flow of the tide through it up and down removed much obstruction without artificial help. There is now an almost moral certainty that the great end contemplated by these operations, the removal of all impediments to navigation for vessels which can come over occacock, may be accomplished if these operations be but prosecuted with vigour, skill and perseverance. It is impossible for any man to foresee all the consequences which would result from the accomplishment of this great object. It is enough to say that the removal of the main obstacle to the commerce of three fourths of the maritime country of North Carolina must give to the whole State a most powerful impulse in the career of prosperity.

In behalf of those by whom I am commissioned to address you, as well as in my character of a citizen of North Carolina, I trust that I shall be excused for strongly inviting your attention to this interesting subject, and requesting that you will use your best exertions (so far as your sense of duty will justify) in having such appropriations made, and causing such energetic measures to be taken, as will procure for our State this inestimable benefit as soon as may be.

I have the honor to be, Sir, respectfully,

Your obt servant

WILL: GASTON

[Addressed:]

Hon. W. P. Mangum

U. S. Senate.

WPM-LC

Colin McIver[70] to Willie P. Mangum

FAYETTEVILLE (N. C.) 21st November 1833

Dear Sir,

Although I have not had the pleasure of often meeting with you, in person, since the period at which you were a student, & I was a Tutor, in the Fayetteville Academy, yet, I take it for granted, that you have not altogether forgotten me. Presuming on the slight acquaintance then formed, I take the liberty of addressing you, on a subject in which I feel some interest; & which, I persuade myself, you will not regard with indifference.

For reasons which, perhaps, it is not necessary now to state, I am desirous to spend the time of the approaching Session of Congress, in the City of Washington. It would be a convenience, & some advantage to me, therefore, if, through the influence of a few personal friends, I could obtain the appointment of chaplain to one of the Houses of Congress, during the approaching Session of that Body. It is my intention, should I have an opportunity of seeing my friend, Mr. Deberry on his way to Washington, to request him to put me in nomination. In the event of his doing so, should it comport with your inclination, & your views of duty, to favour me with your vote, together with all the influence you can command, in relation to this appointment, I will esteem such a favour, as a singular kindness.

---

[70]Rev. Colin McIver, who tutored Mangum while the latter was a student at the Fayetteville Academy, was a Presbyterian minister. In 1823 he published the *North Carolina Register and the United States Calendar*, which is a storehouse of information, and in 1828 he added the *Evangelical Mission* and *The Virginia and North Carolina Presbyterian Preacher*, two monthly pamphlets. Johnson, *Ante-Bellum N. C.*, 747, 802, 811.

Excuse this trouble; & believe me to be, with much esteem
Dear Sir, Yours truly,

COLIN MCIVER

P. S. Should you be favourably disposed, in relation to the within request; & should you find, on conversing with other members, that there will be a greater probability of success in the Senate than in the House of Representatives, you will oblige me, by putting me in nomination,

Yours again,
C. McI.

[Addressed:]

The Hon[ble] Wyllie P. Mangum. M. C.
Hillsborough
Orange County
North Carolina

If Mr. Mangum should)
have started for Washing-)
ton before this reaches)
Hillsborough', the Post-)
master will please to)
forward it.)

WPM-LC

William S. Fulton[71] *to Willie P. Mangum*

LITTLE ROCK, [ARKANSAS] Novr. 23rd, 1833.

Sir.

May I presume upon the acquaintance made last winter, to ask you to read the enclosed appeal to the Public. I think I have been most unjustly treated by a majority of the House of Representatives of our Territorial Legislature & by the Governor.[72] I am to be assailed before the Senate for presuming to question the

[71]William Savin Fulton, a native of Maryland, moved to Tennessee and later to Alabama, where he practiced law and became a judge. In 1829 Jackson made him secretary of the Arkansas territory to replace Robert Crittenden. In Arkansas he served as governor from 1835 to 1836 and as United States Senator from 1836 to 1844, when he died. *Biog. Dir. of Cong.*, 994.

[72]At the same time that Fulton was appointed secretary of the territory, John Pope, of Kentucky, was made governor. The latter was authorized to build a state house, but the legislature refused to appropriate the money. Pope lobbied in Washington until he was promised 6400 acres of public land to pay for the state house. Thereupon, Crittenden, whom Fulton had replaced as secretary, offered to sell his own house for a state house in exchange for the 6400 acres of land. The legislature agreed, but Pope vetoed the legislature's action. Pope was then authorized to sell the land. He sold it for $5 an acre. By this time Crittenden had become the Governor's agent. Fulton opposed the sale. D. Y. Thomas, *Arkansas and its People: A History, 1541-1930*. New York, 1930, I, 80-83.

powers of the Governor under the acts of Congress granting ten sections of land to this Territory for a Legislative House. You will I think be astonished that so much violence could grow out of such a question. But when I tell you that the Governors Agent is the man who was principally interested and *deeply implicated* in the attempt to defraud the Government of 60,000 acres of public lands; to defeat which I attended the two last winters at Washington, and succeeded in so doing in the Supreme Court, last March, you will discover a motive for the war which is waged against me, and the reason why a simple law question has been converted into a theme for abuse. This man is all powerful in a pecuniary point of view, & has the Governor I fear in his power. I am determined to do my duty faithfully without regard to the efforts made against me, & ask to be sustained by the Senate if I deserve to be sustained. I shall be much indebted to you if you can give me your support.

Your obt st
WM. S. FULTON.

The Honble Willie P. Mangum
Senator from North Carolina.

[Addressed:]
The Honble. Willie P. Mangum
Senate, Congress of the
United States,
Washington City.
D. C.

WPM-LC

T. B. Littlejohn[73] *to Willie P. Mangum*

OXFORD 4th. Dec. 1833

My dear Sir

I had promised myself the pleasure of seeing you before you went on to Washington, supposing you would pass through this place on your way there—but I learned yesterday only that you had gone on through Raleigh— The object of this letter is to remind you of my *anxious* wish to obtain a warrant for my son James Thompson Littlejohn[74] to enter the institution at West-

[73]Thomas B. Littlejohn was a justice of the peace of Granville County and a trustee of the Oxford Academy. McIver, *N. C. Register,* 29; Coon (ed.), *N. C. Schools and Academies,* 133, 150, 554.

[74]He did not receive an appointment.

point, and to request your friendly aid in his behalf *as early as possible,* before the vacancies are filled, as it is presumeable there will be many applications.—You were kind enough to promise me that you would endeavour to secure the co-operation of the Honbl. Bedford Brown in pressing the Claims of my son, provided he was not committed in favor of some young friend of his own, and it was on this account I did not write to him myself; which I would otherwise have done, and I hope you will be good enough to assign to him the reason for my not doing so.—I am aware that it requires the aid of strong friends to succeed in such an application, unless the *influence* of some part of the representation in Congress from one State should be exerted in favor of the applicant, and I had intended to have requested the recommendation of a few intimate & influential friends to the Secretary at War—say Gov. Stokes,[75] the Honbl. Nath. Macon, Gov. Burton[76] & one or two others, which might probably have had considerable weight, but relying mainly on *your influence,* aided, as I hoped it would be, by that of your Honble. colleague Bedford Brown Esq., I have neglected to solicit letters from them, although I have good reasons to believe they would readily give them on application—the removal of Gov. Stokes to Arkansas might *now* render it difficult to obtain one from him; but if you think it *important* that I should procure letters to the Secy. at War, and that I could have time to obtain them after hearing from you, I will thank you advise me immediately, and will be glad you would refer me to such persons as you conceive would be most likely to render me the most effectual aid, provided I should be able to obtain letters from them.—I have supposed the privilege you would have a right to claim in filling some of the vacancies in that institution, added to your influence with the War & other departments of the Government, would supersede the necessity of any other recommendations than from the State delegation in Congress—I have no doubt my friend Mr. Rensher;[77] if you will mention the subject to him, will join you heartily, in behalf of my application for *James,* so will Mr. Shepard from the Edenton district, if you desire it, & will inform him that I will feel thankful to him for his aid & influence in this

[75]Montford Stokes was governor of the state and a member of the board of visitors of the Military Academy. In 1832 he was appointed by Jackson to an Indian commission in the Southwest. William O. Foster, "The Career of Montford Stokes in North Carolina," *N. C. Hist. Rev., XVI* (1939), 237-272.

[76]Hutchins Gordon Burton was governor from 1824 to 1827. See above, I, 154n.

[77]Abraham Rencher. See above, I, 322n.

behalf—although not personally acquainted with Mr. Shepard,[78] I will presume to take this liberty, as he is a distant connection, with whose father I was *very intimate & friendly*— Maj. Balie Peyton[79] representative from Tennessee, although a *new* member, & not of *our* State, is a *thorough going Jackson man,* & may possibly, in some form, throw some weight in the scale—If you can profit by any influence which he should be able to exert, you may let him know that I have informed you, he had been good enough to say to me he would cheerfully promote the object of my application in any way he might be able to do.—I have not yet written to the Sec^y^. at War, requesting the name of my son to be placed among the Candidates—If it is necessary that I should write myself to that effect, please inform me, or if it can answer the same purpose, will you have the goodness to have James Thompson Littlejohn (aged 17 years) enrolled among the candidates for admission at West point—You will confer a favor upon me by writing me as soon after receipt of this as you can find leisure, and giving me such information & directions in the premises as you think it important I should have—

I am very respectfully & truly Yr. obt. Svt.

THO. B. LITTLEJOHN

N.B. I am sorry to inform you that Doct. B. Bullock's son *Peter*[80] was accidentally killed in Mississippi, very recently, by your brother Mr. Walter Mangum, who discharged his gun at a Deer, not seeing young Bullock, who unfortunately was in a range with the Deer.—Doct. William Jones of this County, who was at my house this morning, on his way home from that State, brings this melancholy intelligence—he did not see your brother Walter himself, but Col. Wm. H. Bullock of this county, his travelling companion, was either at the house, or in the immediate neighborhood of your brother about 3 weeks ago, when he & his family were well, except the distress produced by the above unhappy event.—

[Addressed:]

The Honorable

Willie P. Mangum Esqr. Washington City

[78]William Biddle Shepard, a graduate of the University of Pennsylvania, read and practiced law in Camden County and Elizabeth City. In the latter place he also became a banker. In 1829 he entered Congress as a National Republican and served until 1837. A Whig in the latter period, he served in the legislature and on several state boards, including the board of trustees of the state university. *Biog. Dir. of Cong.*, 1517.

[79]Peyton was born near Gallatin, Tennessee, in 1803. Although in his early days a Jackson supporter, he soon became a Whig. Serving in Congress from 1833 to 1837, he refused a cabinet post in Tyler's administration. He moved to New Orleans and became the United States attorney. After serving in the Mexican War, he was minister to Chile and, subsequently, prosecuting attorney in San Francisco. *Biog. Dir. of Cong.*, 1406.

[80]See above, I, 444.

WPM-LC

Ezekiel Brewer[81] *to Willie P. Mangum*

December [torn] - - - 1833 Dear Sir I applide to [torn] [Mo]rris the brother of nat morris henry morris andison morris and he told me he was about twelve years of age when they in Sistted you wood be So Cind to apply to the old ginrel for he Command them nat and andeson at the battle at the hawshew and march nat anderson down to new alleans and fout the battle there they parted with the old ginral [torn] they twook Sick and dide henry morris dide on missurry River a garden the fruntteer part they enlisted under James rheagin I am with Respect your umble Sarvent

EZEKIEL BREWER

W. P. Mangum

[Addressed:]
Hon. Wilie P. Mangum
Washington Citty

WPM-LC

——— *to Willie P. Mangum*[82]

Talberton
Georgia

DECEMBER 14th 1833—

To the Honorable Judge Wiley P Mangum
I wish you to Recollect me when I met you at Upchurches in Wake county and I done all I could for you according as I promised you I now call on you for Some Information consering

[81]See below, a letter of Ezekiel Brewer to W. P. Mangum, Jan. 19, 1835.

[82]A typed copy of this letter is in the Mangum Papers, State Department of Archives and History, Raleigh, N. C. The original is not available. The author of this letter is not given.

the Treaty made with the creek nation of Indians[83] The President has ordered out all Intruders forth with and all Peacefull Settlers to leave as Soon as their crops is gathered Say 15th of January next: now the locating agent is ingaged in laying out their claims and it is thought that it will be completed by the 15th of January and as Soon as the Indians gits the locations Run out they wish to sell and the nation is crowed with Speculators and I am at a loss to know how the Rits is to be come at I beg of you that Information and whether the Settlers [torn] be forced to leave those that has peaceable [torn] and made their own farms and whether after the locations, is made we have a Rite to [torn] on the publick lands or not I have lade in goods at New York to take in the nation owing to the low warters my goods are at the appalatchacola bay and Request of you immediate information if you will be good a nuff to do it for me—as I am not acquainted with our Representative in this State as they are Ellected by a Ticket of The whole State So they all live in the Eastern part of the State and we have no Information—only News papers and they differ on the Subject all I wish Is to know how we are to come at an Indian clame and what Steps we are to Take and wheather we Shall after they clames is established have a Rite to Settle the publick lands We are a [illegible] in our Union cause in this State our Ligeslator have a large majority of union Men and all our officers is of that party—the nullifyers is at the end of theer Roe and So much for nullification—

N. B. I hope you will
write me on the Re[t]
of this—

WPM-LC

William Montgomery to Willie P. Mangum

RALEIGH N. C. Dec. 18, 1833.

My dear Sir

We are all, or Nearly so, Mortified at the News from Washington, there is great Excitement and resolutions are before the

[83]By a treaty made on March 24, 1832, the Creeks ceded all their lands east of the Mississippi except individual tracts which were to be held by the Indians for five years or until sold. All intruders were to be removed during this period. Indians were free to migrate or remain on their lands. Whites rushed in and tried to trade Indians out of their reserved lands and the money the government had given them. The Federal government failed to remove the intruders, although the President issued such an order and feebly tried to enforce it. Confusion and strife continued for a year. The governor of Alabama and the county officials defied the Federal enforcement officers. In November, 1833, Francis Scott Key, as the President's representative, worked out a compromise which resulted in the rapid removal of the Creeks and the legalization of the claims of many of the intruders. Foreman, *Indian Removal,* 111-126.

Commons to Instruct, you to vote for [torn] of the [B]ank.[84] I think they will be Lost. But some are sanguine of there success, there is Mutch Feeling as to the Course the Senate[85] are taking at Washington, and I think Before we leave Here Some action Decisive of the strength of the parties will be Had, and I do believe that the Administration will be well sustained I myself Have Nearly dispareed of the union. A House Divided against itself Cannot Stand, the Senate seems to be determined to put down the Administration and support the opposition Men, & it seems now only to be a struggle Between the Bank and the people.

Do write Me soon. Yours &c.

W. MONTGOMERY.

Willie P. Mangum to David L. Swain[86]
Confidential.

WASHINGTON 22nd. Decr. 1833.

My dear Sir.

The present state of parties, and the great results that may be achieved by the efforts of this Winter, & knowing that those efforts on the part of the *Kitchen* are prodigious, lead to this communication.—You will pardon me for addressing you with the purpose I have in this matter.—I know that your position makes it matter of great delicacy to touch general politics.—Nor would I, if I could, have you to violate in the slightest degree the decorums of your station[87]—& yet I feel that the country is entitled to the influence of your great popularity & weight of Character in the pending struggle.—The next six or eight months will probably settled the question of the next Presidency—& with that question every thing else is fixed—For it is obvious, that the whole policy of the Country to a very great extent is controuled by that result. The Campaign this Winter on the part of Mr Van Buren's friends will be exceedingly active—All

---

[84]On December 14, 1833, John S. Guthrie, of Chatham County, introduced resolutions in the state House of Commons to instruct the Senators and to request the Congressmen to use their best influence to secure the recharter of the United States Bank. The resolutions were laid on the table. *Journal of the House of Commons*, 1833-1834, 184.

[85]He refers to the Clay-Calhoun-Webster coalition formed in the Senate in December 1833 to defeat Jackson. This coalition took over the appointment of Senate committees and began its attack on Jackson's removal of deposits. Van Deusen, *Life of Clay*, 278.

[86]The original is in the "Epistolary Correspondence of David L. Swain," IV, North Carolina Room, University of North Carolina, Chapel Hill, N. C. Compare this letter with Swain's reply December 22, 1833.

[87]Swain was governor from 1832 to 1835.

the resources of that bad influence *around* & *under* & *over* the throne will be actively employed.—Every State Legislature, where doubt exists, will be the theatre of active intrigues—And in none, save Pennsylvania where the Kitchen has already met a signal defeat, will those efforts & intrigues be more active or so active as in Virginia & North Carolina.—Gov. Floyd's want of discretion, as well as temper has given & will continue to give the adversary great advantage over him.—But still judging from the best information I can obtain, & my opportunities here are good, I deem it impossible for Van Buren to obtain the vote of that Common Wealth, unless we shall be signally unfortunate in bringing a Candidate into the field.—At present I suppose either Clay or McLean[88] will be the Candidate of the party opposed to Van Buren in the South—My own opinion is unchanged on that subject—I think Clay the best chance in the event he shall place himself in a position not to tread upon our principles,[89] which I think he can honorably do & will do.—Others however, & the number is not small, look with more confidence to Judge McLean.—His politics are not known, & with many, there is strong disinclination to take hold of him, until *they* shall be well understood.—I think either can beat Van Buren, if the contest were single—And if we sustain defeat, I have no doubt it will be occasioned by our divisions.—Our friends[90] to the South I fear, will make difficulties.—I have said & others have said frankly & strongly to their leaders that they must come into the views of the other Souther-States, or the result will be I fear, that they will be cut off from the sympathies of the whole South. They having no views of their own, will be obliged to come in—I think they will, tho not without some difficulty.—This then is the State of the Case at present.—

All opposition here to bad influences, is attributed to *enmity to the hero,* to National republicanism & to nullification.—In these bad times, no man can be honest without being denounced with the sins of hatred of Jackson, nullification &c &c—

The popularity of Jackson on the one hand & the unpopularity of nullification on the other, give the party in power great advantages in the South—& they rely upon them for success—

They will have no one in their ranks unless he go the whole

[88]Judge John McLean, of Ohio, was a perennial candidate for the presidency. He had strong support in the South, especially in North Carolina.

[89]Mangum refers here to the state's rights principles. At this time Mangum was quite friendly to Calhoun.

[90]He refers to South Carolina.

length of sustaining their profligacy. He is not suffered to be friendly to Jackson unless he be likewise friendly to Amos Kendal, Martin Van Buren & all the others & their views—

They hold the terrors of denunciation over the heads of all, & they have to choose between submission to the meanest uses, or to be denounced as the enemies of the President, & as Nullifiers.—You can easily percieve that this terrorism is decisive with many of feeble purpose.

This is the plan of the Campaign in the South connected with Banking &c, which I think is *essentially* weak before the people.—

Prodigious efforts are making, as I have reason to know, to produce an effect upon our Legislature—The object of this letter is single—It is to invoke in the name of all that is dear to us, your influence in counteracting these efforts—I know you can do more than any man in No. Carolina, & that too without seeming to mingle in the strife.—

Certain leaders & through them, the Legislature are constantly plied with the correspondence of the Kitchen—Gen Saunders[91] goes home charged with plenepotentiary powers.—And unless there be effort to counteract, theirs will be decisive—Their object is get an expression of the Legislature favorable to Gen Jackson— & from that, to say & argue all that they desire, to produce effect elsewhere.—Our friends ought to join them as to Jackson cordially, but but [*sic*] *amend* so as to strike a blow at the Kitchen & the *policy* of the Kitchen.—

As the U. S. Bank will not apply this session & probably not to this Congress, for a recharter, I regret that the Bank question has been thrown before the Legislature[92]—The naked question of recharter is much weaker, I presume, than the *Deposite* question[93]—The battle should be fought on the *latter*.—The removal deeply involves the question of *good faith*, as well as all the considerations of policy, & upon the question of faith, I think N.C.[a] will be found strong, if sufficiently enlightened.—I predicate this upon the belief, that we are less corrupted than are the most of our neighbours.—My opinion is, that North Carolina dis-

[91]Romulus M. Saunders was an ardent Jacksonian.

[92]He refers to Guthrie's resolutions.

[93]Secretary Taney issued his order for the removal of deposits in October, 1833.

agrees with the Adm^{n}. in reference to the *public domain*[94] —Clay's Bill[95] upon its great principles, I speak not in reference to all its details, I think falls in with the views of the State generally—

I have twice voted against the measure, upon the ground that until the Tariff was adjusted, I would not *without instruction* entertain any question, that by abstracting from the public revenue, would to that extent be a sort of make-weight in aid of the continuance of the Tariff—No vote of mine has been given on the *merits*—Might not the Legislature, in the event of a movement, such as I anticipate, move that question advantageously?—

Your position before the people of N.C. necessarily connects you to a great extent with all these questions.—If the system of In: Improvement, shall find sufficient favor with the public, which by the bye, I greatly doubt, to go onward with spirit, you may find it to the advantage of the public, as well as most conducive to your own reputation & fame, to which no good man can be insensible, to remain in your present position.—If there shall be a failure, your friends will most probably turn their eyes upon you to take your position in the Senate of the U. States—

What are or may be your personal inclinations in reference to these subjects, it is not my purpose to enquire.—But you must feel well assured that I cannot but feel an interest in having in the Senate one who holds your principles in the main.—You perceive that I take you to hold sound principles in reference to the rights of the States, as well as to this Central machine.—Your public duties have not lead to any public exposition of your views, I know them only from your own conversations, public rumor & principally through Gen. Barringer.[96]—

Though on the one hand far short of So. Ca. nullification yet on the other equally adverse to the antagonist principle of Consolidation.—I foresee that in No. Ca. *The Independents*, as I presume to call myself, or the absolute *submissionists*, (I mean submission to the bad influences here) will wage the war.—There

---

[94]In 1829 eight of the thirteen North Carolina Congressmen had voted for distribution. On the Clay bill of 1832-1833 only three voted for it because the bill did not allow the old states the proportion of the proceeds they desired. When the state legislature met in December, 1833, Governor Swain endorsed distribution. As a result, the lower house passed resolutions memorializing Congress to pass a distribution bill. The state senate tabled it. Distribution soon became a cardinal principle of the North Carolina Whigs. Pegg, "Whig Party in N. C.," 20-25.

[95]On December 10, 1833, Clay proposed the same land bill with minor changes which had been vetoed by Jackson in the previous session. Jackson's veto of the earlier bill was not given to the Senate until December 5. This enabled Clay to attack Jackson for not giving Congress his veto message in time to pass on it during the previous session. *Register of Debates*, 23 Cong. 1 sess., 14-18.

[96]D. L. Barringer.

are fearful odds on the side of the submissionists—all the holders, & hopers for office, will be with them, & besides the power of Gen. Jackson's name will be so used, as to be a tower of strength with the multitude.—The giving of light in active Canvasses, will dispel much of that power, which is the result of an undefined idea that he is as to all his policy, invincible.—In a word—Every man who does not go in for Van Buren, will go down, if he shall go up in N. C.—I have made up my mind.—Though very far from being indifferent to the result. It is exceedingly desirable that nothing shall be done by the Legislature, that will give the appearance of more strength than they have.—In this emergency, I think the Country has a right to the influence of your name and character, as far as is compatible with your duties in other respects.—

It is designed to bring a powerful pressure on me personally, I am feeling it now—My course is taken—I shall give a cordial support, where I can to the admn: But I shall also give what aid I can to the exposure of abuses.—It is on this latter point where there is most sensibility.—I clearly see now, as I have clearly foreseen for several months, that my course would subject me to the most unsparing vituperation of the Collar press here & in No Carolina.[97]—

The only check to as absolute power, as that in Russia is found in the Senate.—The policy of men in power is to destroy that body in public opinion.—Every other branch of the Gov[t]. is unquestionably & almost unqualifiedly subservient to the will & passions of One Man—or to speak more truly, to the will & passions of a Cabal that gives a decided direction to the Executive.—

The daily papers give you all of the Legislative proceedings.—The public men are active—Clay came here under a high pressure—evidently highly charged with the opposition sentiment to North. Webster has been on the point of desertion to the admn. —*There is no mistake in this.*—He insisted upon displacing Clay from the head of the Finance Comm[ee].—The whole admn. force w[d]. have gone for him ag[t]. Clay—and three or four other votes, his own included—Clay, I think, weakly yielded—He says now, that he fears his friend M[r] W. has given himself a fatal stab

[97]The nullification fight had turned Mangum against Jackson, although he had not made an announcement of his change in party alignment. Finally in February, 1834, he announced in a speech in the Senate his shift. In this revealing letter he shows that he was a party to the alignment which would soon make the Whig Party. Mangum soon became an ardent supporter of the Clay program, although he continued to have an attachment for his original state's rights tenets.

among his own friends, but that now if "he deserts, it will be with infamy."—You will perceive that this is a delicate subject, & the expression perhaps, ought not to be repeated.—It is believed that M^{r}. Webster for the residue of the Session, will play in the character of the bat in the fable.—Calhoun absolutely refused to go in for Webster—and altho he (Calhoun) w'd have been elected at the head of the Comm^{ee}. of Foreign Affairs, he said, as the whole matter seemed to be a matter of arrangement, that he w^{d} not accept, and insisted strongly, upon considering it in the light of an injury, if his friends sh^{d}. vote for him.—

He voted for the most of the Comm^{ees}. but says the Northern troops will not fight, that they are interested in perpetuating abuses, that their system in truth, has engendered.—In the Ho of Rep^{s}. there is evidently *at present* an admn. majority, that it is getting weaker daily & less confident, seems to be generally believed.—The great test question will be the displacing of Gales & Seaton—It is not as the News papers say, abandoned—It will probably be moved tomorrow—If they move, they will probably succeed—They count noses closely.

The only obstacle is found in the obstinacy of the South—Some of our people yet retain the antiquated notion, that there ought to be honesty among public men.—

The leaders of the Kitchen Cabinet have day by day, until yesterday, been hanging on & around the H. of Rep^{s}. The day before yesterday, a motion was indignantly made to exclude them from the floor of the House & was lost by a few votes only—They took the hint & yesterday were not in the House.—

Pardon this long affair—I have marked it confidential, meaning *only* that the great freedom with which I write, shall not be exposed, so as to subject me to misrepresentation among my enemies.—All that I say or write is open to friends or candid men.

Accept D^{r}. Sir my high respect & regard & best wishes to all y^{r}. enterprizes

WILLIE P. MANGUM

To
His Excellency
Gov. Swain
Raleigh
N^{o}. Carolina

Silk top hat and leather hat box. The originals are in the possession of Mangum Turner, Winston-Salem, N. C.

Mahogany walking stick with "Mangum" inscribed on the silver head. The original is in the possession of Mangum Weeks, Alexandria, Va.

WPM-LC

C. L. Hinton to Willie P. Mangum

RALEIGH Dec 26th 1833

Dr. Sir

Yours of the 21st I recd yesterday, I regret that my engagements this evening compel me to write in haste, but you shall hear from me in a few days more fully—If there has been much feeling in this place about the course in the Senate I have not heard of it, nor do I believe it, the fact is there is an *apathy*, an *indifference* among the members upon National politicks that I have never witnessed before. You have no idea of the backwardness in expressing of opinions even in private, every one seems as tho he was afraid of committal. The course of Genl. Jackson with regard to the Deposites has but few advocates. Van Buren is not nor cant be a favourite in N. C. Mr. Clay has been and is still growing but the members of the Legislature are not prepared to come out openly for him. I dont think there is any one man that is a favourite at this time if Mr Clay was the opposing Candidate it might drive many back to the Van Buren ranks but I am inclined to think he is much the stronger of the two. I have heard nothing said of any resolutions being about to be brought in upon the subject, I should expect they are unwilling to risque it—

There is an effort making this evening to compromise to Convention question. I am in hopes it will succeed. the object is to give the East the ascendency in the Senate and the West in the other branch.

Lawrence & Lemay[98] request me to say to you they should be pleased to hear from you.

In haste
Your friend
C L Hinton

[Addressed:]
To the
Honble. Willie P. Mangum
Washington City

[98]Editors of the Raleigh *Star*. They were also state printers.

WPM-LC

D. L. Swain to Willie P. Mangum[99]

RALEIGH 27. Dec. 1833.

[Torn]

Your favour of the 22d inst. is before me. I have no leisure to answer it now, & cannot promise myself an opportunity of doing so, until the close of the Session. I write this merely as a note of preparation, for a more free and explicit correspondence on all the topics embraced by your letter.

If you were here, the conversational talent which you possess so preeminently and exercise so fully, might enable you to elicit something from public men with respect to national politics. But I cannot. No man mentions the names of the aspirants to the purple—A listlessness prevails to an extent that I have never before witnessed. If I were to hazard a guess, I would say that one fourth of the members of Assembly seem for Van Buren & a fourth for Clay & that the [torn] half do [torn] whom theyd [Several lines are missing because the letter is badly torn]

much doubt w[hether] any friends of Mr. Van Buren will even risque the introduction of a resolution laudatory of Genl. Jackson, & it is certain that no descreet man will venture to obtain an approval of his course with respect to the Bank.

Genl. Saunders is here—With what object he may have come on I do not know. If for the purpose you suggest, he has arrived at the conclusion that the better part of valour is discretion. He holds communion with few, & will not have the temerity I imagine either to make or advise a demonstration. It is very certain that Mr. Van Buren is not a favorite in North Carolina;—Nullification & he are in decided minorities, & the latter can succeed only when the contest shall settle down, between him & a disciple of that doctrine.

As before [Several lines are torn out of the letter]

Yours very Sincerely,

D. L. SWAIN.

I shall be glad to hear from you at all times & the sooner & oftener the better.

[Addressed:]

To The Honble. Willie P. Mangum,
Washington City.

---

[99]Compare this letter with Mangum's letter to Swain, December 22, 1833.

WPM-LC.

William Montgomery to Willie P. Mangum

RALEIGH N. C. Decm 27th 1833

My Dear Sir

We are getting along — Here Badly — the State bank Has Failed in the Commons, a Bill passed its Last Reading—this Day in the Senate with a Capital of $1,,600,,000, Individuals to take $900,,000, and the State $600,,000, if she will, the Commons passed Finally this Day a bill to Recharter the Capefear Bank, and a Bill to Create a Bank in Newburn, and one in Edenton all these and perhaps More Will pass; some 4 or 5 Railroad Charters are before us, and resolutions Before the House of Commons,[100] to Instruct and request, our Members, in Congress to go for a recharter of the U. S. Bank, should they Be Called up, Mutch Warmth Will be Excited, they are spoken of in the Senate We are ready and Waiting, there is Mutch Excitement Here about the general politics of the Country, and We are (your old Friends) More than Mortifyed at the Course you are taking in the Senate, and many severe anathamas are Made against you, and your Friends Reproached, For your Course, they all say you, were Elected by the Administration Men, and to support the Administration, and that you Have, gone over to our Enimies; it is believed Here, that, the Majority of the Senate are determined to parilise the government, and thereby Make it unpopular, and it is useless to say What Feelings sutch a belief is Calculated to produce, Mr Calhoun and Clay are Now Considered as Insepperately alliied associated and Bound together as the Simese twins, and Set out to distroy this government, or rule it.

[100]The following banks were chartered by this legislature: Bank of Cape Fear (rechartered), Merchants Bank of New Bern, Albemarle Bank of Edenton, and the Bank of the State of North Carolina. The following railroads were chartered: Campbellton and Fayetteville; Greenville and Roanoke; Halifax and Weldon; Roanoke and Raleigh; Roanoke and Yadkin; Portsmouth and Roanoke (amended); and the Petersburg R. R. Co. *N. C. Laws*, 1833-1834, 88-142.

In the Former of which they May succeed, But Success in the Latter is Before the people Impossible; I again repeat What I Before wrote you, that I dispair of the union, the people the presidant and the House of representatives go For the government, and the Senate, (With the power to do so,) Seem determineed to parilise all; its apperations, It is useless to disguise the Fact, that there does Exist Here, a strong Feeling, against the Course, the Majority of the Senate is taking and it daily Increases, and it is By No means Certain that it Will not yet Be the subject of action before the assembly; it is threatened; I Have written In strong Language, but not Stronger than Here Expressed; I would Like to Hear From you, By Letter, soon; I Have to acknowledge the receipt of several Favours From you since Congress Met, With great regard and High Esteem

Yours. &c
W. MONTGOMERY

[Addressed:]
Hon[bl]. Wiley P. Mangum
Senate U. S. Congress
Washington City- D, a,

WPM-LC

A. W. Mebane[101] to Willie P. Mangum

RALEIGH Decm. 30th 1833

Hon. W. P. Mangum
Dr Sir

I hope you will excuse me for the liberty I now take of making a few inquiries, in relation to the very important matters now transpiring or about to transpire at Washington. A great deal of interest is felt by many persons here, as to the course the Senate will take on the subject of the deposites, Will they reject Mr. Taney? Will the consequences of Van Buren's rejection have no Warning influence? Will the Nullifiers & Nationals unite & form a second Holy alliance—? Will the men who were ready to go to extremities because of the Tariff—now unite with the tyrants (as they called them) who imposed it on them—merely

[101]Alexander W. Mebane, of Bertie County, was a member of the state legislature in 1829-1830, and 1833-1837. *N. C. Manual,* 503.

to gratify their unhallowed opposition to Gen. Jackson— & thereby lend their aid to an institution long [si]nce denounced as unconstitutional & inimica[l] [torn] Government—by the immortal Jeff[erson]. A resolution was introduced in the house of Commons early in the session instructing our Senators &C. to do what they could to get the deposites restored—it was laid on the table—to take a Van Winkle nap—So far from its passing the legislature—I am satisfied that the reverse of it—can be passed by a large majority I have no knowledge of your Views on this subject—as I had not the pleasure of your company during your stay in this place—but I have a distinct recollection of the pleasure with which I heard you descant on such general questions in 1830—It is but justice to myself to say—that with me, you have always been a favorite & that I have not been backward in denouncing such insinuations as were levelled at you during the summer of 32— & candour compels me to say that wanton rumour has not been idle since you left here— The reports that—during your stay here—you gave strong indication of entertaining different views—very different, from those of your friends—who stood by you in 1830—

I Sir—claim no right of interrogation on these matters other than that of a constituent—. I have often heard you speak in high terms of commendation of the Ronoak Country—of their firmness & republicanism—. they are equally firm now—equally republican & equally ready to support the [torn] -ure they believed themselves supporting in 1830

We shall adjourn about the 10 Jan— I hope you will receive the few remarks I have made in the friendly Spirit that dictated them— & excuse the haste that has presented them in so rough a garb

I am very respectfully your obt. St.,
A. W. MEBANE.

[Addressed:]
Hon Willie P. Mangum
Washington City.

WPM-LC

C. L. Hinton to Willie P. Mangum

RALEIGH Dec 30th 1833

My Dear Sir

A few days ago I wrote you in haste in answer to yours of the 23d, I believe, promising at the same time a more detailed statement of affairs here when an opportunity offered. I have leisure this evening, but dont know that I could give you any additional information with respect to the political feelings of our Legislature, but from my associations on yesterday (Sunday,) am the more confirmed that there is a listlessness that is very unusual—as an evidence of it I neither hear censure or approval of the votes of yourself or Brown,. Mr Clays speech reached here last night in the daily Intelligencer, I have not seen it but those who have speak of in the most extravagant terms, as they do also of Mr. Mc Duffee,s[102]—If there be a design to bring any political question before the Legislature I have not heard of it, nor do I believe that it would be permitted thus late in the session—Should it be attempted the removal of the deposites shall not be overlooked—. Our Supreme court met to day, to the disappointment and *great mortification* of many of the members, Judge Ruffin was appointed Chief Justice, there is a great deal of murmering among Gastons friends. It was what I expected. Upon the meeting of the court Daniel[103] broke silence—Well Gentlemen the Court must be organized a Chief Justice must be appointed, I would not have it, Mr Gaston is the oldest Lawyer, Judge Ruffin the elder Judge—Neither R nor G spoke—Well I'll draw lots, so putting the two names in the hat, he drew out Ruffin—

Our Legislature will do nothing with Internal improvement more than to grant Charters to private companies, she will not even employ Engineers to make the surveys—I expect we shall make several Banks, the Bank of the State upon the mixed principle has passed the senate and the extension of the Cape fear has passed the House, the private Banks of Newbern and Edenton may possibly pass—The Governor gives a great *to do.* tomorrow night, he has invited about 500, persons—he favoured me with a perusal of your letter, he says your *skin* is *too thin.* he intends at a more leisure time to give you his opinions and principles in full, notwithstanding I believe I understand him, I should like to see them committed to paper

Say to Barringer that we have not reported on remodeling the districts nor do I believe we can do it time enough for the present Legislature to act—Let me hear from you occasionally

Your friend
C L H

[Addressed:]
Jan 1 To the
Honble Willie P. Mangum Washington City

[102]George McDuffie, of South Carolina. See *D. A. B.*, XII, 34-36.
[103]Joseph John Daniel.

WPM-LC

John G. Mosby[104] *to Willie P. Mangum*

RICHMOND Decr. 31st 1833.

Sir,—

By the directions of my brother Richd H. Mosby of North Carolina, I take the liberty of forwarding you the case of Lieut James Scurloe of the Continental line of N. Carolina in the Army of the Revolution; accompanied by a Petition of his administradetrix & widow for his Commutation pay, which my brother desires you will lay before Congress in the manner you may deem most conducive to its success

The *strength* of the claim rests on a Report made to the Senate in 1828, under a Resolution of that body of the 16th of January of that year—This Report shows all of the Conti^l^. Line who at that time were entitled to Land Bounty from the U. States. Now no one was entitled to Land Bounty, but those who served to the *end of the War* or *were supernumerary,* and Scurloe's name is returned on this report it is held conclusive of his right to Com: pay.

If the view taken by me of the subject should be erronius, or if you have any doubts of the success of the application, you will do me a favour by saying so in answer to this. I shall feel myself much your debtor if you will acknowledge the receipt of this, and say what are your opinions of the case.

I have the honor
to be with great consideration
& respect your hnmble. srvt.

JN^o^. G. MOSBY.

Hon. W. P. Mangum.
[Addressed:]
To the Hon.
W. P. Mangum
Washington City

[104] See above II, 40.

1834

WPM-LC

Sam P. Carson to Willie P. Mangum

BRINDLETOWN 1st January 1834.

My dear Sir:—

I was particularly gratified at the manner which you brought to the notice of the Senate the Message of the President in answer to your call upon him &c—his answer is viewed by all here, both friends and foes, as *extraordinary* & as unexamplified in the anals of our history

I solicit a copy of your Report so soon as made, and shall expect it with much anxiety—Shall be much pleased to hear from you as you can give me *indications* &c, &c—that does not find way to news papers more anon—In haste your

Friend,

SAM P CARSON.

[Addressed:]
Honble. W. P. Mangum,
U. S. Senate,
Washington City,
D. C.
Stage writing

WPM-LC

.................................*to Willie P. Mangum*

RALEIGH, N. C.
Jany 17th 1834.

Dear Sir,

I have long intended to return you my own & the thanks of my family for the warm and generous manner you took our Connexion, Mr. Dasheill by the hand on reaching Washington. He is most grateful to you for your kindness, altho' he did not avail himself of all its benefits, by a competition for the place he intended to seek. Be assured, my dear Sir, we will not forget to requite your goodness to him, when it may be in my own or in the power of any of us to do you honor or service.

You have seen a momentary essay made by me to resussitate the Constitutionalist.[1] Alas, it was dead, shrouded coffined & entombed—aye & stunk too badly to infuse life or animation into it—and I have abandoned it to its fate. I did not know the worst of its condition, until after I had committed myself to its fortunes. Peace to its ashes.

The last Star[2] of this City will tell you much of some startling measures projected at the close of the Session. But the whole has not met the public eye. Mr. Mears's compromise,[3] as it was called, would have gotten through, had the managers not been quite so greedy of expected power. They lifted the curtain too high—and revealed some movements which were to follow in the train, when the platform should be fairly laid for them to stand upon. Such a general ticket for Congress—Gerrymandering of the Dists for the accomodation of particular partisans—the location at Raleigh, of a central Junto of Seven—it is said—to Act as the Raleigh regency,—& tell the people over the State, which was the *regular* ticket & so put up & put down whosoever they would. Certain would-be U. S. Senators—and two or three traders in politicks belonging to these cases—have the credit of standing God fathers to these atrocious schemes. But a seasonable discovery—of consequences—destroyed all.

You have no doubt learned that Genl. S.[4] has had to run the gauntlet for his Atto, Genl.ship—aye—and

[The last of letter is missing]

---

[1]In 1831 *The Raleigh Constitutionalist and Peoples Advocate* was established by William S. Ransom and William Patterson. In the latter part of 1831 Charles R. Ramsay became a partner and continued as one of the editors until 1832 when the paper ceased publication. *Union List of Newspapers*, 505; *N. C. Free Press*, Aug. 23, 1831. See also above, I, 474-476, 578-579.

[2]Several motions were made in the legislature to test the strength of the Jackson and anti-Jackson forces. John Guthrie, of Chatham, proposed resolutions favorable to a recharter of the Bank. After sidestepping this resolution, others presented resolutions endorsing Jackson's earlier conduct in the nullification fight. Resolutions denouncing the Force Bill, endorsing the removal of deposits, and questioning the conduct of Mangum and Brown were also proposed. None of these passed, but they gave occasions for speeches. *Raleigh Register*, Jan. 21, 1834; Pegg, "Whig Party in N. C." 33-35.

[3]In the debate over a constitutional convention, William B. Mears, of New Hanover, January 7, proposed in the state senate to amend the bill by substituting for the referendum clause a plan which would have given the eastern part of the state control of the senate and the west control of the House of Commons. His motion was tabled. *N. C. Free Press*, Jan. 17, 1834.

[4]Romulus M. Saunders was attorney general until 1835.

WPM-LC

D. L. Swain to Willie P. Mangum

PRINTED CIRCULAR
EXECUTIVE DEPARTMENT, NORTH CAROLINA

RALEIGH, January 19, 1834.

Sir,

In compliance with the request of the General Assembly of this State, I have the honor to transmit to you the [accompa]nying Report and Resolutions of that body, adopted at the last Session.

I am, sir, with high respect,
Your obedient servant,
D. L. SWAIN

To
The Honble
Willie P. Mangum.

REPORT

The Joint Select Committee to whom was referred the message from the Governor relative to the militia and the public defence, together with the resolutions of the Legislature of the States of New York and Illinois upon these subjects, respectfully submit the following REPORT:

The committee concur entirely with the opinions expressed by the Governor of this State and the Legislatures of the two States referred to, that the present militia system is unnecessarily burdensome and unequal in its operation upon the different classes of society; and that these very causes, instead of increasing, diminish its efficiency. No one who has paid the slightest attention to the militia trainings, as practiced in this State, can have failed to perceive that, except in a few volunteer companies, military science is little understood, and discipline rarely enforced. It may well be doubted, indeed, whether the evils growing out of these periodical assemblages of the whole body of the community, which are too apparent to require illustration, do not more than counterbalance all the improvements which are made in the military art.

The committee are decidedly of opinion, that these evils can be remedied only by an entire change in the organization of the militia system by Congress. That the present term of militia service is entirely too long; that it should be confined to the young and robust; and that proper measures should be adopted to render the training of this class effectual; that a well organized and disciplined force, though comparatively small in point of numbers, would be much more efficient in its character than the unorganized multitudes to which we are accustomed. Such a system would be calculated to beget a spirit of military pride, which could not but have a happy effect upon the country.

There can be no difficulty in pronouncing that the spectators who might witness the evolutions of a well trained corps would acquire much more correct notions of true military science as now regulated, This order of things would [be much less] expensive than that now pursued, and the expense would fall where alone it ough [torn[those who render the service, but on those whose persons and property are pecu[torn] of its protection.

The com[torn] end the adoption of the accompanying resolutions.

WILLIAM P. DODSON, Chairman.

Resolved, [Torn] Congress be instructed, and our Representatives requested to adopt the nece[ssary] [torn] der the system of militia decipline of the United States less burdensome [torn] and more efficient in its organization.

Resolved, That [his Excellen]cy the governor be requested to transmit copies of these resolutions and this report to the President of the United States and the Governors of the several States, and to each of our Senators and Representatives in Congress.

WPM-LC

J. A. Cameron[5] *to Willie P. Mangum*

PENSACOLA Jany 22nd. 1834

Hon: W. P. Mangum,

Dear Sir:

Will you oblige me by turning to your Congressional Library, and look to the printed copy of the acts of the Legislative Council of Florida for the year 1832. In the appendix of those Acts, at page 101, you will find a Memorial presented to Congress, on the subject of the Courts in [the] Western District. You will see that the Council [torn] Congress to make 2 Dis-

[5]See above, I, 260n, 548.

tricts out of the *then* and *now* Western District. Congress did right in resisting the application: there is no *necessity* for a new District, Although the duties required of the Judge in the W. D. are much more than those required of any other Judge in the Territory, and are indeed arduous and difficult of performance, yet they *can* be performed—they *have* been performed by me, and *will* be performed by me, as long as it is my duty to perform them. I call your attention to this Memorial, and hope you will call the attention of Congress to it, for the purpose of showing you, that the Council of 1832 (before I came to the Territory, and when the Salary of the Judge was $2300) thought the Western District so large, and the duties required of the Judge so arduous, as to call upon Congress to make *two* Districts out of his *One*.

I have the honor to be
Most respectfully
Yr. friend & ob^t. Sv^t.
J. A. CAMERON

[Addressed:]
To
The Hon: W. P. Mangum
Senate Chamber
Washington City.

WPM-LC

Step. K. Sneed[6] *to Willie P. Mangum*

OXFORD 25th Janurary 1834.

My dear Sir

I have taken the liberty of enclosing to you the within bundle for my brother William which you will please to hand him. From appearances I think you will have a very long Session, and I hope and trust that you all will never leave the sod untill Genl Jackson is brought to his proper senses; "peaceably if you can but forcibly if you must". If my representative Genl. Hawkins[7] sticks to the old *Gineral* on the deposite question, he will vote against the opinions of ¾ of his constituents. The longer I live and the more I see and hear, the more convinced I am that there never was but one honest party in this county; and that was

[6] See above, I, 5n.
[7] Micajah T. Hawkins.

the old Federal party. I should be glad to hear from you. Your family I have not heard from, since my mother left here.

I remain yr friend
STEP K. SNEED

[Addressed:]
Hon.
Willie P. Mangum.
Washington City

WPM-LC

Richard S. Clinton[8] *to Willie P. Mangum*

CAHABA, Jan. 25th, 1834

Hon. W. P. Mangum
My dear Sir.

A gentleman a few days since of considerable wealth, made a proposition to me, to embark with him, in a land speculation in Austin's Colony in Texas, he seemed to entertain the opinion that the Country in a few years would be owned by the United States, indeed that a secret negotiation was going on at this time touching the matter. Will you do me the kindness to state what in your opinion is the feeling of congress upon this subject, and what in your opinion will be the ultimate fate of that Country from whom do you think the best titles [are to be] had to Land in Texas. Any opinion you may have the kindness to render me will be duly appreciated, and shall remain solely *inter. nos.* I have viewed with much satisfaction your high minded and independent course in Congress, and I trust my dear sir you will yet meet with the reward you deserve.

Your friend
RICHD. S. CLINTON

[Addressed:]
The Hon. W. P. Mangum
Washington City

Cahaba, Ala
28 January

---

[8]He became a judge of the probate court in Alabama. Grant, *Alumni Hist. of U. N. C.*, 116.

WPM-LC

William Welborne[9] *to David Crockett*

CLOVER CREEK T.[ennessee]
27, Jany, 1834.

Colo. D. Crockett,
Dear Sir,

A few days since I recd. your report and Bill on our Ocupant Lands,[10] The people are all Satisfied with your endeavors, and if it passes into a Law it will render more general Satisfaction than any thing you have ever attempted to do for us, those who own Ocupants in our Country have pride and would rather pay 12½ Cents per acre than it should be said it was given them. I saw yesterday in Jackson Adam Huntsman[11] and told him, you had if your Bill passed immortalized yourself—he said yes, By Gd. you had touched upon the right string at Last and spoke favorable of the Report—

Mr. Huntsman is a candidate for the convention and Colo. Tho. Henderson,[12] and Maj. A. L. Martin would be, if we thought we could elect him, but the others are out and the inclinations of the people are set and I hardly think we could erase them, Martin is anxious to run if we could succeed, but as they have such a start of him, it is better he should not be beaten Henderson in my opinion will be elected easy, Huntsman has destroyed himself by writing so much stuff against you—even your enemies in Politicks became disgusted at it, he has therefore in this County lost hundreds of votes, I think.

The Rail Road from Jackson to Mi. River will certainly go I think, 80000$ or upwards is subscribed in the Town of Jackson alone,[13]—I have unstood that Saml. Dickins[14] together with some others would take One hundred thousand dollars in stock, It will in all probability go to Randolph.

My Father Lewis Welborne was a Militiaman in the Revolutionary War and Served two three months Tours as his report

---

[9]Possibly William Welborne, who was in the North Carolina legislature from Rowan County in 1809. *N. C. Manual,* 791.

[10]Crocket's land law 1832.

[11]He was a Whig congressman from 1835 to 1837. *Biog. Dir. of Cong.*, 1134.

[12]See above, I, 76n, for Henderson. I am unable to identify Martin.

[13]In 1833 citizens of Jackson, Tennessee, held a meeting to create sentiment for a railroad from Jackson to the Mississippi. As a result the legislature incorporated the Western Railroad Company. The state paid for the survey, but the road was not built. Phillip M. Hamer, *Tennessee: A History, 1673-1932,* New York, 1933, I, 406.

[14]See above, I, 250n.

will Shew when it comes to hand, he employed Mr. Wolf[15] of Bolivar, a Lawyer to draw all the necessary writings and have had it as legally attested as possible, he has also said in his report that he is acquainted with you, I wish you therefore to assist the old Gentleman as much as you can in obtaining his Pension as he certainly comes under the perview and meaning of the law. Mr. Mangum the Senator from N. Ca. he has also named in his report please speak to Mr. Mangum, Judge Mangum knew a Brother of my Father's as well as he knew any man in Orange County N. Ca. whose name was John Welborne my Father Previous to his comeing to Tennesse lived in Johnson County, which on reflection Judge Mangum will recollect, he has also named the Hon. Danl. L. Baranger who has known him and me for many years.

Please, Colo. Crockett Shew this letter to those Gentlemen or inform them of what my Fathers wishes, that he to the end may obtain his pension, as he most certainly did serve as he reports, he knows he suffered, as (being) very young, as willing to receive some of the loves and fishes while they are going, the old man is in good easy circumstances and it was with some difficulty I and his neighbors could induce him to make application. My compliments and best wishes to you.

WM. WELBORNE.

write to me as soon as you can, what you can do—
I like to hear from you—
Say to Mr. Barenger we will elect Henderson
like a flash—

[Addressed:]
Hon. David Crockett,
Washington City

WPM-LC

Thomas B. Littlejohn to Willie P. Mangum

OXFORD 29th, Jany, 1834.

My dear Sir

I have the pleasure to acknowledge [the] receipt of your kind favor of the 22nd instant, and tender you my thanks for the interest you appear to take in behalf of the [appli]cation on the part of my son—although you represent the prospects as being

[15]Possibly James M. Wolf who went to Texas in 1835, and in 1836 became the secretary of the Texas legation. Garrison (ed.), *Diplomatic Correspondence of the Republic of Texas with the U. S., A. H. A. Reports*, 1907, II, 67, 86, 87.

rather unfavorable, I still flatter myself that the [torn] with which you will urge your influence in his behalf [may] prove successful in obtaining a warrant for him.—you [ju]dge rightly when you say "I have this matter much at heart"—

I presume you have caused by son's name to be entered as a candidate for admission in the M: Academy, but in the event that it should be considered *indispensible* for the application to be made *by myself* to the Sec.y at War, I have enclosed a letter to him, which you will be good enough to have delivered *if necessary.*—it may be considered more respectful.—

I feel very anxious to know the issue of the discussion, now going on in Congress, of the all absorbing subject of the removal of the deposites—it is certainly the most atrocious, high handed despotick measure, that ever was before assumed by the most absolute monarch, and unless it be counteracted by the prompt action of Congress, its baneful effects will speedily be manifested, by the most widespread ruin throughout our whole Country—

I trust there is a sufficient amount of sterling virtue, and patriotism in your great body to crush this monster in its infancy, and if the President should have the hardihood to interpose his *veto,* he ought to be immediately *impeached.*

It will give me pleasure to hear from you as soon, and as frequently as your leisure permit—

I am with much regard
Yr. Mo. Obt. Servt.
THO. B. LITTLEJOHN

[Addressed:]
The Honorable,
Willie P. Mangum Esq.,
Washington City.

Willie P. Mangum to Duncan Cameron[16]

WASHINGTON 7th Feby 1834

My dear Sir.

I enclose you the very able, and as I think the conclusive report from the Comme. of Finance upon Mr. Taney's report—It

[16]The original letter is in the Cameron Papers, University of North Carolina.

is as you will readily preceive from the pen of M^{r}. Webster.[17]—The discussion still continues in both houses—There are indications on the part of the adm^{n}. forces in the House forces to bring it to a close either by long sittings or by the previous question.

The discussion will be prolonged in the Senate until the week after next.—It is not expected to effect any change in the vote; but it is believed that good will grow out of drawing the public eye long & steadily upon the question.—The vote in the Senate for restoring the deposites will be 28-20 being with the adm^{n}.—

In the House by the most incessant drilling & the severest discipline ever known here the administration will probably prevail by a small majority.

It is said there are not 40 members in the House who approve the conduct of the adm^{n}. yet it will be probably sustained by a majority of from 7 to 10 votes.—having already been reduced from 26 to about that number.—

The exposition of Wright[18] of N. Y. may be regarded as the definitive & settled course of the administration, or rather of the Albany school, which has practically the administration of the Govt. as to lands.—You see from that, that the Bank is not to be reachart[er]ed, nor any new bank to be established in either of the States, but a fair experiment is to be made of the affiil-iated pet Banks, and if that shall fail and failure in the still more impracticable & chimerical scheme of returning to *hard* money altogether, as far as the Gen: Govt. is a money dealer, then they will consider of the establishing a Bank in the District of Columbia; or if their [illegible] scruples of a constitutional nature shall be insuperable apply to the States for an amendment of the Constitution—

Upon the whole I regard it certain that the Country is to be exposed to all the evil of a deranged currency for the next two or three years, & the pressure consequent upon destruction of confidence—That the affiliated Banks will be used in this Presidential campaign; & that ultimately if Van Buren shall succeed a district Bank will be established controulled by a control regency & by combination with the power & patronage of the government, controlling & corrupting every thing—nothing can prevent these disastrous results, but a powerful uprising of the people, of which by the bye I have scarcely any hope.—

[17]Webster as chairman was assisted by Tyler, Ewing, Wilkins, and Mangum.

[18]Silas Wright, who had just resigned as comptroller of New York state to become United States Senator, was Van Buren's chief adviser in this controversy over the deposits. Through Van Buren he became one of Jackson's advisers on financial matters. *D.A.B.*, XX, 565-567.

The President is said to be up to that high pitch of excitement that might be expected in a real war campaign.—The north has been so thorough[ly] corrupted by the patronage of the Executive, that it is wholly incapable of making resistance. —To a southern man the statement seems extravagant and in truth, almost inconceivable & yet I doubt not it is sober fact.—Penn[a]. that has twice through the Legislature, instructed her Senators almost unanimously within two years, to vote for the recharter, changes front at Executive Command, & now lies at the foot of power,[19] hopeless & helpless.—The discipline of the Albany school now holds in chains, Maine, N. Hampshire, N. York, Ohio & Penn[a]. and is rapidly seizing after the other northern states.—

Old Massachusetts is the only state that may be expected to resist the infection—Even there, it is acquiring power.—It is perfectly certain that the best men of the north look with most hope upon the disinterestedness & gallantry of the South. They little perceive how weak we are as growing out of the recent bitter political divisions, & how powerless our efforts made in opposition to Jacksonism.—The events of the last winter have given boldness & insolence to power unknown to us in our former history—And in truth (tho I know we differ in that) I think the present suffering to the North will not be without its wholesome uses—The Tyrant that they armed to enforce their unjust exactions, has turned & fixed his grip upon them.—The sentiment is rapidly increasing among the old Federal party to the North, that the usurpations of the Gov[t]. can be guarded against only, by strengthening the States—A few years more & I think it probable that all wise men will regard with amazement the apprehension existing at so early a period & continued to this time, that the danger in our system lies in the States & not in the usurpations of the Central Gov[t].—

Nothing definitive seems to be settled in the public mind as to a candidate to be run ag[t]. V B.—There are many pretenders.—My opinion remains unchanged—The only hope of successful resistence is in M[r]. Clay.—

The South ought to give out its sentiment upon that subject.—But we are in fetters.—

---

[19] Before the end of March, Governor Wolf, of Pennsylvania, denounced the Bank, although he had previously supported it. The senate of Pennsylvania adopted resolutions 19 to 13 against the Bank, and both Senators who had previously supported a recharter were, by the end of March, against it. Scarcely a member of the House from Pennsylvania continued to support the Bank. Catterall, *Second Bank of the United States*, 339-340.

I wrote to Raleigh, especially to the Govr.[20] & many others.—They are obviously alarmed at the responsibility of unfurling the flag.—

Many in No Ca. are looking to Judge McLean.[21] It is a miserable chance—weak in ability, & weaker in purpose, he is almost every way unfit—Yet I w^d^. prefer him to V. B.—

I fear we shall have some difficulty further south, in bringing out Clay.—If Virginia & N.C^a^. shall make a strong demonstration for him, they must go likewise.—

Virginia is almost ready to take him up—V. B. has the sympathy of the people no where—Twenty years ago he could not have got up at all.—It is one of the alarming signs of the decay of public virtue, that a man may hope to attain that office without public service, high talent or any thing strongly to sustain him, except simply the patronage of the Ex: Gov^t^.

Be pleased to present me most respectfully to M^rs^. Cameron, and accept for

yourself the assurance of my
entire respect & esteem
WILLIE P. MANGUM

Dun Cameron Esqr.

Willie P. Mangum to Duncan Cameron[22]

WASHINGTON CITY 9th Feby 1834

My dear Sir.

I enclose you a memorial[23] from the city of N. York that will give you a truer conception of the state of feeling and distress in the north than perhaps any thing you see in the newspapers. This paper, though stronger, is but little stronger than scores that have been presented to Congress.—I send it as a specimen, these papers but rarely finding a place in the public prints.

My committee duties[24] bring me into almost daily intercourse with M^r^. Webster, who is the real representative of the great manufacturing and capitalist interests of New England & the North generally; and judging from his representations the se-

[20]See above, Mangum's letter to Swain, December 22, 1833.
[21]John McLean, of Ohio.
[22]The original letter is in the Cameron Papers, University of North Carolina.
[23]The memorial was not found in the Cameron Papers.
[24]Mangum was on the Foreign Relations and Finance committees. Webster was the Chairman of the Finance Committee. *Register of Debates*, 23 Cong., 1 sess., 43.

vere distress, and apprehension of rapidly approaching calamity in some quarters are appalling.—I meet with no gentleman who seems so deeply impressed with a sense of impending general disaster.—Very much yet depends upon the course of the Penn[a]. Legislature.—A majority of both branches is with the adm[n]. and against the Bank.—The great pressure in portions of that State & the failure to complete loans for internal improvement & the apprehension that the State adm[n]. will have to resort to new taxation thereby hazarding their power & popularity, it is said, have brought the members to a stand.—They have had under advisement for several days a proposition to *unite on all sides* and move en masse to the reserve of the country.—The proposition is as flattering to their vanity as it is suitable to the genius of Penn: politics.—

M[r]. Webster who is in close correspondence with many of them entertains a strong hope of favorable results.—

If they move at all, they will move in solid columns. Yet I think, they will find difficulty in either breaking or slipping the adm[n]. collar.—The issue will be known here in a few days. There is no sign of yielding at any other point.—It is confidently stated and believed that the Cabinet will undergo change.—M[r]. McLane,[25] the secretary of State will resign next week, it was expected.—It is now said, it will be deferred to a later period.—He is anxious to resign & bring before the country his written opinion against the late measure of the Executive, and also the fact that he tendered his resignation.—These circumstances tend to restore Mr. M.L. partially to the good opinion of some of his old friends—Yet it is too true that he has made sacrifices from the effects of which nothing I believe can relieve him.—

Forsythe[26] of Geo. or Rives[27] of Va. will succeed him—most probably Forsythe.—It is said Taney will not be nominated to the Senate—He cannot pass—and probably Rives may succeed him.—Rives & the adm[n] both being down in Va.—to remove Rives is to bring in B. W. Leigh.—a consideration not to be disregarded by the adm[n] in the present state of parties.—Barry[28]

[25]In the summer of 1833 Louis McLane as Secretary of Treasury had refused to carry out Jackson's command to withdraw deposits from the United States Bank. He was, therefore, transferred to the State Department, and Taney was made Secretary of the Treasury. McLane never was confirmed by the Senate, and so on June 18 he resigned. Wiltse, *Calhoun: the Nullifier*, 232.

[26]John Forsyth, Jackson's floor leader in the Senate was, upon McLane's resignation, appointed Secretary of State. Since Taney was not confirmed by the Senate Levi Woodbury was nominated for the treasury post. Wiltse, *Calhoun: the Nullifier*, 232-233; *D.A.B.*, VI, 533-535.

[27]William C. Rives.

[28]William Taylor Barry, member of the Kitchen Cabinet and Postmaster General until 1835.

will go out most probably & yet the President will save him if possible—In that event Wilkins[29] of Penn: will be P. M. Genl.—Free Tom Moore[30] w^{d}. unquestionably be nominated were it not that he w^{d}. be as unquestionably rejected by the Senate.—

Wilkins is incompetent—not preferable even to Barry—It is believed that the deficit in that Department is little short of 12 or 14 hundred thousand dollars. It may not be more than one million.—

Everything almost is practically in utter disorganization and but for the popularity of Jackson, a storm of public indignation would drive the whole concern from power.—

Webster will probably introduce as a measure of present relief a proposition to extend the charter of the U. S. Bank for 2 or 3 years & give more time to wind up.[31]—He hopes for the Cooperation of the Executive.—The measure was mentioned by him yesterday for the first time.—I do not think it will meet with general favor on any side.—I should go for it—if there be no prospect of any thing better yet I am sure it will meet with no Executive favor.—

There is a degree of uncertainty in all things in men's minds without example heretofore in this country. If the Executive shall be thrown into the minority in the Ho. of Reps. you need be surprized at nothing.—The President speaks of the whole south with great asperity—his passions are gradually maturing into a settled hatred—He says Virginia is the most disgraced state in the Union except So. Ca.

If he shall be thrown into a minority and that too (as it w^{d}. be) by the disaffection in the South, I believe the whole policy of the adm^{n}. will be instantly changed—M^{r}. Webster on friday recd. a letter from N. Y. as he says from a source of good authority, that a bill was in that City for *calculations* drawn by Cambreleng,[32] that goes to repeal all subsequent measures & restore the Tariff of 1828 with such modification as the State of the Revenue shall require.—The Revenue from various causes more or less

[29]William Wilkins was a member of the Senate until 1834 when he was appointed by Jackson as minister to Russia. *D.A.B.*, XX, 221.

[30]Thomas Patrick Moore had just returned as American minister to Colombia, where Jackson had sent him in 1829. *Biog. Dir. of Cong.*, 1330.

[31]Disappointed with Clay's leadership on the Bank, Webster and Calhoun broke away in February, 1834, and supported the idea of a recharter. Webster wanted to recharter the Bank for six years and Calhoun for twelve. Friction between Webster and Clay prevented any progress. Catterall, *Second United States Bank*, 336-338; Wiltse, *Calhoun: Nullifier*, 225-227.

[32]Churchill Caldone Cambreleng, a native of North Carolina, moved to New York in 1802 where he became a merchant. From 1821 to 1839 he was in Congress and from 1840 to 1841 minister to Russia. *Biog. Dir. of Cong.*, 779.

connected with the high handed measures of the admn. is likely to fall far short of the estimates.—This with the unexampled increase of expenditure, will produce deep & dangerous difficulties.—All this connected with alarming views imputed to the President touching immediate emancipation &C. has produced uncertainty in men's minds here of anxious portents.

Webster requested that the fact sh^{d}. not be mentioned—He immediately introduced a reso: of inquiry by the Comm: of Finance—

He thinks any thing may be expected—& says touching this matter that they are *mad*.—V. B. must be elected—That is paramount to every thing.—Driven out of the south as they began to think that a union of the north on these questions may be regarded as practicable.—V. B. is too timid for such an experiment. But Jackson lives only by the spirit of pugnacity.—It wd. exactly fall in with his bent of mind—relying as he wd. upon subduing by militray force the south if it shd. prove refractory. —I wish he may not live to be regarded as the most dangerous, as well as the worst man in the Country.—These reflections will fall upon your quiet, as every way extravagant.—Yet they here disturb the soundest & steadiest minds.—The Presidents reception of the N. Y. Committee was to the last degree disrespectful[33]—They actually declined saying what they intended & what was necessary to their purpose in apprehension of his explosive violence.—

All men begin to think here, that they cannot get on—that they will die in their tracks.—Some sudden movement is necessary for them,—and the fear of the effects of change is as strong as the sense of present difficulties.—

Those men who know the President best can most easily conceive of the possibility of these views being realized—

McLane thinks I learn, that the Admn. cannot get on with a currency deranged, faith destroyed & confidence shattered to the extent that he believes will happen.—No. Carolina gives one vote in the Senate & five in the House with the admn.—Hall, Hawkins, Speight, Bynum, & McKay.—Va. will give in the Ho. only 2 Or 3 with the admn. Possibly only Loyall & Stephenson[34] —there may be 2 others.

[33]A commttee of New York merchants presented memorials to Jackson asking relief from the conditions which the removal of deposits had created. Refusing to listen to their arguments, Jackson told them that he would not approve any recharter of the United States Bank until he discovered that the local banks were unsatisfactory. *National Intelligencer* quoted in the *Raleigh Register*, Feb. 2, 18, 1834.

[34]George Loyall and Andrew Stevenson.

I have troubled you at great length.

(Of course Rives in the Senate)

With great respect & regard

I am Dr Sir Yours truly

WILLIE P. MANGUM

[Addressed:]

The Hon:

Duncan Cameron

Stagville

No Carolina

WPM-LC

Samuel D. Morgan[35] *to Willie P. Mangum*

MACON GA Feby 10th 1834

Honl Willie. P. Mangum

Dear Sir

My collections, I fear, will be bad. your notes made last year are all good. But there seems a prevailing disposition, or indisposition, not to pay debts in Georgia at present.

Money is very scarce and a great many failures taking place recently. I have been several days, waiting, or rather trying to get something to write, in the way of settlements &c., that would afford you a more diffenite understanding of your buisness in Macon.

I have thought it best to hire out your servants in Ga as I could see no way of gitting them home I could see no suitable person going to No. Carolina and to hire some one expressly to take them home, to North Carolina would cost two much, though would be glad of your preferance. I would bring them with me by publick conveyance, Knowing that you had as live have them at home. but I am compelled to go to Florida Your Negroes are all well & doing very well and desire to be hired again in Ga. And their hire will bee quite enough more than North Carolina wages to take them home next winter. Wages are something better than last winter. or at least promises are better, besides I

[35]Mangum, as well as other North Carolina planters in the 1830's, had difficulty making money from farming. Consequently, he had his wife hire out his slaves to planters in Georgia and Alabama. In 1842 he received $1,050 for their hire. Morgan handled his business for him in Georgia. See above, I, xxiv, and below a letter of Morgan to Mangum Jan. 1, 1852.

leave it discassionary [discretionary] with you at your option to take them home at any time of the year that you may think proper to do so. Well realative to the loss of Duncan I am not in possession of as much infirmation as I want. am waiting to see a gentleman, who is now absent for a short while from the City and who was an eye witness to the occurance Saw Duncan drowned and as I am told will tell me all the particulars. after which I will write you more particularly, or at least as soon as I ditermine. which will be the most prudent course to persue. I shall of course endeavour to be prudent. but My feelings are so regidly opposed to any Man or Men that will act so as to cause their better principals to be suspected of Mal treatment to slaves, and especially under circumstances similar to the above I shall spare no pains to understand all the particulars, in hast. I am your Obt. Svt. & friend

Very Respectfully
S. D. MORGAN

Hon W. P. Mangum Sr.

WPM-LC

William Gaston to Willie P. Mangum

RALEIGH Feby. 15th. 1834.

My dear Sir

A few days since I received a letter from Mr. George Cooke,[36] a native of Virginia but at present residing at New York, requesting my good offices with some of my friends in Congress to aid an application to be made in his behalf to be employed as an Artist in executing one of the paintings designed for the Rotunda. The subject which he would propose is "the Battle of the Cowpens" which he represents as the only one South of York Town in which the American arms were entirely triumphant, and he informs me that for this purpose he has procured the portraits of the principal actors on that occasion Morgan[37] Howard & Washington.—I am concious that I am but poorly quali-

[36]A native of Maryland, George Cooke studied art in Italy and France. He painted in Alexandria, Richmond, and New York. One of his pupils, John Gadsby, got the commission to paint the "Baptism of Pocahontas" for the Rotunda of the Capitol. William Dunlap, *History of the Rise and Progress of the arts of design in the United States;* new ed. with additions by Frank W. Bayley and Charles E. Goodspeed, Boston, 1918, III, 133.

[37]General Daniel Morgan and Lieutenant Colonels John Eager Howard and William Washington.

fied to give an opinion respecting the competency of any artist to execute such a painting, and therefore beg that whatever I say may be regarded as expressed with much diffidence and distrust of my own judgment. I feel it due however to Mr. Cooke to say that having been exceedingly pleased with a portrait of my eldest daughter which he executed more than a year ago I felt a strong desire when I was in New York to see more of his works. When my leisure permitted I frequently visited his rooms and every visit increased my respect for the talents of the artist and the good qualities of the man.—So far as I am qualified to judge my opinion is highly favorable to him and to his application.—

You are at liberty to make this communication known to whomever you think proper, and will I am sure excuse me for having troubled you with it.

Our Court will I fear have a month more before it can close its session. The business has been permitted to accumulate until it has become oppressive.—

I pray you to believe me respectfully & affectionately,
Your friend & obedt Servt.,
WILL: GASTON.

[Addressed:]
Honble. W. P. Mangum,
Senator
In Congress.

WPM-LC

Saml. Hillman to [*Willie P. Mangum*]

MORGANTON N. C.
16th February 1834

My dear Sir,

Although I have not for a considerable time, had the honour of receiving any letter or other communication from you, I have thought a few lines from me upon the subject of public feeling in this quarter, would not be otherwise than agreeable to you at this time—We have indeed fallen upon evil times; and unless something be effected by the action of Congress during this session to rescue its legitimate powers from the grasp of usurpation, our Constitution is gone—In the Circuit in which I practice, among intellegent and reflecting men, there is but one opinion, and that is in accordance with the sentiment above expressed—Twelve months ago the name of Jackson carried with it a spell, a charm and every measure which received the sanction of his name was sure to be applauded and was received with the utmost confidence in its correctness—Now "there are none so poor to do him reverence"—I have never known so complete a change in public sentiment—One year ago the man in this County who in public and promiscious company would dare to say any thing against General Jackson would have benn insulted. —Now you can hardly go into any crowd without hearing him denounced in the most unqualified terms—Among those who are most bitter against him, are those who have heretofore been his most devoted friends—Before this reaches you, you will have received the proceedings of a meeting held at this place during Court week[38]—It was gotten up on a very short notice, the notice having been given only about twelve O'clock and the meeting held immediately after the adjournment of Court on the same day—It was nevertheless attended by the intelligent and business men from every part of the County—The resolutions as you will have preceived were carried without a dissenting voice and strong as they are I was somewhat censured by some for not having seasoned them still more highly—I admit with you that the question is "law or no law, constitution or no constitution."[39] But it is the pecuniary embarrassment, the great and over-whelming distress consequent upon the removal of the deposites; which comes home to the people—It is this end and this alone I believe which has removed the film from the eyes of the people—It has appeared to me that nothing short of touching their pocket, and that rudely would induce the people or a considerable portion of them to doubt the infallibility of Jacksonism—The circumstance that our local banks are winding up their business, that the U. S. Bank is calling in its notes and curtailing its discounts and the effect which the removal of the Deposits has had by compelling the U. S. Bank suddenly to draw

[38]Early in 1834 the champions of the Bank in North Carolina began holding meetings to protest against the removal of deposits. At such a gathering in Burke County, January 28, Hillman proposed resolutions condemning Jackson's action as unconstitutional and unwise. After favorable speeches by Hillman and S. P. Carson, the resolutions were adopted without opposition. *Senate Documents*, 23 Cong., 1 sess., Doc. 121, pp. 1-2; *Raleigh Star*, Feb. 20, 1834. These resolutions represented the sentiment of a large part of North Carolina, where the Bank had many supporters.

[39]In his speech in the Senate February 3, 1834, Mangum definitely broke with Jackson. He emphasized the point that the fight was not a question of "bank or no bank," but of "constitution or no constitution." For this speech he was severely criticized and warmly praised in North Carolina. Pegg, "Whig Party in N. C.," 15-16.

upon the Georgia [and] South Carolina Banks for the debts due from them [torn] a general depression in the price of produce and [torn] produced a scarity of money in this Country altogether unexampled—The spirit of inquiry is abroad and there is intelligence enough to direct the minds of the people to the true cause of this State of things—Your friends are much gratified at the course which you have chalked out for yourself but they expect to hear from you in Congress more fully upon this interesting and important question. Mr. A. L. Erwin[40] desires me to return you his thanks for Calhoun's Speech and joins me in the request that you will forward to us the report of the Committee of Finance and the Speeches of Mr Clay Mr McDuffie Mr Binnie[41] and others which are distinguished for ability—

I am very respectfully your friend

SAML HILLMAN

WPM-LC

James S. Smith[42] to Willie P. Mangum

HILLSBOROUGH Febry 16th 1834

Dr. Sir

Agreeable to the understanding we had before you left here—I now beg the favour of you cause to be paid to the House of Lawrence, Keese & Co druggists the sum of one Hundred dollars. This is a small sum over the amont of your note and interest but I prefer it being an even sum and I will settle it with you. I received a proper application from this house for a payment on yesterday and they have been at all times so indulgent and obliging to me that I am very desirous to make them payment—I beg you not to forget to attend to this—If you have to transmit any funds hear you would much oblige me to pay an additional Hundred for me at New York and draw on me for it at any time you please and it shall be met promptly—Draw in favor of your Brother[43] or Cain[44] not the Hillsborough Banker[45] I want but little to do with him in any way—I would not

---

[40]An attorney of Burke County who participated in the Burke County meeting. McIver, *N. C. Register*, 46; *Senate Documents*, 23 Cong., 1 sess., Doc. 121, p.2.

[41]Horace Binney, who had served as director of the Bank before he entered Congress in 1833. *D.A.B.*, II, 280-282.

[42]See above, I, 8n.

[43]Priestley H. Mangum.

[44]William Cain.

[45]He probably refers to James Webb, who was the agent for the Bank of Cape Fear.

trouble you with this request was it not that it may be a convenience to you as well as my self—

I have nothing in the way of news to offer you—all your friends are well at this time—

It may be gratifying to you to lear[n] that all the inteligent part of the people approve the course you are persuing so far as it has been yet developed on the Bank Question—

I think as far as I am able to fathom public sentiment a counter current is begining to tell againts the Hero & Co—O! how the folks are repenting of their political sins here, — Nash[46]—Waddell—Scott—Jones—Moore &c &c—I do believe that if Hillsboro was polled tomorrow that Jackson would get but one vote in it—and that would be Child—

Go ahead Judge (as Davy Crocket says) you will find N. C. with you in due time in my opinion—

Say to Mr Calhoun that his speach[47] has almost made nullifiers of us here, even Dr. Webb[48] says that nullification is not half so bad as he thought it was at first—

I Dr Sir am very Respectfully
Your Obdt Svt
J. S. SMITH.

Hon. Willie P. Mangum

[Addressed:] Hillsborough N. C
17 Feby 1834

Hon. Willie P. Mangum
Washin[g]ton City

WPM-LC

William Watts Jones[49] to Willie P. Mangum

WILMINGTON Feby. 17—1834

Dear Sir.

I have it in contemplation to settle some of my negroes on Red River in Louisiana, and am therefore desirous of obtaining all the information I can previous to my doing so.

Will you be so good enough to obtain all the information you

[46]Frederick Nash, Hugh Waddell, John Scott, Allen C. Jones, and George Moore.

[47]On January 13, 1834, Calhoun spoke in the Senate against the removal of deposits. His chief emphasis was on the usurpation of authority by the President. He included a defense of state's rights. Wiltse, *Calhoun: Nullifier*, 219-220.

[48]James Webb.

[49]See above, I, 410n.

can relative to the country and send it to me; there may be Gentlemen in Congress from that part of the country from whom you may be able to obtain the necessary information.

at what places on red river can lands be purchased to most advantage, and on what terms, and at what prices, for cleared, and for wood land.

What are the facilities of obtaining money from the Banks and whether they will take a pledge of the lands or require personal security—and on what credit.

Is it better to setle on Government and run the risk of purchasing when sold or purchase from individuals—Where are the Government lands—how far above Alexandria—when is the next sale (can you procure for me something like a description made by surveyors on a plat or map or history) what is the government price—Is the river open as far up as the Government lands—

Are there any settlers there—

What kind of settlements can be made on them, as respects *health, water musquitoes*

What is an average product of the best lands and what distance is the pine land from the river—is the water good in the pine land are the low grounds subject to the overflowed by freshets—

Do the pine lands furnish a safe retreat in the summer for the little negroes.

Is there a good steamboat navigation on the red river and how far up. If I can succeed with a portion of my negroes, I will send all my force out—unless there should be a general war in Europe, which seems to be brewing—Jackson or rather Kendall[50] is runing the people here as fast as possible—to hell & pitch [?] the gang.

Yours sincerely
WM WATTS JONES

[Addressed:]
The Honble Willie P. Mangum
Washington
City

[Endorsed:]
Answered
27. July 1834.

[50]Amos Kendall of the Kitchen Cabinet.

WPM-LC

Spencer O'Brien[51] *to Willie P. Mangum*

OXFORD 17th Febry '34

My dear Sir;

We have never, before this time, felt the same interest, in the deliberation of Congress, as we now now [*sic*] Men, who have, heretofore been indifferent or, rather, passive lookers on, in the great drama, are now beginning to inquire for themselves! You need not be told that, this is rather characteristic of our State & our People—or as Col. Boston would say, we have been too like, Rip-Van-Winkle.[52] The rebuke was a severe one, and its severity told with a tenfold force, because of its truth.—I trust in the sequel the Col. will have ample cause to do us justice—tho' we are slow to anger, and not sudden & quick in quarrel!

You are doubtless anxious to know how far we approve the act of the Executive in the removal of the deposites.—In three words I can tell you, so far as my acquaintance extends. Genl. Bryan,[53] A. P. Venable,[54] *& your friend* Sandy!![55] Besides these is none else.

The first, glories in his hate for Mr Clay—The second named, avows himself a collar man, & the third delights in being in a minority—More especially, when he thinks he does you a spite.

I wrote a long letter two or three weeks since to your Colleague & my friend Mr. Brown,[56] and went as far with him as I could venture. I regretted extremely to find that one who had taken so noble a stand in opposition to the 'force bill'—refusing the sword—should be willing to—'give the purse.' Either one, is sufficient to alarm—both united, may destroy the hopes of us all. My letter to him was written at the request of many of his former & present friends, and not a few of his late bitterest

[51]See above, I, 379.

[52]During the Ante-Bellum period national journalists and local political leaders frequently referred to North Carolina as "Old Rip" because of its lack of progress. In 1833 Governor Swain, in his message to the legislature, likened the state to Rip Van Winkle; and the *New York Evening Star* added that like Rip Van Winkle North Carolina had "grown poor and ragged from permitting her native energies and strength to lie for so protracted a period dormant and unemployed." In the decade of the 1830's population increased by only two per cent. A change came in that decade, however, when a system of public education and railroad building began. Johnson, *Ante Bellum N. C.*, 20-21, 25, 764, 827-828.

[53]Joseph H. Bryan.

[54]Probably Abraham Watkins Venable, who moved to Oxford, North Carolina, from Virginia in 1829 and became an ardent supporter of Jackson and Van Buren. He was presidential elector on the Democratic tickets in 1832 and 1836 and Democratic Congressman from 1847 to 1853. *Biog. Dir. of Cong.*, 1648-1649.

[55]Sandy Harris.

[56]Bedford Brown remained loyal to Jackson in the Bank fight. Up to 1833 he and Mangum had usually worked together in the Senate. After that date they were usually on opposite sides on political issues, although they continued to have good personal relations and to respect each other politically.

enemies, who would have taken great pleasure in this opportunity to testifying their favourable change of sentiment towards him.

You know the relation in which I have hitherto stood towards this gentleman, and the part which I took in his elevation—it would even now take much to alienate me from him—More especially when David L. Swain is to be the man who is to supplant him. I know you disapproved my course towards that *Judas* in the Hillsborough Convention—but *I* know I was right. When you come to act with him as it has been my fortune to do—and which I fear it will be yours ere long—you will then have realized all I have said of him, and to him.

I yet trust that you & Mr Brown may be brought to act in unison, on this great question. ☞ Show this to Mr. Brown, and confer together.

In the debate on the deposite question I think Messrs. Clay & Webster have given their opponents a decided advantage over them in mixing with it the question of a recharter—and although they disclaimed—Yet they said it, & did it. Mr Calhoun in this—as indeed in all other things, which come from him—showed the Master Spirit. He presented himself in one unbroken front, nor has a single speaker on the other side so far as I have seen touched him. Mr. Rives unquestionably the ablest champion of the Executive, and who, it seems was pitted against Calhoun in particular, was constrained to level his batteries against Clay. Would to God, that Calhoun had led in this debate—! There is no such leader. Benton, Rives & Forsythe might there have been demolished in detail, by Clay, Webster, Preston & *others*.

Rest assured that if any attempt [be] made at the present session to re-charter the U. S. Bank, all is lost. In the first place it is vain & impossible—in the next, it is unwise & impolitic.

Mr. Calhoun's franks here are well received and if he is disposed to keep it up, I will furnish you, with a list of names of gentlemen, who would be much gratified at receiving anything emanating from him.

In spite of the prejudice heretofore existing against him & his cause (now fast wearing away) his speeches are devoured with much avidity.

We anticipate a great treat in his speech for a repeal of the 'force bill.'[57] That is a question which, above all others, ought not to be permitted to slumber for a moment. Keep that question constantly alive. It can lose nothing to the friends of State's rights, by discussion.

Very respectfully
Your Friend
SPENCER O'BRIEN

P.S. I should like to hear from you, & have your opinion as to what will be the end of these things.

Hble. W. P. Mangum
Washington City

[Written on margin]

I have heard some of your friends complain that you are remiss in giving them information. Our district is in a deplorable situation as Hawkins[58] delays every office with Benton & Rives. Mr Calhoun's speech ought to lie in the hands of every man that can read, but we do not expect that of you.

On reflection, perhaps it would not [be] proper to shew this to Mr. B.—He might not take it kindly. You may read such parts of it to him as you like, at your discretion, if it comes in the way appropriately to do so.

[Addressed:]

To
The Hble. Willie P. Mangum
(of the U, S. Senate)
Washington City
D. C.

Mail.

WPM-LC

P. H. Mangum to Willie P. Mangum

HILLSBORO' Feb: 20th. 1834.

Dear Sir,

Some weeks ago, I wrote a letter to Genl. Barringer, requesting his attention to the application of several revolutionary soldiers for pensions—which had been made, thro' me, to the pen-

[57]Although Calhoun worked with Clay and Webster against the removal of deposits and the usurpation of power by Jackson, he never accepted their nationalistic ideas. He kept his state's rights party as a unit and in April proposed the repeal of the Force Act. *Wiltse, Calhoun: Nullifier,* 229.

[58]Micajah T. Hawkins.

sion office months before. Since I wrote to our Representative, abundant time has elapsed for a thorough investigation: if it has been made, the result has not been communicated.—I have thought that the rights of those old men may be attended to, with a little more despatch & certainty—by invoking the aid of a Senator, in conjunction with our immediate representative in Congress—whose attention, in the first instance, was asked, because, it was thought, such matters peculiarly belonged to his province.—The letter I addressed to our representative, contains the names of the applicants, the history & circumstances of the several cases—with more accuracy, than my memory at this distant period, will enable me to pretend to.—Will you call on Genl. Barringer for that letter, & aid by your attention in effecting a speedy & safe result? Old Capt W^{m}— Ray's case is one of importance, and I fear the Department is disinclined to give it a favourable reception—altho' I think that his case as made out by the *second* file of proofs forwarded, is *a very strong one.* Genl. Barringer has disregarded one of my requests contained in my letter to him—and it may be, that a similar disregard may obtain throughout, as far as may be compatible with his supposed accountability to his constituents.—Hence the increased importance of your attention in communion with the Genl.—

The signs in the political heavens are to my mind ominous. It is my fortune to differ in opinion with both parties in some degree—& with my intelligent acquaintances generally, in regard to the topics of the day. The doings of our last Genl. Assembly taken in connexion with the known expressed public voice for ten years before; and the struggle now going on between the Administration & the U. S. Bank, & in Cogress—prove to my mind that this world is awfully governed by money.—We are all bought & sold to that influence by the force of our necessities.—The power of money is in the ascendant in N. C. at this time; and I suppose your course will be approved by a majority for awhile, untill my friend B. Brown shall be beaten by Govr. Swain—& then it will not be long before a large portion of the same party will turn round & elect Govr. Owen over you. I confess I am no prophet—but the course of things has formed & is forming such unnatural *unions,* that I have little hope from the influence of sound principles, in this time of prejudice, necessity, & predominance of a class of men who love money as well as they love the Government, not of their choice, but which they live under.—Most persons think that Genl. Jackson has acted unwisely, rashly & perhaps unlawfully in removing the deposites; I think so too, but I am in some doubt after all, whether it is not right to abate an institution altogether, which has so much power over the property of the country—conceding as I do, the great convenience the Bank affords in transmitting money & equalizing exchange. I have no doubt that a great *stir* will be got up in such parts of N C as it may be practicable to do so, on the subject of the removal—for the purpose of electing Gov. Swain. Now I want to know Gov: Swain's political principles: but others will not think of such a m[in]or matter—& by an union of all sorts & sizes, p[torn]hed up for the special purpose, I see that B. Brown, an honest man & a sound politician, is to be thrown over board—to make room for a man, who may be worthy & talented, & who I think would make as good a Gov[r] as a Senator.—

Your family were well a few days ago—mine are well. I have had ague & fever, but am now well.

Yrs

P. H. MANGUM

[Addressed:]

The Honl.

Willie P. Mangum

(Of the Senate)

City of Washington

D. C.—

Mail.

Patty Taylor's Bill of Complaint[59]

[20 Feb., 1834]

To the honorable the Judge of the Court of Equity for the County of Franklin[60]

The Bill of Complaint of Patty Taylor Widow of the County of Franklin Plaintiff

Against

The honorable Henry Seawell of the County of Wake Defendant

---

[59]The original is in the possession of Mr. Mangum Turner, Winston-Salem, North Carolina.

[60]General Thomas Person's sister, Lucy Person, was Willie P. Mangum's grandmother. In 1819 when this land claim was brought into court, Mangum helped Seawell with the case. See above, I, 14.

Humbly complaining Sheweth unto your honor, your oratrix the said Patty Taylor, that in the year 1819 she having then Several Suits pending in this honorable Court in which she as plaintiff sought to recover against William Person the elder,[61] then of Warren County and now of Tennessee & others very large demands for and on account of matters set forth in the several Bills and remaining of Record before your honor, she applied to the defendant the said honorable Henry Seawell to appear for her, therein as her Counsel & Solicitor—Your Oratrix shews that the said Bills had been exhibited for her by the late Leonard Henderson Esquire and in the Winter of 1818 the said Leonard had been appointed a Judge of the Supreme Court then newly organized and the said Henry Seawell who had been for several years preceding as Judge of the Superior Courts in the Spring of the said year 1819 resigned his office and resumed practice at the Bar, bringing with him a great reputation for ability and learning and your oratrix was desirious to secure his Services in her behalf believing them of the last importance, to the successful prosecution of her said suits, and retained [?] him to appear for her, she agreed to give him the large fee of one thousand dollars—It was however expressly understood that this fee, was only to be paid as a reward for the defendents attention & services in the prosecution of all the said suits and that if he should fail (for any cause) to prosecute any one or more of them he was to be paid only in proportion to her Services —Your Oratrix shews that the said Henry Seawell, took from your Oratrix her Single Bill on Sealed Notes for the payment of the said sum of one thousand dollars as for a debt due and without any qualifications or conditions whatever, either in the body of the said Single Bill or written thereunto, or in any way attached to the said Bill—but he caused to be written a memorandum in Some form of a very unusual discription (as your Oratrix is advised) by which it is in substance stated (as well as your Oratrix is able to state) that the said obligation for one thousand dollars was intended as a fee in all the Suits, was to be paid as a Compensation for the said Henrys Services in prosecuting them all and that should he for any cause, not attend to

[61]In 1784 General Thomas Person acquired ten large tracts of land in western Tennessee. Upon his death in 1800 his brother, William Person, the administrator of the estate, took over his warrants and land titles. General Person left no children and only one brother, William, and two sisters, Mary Anne Little and Patty Taylor. William's sons, William, Jr., and Thomas, soon gained possession of the titles to the land. By 1818 Patty Taylor, wife of Major Francis Taylor who died in 1816, brought suit against William Person, Sr. and his sons to reclaim her part of the estate. "Patty Taylor vs Thomas Person and Others," MS, Franklin County Estates, Person, T-W, Department of Archives and History, Raleigh, N. C.

them or either, or any of them, then a proportionate deduction was to be made from the said Compensation, this paper was Signed by one Green Hill, then a Citizen of Franklin and by your Oratrix & the said Henry and was deposited with the said Hill as the mutual friend of the parties to be kept by him, & faithfully preserved as a memorial of the agreement aforesaid — Your Oratrix shews that this mode of reducing to writing and perpetuating the real agreement & transaction between herself and the said Henry Seawell, was one of his own devising to which your Oratrix made no objection, for reasons sufficiently manifest amongst which was her want of Knowledge of the extreme disadvantage of the situation in which she was thereby placed, she is advised, that the said memorandum, being intended as in nature of a defeasance or qualification upon the absolute engagement, contained in her bond and the bond being debarred to the said Henry and remaining with him, she ought in common fairness and according to the General practice in all like Cases, to have had the possession of the said memorandum, and that as the said Henry had assumed the relation of her Counsel in the said Suits & was a man of great, Knowledge, experience and ability and your Oratrix a Woman both weak & ignorant of the legal rights, he ought to have had the same delivered to her & was bound to see that the same care was taken to preserve to her the full and complete possession & controul of adequate evidence of the fact of the agreement, the preservation of which was of importance to your Oratrix as to perpetuate & Keep in his own power & hands the evidence of your Oratrixes obligation to pay the fee to the defendant—Your Oratrix shews that soon after to wit, in the year and whilst the suits remained almost entirely in the same Situation as when the said Henry was retained and before he had rendered any service whatever in them, or any of them, the said Henry brought suit upon the said bond against your Oratrix in the County Court of Franklin & the same came on for trial at Term of the said Court which was in the year and your Oratrix shews that before the trial of the said suit the said Green Hill had removed from this State and on his departure, deposited the above mentioned written memorandum, with one Daniel Sheni, and on the trial the said Daniel Sheni being summoned, by your Oratrixes Counsel, or otherwise required to produce, the same, came to Court and brought with him the paper, for the purpose of being given in evidence to the Jury on behalf of your

Oratrix and having placed the paper on the Clerks table or some table or desk in the Courthouse and within the bar the said Henry Seawell, (who was personally present in Court) took up the said paper and put it in to his pocket and refused to surrender it to your Oratrixes Counsel, but bore it off in Triumph and has continually since retained it from your Oratrix—By which most unjustifiable act on the part of the said Seawell, the said memorandum instead of being where it could be used for the benefit of your Oratrix in any way was placed beyond her reach and she became dependant for the safe keeping and production of a paper essential to her interest upon the only person in the World, intrusted to destroy suppress or withhold it — Your Oratrix shews that the standing of the said Seawell either by detering her Counsel from an interference with adequate decision & energy or by overawing the magistrates in the County Court, enabled him successfully to carry through this bold effort, to possess himself of and suppress her evidence, and he obtained a Verdict & Judgment against your Oratrix for the full amount appearing due upon the face of the Bond and afterwards having received a very large payment on account thereof send out (execution from time to time for the residue due therefrom Seised & Sold the property of your Oratrix at great Sacrafise and by his agent or agents purchased the same or a Great part thereof at reduced prices & afterwards Sold out his purchases at considerable profit to himself—for which your Orator prays to refer to the said proceedings in the County Court & other proofs be by him exhibited in due time according & according [*sic*] to the Course of the Court,—Further complaining your Oratrix shews unto your honor, that although she had good reason to hope, from the large fee secured to the said Seawell, the unrelenting spirit in which its collection was enforced, the great value of the property involved in the suits and the professional obligations resulting from the relations between them, that he would pay strict & even unusual attention thereto yet she was altogether and most cruelly disappointed them — The said Seawell received from the Government of the United States in the year [—] some office of large emolument which required his attention at Washington City that he was often in Consequence thereof absente from the Court in which her Suits were pending, that he neglected to give such attention to them as his offices would have permitted, took no measures for the prosecution of said Suits for trial, was always impatient of any intercourse with your Oratrix & studiously avoided her, when she sought interviews with him, for the purpose of Consultation with him upon the State of the Suits and obtaining advice and instruction and when he attended the Courts, from time to time neglected to examine the papers and inform himself of the Condition of her business—In short your Oratrix charges, that he grossly disregarded her interest & his professional obligations as her Counsel & attorney not only in one, or in some, but in all the said Suits and Seemed only anxious to let them, one after another be dismissed, either from want of due prosecution or upon hearings necessarily resulting in defeat, because brought on without any adequate preparation and then to leave your Oratrix without any redress—Your Oratrix shews that the issue of her Suits has been what under such neglect and mismanagement might have been expected most of them have been dismissed and one of them was within a year or two past, removed at the instance of the said Henry to the Supreme Court for trial when inasmuch as your Oratrixs Case was by no means made out, and that fact was well known to the Said Henry, he must have expected, that the same would like the others, be heard & dismissed which would have been the case, but your Oratrix is informed, that in the Supreme Court it was ascertained, that a most necessary party was dead—and the suit was abated, a fact which had existed for more than two Terms previous to the removal and yet the same had not been suggested, nor any steps taken to bring his representatives before the Court and your Oratrix shews that the said suit was upon that discovery, remanded to this Court in order that further proceedings might be had, and the same is now pending here, and shortly after the said Cause was remanded the said Seawell hath been appointed & hath accepted the office of a Judge of the Superior Courts—

Your Oratrix therefore charges that her business in and about which the said Seawell was retained was by him Shamefully neglected and she is advised that she is entitled in this honorable Court to have the said sum, so collected upon the Judgment aforesaid refunded to her, and to have an an[*sic*] account of the profits made by the said Seawell & his agent or agents upon the resale of your Orators property so bought at Execution sale and for that purpose to have a discovery from the said Seawell of the purchases and the profits made, upon the resales.

Your Oratrix charges, that the said Seawell had the said written memorandum, in his possession within a few months past and now has it, and she is advised that she is entitled to have the same discovered & produced—Your Oratrix is advised that in this honorable Court, the said Bond & Judgment under the special circumstances herein before set forth is considered, but as a Security for such sum or sums of money as the said Seawell may have reasonably deserved, to have for his professional Services in the premises, that although the said Judgment hath been collected, yet that in this honorable Court, the said written Memorandum, under the circumstances herein before stated, will be considered, either as explanatory of & part of the said bond & Judgment, or as in the nature of a defeasance or qualification thereof and the case having happened in which it is clearly ascertained, that the said Judgment ought not to have been inforced, either in whole or in part your Oratrix is entitled to relief in this honorable Court,—To the end therefore that the Said Henry Seawell may upon his Corporal Oath, full true & perfect answer make to all & singular the premises and that in the same full, ample & specific manner as if the same were repeated and he thereunto specially interrogated, that he may produce & exhibit the said written memorandum, that your Oratrix may have an account of the profits made by the Said Seawell on the resale of the property purchased by him & his agent as above stated That the said Bond & Judgment may by a decree of your honor, be declared to have been only in nature of a Security, for anything which might be found due, the said Henry,—that he may be decreed to refund & repay to your Oratrix, not only all the profits so made as aforesaid, but also all the monies collected on the aid Judgment or the Value of any other thing received in Satisfaction thereof, together with interests, thereupon and that your Oratrix may have such other further & adequate remedy & and [*sic*] relief in the premises as the nature of her case may require and to your honor may seem meet and equitable—May it please your honor to grant to your Oratrix, the states most gracious writ of Subpoena, to the said Henry Seawell, to be directed commanding him to be and appear before your honor at the Court of Equity to be held for the County of Franklin at the Courthouse in Lewisburg on the 2nd Monday after the 4th Monday in March 1834 then & there to answer the premises and to abide by and perform such decree as to your your [*sic*] honor shall seem meet —and your Oratrix as in duty bound will pray &c

G E BADGER for
plft

State of North Carolina
Franklin County

Patty Taylor makes oath that the paper writings, whereof in the foregoing she doth seek a discovery is not in her possession or under her controul in any way, but she doth believe the same is in the possession of the defendant, or is under his controul or else the same has been destroyed by him

Signed PATTY TAYLOR

Sworn to & Subscribed
before me this 8th day of
October 1833.

N Pattison OSC

State of North Carolina
Franklin County I Samuel Johnson Clerk Master of the Court of Equity for the County aforesaid do hereby certify the foregoing writing to be a true Copy of the Original filed in my office in the Case therein stated Given under my hand & Seal of office at Lewisburg this 22nd day of February 1834.

SAMUEL JOHNSON CMC

[Endorsement:]
Patty Taylor vs Henry Seawell
Original Bill in my office the 20th February 1834
A Copy for Henry Seawell Esqr.

SAML. JOHNSON CMC

WPM-LC

James Lea[62] *to Willie P. Mangum*

LEASBURG CASWELL CTY N. C. Feby 21st 1834

Dear Sir.

I think it may be truly said that we have fallen upon evil times, or rather evil times have fallen upon us, when an honourable Senator will get up in the Senate of the United States, and state that his State N. Carolina. has received no benefit from the Bank

[62]A merchant at Leasburg, Caswell County.

of the U. S.[63] it shows how far men of the highest standing for personal worth and integrity can be led astray by party feelings, regardless of the welfare of their country: such [language] your colleague is represented as using. I for one can safely [s]peak, that I have been greatly benefited by the Bank of the U. S. and I believe together with thousands of my fellow Citizens, that the whole mercantile class of the community have been greatly benefited by that institution I have no doubt and that the benefit has been extended in a greater or less degree, to the whole community is equally evident to me. What was it that restored our local Bank paper to credit? from an unwarrentable discount even in our State, it was the simple fact of the branch Bank of the U. S. at Fayetteville, taken it in deposit, and in payment of debts due the Bank, thereby placing our local Bank paper at once upon par with its own, yes untill that period I was together with others engaged in the same business with my self in the habit of paying from 3 to 5 per Cent, and even sometimes more, in our Bank Notes to get Northern funds, but what has been the consequence from that time untill the late unfortunate removal of the deposits? you could at all times obtain from the Branch Bank of the U. S. of Fayetteville drafts on Philadelphia or New York for ¼ to ½ per Cent premium, I never paid more than the former, and that too with our local Bank paper, instead of paying a Broker from 3 to 5 per Cent, and yet we are told the Bank has been of no benefit to us. there is not an individual in the State who has spent one dollar for the ordinary merchandise of the Country, who has not been benefited by it, for it is presumable that no merchant who pays 5 per Cent discount on such money as he receives in payment for his goods, will not take that loss into consideration when he comes to sell those goods to his customers, and further how many thousands of dollars has it not saved to those of our fellow Citizens who have emigrated to the South and West, since the location of the Branch Bank of the U. S. at Fayetteville in enabling them to ob[tain funds] at par which would answer them the same purpose, as Gold & silver, it is idle to reason the question with those who cannot see the benefit, I know that the constitutionality of the Bank of the U. S. is a question in relation to which the ablest men of our Country differ in opinion, and it is an honest difference of opinion too,

[63]When Mangum began presenting resolutions and petitions from various parts of North Carolina in favor of the Bank, Brown declared in the Senate that these resolutions did not represent North Carolina sentiment. McDuffie, "Willie P. Mangum," 51.

that is a question on which I feel myself incompetent to give an opinion, but as to the expediency of the institution, I should think, there ought to be no difference of opinion.

There is no act of Gen[l]. Jacksons publick life which has had so great a tendency to impair his popularity in this part of the State, as his unwarrentable assumption or abuse of power, in the removal of the publick deposits, I have scarcely seen an individual of any party who does not regret the measure, however you will always find some few who are ready to sustain all the measures of the "Sainted Chief" wright or wrong, and there are some of our prominent politicians who abused the old General so vilely, when he was first before the people for the high office he now fills, with so much discredit to his country, that they think the only atonement now in their power. is by the most servile adulations, you well know that this county has heretofore been more united in favour of Gen[l] Jackson than perhaps any other county in the State, but not so at the present time the recent course of the administration, has and is producing a wonderful change.

I have been prompted alone in this communication from our early acquaintance, and the high regard I have ever [torn] your character both as a private and publick citizen.

With Much respect
Yours truly
JAMES LEA

[Addressed:]
To the
Hon W. P. Mangum — Leasburg N. C.
Washington City. — Feb 22d 1834

WPM-LC

Frederick Nash to Willie P. Mangum

HILLSBORO the 21st Feb. [1834]

My dear Sir

Last week I received Mr. Websters report on the deposits,[64] franked by you—& to you also I was indebted for a copy of the

[64]On February 5, Webster, as Chairman of the Finance Committee, of which Mangum was a member, reported to the Senate that Taney's reasons for removal of the deposits were not sufficient. He recommended the adoption of Clay's resolution of censure of the President. Six thousand copies were printed for distribution despite the bitter opposition of the Jackson forces. *Daily National Intelligencer*, Feb. 10, 1834; Catteral, *Second U. S. Bank*, 335.

mad proceedings of the liberating fanatics of the North—For each of these I beg you to accept my acknowledgements—for the first particularly—It does Mr. Webster great honor not only as a sound politician, and as a cool, skillful logician I presume that all its coolness however is attributed to the station he occupied in making—Well may Mr. Forsythe express his surprise at the character of the report—it gives to him and his coadjutors nothing upon which they can seise—to lead the Public mind from the one, sole important object before them—It is a plain powerful argument, & how to be met except as heretofore—by a blind & furious denunciation of the Bank I can not perceive—I can not say, this report has raised Mr. Webster any higher in my estimation, for he stood before as high as he could—but it has done another thing—placed his political integrity beyond cavil or dispute—If Mr. Webster could have been induced to forget what was due to his country—here was ample opportunity to have sold himself to advantage—Pressed as the administration is—beset on all sides by the ablest & most eloquent men of the nation—driven to depend for defense on talents of an inferior grade —& for safety, to the ignorance & blind passions of the mob—what a principl it would have been to have enlisted the [illegible] of the North in its course—what office could or would have been denied—And I think I have heard a gentleman not very far from the Honorable Senator who is now reading this—hint that such things might be—For my own part I never for an instant doubted the course Mr. Webster would pursue—I know nothing of him personally—I judge him by his public life—He has raised too proud a monument to his own & his countries fame to tarnish either by truckling to power or pandering to vice—

Mr. Calhoun was so kind as to send me his speech—with his compliments—will you do me the favor to say to him, I have received the speech & duly estimate the kindness, which permitted him to think of an individual obscure as I am, when distributing it—I would have written to him, immediately—but I know very well that it is neither expected or wished, that such marks of respect should be repaid by an unnecessary consumption of the time of him conferring them—To you I may say, what to him, I might not venture—it is a masterly view of the ground & the whole ground—the argument is close & logical— & to my apprehension, perfectly irrefutable—With him I entirely agree after the first stage in his argument, that there he might in perfect safety have risked his case—It is thro'out a powerful argument—strongly characteristic of the speakers mind—I rejoice greatly to see him erecting his manly front among the zealous defenders of the constitution and if he will only say nothing more at *present* about nullification—I for one am willing to forget & forgive—I can not for my part consent to throw away such a man as John C. Calhoun—Mr. Mangum I tremble more for the permanency of our inhabitants now than I did twelve months ago—I believe they are in more danger—The danger, it is true, is of a differenct kind—but more insidious & therefore an entire change of our government from a Representative to a pure democracy — the stepping stone — the connecting link between freedom & Tyranny—If we are to have a master, in Gods name let us have him—without the agonies & convulsions of the government of a mob. To such results the present administration is leading us—& nothing under Heavan, can save us but the people themselves—But why say all this to you—you know it & feel it all—As your personal friend I feel rejoiced in the stand *you* have taken—and can not & will not believe but what it will meet with the unquallified aprobation of those who placed [you] where you are not to support & sustain Genl. Jackson but to sustain & support & defend their rights & interests as guaranteed by the constitution—I have heard but one opinion, here, in Granville & at Raleigh as to your course—

Have you any hope of the House of Representatives—Is it possible that if the two houses agree in ordering the deposits to be restored that the Executive can defeat their action—by his veto? is that the opinion of the intelligent with you—If it is so—it was very idle in those who granted the Bank charter—to require the secretary to report to *them* his reason in removing the deposits—of what importance is their opinion if subject to the revising control of the President—what Secretary will or *can* remove without the aprobation of the chief magistrate—and if by the constitution the President has all the power he choses—our forefathers were fools—as have been all who have administered the Government since—for all have tho't that the sword & purse were entrusted to different departments—& they were blockheads enough to support the principle essential to a free government—

And now after all we are told sapiently by King *Stork* it is an experiment—the country is to be convulsed from one end to the other—confidence destroyed—ruin entailed upon thousand[s] the government shaken to its base—and all for an experiment—nor can he say as was said by another such experimenter upon the bare passions of the mob—we are in the full tide of the *successful* experiment—for all-ready the cracking of the timbers of the social edifice—& the tears and groans of its terrified inmates are sounding in his ears—but he consoles them with—it is an experiment—I know you dislike political writing—there is something dangerous in it—but pray let me know if you can find time—is there any hope—

Your friend,
F. NASH.

[Addressed:]
Honorble,
W. P. Mangum
Washington City
[Postmarked:]
Hillsborough N. C
22 Feby 1834.

WPM-LC

Willie P. Mangum to Duncan Cameron[65]

WASHINGTON CITY 24th Feby 1834

My dear Sir.

The enclosed[66] I received this morning from Mr. Chauncey of Phila.—as it contains an authentic account of the interview of the Comm: with the President (excluding of course much bad grammar & violent, not to say coarse language) it will convey to you the best conception of the profound unacquaintance on his part with whole subject & the recklessness with which he will persist in his present lawless course.—

A plan is under advisement coming from the South, approved by the Bank and likely to have the entire cooperation of Messrs. Clay & Webster to settle the great question of currency upon a sound & permanent foundation.—It is the conception of Mr. Cal-

[65]The original is in the Cameron Papers, University of North Carolina.
[66]This enclosure was not found.

houn who[67] is unquestionably the ablest man here upon questions of this character.—You know he thought much & profoundly on these subjects immediately after the war.—Some preliminary difficulties have to be removed—and it will be offered as soon as that can be done.—It is deemed of much consequence to bring Gov Tazewell into its support, and thereby secure Virginia.[68]

It will probably be done, though Mr. T. is rather timid as he grows older.

Mr. T's present view is to leave the admn. the proposing of some course—It is hoped Va. may be brought to its support.—

If it shall be introduced—it will carry more than 2/3rds of the Senate—& it is believed a majority of the House—& in case of veto, a heavy responsibility will be thrown on the minority in the House.—

I am not at liberty to be more specific in reference to details.—

I write in haste in the Senate Chamber.

I am Dear Sir

Yours Mo. truly

WILLIE P. MANGUM

WPM-LC

Willis Alston to Willie P. Mangum

BUTTERWOOD Feby 24th 1834.

My Dear Sir $17 Send recpts to Judge Mangum.

I received an account of Duff Green under cover from you and now take the liberty of enclosing a Ten dollar bill for and on account of my subscription to his paper.

I also send you seven dollars for C. F. Rencher both papers being sent to Gretna Green, Mr. Rencher having left this part of the country, his paper must in future be sent to Stirling Gee, one of our best citizens. The seven dollars inclosed agreeably to a stated a/c sent will pay for Mr. Gee until the first of December next, get our receipts and enclose them, you see I dont mind

[67]While the debate was continuing on Clay's resolutions against the removal of deposits, Webster, Biddle, and Calhoun tried to save the Bank rather than win a political fight. They worked out a plan to return the deposits and extend the charter for a few years until the Bank could be liquidated. Calhoun and Webster disagreed on the length of the charter and as a result the plan never materialized. Catterall, *Second U. S. Bank*, 336.

[68]Virginia had become lukewarm toward Jackson as a result of the Force Bill. In January, 1833, Tazewell was elected governor to succeed Floyd. A few weeks later the legislature passed resolutions instructing the Virginia Senators to work for the restoration of deposits. Rives, who could not follow these resolutions, resigned and B. W. Leigh took his place. Wiltse, *Calhoun: Nullifier*, 217.

troubling a Senator when we have no Representative.

Tell Calhoun I shall send his apple grafts as he di[rected].

So far as I am informed your political [conduct] is most approved in our part of the country, we are a quiet People and bear with arbitrary measures some time before we break out.

I am your friend
WILLIS ALSTON.

P.S. No one Clay or Van Buren man can be found in our whole county

[Addressed:]
Honble
Willie P. Mangum Gretna Green NC
Senator
Washington City

WPM-LC

John Chavis to Willie P. Mangum

WAKE CTY N. CAROLINA
Feby. 26th 1834—

My dear Sir/

No person could be more intensely solicitous to know [what] would be your course respecting the removal of the deposites than I have been. Knowing you to be the friend of G. Jackson, I could not decide with certainty what you would do. However I could not avoid believing any other than that you would disapprove of his outrageous proceedings. In the mean time I thought I would not write until I was convinced of your course. This I never discovered until last night and finding that you [Several lines are faded.]

I am perfectly satisfied, and do rejoice that I can speak to my neighbours with freedom & confidence respecting the course of my friend Judge Mangum—

Mr. Brown ought to be at home grubing or frying pancakes for his wife (if he has got one) instead of having a seat in the Senate of the United States—

What noble fellows are Clay & Webster are! Cahoun would not be far behind them if his brains did not contain so much of the fruits of Nullification, which he intends at a future day to let out by bring[ing] up again state rights; but it wont do the union must be supported if not the welfare of [torn]

While I was in doubts what course you would take I was of the opinion that you were preparing to make a dead set upon the conduct of the Executive & to show not only the propriety but the absolute necessity there was that the deposites should be restored & I now think I was not mistaken that I was not mistaken—[*sic*].

Should your speech[69] upon that subject be published in *Pamphlet* form please to send me a copy to Rogers store—

Please to give my respects to Gen. Barringer & my son Abraham Rencher & tell them I am anxious to know their course respecting the deposites But that I entertain a hope that they will be in favour of these resolutions—

I was much gratified at hearing that you spent four days in Raleigh on your way to Congress, supposing that you had the pleasure not only of meeting a number of your friends but of showing your enemies [Several lines are faded.] coming to Teach for you [faded] I wrote I had determined to break up house-keeping & board my wife at a neighbours house & had made arrangements to do so, but when I was about to bring the matter to the hearthstone my wife refused to be boarded out, but I still determined that i[f] you wanted me I would have some person to stay with her & come. Col. Horner having written to me that you had let him know that you would write to me shortly upon the subject I waited for your letter with much impatience, but none came to hand. In the mean time Doctor Parish[70] wrote to me that he wished me to come & break in his [Several lines are faded.] was still waiting for you; but conved in his letter that I must not let any person know of my coming to his part of the neighbourhood. That I did not like because its a sly ungenerous appearance in some way unknown to me therefore I wrote him that it was quite unnecessary for me to come about making the school, as my character as a Teacher was know to you & the Col & to you & him neighbours

[69]In the heated debate that continued for the first three months of 1834, Mangum said little. On January 23 he presented memorials of "sundry citizens" of the state. Later he added those from Burke, Fayetteville, Wilkes, Washington, and Lenoir. On February 25 he made his main speech against the removal of deposits. The "Young Men" of Hartford, Connecticut, published it in pamphlet form. After denying Senator Brown's contention that the memorials did not represent the sentiment in North Carolina, Mangum made a strong attack on Jackson for deserting the South on the tariff. He condemned those who blindly followed the President. Finally he emphasized the unconstitutionality of removal of the deposits. The money, he said, was placed by law in the U. S. Bank and Jackson had removed it for the gain of his supporters. *National Intelligencer*, Mar. 6, 1834; *Raleigh Star*, Mar. 27, 1834.

[70]The Parishes were Mangum's close neighbors.

Chess and draughts pieces and board. The originals are in the possession of Miss Sallie Alston Turner, Washington, D. C.

must have reference, & I have heard nothing from him since—

Last year I made about $30. by Teaching & this year, perhaps I may make 6[torn] Thus you see what a miserable neighbourhood I live in—

My wife has been dying slowly for about fifteen months. She is not completely comfortable [in] her bed, but has not been found of disadvantage to the family during [Several lines are faded.]

I should be glad to receive a letter from you or anything else you think I will be glad to see—

I am sincerely yours &c

JOHN CHAVES—

P S.

Please to tell my son Rencher that as soon as I find out his course respecting the deposites I will write to him—

[Addressed:]

Hon. Willie P. Mangum
A member of Congress
Washington City
Mail) District of Columbia

WPM-LC

E. L. Winslow[71] *to Willie P. Mangum*

Honble Willie P. Mangum
Dear Sir

FAYETTEVILLE February 26, 1834

I take great pleasure in being the organ of communicating to you the desire of Your fellow citizens in this part of the State, that you would receive & take charge of the enclosed Memorial[72] to the Congress of the United States, on the subject of the re-

[71]Interested in internal improvements and business affairs, he represented Fayetteville at the internal improvements convention at Salisbury in 1833 and one at Raleigh in 1838. In 1850 he was president of the Fayetteville and Western Plank Road. *Raleigh Register*, Nov. 5, 1833; *Hillsborough Recorder*, Dec. 20, 1838; *Report of the Board of Internal Improvements of the Legislature of North Carolina at the Session of 1850-1851*, Appendix E.

[72]These resolutions were presented to Congress by Mangum March 5, 1834. After asserting that the country was prosperous before removal, the proposers of the resolutions stated that removal was a mistake and asked Congress to relieve the distress caused thereby. *Senate Documents*, 23 Cong., 1 sess., Doc. 143, pp. 1-2.

moval of the public deposites & the course of the Executive, in relation to that subject.

They have generally admired the high, dignified & independent course You have taken in the Senate on this subject.

The names to this Memorial are 237 in number & embrace among them many of the most respectable influential & wealthy of our citizens, & many who I believe voted for the President of the United States. There are also, many of that class of our citizens, who are engaged in the different mechanical employments, there are others who are Farmers, We do not know that any good will arise, but we think that if the citizens of this State could be made to speak out on this subject, North Carolina would be found not to have lost any of the Spirit that animated her in 76.

Very Respectfully & truly
Yours
E L WINSLOW.

A copy of the Memorial will be Enclosed to Mr. Deberry this day by another gentleman.
The President, cashier & officers of the Bank of Cape Fear have signed—but no one who is connected with the Bank of the United States.
[Addressed:]
Honble
Willie P. Mangum
Senate of the
United States.

WPM-LC

Johnson Busbee[73] to Willie P. Mangum

N. C Wake County 27th Feby. 1834

Hon. W. P. Mangum Esq. My dear Sir, I see in the papers that you have taken an independant stand against the enemies of our Constitution and Liberties of the people, to which I say well done thou good and faithful servant. I do think that it is time for the American people to speak out. I have lately been three days, in large collections of people a great Many of them of the first order of interest, & I can say with truth that I heard

[73]See above, I, 559.

only one Man advocate the removal of the deposits & he admitted that it was a high handed Measure. You know that our Banks are winding up their business & of course lend, no Money, & the Branch of the U. S at Fayetteville has stoped loaning which places the N. Caroliana in an unpleasant situation, without flattery you stand higher in the estimation of the Citizens of your State than you ever did & Genl, Barringer is also more Poppular in his district than he ever was. I think he would beat Williamson[74] at this time—in the district 1000 votes at least. I think my old friend Genl. Hawkins is paving his way to stay at Home. I should like to know what you think will be the final result of the removal of the deposits and if you think there will be a compromise to recharter the U S Bank. & who you think will go to England as Minister & if the President intends to have a Secretary of the treasurer or not, (if I have asked an unfair question I ask pardon) if not when you have time I should like to know your opinion &c

Yours truly,

N. B. Direct yours letter

J. BUSBEE.

to Busbee's Store, Wake Co.N.C.

[Addressed:] J. B Busbee's Store Wake Co.

N. C. 27th Feb'y.

Willie P. Mangum Esq.,
Senate U. States
Washington City

WPM-LC

Isaac T. Avery[75] to Willie P. Mangum

SWANN PONDS BURK CO NO. CA.
Febuary 28th—34.

The Honble Wilie P. Mangum,
Dear Sir,

A sketch of the debate in the UN. States Senate, on the introduction of the Burke resolutions,[76] has just reached us. I am happy in having it in my power, to assure you that your course meets the approbation of this Community—

---

[74]Possibly John G. A. Williamson from Person County.

[75]See above, I, 382n.

[76]See above, II, p. 82, for the controversy over the Burke Resolutions.

The call for the meeting was made, by the Friends of Mr. Graham[77] and the original Friends of Genl. Jackson, whole hog men, who had opposed Saml P. Carson, because as they said, he had deserted Genl Jackson. Of the Presiding officers Coln. Dickson,[78] Greenaway,[79] and Kincaid[80] two of them had been warm supporters of Genl. Jackson; and two decided Friends of Mr. Graham, myself, and others, who were not of this class, refused to have any thing to do in getting up the meeting; or in its proceedings. Samuel P. Carson I verily believe did not know of the call; he was accidently there attending Court. and after the introduction of the resolutions by Colo. Hillman,[81] was called on I think by the Presiding officer, to give his views. It was the largest political Meeting I have ever seen in this place (with one exception). & a more sober, orderly, or respectable assemblage, I have never seen; or one in which there was more unanimity, although composed of men of all parties.

Mr. Forsyth[82] calls it a *miserable Petition,* got up by Pot House Politicians &c. we know Mr. Forsyth. if we are miserable, we had not calculated on his sympathies, his selfish, Partizan course, his disregard of Southern feelings and Southern interests. I may add of the Country & Constitution when they come in conflict with the views of the *Party* had not prepared us to expect any thing milder from his tender Mercy, than the force Bill—I will say nothing of the mass of the Citizens of this County, you personally know a number of them. It is also known to you Sir that the Mines[83] in this County have attracted hither, a body of Men who taken collectively will perhaps be found, to possess as much enterprize, and intelligence, as can be found among an equal population any where—there are men engaged in this business, who have filled the highest offices in our State. If not as capable of forming correct opinions, on Constitutional Questions as this Ex. Minister; they are, from the pure air they breathe, more likely to be exempt from Party, and Political Prejudice—they have received neither outfits or Salaries to

[77]James Graham, brother of William A. Graham, was a lawyer who represented Rutherford County in the legislature in 1822-1824 and 1828-1829, and his district in Congress in 1833-1843 and 1845-1847. *Biog. Dir. of Cong.,* 1027.

[78]Col. William Dickson represented Burke County in the legislature in 1812-1814. *N. C. Manual,* 521.

[79]Col. William Greenway was vice president of the Burke County meeting.

[80]John Kincaid presided at the meeting.

[81]Samuel Hillman.

[82]John Forsyth.

[83]Burke County was a part of the gold mining district of North Carolina. F. M. Green, "Gold Mining: A Forgotten Industry of Ante-Bellum North Carolina," *The N. C. Hist. Rev.,* XIV, 12.

sooth the past. they have none in prospect to Gild the perspective—They are engaged in a business, in which they are compelled to purchase everything, Pork from Kentuckeans, Bacon and Flour from Tennessee. large quantities of Iron, and castings, Spades & Shovels from the Manufacturer at Philadelphia. Shoes and Negro Cloathing from the North. Corn, and beef vegtables &c from the neighbouring Farmers to pay Negro hire to Citizens of this State, Virginia, and South Carolina. from having been a purchaser of Bullion, I can safely state the amount of exchanges necessary to carry on this business for the last two, or three years, at from 10 to $20.000 pr. week. The State Bank of North Carolina had purchased Bullion at the Mint value, taking the premium on the Mint Certificate, as compensation for interest, on advances, and risque of transportation, untill the term of the charter, had so nearly expired that the trade ceased to be an object—she very liberally paid out, UN. S. Paper in the proportion, that was required to meet engagements, out of the State. in the mean time, Speculators were largely concerned in the trade with Georgia Money; the Bank of Macon, after throwing into circulation perhaps to the amount of $100.-000 failed, and left this amount a dead loss in the hands of our, Mining & Farming Community since then, it has been impossible to force into circulation the Paper of these local Banks. Notes of the Banks of the State, a UN. States, with the exception of some So. Ca. Paper, is all that will circulate here. up to the first of October, Speculators were induced to continue the trade; and to furnish the funds, on terms a little less favorable, than those on which the Bank had purchased, since the fall on the premium they had ceased to purchase—Some wealthy and respectable Individuals who were engaged in the business; the Messrs. Hamiltons, Turner, and Robards, seeing, and feeling the situation of the Community, have endeavored to supply a circulating medium, by Issuing small checks, on New York, they have aleivated, but not relieved us. they are not receivable for Taxes or Bankable, and cannot be got off except at a Discount—A Miner would perish in this Community, with his pockets full of Chatahooche Notes, allthough this Institution is said to be a Pet, and favorite of the Senator from Georgia.

Is it wonderful, that a community situated as ours, should condemn an act, which put them to great and daily inconvenience; and subjected them to positive loss, in allmost every monied transaction, for they are not only compelled to take less than the Mint value of their Bullion, but in every purchase, or payment, to lose the difference in exchange. the consequence is that the business is declining, and Capital and labour, withdrawing from it—the letter writer whose letter you introduced, was mistaken in stating that the Notes of our State Banks were at a Discount here. they are at par except when wanted for purpose out of the State, it was stated at the meeting, and correctly that the Notes of our Banks all of which pay specie were up to the 1st of October convertable into Northern funds at ¼ of one pr ct. and since then they had fallen in New York, and were then at from 5 to 8 pr. cent Discount.

Your Colleague Mr. Brown, will find himself I conceive greatly mistaken in his calculations. find as to public opinion—the press, is after I take it to follow, than lead Public Opinion, there is not as far as I know a paper in the State, that Justifies the removal of the Deposits, like some other acts, it was easier committed than Justified—

The little Van Buren paper in Rutherford publishes extracts from the Adm. papers; such articles as are manufactured for it at Washington, and the Homiles of Judge Foreman, the only Man I have ever seen in No. Ca. who openly avows the Doctrine that in Political contests the spoils of the vanquished, rightfully belong to the Victor, and are the only object worth contending for. But Mr. Elmer does not come out Editorially; and Justify the Act; if he attempts it he will sink at once.

Mr. Brown appears disposed to lean, on the Western part of No. Ca. for countenance, and support, let him not lay that flattering unction to his Soul I can find one hundred Men, who would sighn an address, requesting him to resighn, for every one he could get who approbates his course, he must look to the Kitchen Cabinet, and not to the freemen of No. Ca. either for support or reward. He adduces the fact, of the State having chartered new Banks, as an evidence of prosperity. what is the fact, is it not the scarcity of the money, the hope of relief, from the debts due the State and UN.S. Bank, by our Citizens, that has extorted these charters from our Legislature, is an increase of Banks in an Agricultural State evidence of prosperity, or when chartered as the means of Relief, have they ever afforded it, what is the History of Kentucky with her 50, and Penysylvania with her 100 Banks in 1819, but one of wide spread

Bankrupcy, and ruin. Even in Tennessee where even the system was not carried so far it was but little better. I speak from painfull experience having lost 25 pr. Cent on debts due me there, to an amount which injured me seriously, after making collections, I could not exchange the money which had been forced on me by tender laws, but was compelled to seek out, and purchase bonds not due, on men residing in No. Ca. and give 25 pr. Cent.—but History has no warnings for our present rulers, nothing but an experiment will satisfy them, they are making one, that I fear is deeply to injure the prosperity of our good old Mother No. Ca., she may be oppressed and impoverished, but I hope she will allways be able like the Illustrious Mother of old, to point with pride, and pleasure, to some of her Sons, in our National Annals, and claim them as her Jewels. While we Southerners have you, Calhoun, Preston,[84] Poindexter,[85] with many others I could name, we will not give up the Ship or believe but the Constitution, and the Country, will be saved may your exertions in the cause of both be crowned with success, and secure you the Statesmans richest reward the continued confidence and approbation of your Constituents

Accept assurances of respect and esteem from your friend and
Obedt Servt.
ISAAC T. AVERY

P. S. On looking over this hastily written letter, it strikes me that I may from excited feelings, have abused Mr. Forsyth more than I ought but he has excited strong feelings here, where he was no favourite as I am writing to you alone—believe I will not copy or retract what I have said.

[Addressed:]
The Honble. Wilie P. Mangum
U. N. S. Senate
Washington.

[Postmarked:]
Morganton, N. C., Mar. 3.

[84]William C. Preston, of South Carolina. *D. A. B.*, XV, 207-208.
[85]George Poindexter, of Mississippi.

WPM-LC

Saml. Hillman to Willie P. Mangum

MORGANTON N. C. March 1st. 1834

My dear Sir,

I stated to you in my last that the notes of the Bank of United State's were fast receding from circulation among us,[86] that our local banks are on the eve of winding up their business and had been for some years collecting in their notes, that the agency of the State Bank at this place had been discontinued—and that a note on either of our State Banks was now rarely to be met with—I stated further that our principal markets were Charleston and Augusta and that for some time past our principal circulating medium in this part of the State had consisted of Georgia and South Carolina Bank notes— That since the removal of the Deposits the usual Bank accommodations were withheld at both those market towns the consequence of which had been a great depression in the price of produce and that Southern money was becoming very scarce and that we were left almost entirely without a circulating medium—Even gold in consequence of the reduction of the premium, sustains a loss of three cents on the cwt or 80cts—Can all this State of things exist and yet one of our Senators be found declaring on the floor of Congress that North Carolina was never more prosperous? That this section of the State is labouring under no grievances? That the meeting was gotten up for political and party purposes? It is true our Banks are Specie paying Banks but what evidence have we that they will continue to be so even for the short period which their charters have to run—Mr Brown argues as if he thought the rechartering the Cape Fear Bank and the chartering other banks was evidence of the prosperity of the State—This action on the part of the Legislature was loudly called for by the necessities of the people, not for the purpose of extending the commerce of the State, not for the purpose of encouraging commercial enterprize but for the purpose of creating a circulating medium with which the people of the State may be enabled to pay their debts without being ruined—From a statement which I have seen taken from the Raleigh Register it appears that the people of this State owe to our local Banks

[86]As a result of Jackson's removal of the deposits the value of the Bank's stock declined. A panic was precipitated by the shock. At the same time the tariff was reduced and the Bank contracted its loans. Catterall, *Second U. S. Bank*, 287-297.

and to the United States Branch at Fayetteville the sum of $2:971:465—while the amount of their notes in circulation is $1.497:454 making the people indebted to them beyond the entire amount of their notes in circulation $1:971:465 or nearly half a million more than two to one of debts due these banks to the whole amount of their notes outstanding—In this estimate no notice is taken of the supposed amount of these notes circulating beyound this State which must be very great, for as the Banks expire by their Charter in 1835 (Jan^{ry}) and have been winding up their business and calling in their notes for several years, the notes of our local banks have been sought for with the greatest avidity for the purpose of paying instalments—There can be no doubt I think that the amount of our notes abroad is much greater than the amount of Bank paper of our sister states circulating within this State—If so the disproportion of debts due the banks compared with the currency of the State will be encreased in the same proportion and will probably not fall short of $3:00 to $1:00—I have before me the Charter of "A Bank of the State of North Carolina" which requires the stock of that Bank to be paid "in gold and silver coins of the United States, or Spanish milled dollars or *their equivalent*—The other Charters I have not at hand but do not doubt but they contain provisions similar to those which Mr Brown alluded to in the debate in the Senate on our resolutions to wit that they authorise subscriptions of Stock to be made in the notes of the State Bank of North Carolina; but if I am correctly informed the provision goes a step further and authorises the stock to be subscribed for and paid in North Carolina Specie paying Bank notes and in notes of the United States Bank—and that I think is the true construction of the words "*or their equivalent*" in the Charter of the Bank of the State—Unless Mr Brown can tell us how $1.00 can be made to pay $2½ or $3:00 I am unable to understand by what system of financiering by what political Arithmetic he can prove that the people are to be benefited by the privilege granted to the Stockholders of subscribing in the notes of these specie paying banks—The charters of the State Bank and of the Bank of Newbern expire with the present year and the debts due them must be paid—Suppose the people who are indebted to these banks could collect every dollar of their notes which is circulating in the State it would not enable them to pay one half, if it did one third of the debts which they owe to the banks alone to say nothing of debts to Merchants and others —It is admitted that these provisions are a considerable convenience to large capitalists who may be desirous of taking stock in the new banks and also to the old banks who may have an interest in having the debts due them transferred from them to the new banks, and thereby be saved from the necessity of coercing their debtors—It may also be of advantage to the private capitalists who has money which he is willing to lend at exorbitant interest or to invest in property at very reduced prices—The scarcer the money the higher the interest and the more depreciated the property—But in God's name I ask how are these provisions which are made in favour of subscribers of new stock and of the old banks to benefit the people? As I have said before the people probably owe about $3:00 to the banks for every $1:00 of bank paper which is circulating among them —Will not every dollar then which may be subscribed in the money of the old banks for the purchase of stock in the new banks, be so much withdrawn from circulation; at least until the new banks get into successful operation? And will not the inability of the debtor to pay be encreased in the same proportion? But suppose the stock in these new banks to be taken to any considerable amount in the bills of the old banks and that they go into full operaion? Who will be most urgent in their applications for loans? Will they not be the debtors of the old banks and of the Branch Bank of the United States at Fayetteville? What will they do with the money which they must thus borrow, but pay it back into these very banks in discharge of instalments due them? Thus these banks will be always fortified against any runs which may be made upon them for specie; and as the debts due them greatly exceed the amount of their notes in circulation both in and out of the State, they will soon commence running on them for their notes which may have been paid in as *an equivalent* for Gold and Silver, or for Gold and Silver itself, until the ability of these new banks to pay specie will be "as baseless as the fabric of a vision"—The Charters of our banks expire on the 1st. day of January next and the United States Bank about two years from this time—From the time of the expirations of their charters they cease to discount—It is true they have two additional years to call in their debts and wind up their business—But if the present State of things exists those two years I apprehend will be employed by the banks in collecting their debts by legal coercion—If so we are to witness the gloomiest periods which have ever overshadowed the prospects of North Carolina—Had the currency of the Country remained undisturbed by the wild ruthless and vindictive spirit which has assailed it a spirit of confidence would have existed by which an arrangement might have been made by the new with the old banks and the branch of the U. S. Bank at Fayetteville by which the new banks might have gone into successful operation and the people, by gaining a little more time, might have been saved from ruin, which now seems impending over them—What will be the consequence of the present high handed and lawless measures God only knows—United States Bank notes are equivalent to gold and Silver Coins and therefore our Legislature have said substantially that stock in these newly created banks may be subscribed for in these notes—But Mr. Brown by swelling (he ought to read Aesop) and fulminating eternally, nolens volens, against the U. S. Bank he trying to ape his great prototype Genl. Jackson and because his master has repealed an act of Congress, he is trying to repeal an act of our General Assembly—The public here Sir look to you and those of their representatives who think with [you] to strain every nerve in defence of the Country The course which you have pursued meets with the most cordial approbation of all parties—

Adieu—

SAM[l] HILLMAN

Hon[l]. Willie P. Mangum

[Addressed:]

Hon. Willie P. Mangum
U. S. Senate
Washington

WPM-LC

Geo. W. Jones[87] to Willie P. Mangum

GRANVILLE COUNTY 1st. March 1834.

Dear Judge,

I believe that I have written nearly a quire of paper in letters to you since you left home; but I have not received the first answer from you—

[87]George W. Jones, who lived in Granville not far from Mangum's home, was a lawyer and planter who was a member of several Whig committees. *Hillsborough Recorder*, January 8, June 6, 1844.

That you have not received them, owing to the management of the post Office departments I have concluded to write you again; and have it mailed at Oxford—I hope that you will answer this letter and let me know what I must do, for I am here at nothing, I am unable to know, what to be at until I receive an answer from you—I have written this letter merely to remind you of writing to me—There is no news of importance in this section at present—I was at your house the other evening, and your wife and family were well—Your wife stated that she had lost a negro girl a few days previous—Excuse my bad writing—as I am in haste—I do hope that you will write me immediately; as I would be exceedingly rejoiced to receive one from you—

Yrs very respectfully
GEO: W. JONES

[Addressed:]
Hon
Willie P. Mangum
Washington City
D. S. of Columbia

WPM-LC

John A. Anderson[88] *to Willie P. Mangum*

WINTON 4th March 1834.

Dear Sir

Enclosed I hand you a communication to Genl. Green.[89] please hand it to him.

Our County has been one of the strongest administration supporters in the district. It has heretofore been Repty [reputedly] aroused in its Support by one or two office holders shoveing a head a lot of demagoge who could not believe the administration Could err. in the administration of his Goverment—They have become languid and renounce the removal of the deposits, the pressure is hourly increasing—and the old hero. with the administration of *his* government must go down with it. I can assure you Sir the Course you are persuing at the present crissis

[88]John A. Anderson was later a member of the Council of State and chairman of the Hertford County court. Benj. B. Winborne, *The Colonial and State Political History of Hertford County, N. C.*, [Raleigh], 1906, p. 237; *N. C. Manual*, *436-437*.

[89]Duff Green.

caused us in this Quarter to be proud to acknowledge you as our Statesman.

Very Respectfully
Your obt srvt
JOHN A ANDERSON

[Addressed:]
Honble. Willie P. Mangum
Senate United States
Washington City
D C

WPM-LC

P. H. Mangum to Willie P. Mangum

OXFORD, N. C. March 7th.. 1834.

Dear Sir,

I came to this place by way of your house: Your family was well. There is nothing doing here this week, except trying the validity of Jno. G. Smith's will—which closed last night after two day's labour. The will is set aside.—No new business afloat. The profession goes begging. I have no news of importance to give you, & write now principally to touch on the pending Indictmt vs Sandy Harris.[90] Do you remember my telling you, that you had better be present on that trial, if one should be had? You replied that Mr. Nash[91] & Mr. Waddell[92] would take care of your feelings & character, so far as either were connected with that matter.—

That Indictment is contd. by Consent. To-day the State Docket was taken up—& this morning, it being then the first opportunity this week, I asked Mr. Nash in my room, & remarked that "Willie has committed his honor to you & Mr. Waddell, in the matter of the Indt- vs S. Harris." He replied that "a Court of Justice was not the place for the Honor of a man to be protected—that if Mr. Mangum's Honor had been assailed, it was for Mr. Mangum & in another way to repel the assault"—that he did not know the Honor of the world &c or words to that effect, with an indifference & coldness that absolutely shocked me. Mr. Nash was under the impression that Harris stood In-

[90]See above, I, 585n; and below, II, 177.
[91]Frederick Nash.
[92]Hugh Waddell.

dicted for a *Libel,* & said that if he had his way with it, that he would recommend a Nolle Prosequi:—Mr. Nash & Waddell were got together:—Mr. Waddell expressed his interest in every thing that could affect Mr. Mangum:—& said that he had supposed the prosecution was not to be carried on—as he supposed the witnesses were not here.—After some conversation, I remarked that in justice to you the Indictment should not be tried unless the Witnesses were present—that altho' I had in common with you, relied on them to attend to the pros: & had supposed that their attention had been directed to it with some particularity, & for that reason in connexion with the delicate relation I stood in to the matter—I had declined attending to it;—Yet I should see that the matter should not be tried unless the Witnesses were present—& that "a nol: pros:" should be entered, if the matter could not be explained correctly—I then went to Scott & talked with him: he s^{d}. that deft—would deny the ass^{t}, & if pressed he Harris should continue the Ind^{t}. on acc^{t}. of your absence, as he wanted your evidence— Whereupon they agreed to continue by Consent.—I told Scott that if tried, the Witnesses must be present—otherwise there must be a nolle pros—He s^{d}. if I—Nash & Wad—said a nol: pros: he would enter it—At all events he would not try in the absence of witnesses.—As the matter was to be cont^{d}. I s^{d}. it had better remain untill you came home: so it rests.—

I hold that a man's Honor is always safest in his own hands.—Friends are sometimes forgetful. If that matter is to undergo a Judicial investigation, I say "Be present"—and trust to "Nobody".—

I am making *no money*—& will leave this Country, if my poverty will admit of it.—

I expect a meeting at Hillsboro' next week, on the Deposit question—of old Fed's, young Feds—Bank men & merchants.—The great body of our People would sustain the President—but the above descriptions of people, & generally the intilligent, would condemn.—

Yrs

P. H. MANGUM

[Addressed:]

The Hon^{l}.

Willie P. Mangum

WPM-D

Isaac T. Avery to Willie P. Mangum

MORGANTOWN March 8th 1834

The Honble Willie P. Mangum.

Dear Sir,

I take the liberty to enclose to you a letter to Genl. Green; covering the amt of my subscription to the Tellegraphe. may I ask the favour of you to hand it to him. very respectfully your friend and

Obedt. Servt

ISAAC T. AVERY.

P.S. while writing the above I learn that the Newland, Stage Contractor,[93] have stopped payment owing to the pressure of the times and the embarrassments of the P. O. Department.—Their Father Benjn Newland, in whose name I believe the contracts are still made, is perhaps the oldest Contractor, in the U. N. States, and has allways, stood for

I [illegible] the young men, their property is under [illegible] I sincerely hope Congress may m[ake] an immediate appropriation to relieve the Contractors.—If they [illegible] leave the [illegible] which the department has Contracted, untill after an investigation takes place [illegible]

[Addressed:] The Honble Willie P. Mangum
cr the U N S Senate
Washington

WPM-LC

C. P. Mallett[94] to Willie P. Mangum

FAYETTEVILLE 11th March 1834

My Dear Sir,

The knowledge I have of your character induces me to intrude upon you a matter of business in which I have no other interest than a will to serve an old widow: who is the relict of an officer of the Revolution her husband was possessed of a tolerable living entered the army as Lieutenant—was promoted to Captain—

[93]They received a mail contract in 1833-1834 for $1,516.24. *Senate Documents*, 23 Cong., 1 sess., Doc. No. 422.

[94]See above, I, 527.

in which capacity he served through the War—shortly before peace being in bad health, from severe exposure—he returned on furlough but never left his bed untill the troops were disbanded—the disease fell in his limbs and he became a cripple for the residue of his life—and his little patrimony soon wasted away in the support of himself and family—when the Pension Fund was first raised—he made an attempt to get to Washington—but was unable—he sent his papers—to Mr. McBryen—who said he left them filed—and who told him from time to time that all would be right—the old man lingered out a life of suffering (no doubt from early exposure for his character can be readily shewn to have been correct.) his widow has now a helpless family about her—and but for an appropriation from our State of $40 pr year she would actually want. Now My Dear Sir the object of this present is merely to know if any special provision could be made by having all the facts set forth by way of petition—and whether you could come down from your higher engagements—to undertake the widows cause. I will do all the work if you will only point out the mode.

With sentiments of very high regard
I am Respectfully
Your Friend
C. P. MALLETT

[Addressed:] To/
The Honble
W. P. Mangum
Washington.

WPM-LC

Henry T. Clark[95] *to Willie P. Mangum*

TARBORO N C
March 12th 1834

Dear Sir

Having received a few days since a communication from Duff Green under your frank—I must ask the privilege of reply thro the same channel.

[95]Henry Toole Clark, 1808-1874, a graduate of the state university, was a planter of Edgecombe County. A member of the state senate from 1850 to 1861, he became speaker and lieutenant governor in 1859-1861. In the 1840's he was clerk of Edgecombe County Court. Grant, *Alumni Hist. of U. N. C.*, 111; Ashe, *Biog. Hist. of N. C.*, IX, in MS. at Duke University.

Archibald DeBow Murphey. 1777-1832. From the original oil portrait by Weisman and now in the possession of the Dialectic Society at the University of North Carolina, Chapel Hill, N. C.

I cannot omit this opportunity of adding a "well done" to your course as a North Carolina Senator. Disdaining the "shackles of party" at home and abroad you have acted as a highminded independent Representative of a *Sovereign State* However such a course may draw on you the rancour of thos who are thwarted, it must ultimately prevail and gain you the commendation of your people—The freedom of these remarks may subject me to the suspicion of flattery or pertness as my acquaintance with you is so slight. But Sir you are executing a public trust, and it certainly is becoming to express our satisfaction & opinions about public acts.—And I much mistake your character if you dont hold yourself accessible to any citizen of Carolina however humble or remote he may be—

I live in a strong Jackson county, the Politicians aware of the influence of Jacksonism nourish it for their *own support* & protiction and endeavour to spell-bound every subject by the magic of a name—But the future is more promising to freedom of opinion. for which we may feel indebted to the example *set us in high places.*

I myself belong to the school of "States-rights and State-remedies" — and the proclamation formed the epitaph of my Jacksonism—So I cant speak "By authority on the subject of "the party". But if an alternative which can possibly be acceptable to No. Carolina is presented, the influence of Jackson will certainly expire with his term—and the "malign influence" K. C. Regency et id omne genus will cease.

Yours very Respectfully

The Honble HENRY T. CLARK

W. P. Mangum.

[Addressed:] Willie P. Mangum

Senate.

Washington City.

WPM-LC

James Wellborn[96] to Bedford Brown & Willie P. Mangum

MOUNT TREAL WILKES N. C^{a}.

March 13 1834

Gentlemen—I herewith transmit to you a Memorial to the Senate and House of Representatives of Congress with a Request

10 [96]See above, I, 586n.

that you will furnish our Representative with a Copy thereof, in order that the memorial may be Presented to both House, our Representative can inform you as to the Respectability of the Signers as most of them are his personaly accquaintances. it is also true that three out of ten were original Supporters of the President, and opposed to Rechartering the bank of the U N. S. I am—gentlemen with due Respect and Esteem your most obedient Servant

J, WELLBORN

Hon[rl]. B. Brown & W. P. Mangum Senators in Congress
[Addressed:]

The Honbl. Wiley P. Mangum & Bedford Brown
Senators in Congress of
the United States
Washington City
D. C.

For
mail

WPM-LC

John Branch to Willie P. Mangum

TALLAHASSEE
March 16th 1834

My Dear Sir,

I have for some time intended to write you. If for no other purpose to express my decided approbation of the fair, independent, and patriotic course, which you have pursued in the Senate of the United States. [torn] men with [torn]ls, and tens of thousands of [torn]est planters of the south. If [torn]

[S]ensible of the debt of gratitude which your *noble bearing* in the peoples' cause, justly entitles you.

And when contrasted with the sycophancy of some few of our southern representatives your disinterested and able defence of constitutional liberty, merits and must receive the lasting plaudits of every sincere friend, to our free, and hitherto prosperous Institutions.

But I have been so much engrossed with the adjustment of my private concerns, that I dare say I should have postponed this tribute of respect & esteem, untill my return to N. Carolina, were it not for the indignation I feel f[rom] the reading the enclosed[97] extra [which I h]ave cut from a Boston Paper [sent] to me by some unknown f[riend] If anything could astonish me in [these] degenerate days, the *barefaced libel* which it contains on my administration of the Navy Department, connected with [an] unmerited wreathe which is attempted to be entwined around the President's brow *at my expense,* would excite this sensation to its highest pitch. But I have long since ceased to wonder at any encroachment on private, or public justice which proceeds from this corrupt and despotic dynasty. I nevertheless feel that I am bound by the highest considerations [to] defend my good name, from [unmer]itted odium. It is the property [of my] numerous offspring, and none [torn]el and vindictive tyrant, [torn] [un]principled band of base retainers, would take a pleasure in tarnishing it. Will you therefore my Dr. Sr. call on the President of the U. States, or the Secretary of the Navy for a copy of the correspondence which passed between the Navy Commis[sion] and myself, in 1830, in relation to the rebuilding of the Sloop John Adams? When this is obtained, I will thank you to forward to me a copy, and I pledge myself to prove to the satisfaction of every unprejudiced mind, that Genl. Jackson is as little entitled to the honor which is claimed for him in this affair, by his parasites as he is entitled to be considered the *faithful* guardian of *Constitutional* liberty—and fur[torn] little merit, the charge of a [torn] to cast in the shade, the splend[torn] glorious victories of *Old Ironsides* [torn] the command of the gallant Hull, Ba[i]nbridge, and Stewart, as Genl. Jackson and his myrmidons merit to be esteemed, wise & upright Statesmen

Will you present me to Tyler, Calhoun, and Clay in the most cordial terms and at the same time offer to them my sincere

---

[97]Because of its bad condition, the ship *Constitution* went out of commission in 1828. In 1830 the Navy Department ordered its demolition. When this order became known, public sentiment was so aroused, partly because of a poem, "Old Ironsides," published by Oliver Wendell Holmes, that the order had to be countermanded. Congress made an appropriation and the ship was repaired. In the spring of 1833 Captain Jesse Elliott, who was in charge of the repair, decided to place a figure of Andrew Jackson on the bow of the ship. News of this plan leaked out and caused a howl, especially from the Whigs. Elliott had as a precedent the frigate *John Adams*, which carried not only the statue but the name of John Adams. After the figure was placed on the ship, Samuel W. Dewey wantonly cut it from the bow and later turned it over to the Secretary of the Navy. Later it was replaced and stayed on the ship for forty years.

The enclosed clipping which Branch refers to in this letter was not found. Since he had gone over to the Whigs this was probably an effort of the Jackson paper to blame Branch for the order to demolish the ship. Ira N. Hollis, *The Frigate Constitution: The Central Figure of the Navy under Sail,* Boston, 1931, 218-227.

thanks for their *coalition* in defence of *virtue, liberty* & *law* assaild. as all are, by a *banditti* clothed with power & patronage.

Accept my assurances of
respect & esteem
JN BRANCH

Hon. Willie P. Mangum
Washington City.

I expect to leave this for Enfield [N.C.] in a few days where I should be happy to hear from you

---

Enclosure

Clipping from the Morning Post[98]

Monday, February 24th, 1834.

Figure Head—"We learn that by order of the Navy Department, the cut-water of the U. S. Frigate Constitution, (a ship dear to every American,) now repairing at the Navy Yard in Charleston, is to be surmounted with a colossal figure of Andrew Jackson. The work is to be executed by Laban S. Beecher, of this City, and is already in a state of forwardness. It will represent the General dressed in his ordinary riding cloak, holding his hat and cane in one hand, in the other a scroll of the Constitution."—*Mercantile Journal.*[99]

We copy the above for the purpose of correcting an error, and to append a statement relative to the repair of the Constitution. Some time since, during Mr. Secretary Branch's administration of the Navy Department, he reported to President Jackson, that the Constitution could not be repaired, and must be broken up. Gen. Jackson, knowing the patriotic recollection associated with the name and fame of old "Ironsides," promptly said, as he did of the Federal Union, on another occasion, "THE CONSTITUTION MUST BE PRESERVED"; and directed that she should be thoroughly repaired, and restored as nearly as possible to her original model. The repairs now making are in obedience to these orders. The ornaments put upon the ship, are not by the order of the Navy Department, but by the order of the Commandant of the Navy Yard. The old figurehead was originally a colossal wooden figure of a man O after that, a common billet head was substituted. In ornamenting her anew, the Comman-

[98]Boston *Morning Post.*
[99]Boston *Mercantile Journal.*

dant of the Yard, that brave and excellent officer, the gallant Commodore ELLIOT, has ordered the stern to be decorated with the likenesses of her former brave commanders, HULL, BAINBRIDGE and STEWART, and the bows, with the figure of GEN. JACKSON the Commander of the Army and *Navy* of the United States, in the act of giving his positive order for her preservation. Nothing could be more appropriate, and none more popular throughout the Union, we are sure.

The inflammatory placard, relative to this matter, posted up in the city on Saturday, and copied into the Boston Transcript and Evening Gazette, is the offering of some poor driveller, who dare not own his name, or avow the authorship, and is condemned by all the decent part of the opposition.

WPM-LC

E. H. Burritt[100] *to Willie P. Mangum*

NEW BRITAIN, CON. March 20 - 1834

Hon. Wm. D. Mangum—

Dr. Sir: I am one of many in this [reg]ion who feel a deep stake in the institution[s] of our country—who feel the most pain[ful soli]citude in the issue of the Executive Exper[i]ments.

In this land of winters—our people are cool, calculating, and serious. They are not easily moved, nor suddenly excited. But, Sir, the soul of this people is kindling. Their energies are coalescing—meetings are frequent and more and more evincive of a spirit which will not always bare.—We make it our day-labor business to instruct, to animate, and unite our fellow citizens for the rescue. We print and circulate, at our own expense, weekly—many thousands of such powerful missiles as the enclosed.[101] We sincerely wish we had fifty more, equal to it.

Accept, Sir, the tribute of a patriot's heart, for the language and the arguments which you have enabled us to lay before our fellow citizens. With unfeigned respect.

E. H. BURRIT

---

[100]Possibly the brother of Elihu Burritt, the "Learned Blacksmith."
[101]No enclosure has been found.

WPM-LC

Joshua Tayloe[102] *to Willie P. Mangum*

WASHINGTON NO CAROLINA
March 22d 1834

Sir

— Herewith I have the honor to enclose[103] you the proceedings of a public meeting held in this place on the evening of the 11 Inst. disaproving the removal of the Government deposites from the United States Bank; also a memorial Signed by Citizens of this County petitioning for their restoration, which you are requested to have presented for the consideration of Congress.

The *original* signatures to the Memorial have been transmitted to the Honble Thos H Hall our representative.

Very respectfully Your
obt Servant.
JOSHA TAYLOE

To the
Honbl. Willie P Mangum
Washington City

WPM-LC

Edward B. Dudley[104] *to Willie P. Mangum*

WILMINGTON N. C. March 23, 1834

Dear Sir

Having some days since received, under your frank, a communication from Genl. Green, I presume I am authorized & invited to reply through the same source; will you therefore do me the favour to hand or send to, the Genl. the, enclosed, letter addressed to him—You will pardon me for asking a similar favour as regards the, enclosed, letter addressed to Mrs. A. Royal[105]

---

[102] Joshua Tayloe held several state offices: he was a member of the legislature in 1844-1845, the Constitutional Convention in 1835, and the Council of State in 1848. *N. C. Manual*, 437, 498, 867.

[103] The copy of the proceedings is not in the Mangum Papers.

[104] Edward Bishop Dudley was one of the most prominent North Carolina Whigs. He served as a legislator, congressman, and governor. He also helped organize the Wilmington and Weldon Railroad. *Biog. Dir. of Cong.*, 922.

[105] Anne Newport Royall was one of the most talked about women journalists of the Ante-Bellum period. After her husband's death in 1824 she tried to support herself by writing accounts of her travels. In all she published ten volumes of travel. In 1831-1836 she produced *Paul Pry* and *The Huntress*, two small independent newspapers. She advocated the veto of the Bank, a non-partisan tariff, internal improvements, and non-interference with slavery. In the Mangum Papers are several references to her. *D. A. B.*, XVI, 204-205.

—A small matter of postage goes a good way with the Old Lady —She has been sending me her paper for some time for which I have remitted the pay & *begged* the discontinuance of the paper—

As far as I have seen or heard, our State is undergoing considerable change—General Jackson's tyranny & folly has alarmed & disgusted many of his old friends—among the intelligent part of the Community a Jacksonian is a *rare bird.* This section of country too is not exempt from the pressure so loudly Complained in the large cities—business exceedingly dull & produce low priced & dull sale

I am with great respect

Your ob St.

EDW. B DUDLEY.

[Addressed:]
Honble. Willie P. Mangum
Senate U States
Washington
City

WPM-LC

Copy of Burke County Resolutions[106]

[March 27, 1834]

A meeting of the Citizens of the County of Burke convened according to previous notice at the Court House in Morganton on the 27th day of March 1834 being the Thursday of the Superior Court week for the purpose of taking into consideration the treatment which certain resolutions adopted at a public meeting held at the Court House in Morganton during the week of the January Court by a numerous assembly of the Citizens of Burke have received from their representatives in Congress and certain opprobrious and disrespectful epithets cast upon them by an Honorable Senator from the State of Georgia.[107] The meeting was organized by appointed Col. William Greenway,[108] President Col. William Dickson Vice President and Joseph Jay Erwin Secretary.

---

[106]On January 28, 1834, at an informal meeting at Morganton, resolutions against the removal of deposits were adopted. After Mangum presented these to the Senate, Bedford Brown denied that they represented the sentiment of Burke County. John Forsyth and other Jackson supporters agreed with Brown and denounced the resolutions. Consequently, at a second meeting on March 27, these resolutions were adopted.

[107]John Forsyth.

[108]These were the same officers as in the first meeting.

The objects of the meeting having been explained by William Roane Esquire in a few appropriate and [torn] remarks and on his motion a committee consist[ing of] William Roane Esqr.[109] Col. Isaac T Avery Col. John [torn] Capt. Charles McDowell Burgess S Gaither Esq. Da-[torn] Corpening and William B Hawkins were appointed [to] take into consideration the subject for which the meeting had been called. The committee retired for a short time & returned with the following report towit That in a Republican Government all political power emanates from the people. The representative as such is bound to consult the interests of his constituents not his own. Any measure which materially effects their interests presents a case in which those who have delegated powers to others to act for them for their benefit have a right to present their grievances either existing or anticipated through their representatives to that body which alone can grant relief As all the parts constitute the whole every portion of the community has a right to be heard either by petition or remonstrance in regard to any meas[ure] which they may deem important to thei[r] [torn] such petition or remonstrance is entitled to a respectful consideration and should not be treated as coming "in a questionable shape" without investigation and proof That the present deranged State of the currency the depreceation of property and the general want of confidence in the community produced as we believe by the unauthorized illegal and unconstitutional act of the President of the United States through his Secretary of the Treasury in the removal of the public deposits from the United States Bank where they were deposited by law to certain favourite local banks has created embarisment distress and consternation throught the land presents a proper case for petition and remonstrance

Therefore

Resolved That this meeting do highly approve the proceedings of a public meeting held at this place [torn] January last on the subject of the removal of the [torn] deposites.

Resolved that the thanks of this meeting [torn] presented to the Honorable Wilie P Mangum one of our Senators in Congress for his prompt and manly vindication of the characters and motives of the persons who met in January last from the offensive imputations which were cast on them by a Senator from Georgia and for the dignified and eloquent manner in which he exposed

[109] See above, I, 376-377, for brief sketches of Roane and Gaither. See above, II, 82, 107-111.

the encroachments of executive power

Resolved That the Honorable Bedford Brown by representing the proceedings of the meeting in January last as coming before Congress "in a questionable shape" has manifested a dereliction towards and a want of respect for his immediate constituents and by trying to thwart instead of seconding the efforts of the meeting he has shown a much greater devotion to "the powers that be" than to the interests of those whom it is his [torn] to represent

Resolved. That the opprobrious epithets cast upon the proceedings of the meeting in January last by the Honorable John Forsyth a Senator from Georgia a Gentleman of known courtesy in debate can only be accounted for by supposing that the Honorable Senator was more than ordinarily exhilerated but whether from the influence of a "pot House" or the Palace this meeting deem immaterial

Resolved That we approve the vote of our immediate representative in Congress the Honorable James Graham upon the deposite question

The report and resolutions were warmly advocated by several Gentlemen In the course of their remarks the Honorable Wilie P Mangum was highly complimented for his manly and independent course and not a little of censure was thrown upon the Honorable Bedford Brown for representing the proceedings in [torn] last as coming before Congress "in a question [t o r n] The right of petition and remonstrance was [t o r n] as the birth right of every freeman and not [torn] even to the slave —that when emanating from the people any petition or remonstrance clothed in respectful language towards the representative was entitled to a respectful consideration and any representative who took upon himself to say that the petition or remonstrance of his constituents did not speak the sentiments of those who adopted it was regardless of the interests and the characters of those whom it is his duty to represent and whether the extreme zeal with which the removal of the deposites is justified in Congress be the result of honest sentiment or party feeling it is obvious that a peculiar influence exists in our legislative councils when we see an Honorable Senator sacrificing native partiality and State pride and joining in a tirade against a portion of the free citizens [torn] the Country connected with the obnoxious petition The Honorable John Forsyth came in for his full portion of wit and sarcasm. The speakers held that it was insulting and degrading to a free people when presenting their grievances to Congress that an Honorable Senator should feel it his duty in his place to characterize the proceedings of a public meeting convened according to previous notice at the Court House during Court and to which every body was invited and held without distinction of party as a "miserable petition gotten up by pot house politicians"

The vote was taken upon the adoption of the preamble and resolutions and were carried with but two dissenting voices

The following resolution was then offered by Burgess S Gaither Esqr. and carried by a large majority

Resolved That this meeting approve the bill [torn] the charter of the United States Bank as introduced [torn] Senate of the United States by the Honorable [Dani]el Webster

Resolved. That copies of the proceedings of this meeting be forwarded by the secretary to each of our Senators and our representative in Congress from this district

Resolved. That the secretary transmit official copies of the proceedings of this meeting to the Editors of the Journals in Washington who publish the proceedings of Congress and to those in this State who are opposed to the removal of the deposites with the request that they give them an insertion in their respective papers

WILLIAM GREENWAY President
WILLIAM DICKSON V President

J. J Erwin Secretary

WPM-LC

William A. Blount[110] *to Willie P. Mangum*

[Post mark: "WASHINGTON, N. C. Mar. 27" c.1834]

My Dear Sir—

Some days Since I received a communication from Genl. Green[111] under cover of your frank. this affords me an opportunity of saying to you, that in this part of N. C. your course in relation to recent events in the Senate has been noticed & is very

[110]General William Augustus Blount, 1792-1867, was from the prominent Blount family of Beaufort County. He was commander of the sixth division of the North Carolina militia. A member of the legislature in 1824-1827, and 1838, he served on the State Board of Internal Improvement and for nearly forty years as a trustee of the University. Ashe, *Biog. Hist. of N. C.*, I, 164-166.

[111]Duff Green was already preparing the way for the nomination of Calhoun for President. Wiltse, *Calhoun: Nullifier*, 225.

generally approved—I have, you are aware Sir, been a representative of the People Myself; & the high pleasure I recd. in that capacity to know that by evidences approved, induces me at this time by the mention of the above fact, to give you the same pleasure that I have myself experienced—Senator Brown or Yourself must Fall. I am a private man, but still I hope I may be enabled to assist to some extent to sustain the man who has so fearlessly & permit me to add ably, Sustained the reputation of N. C. & the interests of our Country—

With high respect
WILL. A. BLOUNT

[Addressed:]
The Honble...
Willie P. Mangum
Washington City
D. C.

WPM-LC

John Hill[112] to Willie P. Mangum

WILMINGTON NO CAROLINA
1st April 1834

Dear Sir,

Will you permit an old classmate after the lapse of twenty years, to renew the acquaintance of happy, by gone days?—My Wife's Father Richard Bradley Senr.[113] died on saturday last, holding the office of Surveyor & Inspector of the Port.—and my object is, to ask your interest & friendly assistance in behalf of his Son Richd. Bradley Jr.

The infirm health of the Father for the last 18 months or two years, has thrown the duties of the office almost entirely on the Son Richd. and I presume from the satisfaction he has given here, that he has discharged them faithfully, correctly, & to the satisfaction of the department at Washington—Mr Bradley has left a large family once easy & independent. now I fear crushed & involved, and requiring all the aid which the senior members of the family by their industry can afford.—

---

[112]After graduating from the University in 1814, he practiced medicine in Wilmington. Grant, *Alumni Hist. of U. N. C.*, 281.

[113]He was President of the Bank of Cape Fear before he became surveyor and inspector of the port. McIver, *N. C. Register*, 83.

The inhabitants of the Town, I understand are preparing a petition for Richard, with the same object, which will be forwarded to your city in a day or two. But as an intimation has been given me, that an application for the same office, but from a defferent quarter, was made weeks ago, even before the death of the late incumbent. I would suggest to you the necessity for dispatch lest you be forestalled.—

Genl. McKay[114] I learn is not at Washington. Should he arrive in Season will you be good enough to consult him upon the subject.

I will not encroach further on your time, which I am happy to see is so honorably & zealously employed But have the honor to be, very respectfully

Your friend &
Obt Srvt
JOHN HILL

[Addressed:]
Hon[ble] Willie P. Mangum
Senate, United States
Washington City

WPM-LC

R. H. Mosby[115] to Willie P. Mangum

WARREN COUNTY April 2d: 1834

Dr Sir,

My inability to get on to Washington compells me again to trouble you in reference to matters in which I feel in common with others great interest—I am sensible these drafts upon your time and attention in the midst of matters which effect not the rights or interest of one or two But millions can scarcely be excused by any circumstances and I beg you will be assured nothing but a necessity which cannot be otherwise disposed of would induce me to do so—

I am interested in a claim which has past the H. of R, and is now before the Senate, and it is absolutely necessary for me to know what its present situation is, and when it will be considered by the Senate—These facts are necessary for me to know that I

---

[114]Congressman James J. McKay. See above, I, 448.
[115]See above, II, 40.

may take the necessary steps to secure the interest I hold in the claim—as others may draw the money and give me trouble—The case is that of Butler Claiborne a captain or Major in the Va: State Line and for commutation pay—Mr. Davenport of the House has had the management of it—You will do me a great favour by looking into the case and apprising me of its exact situation, and if not already acted on be so good as to let me know when it will be—and if necessary I trust your friendly aid will be given to it should any difficulty occur when it is before the Senate. By applying to Mr. D. he will at once put you in possession of the facts of the case and show it is just & should be allowed.

I cannot close this scrall without tendering you my thanks as an American citizen for your efforts in the Senate upon what has and is truly called a struggle for the lost principles of the Constitution for the party itself.

The earthquake voice of the people is beginning to be heard on all hands— You may rest assured it will sustain you in the course you have taken—and consign those who have abused the confidence reposed in them a place in strict accordance with their deserts—Nothing but the influence of a few individuals here prevents the member from this district from being instructed upon the question of the removal of the Deposites in a way that would place him and his idolatry for the General in strong, and to him [unanswerable] conflict—The indications of an intention on the part of the President to make an issue before the people upon the various questions now before the Senate, has alarmed many of his friends—as it is well calculated to do—and shows clearly that he has no talent but that of producing mischief—I am recovering from my long indisposition, and trust by the 1st of May I shall have the pleasure to see and acknowledge the many acts of kindness which you have extended to me. By that time the climate of Washington will be mild enough for me to venture on—In the mean time I trust you will let me hear from you with as little delay as practicable.

I remain your friend

R. H. MOSBY

[Addressed:]

The Hble

Willie P. Mangum

Senator of the U. States

Washington City

Mail) (D- of C)

Ellisville N C.

8th April

WPM-LC

A. M. H.[116] *to David Crockett*

DRESDEN, TENN.

April 2nd. 1834

Col. David Crockett

Sir

I wrote you the other day, but as I am anxious to hear from the scene of action often I again write you. I have read yesterday the speech of Mr. Mangum of N. C. in the Senate upon the presentation of a memorial & resolution of some of the citizens of his state, in favour of the [removal] of the deposits. I should like to see a good many of these speeches distributed in this section of the State. He stands high with the North Carolinians. If you could induce him to send copies of these himself it would have a powerful influence—say that he send copies of it to Majr. W. G. Bowers, Col. Jas. W. Rogers, Perry Vincent Esq. Dr J Rogers, Capt Nelson Nailing. Robert Giter Esq. Caleb Brassfield Esq. & to such others as you may think of—If the addresses of Webster & Clay upon the presentation of the memorial & petition of the Philadelphia delegation of [work]ing men is printed in [pamp]let form you could not send too many [torn] here. The speech of Mr. Clay on that occasion [torn] not fail to convince wherever its read [torn] Soul stirring eloquence and lofty patriotism of the noble Kentuckian must—it will open the eyes of the people of these States to their true situation. Tender to this highminded patriot my best respects—Tell him to go on conquering & to conquer—That he has the *law* & the *Constitution & right* on his side—and that he has the entire south with him & before six months more [s]hall roll around the whole people from [East to] West, from North to South will be found

[116]Unable to identify.

arranged on the side of liberty & law, and against the unjust encroachments of Executive usurpations. The people must—they will Veto Andrew Jackson. They cannot—they will not sustain him in his despotic course, on the deposit question. If they do farwell a long farwell to our liberties.

Let me hear from you upon all subjects of interest—Calhoun & his party have in a great degree redeemed themselves from their *herecies* by the lofty & independent stand they have taken upon the subject of executive ursurpations—they in this case stand up [as] strong as any others for the constitution & [torn] of the laws.

I think these reports [of the] New York, Philadelphia & Baltimore Conven[tion]s to their Townsmen will have a mighty influence in opening the eyes of the American people to the true character of Andrew Jackson—His treatment to those committees—the rough & insulting manner in which he spoke to them is enough to disgust all highminded independent & honorable men with *the man.*

Mr. Fitzgerald is about selling out here and intends moving to Paris. He perhaps intends locati[ng] himself there for your benefit at the next electi[on when] Mr. Huntsman will run against you.

No news of a local nature worth w[riting] about. You are well informed of the hardness of the times and "know the sour[ce] & course of i[t."]

Yours truly
A. M. H[torn].

[Addressed:]
Col. David Crockett,
of the U. S. house of representatives
Washington
(D C)

WPM-LC

John W. Carson[117] *to Willie P. Mangum*

PLEASANT GARDENS
Apl 6th 1834

Dr Sir— I have read Mr. Calhouns speech on Mr Websters proposition to extend the Charter of the U. States Bank 6 years;

[117]Brother of Samuel P. Carson.

and altho my oppinion of his talents was such as to place him first upon the list of highly gifted men, yet his late effort on Mr Websters motion surpass the Conceptions I entertained of the great & comprehensive powers of his intellect—

We had a meeting at Morganton the week of our Supr- Court numerously attended, convened in consequence of the debate in the Senate on the resolutions from Burke in January last, and further stimulated from the indignant feelings felt at the course our Senator Mr Brown took on that occasion. It was to disabuse the meeting (in Jan.ry) of the aspersion cast upon it by Mr Forsyth followed up by Mr Brown. The vote on the resolutions were unanimous save 2.

After we had pass[d]. the Resolutions which was the principle object of the meeting. Mr Gaither offered a resolution approving of Mr. Websters Bill for the extensions of the Charter—Col. I. T. Avery & my brother, S. P. Carson, requested that he would withdraw his resolution. Col. Avery not deeming it appropriate to the Occasion, and my brother not satisfyed as regards constitutional principles—Yet Mr Gaither persevered in his motion to offer the resolution which was carried by a large majority myself voting with the majority—But I think that our Vote on that resolution was premature Tho, we had not heard of Mr Websters proposition Untill it was read in the meeting and my being in favour of a renewal of the Charter under certain restrictions I voted for Mr Websters plan—But I have a decided preference for Mr Calhouns—so clear, comprehensive, & conclusive, that the more I read, the more were my convictions, of its correctness & truth confirmed—

I take pleasure in informing you that your speech on the Burke memorial is received by all who I have heard speak of it with praise & approbation; And I cannot but express to you that I feel proud that We have one from our State, who has the fearless [in]dependance to march forward in the vindication of principle, and the ability to sustain himself, in the high honorable course, which you have adopted—

Present my respects to Mr Calhoun, Col Preston, &C. and accept for yourself the assurance of my best wishes & esteem.

JOHN. W. CARSON

P. S. altho we dont feel the pressure here like many other parts of the Union yet to a certain extent it affects us. Our gold does not bring by 2 cents in the Dwt as much as it did 3 months ago.

J. W. C.

[Addressed:]

Honb[l]

Wiley P. Mangum

Senator in Congress

Washington D. C.

WPM-LC

Henry T. Clark to Willie P. Mangum

TARBORO N. CAROLINA

April. 8th. 1834.

Dear Sir

A few days since a public meeting was held in this place, among other resolutions which were passed was one denouncing your recent opposition to the administration.[118] Approving as I do your course and knowing how many of the intelligent and high minded voters of this county who coincide with me—I feel it an act of Justice, to give you the following explanation, that you may be your own Judge of the force of the censure

At the last Presidential election. Edgecombe might be called an unanimous Jackson County. as he lost but 3 or 4 votes—Since that he has gradually lost ground and cannot now command two thirds. So it is still a Jackson County and it is so. because the measures of the administration have never been canvassed or even questioned in the county. and the Mass of the People are without information relying upon their leaders, who on their side rely on the magic of Jacksonism to perpetuate their influence thus the delusion is kept up. The reading of impartial and opposition newspapers are the only source of information for the mal-administration of the Government, and unfortunately they are of limited circulation.

The Globe and Richmond Enqr. are in abundant circulation and they act as "Glorification Spectacles." But this is a digression—My reasons or apology for a majority of this county still *hurrahing* for Jackson But I am gratified to know that Independent thinking and acting on Jackson is rapidly progressing here

---

[118]On March 31, 1834, at the county court house, resolutions were adopted endorsing Jackson's action. These resolutions stated that the President had the authority to remove an officer such as Duane and that the removal of the deposits was legal and for the public interest. The Bank, they continued, had provoked the economic stress and Mangum had followed a course toward the administration that was marked by "captiousness and an asperity which we are bound in candor to condemn." *Senate Documents*, 23 Cong., 1 sess., Doc. No. 252, 2 pp.

The public Meeting above alluded to, was a call on "the *friends of Jackson*" which insured a packed Jury with a verdict responsive to the call But one ante-man attended (Mr Hines)[119] who asked permission to speak and twas granted as a *favor* as he was an uninvited guest—Dr Potts[120] who figures as sponsor for the Resolution is a zealous partizan of the administration (of President & *Vice-President*), and a warm supporter of Bedford Brown —and is doubtless so aiming to shape public opinion as to operate as instructions to himself & colleagues in the next legislature to support the course of Mr Brown

The above meeting has been proclaimed abroad as a general meeting of the citizens and the *largest* ever held here—But the fact is it was an express invitation to the "Friends of Jackson" and altho the meeting was called and published for fortnight, before, & due diligence & notice employed, the meeting did not exceed 75 or 80, and the *same* persons who *drafted* and organized the meeting here & in part composed it, have performed the same manoeuvre in the upper part of the county.—and succeeded in getting up a *still smaller* meeting.[121]—the leaders and most of the component part being the same—

Thus they manufacture public sentiment, and large meetings here—and thus the notes of Praise and censure with the powers of ventriloquism are wafted from the various part of Edgecombe

The lower counties of this Cong. District is or said to be in decided opposition to the administration on the Deposite question from three of them you have already presented memorials. A piece in a late Star from Pitt Co. signed "A Voice" was written by Henry Toole[122] who informs me that your course is generally sustained there.

My friend Dr Hall differed from many of his constituents on this immediate question. but his political principles are sound and always command the support of his District — We place great reliance on him—

I hope you will pardon this trespass on your attention—I considered it due to yourself and your friends here that this matter should be fairly represented to you that you may properly estimate both the *quantity* & *quality* of censure which has been

---

[119]Richard Hines.

[120]Dr. John W. Potts was a member of the state legislature from 1832 to 1834. *N. C. Manual*, 602.

[121]On April 28, a meeting of the militia drew up resolutions similar to those on March 31. *Senate Documents*, 23 Cong., 1 sess. Doc. No. 310, 2 pp.

[122]Henry Toole was a member of the state legislature from Edgecombe County in 1831. *N. C. Manual*, 763.

aimed at you. by some of our "Cantankerous" politicians (as Mr F would say—) and that the "Captiousness and asperity" they have thrown at you may be fairly retorted on themselves—

Your independent course deserves the support of every No Carolinian

With Great respect
Yours HENRY T. CLARK

Honble
W P Mangum

WPM-LC

E. B. Smith[123] to Willie P. Mangum

NASHVILLE, TEN: Ap[l]. 8. 1834

Dear Sir,

Permit me so far to trespass on your goodness as to request the favor of you to call at the office of the National Intelligence & receive my subscription to that print—Since I have been here I have almost lost the run of the politics of the country—I must begin to read again and think I shall be as likely to get the truth from the Intelligencer as any of the papers.—and perhaps more so.—The times seem to be portentious, and the political horizon begins to be troubled.—

Your course in regard to the Deposite Question I cordially approve and hope the good people of N. Carolina will sustain you—.

After all I begin to think our native State has more virtue and modesty than almost any of her [torn], little as they may esteem her.—I should be glad to hear from you—

Respectfully yours
E. B. SMITH

[Addressed:]
Hon: Willie P. Mangum
City of Washington

WPM-LC

C. L. Hinton to Willie P. Mangum

Apl 11th 1834

My Dear Mangum

This has been with us a dark cloudy day with a stormy N. E. wind which has confined me to the house without any company

---

[123]He was clerk of the court in Halifax County, North Carolina, before he moved to Tennessee.

save my smallest boy—I have read over Mr Calhouns speech, Mr Wrights speech and Mr Websters Bank speech of 32—I have reflected on them—and am reminded of old Zadock Bells sermon when he told his congregation if they did not all repent they would be in a most *damnable predicament.* So I think of the friends of your friends Andrew, & Martin, who I suppose are not insensible of your indefatigable exertions in elevating them to their present enviable stations—If you are still enjoying their smiles and their confidence, but m [Several lines are torn.] believes his feelings are perfectly in unison with thousands & thousands of his old supporters—The General may weather the storm, but the heir apparent has neither *fought, bled,* or *died,* for his country— But to be serious—

Mr Calhouns speech I have read with a great deal of satisfaction, and am pleased to have it spoken of by more competent judges in terms of the highest approbation, it must have a strong tendency to quiet old prejudices—. I am prepared to forget past political differences of opinion, and to pay to him that tribute of respect which his merits and *unrivaled* talents eminently entitle him—I cant say I am prepared to go for him for President —indeed I cant say who my choice would be, but I *think* I can *say* I am prepared to go against Van Buren—And it must be bad management among the [Several lines are torn.] d to have the benefit of the patronage of the Genl Government—[torn] other states must be blinded indeed if they [are] not roused to a sense of their interest t[hat] at least is the light in which we view [all] things in this quarter—and we think as ma[tters] progress they must become more apparent to [the] most common understanding—

I regretted to find so decided majority in the [H.R.] against the recharter of the U S Bank, to me [that] appears one of the plainest political questions [that] presented to the American people—but those who a[re op]posed to the policy cannot be unapprised of [torn]—dency—

I have written thus much not that I expected to interest you—but for employment—local n[ews] we have none, such as we have you will coll[ect] from our old friend Alfred Jones who will be on a few days, with Gov Burton

Adieu
C L Hi[nton]

[Addressed:]
To The
Honble Willie P Mangum
Washington City

WPM-LC

Joseph Loftin[124] *to Willie P. Mangum*

CASWELL April 11th 1834—

Dear Sir

E[nclosed] I send you the proceedings & Memorial of Citi-[zen]s of Lenoir County. It is desirable that the memorial should be presented if you shall think that it is not too late. A larger number of signatures could have been obtained, if the memorial had been handed about through the County—Nineteen twentieths of the signatures were obtained in this village. The language of our memorial may seem strong, but it is not too strong to express the feelings & opinions of the intelligent freemen of Lenoir, or at least that portion of them unbiased by party zeal or prejudice—

Respectfully Your Obt. Sert.
JOSEPH LOFTIN

[Addressed:]
Wilie P. Mangum
Washington City
D. C.

WPM-LC

John F. Buie[125] *to Willie P. Mangum*

Near LAUREL HILL Apl. 11th, 1834

My Dear Sir

Although not Personally acquainted with you & having nothing more than a mere formal Introduction to you in Chas. Manlys office in Raleigh during the week of the County Court in

---

[124]Joseph Loftin was a member of the legislature in 1812-1816, and 1819-1820, and sheriff of Lenoir County in 1823-1826. *N. C. Manual*, 679; *N. C. Laws* 1826, appendix; McIver, *N. C. Register*, 44.

[125]John F. Buie, who lived in Fayetteville from 1816 to 1824 as a counting house clerk, became a justice of peace in Richmond County and in 1827 sought from Thomas Ruffin the position of clerk of the court. Hamilton (ed.), *Papers of Ruffin*, I, 409-411.

Novr. 1819 (I think it was) I take this method of communicating to you the Pleasure it gave me & others (& I think I may say 3/4 of the People of Richd. County who lent their aid in 1828 in Placing the Present Executive in the Chair of State) to see the stand you have taken on the Deposite Question

I know of but few in this section who Justify the Executive. You may be surprised that there has not been any expression of Public opinion on that subject in this County Such a thing was spoken of at our Supr. Cts. but it was deemed entirely unnecessary as our Highly Respectable Representative Mr. Deberry so fully Represented the feelings of the great Majority of the People, Not only of this County but of his entire District that Consequently the Meeting was dispensed with—I have myself the N. Inteligencer & Richd. Whig & If I choose the *Globe* to inform me what is going on there—It gave me great Pleasure to see the Result of the vote on Mr. Clays Resolutions[126] & I greave to say that I feel much mortified at the Result of the vote in the H. R.—The only redress the People have now is at the Polls at the ensuing Election—I may venture to say that the most Talented Man in this Dist. could not be Elected Provided he approved of the Executive Measures in removing the Deposites &c as regards my own views—I am for a Ren[l] of the charter with certain modifications & If that cannot be effected for a New Bank—I trust the majority of the ensuing Congress will be sufficient *Veto* or *no Veto,* to make some Permanent arrangement with the currency of the Country—For my own Part although a Strict States right man (even unto Nullification If you Please) I could never see or view any constitutional objection to a Bk. Established by Congress—Permit me to thank you for Mr. Calhouns speech. I would indeed like to get Prestons, Leighs & your own If they are to be had also one of the *Blue Books** shewing the contracts of Mail Contractors with Extra allowance &c

Your Colleague Mr. Brown may make the most of his time—His days are numbered—It will be made a Test Question for Members to the ensuing Legislature — I have now communicated to you freely (although in brief terms) my own views &

[126]In December, 1833, Clay led the fight against the removal of deposits by introducing resolutions condemning the President's action. Clay spoke for three days on these resolutions. A debate of three months ensued before the resolutions were passed by a vote of 26 to 20. Thereupon, Clay proposed joint resolutions in favor of restoring the deposits. These passed the Senate but were defeated in the House. Van Deusen, *Life of Clay,* 278-284.

I may safely say the views of the great majority of the People of Richd. Cty. on the all engrossing subject of the Deposites Bank &c

While I Remain
Yours very Truly
JNO. F. BUIE

*The Book spoken of by [Benjamin Watkins] Leigh & [Felix] Grundy

[Addressed:]

The Hon. Willie P. Mangum
(Senator from N. Ca.)
Washington City
Dist. of Col.

WPM-LC

Isaac Croom[127] to Willie P. Mangum

MANTUA, LENOIR CY. April 13th, 1834

Dear Sir,

[torn] this letter shall reach you, you will probably ha[ve rece]ived the memorial sent from this County, [torn] of the continuance of the Deposits &c. &c—It is to be [re]gretted that our Memorial was not sent before the vote was taken, but perhaps as it was principally intended to be an expression of public sentiment, it is not of so much importance. Had proper exertions been made I hazard nothing in saying that a majority of the County would have signed the memorial, altho heretofore the vote has been 3 to 1 in favor of Jackson. Many of the signers were even zealous supporters of Speight[128] & Old Hickory, but who now regarding principles rather than men, denounce both of these worthies with a singleness of good will, which does equal credit to their discernment & patriotism—The weight of intilligence & of numbers too in this County will I believe be found opposed to the 'malign influence'. There are still some respectable men of the Jackson, Van Buren drill[?] who hold [o]n, but they do it with a bad grace & are not therefore ver[y form]idable—

[127]A contemporary of Mangum at the University, Isaac Croom was in the state legislature representing Lenoir County in 1823 and 1826. Later he moved to Greensboro, Alabama. *N. C. Manual*, 679-680; Grant, *Alumni Hist. of U.N.C.*, 143.

[128]Jesse Speight, member of Congress from North Carolina.

I believe the foregoing remarks will apply [more o]r less to the surrounding Counties. But Sir you cannot [torn] to be apprised of public sentiment in any part of [Nor]th Carolina—I will however take the liberty to say [to y]ou that your course during the present session of Congress has the cordial approbation of a large majority of the intelligent & independent freemen of Lenoir C I trust of N Carolina—

Rely upon it Sir that we will understand the nature of the Contest that is now waging—a contest of power corruption, selfishness & intrigue against liberty, the Constitution & laws of the republic—We are deliberately prepared too, to go to the rescue, with such means as the laws of God & nature will justify —We are at present under a practical despotism & unless the ballot boxes shall vindicate a violated Constitution, it is fearful to think of our Country's doom—My only hope then will be in the sovereignty of the [torn] & the independence, honesty, republicanism & intelligence [of] the South—Virginia & the Carolinas would present form[idable] barriers to any usurper.

The Chairman of ou[r committee] feeling himself bound by one of the resolutions has tr[ansmitt]ed a copy of the memorial signatures to Jesse Speight [and has] referred him to you for the originals—He is howev[er not to be] expected or relied on, or so far as I know was requested to pre[fer] the memorial—It was respect for themselves only that [induc]ed the meeting to notice Speight at all, for they have [not] the slightest confidence in or respect for him & view him not as their representative but the obedient servant of Jackson Burenism, alias the Kitchen cabinet [torn] Scullion—If there are any prospects [torn] for weal or for woe', not elicited by the press, I should be [torn]-d by a disclosure—what will probably be done by the [torn] Congress for relief & what its period & manner of [torn] ment?

With much regard your
friend & Ob[t] Ser[t]-
IS. CROOM

[Addressed:]
Honb[le]—
Wilie P MAngum
Washington City

WPM-LC

..................................[129] *to Willie P. Mangum*

BONA VISTA near Smithfield N-C^{a}. 16th. apl.
1834

My Dear Sir

For the reasons that may arise out of the context of this Letter you will I have no doubt readily excuse what possibly may wear a feature of presumptive medling, bearly justifiable by our personal acquaintance: but in these *throing* [troubling] times, no earnest of forgiveness is required from the Representative of my State for communicating to him whatever suggestion an humble Individual may believe necessary to disabuse a community already tottering on the brink of ruin by their incredulity and an organised system of imposition upon their lack of political understanding; more particularly, when such suggestions are made to one who has frequently, and specially of late, given every testimony of devotion to a pure and honest exercise *only,* of our abused and violated Constitution. You need not Sir, my gratulations for your [torn]-less, open, and brilliant exposition of the turpitude and m[torn] with which the People of the U. States are now governed for [torn] the independent [torn] our name [A whole line is torn out.]
Congress for some prophetic sign of either a bold and daring Revolution, or a Civil triumph— they know the one or the other is at hand, and in cold and thrilling reflection they are almost ready to give into the opinion that time is once more, and for ever, about to prove that men can only govern themselves "pro tempore" To the servile condition of the Press in this country may mainly be attributed the encroachments of power upon the Laws and the Constitution and so long as its freedom may be purchased by the patronage of Power and with the money of the "*Subject*" so long will it be used, in base hands, to reconcile the People to the urgent needs of Despotism by insideous and gradual moves. Thus its usefulness, as once esteemed "the Paladium of liberty" will be totally reversed in a country so ignorant of public affairs as are the Citizens of ours—a Country and Government in which, the men of intelligence and political under-

[129]The signature is missing.

standing—the honest, private, reading, Yeomanry of which, are designed, by the complexion of the Government, to discharge the duties of an Order useful, if not absolutely necessary, in other Governments, an order of mediation between the ab-[solution of] Power, and the baseness of licentiousness—The usefulness of su[ch I] say is being extinguished by the [torn] servility of the Press [torn] wide spread difusion [torn] and it is a matter of concern to this country if [A whole line is torn out.]
his Lord and political master, the popularity of whose name has borne him to his present station. Although those friendly relations still continue between myself and the "Gineral" yet you know, I must desire, most ardently, to see my Country released from the destructive sway of the present Order of things. To secure a continuance of belief in the infalibility of Genl. Jackson and all his measures my honorable Gen[l]. Speight continues to flood our District with prints, Globes, Reports and Speeches in favor of his Jupiter Mamon, directed, not always to men even, of ordinary comprehension, but in profusion to such as will only read a few sentences and take them to be the very defence of liberty. Your very Colleague also, is not unmindful of some "of our folks" but visits them now and then with a Globe or Speech or Report, or something of the kind. Now my Dear Sir, you can scarcely imagine the *known* effect that all such, has on an ignorant community when connected with the hitherto popularity of Jackson Still I think their offer may now, and hereafter be greatly counteracted [t o r n] mixture of their antidotes if hundreds who see [torn] these things could have the same opportunity of seeing the reverse of the picture no doubt but different conclusions [torn] formed—Can not this be done? [A whole line is torn out.]
If I have herein trespassed upon decorousness, I hope I shall find a pardon in an assimilation of feeling growing out of the present prostration of our country's laws and constitution—
[Addressed:]

Honl. Willie P. Mangum
United States Senate
Washington City

WPM-LC

Mat M. Moore[130] *to Willie P. Mangum*

GERMANTON
April 17th 1834

Honl.. W. P. Mangum
Dear Sir

I had the pleasure of receiving through your kindness and attention, by last mail a copy of Mr Calhoun's speech on Mr W.s bank proposition—with this as with his other speeches I am well pleased & in this as in others when he lays down his premises & draws his conclusions I should say there was an end of argument—

Candour & truth compel me to say that my devotion to the Union & the dread of the frightful and dangerous consequences anticipated from a dissolution have heretofore prejudiced my mind strongly against him—But justice & truth now require that I should acknowledge the fact that I in my opion have done him great injustice on this point—

The chief object however of this letter is to transmit to you an acknowledgment of the great pleasure your course this winter has afforded me—This I am aware can be of small consequence to you—and I regret that in all probability I shall not be able to render you a more valuable return for your able candid & independent devotion to what I conceive to be the best interests of our contry at this critical and dangerous crisis. Should this avowal afford you any pleasure set it down as an off-set to the Tarborough resolutions—but must say that the avowal alone possibly may be its measure of value—

But to return to Mr. C's Speech &C the current here of popular feeling or rather of prejudice as I should say against him is remarkably strong & obstinate with the unreading portion—but the enlightened are willing to render him liberal justice—for instance Mr. Gilmer[131] a lawyer of Greensbr°. has been as violent as any one against Mr. C's Nullification views; on this subject we have often conversed: and last evening he expressed himself to me in terms highly complimentary to both of Mr C's speeches and I will take the liberty of adding also a wish to see you reelected—He however has always been an anti Jackson man—

[130]Mat M. Moore, a brother of Gabriel Moore, was clerk of the court of Stokes County.
[131]Probably John A. Gilmer, who began practicing law in 1832.

It is now Court week here & I have not heard of more than three men who approve the policy of the removal I mean among those who read—Yet all the colar[132] men justify it since it has been done and at the head of this party stands conspicuously your old friend — Hill[133]—

The subject of Nullification is not now mentioned here only by the obstinate & illiterate Jackson men when they cant sustain in argument the removal they endeavour fix the charge of that doctrine on one or they appeal to the gratitude due to the Genl. on that subject as a palliation as they say of error in regard to the deposits—

Say to brother[134] we are all well shall write him this week or immediately on my return home

Yours most truly
MAT M. MOORE

[Addressed:]
Honl. Willie P. Mangum
United States Senate
Washington City

WPM-LC

Samuel Smith to Willie P. Mangum

BALT. 19: April 1834.

My dear Sir/

Confidential

I am glad to hear that poor Dawson has two Messes They tell me the number in Each—The Session will be a long one, and will I hope give him something to live on during the Recess. I was one of his lodgers so long—that I have always felt a deep interest in his Welfare.

I see by the Papers, That you disapprove the removal of the deposites. Whether that be the Cause of the present distress or some other is matter of dispute between the parties, but that there is great distress and total ruin to many is now admitted

[132]The Whigs frequently referred to those who slavishly followed Jackson as "Collar" men.

[133]John Hill, of Stokes, was about Mangum's age. They were at the University at the same time. Hill was clerk of the court for thirty years, member of the legislature for nine years, and Democratic Congressman from 1839 to 1841. *Biog. Dir. of Cong.*, 1097-1098.

[134]Gabriel Moore moved to Huntsville, Alabama, where he held numerous state offices before he entered Congress in 1821. He served in the House of Representatives from 1821 to 1829 and in the Senate from 1831 to 1837. He was governor of Alabama from 1829 to 1831. In 1834 he moved to Texas and died there two years later. *Biog. Dir. of Cong.*, 1327.

by all parties. Two of our Banks have failed. One has occasioned a wide spread ruin. It received deposites on interest, and when it failed it had of that description an amount exceeding six hundred thousand dollars from $100 to forty thousand. It has fallen on the Widow, Lawyer, Doctors, orphans Men out of business, Farmers and the middling and poorer classes. On the heirs of Mr. Carroll[135] nearly $40.000. Its paper had been spread by its Agents over all the West, and it was in debt for the Bonds of the new Tennessee Bank. The U.S.B. is in for at least $200.-000. The Branch here would not take its Paper. the Mother Bank and some of its Branches did.

On the first Run two other of our Banks must have stopped but for the aid given by the Branch, and One in the Interior—One other has since been assisted by the Mother Bank to a considerable amount, and I hope that all will now be safe. There are however doubts of some of those who have received deposites on interest the depositors have notified them generally that they shall want their money when the terms of their loans shall have expired—Now those Banks are perfectly safe. But having lent out the money to government cannot be expected, that they will be in cash to pay the Depositors, and there may be a Crash. which will help the Brokers—some of whom are making fortunes for themselves and those who advance them money—

I Enter not into the subject, that is in much better keeping—I may however say to you, That our people have lost confidence in Bank notes except those of the U. S. B—Those some take for the produce they bring to market, but the farmers generally take home the dollars. In consequence all the Banks begun to feel a decrease of their specie, a constant small decrease in *hourly process* [?] must in the end create serious difficulty.—One good has arisen. The present want of confidence has caused a general retrenchment of Expenses in Every family, and Economy has become fashionable. I save money for I supply my family at 20 p cent less than formerly, and my Rents have not fallen as yet.

Our large manufacturers of Iron are discharging their hands, and they are old men. One has paid off fifty another will after working up the Iron on hand discharge 300 during the next month, for he says—That he knows not who to trust, and has a large quantity of articles unsold—He told me, that the Notes

[135]Charles Carroll, of Carrollton, who died in 1832.

due him he is compelled to renew for that few or none can pay, altho: safe men. He however is rich and can Stagger through.—A great Ropemaker paid off his hands. Locked up his Rope walk & it was burned down a few days after—I write my friend for your information, and do not wish to be quoted for anything I have written or may write—I am now nearly 82 years of age and never knew such universal distress as Exists all around me—May God grant That some mode of alleviating it may be adopted. For myself I can offer none—I know of none

Your Sincere friend
S. SMITH

Mr. Mangum
[Addressed:]
Honble
Wilie P. Mangum
In Senate
Washington

WPM-LC

Anne Royall[136] *to Bedford Brown & Willie P. Mangum*

[April 21, 1834]

Mrs. Royall is sorry to return [torn]
note ($4. State Bank N. C.) to Dr. [torn]
it will not pass here at [torn]
discount. Being in want of [torn]
ful Mrs. R. is grieved to waidt long [torn]
Perhaps it is not the same [torn]
money for which reason Mrs R is [torn]
particular to direct it to the D—himself whom she prays to accept of her esteem & regard.

Washington D. C.
April 21st
1834

Dr. J. G. Hanner
Merry Mills
Randolph Co. N. C.

[136]See above, II, 126n.

[Addressed:] Hon.'s
Bedford Brown
&
W. P. Mangum
U S Senators

WPM-LC

Gales & Seaton to Willie P. Mangum

[April 21, 1834]

Dear Sir

We have just come to your speech on the Force Bill[137] of last Session, & could now if we had it, insert it in its place in the Register of Debates, which we should be very glad to do. Have you had time to prepare it, or can you shortly.

Yrs. truly
GALES & SEATON
Ap. 21 '34

[Addressed:]
Hon. W. P. Mangum
Senate.

WPM-LC

Henry Gariet to Wadkins Lee[138]

FORT GEORGE[139] April the 23th 1834

Dear Master—for the first time Since I left you that I have wrighten to you and i hope whin thes few Lines Come to hand thay may find you well as they leve me at this time but I have been very on well for Some time and I must confes to you I am Sory that I Lefe you—and would Be Glad to come home If I had the means—. thire for [therefore] If you will Send me Some money to pay my way home I will Return—I think it will take the Some of 60$ for why I shall be Glad to bring my wife

---

[137]Several brief statements by Mangum were published in the *Register of Debates* but his longer speech on the Force Bill was not included.
[138]Probably Benjamin Watkins Leigh.
[139]This letter was postmarked Youngstown, New York.

with me—but I am in hopes that you will not put me to any thing more than i am a coostom to. Send it as Soon as you can, Give my Love to wadkin^s and the Rest of the children

Nothing More I Remain your umble
Servant henry GarRiet

Dear Mistress. I am very Sory for what i have don—thirefore i hope you will forGive me for what I have don. dear mam vey anchus to See all of you—in this life aGian and that i hope well be in a few dayes Kiss all of your children for me and tell them howdy for me I Remain your SerVant

HENRY GARIET

[Addressed:]
Mr. Wadkins Lee—
RichMond Va
[Postmarked:] Youngstown, N. Y.

WPM-LC

J. J. Daniel[140] *to Willie P. Mangum*

HALIFAX, April 24th 1834

Dear Sir,

Permit me to introduce to you Mr. A. Austin,[141] the young gentleman who will hand you this letter—He is about to make [torn] to Washington City, and I have taken the liberty to ask for him a small portion of your attention. He is the son of Col. Austin of Virginia, and the nephew of Mrs. Thomas Burges of this place. Be so good as to make him acquainted with some of the N. C. and Virg. delegation in Congress, and oblige your obt. Servant,—

J. J. DANIEL.

[Addressed:]
Hon. Willie P. Mangum,
Washington City.

WPM-LC

Hugh Waddell[142] *to Willie P. Mangum*

HILLSBORO, April 30, '34.

My dear Sir;

I have been anxiously expecting to hear from you for some

[140]At this time Joseph J. Daniel was serving as judge of the state Supreme Court.
[141]Archibald Austin, of Buckingham County, Virginia.
[142]See above, I, 42n.

days past, as your last favour of March 28^h, intimated that I should do, but I feared that the excitement at Washington would prevent the action of the Ho. of Representatives on any other subject than that of the pecuniary condition of the country—and I doubt not it would be necessary to have the report of the proper Committee to the House, before you could suggest any thing as to the result & this of course must take time.—

One of the principal reasons of my anxiety was, that it might depend on what I should hear whether I should visit the City—While in this State of anxiety I have received intelligence, which will make it necessary for me to visit Washington on another subject.—

The recent conduct of the British authorities at Nassau, New Providence, in forcing from my brothers,[143] who had been *shipwrecked,* 20 or 30 slaves & *liberating* them, is regarded by the whole South as such an outrage on the laws of Nations, that we cannot doubt the ready interposition of our own Government to redress it.

If it be known to the Slaves of our Southern Atlantic States that a two days voyage to the British Islands is all that is necessary to effect their freedom, I think it will be holding out a premium to *insurrection.*

My brother John who was one of the sufferers will accompany me to Washington—He has all the Documentary evidence necessary to lay our case fairly before the proper authorities at Washington.—

We expect to leave this on Saturday next & hope to see you about the 8th May, but I fear a *man out of the woods* as I am, will receive anything but pleasure from *sojourning* among the great.—Among the consolations which I entertain in my *pilgrimage* to the Modern Babel is the confidence that I shall meet yourself & some other friends who will make me ample amends for much of what might be disagreeable.—

I will not ask too much when I desire to see you as early after my arrival as your engagements will permit—

Accept My dear Sir, the sincere tribute of my affectionate

---

[143]John Waddell lived at "Bellville" in New Hanover County and Moses Q. Waddell lived most of his life in Chatham County. The facts of this case are similar to those of the famous *Creole* case. See John B. Moore, *Digest of International Law,* II, 35.

regard & believe me

Yr. friend & servt.

[Addressed:] H. WADDELL.

Hon. W. P. Mangum,
U. S. Senate,
Washington.

WPM-LC

Thomas Jef. Green[144] *to Willie P. Mangum*

TALLAHASSEE May 5th. 1834.

Dear Sir:

I have to-day understood that there has been some objections raised in the Senate against the confirmation of James D. Westcotts[145] appointment as District attorney for the middle district of Florida, upon the score of qualification &c.—I have know Mr. W. Since he first came to the Territory and take great pleasure in Stateing my belief that this appointment is entirely judicious—As to his qualifications as a lawyer, I believe he has no superior at our bar, and but few equals,—& he has at this time the best practice in our court which is of itself sufficient evidence of that fact. I should like much to see Mr. *Westcott's* appointment confirmed upon the score of public benefit, believeing him every way qualified for the Situation.

If from our Long personal acquaintance—you think this testimony is worth aught, you will be so good as to hand it to my friends Judges H. L. White & Grundy, as some evidence of Mr. Westcotts Standing with us

Very respectfully your obt.
hul. Sert.
TH: JEF: GREEN.

The Hon.
Wiley P. Mangum
Washington,)
)
City.)

[Addressed:]
The Hon.
Wiley P. Mangum.
Washington City.

---

[144]See above, I, 331n.

[145]James D. Westcott, a lawyer from New Jersey, served in the consular bureau at Washington before he was appointed as secretary for the Florida territory. From 1834 to 1836 he was United States attorney for the Middle District of Florida. He served as United States Senator from Florida from 1845 to 1849, at the close of which time he moved to New York and then to Canada. *Biog. Dir. of Cong.*, 1684.

WPM-LC

Bill of Willie P. Mangum

[May 11, 1834]

Honl. Willie P. Mangum

Bot of Tucker & Thompson[146]

1832			
Dec	1st.	Sup Blk Velvet Vest	$ 8.
	3	" " Cloth Pants	" 18.
	"	3 " Silk Hdkfs @ 1$\frac{50}{100}$	" 4.50
1833		.................[torn] do.	" 0.50
Nov	25th	Sup Blk Cloth Coat	" 38.
	"	" " " Pants	" 18.
	"	" " Mohair Vest	" 9.
	29	2 " Silk Hdkfs & Heming	" 4.25
	"	1 " Blk Mohair Stock	" 3.
Decr.	11	" Blk Casse Vest	" 8.
1834	4	" [torn] Wool Shirt	" 3.50
Jany	4	" Blk Satin Vest	" 8.
	6	" 1 pr White Castor Gloves	" 1.
April	24	" Raven Green Cloth Coat	" 32.
	"	Blk Bombazine Pants	" 9.
	29	Silk Gloves	" 1.
May	3	1 pr Sup Green Elastic Suspenders	" 2.50
	11	Repa[torn] Pantaloons	" 1.00
		[torn]	

[Endorsed:]

Honl W. P. Mangum

WPM-LC

Wm. Horner[147] to Willie P. Mangum

May 21st. 1834.

Dear Sir

I am requested by old Mr. William Hopkins to write to you respecting his pension, he complains on account of his drawing less than any others who served no longer than himself, I promised him I wou'd write to you on the subject, but told him I did not expect you cou'd change the thing now, but he rather

[146]The well known tailoring firm of Washington, D. C.

[147]A justice of peace and neighbor of Mangum.

seems to think that you can, and if you can have his pension raised it will help the feelings of the old man very much, as well as his actual need, you will therefore think on the subject & please write to the old man as early as possible; I have no particular news of the neighbourhood to inform you, corn is scarce and ready sale at $3.50 cash, our wheat crops looks very prosperous at the present, we had a frost on the nights of the 15th. & 16th. Instant which killed our cotton very much, some people had to plant entirely over again though yours I understand escaped by reason of its not having come properly up I see your overseer Stagg on yesterday, your family are well, & people of the neighbourhood are generally well. Though a great many death among the old have occured since you left home Old Capt William Ray died some little time back he Just lived long enough to make his draw [of a pension] & a great many others I cou'd name but as you will certainly be at home shortly I dont deem it necessary, you have had a long & tiresome time of it there, & I expect begin to want to see home nothing more at present, I am in a hurry otherwise I would extend my letter to greater length by giving you & full detail of all the transactions of the neighbourhood which might be some satisfaction but no profit. Old uncle George is well pleased with you for the trouble you took on yourself for him but says he has always been your friend so I quit

Respectfully your most Humble Sert.
WM. HORNER

Willie P. Mangum Esqr.
[Addressed:]
Hon. Willie P. Mangum
Washington
D. C.

WPM-LC

J. Wallace Griffith[148] *to Willie P. Mangum*

[NEW YORK
May 28, 1834.]

Hon. W. P. Mangum
Sir

In connexion with another gentleman of this city I intend publishing in pamphlet form a connected narrative of the

[148] J. Wallace Griffith, 1809-1882, a naval architect, was largely responsible for the development of the clipper ship. W. T. Bonner, *New York: the World's Metropolis . . .*, New York, 1924, 274.

Deposite & Protest controversies, embracing in regular order the official documents the proceedings of Congress, and the speeches of leading members on both subjects.—The plan was designed with the concurrence of Chancellor Kent and G. C. Verplanck, who have given us their written recommendations, and the work will be issued under the auspices of the Whig General Committee of Young Men, and a sufficiently large edition will be printed, so that it can be circulated in any part of the country where it may be useful, to effect which object we intend writing to the committees of the different cities requesting them to order such number of copies (at cost) as they may think proper for gratuitious distribution

My object in addressing you Sir, is to request authentic copies of speeches delivered by you on the above mentioned questions or if it should be inconvenient for you to transmit such copies, that you would apprize us from what source you would prefer our procuring them

I hope sir you will find a sufficient apology for the liberty I am taking in addressing you in the object we have in view

I have the honor to be Sir

Very Rest. Your Obet. Sert

J. WALLACE GRIFFITH

New York May 28th 1834

[Addressed:]

Hon. W. P. Mangum

WPM-LC

Resolutions of Hillsboro Citizens

[HILLSBORO, N. C., May 30, 1834.]

At a public meeting of citizens held in the court house of Orange county N. C. on friday the 30th. of May 1834 the following preamble & resolutions were adopted— viz— [A whole line is torn out.]

demands a free expression of opinion in every section of our country, lest silence on the part of any portion of the people should be construed into acquiescence in measures subversive of the constitution, and deeply injurious to the prosperity of the whole nation; therefore

1 Resolved, as the sense of this meeting that the removal of the deposites of the public money from the bank of the United States in October last by order of the President of the United States was unauthorised by the constitution & laws—

2 Resolved, that the President of the United States has no such control over the public money & other property of the people of the United States as he claims in his late message to the senate, usually called his protest—

3 Resolved, therefore, that we do respectfully, but most decidedly condemn each of those measures of the President—

4 Resolved, further, as the deliberate opinion of this meeting, that a bank of the United States is absolutely necessary in order to ensure to the people of the United States a sound currency & a fair, equal & successful operation of the revenue laws & the financial system of the government—

5 Resolved that we highly approve of the conduct of our S[enator] Honl. W. P. Man[gum] [torn] & the other representat[ives] [o]f the state who acted with them, in relation to these subjects, during the present session of congress—

6 Resolved that the foregoing preamble & resolutions be signed by the chairman & countersigned by the secretary & a copy of them be forwarded to the Honl. W. P. Mangum our Senator & D. L. Barringer our representative in Congress—

CADr JONES[149] Chairman

Ed. Strudwick

WPM-LC

M. St. Clair Clarke[150] *to Jno. C. Calhoun*

[May 30, 1834.]

Mr Colhoun,

Allow me to occupy your time for a few moments, while I tell a short story of my own troubles—

[149] Cadwallader Jones, a colonel in the militia, moved from Halifax County to Hillsboro where he accumulated considerable wealth and was active in civic affairs. He was prominent in the Whig party councils in 1836. Johnson, *Ante-Bellum N. C.*, 149, 685.

[150] See above, I, 562. See also M. St. Clair Clarke and Peter Force, *Report Made to the Hon. John Forsyth, Secretary of State of the United States on the Subject of the Documentary History of the United States now Publishing under an Act of Congress*, Washington, 1834, 39 pp.

The Item of Appropriation for the "Documentary History" is objected to by some Senators—perhaps without being well understood—

In our memorial we proposed to subject the matter for publication, before being printed, to any tribunal Congress might create—They did not do so—nor did the Act place any limit to the work, except as to price—

There is an alternate in the Act, as to cost—

First the "Diplomatic Correspondence heretofore printed" meaning Sparks work—

Second "that now printing" meaning t[he] continuation by F. P. Blair—

The Secretary in preparing to make the contract directed the Agent of the Department to furnish him with the exact cost of these two works—

Sparks	cost per Vol. Octavo	$2:57–1/3
Blairs	Ibid	2.20
	excess in favour of Sparks	.37–1/3

The Secretary selected *Folio* as the form of the work and the page to contain four times as much matter as the others—

We proposed to execute the work for the cost of Sparks—The Secretary refused, saying that he considered himself bound by the *lowest* alternate—A statement was made out and the whole submitted to the Attorney-General who said as the case admitted of a doubt the Secretary had better adhere to his first impressions—

We submitted—

The Secretary finding there were no indexes to either of the works, and requiring them to be put into ours—allowed us the average cost of the Indexes made for Gales & Seatons work, making the cost $2.31—being still within the cost of Sparks 26–1/3/100—per vol—Thus then it is respectfully submitted that the Secretary guarded the public interest so far—

As to the want of limitations in material or number of Volumes I make the following remarks—When the Secretary enquired how many volumes there would be, we answered him as we now say—that it appeared very possible to us each colony or old State might take a Vol—being 13—and that for the Continental Congress from 76 to 83, and then to 89, might reach to make 20 Vol in all—but that it might be less—The Secretary observed, Gentlemen, the Law does not require me to limit the work, I do not know how it well could be, in consequence of the nature of the material, do your duty faithfully, for if you print nonsense you would injure your expectation and get into difficulties with Congress—

Under all these circumstances we entered on our work and have already expended in one thing and another about 12,000$—ten of which I borrowed out of Bank and have of course to repay—You can well imagine how I feel—I cannot make the same exertions for myself as I could for others—

Might I venture to ask you to ascertain from Mr. Mangum, whether, if we file in the Department of State an additional covenant that the work shall not exceed 20 Vols, he would be satisfied—or what course he would advise—I will do any thing that an honorable and just man can require.

By next year a volume will be in the hands of Members and they will then be able to judge of the merits—but [torn] pray them not to bring ruin double refined at the end of a Session which began in proscription in the other house—

Very respectfully
Your Obt Servt
M. St. Clair Clarke

Friday 30 May 1834
Capitol
On reflection I have retained the papers as they are long—
[Addressed:]
Honb. Jn° C. Calhoun,
Senate U. S.

WPM-LC

James Seawell[151] to Willie P. Mangum

FAYETTEVILLE 1 June 1834.

Dear Sir,

I had not when at Washington last anticipated that entire suspension of communication between us as has since occured, and so far as the cause may be attributable to me I am Prepared to make atonement by a more ridgid observance of Punctuality in

[151]See above, I, 592n.

the future.—The truth is, for the last two months I have been up to the hub, engaged in matters relating to Internal Improvement which has required my undivided attention.

We have commenced our Railroad (the Cape Fear Yadkin & Pedee) and although with limited means we intend to keep the work in a state of successful Progress untill we Penetrate the centre of the Western region of our State,—can't you contrive for us to borrow from Uncle Sam a couple of hundred thousand dollars, we will accept of it even from the "Deposit fund,"—with the aid of that amt. it would enable us to accomplish the undertaking speedily.—

Notwithstanding my engagements in Rail Road affairs I have kept a steady eye upon the movements of the dominant Political Party of the times, it is apparent they are Playing a game with two Kings on the same side, Jackson and Van Buren, and the Policy of the game is, to afford Van Buren an opportunity to bring up the rear for his own benefit, at its turmination, but all to no Purpose, they have manoeuvered themselves in a Position which the next move by either, will put each other in check;—at any rate such will be the result of things with regard to the next President in No. Carolina.

A great and desperate effort however will be made by the Administration Party in this State at the approaching election to gain the ascendency in the next genl assembly, their object is to test their strength by placing the election upon *Political grounds* —this they have deturmined upon whither they gain or loose by it—In this Town their plans were convurted under the auspices of a caucus convened during our Supr. Court term,—Wm. H. Haywood Jr., from Raleigh was here and upon his return home became a candidate for Wake.

My opponent Mr. Hybart[152] has again come forth with renewed & imposing confidence of success and has entered the field under the Jacksonian banner, the "*Battle of Orleans and the Indian War*"—we shall meet them upon their own ground and from the word go, contest every inch they now occupy, They will doubtless however have it in their Power to command more formadable appearance than was shown during the contest of last election, but the result I think will not vary much from what it was then.—The campaign will be opened without much rancour of feeling and I trust continue so till its turmination.

[152]Thomas L. Hybart was elected over Seawell.

I notice in some of the News Papers a Statement of the difference of the expense between the Present Administration and former administrations, should there be any Documents Published upon that subject will you do me the favor to send me one.

Will any movements be made by either Party at the Present Session of Congress towards a nomination fir the next Presidency?

When do you expect to rise?—How does the old President like the present appearances of things?

Will you Please Present me to Mr Calhoun, Mr Leigh, Genl McKay and Mr Brown, and to Mr Deberry, and say to Mr D. that I hope soon to find a leisure moment when I will write him.—I tender you the salutations of a friend

J. SEAWELL

Honl Willie P. Mangum

[Addressed:]

The Honorable

Willie P. Mangum

Mail. Washington D. C.

WASHINGTON CITY 13th. June 1836

Willie P. Mangum to James Webb[153]

Sir,

I have received your letter[154] of the 10th instant in relation to the Post office & the Post Master at Hillsbor^{o}..—I have shown it to Mr Brown of the Senate, and enclosed it to the Department with the following endorsement, to wit—

"Senate Chamber
13th June 1836

"To the Hon: Post Master General

"Sir.

"I feel it my duty to enclose this letter to the Department—The veracity of the writer is unquestionable.—He is a gentleman of the highest standing as a man of business & for personal character.

"I have neither personal nor political inclinations in this matter.—I refer the matter to you from a sense of duty to a respect-

[153]The original is in the James Webb Papers, University of North Carolina.

[154]The letter was not found in the Webb or Mangum papers.

able constituent, & from a desire that actual grievance in the Post office alluded to, may be corrected.—Being apprized of the complaints, I doubt not that the usual investigation will be had, & an appropriate remedy applied.

"Your obt servt.

WILLIE P. MANGUM" I have little expectation that you will be able to get a better postmaster than Mr Clancy,[155] especially if the citizens can manage to get him a good deputy.—

Clancy is honest, & that is a great matter—A change may give you one, to whom even greater objections may lie, than to Mr Clancy.—That any man opposed to the admn. will be appointed is not to be expected; no, not even if every man in Hillsbor°. should request & urge it.—

No one feels more strongly than I do, the wretched condition of the public service, when things come to this pass.—What cannot be remedied, must be endured.—

Mr Brown does not indicate any inclination to interpose in this matter, further than to request the Dept. to look to that office, & have an eye on the manner in which it may be conducted.—

With him & the representative is all power on this subject.— I need not say, that my opinions & wishes can form no motive for the action of the Department.

Your obedient

Sevt.

WILLIE P. MANGUM

[Addressed:] Doct. James Webb
Hillsborough No. Carolina

Free
Willie P. Mangum

WPM-LC

James Whitaker[156] to Willie P. Mangum

FRANKLIN June 13th 1834.

Dear Sir,

Permit an obscure friend, to drop you a few lines. to you by way, rather of enquiry. and first, we live bordering on the Chero-

[155]Thomas Clancy. See above, I, 55.

[156]James Whitaker was born in Rowan County. For many years he served as justice of the peace there. In 1817 he moved to Buncombe County and then to Macon County. He served in the legislature in 1818-1821, 1823, 1829-1832, and 1842-4843. *N. C. Manual*, 576; John P. Arthur, *Western North Carolina: a History from 1730 to 1913*, Raleigh, 1914, pp. 177-178.

kees, and feel a deep interest in every thing Connected with that people. if you therefore, have any information about them, either as regards a Treaty, or otherwise, we wou'd be thankfull to get it. —

we receive but few Documents, and but little information from Washington, except Newspapers any how.—Unfortunately for some of us, we are too strong friends to the Republican Doctrines of 98—and of state Rights now. to receive much from the Dominant party. for my dear Sir, we have many in our County, who seem to think that Andrew. Jackson, can do no rong—and I verily believe, woud applaud his Conduct, even if he should, (as Maj. Jack[157] says,) Kick the whole Senate, into the Potomac,—Sir, send us something, if nothing better, send Jacks Letters.

Many of my acquaintance in this county,[158] Haywood, and Buncombe, wish to know something of the encouragement, given by Government, (if any.) to Emigrants, for the Columbian River[159] Many families in my acquaintance, would go—if they knew, something more on the subject. i,e, if encouragement worth Notice is held out &C.—

Sir, you ought to pay some little attention to us in this County, if, for nothing else than to keep up our Spirits, Many of us, are Decidedly your Political friends, tho a Majority, go against you, some from principle; and some through ignorance; and some through fear. But the State Right party, are pleased with your Course in the senate, particularly on the Depossit question.

Sir, excuse the hasty remarks of a friend, and partial acquaintance.

JAMES WHITAKER—

[Addressed:]

[W. P.] Mangum. Esqr—
) Washington
City

---

[157]In 1834 "Maj. Jack Dowling" wrote a series of letters to the *New York Daily Advertiser* attacking the Jackson administration. *Daily National Intelligencer*, Feb. 7, 1834.

[158]Macon County.

[159]By 1832 there was great interest in the settlement of Oregon. A number of expeditions were organized including some immigrants from France. Missionaries, especially Methodists and Jesuits, and Marcus Whitman were actively engaged in the development. Unlike the fur traders their settlements were permanent. Frederick J. Paxson, *History of the American Frontier, 1762-1893*, Boston, 1924, 332-334.

WPM-LC

Mathew Carey[160] *et als. to Willie P. Mangum*

PHILADELPHIA June 14. 1834

Dear Sir—

A large and respectable meeting of the citizens of the city of Philad^a. held on the 11th inst—impressed with a sincere respect for the devotion of your talents to the interpid defence of the laws and Constitution, of our common country have devolved on us the agreeable duty of requesting the pleasure of your company at a dinner on the 58th anniversary of the declaration of independence of our country.

Hoping that a compliance with the request may comport equally with your convenience and inclination We remain

Respectfully yours
Mathew Carey
J. Randall
G: Scull
George W. Jones
John Scholefield
James L. Biddle
J. S. Riddle

[Addressed:]
Hon: Mr Mangum
U. S. Senate
Washington.

Willie P. Mangum to James Webb[161]

WASHINGTON CITY 16th. June 1836

Dr Sir

I have just received your note of the 11th. inst. in relation to Mr. Crabtree's certificate.—

I have forwarded it to the office, & hope to get a duplicate before leaving here, by guaranteeing its' non-delivery to Mr. C. until he shall comply with the usual requisitions of the office.—

[160]Mathew Carey, 1760-1839, an immigrant from Ireland, had little formal education but read extensively. He published the *Republican*, a number of books, and developed considerable interest in politics. He favored the tariff, universal education, and internal improvements. *D. A. B.*, III, 489-491.

[161]The original is in the James Webb Papers, University of North Carolina.

In that case, it will be forwarded to you, with the expectation that you will see that the usual affidavits shall be made, & forwarded, to the pension office.—In case that cannot be done, I will immediately transmit the requisite information.—

Your obt. Sevt.
W. P. MANGUM

[Addressed:] Doct. James Webb
Hillsbor°
No. Carolina

Free
Willie P. Mangum.

WPM-LC

Saml Black[162] *& others to Willie P. Mangum*

PHILADA. 19th June 1834

Dear Sir

The Citizens of the first Congressional District of Pennsylvania opposed to Executive usurpation have made arrangements to celebrate the approaching anniversary of American Independence.—On their behalf, we, their Committee Cordially invite your participation with us in the festivities of the day—and should it not be inconsistent with your convenience and engagements to unite with us on that occasion, it will confer an honor and obligation on those whom we repesent, and

Dear Sir
Your Obedt. Servts.
(Saml Black
(
(Geo. Norton
(
(Geo. G. West
(
(R. M. Anners
(
(Henry Flickwir
(
(Jas. Cavenaugh

[162]An eminent lawyer in Philadelphia. John Livingston, *Biographical Sketches of Eminent American Lawyers Now Living,* New York, 1852, p. 548.

Pr. (
Sam[l] Black (Jas. Maxwell
chairman. (
(T. M. Hubbell
(
(W. C. Donaldson
(
(N. C. Foster
(
(
(
(
(

Honble. Wm. P. Mangum.
U S Senate
[Addressed:]
Honble. Wm. P. Mangum
U. S. Senate
Washington City
D. C.

WPM-LC

John D. DeLacy[163] to Willie P. Mangum

NEW YORK June the 20th. 1834

Wyllie P. Mangum Esqr
Dear Sir

It is with pleasure I see that you at present occupy a seat for which your telents and turn of mind eminently fit you: certainly far more than for the drudgery Dust, labour and brain racking details of a law shop

I have taken up my pen to tell you that should you wish to relax after your legislative labours after a laborious and truly singular session and recruit your self after your fatigues, You had better visit this city and the Saratoga Springs and see what stuff we are made off; for be assured there are very many here would be glad to see you and among them none more so than him who is Respectfully and sincerely

Your Most Obed[t].
JOHN D DELACY
No. 1 Chamber Street

[163]See above, I, 13n.

Please to present my respects to Col. D. Crocket. He told me when here that he was acquainted with you—

[Addressed:]

Honbl, Wyllie P. Mangum
U. S. Senate
Washington City

WPM-LC

R. H. Bradford[164] *to Willie P. Mangum*

WASHINGTON CITY
21st June 1834.

Sir

I took the liberty the other day to request you to enclose to Mr. Minor of (N. Y) Editor of the R. Road Journal some little information which I had procured at his request "on the progress and present condition of the internal improvements of Vrgn. & No. Carolina, particular as related to canals & R. Roads".

Since the date of my note I have recd. some further intelligence on these subjects especially as to the Road from Portsmth. Vrgn. to Weldon No. Ca. which I have to ask the additional favor of you to forward to Mr. Minor, who has requested that I would adopt this mode of transmitting the same to him—

I hope I shall not have occasion to give you further trouble in this way, hereafter tho I confess I feel very desirous to aid the very meritorious Editor of this Journal in his efforts to obtain correct intelligence in relation to the subject mentioned.

I have the honor to be very resfy,
etc. etc.

Honble W. P. Mangum,

R. H. BRADFORD

[Addressed:]

Honble W. P. Mangum
U. States
Senate.

[Endorsed:]

D. K. Minor
Edi R. R. Journal
N. Y.

---

[164]He was in one of the Federal offices. Bassett (ed.), *Cor. of Jackson,* IV, 291n.

WPM-LC

C. A. Alexander[165] *& others to Willie P. Mangum*[166]

LEESBURG LOUDOUN COUNTY VA.
June 21st 1834

Dear Sir,

A Number of the Citizens of Loudoun County, who regard with deep interest the course of public affairs, and who percive in the recent demonstrations of popular opinion in Virginia, anomen of future success, to the great principles of Civil Liberty, desire to signalize the occasion by some suitable and public expression of their feelings at so auspicious an event.

To promote this purpose, they have appointed the undersigned a Committee, to silicet the presence of certain of our distinguished friends at a dinner, to be given in the town of Leesburg on the 26th of the present month; It is in pursuance Sir, of instructions to this effect, that we present the request to you, and beg leave to add an assurance of the great satisfaction with which your compliance will be received by a numerous body of your fellow Citizens and friends.

Respectfully your obt. Servants.
C. A. Alexander

Wilson C. Selden Senr.)
John Rose)
Presley Cordell) COMMITTEE.
Wm. A. Powell)
Wm. Elsey)
Fleming Hinon)

Hon. Wilie P. Mangum.
[Addressed:] Hon: Willie P. Mangum
Washington City.

---

[165]Unable to identify.

[166]This letter is one of many which Mangum received in 1834 asking him to participate in Whig rallies outsde of the state. His important part in the fight against Jackson in the first session of the Twenty-third Congress increased his reputation in other sections of the country.

WPM-LC

Samuel Branch[167] *& others to Willie P. Mangum*

FARMVILLE [Va] June 24 1834

Honl. Mr. Mangum

Dear Sir,

The Citizens of this vilage and its vicinity have determined to commemorate the ensuing Fourth of July by a public celebration. Believing that the day which conferred such lasting honour on our sires should be held in perpetual remembrance by their decendents, we should deem ourselves unworthy inheritors of the fruits of their labors, if we failed to celebrate the day on which they pledged their lives & fortunes in the cause of American Liberty, by Suitable marks of respect. The people of this district are, also, urged to this duty, by another consideration. The genius of misrule and monarchial principles seems to have taken advantage of the death of the lamented Randolph[168] & Bauldin[169] to inthrone himself in that seat on which during the lives of those gifted spirits sat only the genuis of Liberty and Law. Doctrines then breathed only in secrecy and in the ear of friendship, are now proclaimed on the housetop & declared to be the true Southern principles. we believe the expression of opinion on the ensuing "fourth" will show that the spirit of our lamented representatives still glows in the hearts of their constituents.

With gratitude to you and your coadjutors in the Senate for your exertions in arresting usurpation, in be half of the Citizens of this vicinity, we respectfully solicit you to join with us in person, or by a sentiment in honouring that day so dear to American freemen.

We have the honour to be
Your Obt Servts.

Committee of Invitation.	Saml. Branch	F. Hobson
	G Wilson	E Booker
	B F Wilson	Thos. W. Morton
	T M McRobert	J. W. Wood
	J Lyle	W B Gholson.

[167]For many years he was a trustee of Hampden-Sidney College and a resident of Buckingham County. *Virginia Magazine of History,* VI, 182.

[168]John Randolph died in 1833.

[169]Thomas T. Bouldin died in the early part of 1834. *Biog. Dir. of Cong.,* 719.

[Addressed:]
Honl. Mr. Mangum
U. S. Senator from the State of N. Carolina
Washington City
[Postmarked:] Farmville, June 25.

WPM-LC

Wm. D. Amis[170] *to Willie P. Mangum*

BLAKELY June 24th 1834

Dear Sir

At our last court, I consented to become a candidate to represent, this county in the senate, on the ante-administration ticket, contrary to all expectations, I found an oponent, in my friend & neighbour Col Wm B Lockhart.[171] I think I shall beat him in the election, owing to his politics, which are administration, altogether, and has promised the people, that he would satisfy them that the Genl. administration had been one productive of great good & more particularly this section of the country.

I have travelled some in this state since I saw you, in Washington city and am happy to inform you, that your decided stand that you have assumed, in opposition to the usurpation of the laws & constitution by the present Executive, meets the warmest approbation of your fellow citizens of this state.

From my mingling with the people, they appear to be appraised, that "there is something rotten in Denmark" and are more open to conviction, relative to the conduct of the present mal-administration of the Executive, than I have ever known them before.—Mr. Bynum[172] has been industrious, in giving publicity to all congress documents, which have a tendency to eulogize & forward the views of the administration.—I think it advisable (for really I consider the present, a mal-administration) to counteract those, by some from the whig party, by sending us a few of Mr. Calhouns speeches, the report of the majority on the post office department. This may incur a little expence & considerable trouble, The former, I am willing share

[170]In 1832 Amis was a delegate to the state Democratic convention which endorsed Jackson, but he later joined the Whig party. *N. C. Free Press,* July 3, 1832.
[171]Col. William B. Lockhart won in the election. He was also a member of the Council of State from 1826 to 1829. *N. C. Manual,* 433-434.
[172]Jesse Bynum.

with you on sight. The latter the interest of your state, and to promote its inhabitants demands of you—Par & myself were much pleased with Mr Calhoun's speach, for which he has our warmest respects.

The people are more pleased with the doctrine of nullification, than the word itself Below I send you the names of some of our most respectable inhabitants, with their respective post offices.—

Jesse Bradley	Jackson, N. C.	Bryan Randolph
D. H. Clements	Wm Bottom	Jas. Rutland
Edmund Jones	Thos. Branch	Nathan Wootten
James Vincent	Wm Deloach	*Richs. Square*
Bulladmons' Store	Britton Doles	Geo. Benn
Jos. Collier	Alfred Eldridge	Jordan Beall
James Gowing	Herod Faison	Eli Cook
Wm Harding	Henry W. Ivy	Wm. Futrell Sr.
Wm Moody	John L. W. Long	Willie Futrell
Sykes Store	Jos. M. S. Rogers	Henry Joyner
Henry P. Barkly	A. P. Smith	Thos. Joyner
D. B. Boykin	*Diamond Grove*	Jas. W. Moore
Doct Jas. R. Crump	Allen Barkley	John Outland
Robt. Ellis	Nicholas Magett	Jesse Woodard
Blakely Depot	Shad. Grant	*Futrells Tavern*
Doct C. Cross	Edmund Jacobs	Simmons Burns
Dempsey R. Gamp	Norman Branch	C. W. Barnes
Arthur Jordan	*Jackson N. C.*	A(le)x Moore
John Jordan	Lem. Bowden	John D. Maget
Pleasant Hill	Elijah Futrell	John B Sharrod
Jas. Exum	Wm Josey	Nicholas Tyner
E. J. Peebles	Jno. Lambertson	Jas. Woodard
Jas. H Grant	Jos. Outland	*Martins' Tavern*
John White	Thos. Peele	*Near Murfreesboro'*

The above are the most respectable & influencing men, in the different neighbourhoods.

Respectfully yours'
truly
WM. D. AMIS .

[Addressed:]
Hon: Willie P. Mangum
Washington City
D. C.

NO ampton
29 June

WPM-LC

Thomas W. Gilmer[173] *et als to Willie P. Mangum*

CHARLOTTESVILLE
June 25th 1834

Sir

A number of the citizens of this county, who are opposed to Executive usurpation and misrule, have made arrangements for a public dinner at this place on the approaching 4th of July—We have been desired in their behalf to invite you to attend on this occasion, and to assure you of the satisfaction with which those, whose organs we are, have witnessed the independence and ability you have so conspicuously manifested in the Senate of the United States—It will afford us very great pleasure if you can unite with us—

We are with the highest regard
Your fellow citizens
Thomas W. Gilmer
V. W. Southall
C. Everette
D. F. Carr
H. Massie
G. M. Lewis
& others

To W. P. Mangum Esq.
committee

[Addressed:]
Wilie P. Mangum Esq.
U. S. Senate
Washington City

WPM-LC

John Branch to Willie P. Mangum

ENFIELD June 25th 1834

My dear Sir,

Will you do me the favour to forward to my address a *fair proportion* of the reports of the Post Office Committee?[174]

---

[173]At this time Gilmer was a member of the Virginia legislature. Later he was governor of the state, a member of Congress and Secretary of the Navy. He was killed in the explosion on the *Princeton* in 1844. *Biog. Dir. of Cong.*, 1014; *D. A. B.*, VII, 308.

[174]On June 9, 1834, the Senate Committee on Post Office and Post Roads made its report. According to this partisan report the postmasters borrowed from banks without authority, granted contracts on bids which revealed that undue advantage was given to favorites, and allowed extra allowances without requiring an increase of service. It further stated that steamship lines were authorized to carry mail contrary to the law and that public credit was provided for the benefit of mail contractors who were deeply in debt and whose affairs were in disorder. The Committee recommended that 30,000 copies of the report be printed. *Hillsborough Recorder*, June 18, 1834.

We have flattering prospects in our State, and I cannot doubt but that the reign of tyranny & Corruption is drawing to a close.

JN BRANCH.

We must not however, be lull^{d}. into a premature security.

Accept my friendly assurances & best wishes.

Hon. W. P. Mangum.

[Addressed:]

Hon. W. P. Mangum,
Washington City,
D. C.

Enfield N. C.
26th June 1834

WPM-LC

Jno. B. Muse[175] *to Willie P. Mangum*

ELIZABETH CITY June 28th 1834

Dear Sir.

Yours of the 18th did not reach me until the day before yesterday, the 26th Inst, and according to your request, I seize the earliest opportunity to reply. You will readily perceive, that owing to the lateness of the period at which your letter was received, I could not, even if I were to accept the proffered honour, by any possibility, reach the City of Washington by the 30th Inst., tomorrow morning being the first Stage northward, since its receipt.

Though I feel highly honoured in being thought worthy of such a trust & much obliged to you for the kind & flattering manner in which, you addressed me, yet my duty to myself dictates, that I should remain at home, And attend to my professional engagements. In the month of August our County Courts commence, and in the two or three succeeding months, my time will be entirely occupied with attending the Superior Courts; with but very few leisure weeks. These considerations will, I trust, satisfy you of the prudence of My course; and I hope at a future period to shew the friends of Liberty and the Constitution that my heart is with them in the cause & that in thus declining to act in the capacity you wish, that my motives are of a nature not entirely selfish.

I here take occasion to say, that if General Green will send me two or three copies of his prospectus,[176] it will afford me much

---

[175]See above, I, 355n.

[176]He probably refers to Duff Green's effort to issue one of his extras in support of Calhoun's candidacy for the presidency.

pleasure, to assist him, as much as is in my power, by procuring subscribers in those counties where my profesional engagements shall lead me.

Gen William Gregory of this place, with whom I believe you are acquainted, would I have no doubt, be perfectly willing to undertake the trust for a suitable compensation—He is Post Master of This place, & tho' compelled from the nature of things, to keep his zeal within due bounds, he is not on that account the less firm & staunch on our side.—He has a high regard for Gen Green, tho' unacquainted, & is a constant reader of his paper. He intends spending the summer months in the western part of our State, & could without inconvenience to himself be of material service to the cause of State Rights—

If Gen[l] Green & yourself should concur with me in this matter, you will please address a letter to Gen[l] Gregory or myself & I will with pleasure do all in my power to further the matter.

I am, Dear Sir

Very Respectfully etd.

JNO. B. MUSE.

P. S. Mr Bailey desires me to present his respectful compliments.

[Addressed:]

Honorable

Willie P. Mangum.

U. S. Senate.

Washington City.

WPM-LC

Senate Finance Committee to the Officers of U. S. Bank[177]

PHILADELPHIA, July 7, 1834.-

To the President and Directors
of the Bank of the United [States]
Gentlemen,

We enclose you a copy of a resolution passed by the Senate of the United States on the 30. June by which you will perceive

[177]On June 30, 1834, the Senate adopted resolutions authorizing the Finance Committee to investigate the conditions of the United States Bank and of the state banks in which Federal deposits were placed. Webster, the chairman, asked Tyler to act as reporter. Mangum gathered most of the information for the Committee. After traveling to Philadelphia, New York, and Boston, and after gaining from replies to letters to the officers of the other branches of the Bank, the Committee rendered its report to the Senate December 18, 1834. Mangum, Ewing, Webster, Tyler, and Wilkins were the members of the Committee. Wilkins, the only member who favored Jackson, refused to serve. *Daily National Intelligencer*, Dec. 19, 1834.

it is made our duty to execute certain enquiries respecting the Bank of the United States.—These enquiries are.—

1. Whether the Bank has violated its charter;—
2.- Whether the monies of the United States, now remaining in the Bank are safe.—
3. What has been the conduct of the Bank, since 1832, in regard to the successive extensions and curtailments of its loans and discounts and its dealings in domestic or internal bills of Exchange;—
4.- And what has been its General conduct and management since that period.—

We shall enter upon these enquiries at some period before the next meeting of Congress and shall endeavour to obtain the most full and ample information upon all and each of the points enumerated in the instructions of the Senate.—

To this end it will be necessary that the Books of the Bank should be freely subject to our inspection and that we should be furnished with all such accounts, statements, abstracts and exhibits as we may deem useful and proper.—The time of commencing the examination will be hereafter communicated to you, but in order to facilitate our labor and to enable us to go through it with more despatch when we shall again meet, we have now to request that the following statements or tables be made out and forwarded as soon as convenient to the chairman of the Committee.—

I.- A quarterly statement of the affairs of the Bank and its Offices respectively for the several quarters of the years 1832 and 1833, and the three first quarters of 1834, this statement to contain

1. Amount of notes discounted.
2. Domestic Bills of Exchange purchased and discounted.—
3.- Foreign Bills of Exchange purchased and discounted.—
4.- Balance due from other Banks including their notes.—
5.- Balance due to other Banks.—
6.- Amount of specie; specifying how much in gold and how much silver, how much coin and how much coin [*sic*] and how much bullion.—
7.- Amount of public Deposits.—
8.- Account of private Deposits—

II. Statement of all the dividends of the Bank; with the amount of any existing surplus fund or contingent fund.—

III. Statement of the real estate and Banking house held by the Bank with an estimate of their value.—

IV.- The debts due the Bank; with an estimate showing what part is regarded as bad or doubtful, and what funds, if any, are relied on to meet any deficiency arising from such causes.—

V.- Copies of all the bye laws and rules of proceeding adopted by the Directors.—

VI. Statement of the rates of Exchange on domestic bills for the several quarters before mentioned between the principal cities in the United States and tables of the rates of such exchanges yearly since 1816.—

Signed by the Committee

WPM-LC

L. G. Watson to Willie P. Mangum

[Oxford]
Tuesday night July 9th [1834]
8 o'clock.

Dear Sir:

Enclosed[178] you have a precious morsel from our County-man which has this moment dropped from the press—Thro' the Courtesy of the editor I have been permitted to take this circular without the knowledge of the writer, as I was anxious you should be in possession of it as early as possible, and if you are disposed to notice it, I must beg that you will not speak of the manner in which you obtained it. Mr. Harris has asserted & reasserted that you gave evidences of great affright, & took refuge behind Col Jones, notwithstanding Thomas B. Littlejohn, esq. & John Bullock esq. both declare it false In stating what these Gentlemen told me, Mr Harris stated that Col. Iverson Hicks saw you do so, I took occasion this evening to enquire of Col H. who is Mr Harris' most particular friend He stated that Mr H had made an incorrect statement "that you arose suddenly displaced a man by the name of Barnet, & jumping behind your chair grasped it firmly when instantly John Bullock interposed" —

[178]The enclosure is not in the Mangum Papers.

Sandy Is playing a desperate and I apprehend a ruinous game at least so in the estimate of 4/5 of the intelligent community—For my part I have no wish to interfere with or have anything to do with him in any shape We know one another, and altho' we are distantly nay sometimes genteely polite to each our respect for one another falls little short of bitter aversion—It is however desirable in these little villages to get along as well as we can—so we go. Tomorrow the "Campaign" commences, & Mr H will take the grand rounds for the Clerks office & will send forth as much venom as his little system is capable of generating—The mail closes in 10 minutes & I have no time to write you more at large—You will excuse the haste & imperfections of this scrawl & believe me to be

Truly yr. friend

L. G. WATSON

[Addressed:]

Hon. Willie P. Mangum

Red Mountain

N. C.

Col. Parker is respectfully requested to forward this immediately as the writer is anxious that Judge Mangum should receive it *immediately*. L. G. Watson.

(Oxford, N. C. July 10).

WPM-LC

Henry N. Jasper to Willie P. Mangum

FRANKLIN COUNTY N. C. July 17, 1834.

Sir,

A slight personal acquaintance with you, & being a constant admirer of your political principles & conduct as they were to be understood by me & most of those with whom I usually accord in sentiment & action, have emboldened me to address you on the present occasion. I have heard it asserted by a conspicuous candidate for the State Legislature in the Senate in this county, that there was a difference between you & your colleage Mr. Brown on the subject of the *constitutionality* of the U. S. Bank as well as to the expediency of re-chartering it. The only inference that could be drawn, from such a declaration by those at all acquainted with the whole hog collar principles of Mr.

Brown was, that you admitted the constitutionality of the measure, & thought it expedient.[179] Ever having entertained, I may say, *a positive* conviction that your political sentiments were of a different cast, I felt no hesitation in assuring the gentleman who made the declaration that he must be mistaken. But in no long time afterwards, it was publicly asserted by the Hon. M. T. Hawkins, the representative of this district that you had declared to him that if you had been present or in Congress (my memory does not exactly serve me as to the precise expression of Mr. H.) you would have voted for the re-chartering the U. S. Bank coming from such a source, I could not deny it; yet I could not hesitate to declare to Mr. H. that either he must have greatly misconstrued your expression, or, I must have entirely mistaken your political sentiments. At the same time I pledged my word to the people that I would ascertain from the best possible source, viz, yourself, who was mistaken with regard to your political principles in that particular measure. Therefore Sir, if you should not view the request as impertinent, you will greatly oblige one who has been a uniform admirer both of your principles & the ability with which they have been set forth, if you will do me the favor to inform me of your sentiments on that subject. At the same time I can assure you that you will highly gratify many in this county who have heretofore entirely coincided with me in approving & admiring your principles as made known by your previous declarations & conduct, should you think it not too great a sacrifice of time to place us on the 'vantage ground' of those who are disposed to condemn without knowing the why or wherefore, your course of conduct, as a Senator, by combining with the answer to the original request, a brief sketch of general politics & political matters. I remain Sir, with the most profound respect,

Your Obt. Servt.
HENRY N. JASPER

P.S. I wish to apprize you of the fact that in making this request I have no interested motives to influence me—being no candi-

[179]For Mangum's position on the Bank see above, I, xxvii, xxix, xxx, 455-456, 480-481.

date for public favor, & thinking it doubtful whether or not I ever shall be.

H. N. JASPER

[Addressed:]

Hon. Willie P. Mangum
Red Mountain via
Orange County
Stagville

By Mail N. Ca.

WPM-LC

Bill of Willie P. Mangum

RED MOUNTAIN July 19th 1834

Willie P. Mangum Esqr.

Bot of a Parker & Co[180]

3 lbs Coffee	1/9–$,,		53
3/4 yd. Buckram	2/–	..	15
1½ yds Nº Homespun	1/–	,,	15
3/4 Yard. padding	5/–	,,	38
1 Stick Twist			10
1 Set L. Buttons			20
			$1.51

pr. willie Stagg)[181]

WPM-LC

Walter Lowrie[182] to Willie P. Mangum

WASHINGTON July 19 1834

Dear Sir

From the business which I must dispose of in the office, I find it will be impracticable for me to be with you in Philadelphia[183] as you proposed when you were here. As soon as the clerks bring up the current business of the office, I must join them in preparing the State Papers. The work cannot go on without me. The responsibility of deciding what papers are to be printed, & what not printed is too great for me to leave to others, when the law makes that my duty.

---

[180]Colonel Abner Parker, who lived near Mangum.

[181]Mangum's overseer.

[182]Secretary of the Senate. See above, II, 23n.

[183]With other members of the Finance Committee, Mangum went to Philadelphia to investigate the U. S. Bank.

As it will be impossible for me to be with you, I take this early opportunity of informing you of it that you may look out some other person.

I have also written to Messrs Tyler & Webster.

I respectfully
your friend & Svt
WALTER LOWRIE

Hon. W. P. Mangum.

[Addressed:]

Hon. W. P. Mangum
Orange County
Red Mountain
North Carolina.

WPM-LC

Henry A. Donaldson et als. to Willie P. Mangum

WAKE FOREST 26 July 1834.

The Honble
Willie P. Mangum

[torn] number of the Citizens of Wake Forest and vicinity propose having a public Dinner at the Falls of Neuse on the Seventh of next month—We have been desired on their behalf to invite you, and to bear to you the assurance of the high regard which they entertain for your important public Services and your devotion to the great principles of Free government and equals rights

We are with great respect
yr ob Servants
Hy. A. Donaldson)
John Y. Young)
) Committee.
Jesse Powell)
Turner Pullen)
John Ligon)

[Addressed:]

The Honble.
Willie P. Mangum
Red Mountain,
N. C.

WPM-LC

Nathaniel J. Palmer[184] *to Willie P. Mangum*

MILTON, N. C. Aug 4th 1834.

Dear Sir,

Yours of the 31st ult. came to hand by yesterday's mail. Agreeable to your request the paper sent to you will be discontinued. You will find enclosed your account and the balance due stated.

It is I assure you a source of deep regret to me, that we differ in opinion so widely, in relation to the late measures of the Administration. But with me as I have every reason to believe with yourself an honest difference in political matters shall never violate private & personal friendship. I have but little doubt but that some of the Administration prints have done you great injustice, and while I have not followed their example in personal abuse and slander, I have not been able conscientiously to approve of your recent course in the Senate [torn] you person [torn] I shall never [Several lines are torn out] gree than I feel towards your colleague Mr. Brown. You know that I have ever been a supporter of Gen. Jackson and his Administration, and I hope I shall never have sufficient cause to withdraw that support. I am aware that he has committed some errors but if the measures of his Administration are properly weighed, and appreciated the preponderance will be found in his favor.

With sincere regards, yours, &c.

NATHANIEL J PALMER.

Hon. W. P. Mangum.

[Addressed:]

Hon. Willie P. Mangum
Red Mountain
Orange County, N. C.

[184]See above, I, 414-415.

WPM-LC

Willie P. Mangum to Charity A. Mangum

STATE OF RHODE ISLAND.[185]
TOWN OF NEWPORT.
19th of August 1834.

My dear Love.

I wrote to you from Washington on the 15th.—I was then unwel, having suffered excessively from the intense heat.—on Saturday morning the 16th. I set out for Baltimore, where I arrived in the evening and met with Govr. Tyler, his lady, daughter & family of children. They took me to task for your absence. —I staid at Baltimore saturday night, & we all took the steamboat for Philadelphia on Sunday morning.—That evening at three oclock we reached Philadelphia—spent the evening and night there, and on Monday morning we took the boat for New York.—Having heard that the cholera was raging in New York and from 20 to 30 deaths a day taking place, the company felt afraid to stop there—We arrived at 2 oclock in the evening, and the boat was to leave there at 5 oclock, giving us only three hours to stay.—The company left one boat and went into the other, without going into the City.—I hired a coach, as I felt no fear, and drove throughout the City, visiting every place, that a stranger would like to see—I paid $1.50cts & did not regret the expense.—Take New York alltogether, its bay, its rivers, its city & its heights about it they form the most picturesque & delightful spot I ever saw—except some scenes of the mountains; which I admire above all things. I was tolerably well.—

STATE OF RHODE ISLAND
CITY OF PROVIDENCE 20th August
1834.

I had written yesterday evening as far as the above, when I was called off by company, and to day I resume the letter from Providence, which is thirty miles from New-port.—

We left New York at 5 oclock in the evening on Monday—& took Long Island sound, and passed through Hell-gate, sometime called Hurl-gate or the boiling pot before sunset.—These

[185]Mangum, with the other members of the Senate Committee on Finance, was on a trip to investigate the U. S. Bank.

waters are the terror of mariners and many vessels have been lost there.—Cooper the novelist describes them in his "Water Witch"—and as you have the book let me ask you to turn to the novel, and read the account of these dangerous narrows—

The tide happened to be full, and I saw none of the dangerous & peculiar features of this pass—I regretted it, and had much rather the tide had been ebb or ebbing, so that I might have formed a juster idea of those dangers that have so often appalled the heart of the sailors.—I cannot convey to you an idea of the beauty of many of the residences on the Deleware above Philadelphia, and especially of those on both sides of Long Island sound east of New York—Many of them seem to be the spots that Calypso would have chosen as the seat of the Muses, or as the lovely retreats of the Nymphs of the sea.—

The moon rose that evening in her full majesty and shone all night, bright in the midst of Myriads of stars.—I remained upon deck until late, tho the east wind was fresh & chilling—After passing the narrows, we went into a sound 10 or twenty miles wide, swept along the Connecticut shore, which lay in its loveliness, on the borders of the bright & sparkling sea waters—

I turned into my cot, but was the earliest to rise in the morning—When I looked out we were at sea, with Rock Island lying in the distance to the east, and the main to the West—That Island soon disappeared and we were on the broad bosom of the Ocean for 15 or 20 Miles, until we arrived at Newport a pretty town of 5 or 6,000 inhabitants in a pretty island.—It is the resort of all the Cities for a pure & bracing air, and for sea bathing—Every house public & private is now full—We got lodging with difficulty—I went up four pair of stairs into a small room, without bells, & where I had not the honor to see a servant but once during my stay there.—I cursed and have quit, though not until I walked over the island & upon the sea shore, seeing all that one w^{d}. care for.—This morning the accommodation was so badly attended to, that I determined to take the steam boat for Providence—Govr. Tyler & his family are at Newport, where the family will stay—I turned a deaf ear to all their pursuasions to stay a day longer & sent my baggage to the steamboat at 7 oclock in the morning—It was put aboard, and as I was behind it a few minutes, the boat left me, carrying my trunk & clothes bag and all my clothes.—You may be sure that even my mild & patient temper was a little ruffled.—

I returned & swore I w[d]. not stay an hour longer—I was left, by mis information from the bar keeper which was designed to mislead me.—

I went to the stage office & took my passage by land, except an arm of the sea, a mile & an half wide that I had to pass in a sail boat that I thought several times would upset—the wind being high,—It became cloudy yesterday has been so to day & is still so, with every appearance of a north east storm.—

I saw much of the country, the comfortable farm houses, the beautiful orchards & nurseries, the green grass meadows, flats & pastures, the strong stone fences & pretty hedges.—Altogether the day has been very interesting—Besides I passed through the flourishing towns of Bristol & Warren in the first of which I dined.—

On my arrival here, which is a flourishing City of thirty thousand inhabitants, I found my baggage in the steam boat, and am now writing in the City Hotel, a splendid establishment, at 8 oclock in the evening.—Tomorrow I think I shall go to Boston the whole of which distance about 50 miles, is land travel

I have been tolerably well, except the tooth ache which I got in Long Island sound.—And to day some disturbance of my bowels by the change of water.

I intend to return by land to New York—the travel is longer & more laborious; but as it may be the only opportunity, I shall have to see New England, I wish to avail myself of it, to see all that I can.—It is a wonderful Country, and they are a wonderful people, and one is constantly reminded that he is amongst strangers.—

I am now more than eight hundred miles from home, the greatest distance I have ever been from home & from you My dear Love.—

I think of you much my Love, and feel that you were never dearer to my heart & my affections, than at this instant.—My heart throbs as warmly with love & affection for my dear Wife, as when I hug her to my bosom, perhaps even more so.—As a tinge of melancholy that I feel in this strange & distant land, heightens the interest with which I feel & think of you & our dear children

May God bless you all,—Remember me often My Love For in your love, I have a treasure dear to the heart—that I trust neither time nor chance shall deprive me of while we both live.

Your affectionate husband

W. P. MANGUM.

Kiss our dear children for me.

[Addressed:]

Mrs. C. A. Mangum
Red Mountain
No. Carolina

[Postmarked:]

Providence

WPM-LC

Robert H. Jones[186] *to Willie P. Mangum*

WARRENTON [N. C.] 22. Augt. 1834

My dear Sir,

I had intended to give you my candid opinion upon sundry points, presented in the course of General Jacksons administration, as they were believed to impugn the rights of the States, of the people and of the Senate of the United States, by the party to which it is manifest you have attached yourself. It was this opinion which you invoked at the moment of our separation, and it is the opinion, I wou'd most gladly submit to your examination and your most rigid scrutiny. But I regret that a continued indisposition, and the pressure of my Court business, renders it impossible for me enter upon a field of Argument, so expansive, and as it wou'd seem from the failure of Mr. Webster, Mr. Clay, Mr. Calhoun and others, is so beset with difficulties—with the least hope of doing justice to myself, or gratifying you. You therefore my friend, must indulge me in passing over the ground lightly until a more favourable opportunity shall offer, of going at length and into details upon all matters embraced in your request.

I fear you will think me adventurous, in imputing to Mr. Webster a failure in argument, after hearing my eulogism on his intellectual endowments. I however sincerely believe his last speech in the Senate upon the removal of the deposites, *was a*

---

[186]See above, I, 36n.

signal failure; not to be accounted for upon any principle except his fervid anxiety, to serve a party to which unfortunately for his country and himself, he belongs, and to wound a hated administration. But that modesty for which you know I am much prized and esteemed induces me to say,

Nam neque adhuc
Var[i]o videor, nec dicere Cinna
Digna: sed argutos inter strepere anser olores.[187]

Taking an affectionate leave of Mr. Webster and his coadjutors in promoting modern Whiggism, composed as it seems to be, of Bank fragments, nullification fragments—the patches and shreds of the federal party, and those who clamor about state rights, without knowing or being capable of understanding state or federal rights—I will rehearse to you some at least of the articles of my political creed.

First—I believe, no state has the right to nullify an Act of Congress.

Secondly—I believe no state has a right inherent, to secede from the other states of the Union.

Thirdly—I believe that both Nullification and Secession are revolutionary measures, and that neither of them are comprehended within the reserved rights of the States—if they are, civil war, blood shed, anarchy and insecurity, are reserved as portions of state sovereignty and supremacy, and with great submission to you and Mr. Calhoun, this seems to me most absurd.

Fourthly—I believe that Congress has no right founded in the Constitution to pass any law violating any, or the least of the "rights, reserved to the states or to the people"—and if they pass such a law, it is void and therefore no law. Prudence however suggests before such an enactment is resisted, that its validity be tested before the Supreme Court of the Union. This Court is the property of the people and the states—it is the work of their hands—if the enactment be here sustained, the ballot-box is the last pacific tribunal to which an appeal is to be made—and if this fail, and the people or community be degenerate, and determined to destroy liberty and their Country — then must come, Nullification and Secession, et bella, horrida bella.

Fifthly—I believe that Congress possesses no authority under the Constitution to create a Bank or other Corporation, and I

[187]Virgil, *Ecologues*, IX, 35-36, in which Virgil compares himself to a goose among swans.

go farther and deny that any state in the union has the authority to incorporate a company for banking purposes. But if I cou'd admit that Congress possesses the power in question—the agitation created in the Country and in the Senate of the United States, during the last winter and spring, wou'd admonish me, that the power ought never to be exercised—The public money shou'd rather be kept in dpo: with Mr. Campbell, guarded by a Battallion of soldiers.

Sixthly—I object not to the presidents proclamations, (except as to its length, for if I remember right it was printed upon a most terrific sheet) because it seemed well to me that the unsuspecting, ignorant and credulous parties of the South, shou'd be guarded in time against the dangers of Nullification.

7thly.—The force bill seemed well to me also—because if freemen will not observe order and respect and obey the laws of the land, they ought to be flogg'd like slaves—that they may be kep't free and independent citizens of the United States—a title I am always prou'd of "Hic domus, hac patria est."

8. I believe the Senate of the United States has no authority or right to adopt Mr. Clays resolutions—for diverse reasons. 1st. they asserted that the late executive proceedings in relation to the revenue were derogatory to the laws and Constitution of the United States—now I hold, that the president had a right to dismiss Mr. Duane—as he had a right to cause the successor if were necessary to remove the deposites. Now I did not approve of the removal, because it seemed to me unnecessary and inexpedient, but I cou'd never deny to the president the power, under both law and constitution, that he exercised.

But the Senate Sin'd against something more than facts—they assumed power which did not belong to them in adopting Mr. Clays resolution—Let us for a moment inquire what functions the Senate are inbued with—they have an Executive—a legislative and a judicial capacity. No body pretends that the resolution was legislative, or Executive—but if it is so pretended, it is sheer pretence—for it prescribes no future action or such to the president or any officer of the Government. If it is to be regarded as judicial, then it is a void sentence or judgement and wou'd be reversed upon a Writ of Error, if there were any supervising tribunal to take cognizance of the subject. The Senate wou'd not have sin'd or err'd more hugely, had they have resolved the same offences against the Supreme Court, or the other House of Congress But my farourite Mr. Webster cites a precedent—the resolution introduced by Mr. Branch, but not argued by him except in a *shilly-shally* way. Now if the journals of the Senate of that Session—I mean the session of the Panama debate are looked at—it will be found that the Senate were engaged in strict Executive business. the Precedent I regard as an unfortunate one for Mr. Webster. I pray you not to understand that I am a man worshipper—I know nothing of General Jackson personally—I only defend some of his measures, feebly I know—and condemn unhesitatingly the Course of the Senate in a variety of instances.

Iliacos intra muros peccatur, et extra.[188]

Both have sin'd, passion and prejudice have prevailed too extensively—the Country will feel it, and therefore not forget this wayward course of their rulers for years to come.—By strife and disunion within and without, the Trojan towers fell—so may it never be with the Citadel of our liberties!

My nephew Jo. S. Jones is somewhere to the north—I cannot hear from him—If you find him out write me what he is doing and what his prospects. Give him good advice for my sake and believe me allways in truth and sincerity Yr. friend

ROB H. JONES

Hon.

Willie P. Mangum

Memorandum in Conclusion.

I mention for your satisfaction, and I am grieved at the thought, that the next Legislature of this state will be Anti-administration, and I as little doubt it will be anti Van Buren. I am as confident it will be Anti McLane—Anti Calhoun—Anti Clay—aye, and Anti Leigh.

I desire to be understood that I am not grieved at the legislatures being *Anti* in the four last instances—On the contrary I am delighted with the anticipation.

I repeat my feelings toward you—But take heed of yourself allways—as for the Country and my notions about politics they will allways take care of themselves.

I have given, as our old friend Mr. Macon says, some tests and if you dispute my orthodoxy, I propose that we discuss them

[188]A Roman proverb. See Horace, *Epistles*, 1, 2, 16.

seriatim before the next rail road-meeting we shall happen to be at.

By-the by—Mr. Macon is in very good health—if there shou'd be a Convention in this State, he will be a member. He is too popular to be harmless—His errors are always dangerous—so it allways has been with great popularity.

ROB H. JONES

So fare well.
[Addressed:]

Hon. Warrenton N. C.
24 Aug. 1834.

Willie P. Mangum
Boston
Massachusetts.

If Mr. Mangum shou'd have left Boston before this letter—the postmaster will oblige the writer by forwarding to him wherever his duty may carry him.

WPM-LC

Daniel Dickson to Willie P. Mangum

TREMONT HOUSE Augt 26. 1834

Hon. W. P. Mangum
Dear Sir

As you arrived here since I did, I have thot you might have left home since the Elections,[189]—I should be verry much pleased to hear the result of the Fayetteville Election[190]—Yesterday I recd. a letter from home (Wilmington) containing the pleasing intelligence of the election of Genl. E. B. Dudley to represent our town, he is opposed to the reelection of Senator Brown & will have considerable influence with the members of two of the adjoining counties. If convenient a personal acquaintance would be agreeable, as I have no acquaintance in this house & do not know of any other from our State.

Very Respy
DANIEL DICKSON.

[Addressed:]

Hon. W. P. Mangum
Tremont House

---

[189]The campaign for the North Carolina legislature was a spirited one. The Whigs were made up of different elements who were hostile to Jackson. The western part of the state voted for the Whigs and the eastern part for the Democrats. All of the boroughs were in the Whig column. Nevertheless, the Jackson forces controlled the legislature. Pegg, "Whig Party in N. C.," 35.

[190]James Seawell, a Whig, was elected in Fayetteville.

WPM-D

Henry Clay to Willie P. Mangum

ASHLAND 26th Aug. 1834.

My dear Sir.

You will have heard the result of our K. election. We could not desire that it should have been better—76 out of the 101 members of the H. of R. Letcher's re-election, and 11 of the 12 Senators to be chosen elected on our side. Indiana has done nearly as well; and Illinois and Missouri are not much behind her. Ohio will bring up the rear gloriously in the West.

How have you fared in N. Carolina? Do tell me. I have seen no satisfactory account; and the Intellr. says we shall know nothing until the Legislature assembles; but I presume you are better informed.

Have you not been shocked with the impudence of D. Green?[191] To stir *such* a question as that of the Presidency at such a time as this! And to stir it as he has done! Poor fellow how much he professes to be devoted to his principles; as if others were less attached to others! Now it is clear that if each element of the opposition comes to the resolution (and one has just as much right to do it as another) that it will support no Candidate who does not entertain its principles, there can be no union or harmony.

Let me hear from you soon, and say when you go North.

Your friend
H. CLAY.

Willie P. Mangum Esq.
[Addressed:] The Honble.
Willie P. Mangum
Red Mountain
Orange
No. Carolina.
[Postmarked:] Lexington
Aug 27

[191]In the spring and summer of 1834 the different anti-Jackson factions tried to get together on a common policy. Calhoun insisted on his state's rights party keeping its own tenets. In the midst of these maneuvers of conciliation, Duff Green began writing letters and carrying articles in the *Telegraph* praising Calhoun. In August, when it was evident the factions of anti-Jackson men could not get together, the Richmond *Whig* offered to give up Clay for the good of the party and asked Green to give up Calhoun. For a month the two editors argued. Green finally agreed to support anyone who endorsed the ideas his paper upheld, but in offering this he practically said Calhoun was the only strong candidate who held the paper's views. Wiltse, *Calhoun: Nullifier*, 228, 230, 235.

WPM-LC

Invitation of the Harvard Chapter of Phi Beta Kappa
to
Willie P. Mangum

[August 27, 1834]

The President of the society of Phi Beta Kappa invites the Hon Mr. Mangum, to attend the literary exercises of the society, at Cambridge tomorrow at 12 o'clock & afterwards to honor them with his company at dinner.
Wednesday 27 Aug 1834

[Addressed:]
Hon. Mr Mangum
of U S Senate
Tremont House

WPM-LC

John Davis[192] *to Willie P. Mangum*

[August 27, 1834]

My Dr Sir

I have to ask the favor of your company with the Executive board of the Govt. to Cambridge this morning to attend the annual commencement—I have this moment learnt that you are in the city. We start from *here* between 8 & half past 8 oclock this morning & shall have a spare coach in readiness for you—The mesenger will wait for an answer.

Very respectfully Your Obt Sert

J DAVIS

State House Augt 27th

[Addressed:]
Hon Mr Mangum
of N. Carolina

[192]John Davis, of Massachusetts, who had served in Congress from 1825 to 1834, had just become governor, a post which he held for one year before he returned to Congress as United States Senator. Later he was nominated for Vice President on the Whig ticket. *Biog. Dir. of Cong.*, 886.

WPM-LC

Willie P. Mangum to Charity A. Mangum

BOSTON 2nd. Septr. 1834.

My dear Love

I have not written to you since I was at Providence Rhode Island, now almost two weeks—The reason is, that I wished to be able to tell you where to write to me.—I hope you will write to me at *Philadelphia* "Philadelphia"—I am very desirous of hearing from you, My Love.—In this strange land, I seek to shun the attentions & hospitalities that are daily pressed upon me, to think of you My Love, and our dear children.—At no period of my life, have my affections been fresher & stronger for you, than they are now.—As your natural friends & protectors drop off, one by one, I feel that the chords of our affections are drawn closer & closer.—And altho, I feel, that in my course of life, we have been so much seperated, that you must feel that you are almost alone, yet in my heart I wear you, as not only the dearest object in this world, but also as deserving to be so—And if in the course of human events, I should cease to feel that sentiment, I should at the same time, cease to feel self respect.—Whatever of change & disaster may come, I trust, that I shall not only possess but also deserve to possess all the love of my dearly beloved, virtuous & angel wife.—These are strong terms—Yet I believe them to be just—When I look over the world, see the conduct of others—& then look to my own frail & often violent bursts of temper—& consider your steady & unruffled temper, & the constant flow of your affections; I am not only justified in calling you, but constrained to think of you as my dearly beloved angel wife.—May God grant, that it may always be so.—Let what may come, I know, that you may always consider yourself dearer to me, than every thing else.

I left Providence on Thursday the 21st. August, & travelled to Boston a little short of 50 miles, through a succession of towns & villages, & through the most highly cultivated country that I ever saw.—It is not the best part of Massachusetts, & yet the beauty of it, far surpasses my former conception of it—In this climate every thing is green—every hill & dale as beautiful as our lovely yard in the best season & with the best care.—I arrived at Boston that evening at one oclock.—I called at Tremont House the fashionable Hotel and the very best in the United States—it was full and I could not get in.—I went to the New England Coffee house, it was full, I could not get in.—Then I went to "The Exchange Coffee house," it was full & Ic^{d}. not get in—The entire South seems to be here—I then enquired for a respectable private boarding house, & went to Miss Lecair's in Pearl street—I found the house spacious, richly furnished & the accommodation good.—Here I rested that evening without seeing any one—

The 22nd. Aug^{t}.

I called on Mr. Webster—He received me with great cordiality—These seem to be the most civil people in the world & the kindest.—They only differ from the South, in this, they are always attentive to persons of distinction, a stranger might be here for weeks, if unknown to the world, & remain unknown to Bostonians.—Mr. Webster had procured me lodging at "Tremont House," & the reason I missed was that I had not given my name. He insisted that I should go to "Tremont."—As is is the fashion here, I had to do so; tho I greatly preferred my comfortable lodgings & my kind & attentive hostess.—Yet fashion here, is a much greater tyrant than it is with us, or even than Gen Jackson himself.—I had left Govr. Tyler with his family at New Port.—Mr. Ewing of Ohio had not arrived.—Mr. Webster after taking me from his office to his house walked with me to the most interesting portions of the City. Mrs. Webster was at their country seat on the sea shore, "Marshfield," some 25 miles from Boston.—

This city has the largest & most costly houses in the United States. It is not only beautiful, but grand—Yet all Cities are rather vulgar things—When you see one great city, you have seen nearly all, they are so much alike.—

The Bostonians are especially proud of their city, the ladies & all & when I say to them with great apparent indifference that cities are "vulgar things," they look at me with infinite surprize—When they talk of Cities—I talk of the magnificent scenery of our mountains, & affirm that the city compared with

"Negro head,"[193] is no more than a mouse trap compared with a regular fortification.—so we go.—

Saturday 23rd. August—

This day Gov. Tyler arrived, and I left my private boarding house & went to "Tremont House."—I left an agreeable mess—and gave up comfort for show.—I met a gentleman by the name of Bailey with his lady from Charleston So. Ca.—I had known him when we were both boys.—

At Tremont House—We have a private parlour where we dine & do not go to the public table.—The parlour is for our committee, where we live as well as one could desire.—Ewing not yet arrived.—

Sunday 24th. Augt.

This day I went to Brattle Street Church, with Mr. Webster, and heard as fine organs, & vocal musicians as I ever heard in the Catholic church of Washington City— The sermon only tolerable.—I returned to dinner & at 3 oclock took Mr. Websters coach—the whole committee, & went 5 miles to Col. Perkins' one of the oldest & wealthiest gentlemen of this Country—The Country about Boston—an amphitheatre—is absolutely enchanting.—I have seen nothing like it—At Col Parkins'[194] we took a glass of wine—in the dwelling embowered in trees, with walks pebbled, around the dwelling—altogether exhibiting the finest specimen of the magnificent cottage in the United States.—His gardens, warm houses, & graperies with biliard table in the midst.—are, by far, the most costly and elegant in America.—After passing thro we returned to the Cottage, partook of a collation & returned to the city after dark, passing over a stone wall over an arm of the sea, more than one mile in length.—

Monday 25th. August.

On this day the Committee had a formal meeting & proceeded to the business with which they are charged—In the evening a large party was had at Mr. Webster's—Many Gentlemen & ladies from the South—Mrs. Webster was detained in the Country by a "pain in the face" in our country known as the tooth ache.—The party was agreeable.—This evening the balloon went up from the Common—20,000 people seeing it. the whole magnificent.

[193]"Nigger Head" is a mountain peak in Clay County, North Carolina. In 1819 when Mangum rode the western circuit he was tremendously impressed with the mountains, and he frequently recalled their beauty.

[194]Probably Colonel Thomas H. Perkins, 1764-1854, who made a fortune in commerce, especially in his Chinese trade. He served several terms in the Massachusetts legislature and, as an officer, in the state militia. He was noted for his good living and for his philanthropy. *D. A. B.*, XIV, 477-478.

Tuesday 26th. August—

This day we worked until late, & upon my proposition, we rode into the Country 10½ miles to the Town of Quincy to pay a visit of *respect* to Mr. Adams & his lady—the late President Adams.—Here the roads are so good, that 10½ miles are not more than 3 in our country—We called, sat an hour in the residence of the first President Adam's.—eat cake, drank wine but declined staying to Tea.—Mr. Adams lives in the old & venerable seat of his Father, though in less than ½ a mile, he has a modern house of much more taste & spendour.—I was glad to meet Mrs. Adam's who is a good lady, & not spoiled by the world.—

We rode around the Town of Quincy—looked at the noble church founded & mainly built by the elder Mr. Adams, of Quincy granite, under the portico of which, lie his remains.—This is the land of churches—in this City & 20 miles around, there are more churches, than in the whole of N°. Ca:

I never enjoyed a ride more than this, & to make me happy: I wanted nothing but you, My Love, sitting at my side with your quiet & affectionate look, tone & manner.—We passed over "Milton Hill"—The highest land in the vicinity—presenting a greater variety in the scenery, than I ever saw—In the west, scenery not unlike the mountain country of our beloved State, & in the east the finest combination possible of Bays, arms of the sea, heights—islands—ships, bridges, marsh meadow, & all that; speckled with villages & sprinkled with pretty dwellings—every thing painted, pretty, neat, white, & lovely—Altogether, the country about Boston, is the finest in America in the summer—But in the winter intolerably cold—We returned to the city a little after dark.—The invitations had crowded on us in numbers large enough to detain us a month.

These invitations were to *Senator Mangum*—poor Willie P. Mangum might have been here years, & not seen so many.—No one could see the emptiness of all this, more than I do—It is the difference between the *world* & *home*—I never felt it stronger. —If the world were to desert me, In this City I should be a Cypher.—But in the bosom of my dear wife, as dear, if not dearer, than if the world were kind to me.—You see how much & how strongly I believe in your virtuous & disinterested love—I dont doubt it, & should be amongst the most miserable of men, if I did.—The most of husbands could not believe so strongly—They might have a shadow of doubt.—I have none—I think, I know, you & your heart & your ever abiding love; as well as I know my own—& whatever storms, clouds, & dreariness may occasionally pass over the disk of my heart & affections—they do pass—& to you the needle of my heart & affections is ever steady & true.—I do not know which would render me most miserable to loose your affection; or to loose my affection for you.—Either would make me a miserable man—& I pray God to continue to us life health & love, & above all, to continue to us mutual love, during our lives.—I have so much confidence in the honesty & tenderness of your heart, & the steadiness of your affections, that I doubt you, even less than myself.—And myself, I will not doubt, for when I shall, I shall not only be miserable, but feel that I am unworthy of myself & of life.—To love you, is the delight of my heart, knowing as I do, that except my dear Mother, no human being ever loved me so well so steadily & so disinterestedly.—& none ever—ever will or can.—But I must stop this—Distance, the poets say, lends enchantment—And I fear that I shall become a love sick swain.—& yet, My Love, this short summer, *with you,* was about the happiest of my life.—But that I may quit this strain I go to.

Wednesday the 27th. Augt.—

This day we worked in the morning, and at 9 Oclock the Governor of the State,[195] sent us an invitation, to meet him at the Council chamber at the State house, & to take a coach, which was prepared for us to go to "Harvard College" the oldest & most celebrated university in the country, to attend the commencement—We went, heard the speeches as at Chapel Hill.—The College is three miles from Boston in the Town of Cambridge.—The buildings are old & venerable—The grounds enclosed, & beautifully set in grass & trees, with serpentine walks, well graveled.

The exercises were in a new church, beautifully built of Quincy granite—attended by all the fashion & flash of Boston—We were placed in the seats of honor, and were the *lions* of the day.—during the exercises we (the Committee) left by a back door, & walked over the town, & looked into the House, where Gen: Washington had his head quarters, immediately after the Battle at Bunker's Hill.—The House is still owned by the widow, Mrs. Craiggee—We then went to a friend's of Mr. Webster's, Mr.

[195]John Davis.

Buckingham's,[196] where we drank wine, partook of a collation & then returned to the College Chapel.—The exercises were concluded at 3 oclock—We then marched, with a band of the best music to the college dining room, where 4 or 500 people, consisting of the elite of Massachusetts took dinner after a prayer.—The dinner was good—after the dinner a psalm was sung, which has been done every year for nearly 200 years, which was an institution of the old New England pilgrim—The whole of it was strange, venerable & deeply interesting to me.—after the dinner, we adjourned to the dwelling of the President of the College Mr. Quincy's,[197] where we met many ladies, examined pictures, drank tea, conversed, gallanted, & then we took our coach & came home at sunset.—

Thursday 28th. Augt.

We worked this day closely in the Bank—at four oclock in the evening, we dined with Mr. Webster & his company consisting of a dozen of the most distinguished people in the City & country—Mr. President Adams of the number—Mrs. Webster at home.—We sat late, talked much, & got home between 8 & 9 oclock—The whole interesting and agreeable.—

Friday the 29th. Augt.

This day we worked closely—In the evening we were to dine with the Mayor of the City The Hon Mr. Lyman,[198] given as a compliment to the Committee,—being tired out, I sent my apology, staid at home close, thought of my Dear Love & our children, went to bed early & slept sweetly.—

Saturday the 30th. August.

This day we worked the morning—Went at 1 oclock to Nahant, 10½ miles from Boston—a tongue of land that runs into the sea, several miles—the summer resort of the Boston gentry—where no trees grow—& lashed by the angry wave of the atlantic Ocean —Many pretty buildings—and at this season of the year the resort of several hundred of rich idlers who kill time in the best way they can.—We were invited to dine there with Mr. Appleton,[199] who had 15 or 18 of the *distinguee's* as they are called

---

[196]Probably Joseph Tinker Buckingham, who for several years was a Whig member of the state legislature. *D. A. B.*, III, 227-228.

[197]Josiah Quincy, who after serving several terms as state legislator and as mayor of Boston, became president of Harvard. He remained in that post until 1845. *D. A. B.*, XV, 308-311.

[198]Theodore Lyman, in his early years, was a Federalist and then a supporter of Jackson. In 1833 and 1834 he became the Whig mayor of Boston. *D. A. B.*, XI, 518.

[199]William Appleton, a merchant and president of the Boston branch of the United States Bank, was a member of Congress and president of the Massachusetts General Hospital. *Appleton's Cyclopedia of American Biography*, I, 85.

here—The whole of it, very unique, picturesque & agreeable—We returned[200]

WPM-LC

Willie P. Mangum to the Arcade Bank Officials

COPY

PROVIDENCE
CITY HOTEL 10th Sept 1834.

To the President & directors
of the Arcade Bank
Gentlemen

The finance Comm. of the U. S. Senate among other things, have been charged with Certain enquiries touching the condition of the Banks selected by the late secretary of the Treasury for the deposit of the public moneys—The Comm: propose to proceed in the execution of that duty in this City as soon as it shall be agreeable to the officers of the Deposit Bank.

The Comm. will have the honor to wait upon the officers of the Arcade Banke, at a time & place, that may be designated. [Torn] will be gratified to meet them in the [torn] of this morning. When they will more fully disclose the scope & object of the investigation proposed

I have the honor &c
W. P. Mangum
in behalf of the
Committee.

[Endorsed:] Copy of Letter
to
Arcade Bank
Providence.

The Committee desire among other things—

1. The state of the Bank the first week in August.
2. The account of the Bank, at the same time, with the Treasurer of the U. States, & every other officer of the Government.
3. Information of any loan, made by the Bank to any Department of Government, or any officer of Government, in his official capacity, setting forth fully its amount, the time of making, its reimbursement, in whole or in part, if any such re-imbursement has been made; together with all the cor-

[200]The rest of the letter is missing.

respondence, between the Bank, or any of its officers, o[r] persons writing, or written to, in its behalf, and any Department or officer of the govt.

4. Information of any security, given by the Bank, to Govt, or to any public officer, for the public monies, deposited in the Bank.—
5. Information whether the Bank has paid or contributed any sum of money, or been asked to do so, to defray charges or pay expences of any person, or to make compensation to him, for examining the State of the Bank, or any other service rendered by the authority or at the request of any officer of the Govt.
6. Copies of all transfer drafts, made on the Bank, or in its favor, or in its employment, as a Deposite Bank
7. An account on the first monday in each month, (beginning the month of Septr. 1833 to Jan: 34 inclusive) of the amount of deposites distinguishing those by the Govt to its officers, from those by individuals—the amount of discounts &c. at same times, exhibiting the extension or contraction of the business of the Bank prior to & subsequent to the receiving of the Govt. deposits covering the time before mentioned.—

[Endorsed:] Copy of Questions
to be answered by the Bank.

WPM-LC

Willie P. Mangum to Charity A. Mangum

LONG ISLAND SOUND
Saturday morning
13th September 1834.

My dear Love.

I am in a steamboat returning to Philadelphia—The boat has so strong a tremulous motion, that I can scarcely write legibly.—It is now eight or ten days since I wrote to you.—It was the 2nd of the month, as well as I remember, that I wrote to you from Boston.—I received your letter the day after—& was greatly rejoiced to hear from you.—

My health has been uniformly good, with the exception of a slight cold.—The Weather for two days has been so cold, that there has been a slight frost.—

On Wednesday the 3rd Sept.

I went from Boston 15 or 16 miles to Salem a pretty Town on the North East of Boston, on the sea shore to dine with Mr. Silsbee[201] one of the Senators from Massachusetts.—His residence is beautiful & magnificent.—He had some 18 or 20 Gentlemen of his Town to dinner.—I went down in the morning & spent two hours or so, in the Museum with much interest—The collection is large, rare & tasteful.—We sat to dinner at 2 oclock. —the hour being early to enable us to return to Boston that evening. The party was extremely agreeable, enlivened & sustained as it was by the frank & warm cordiality of Mr. Silsbee's very agreeable family.—We returned that evening to Boston at ½ past 8 oclock—& went that evening at 9 o clock, to a party at Mr. Sullivan's;[202] a Gentleman whom I mentioned to you in my last.—The party was large & I suppose agreeable—I did not stay more than ½ an hour, being much fatigued—& should not have gone at all, but that it was made as a compliment to our Committee.—The society here is gay, polished & refined—but the ladies generally are not pretty—far from it—much less so than at the South.—I went to sleep at 10clock—as on—

Thursday the 4th Sept.

I set out for Lowell, the great manufacturing town 28 or 30 miles north west of Boston—It is the "Birmingham" of the United States.—Mr. Nathan Appleton formerly a member of Congress, & one of the wealthiest proprietors at Lowell, set out at ½ past 5 oclock in the morning with Mr. Ewing Mr. Wilde of Geo. & myself.—We arrived before 10 oclock, & for 6 (Six) hours, we were constantly engaged in examining the machinery &c.—The Capital invested here is prodigious—& the ingenuity & enterprize are truly admirable.—

Everything indicated a prosperity leading rapidly to wealth & was every way agreeable except the thousands of Girls from 12 to 18 years of age, that labour here.—They look unhealthy & unhappy—& altogether, presented to my mind a melancholy & painful spectacle.

[201]Nathaniel Silsbee, a Boston merchant, served as a member of the Massachusetts legislature, national House of Representatives, Senate, and as presidential elector. He was in the Senate from 1826 to 1835. In 1836 he supported Webster for President. *Biog. Dir. of Cong.*, 1524; *D. A. B.*, XVII, 165.

[202]A Harvard graduate, lawyer and Federalist, William Sullivan was from 1804 to 1830 "in almost continuous service as representative, senator, or member of the executive council of the state." He wrote a number of "class books" to spread popular education. *D. A. B.*, XVIII, 199-200.

I had rather my daughters should go to the cornfield with their hoes, incomparably rather than that they should go into a factory.

We returned to Boston at 8 oclock, & that evening, went to a party at Mr. Crowninshield's[203] who was formerly secretary of the Navy & a member of Congress—It was like all other parties. I staid but a short time & went home to bed—

On Friday the 5th

We were to have gone to Mr. Websters residence on the sea-shore at Marshfield, but rained & we staid at Tremont house—I visited this day the Athenaeum, saw many very interesting paintings and a large Library—In the evening I visited the wharf & the shipping, & saw & went through the whole.—I got tired of sight seeing—& retired to my chamber to ruminate on my dear wife & children & my distant home.—

On Saturday the 6th.

The Lafayette celebration took place—The whole City turned out.—The Gov. sent his aide for us.—We joined the procession at 10 oclock & marched with it 2½ hours, but before entering Faneuil Hall Ewing & myself escaped.—Mr. Everett[204] delivered an eloquent oration—That evening at 4 oclock, I went into the Country 5 miles to dine at the Country seat of Col. Perkins[205]—a magnificent seat it is—& the country about it the most beautiful I ever saw—We sat until 8 oclock & returned to the City at 9 oclock,—& went to bed.—

Sunday the 7th.

I went with Mr. Appleton[206] to the Unitarian Church heard fine music with organs, an ordinary sermon—went to his house after church eat some cake, drank a glass of wine, talked an hour with him & his daughters—went home to dinner—read in the evening—& staid at home—

Monday the 8th.

We waited for Mr. Webster who was in the Country, he did not come. I staid at home all day, &

[203]Benjamin William Crowninshield, a Boston merchant, served for many years in the state legislature and the national Congress. From 1814 to 1818 he was Secretary of the Navy. *Biog. Dir. of Cong.*, 865; *D. A. B.*, IV, 577-578.

[204]Edward Everett.

[205]See above, II, 195n.

[206]See above, II, 198n.

Tuesday morning the 9th

set out for Providence, Rhode Island, & arrived there in the evening—We attended a party that evening at Mr. Knight's[207] who is a Senator from Rhode Island—All parties are very much alike, & to me are often very dull things.—

Wednesday the 10th.

We examined the Banks at Providence rode around the town in the evening, many views of it are beautiful—& that evening went to a party of Gentlemen at Mr. Ives,[208] a wealthy man—The members of a Convention now sitting in Rhode Island were generally there. The evening was spent agreeably.—

Thursday the 11th.

Gov. Tyler, his family & Mr. Ewing took the Steamboat for New York—& thence to Philadelphia, Where we shall be for some time. The Cholera at New York prevents our going there at this time—I determined to leave them & take a land passage to New Haven in Connecticut, a distance of 120 miles—They were unwilling—But at 4 oclock in the morning, I got into the stage coach & travelled 80 miles to Hartford on the Connecticut River through a broken Country, as much so as ours near the Mountains. I got to Hartford at dark. The next morning looked around the beautiful town, went into the Cupalo of the State House, looked down upon the City & the highly cultivated valley of the Connecticut River 20 miles wide & the high lands rising into mountains on either side—altogether presenting as lovely a view as one could desire. I have heard much of it, expected much & was not disappointed.—

Tuesday the 12th.

at 10 oclock set out for New Haven 40 miles through a lovely Country—the day lovely but a little cool—At 4 Oclock arrived & saw the most beautiful & tasteful town in New England—The whole City is overshadowed with beautiful & venerable elms.—It is on a beautiful plain—the back ground rising abruptly into mountains—

I had not arrived at the Tontine House more than 3 minutes before I saw Mr. Smith[209] one of the Senators pass the door—a

[207]After holding several state offices, including the governorship, Nehemiah Rice Knight, a banker, became United States Senator in 1821 and served until 1841. *Biog. Dir. of Cong.*, 1192.

[208]Possibly Moses B. Ives, a lawyer of Providence. John Livingston, *Law Register*, 1851, 554.

[209]A graduate of the Litchfield Law School, Nathan Smith became a successful lawyer, prosecuting attorney, and United States district attorney before he became Senator in 1833. He remained in the Senate until his death in 1835. *Biog. Dir. of Cong.*, 1540.

venerable & high spirited gentleman—in shorts, fair top boots & powdered hair—I spoke to him, he seemed very glad to see me, took me right off to his house in a beautiful position, of ample & elegant dimensions & richly furnished—Carried me thro his gardens—Had his carriage got, carried me all around & thro this beautiful city—took me back to his house where in the evening some of the most distinguished Gentlemen of the place met—& in that interesting family of Wife grown sons & daughters I spent a most agreeable eveing.—I left at 10clock, went to Bed—rose this morning at 5 oclock—rode a mile to the Boat—& am now on my way to New York, where I shall arrive at 10clock, & I shall instantly leave for Philadelphia—

Tho I feel no fear of cholera, yet perhaps, it is best not to go where it is—

Thus have I given you some notice of the time that has intervened since I wrote to you—My time altogether has been pleasantly & I hope, usefully spent—I wanted nothing to make me happy, but the company of my dearly beloved wife—

I hope you are well—& I hope to see you before long—I think of you almost constantly, & always with a heart warm with love & affection—may God bless you & our dear children & restore you to the arms of your most affectionate husband,

W. P. MANGUM

[Addressed:]

Willie P. Mangum
U. S. Senate.

Mrs. C. [A.] Mangum
Red Mountain
North Carolina

WPM-LC

Thomas Ewing to Willie P. Mangum

WASHINGTON CITY
Sept 22nd 1834

Dear Sir

I enclose you the answers from the Norwalk Bank which you will cause to be copied into your books, & return the original to me—

We have been going on slowly thus far smoothly in our Post Office investigation—We shall find matter enough to occupy us here about 2 weeks & we will then adjourn to Philadelphia.—

What are you doing? Write me—Have you heard from Webster?

Southard,[210] is sick this morning not severely but so as to be unable to attend to his duties—

Your friend
T. EWING

Hon. W. P. Mangum.

Willie P. Mangum to William Gaston[211]

PHILADELPHIA 24th Sept. 1834.

My dear Sir.

The Finance Comm. in the course of their investigation of the Bank have turned their attention to the facilities & indulgences extended from time to time, to the local or State Banks.—

Your late official connexion with the Newbern Bank, enables you to understand fully the relations formerly subsisting between that Bank & The U.S. Bank.—

I have heard that the Newbern Bank owed, at one time, a large sum to the U.S.B. and at a period when it was hard pressed from other causes.

At the instance of the Comm: I have to ask you to be so good as to turn your attention to this subject; give me the details of the relations of the Newbern Bank with the Bank of the U. States. And the effect of the arrangements of the U. S. Bank upon the prosperity of the local banks & upon the *Currency* of N.C at that time—

I trust, I do not ask too much—I would not draw upon your valuable time, if I could otherwise attain the object of the Committee. I shall write to our friend Mr. Cameron[212] touching the relations of the State Bank with the U. S. B.

Your intimate acquaintance with the deranged State of our Currency a few years ago, & the salutary influence of the action of the U.S.B. upon it, will enable you, if you can command the time, to give us much useful information upon that subject.

May I indulge the hope, that you will gratify our wishes, & enclose to me at Phila. as early as may suit your convenience.

---

[210] Samuel Lewis Southard.
[211] The original letter is in the William Gaston Papers, University of North Carolina.
[212] Duncan Cameron was president of the State Bank of North Carolina from 1829 to 1849.

Be pleased My Dear Sir to accept the assurance
of my very great respect & regard.
WILLIE P. MANGUM

[Addressed:] The Hon: William Gaston
Newbern
N. Carolina

[Endorsed:] *Free*
Willie P. Mangum

Charity A. Mangum to Sally A. Mangum[213]

SEPTEMBER, 28, 1834

My Dear
Daughter.

I have sent Orange[214] with your trunk and some thick frocks for you, and a barrell of flower for your Aunt Rebecca.[215] I am very anxious to hear from your Aunts and Family and to hear how you are doing my Dear little daughter. I hope my child that you are a good obedient child and that you mind your Aunt and uncle Priestly and that you try to be a good obedient Child, as you know how much it would distress your Father and Mother to learn that you would not try to be a good child, and be attentive to your book and learn your lessons well. I have sent you some paper qu[ills] and a pen knife to make pens [torn] must give it to your Aunt and only have it when [she] [thi]nks it right for you to use it. You must be particular [torn] your aunt your key, I wish her to examine [torn] [fre]quently and remember my child to keep [torn] not your own if you find any thing [torn] small it is, shew it to your aunt [torn] what you aught to do with it.

[torn] [lit]tle Daughter to see you soon and [torn] pleasure it would give your [torn] your Aunt and your teacher that you had been a good obedient child and attended to your studies. You must try and perform your promises to Mother if you wish her to love you.

I have sent some cakes four you and your little cousins, I want to see you very much and hope to see you soon if I can learn you are a good child.

---

[213]The original letter is in the possession of Miss Preston Weeks, Washington, D. C. Sally A. Mangum, ten years old at this time, was Willie P. Mangum's oldest daughter.

[214]Household slave of Mangum.

[215]Priestley H. Mangum's wife.

Farewell give my love to your Aunt Uncle and Cousins, and remember always my child what pleasure it would give your Mother to learn you were doing well.

CHARITY A. MANGUM

Sally A. Mangum

I have sent some yarn for you to knit yourself some Stockings, you must get your aunt to send for three sets of needles—and keep one. I want the size that will do to knit the yarn I send you.—

[torn] [th]at you find in you [torn] pocket.

[Addressed:]

[torn] Mangum
[torn] [Hills]borough

William Gaston to Willie P. Mangum[216]

NEWBERN Oct 1st 1834

My dear Sir.

By the last mail I had the honour to receive your letter of the 26th of September, in which, deferring to my late official connexion with the Bank of Newbern, you request in behalf of the Committee of Finance that I would communicate such information as I may possess respecting the transactions and relations of that Bank with the Bank of the United States, and the effect of these arrangements upon the prosperity of the local Banks and the Currency of North Carolina. My desire to aid the Committee of my Country in the ascertainment of whatever facts it may be important for them to know, will not permit me to hesitate in complying with this request—

I accepted of the appointment of President of the Bank of Newbern in June 1828 and remained in office until the close of the year 1833. Before this appointment I had a general acquaintance with the affairs of the Institution, having acted as one of its Directors, but afterwards I felt it a duty to make myself intimately acquainted with them—With regard to the *general* character of its dealings with the Bank of the U States, and the result which the operations of the latter produced upon the currency of North Carolina, I do not know that I can express myself more satisfactorily than by referring you to a copy, herewith transmitted, of a Memorial to the Congress of the United States

[216]The original letter is in the William Gaston Papers, University of North Carolina.

which was adopted by a unanimous vote of the Directors of the Bank of Newbern on the 1st of March 1832—As the Committee however may desire information rather more in detail I proceed to give such statements and explanations as will probably be more satisfactory.

During the War all the Banks in the Middle and Southern States refused to pay specie for their notes—In February 1817, while in Congress, I received a communication from the Bank of Newbern requesting me to proceed to Philadelphia and endeavor to procure from the Bank of the United States a loan for the sum not exceeding (I think) $100,000, to prepare the Directors of the Bank of Newbern to resume specie payments in July following. Immediately after the close of the session, early in the month of March I executed this commission and without difficulty procured the desired loan—By means of the facility thus given and a moderate reduction of its discounts, the Bank was enabled to sustain the credit of its paper and for a year and better punctually redeemed its notes when presented for payment. The reduction of discounts was however an unpoplar measure—In common with the other Banks of the State the Bank of Newbern had thrown out its notes to an injurious and impolitic extent. The debtors had been accustomed to receive an indefinite indulgence—They were to be found among all classes of the Community and exercised a powerful controul over the Directors and Stockholders of the Institution—It was alleged that the notes themselves answered all the ordinary purposes of money—that no one wanted specie but the brokers and that *they* ought not to be favoured at the expence of the great body of the Community and that to diminish the quantity of the circulating medium and compel payments from the Bank Debtors would occasion serious sacrifices of property and produce general distress—While such was the popular cry a meeting took place at Fayeteeville of delegates from all the local Banks and they entered into a compact which was published in the newspapers and hailed with acclamations, that the Bank would refuse specie to Brokers—The precise date of this meeting I do not at this moment recollect but I think that it was in 1819—After this the Bank of Newbern and I believe the other Banks ceased to make any effectual exertions for lessening its circulation or sustaining its credit Debtors were again indulged almost ad libitum indulgences ultimately which not only endangered the Capital Stock of the Institution but utterly ruined a large portion of its debtors and their sureties—The notes were shamefully depreciated, the rates of depreciation fluctuating between five and twelve per cent—Altho the vault had closed assumedly [?] against the Brokers only, in fact these were the only persons at whose command it was opened—The Merchants who wanted specie funds were generally afraid to discard them and unable to endure the delay and expense of compelling payments of them—The Brokers had no such fears and were strong enough to put the law in force. It became necessary therefore to propitiate these and they were propitiated, sometimes by specie and drafts which the Bank bought at a premium and at other times by expedients highly profitable to them and ruinous to the Institutions—The depreciation still continued and the Brokers returned again and again with the notes bought by the funds thus paid over to them—It was manifest to every man of ordinary intelligence in our State that these evils must be cured as the consequences would be most extensively and permanently calamitous—Yet they were not cured not any effiicient bona fide measures adopted for curing them until the contract of the Bank of the U. States upon the issues of the local Bank forced a remedy—For some years after the establishment of a branch of the U. States Bank in N. Carolina it did not return upon the local Banks such of their Papers as it received—Sometimes it would not receive this paper—After it felt itself oblige to taked the notes of the local Banks from its debtors it re-issued them in new loans—The notes nevertheless accumulated and it then became necessary to make occasional exchanges and when the differences were not paid to charge them in accounts Upon these accounts the balances in favor of the Branch became large, and the Banks were notified that these must be paid or put upon interest—A short time before I entered upon the duties of my office the balance in account against the Bank of Newbern had upwards of $350,000, & nearly one half of the Capital Stock of the Institution ($800,000). It was an alarming state of things, and few are the duties which I have been called on to discharge, which occasioned me more anxiety than those which the wretchedly embarassed state of the Bank imposed upon me. The gentlemen however with whom I was associated agreed with me that the emergency must be met honestly and resolutely and by means of an arrangement with the Officers of the Bank of the U. States and a gradual, temperate, and firm reduction of accommodations, we were enabled in a shorter time than I had hoped, to pay off the balance, raise our paper to par, and punctually answer every engagement. The outlines of the arrangements were, to put the balance upon interest and to pay off $20,000 every ninety days—to make exchanges once in thirty days and if upon such exchanges there was a balance which we could not meet to put that also on interest by giving a note for it at ninety days—to receive from us in payment northern notes, notes of good southern banks and whatever could conveniently answer as Specie to the U. S. Bank—and to allow as interest on all sums whatever amount and at whatever time deposited with them designed as payments on our part—The Officers of the U. S Bank had entire confidence that the arrangements would be complied with to the extent of our ability, but at the same time knew that it was scarcely possible with every exertion on our part that perfect punctuality could be observed for some time. *All* our debts were in effect accommodation debts—Humanity, Justice and Policy all forbade too severe a pressure upon the Debtors—The balance therefore instead of an immediate diminution actually rose against us to about $400,000 But we were not dispirited and our Creditors manifested every lenity which we could desire. Both had in view the same object, the payment of the debt with as little distress to the Community as possible and on the 23^{d}. of May 1832 the last dollar was paid viz $49,000—Since that day we have never felt any inconvenient pressure from the Bank of the U. States and all our dealings with it left the most decidedly favorable impressions on our minds of the probity, liberality and honour which marked its conduct—To you my dear Sir much of this strange history is not new—You are probably better acquainted with the dealings of the Bank of the U. States with the State Bank of N. Carolina—The latter from its locality, felt the salutary controul of the operations of the U. S. Bank upon its issues earlier than we did, and therefore began sooner to curtail its accommodations You cannot have forgotten the odium which they thereby encountered nor the popular rage which was thereby excited These were unquestionably among the main causes which in the session of 1828 led to the violent measures against the local banks which had nearly passed and which threatened universal confusion—Your desire for an early answer and the pressure of other engagements have made this a hasty communication but I trust and believe that it is substantially accurate I take pleasure in embracing this opportunity to express to you the respect and esteem with which I am, dear Sir

Your friend and Ob[dt]. Serv—

WILL: GASTON

Honble W P Mangum

WPM-LC

Duncan Cameron to Willie P. Mangum

RALEIGH Octo. 3rd. 1834

My dear Sir,

I have this moment received your's of 24th Sep[t]. last.—its being addressed to me at Stagville, subjected its receipt here, to some delay.

In consequence of excessive issues by the State Bank some years past; and the embarrassed condition of its debtors—it became unable to meet its liabilities with promptness—its notes depreciated—were purchased up by Brokers—suits bro't against the Bank—the Bank embarrassed in various ways—and while the citizens of the state were paying a heavy premium on the depreciation of the Bank notes—the foreign money dealers were realizing enormous profits in the traffic they were carrying on in these.—

During that period, the Bank of the U. States at Fayett. declined to receive the notes in payment or deposite—about 1827—or 1828 being satisfied, that the Bank was perfectly solvent—and that time only was wanted, to collect its resources, to meet its liabilities—the Bank U. States changed its course—it received the notes of the State Bank and all its Branches—shared acc[ts]. with them—sent back the notes as they accumulated—received payment as they were able from time to time to make it,—and Interest on the balances due at regular periods.

During the years 1828-29, the amount due by the State—Bank & its branches to the office Bank U. States at Fayett[e]. was usually from 250—to 300.000 dollars—and sometimes larger than the last mentioned sum—in 1830, the debt was (by vigorous exertions) rapidly reduced—& in November of that year, the whole debt was paid off by myself as President of the State-Bank—since that time, the notes of the State Bank & its Branches have been promptly taken up when presented—and no Interest has been paid.

The effect produced by the conduct of the off: Bank U. States, towards the State Banks, was, to free the Bank from the harassing calls of money-dealers—to restore its notes to credit in general circulation—and to enable it to escape from the ruin with which it was seriously threatened.

The influence of the Bank U. States in regulating the value of the currency and preserving it in a sound and healthy state was most obviously exemplified in this state on this point—no person at all acquainted with the condition of the currency is in doubt its action has preserved both the currency & the Banks.—As soon the [torn] Banks [mani]fested a fixed determination to make [every e]ffort in their power to meet and discharge [their] liabilities—The Bank U. States afforded them [torn]—lity, which the accomplishment of that [object] required.

In the measures accepted by the State Bank to wind up its affairs its capital, it has received important support from the principal Bank at Philadelphia thro its office at Fayett[e].—without which it would have been compelled to procure specie from abroad at much expence and trouble.

It gives me pleasure to [ac]knowledge the obligations which the *new* Bank (just commencing business,) is under to the Bank U- States Philadel[a]. for the friendly assistance it has already afforded it.—The truth is, that neither we, or the country can do without it.

With the highest regard
My dear Sir
Yrs. truly
DUN: CAMERON

[Addressed:]
The Honble
Willie P. Mangum
(U. States Senate)
Philadelp[a].

Willie P. Mangum to John Beard[217]

PHILADELPHIA 7th Octr: 1834

My dear Sir.

Having an evening of leisure I have determined to devote a portion of it, to put you in possesion of some of the views I have

[217]The original letter is in the Charles Fisher Papers, University of North Carolina. John Beard, of Salisbury, was a brother-in-law of Charles Fisher and editor of the *Western Carolinian.* He served in the state legislature from 1833 to 1834. His paper supported Calhoun. *N. C. Manual,* 792.

been compelled to take, during my sojourn in the Eastern & Middle States.—

In a word the prospect before us, is any thing but encouraging.—

In relation to the great struggle going on between the executive & the opposition: the Executive is unquestionably in the minority—and yet the materials forming the opposition are so discordant, indeed, so opposite upon great elementary & vital principles, that I look for nothing but the triumph of patronage and corruption.—

The principles that you and I hold to be the only conservative principles of our Federative system, so far from having taken root in the Centre the North & the East, are scarcely comprehended by the most intelligent of the National republicans.—

It is true, that there is a small band in the City of P^{ha}. headed by C. Raguet[218] but it is so small, that it is not regarded as a distinct party.—It can do nothing of itself.—The basis of all party organization in the North & East is *naked interest.*—Principles are silly things as contradistinguished from pecuniary interest.—In New Engla there is much more of principle than in Penn: or New York—But it is a principle that we abhor, & believe to be destructive ultimately of our system, in case it shall prevail.—

Is it not remarkable that the only paper in New England of general circulation & reputation, that ever condescends to hold parley with our principles, is the paper most devoted to Mr. Webster, his force bill / doctrines & all.? Sir. Our northern brethern know how & when to say pleasant & agreeable things to the traveller from the South much better than we; and almost all that I have seen or heard that favors our views, has obviously been put forth, to soothe & to secure our support to views & opinions alien to the true interest of the South.—I regrĕt to feel compelled to express an opinion that savors so much of uncharitableness.—& to you of all men it is least likely to be agreeable, not because we differ essentially in our political opinion; but because your path in life, has happily, had a direction to make you less censorious, perhaps. I may say, distrustful of the sincerity of professions.—

But Sir. We have nothing for the present to hope from New England.—And deeply as I abhor the treachery & the usurpa-

[218]Condy Raguet, an economist and journalist, edited the *Philadelphia Banner*.

tions of the present administration, I fear their weak & rash excesses, much less than I do the settled, steady & preservering policy of New England.

But let me do them justice—They are highly intelligent, industrious & moral & *patriotic;* but their views of national—(I hate the word)—Federal policy are essentially selfish & in my poor opinion, certainly destructive of the whole system.—

Power, in this Country & age, cannot long remain concentrated in the hands of a single individual or of a cabal, without open resistance & revolution, but what shall save us from the fangs of an interested majority? When I contemplate these majorities, I feel a species of suffocation.—remorseless, heartless and persevering.—nothing capable of resisting them but the highest spirit of Liberty—& where under Heaven is that high & disinterested spirit to be found?—The late history of our Country found us to a great extend debilitated & wholly powerless.—What with false opinions, interested purposes & weakness & vacillation, & ignorance & immobility—the last the worst of all—have we to hope, in future efforts, against this majority.? And that this specific question will come up, none can doubt who travel to the East to enquire for truth.—

That the tariff compromise as a settled policy, will not be suffered to remain, I have not the slightest doubt.—The question will come up again & earlier than the period contemplated by any of those who concurred in that measure.—When it shall come, if we shall prove recreant to the true interest of the country, all may be lost.—*Nothing on the Slave question is to be found.* All looks well in this respect—But as to the Tariff—nothing will save us but a prompt & fearless perilling of all, on the question—New England looks to interest, she will not fight for the policy—But she will push it, if she can get such Myrmidons as those of Gen. J. to do the fighting, or if it can be carried out, without a fight. Our only safety is in a prompt & high & determined defiance—& resistance at all hazards.—

I have sought many opportunities to impress the opinion, that a re-enactment of the Tariff of 1828, *next Winter,* would be the signal for universal resistance throughout the South—That it would, I don't doubt.—But after the lapse of 4 or 5 Years.—when the spirit shall have gone down, & the opiates of patronage shall have withdrawn from their posts many of our public men, what shall we be able to do?—

I was invited to dine at Nahant with a party of the "Exclusives"—You know Nahant is some 14½ miles from Boston on the sea shore—Mr. Webster was of the party & some twenty gentlemen—All these subjects came up—I pressed the view above stated strongly; & among other things had the impudence to say, that the union, on the *practical application* of Mr. W's force bill principles could not endure ten years.—& that no intelligent man at the South, could at this day believe that it would so endure.—Mr. W. had retired at the time of this Conversation—I further stated as my opinion, that even Mr. W. since that discussion, had learnt enough, to be satisfied, that the Union could not endure under the aplication of *force* to the *States*—

These seemed to be new views to many of these gentlemen.—& I was amused at the startling effect produced by such opinions, in this strong hold.—& yet they seemed to think that all I stated, was very probable,—& sd many kind things etc. Light [illegible] in reference to our peculiar views, is not permitted to penetrate N.E.—The managers attempt (& thus far have succeeded) to govern by excluding light.—

The only papers from the South that can be found, are the *base* papers from S°. Cª. that have the unparalelled impudence to claim the name of "*Union papers.*"[219]—I regard that party in S°. Cª. as the most atrocious that this Country has produced—The reasons for this opinion, I have not time to give—"The play, is not worth the Candle."—

But this is due to Boston—They are the most civil people to strangers, in the world.—& yet you feel all the time— that there is a slight incrustation of ice about them.—But little of that frank (I have almost given up the word "frank." Gen. J. has given it a new & strange meaning) I say, but little of that frank, open & cordial feeling that enables one to look at once into the heart of our southern people.—I never spent three weeks, more pleasantly than at Boston.—I hope, I feel a due degree of gratitude.—& yet the pleasure was derived as much from the fine weather, the highly, the most highly cultivated country, & the beautiful City & bay & heights around, & the fine &c. &c. as from the *frank cordiality* of the people.—And yet, I believe, as I ap-

[219]In the campaign in the summer of 1834 for the election of members of the South Carolina legislature, the State's Rights party tried to discredit the opposition by forcing a test oath of first allegiance to South Carolina. A compromise was worked out by which the Union party members could take the oath without violating their oath to uphold the United States Constitution. C. S. Boucher, *The Nullification Controversy in South Carolina*, Chicago, 1916, 348-352, 356-360.

peared in the character of *one of the Whigs of the Senate;* I received rather more attention than I have been accustomed to.—I like that open, sincere & hearty welcome, that none can question.—Whigs!!![220]—now My Dear Sir. suffer me to say that no man has more respect, than I, for the Whigs of the *revolution*—But as to our modern Whigs tho, I quarrel with no man for calling me Whig—yet I feel it no compliment.—God save the mark—The Whigs of New England!!—What say you?
The south has before her a high & glorious destiny, if our people have the virtue to achieve it.—It is a high destiny—& more than all, it is a virtuous one.—

Forebearance and self-denial are our lot.—If we have virtue enough for this high destiny, we may be happy.—

We are, in truth, the real conservators of our political system.—If we shall love Liberty enough to seek & defend her; regardless of the usual *official* bounties & honors; Liberty may be preserved.—

Nothing can more contribute to the virtue of our people & our *public men,* than to stamp with some *suspicion,* not to say, *disgrace* any public man who shall accept any honor or emolument, except *that* which may be necessary to aid the Gov^{t}. in his immediate *region.*—I mean *local* office.—If such public opinion, we should have much less of servility & much more of purity.—

"Off with the heads" of *all* who seek office by the slightest sacrifice of their own, or their country's principles.—The press of the South, should lose no occasion to impress this opinion on the public mind.—

I know only two classes of *public men* in the South who support the measures of the adm^{n}. of recent date—1st. class— Venality—*expectants*—2nd stupidity.—no particular motive, save that of popularity.—Did you everknow a man of weak mind, who had moral courage? I have known *obstinate* men of fixed purpose & yet—generally weak minds But, in the general, the man who sees clearly will feel strongly, & act firmly.—
As to the Presidency—The views, I expressed to you last winter at Raleigh, were *then* practicable—I fear, they are no longer so.—I see no prospect of success for the views of our party—The want of Patriotism is great among the leaders—A question of personal ambition supersedes all others among them.—

[220]By 1834 considerable opposition to Jackson had developed in North Carolina. Elsewhere, the opposition party took the name of Whig, but in North Carolina that name was not too popular. By the summer, however, the name was frequently used in the state. Pegg, "Whig Party in N. C.," 32-35.

Duncan Cameron, 1777-1853. From the original oil portrait by J. A. Elder and now in the possession of the University of North Carolina, Chapel Hill, N. C.

Mr. Calhoun has no more chance for the Presidency than you or I have.—It is in vain for me to say, that if he c[d]. command a majority, I sh[d]. prefer him to any man in the country—The reasons are numerous, & in my view, Conclusive—But he has no chance—& yet his friends urge him—Their views are, that we must go for *our principles* or not go *at all*.—This is all well in the *abstract*.—But it is not clear, practically—That this course will throw both Virginia & N°. Ca. into the arms of Van Buren —I am sure it is—Mr C. cannot get the vote of either State, & you & I, may cry our eyes out, yet he cannot get either.—

Clay could have been brought to compromizes that would have rendered it not incompatible with the principles of the wildest nullifier to vote for him. I fear, it is now too late—If so—V. Buren will be the President.—For the question will come. Whether the people, "prefer an Election by the House or to yield to the dication of the national Convention.[") They will prefer the latter, as the former has been already deeply disgraced.—The result of all which, is the election of M. V. Buren, from which I pray God to deliver me & my country.—I have no hope but it is now practicable to carry out the views that I disclosed to you last winter.—

I *cannot now* vote for Mr Clay under *present* circumstances—He must first come to the grounds that I can support him.—To effect this, His friends must feel the necessity of doing so to elect him & therefore must place him upon grounds, that we can approve.—

That they w[d]. have done so, I don't doubt—I believe it is *now* too late— & I believe the failure is attributable to the want of patriotism in the South.—

These views have all been given to Mr. Calhoun & his friends & by me too.—They are familiar with them—& tho they assent to their propriety, as far as I understand, yet they thwart them.—

The struggle then will probably be, between McLean & Van Buren—& tho, it is next to impossible for me to go for V.B. yet to go for McL. is but little better—I suppose I sh[d]. go for him—yet I greatly doubt, whether he has any principles, to which he will stick.—When I think of him, I think of a Gentleman in wooden patterns on a pedestal of ice, who moves N°. S°. East or West on the slightest external pressure.—

You perceive that I am a *Non-Content*—And though I will go for no man who does not either *profess* my principles—or place himself in a position not to trample on them—yet I will not aid a scheme wholly impracticable, & which, in my judgment, inevitably leads to the result, above all others, by me deprecated.—I am willing to quit public life, & shall probably do so this winter—Yet I will not, under any pressure, pursue a course condemned by my judgment. & my clear convictions of the public interest.—

To remain in public life an instant against the wishes of the States Rights party, I would not do.—That is the party to which I belong & which has all my sympathies. Judging from the views of Mr Fisher, I cannot represent them—that is—I cannot be guilty of the rashness & suicide to our party in N°. Ca. to take up Mr. Calhoun under present appearances. To carry him is impossible, tho I repeat, that I w^d^. prefer him to any man in the union.—

You are the first man, I have written to on the subject—I have all confidence in your honor & sincerity—I wish you to write to me as fully, as I write to you.

The first thought that comes up, I write, simply, because I feel that I write to a man of principle—Will you do me the favor to write to me as freely & unreservedly. I am writing at 12 Oclock at night, and have scarcely read, what I have written.

I have been denounced as an *"apostate"* I feel the injustice of it—I have abandoned no principle upon which I was elected.—& yet I had rather go home & *eat straw* than to remain in public life at the sacrifice of my own self respect. My friends are intitled to be consulted, & if they shall even *doubt*, I shall feel it my duty to resign.—

How the majority of the State is, I feel great doubt—If against us, without recognizing the principle, I have said that I will not remain an instant against the public will.[221]—This, I must comply with Will you write me freely & unreservedly on all these matters.—

I hope you will show this hasty letter to no one—I sh^d^. be ashamed of the literary execution—The principles contained in it, are free for all the world.—I give you a mark of my highest confidence in your honor & right feeling, in sending you a pro-

[221]In the legislature of 1834-1835 Mangum was instructed to vote for the expunging resolutions. For months he refused to resign on the grounds that the legislature had no authority to instruct and that the legislature did not represent popular sentiment. Later, after a new election and the party opposed to Mangum won, he resigned.

duction, every way, so incomplete & exceptionable.—I do not mistake you.—Write me to Baltimore—I go tomorrow to New York—return here in a few days—stay here—say 2 Or 3 then go to Baltimore & thence home—

Our examination has been such as I expected—not much varying *anything* from what has already appeared.—

I but rarely see your excellent paper—I could desire to see it oftener.—I hope, you are doing well with it—Your entrepidity deserves well of the public—But deservings are not always appreciated.

May God bless you & yours
Your friend.
W. P. MANGUM

Mr Websters friends in Mass. are determined to push him for the presidency.—They are willing to give up Clay—His Compromize is unpopular.—Webster cannot & [*sic*] possibly go & must not. Oh: for a prophet to tell us what we ought to do.

W.P.M.

John Beard Esqr.
Salisbury

[Addressed:] Major John Beard
Salisbury
N°. Ca.

WPM-D

Daniel Webster to Willie P. Mangum

BOSTON Oct. 7. 1834.

My Dear Sir.

On my return from N. Hampshire, I recd your letter of the 24th Septr. & am glad to learn that my attendance with you is not deemed indispensable at present. The state of my health has been such, ever since I saw you, that I have been capable of very little business. I took a cold,—I believe the night we came home from Quincy—which attacked my head, & very severely affected my *eyes*. I hardly know whether I have written two letters, of three pages, since I saw you. Once or twice, I have been apparently well; but the cold returns again, upon the slightest exposure, & drives me to my room & sometimes to my bed. I hope much from the present dry & settled state of the atmosphere.

I shall set off, I think, in three or four days, in the expectation that I may probably meet you & the other Gentlemen in N. York about the end of this week, or the beginning of next. In the meantime, I may probably hear from you again.

Be kind enough to present my best regards to the other Gentlemen. I am glad to hear that every thing is so readily communicated by the Bank, & is found so fair & favorable.

I am, Dear Sir,
With entire regard
Yours truly
DANL. WEBSTER.

Honble Willie P. Mangum,
of the Senate of U. S.
Philadelphia.

WPM-LC

Daniel Webster to Willie P. Mangum

BOSTON Oct. 8. 1834

My D Sir,

I wrote you yesterday, & observed that I should leave home in a few days to join you. Such is my purpose; but I have so many engagements on hand, that it would suit my convenience quite well to know, with some accuracy, the *day* on which it would be desirable for me to be in N. York. If you shall not have already written, be kind enough to say a word on that point.

At N. York, I usually go to Washington Hall, as a place where rooms may generally be had.

Yrs as ever,
DAN[l] WEBSTER.

Hon. Willie P. Mangum,
U. S. Senate
Philadelphia.

WPM-LC

Daniel Webster to Willie P. Mangum

BOSTON Oct[r]. 9, 1834

My Dear Sir

I recd your second letter, two days ago, and was now just on the Eve of departing for New York when I recd. a letter from

Ewing, of which I enclose extracts. As Mr. Ewing expresses a wish to be with us, at N. York, & canot join us till Nov. 1st, I now wait your pleasure to say whether I shall come forwith to N. York, or whether I shall postpone the visits to the first of Novr.—of course, we shall both feel a strong disposition to meet his wishes. I wrote you on the 7. and the 8th—addresed to Philadelphia . .—

Yrs very truly,
DANl WEBSTER.

Hon W. P. Mangum,
U. S. Senate
Now at N York.

ENCLOSURE

Thomas Ewing to Daniel Webster

"Mr Mangum will write requesting you to meet him at New York—I have dropped him a hasty note requesting the postponement of that meeting to the 1st of Nov—I wish that could be done for various reasons—

Now I wish to be with you in N. Y. & I attend the P. O. Committee[222] there on the 1st Nov. There are some inquiries which can be better pursued by the two committees than by one—Write me on the receipt of this & your letter will find me in Lancaster Ohio.

Your friend,"

WPM-LC

John L. Smith to R. E. DeRussy[223]

GOVERNORS ISLAND N. Y.
Oct. 13th, 1834.

Dear Colonel

Judge Mangum of North Carolina proposes to visit West Point —Allow me to introduce him to you—He is a member of the U. S. Senate—Should he desire to examine the Military Academy I hope you may find it convenient to explain to him the organi-

[222]This was a Senate committee authorized to investigate charges of corruption in the Post Office Department. The Postmaster General refused to furnish to the committee the desired information. Instead, he tried to discredit the committee by attacking it in the press. *Daily National Intelligencer*, Oct. 8, 1834.

[223]I am unable to identify John L. Smith. Rene E. De Russy was a student at West Point from 1807 to 1812 when he graduated. He entered the engineering corps and in the War of 1812 had charge of the construction of defenses at Sackett Harbor, New York. From 1833 to 1838 he was superintendent of the Military Academy. Cullum, *Biog. Reg. of Officers of U. S. Milt. Acad.*, I, 109-110.

zation discipline exercises and course of studies.

I remain with respect & regard,

Yrs. truly

JNO L SMITH

Colo. R. E. DeRussy
Supdt. Mil. Acady
West Point

WPM-LC

John Tyler to Willie P. Mangum

[YORKTOWN] Wednesday Oct: 22. 1834

My Dear Sir;

Your letter of the 13. reached me this morning in which you enjoin it upon me to meet you [in] Washington by this day at the latest—I know not where it has lingerd on the way and deeply regret the disapointment which you do not feel more sensibly than myself—What can I now do but regret the delay, since it finds me wholly unprepared and no conveyance to Washington except by the mail stage which will bear you this, and which would keep me on the road two nights in succession and would literally incapacitate me from labour for a week—The earliest steam boat for Washington occurs on Sunday which I shall take, if nothing out of the usual way occurs, and will be with you either on Monday or Tuesday as her speed will permit—Had you not better give up your trip home until we return to New York and Baltimore where if you will unite with me in pressing matters, we can get our discharge in a week from both places—and you and myself having in the mean time prosecuted all enquiries at Washington—we can return to our families in tranquility until Congress meets—In the mean time write to Webster to meet us beyond doubt on the 1. Novr. in New York, so that no delay shall occur—I know your solicitude to visit your family must be great, and I think that this is the best mode of accomplishing that object—a fortnight longer will restore you to them, and acquit us of our duty to the public. My report[224] cannot be prepared sooner than the meeting of Congress

[224]Webster agreed to let Tyler write the report of the Committee on Finance. According to the *Daily National Intelligencer*, Mangum gathered most of the information and Tyler wrote the report. Since Tyler had not been a champion of the Bank and Webster had, it was felt the country would feel the report was impartial if it came from Tyler. Tyler presented the report to the Senate December 18, 1834. In this report he stated that the Bank was safe prior to the removal of deposits, that it had not used its money to corrupt the press, and that it had curtailed discounts because of a loss of deposits rather than because of political reasons. Lyon G. Tyler, *The Letters and Times of the Tylers*, Richmond, 1884-1896, I, 503-505; *Daily National Intelligencer*, Dec. 19, 1834.

which will be time enough—The papers give you some account of the Leigh dinner[225] at Petersburg and of myself as present—I have much to say to you and hope I shall find you in Washington on my arrival there—

My family join in sincere regard to you—Robert leaves home for College the day after to morrow

God bless you
Yours Truly
JOHN TYLER

Mary wishes to know whether your new frock coat was greatly admired in N. York or not—

[Addressed:]
Hon: Willie P. Mangum
Washington City
D. of Columbia

Yorktown
Oct 22th

WPM-LC

Daniel Webster to Willie P. Mangum

NEW YORK Nov. 4. 1834

My Dear Sir,

I arrived here this morning, & found Mr Ewing in the City, & learn that Govr. Tyler is in Philadelphia. Being much of the same opinion as was expressed by you in your last letter, I doubt whether it is advisable for the Com^{ee}. to assemble again, until the commencement of the Session. Mr Ewing inclines to that opinion, & I have written on the subjects to Gov. Tyler. We need not report the first week of the session; indeed it will be difficult to have any of the Reports ready by that time. And as the first week of the session is not usually very much occupied with the ordinary business of the Senate, we can then examine the Deposite Banks of Baltimore, if thought advisable. It will be necessary to continue the power of the Com^{ee}; & the same course is expected to be adopted, in regard to the Com^{ee}. on the Post Office.

I shall write you again, before Mr. Ewing & myself separate, & after I shall have heard from Govr. Tyler. I will write you to-

---

[225]As a result of resolutions in the Virginia legislature in favor of the restoration of deposits, W. C. Rives, a Jackson man, resigned his seat in the Senate, and Benjamin Watkins Leigh was elected to take his place. Soon the Jacksonians campaigned vigorously to defeat Leigh for reelection. Wiltse, *Calhoun: Nullifier,* 235, 236, 245.

morrow, also, on other subjects; & am always, very truly & cordially,

Yrs & &
DAN[l] WEBSTER

Hon Mr Mangum

WPM-LC

BOSTON Nov. 27, 1834

Daniel Webster to John Tyler

My D Sir

As I may not arrive, until the Session shall have begun, I send you the following papers, obtained at N. York, or lent to me from that place, according to request.

I am now ready for my departure, I shall set forth as soon as the weather encourages me to try the Sound.

Yrs ever, very sincerely,
DAN[l] WEBSTER

Hon Jno. Tyler,
U. S. Senate
Washington.
[Addressed:]
Hon. Mr. Tyler

WPM-LC

R. H. Alexander[226] *to Willie P. Mangum*

RALEIGH, Nov. 29, 1834.

My Dear Sir.

The result of the Senatorial election and the consequences necessarily resulting from it—are alarming—to every man who loves his Country—and who wishes to see its councils conducted with purity and administered with ability Swain might have been elected—if Branch and his friends had united—some time before the meeting of the Legislature—with the great body of the opposition and if certain members—from Grahams district had not betrayed—the wishes and feelings—of their constituents, in preferring Brown—to Swain—had he been a candidate.

---

[226]Richard Henderson Alexander, a graduate of the state university, was a member of the Baltimore National Republican Convention in 1831 and the state legislature in 1833-1835. *N. C. Manual,* 789; Grant, *Alumni Hist. of U. N. C.,* 6.

Could the people—of Rutherford—Macon and Haywood—have voted at the polls—for Senator, who can have a doubt as to the result—The truth is, that Durham,[227] the Senator from Rutherford—& Quinn[228] of Macon—Brittain[229] and Edmondson[230]—all wish to be opposing candidates to Graham—for Congress—and he being considered in the opposition—they suppose that they can only succeed—by identifying themselves—with the administration.

Much art and cunning—and trick—were resorted to—for the purpose of uniting the party—and the thing was managed under the auspices—of their main leader—Haywood[231]—in a manner not unworthy—of their new desciple of the Van Buren School.

Theirs is a decisive majority of about 20—in favor of the administration.

The battle has yet to be fought in this State—and it is time—commence operations—and we never are commence operations—with success—without a candidate in the field—for the Presidency. I have talked—much—with the opposition members—here—with some members of *Congress* and I know—something—of the sentiments of the people—by actual conversation with them—upon the Circuit—and I have come to the decisive conclusion—that neither Calhoun or Clay—can compeat—with Van in this State—and that the only man—who can beat him—provided he is taken up by the great Whig Party—in the several States as the candidate of the opposition, is Judge MacClean—this may be deemed by *you*, a singular opinion—but still *it* is the *truth*. The sooner a candidate is brought out the better—no person who has the least intelligence can doubt but that *the party*—will select Van Buren—as their candidate—and that he is now so considered

Resolutions were introduced by Dr. Potts[232] yesterday one of them asserting the right on instruction[233]—the other instructing you to expunge from Journals of the Senate—the Resolutions of Clay—charging that the President had acted—contrary to the Constitution—and in derogation of the laws when he removed Mr Duane and removed deposites—The resolution is a similar one to that passed by the Legislature of New Jersey We shall

[227]Brennen H. Durham.
[228]James W. Gwinn.
[229]Benjamin S. Brittain.
[230]Ninian Edmondson.
[231]William H. Haywood.
[232]Dr. John W. Potts, of Edgecome County. See above, II, 138.
[233]See below, II, 232, 269-270.

make a death struggle—against them at least the last one—and shall introduce resolutions—*censuring*—the administration in some of its most objectionable features Your presence here—before going on to Congress was desirable, in many points of view—for the purpose of arranging matters—and organizing the opposition.

The party have a dirty tool in Philo. White[234] the new undertaker—to report what was said when Browns nomination was under discussion. He garbled and misrepresented every thing that I did say—I took occasion—yesterday—in the House to comment—upon his publication and it was admitted—on all hands—that his report was false and incorrect.

I should like to hear from you in full—and any communication you may make—shall be considered confidential—if so desired—I shall be obliged to you—if you would inclose me a copy of Websters speech—on the Protest. Strange it cannot be procured in this great City from the Editors.

Julius is improving in his health.

I am with Dear Sir Yours
R. H. ALEXANDER

[Addressed:] The Honorable
Willie P. Mangum
Washington City
District of Columbia.

WPM-LC

Memucan Hunt[235] to Willie P. Mangum

BLAKELY N—Ca DEC^r^. 2nd 1834
Ans

My Dear Sir:

I set out for Mississippi in a few days and should be gratified to procure through you some letters of acquaintance from

[234]Philo White, a native of New York, moved to North Carolina in 1820 to help edit the *Western Carolinian* at Salisbury. From 1830 to 1834 he was a naval agent in a Pacific station, at the end of which period he returned to Raleigh to establish the Jackson paper, the *North Carolina Standard.* Elected state printer and supported by his party, he made the *Standard* the chief Jackson newspaper in the state. In 1836 he sold out to Thomas Loring and in turn became naval purser, consul, and United States minister. Johnson, *Anate-Bellum N. C.*, 770.

[235]Son of the Revolutionary treasurer of North Carolina and brother of Dr. Thomas Hunt, Memucan Hunt, of Granville, moved to Mississippi in 1834 and then to Texas, where he participated in the Texan Revolution as a major general. He became the Texan representative at Washington in 1837.

Messrs Black[236] and Cage.[237] I shall take with me one of the best American bred stallions, in which I own one half an interest the other belonging to our mutual friend W. D. Amis Esqr. with whom I am spending a day and who desires me to present his respects to you. I shall be glad to get letters in and near Jackson and Woodville and Natches. I shall settle a plantation near Livingston and already have acquaintances there and at Vicksburg.

Please enclose any letters you may get for me to Livingston Mississippi as early as convenient.

I have nothing to say on politics.

I have the honor to be your

political and personal friend

MEMUCAN HUNT

[Endorsed:]

Col. Hunt: is a fine clever fellow, in every respect a most amiable gentleman & a man of fortune—

W. P. MANGUM.

[Addressed:]

Honble Willie P. Mangum

Washington City

D. C.

[Endorsed:]

ans^{d}/ 9th. Dec^{r}.

1834

WPM-LC

William Gaston to Willie P. Mangum

NEWBERN DEC^{r}. 3rd, 1834

My dear Sir

Mrs. Clitherall[238] a widow lady of this town of great respectability, the sister of Mr. Burgwin[239] Judge Nash's[240] brother in law, is deeply interested in some bill before Congress remuner-

[236]Judge John Black, a native of New York, moved to Mississippi where he became judge of the state court and from 1832 to 1838 United States Senator. *Biog. Dir. of Cong.*, 705.

[237]A native of Tennessee, Harry Cage moved to Mississippi where he practiced law and became a state judge before entering Congress in 1833. After one term in Congress he retired from public life and settled on a plantation in Louisiana. *Biog. Dir. of Cong.*, 774.

[238]See below, II, 277.

[239]George William Bush Burgwyn.

[240]Abner Nash.

ating the family of her deceased husband. I know nothing of the claim, but understand it has passed through the ordeal of a Committee. All that I know is, that the family is in urgent need of whatever it may be entitled to, and therefore I take the liberty of begging of you to examine the claim, and if you find it well founded to take it under your patronage.

I can scarcely trust myself to write any thing about Politics, as I shall not know when to conclude if once I enter upon them. It is not permitted to a good citizen to despair of the Commonwealth, and therefore I will not abandon the hope of our ultimate deliverance from the thraldom of corrupt and factious misrule. But indeed the prospect of this consummation seems to me exceedingly unpromising. Popular infatuation, the discipline of party and the bribes of office combined, are I fear too powerful for reason patriotism and eloquence.—Yours is emphatatically a *trying* situation. But you will undergo its probation I trust so with that firmness without which virtue loses all its claim to respect.—

I pray you to believe me my dear, Sir
Very respectfully
Your friend & obedt Serv[t].
WILL: GASTON

Honble. W. P. Mangum.
[Addressed:]
Honble. W. P. Mangum
Senator from No. Carolina
In Congress.

WPM-LC

Paul Barringer[241] *to Willie P. Mangum*

CONCORD 4th DECR. 1834

My Dear Sir

I supose you will have Lernt eare these Lines reach you that Bedford Brown has been Elected to the Senate of the U. S. for six years from March next and as the Hasa[?] Boys of the present Legislature of N. C. will make an attempt to discourage

[241]General Paul Barringer, 1778-1844, the father of D. M. Barringer, was educated in Germany and at an English classical school. He accumulated a respectable fortune; became active in the Lutheran Church; subscribed liberally to railroads and cotton mills; and served as a general in the War of 1812 and later as a member of the state legislature. Ashe, *Biog. Hist. of N. C.*, I, 95-100.

you by passing Resolution[242] disaproving your couse in the U S. Senate or as they stile it give you a polite invitation to resigne. I take this meathod of giving you some Idia of the situation of parties (I mean Political) of this sextion of the State depend upon it a large Majority think with you & I hope you will hold on & serve out your Constitutional term Sir when even another Name is brought before the publice in place of Andrew Jackson there will be a Verry Large falling off and an event of that kind will & must certainly take place within your constitutional term Martin Vanburan can not stan the current in N. C. I am verry certain & old Andy must & that in a verry short time tou get off the Public stage

I hope sir you will hold on as I have little doubt Sir that there will be a revolution in the politicks of this State in a yeare or two at furthest nothin more but remain

yours
Verry respectfully
P. BARRINGER

[Addressed:] Concord N. C.
Hon. W. P. Mangum Dec 5
Washington City
D. C.

WPM-LC

William A. Graham to Willie P. Mangum

RALEIGH DEC[r] 8th 1834

My dear Sir

You have doubtless been apprized of the Resolutions which have been introduced into the House of Commons relative to yourself—I had not anticipated any such movement before my arrival here, & for several days afterwards—The senatorial election first gave full confidence to "the party" in their strength, and I believe it was not untill after that, they determined to embarrass you if possible—The Resolutions you have no doubt seen in prints—The discussion of them commenced on Thursday last, & has been continued untill this evening with a good deal of warmth—tho' with decorous language towards you personally—

[242]The legislature passed resolutions instructing Mangum to vote for expunging Clay's resolution of censorship to Jackson for removing the deposits.

Every evening we have had a scene of confusion, on the question of adjournment—"The party" first endeavoured to force a silent vote on them, and with the previous question, among our rules of order, they would have sacrificed you without a word—To-morrow, I think, they will make a desperate effort to bring the debate to a close, attempting to fatigue us into a decision, by refusing to adjourn—The discussion has been conducted by Messrs Potts,[243] Daniel,[244] Jordan,[245] Harris,[246] Potter,[247] in favour of the resolutions, & against the motion to postpone indefinitely—and Messrs Craig,[248] Fleming,[249] Manly,[250] R. H. Alexander, Outlaw[251] & Barringer[252] on the other side—Messrs Haywood[253] & Bragg[254] have spoken on the motion to lay on the table which has been twice made—but have as yet reserved themselves in the main debate—The former[255] setting at a table & taking notes of every speech which has been delivered—By advice of Messrs Iredell[256] & Swain,[257] I have waited for him to come out, before I should say any thing—I fear it has not been the wisest course—By the collissions every evening on the motion to adjourn—the party is knitted together by new irritation—With the exception of the speeches to-day I don't think the questions involved in the resolutions have been elucidated at all—It has been mere wandering in the fields of party politics.

I think I am prepared to present some views not yet mentioned in the house, but as many of our friends insist upon being heard, I am afraid, that only a scanty allowance of time will be afforded me—With three or four friends whom I could select I should not despair, of being able yet to defeat them, were the matter left in our hands, but undisciplined as our forces are every man fights on his own hook. If possible I will take the floor to-morrow, whether the Ajax be in the field or not—I am convinced that delay will only render the minds of members more inaccessible to truth—I deny the right of the Senate to expunge any thing from its Journals after they have been published—Or if

[243]John W. Potts, of Edgecomb County.
[244]John R. J. Daniel, of Halifax County.
[245]Dillon Jordan, Jr., of Granville County.
[246]Sandy Harris, of Granville County.
[247]Robert Potter, of Granville County.
[248]Burton Craige, of Rowan County.
[249]Samuel Fleming, of Burke County.
[250]Matthias E. Manly, of Craven County.
[251]David Outlaw, of Bertie County.
[252]Daniel M. Barringer, of Cabarrus County.
[253]William H. Haywood, Jr., of Wake County.
[254]John Bragg, of Warren County.
[255]Will H. Haywood, Jr., was the leader of the Jackson forces.
[256]James Iredell.
[257]David L. Swain.

they had the constitutional right to do so, they could do it only by motion or resolution which they would have to record—& thereby perpetuate the thing expunged—

I should have been pleased to hear from you before these proceedings were instituted, and had supposed, that I certainly should have heard from you after they were published—Be assured however that I shall not relax in any degree my efforts, such as they are, in your defence—since it is demanded of me not merely by the obligations of a friendship which I value, but by my regard for the constitution & the Laws—You know that I am but little addicted to politics, and have differed from you on some subjects—Were your course the very opposite to any thing I could approve, I never could consent to the disgraceful proceedings, on which I am called now to act—I will write you again as soon as the subject is disposed of in the Commons—

With assurances of high
regard & Frienship
I am Very Truly
Yours
WILL. A. GRAHAM

Hon. W. P. Mangum)
[Addressed:]
Hon. Willie P. Mangum
City of Washington
D. C.

WPM-LC

James A. King[258] *to Willie P. Mangum*

RALEIGH DEC^{r}. 8th., 1834

Dear Sir

I have been requested by some of your friends to write to you besides I perceive from your letter to Mr. Alexander[259] that you

[258]He was a member of the House of Commons from Iredell County in 1833-1836. *N. C. Manual,* 662-663.

[259]Richard H. Alexander, of Salisbury.

desire it. Potts Resolutions[260] are now undergoing a discussion of the most angry character in the Commons—J R J Daniel concluded a Philipic in his *peculiarly felicitous* style against yourself, monied Aristocracies, Blue Light Federalists &c. & in favor of *"the* Republican Party"—such farrago lasting as it did on Saturday last for two hours & a half has never been heard. Mr. Outlaw[261] has the floor this morning—You know him—He will say some bitter things & make a good speech—The ground mentioned in your letter has been assumed & your friends all think that you would dishonor yourself & State by obedience & so think the minions of Power, so thinks that *pure & spotless* Patriot W. H. Haywood who is weilding "the Party" here for his own selfish purposes [torn] Personal gratification of Genl. Jackson—Mr. Manly,[262] R. H. Alexander & others have already discussed the resolutions & others of the opposition will do so—Harris[263] of Granville bolted? on Saturday—He rose for the purpose of offering an amendment, the question being on an indef. Post. [postponement] he was out of order—his amendment was a simple expression of disaprobation without requiring you in so many words to vote for expunging &c.—He conceeded that the resolutions as they now stand require you to disgrace yourself & declared that they would disgrace the Legislature & their authors—He wont vote for them in their present shape—The resolutions have been debated to-day by Outlaw and Barringer against—& D. Jordan in favor. Outlaw made a speech which it is considered on all hands would have given him a high reputation in Congress—He gave the President some [torn] blows

[260]The Jackson forces won control of both houses of the North Carolina legislature in 1834 and reelected Bedford Brown as Senator. Wishing to force Mangum to resign, Dr. John W. Potts, of Edgecombe, introduced resolutions in the House of Commons instructing the North Carolina representatives in the Senate to vote for a Democratic resolution to expunge from the Senate journal Clay's resolutions of censorship of Jackson for the removal of deposits.

For many years the right of the legislature to instruct a Senator had been an object of debate in North Carolina and many of the other states. In the first twenty-five years after the Federal Constitution was adopted the only question about passing such resolutions was a matter of expediency rather than constitutionality. In this incident a very heated debate developed over the authority of the legislature to instruct the Senators. The Jacksonians held that the "right to elect implied the right to instruct." They cited English history and the Bill of Rights to support their contention. Mangum, they continued, had gone against the will of the state and, therefore, the body which elected him should instruct him.

Mangum's friends, partcularly W. A. Graham and John Branch, contended that Mangum in voting for Clay's resolution had not gone against the will of the people and to vote for Thomas Hart Benton's motion to expunge would be against the Constitution, since Jackson had acted unconstitutionally in removing the deposits. Nevertheless, after a heated debate in which the press took up the argument, the resolutions of instruction were approved by a vote of 69 to 47 in the House of Commons and 33 to 28 in the Senate. Earl R. Franklin, "The Instruction of United States Senators by North Carolina," *The Trinity College Historical Papers,* Ser. VII (1907), pp. 1-15; Pegg, "Whig Party in N. C.," 35-36.

[261]David Outlaw.

[262]Matthias E. Manly.

[263]Sandy Harris. He had a personal grudge against Mangum. See above, II, 177.

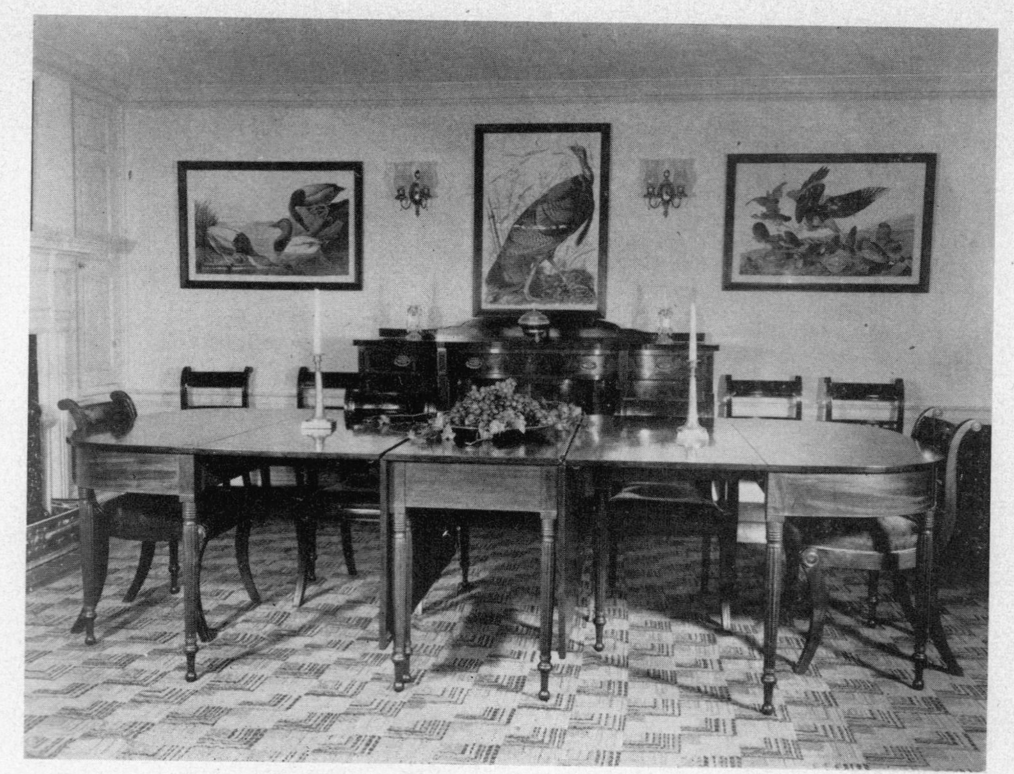

Mahogany banqueting table, brass candlesticks, and brass fire fender of Willie Person Mangum. The originals are in the possession of Mangum Weeks, Alexandria, Va.

Martin Van Buren & the Kitchen are not spared & it seems to me that nothing can be said of them which they do not deserve —The resolutions will pass the Commons in their present shape by a majority of ten or 11 votes[264]—two of our party are sick in bed—Your friends say that in the event you should determine to resign, that you ought to do it to the next Legislature—In the meantime we can make up the issue next August—I know myself, that at least two Counties of the West are misrepresented, the same said of the East—When the issue shall be made between Van and the opposition we can beat him—We know you will demean yourself as a gentleman & a Patriot—I should be extremely glad to hear from you soon—the debate in the Com. will terminate on to morrow I think—

Very sincerely
Your obt Svt
JA. A KING

[Addressed:]
Honl. Willie P. Mangum
Washington
D. C.

WPM-LC

Gabriel Holmes[265] to Willie P. Mangum

WILMINGTON N. C. DECR. 11th. 1834.

Sir:

I have the honor to enclose to you the proceedings of a meeting recently held in this Town, relative to the improvements on Cape Fear River below this place; to which I beg leave to invite your attention.

I am Sir
most Respectfully
Your Obdt Serv Sc
GABL. HOLMES Chairman

Honorable W. P. Mangum
Washington City
[Addressed:]
Honorable W. P. Mangum
Senate U. States
Washington City
D. C.

[264]They passed by a majority of 22 votes.
[265]Probably the son of Governor Gabriel Holmes, who died in 1829.

ENCLOSURE

[Nov. 28, 1834]

At a general meeting of the Citizens of Wilmington and its vicinity, held in the Town Hall on 3rd instant, in pursuance of public notice, Gabriel Holmes was called to the chair and William B Mears appointed Secretary.—

The object of the meeting being made known by the chairman, the following preamble and resolutions were submitted, and unanimously adopted.—

Whereas the completion of the Works for the improvement the navigation of the Cape Fear River,[266] below Wilmington, (now in a state of forwardness, under the management of the Government of the United States) is, of the greatest importance to that portion of North Carolina, trading to the Cape Fear, and whereas it has been suggested, that reports are circulated, calculated to make unfavorable impressions as to the progress of the Work, and the results Contemplated from its Completion.—

Therefore Resolved, that this meeting have full confidence in the report made, some years since, by Major Bache,[267] regarding the improvement—of the Navigation of Cape Fear River; and they believe the Completion of his plan of operations, will insure the results expected from it—

Resolved, as the opinion of this meeting, that the reports above alluded to, are unfounded in fact, in as much as the depth of Water on the shoals of the River, has been increased more than three feet—since the commencement of the Work—

Resolved further as the opinion of this meeting, that said Works ought to be prosecuted by the Government of the United States until said plan is Completed; and to stop their further prosecution would be an abandonment of the best interests of a large portion of North Carolina.—

Resolved, that our Representatives in Congress be requested to urge the prosecution of said Works to their full completion.—

Resolved, that Copies of these Resolutions, together with Copies of the Certificates of Peter Daniels, Henry Rouark & others submitted to this meeting, be forwarded to the Governor of this State, to the Senators of North Carolina, and the Repre-

[266]In 1827-1828 the War Department ordered Capt. Hartman Bache to make a survey of the harbor. Bache recommended the removal of obstructions below the city where the channel was only nine feet deep. Prior to this the state had unsuccessfully tried to dredge the channel. From 1829 to 1839 the War Department continued its work but with little success. In 1847 a new and more successful effort began which resulted in a channel of nine to thirteen feet deep all the way to the sea. James Sprunt, *Chronicles of the Cape Fear River 1660-1916*, Raleigh, 1916, 144-145.

[267]Capt. Hartman Bache made his survey in 1828.

sentative of the District in Congress and to Genl. Gratiat.[268]

Resolved, that in the opinion of this meeting, Peter Daniels Henry Rouark, & the others whose signatures are annexed to the certificates submitted to this meeting, bring Pilots & others well acquainted with the Cape Fear River are entitled to full credit.—

Resolved, that the Editor of the Peoples Press be furnished with a copy of these proceedings for publication, and that the Editors of other Journals, within this State, be requested to publish the same.—

The following certificates were submitted to the meeting—

"Smithfield N. C. 28 November 1834

"We the undersigned, Pilots on the Cape Fear River, hereby certify that the Brig Telegraph was towed over the Wreck, Middle and Bulk Head Shoals, by the Steam Boat Clarendon, on the 24th instant: And that she (the Brig) drew 12 feet 4 inches— There were 13 feet of water on the Wreck Shoal (which we consider to be the Worst in the River) when the Brig Went over, notwithstanding the Winds had been from the West—and Northwest, for two or three days previous, which winds generally reduce the tide about one foot.

Peter Daniels.
Henry Rouark.
Hanson Rouark.

"We are knowing to the above facts, having accompanied the above named Brig over the Wreck, Middle and Bulk Head Shoals, on the day above mentioned.

John A. Wade, Com. Steam Boat Clarendon.
David Blanchard, Com. Brig Telegraph.

"We the undersigned Pilots on Cape Fear River, have no hesitation, in declaring it as our opinion that 12 feet can be carried over the Bulk Head, Middle, & Wreck Shoals at high Water, on ordinary or Common tides.—

John Price.	Peter Daniels
Elijah Todd.	Henry Rouark
Hanson Rouark.	Lewis Craig
Simon Grissom.	James Burriss
Wm. Grissom.	Jesse Craig

GABRIEL HOLMES Chairman.

Wm. B. Meares, Secry.

[268]General C. Gratiot. In 1826 he surveyed the Dismal Swamp Canal region.

WPM-LC

Josiah Randall[269] *to Willie P. Mangum*

PHIL[a]. 12. DEC— 1834

(Confidential)

Dear Sir,

By prejudice in the public mind and great indiscretion in the directors, the Bank of the U. S. is now dead, & cannot be revived. I regret it but I much more regret that it has given its opponents a false power over the public mind. No report from any Com[ee]. can help the Bank. no matter how [torn]. the sooner we get clear of it the better. I think however you & Mr. Tyler stand differently from many of us in relation to Virg[a] & N. Carolina and oposed to the Bank on principle, and I should be sorry to see any report made by your Com[ee]. which would injure the standing of either of you at home. I know either of you would be willing to bear the responsibility of doing what you thought right, but remember that thro' you our cause is attacked and that any thing which wuld injure your standing at home wuld also injure the Whig cause.

I make these suggestions from a conviction of their force, I have no objection to their being communicated to Mr. Tyler and to Mr. Clay (to whom when in Phil[a]. I made the same suggestion) but beyond them I ask this Comm[n]. to be private.

Hoping for improvement in our future prospects

I remain

Your Sincere friend

JOSIAH RANDALL

WPM-LC

Michael Holt[270] *to Willie P. Mangum*

HOLTS STORE DECEMBER 13 1834

Friend Mangum

I have seen the proceedings of our General Assembly—They seem to want to drive you out of Congress—I Hope you will not be drove so easily—our Assembly dances the Green-Corn dance

[269]A close friend of J. Watson Webb, Josiah Randall was an eminent lawyer in Philadelphia. Livingston, *Law Register*, 1851, p. 550.

[270]See above, I, 67n.

after the Tune of Glory, and Philo White plays the Banger—I have lately seen many persons of sound Judgment in our county and adjoining counties The expressed opinion is that the people, many would not vote for B. B[271] altho They voted for our present Members of Assembly—I Hope you will Hold on, and not be drove so easily—Major Wright of Rockingham County on his way to Fayetteville N. C. Informs me that Judge Settle[272] is opposed to the present administration

If you have any time to spare, and any news worth communicating please write me

Will the nomination of Judge White[273] Take or Judge McLean[274]—

With esteem
MICH[l]. HOLT

Hon[le] W. P. Mangum
N. B. I am informed that the Hon[ble]. R. M. S.[275] is very busy in business at Raleigh—
[Addressed:]
Hon[ble]. Wiley P. Mangum
Washington City
D. C.
[Endorsed:]
Ans[d]. 19 Dec[r]. 1834

WPM-LC

Hugh Waddell to Willie P. Mangum

HILLSBORO. DEC[r]. 14. 1834.

My dear Sir.

I have sent by this Mail a package addressed to you, which I beg you will have sent to Messrs. Gales & Seaton, it contains a paper on the subject of the right of "Instruction;"[276] which one of my acquaintances requested me to have conveyed to the Editors of the Nat: Intelligencer.—

---

[271]Bedford Brown.
[272]Judge Thomas Settle.
[273]Hugh Lawson White.
[274]John McLean, of Ohio.
[275]Romulus M. Saunders.
[276]On December 27, 1834, the *National Intelligencer* carried in a two column article the speech of Samuel Fleming, of Burke County, in the North Carolina legislature. Fleming argued that instruction would set a precedent which would curtail the rights of a Senator and make caprice of the party in power and not the Constitution the determinant of his tenure in office.

There may be some improper allusions in it to the men in power, as also to mistakes of other parties, but they are of minor consequence.—You had better send it to the Editors immediately on the receipt of it, as the final question in our State Legislature may not be taken before it comes out.—I assure you I am in deep anxiety on your subject. May the rascals be defeated.—

In very great haste I am

My dear Sir

truly yours

H. WADDELL

Though I approve the opinions, I had not the slightest connexion with the writing of the paper sent.

[Addressed:]

Hon: W. P. Mangum
U. S. Senate
Washington City.

[Postmarked:]

Hillsboro N C
13th Dec 1834

WPM-LC

Benjamin S. King[277] *to Willie P. Mangum*

RALEIGH 15. th DEC^r 1834

W. P. Mangum Esqr.

D. Sr

I think it quite probible that the Resolutions [on] the subject of your vote on the Deposit Question (as it is called here) has called forth a degree of excitement, not excelled by any subject heretofore before the Legislature. It really seems that a perfect mania has gotten hold of the Dominant party, Since they have found out their Strength in both Houses, The Resolutions were carried by a vote of 12 majority in the lower house, and will pass the other house by about 4 or 5. And will be sent on to you requesting you to have expunged from the Journals your vote on the subject alluded—at the last Congress;

It is Intended as a broad hint for you to resign your Seat in the Senate of the United States, I ask you if it follows of course that you will resign. It seems to me that you are not bound to do the one or the other. That is to expunge or resign,

[277]See above, I, 13n, for a sketch of King.

From the views I have (according to my weak Judg[t].) on the subject of resignation, that you are not bound to obey such Instructions, especially when they have come forth from the mear effervesent State of the public mind, [torn] by a strange infatuation characteristic of minds misguided, and when on a calm reflection many would vote diferent, I have heard some of them say that they were sorry they were brought forward but in as much as they were they must vote with the party. I think it Quite likely that the very next Legislature, will approbate your vote, and thus you must be expunging and replacing your vote on such Important subject transversely to ad, Infinitum—It is the opinion of many of your friends here that you should not pay any attention to them, but go on and do your duty as a faithful Sentinel of your Country, and that before the next three years shall have passed away, your conduct will convince all that you have done well for your Country—

I have taken the liberty to drop [torn] hasty note, You will pardon [torn] I have taken, You are well [torn] they flow from a hart & mind, [torn] a Strong [torn] for you [torn] and a public servant. Presen[torn] to Henry Clay Esq.

We are well, y[torn]

B. S. [torn]

[Addressed:]

Hon[l]. Willie P. Mangum
Washington City
D. C.

[Endorsed:]

Ans[d]. 19 Decr. 34

WPM-LC

Robert H. Jones to Willie P. Mangum

WARRENTON 16. DEC[r]. 1834

Dear Sir,

Having understood that the numbers signed "Lucius"[278] which are appearing in the "Standard" are ascribed to my pen and

---

[278]In the *North Carolina Standard,* from November 14 to December 19, 1834, a series of letters addressed to Mangum and signed "Lucius" were published. In this series the author reviewed Mangum's political life. He stated that Mangum entered politics in 1815 as a Federalist and in opposition to the War of 1812; that he was judge of the superior court long enough to obtain the title of "judge" to help his law practice; that he changed from Federalism because he thought it was wise; that he had been elected to the Senate as a champion of Jackson and that he had since then become the President's enemy; that he had been unfair to Jackson by his votes, on committees, and in his speeches; and that since he was elected as a Jackson man and had turned against him, he should resign. This is an able but partisan series of articles by one who knew enough of Mangum's life to make some effective, although exaggerated statements. *N. C. Standard,* Nov. 14, Dec. 5, 19, 1834.

feeling no wish to share in the credit or disgrace of that publication I avail myself of the passing moment, to say to you, that I have had no agency directly or indirectly in preparing the matter they contain for the public eye, nor have I any knowledge of the author of the numbers in question.

If the numbers were in Unison with my sympathies and respect for you personally, a just regard for my own understanding of the language in which I write, wou'd furnish ample instances for disclaiming the production of "Lucius"—Haec scripsi non abundantia otii, sed amoris erga te.

You have been long enough in public life, and the employment of people, to know, that there is but little stability in the popularity of any man who seeks to earn it by administering to the caprice of the people; He who devotes himself to the service of the people, [and] means to sustain himself, must act upon principle, and firm[ly sus]tain his character for consistency and uprightness of motive—[torn] the column of his fame will be proportioned to the base wh[ich supp]rts it. The Wise King of all, somewhere saith—"curse not the King, [torn] in thy thoughts, and curse not the rich in thy bed chamber, for a bi[rd] of the air shall carry the voice, and that which hath wings shall tell the matter." Thus spake Solomon—so I say to you read Solomon, and prosper in Wisdom and in all usefulness to thyself and thy country.

Yours in sincerity.
ROB H. JONES

[Addressed:]
Hon.
Willie P. Mangum
Washington City

Willie P. Mangum to William A. Graham[279]

WASHINGTON CITY 16th. DECr 1834

My dear Sir

I have received your two several favors of the 8th and 12th instant, for which be pleased to accept my thanks.—Before this reaches you, the resolutions of the Ho. of Commons will most probably have been adopted by the Senate.—

[279]The original letter is in the William A. Graham Papers, University of North Carolina.

It now only remains for me to do my duty.[280] Upon that subject I trust you will be assured, that it will cost me scarcely anything to perform that duty without the slightest reference to the consequences to me personally.—

Were I to consult either my pride or my feelings I should resign instantly.—Were I to look to the recovery of any portion of that paltry popularity which now seems so hopelessly wrecked for the present, I should resign forthwith.—But animated by the same spirit that threw me into the opposition to a great and hitherto irresistable power to popularity two winters ago, as well as the last; I stand prepared, and it costs me almost nothing, to do my duty.—Upon that point, I desire, the fullest & most frank interchange of sentiments with those engaged in the same great and good cause & shall weigh deliberately and with due respect every suggestion, coming from that quarter.—Ought not our friends to meet and harmonize their views on that subject?—

That the Senate presents the only barrier to an *absolute power practically* on the part of the Executive, I regard as certain.—That the Senate is to be subjugated by the seduction of Executive favor; or over awed by popular violence, is obvious—Nor is it less obvious that it is an object nearest to the heart of the President & many of his supporters.—How many of those supporters would hope for office during the yet unexpired term of the incumbent, who can scarcely be so sanguine as to indulge a hope with the present Senate. How many debts are yet unpaid? How many are put off with the Certainty that a nomination of them would only subject them to rejection?

Besides these things that lie on the surface yet greater, grander & more fearful enterprizes may disturb a brain never one of the soundest, & now reeling under an intoxication arising from a complete national prostration to the will of one man.—

Hence every effort is made to remove that barrier.—The question is under such circumstances, can any one resign, without giving countenance to a gross perversion of the spirit of the Constitution; & subjecting himself to the imputation of being most discreditably deficient in moral courage? My principles will not suffer me to hold parley an instant with the pretension, that

[280]When the resolutions were received by Mangum he presented them and in a brief speech explained to the Senators that, like himself, the legislature was a servant of the people and had no authority to instruct him. When Benton's motion to expunge Clay's resolution came up for a vote, Mangum announced that he would refrain from voting. He determined to await the results of the next election of the legislature. Finally in November, 1836, he resigned. Pegg, "Whig Party in N. C.," 35-38, 101-103; McDuffie, "Willie P. Mangum," 53-54; *Register of Debates*, 23 Cong., 2 sess., 722.

the Senate which by the framers of the Cons: was designed to be the *most permanent* element in the *Legislative* & *Executive* faculty of the Govt. is by indirection, by mining & sapping to be converted into a mere tenancy at will or at best a tenancy from year to year. The Senate, in that view, w[d]. be less stable than the Ho. of Reps. The pretension can not be sustained by reason & argument.—Yet I have often said, & always thought, that I would not hold place an instant beyond the moment that the power which conferred should express a wish to disrobe me of the trust.—That is a natural sentiment which every man of honorable & elevated feeling, will instantly understand.—It proceeds from a laudable pride & just self respect.—But the question here is, May I under present Circumstances be permitted to consult either pride or any other feeling merely personal to myself?

If they are the proper advisers, the question is settled—But does not a high, & to me a most unpleasant duty require that considerations of self shall be sunk; & that I shall look only to the Constitution & the State of the Country.—Will you Consult our friends freely—& write me frankly—Might not a resignation at the end of the session, or after the adjournment of the assembly give strength to our Cause; & next winter might we not put a stronger & less obnoxious man before the Legislature to fill the vacancy.—

I know Sir, that my personal friends would feel great delicacy in adding anything to the weight that may now be supposed to oppress me, & especially by saying to me that anything *personal to me,* weakens the cause.—But my Dear Sir, I enjoin it upon you, as due alike to me & the Country, to consult with others freely, & communicate to me equally freely.—It will be regarded by me as another title to that high respect & regard, with which I have long regarded you.—That it will in any way embarrass me, is impossible—My strongest wish is to leave *this position,* as soon as I may do it with honor, & the respect of good men.—

But the Cause is far above all personal considerations.—The unit is & ought to be regarded as nothing viewed in Connexion with the unexampled & alarming pretensions on the part of the Executive.

I have no idea of resigning to the present Legislature—as matter of delicacy to the "party itself," I ought to be restrained. —Rumor has pointed her finger to more aspirants in the Legislature, to my *place here,* than would change the *result* in the Ho

of Commons, were their votes deducted from the other & added to our side.—To throw an election upon them, could not but embarrass them, as it might detract something from the purity of their patriotism in the public judgt., & subject them to the imputation of selfish & ambitious purposes.—
Nor have I much idea of resigning to a Council to supply temporarily that vacancy; lest there might be supposed to be ground, for the opinion that the successor to the vacancy might be indebted for the place to the gratitude of a Council[281] Constituted by his management.—

If I shall resign *at all*, my present impression is, that it will be only, when the trust can be surrundered to the *people*.—

It is to that point that I invoke the calm & deliberate consideration of all those members of the assembly with whom I am acting.—I trust, they will take it up as a public question, without reference to any one—And that you will write to me freely.—

You advert to a statement of Mr. Haywood in debate, that "I was the author of the meeting in Raleigh to appoint delegates to the Baltimore Convention."—I do not remember that any meeting in Raleigh took place—But I do remember having written to Gen Sanders[282] & some one else, I have forgotten to whom & recommended the appointing of delegates—at that time The Tariff was the great question. Van B. had been rejected by the Senate, or it was supposed he would be rejected, & *his friends* who held the destinies of the South in their hands, held out the fairest promises to Southern men—I *then* went for Mr. V. B. for Vice P as I would now for the Presidency, if I could believe his policy would be such as to render to his Country as great a good, as I then supposed the satisfactory adjustment of the tariff would be.—

Mr. Haywood[283] forgot however to *tell* that soon afterwards, it was perceived that the Van B party were playing falsely with us, and that I wrote to Saunders or to him (no matter whom for no doubt both saw it) and urged upon him (I think it was Saunders) to have a strong article published in the Van Buren paper in Raleigh, denouncing the vengeance of the State agt V. B. if his friends should *not* aid in the adjustment of the Tariff—The *article* appeared accordingly. & produced much sensation both at home & *here*—The party continued to play falsely. &

[281]Some felt that if the legislature were not in session at the time of a vacancy, the Council of State would select a Senator to serve until the legislature met.
[282]Romulus M. Saunders.
[283]William H. Haywood, Jr., was the leader of the Jackson forces.

the only difference between those Gentlemen & myself, is that I quit V. B. then in accordance with my principles on that *leading* subject—& they (it being the safer course) more wisely perhaps as they think, stuck to him through thick & thin.—

Great public considerations, then determined my course, as I trust, they have Since and ever will.—
Who amongst my enemies supposes me to be so weak, so mere a puling fool, as ever to have been found in *the opposition,* if my object had been my own personal advancement. These Gentlemen I trust & I hope, have as clean a Conscience [as] I have on this subject.—

I have written the whole of this in the Senate, during the progress of unimportant business. Hence its incongruity, its almost illegibility. But it has the virtue of giving out my thoughts as freely as they arise.—

You may exhibit this or any part of it, or communicate it otherwise to such of our friends as you think fit—

Do write out your speech with much care. Outlaw[284] likewise —I hear them both spoken of in the very highest terms—
I hope our other friends will give thier speeches at length & with care to the public.—

With great respect & regard
I am Dear Sir
Your friend & obt Ser^{t}.
WILLIE P. MANGUM

Be pleased to say to my friend Mr J. A. King of the Ho. that I shall avail myself of some early occasion to write to him not about myself, but affairs here.—

WPM-LC

Gales and Seaton to Willie P. Mangum

Dear Sir: We return your friend's letter. We shall have great pleasure in complying with your wish & his request.

Very respy
Yr. friends & Servts
GALES & SEATON

Dec. 17, 1834

Hon. W. P. Mangum.
[Addressed:]
Hon W. P. Mangum.

---

[284]David Outlaw made a strong speech against instruction.

Willie P. Mangum to William A. Graham[285]

WASHINGTON CITY 17th. DECr. 1834

My dear Sir,

In my very hasty letter of yesterday, I purposely omitted to touch one subject of some delicacy: the open avowal of which as constituting a leading motive to the course I may ultimately pursue would only expose me to more exasperated & reckless assaults.—

You will perceive that the information ought to be taken into the estimate in forming an ultimate opinion both by myself & others advocating the same cause.—yet perhaps, prudence would dictate that my name should be kept out of view as much as possible.—The whole therefore is submitted to your sound discretion.

If I resign Jackson will be able to command the Senate in the *next* Congress.—If I stand firmly, the opposition will continue in the ascendancy in the *next Congress*—

That is the proposition—Now for the details—Govr. Moore[286] of Alabama, will be instructed in terms more disreputable to his State, and casting something more of indignity upon him personally than we have just witnessed in N. Ca. in reference to myself.—

Judge Black[287] of Mississippi, will most probably be placed in a predicament in all respects similar to mine.—
My course will be decisive of theirs.—They both have given me the strongest & most satisfactory assurances, that their course will be regulated by mine.—They both say that if I resign, it will be impossible for them to stand up against the storm that will blow upon them.—That if I stand firm, that they will stand by me to the death.—

Moore, by the bye, With Kindness, might have been brought into their ranks.—Jackson violence & the eagerness of expectants have lost that opportunity & have driven him to the wall; & with a dogged resolution he will resist to the bitter end.—

[285]The original letter is in the William A. Graham Papers, University of North Carolina.

[286]While governor, Gabriel Moore had supported instruction, but later as United States Senator he refused to comply with the legislature's instructions to vote for the expunging resolution. He did not resign until 1837. When Senator King, of Alabama, presented the resolutions, the United States Senate laid them on the table by a vote of 27 to 20. *D. A. B.*, XIII, 122-123; Benton, *Thirty Years View*, I, 528.

[287]In January, 1835, the Mississippi legislature adopted resolutions declaring that since John Black, who was elected as a Jackson supporter, had by his vote for Clay's resolution "unfaithfully represented" the people of Mississippi he should resign. Nevertheless, he did not resign until 1838. Dunbar Rowland, *History of Mississippi: the Heart of the South*, Chicago, 1925, I, 609-610.

Black's term runs two years beyond that of Jackson; & therefore he feels the less alarm.—

In the meantime, it is believed, that although we shall be unable to attack Van Buren, successfully in the front, yet that his flank may be turned, his trops thrown into disorder, & he ultimately routed & driven from the field with his base & mercenary retainers.—

The following exhibits truly & accurately the relative strength of parties in the Senate, *in the next Congress,* provided Mr. Leigh of Virginia,[288] shall be reelected, of which at this time, there is the most flattering prospect.—& supposing Poindexter to be leader, which is almost certain.

	Jackson	Opposition
State of Maine	2	0
New Hampshire	2	"
Massachusette	0	2
Vermont	0	2
Rhode Island	0	2
Connecticut	0	2
New York	2	0
New Jersey	1	1
Pennsylvania	2	0
Deleware	0	2
Maryland	0	2
Virginia	0	2
N°. Carolina	1	1
S°. Carolina	0	2
Georgia	2	0
Alabama	1	1
Mississippi	1	1
Louisiana	0	2
Tennessee	2	0
Kentucky	0	2
Missouri	2	0
Illinois	2	0
Indiana	2	0
Ohio	1	1
	23	25

[288]In 1835 the Virginia legislature was against Jackson's policy on removals, but by 1836 it had changed to the point that it passed pro-Jackson resolutions of instruction. In the 1834-1835 session the legislature elected Leigh, although he received a majority of only two. Wiltse, *Calhoun: Nullifier,* 236.

In the foregoing every thing is well defined & certain except as to Indiana.—Both Senators are now as much opposition in their feelings as I am.—Their State is so likewise, & they are as much opposed to Van Buren as any one, and are as anxiously engaged in the endeavour to organize an opposition that may blow up the "favorite."—Yet the patronage in the new States is so powerful & the tone of public men is so low, that no certain reliance is to be placed upon them.—These Gentlemen have heretofore been adm[n]. & may be so again, when they shall deem it expedient.—

In case an opponent judiciously selected shall take the field ag[t]. V. B. these gentlemen may be counted.—

Mark it.—*No opposition Man, can be elected President.*—They may mar, but they can't make. This opinion prevails here almost universally.—Clay is off—Calhoun is off—& Webster, tho anxious for a nomination, must soon find that overwhelming defeat is inevitable.

All that is left to us, is a choice of evils.—& that choice will most probably be restricted to Judge McLean, Judge White, & Van Buren—Of these I most decidedly prefer White—Yet I shall hold myself ready to act with my friends, always provided, those friends take position against V. Buren.—

If White shall be nominated by the Ala. Legislature,[289] as he probably will, in disregard of all caucases, & conventions rely upon it, he will be a powerful competitor & in *my opinion*, strange as you may think it,—will get every *electoral vote* in every slave holding State.—Calhoun was disposed to *take much part in these things*.—I believe he has been reduced to a state of *inaction*—

You may show this to our friend Major Beard, as I have the fullest confidence in his honor & discretion.—

I am My D. Sir y[rs]. Mo. truly.

W. P. MANGUM

W. A. Graham Esq[r].

---

[289]In December, 1834, a majority of the members of the lower house of the Tennessee legislature invited Hugh Lawson White to become a candidate for President. Later Ohio Whigs nominated Judge John McLean. The Alabama legislature followed in January, 1835, with an endorsement of White. J. B. McMaster, *A History of the People of the United States*, VI, 359-360.

WPM-LC

A. Van Hook[290] *to Willie P. Mangum*

DECEMBER 17th 1834

Dear Sir

I drop these lines to let you know the size & age of my Brother Thomas D. Van Hook which I wish to get in at west Point. he weighs about 160 lbs. five feet eleven Inches high. is in his twentyeth year. and is a youth of fine appearance & Steady habbits— [If] I am not mistaken three years ago my father spoke to Gen^rl^. Baringer to enroll Thom^s^. name for the purpose of geting him in at west Point he can inform you whether he did so or not I likewise drop him a few lines requesting him to assist you if he can, likewise informing of how that you will act in concert with him in obtaining the old man [Sp]ringfield,s Pension which I am in hopes you will do. I am sorry that I have no news of importance to write you, no doubt ere this comes to hand you will hear the result of our senatorial Ellection, likewise that our Governor has had a close contest in his last Ellection. I am a [torn] fearful before this time that they have passed resolutions instructing you. the course to pursue—the convention Bill will likewise be killed from what information I can gether to these matters I must yeald though conscientiously believe that the majority is wrong. Since I saw you we have lost too of our nearest & aged Neighbours (Viz) James Williamson & Thomas Hargis. myself & the family is enjoying of tolerable health and I am in hopes these may find you enjoying of good health whilst I remain your friend

A. VAN HOOK

P. S. I want you to write me as soon as you can what the chance will be for Thos.

A. V.

[Addressed:]

Hon^r^. Wiley P. Mangum
Washington City,
D. C.

[Postmarked:]

Van Hook's Store, N C
December 17th

[290]A. Van Hooks was from Person County not far from Mangum's home.

WPM-LC

William M. Sneed to Willie P. Mangum

DEC^r. 21st. 1834.

My Dear Sir,

It is now sunday night about 11 O,clock and I would commune with thee—a Man in bed & asleep—I halt for words to begin with—Well—the infernal resolutions—I suppose they will pass —It is not the first time faction and intrigue has obtained the ascendancy. But suppose they do? will Willie P. Mangum suffer himself to be driven from the Post of Honor—nobly fighting for the Honor of his country, the Welfare of his esteemed fellow citizens, in supporting and defending their violated Magna Charta? I hope and beleive he has too much respect for himself, too much contempt for reckless and lawless demagogues, and too exalted a Sense of True Patriotism to forsake the Station assigned him, when the hopes of all good men rest upon him—What sort of a Politician is he who will not immolate himself, if it be necessary, to save his, country—

In soberness—I think the people ought to know and approve the monstrous course their delegates have taken in this case before a Senator is bound (if at all) to bow to such instructions—Let the matter be considered by them before the next Election and then if the order "Depart, be given, you can, perhaps, ought to obey—

I cannot but think that a great deal of moral courage is requisite to be used in this Crisis; and I trust you will, for you can, exercise it.—I trust you will not lend yourself to the *disorganising* and demoniac attempt to undermine the main stay and Pillars of our Government—

I know you will think much and I trust you will ask & receive the best counsel before you act—

I heard a few days ago, that Mrs. Mangum & the Children were well.—

I will write again in a few days Perhaps from Raleigh—

Your friend & Servant

W. M. SNEED

[Addressed:]

Honl. Willie P. Mangum
Washington City

[Postmarked:]
Oxford, N. C.
Dec 23

WPM-LC

Orlando Brown[291] *to Willie P. Mangum*

FRANKFORT DEC. 21. 1834

Dear Sir

When I was in Washington last spring, [you were] so kind as to express an interest in my welfare [torn] me with friendly attentions. For this I have not been [unmindful] although I have been silent. On several occasions I h[ave taken my pen in] my hand with the purpose of writing you a long [letter but] something occurred to prevent me. I indeed, particul [torn] apologize to yourself and the other truly distinguished [gentleman] by whose courtesy I was permitted to form one of your [torn] seemingly abrupt manner of my departure. No doubt [you have] all forgotten the occurrence—but not so with me. My [torn] a brief one; the stage called for me an hour earlier than [I expected] and hurried me off without giving me time to run over to [torn] or even to write a note. I intended writing from New York [or Phi]ladelphia but the hurry in which I was in kept me from [doing] so, and on my return home I plunged at once into an [elec]tioneering campaign—entered upon the routine [torn] temp speaking—*barbacueing*—going to musters &c and of course was pretty busily occupied. I promised to inform you of the [re-]sult of the election. A competitor from our own ranks took t[torn]ld and produced such a state of confusion that the Jackson men were on the eve of bringing out a candidate who, as things then stood, might have been elected. My opponent would not decline— our friends met & ruled us *both off the track* & brought out a candidate upon whom all could unite. This is the brief outline of my first essay in the [wa]y of political distinction—if it is an earnest of my future success it would be well enough for me to begin to think meanly of popular distinctions & honors. I had, however, one consolation—we carried the State triumphantly—we [torn]ed [torn] as secures to us the ascendency in Kentucky for years [torn] contest with us was carried on as a Whig contest—the [torn] purely of principle without reference to any political [torn] reat benefit of this is felt in our being known as a [torn] untrammelled by pledges of any sort.

---

[291]"One of the most elegant and scholarly gentlemen of the state [Kentucky]; for many years editor of the Frankfort *Commonwealth*, secretary of state under Gov. Crittenden for a short time, and commissioner of Indian affairs under President Taylor." He died July 26, 1867, at the age of 55. Richard K. Collins, *History of Kentucky by the late Lewis Collins, Revised, enlarged fourfold*, 2 vols., 1924, I, 181.

We are ready [to enter] the next great battle for or with any man who [torn] [pr]ospect of "driving the Goths from Rome." We look anxious [torn]t Congress for a settlement of the question—" [torn] candidate for the Presidency." It is all important [that e]minent political men should settle this matter—In [torn] —ht Kentucky much has yet to be done—the party [torn] together without some visible head. You have observed [torn] & the North Western States—there the contest is far [torn] over A judicious selection of a candidate may enable [torn] more effectively and produced a concert when we are [torn] cramped by contrary personal interests. For the men [torn] of the West, the less of *Nullification* the candidate may [torn] will be the better for the Whigs. With Mr. *Calhoun* we c[ould] not get along. Mr. Clay would be our *preference* but [we] do not wish him to hazard another defeat—If Va and North Carolina will support him he will be the strongest man you could start. Judge McClean[292] has only a negative popularity [th]at kind of strength which grows entirely out of being [lo]oked upon as an *alternative.* Judge Marshall[293] is spoken [of here] by many—Mr. Leigh also, and *your own* annunciation by the Evening Star has been much talked of.[294] By the way we observe, with no pleasure, that your legislature wishes to[put the] collar on you or to make you undo the glorious deeds of last winter. My dear Sir, were I in your [place I] would not for the world retract one jot or title of w—[torn] done—last session the Whig Senators *immortalised* them—[They] made their children rich in paternal honor—and [should] not resign—we are out of temper with Sprague[295] [torn] fied with Clayton. Stand firm and before long the [torn] be filled again with good men and true. We will [elect] Crittenden, a host in argument and eloquence, [torn] the brim of those generous qualities which will m[torn] him. He is extremely anxious for an acquaintan[ce with you] and if you do *not fall in love* with each other [torn] both to be turned out of the Senate.—I find my [torn] talking as familiarly to you as if I were a prom[torn] —racter—you must excuse me however for when I li[ke a man] I forget his elevation and think only of the kindness there—

Before I close this letter, I hope you will take no offen[ce] at my making a small request—nor *for offi[ce]* thank God I have not come to that yet but for information In Kentucky we are ex-

[292]Judge John McLean, of Ohio.

[293]Possibly he meant the Chief Justice even though he was 79 at this time.

[294]After this Mangum was frequently mentioned for the presidency. In 1836 he received the electoral vote of South Carolina because of W. C. Preston's and Calhoun's endorsements.

[295]Peleg Sprague, Senator from Maine. *D. A. B., XVII,* 473-474.

tremely anxious to know what is going [on] out of doors at Washington—any thing in the shape of [news] from the *City* is devoured with eagerness. I wished to have gone on again this session but could not do so. Now [Sir,] you will now and then devote an hour to giving me some [of] the *on-dits* and speculations of the Federal City you w[oul]d confer upon me an important favor and gratify a cl[ass] of men who may one day remember your kindness. I repeat it—you would confer upon me a very great favor.

This letter has already extended to a troublesome [length. I] therefore close by requesting you to remember me to [torn] Mr Leigh, Mr Archer and Mr Fulton[296] and also to [torn] who, I am glad to see is again in Washington) and [torn]gy to them which I have made to you.

[I cannot for]bear telling you, that two days before my arrival [torn] my wife had borne me a *son.*—it was [torn] about it. You may tell Mr Preston that I have [torn] hint of his in order to designate the family of Browns [torn]-long, and called the boy *John Preston*—he is, [torn] it, a boy of much promise.

[torn] will you write to me soon.

Believe me dear sir that in calling myself your *friend,* I attach due [me]aning to the word.

Your friend

ORLANDO BROWN.

Honble [W] P. Mangum
[City] of Washington

WPM-LC

William J. Alexander to Willie P. Mangum

DEC. 22 [1834]

My dear Sir

I ought no doubt apologize for not writing to you [ear]lier but this has not for a moment I am sure created a doubt in your mind that I am less sincerely attached to you that I have heretofore professed—I will not stop to argue how the state of things in North Carolina has been brought about. It is our business to endeavor to regain the lapsed ground. In the pending controversy for the Presidency (for I look upon it as having long commenced) if we are prudent here we will be enabled to

[296]John H. Fulton, of Virginia. *Biog. Dir. of Cong.*, 994.

cover the present dominant party with dismay. The difficulty [is] at present to unite on one man, the select[ion] resting between two—White & McLean and Mr. [torn] will carry the day in this State the latter most certainly—I received a letter from Mr. Foster of Georgia and in reply wrote him [a whole phrase is torn out] What are your views on the subject—let me know fully and immediately that we may do all that be [*sic*] can be done before we adjourn—I have seen your letter to Mr Graham received by him a few days since and I for one say to you—act not hastily Your friends here as far as I can learn do not wish you to resign. They do not wish to compromit your honor and will endeavor to feel on that subject as if they were consulting the interest of a brother. We are now in consultation on that subject and we are sure that you will feel yourself bound to act in such way [as] best promote the dignity of the station you fill and subserve the political principles you have [A whole line is torn out]

I am Dear Sir with respects your &

WM. L. ALEXANDER.

[Addressed:]

The Honble W. P. Mangum

Washington City.

WPM-LC

Pro Patria to Willie P. Mangum

DUPLIN, NO. CA. 24. DEC^{r}—1834.

Hon. W. P. Mangum,

With some degree of surprise did I notice the introduction in our Legislature of the resolution in reference to instructing you as Senator, because I thought that Body was convened for the *sole* purpose of enacting, amending, & repealing Laws for the general welfare of the State; elections excepted but was still more surprised at the number who Voted for the passage of said Resolutions—

I confess my information on governmental affairs is limited, but still must be permitted to say that the same number of persons convened in any other place, should have the same influence over your conduct, that this small majority of persons, acting in their dictatorial & not their representative capacity—I ask, has your conduct in that particular been the subject of discussion among the people generally, none so fool hardy as to answer in the affirmative; and shall one hundred persons clothed with *no* authority in this matter, acting entirely without the instruction of *their* constituents, governed by *no* principle but that of party, call upon *you* (one of the Representatives of *all* North Carolina) to expunge "monstrous" yes expunge from the Records of the country a Resolution passed by a deliberative body of intelligent men, the highest & most honorable body known in our government "passed after discussion & reflection, & now expunge it, I say again, because these few calls upon you, are you to listen to them, against the call of the whole balance of the State; are those few violent partizans, all that you represent; if so, attend to their instructions; if you represent the State, hear what *she* says, before you act.

I was honored with a short acquaintance in Raleigh with you, on your way to Washington in 1823.—I expect probably you have forgotten me, or I would enter fully in this subject, lest it be considered presumptuous, I wont give my name (except the initials)[297] but believe me Sir to be your anxious friend & well wisher in this time of trial—

Truly & Respectfully,

PRO PATRIA[298]

The friends to the constitution here, are increasing, & they *all* approve your course,—Fear not, for in due time we shall reap, if we faint not—

[Addressed:]
Honbl—Willie P. Mangum
Washington City
D. C.
Mail.
[Postmarked:] Kenansville

[297]The initials are in parentheses. They are marked out so completely that they are not distinguishable.

[298]The initials are repeated and marked out. They seem to be J. P. The handwriting is that of Jeremiah Pearsall.

WPM-LC

Charles P. Green[299] *to Wm. L. Long*[300]

WASHINGTON D C DEC 26 1834

My dear Sir

I arrived here a few days via Richmond at which place I purchased a press & type an employed a printer who goes on in a few days to Boydton I expect to issue the first number by the 15 of January—I have seen the most of our party who are very anxious to start opposition to the Magician on consultation particularly with Genl Green & Judge Mangum who are of the opion that the people should understand the movements of the Jackson Van buren party. and the best way to effect that is to inform them direct from this place. the old Rip Van winkle must be aroused Judge Mangum & Genl Green is of the believe that there can be more effected by geting some person who will go through the State in every county and to every man house who will take either one of the papers published by General Green he publishes a newspaper at five dollars.[301] the Political Register with the Register of the debates at five—and also an Extra Tellegraph at one dollar. I have written to Craig[302] also has Judge Mangum he intends to write to Sawyer[303] Beard[304] Alexander[305] and others you must get our party to act with great unanimity to put down this delusion. we must organise societies in the different counties throughout the State. and more particularly the the Tellegraph must be sustained or the principles that we have contended for with so much zeal will inevitably remain in

[299]Charles Plummer Green, the brother of General Thomas Jefferson Green, was born and reared in Warren County. With one of his brothers he worked the gold mines of western North Carolina before he went to Boydton, Virginia, where in 1835 he established the first newspaper in Mecklenburg County, Virginia. He called the paper the *Virginia Expositor and Southern Advocate,* which he discontinued in 1836. In the latter year he began the study of law and then went to Texas. He died in 1843 in Warren County, North Carolina, after his return from Texas. Letter of William B. Hill, Boydton, Va., to the editor, Sept. 24, 1951. Charles Plummer Green's letters are among the most valuable in the Mangum collection. Unfortunately, after a careful search, I have been unable to locate his file of letters from Mangum to him.

[300]A Whig leader from Halifax County, he was in the legislature in 1829-1835, 1848, and 1858. In 1840 he was a Whig presidential elector and in 1846 a member of the state Whig convention. *N. C. Manual,* 637, 641-642; *Greensborough Patriot,* Jan. 24, 1846; *Hillsborough Recorder,* Sept. 10, 1840.

[301]Mangum worked closely with Duff Green in this period to further the interest of the state's rights party. At this time his admiration for Calhoun was greater than for Clay. After Calhoun went back to the Democratic Party in the late 1830's, Mangum gave his support to Clay.

[302]Burton Craige represented Rowan County in the House of Commons in 1834-1835.

[303]Samuel T. Sawyer represented Chowan County in the state senate in 1834-1835.

[304]John Beard, Jr., represented Rowan County in the senate in 1834-1835.

[305]Richard H. Alexander represented Salisbury in the House of Commons in 1834-1835.

the minority if we will act with decision we can beat them the next year and sustain Mangum finally carry the State against the old tyrant and his *darling,* the State Rights party are bound by every principle of gratitude to keep up the Tellegraph it is at the seat of government having a better opportunity than every other to defend our course, and expose all corruptions at this place besides he has done more than any other and sacrificed more when at the present he might have been basking in the favour of his Royal Highness King Andrew and could have been worth treble what he is at present—

I know your feelings towards the Editor and I feel fully confident that you are willing to do all in your power to keep up the great organ of our party I have concluded as soon as I get the second number of my paper issued to go through every county in the State soliciting patronage to the Tellegraph the paper at Boydton can go on without my assistance—I will give the whole of my time for one year without any compensation to aid in disseminating the principles that we hold so dear my exertions will do very little good without the State Rights party (with all the opposition) will come forward do their best in their respective counties in geting the ignorant class to take the cheap paper at one dollar per annum. you must see the opposition that is at Raleigh explain to them the plan—get them to agree to assist in the undertaking and request them to write to me at Boydton giving their views *rouse them you can do it,* tell them of the consequences that will of course take place without we are active—Our party have not agreed upon the opposition to Jackson or Van as it is doubtful who will of the two be a candidate,—some say White others say wait for a proper time that there will be a chance for Calhoun or [torn] hold yourselves [torn] time enough—[torn] by a paper in [torn] Genl Green says [torn] he will be compeled to strike his flag soon—it is now very late at night and I am sleepy this is to a friend therefore I shall make on excuse for bad writing &c—you must write to me at Boydton

I am your
personal & political Friend
CHAS P GREEN

P S

A good many of the Nullifiers spoke of the contest between yourself & [Several lines are torn out]

if he has made peace with his God I am willing he should go on as soon as possible

C P GREEN

[Addressed:]
Col Wm L Long
Raleigh
N Carolina

WPM-LC

Charles P. Green to P. H. Simmons[306]

WASHINGTON D C
DEC 27 1834

My dear Simmons

I wrote to you at Raleigh which letter I hope you have received—a few days after I came on to Richmond bought a press & type employed a printer & so I expect to get out the first number by 15 of January. I have had the pleasure to become acquainted with Mr Calhoun Preston Mangum Leigh Pondexter Genl Green and others. I have had free conversation with them all they say the great thing is to regenerate N Carolina which can be done by some active man that will go through the State in every direction to get subscriber to the Tellegraph being the only paper holding the confidence of the State Rights party, the people must be informed before any thing can be effected I have agreed to go on as soon as I get my paper under way to every county in the State to see what can be done in the way of getting subscribers to the Tellegraph at five dollars by the reding part of the comunity and get the more ignorant class to subscribe to take the Extra published at one dollar per Annum I have written to Long[307] Craige[308] Mathews[309] and others judge Mangum will also write we must organize societies in the different counties.[310] I have not time to write to you at length you understand my meaning the Tellegraph must not be neglected if Green retires we are dew to him we are more than to any other his is an

---

[306]A friend of Green from Halifax County.
[307]William L. Long.
[308]Burton Craige.
[309]Thomas C. Mathews was a member of the House of Commons from Pasquotank County in 1834-1835.
[310]The organization of the Whig party was perfected in North Carolina in 1834 and 1835. The first state Whig caucus met in Raleigh in December, 1835.

expensive establishment it must be kept up and shall so far as I am able to assist in any way. I have vollunteered my umble aid to the rescue of liberty from the grasp of the old Tyrant whom I saw yesterday living by the flatery of the Kitchen Cabinet and the fauning smiles of Kinderhook[311] portrait that ordons his *parlor* there is no doubt that he is declining in *health* very fast *God send* him spedily home I also saw his Proclamation in that [torn] hall. Write to me at Boydton also write to Green through Mangum as he can franck and will do all in his power give my respects to your wife & Boys. White is spoken of here by some of our party others say wait we can do better keep our flag flying if the worst comes to the worst the South can draw from the North.

I am your
Most particular friend
CHAS. P. GREEN.

K. P. Willis is here swelling & puffing
P. S. Ask if either of those Editors, of the Advocate[312] can come up to Boydton and spend a day or two in starting the Expositor
[Addressed:]
Col. P. H. Simmons
Halifax
N. Carolina.

WPM-LC

Charles P. Green to Thomas C. Mathews

WASHINGTON D C
DEC 27 1834

Dear Sir

Since I saw you at Raleigh I have made every arrangement to start the "Expositor" by the 15 or January. I arrived here some days ago upon consultation with our friends who says something Must be done in our State to sustain our cause by so doing we shall sustain Judge Mangum—who you know is the only man from the State that gives it any character and more particularly the great machine at this place must have free circulation or our exertions will do no good. you know the progress

[311]Van Buren's birthplace.
[312]*The Roanoke Advocate* was the new name for the *Halifax Minerva*. Johnson, *Ante Bellum N. C.*, 768.

that we have made in two years, and with a good strong pull for a few months all will be right there is no way to effect this without a paper at the seat of government has free circulation through the country, the Tellegraph is the only one here that has the confidence of the State Rights party Genl Green has done more to place Jackson in power than all others, and he can do more to pull down his would be successor I have had frequent conversations with Genl Green Messrs Calhoun Preston Mangum and others. they are of the opion that if some person should go through the State to every county spare no troble nor expence and solicit every man that will either take the five dollar paper or the Extra Tellegraph published at one dollar per annum—knowing the great want of zeal in this cause I have volunteered my services to that effect I also know as you do the injury that the Editor of the Tellegraph has sustained both in a political & pecuniary manner. under those circumstances every patriot is bound to give a helping hand in such a grand cause. I am willing to go as far as any person in my situation, as soon as I get my paper under way I will start to a tour through the State to every county all of which I am willing to do without remuneration than to know that I have done all in my umble situation to promote the great cause that the South is labouring to effect. I feel every assurance that all your assistance will be freely given to so laudable and undertaking you must see the friends of free principles now in the Legislature and get them to do some little to accomplish an overthrow of this hereditary sussession I have written to Craig Long & others, Judge Mangum has written to some others. Mr. Calhoun will also write this is a plain letter in great haste—write to me at Boydton Va do not fail—

I am yours
Respectfully
CHAS PLUMMER GREEN

[Addressed:]
Dr Thos C Mathews
Member of Commons
Raleigh
N° Carolina

Willie P. Mangum to Messrs. Gales & Seaton[313]

SENATE CHAMBER
27th. Decr. 1834

Messrs. Gales & Seaton.

A letter appeared a few days ago in the New York Courier & Enquirer under the signature of the "Spy in Washington;" exhibiting six or more cases under Mr. Adam's Admn. where the senators did not *give out accurately* the party views of their respective States & yet there was no movement in their Legislatures—& notwithstanding all this flagrant outrage, our good Lord & Master Gen. Jackson rewarded four or five of them—McLane of del. Dickerson of N. Jersey—Livingston—Gen. Chandler—& perhaps others[314]—"It was your Bull &C."—Will you republish that letter, when your convenience will admit of it?

& oblige Yrs truly
W. P. MANGUM

Willie P. Mangum to William A. Graham[315]

WASHINGTON CITY, 28th. Dec'r. 1834.

My dear Sir.

I write to give you a fact different from that presented in my last; & which may be of some moment in deciding upon the course I ought to pursue.—Gov'r Moore of Ala. has this morning rec'd intelligence of the resolutions having passed the Ala. Legislature by so large a majority, that the firmness of his friends at home is much shaken; & he in turn is so deeply shaken in his purpose, that I think his resignation at the close of this session exceedingly probable.—He has just left me, & is in great distress. —If there shall be a general yielding, it will settle practically, the Constitution in the South; and in my judg't will be deeply & fatally revolutionary.

In case of his resignation, you will perceive that the power of resistance in the Senate will be probably lost—

My anxious wish is to quit this unpleasant position—& yet I feel the strongest repugnance, & shrink from it as a fearful responsibility, to give my countenance, humble as it is, to a doc-

---

313The original is in the Ford Collection, New York Public Library, New York City.

314Louis McLane, of Delaware, Mahlon Dickerson, of New Jersey, Edward Livingston, of Louisiana, and probably John Chandler, a former United States Senator from Maine, and later consul under Jackson.

315The original is in the William A. Graham Papers, University of North Carolina.

trine essentially revolutionary, & perhaps to be fatally disastrous.—If there were any hope of concert upon the Presidential question, we might yet prevail.—But upon that question the distraction is as great almost as might be seen on board a sinking ship.—The Virginia Legislature will most probably nominate Mr. Leigh—Mass. Mr. Webster—Alabama Judge White. Ohio prrobably Judge McLean—& not the slightest indication of a yielding on any hand.

Defeat under such circumstances, is inevitable.—Things may however take a different turn. They certainly would, but for a signal & apparent dificiency of patriotism—

Will you do me the favor to endeavor to communicate to me the opinion of our friends?—

I shall most certainly take no step before the close of this session.—

Accept My dear Sir
My best wishes
W. P. MANGUM

[Addressed to:]
William A. Graham, Esq.,
Raleigh,
No. Carolina.

WPM-LC

Will. H. Haywood, Jr., to Willie P. Mangum

RALEIGH 30 DECR 1834.

Dear Sir/.

A friend of mine informed me to day that you had either charged me with the authorship of certain essays published in the Standard signed "Lucius"[316] or that you believed me to be the author of them & had expressed that opinion in Louisburg. The communication was made to me not in a spirit of unkindness but because I had declared in the presence of that gent^{n}. that I never wrote an article or essay impeaching either your political or personal conduct. After learning that the authorship of these essays has been imputed to me I have concluded that it is a duty I owe to *myself* to undeceive you and to say to you that *I am not the author of any essay or article of any kind*

[316]See above, II, 239n.

published in any Gazette whatsoever of or concerning you or your political course. And I have perfect confidence that after such assurance on my part you will both see & feel the justice of not imputing to me any thing of the kind.

I am not to be understood to pronounce judgment on the conduct or motives of others while I say that my conduct on the present occasion regulated by my own sense of what is due to my christian profession & since the acrimony of those essays would in my judgment be inconsistent with that profession and others will believe that your suspicions when expressed are well founded it is neither a sacrifice of pride nor honour that I should set you right in the premises. . . If it [serves] no better purpose [torn] assure [torn] which others perhaps *not more friendly to* [*you*] *personally* have endeavored to make. I do not wish to be understood as complaining of injury at your hands in this matter, much less do I write this as a covert means of hunting out the source of this unjust suspicion entertained towards me but I write simply & only for the sake of undeceiving you and thereby protecting myself against unmerited censure. I make to you no warm professions of personal regard I leave it to your own high sense of honour to detect if you can any appearance of personal unkindness through our whole lives— and indeed I might confidently rely upon the same sense to claim the remembrance of a uniform personal regard & a conduct perfectly consistent with it.

I am with high respect yours,
WILL. H. HAYWOOD, JR.

[Addressed:]
The Hon: Willie P. Mangum
Senate of U. S.
Washington City

WPM-LC

J. L. Edwards to Willie P. Mangum

War Department
Pension Office
December 31, 1834.

Sir.

I have examined the declaration of John King[317] who claims a pension for military service during the revolution: but I find

[317]In 1834 only those who had served in the Continental military forces were entitled to pensions.

that none of the services set forth by the claimant can be considered of that character.—

At the age of 12 years he performed, as he alleges, five different tours which consisted of driving a wagon and attending upon some prisoners, amounting to 151 days: this was in the year 1778.

In 1779 he was engaged in several tours in driving cattle for the use of the army in carrying expresses, amounting to 79 days.

He next alleges to have performed 15 months service, from "February 1779 to the fall of Charleston," and was engaged in furnishing provisions for the guard at Camden. It will ready be perceived that the service above recited cannot be considered as Military within the meaning of the Act of Congress, passed June 7, 1832.

Upon this ground the claim is rejected and his papers placed on file.

I have the honor to be
Your Ob. Servant
J. L. EDWARDS

Hon: W. P. Mangum)
)
U. S. Senate.)

[Addressed:]
Hon: W. P. Mangum
United States Senate.

WPM-LC

Henry Potter[318] *to Willie P. Mangum*

FAYETTEVILLE 31st. DECEMr. 1834.

Dear Sir.

The resolutions, so long pending in our Legislature to *instruct* you out of office, have at length passed: and it is rumoured by the manoeuvring party, falsely I dare say, that you are under a pledge to resign. I beg leave to say that all your political friends in this section of the State, and, as far as I know or believe, throughout the State, expect you to remain at your post "unmoved by party rage."

[318]See above, I, 13.

You have doubtless pondered this subject well, and have no need of additional arguments to bring your mind to a proper conclusion: but it may be some satisfaction to know that you are supported by a large & respectable portion of the "good men & true" of N°. Carolina. Yes, I verily believe that a large majority of the citizens of this State, if left to their own unbiased judgments, would be opposed to the instructions.

In all former attempts by demagogues & aspirants to impair the fine framework of our republican institutions, the sovereign people were roused to indignation & maintained their rights: but the present crisis (for it is a crisis) has no parallel in the history of our Government.—The people, in whom rests, very properly, the residue & the reversion of sovereign power have been grossly deceived & hoodwinked by insidious partisan politicians & office seekers; so that they perceive not that their liberties are in jeopardy.

The Senate, that host of patriots, has been our sheet anchor, & has thus far saved the Republic; and my only hope is in that body & in the wisdom & stability of the Supreme Court. But we have need of more than Roman virtue & Spartan courage to stay the plague & repair the breach. Great wisdom & prudence & firmness are necessary to guard our chartered rights ag^{t}. the inroads of a dominant faction. A few more removals from the Senate, & that branch of the Legislature may be as supple as the *House*.

Touching the right of instruction, suffer me to give you a few hints.—Although there is no license for such a practice in the Constitution, there is nothing in that instrument to restrain the exercise of it. And what power but their own mere volition can rule the legislature on this subject? The Judiciary cannot. It is a sort of extra legislation, or rather the expression of an opinion to produce an effect, without any power to inforce obedience; and has become almost as common & has just about the same authority, as political presentments by Grand Juries. The same right might be exercised by any convention of men in the State & with as much power to compel a compliance. It is true that a modest man in any station of life would pay a decent respect to the opinions of any set of intelligent & respectable men, relative to the duties of his station, when offered in the spirit of candour and moderation: but it is at last for the officer, with his best lights, to judge & act for himself. Instruc-

John Caldwell Calhoun. From an original oil portrait by Chester Harding, painted in 1820 and now in the possession of the Library of the University of North Carolina, Chapel Hill, N. C.

tions, though intended as threats, are but empty recommendations. Whatever influence they ought to have, under any supposable circumstances, where the relation between the Legislature & the Senator remains as it was at the time of his election (a mere possible case), it is clear that no succeeding Legislature, composed of other men, can exercise a power, phisical or moral, over the conscience or acts of such Senator. I speak now of ordinary times; but in seasons of political excitement, such as the present, when all plans and events are in the wind & that wind is continually veering about, a politician to keep with the current, must be a complete weather cock. Suppose that A at the present Session gets a majority over B, for the Senate;—that at the next Session, the wind having shifted, A is instructed out of office & B is elected;—and that at the succeeding Legislature, another change takes place, & B is instructed out & A is elected—and so *toties quoties*. Where is the permanence of our boasted charter or the stability of our political institutions? The Constitution might thus be indirectly & insidiously abrogated, & the Senatorial term be practically reduced from 6 years to one year.

It is not the popularity of Genl. Jackson (great as it is) which has so imposed upon the good sense of the people & kept them in check. Had his usurpations & misrule found no support but in his own intrinsic or supposed merits, he might, ere this, have been execrated. But the use & abuse of patronage, with the Bank as the instrument, have done the mischief. To every charge ag^{t}. the administration, however serious & well supported, the only answer by the sycophants, & that rung perpetually in the ears of the honest & confiding yeomanry, is Bank— Bank— Bank—the rich ag^{t}. the poor! But let two brief years pass away & the veil will be rent, & the people will see & lament that they have been so blind, & so reckless of their own liberties. The Bank, that Windmill whose long arms have so excited the quixotian ire of our chief of La Manche,[319] will then be lifeless at his feet, & he, the valliant knight, will ungird his armour & enjoy the triumphs of victory at the Hermitage. And then, my life on it, we shall have a National Bank;—we can't do without one.

[319] This should read "La Munchā," the province where Don Quixote lived.

Excuse the liberty I have taken in these crude remarks. I mean not to obtrude. My country's good is my only aim; and my good intentions must be my apology.

With much respect, I am, Dear Sir,
Yr. Mo. obt. Huml. Servt.
H. POTTER

[Addressed:]
Hon-ble Willie P. Mangum
Senator in Congress
Washington City

1835

WPM-LC

P. W. Kittrell[1] to Willie P. Mangum

RALEIGH Jan. 1st, 1834. [1835][2]

Dear Sir

Though our acquaintance is not intimate yet sufficient to furnish an apology I trust for troubling you with a letter I have been necessarily participant in the strange scenes enacted in our Legislature this session—Early in the session it was ascertained indeed I felt it my duty distinctly announce the fact on the floor, that I was constrained from a sense of duty to my Constituents to vote against the reelection of Bedford Brown & that I was decidedly opposed to Van Burenism in any shape I of course was excluded the Sanctuary & not invited to any of the caucuses in which the extraordinary measures that disgraced the opening of our session were concocted Though I have always been recognized in my county as a friend of the administration & indeed was sincerely so up to the date of the *proclamation* that abominable paper; Yet because I dared be honest here & exercise my right of thinking and acting for myself: I have been proscribed by the *powers that be,* have been condemned as a heretic & doomed to undergo all the tortues of a political inquisition I have the consolation of suffering in good company With those who though now dead will one day have I trust a glorious resur-

[1]A member of the House of Commons from Anson County in 1833-1835. *N. C. Manual,* 488.

[2]This letter should be dated 1835.

rection. I still Sir claim to be a republican I will never bow the knee to Baal or pay a blind and implicit obedience to the Moloch of party without regard to principle—I hope ever to be found fighting on the side of Constitutional liberty

One object in addressing you this letter is to say to you, that as far as I can learn your friends are decidedly opposed to your resigning your seat in the Senate of the U. States. They have entertained some fears lest the passage of some political resolutions in our legislature in reference to yourself might operate so far on your sensitiveness as to cause you to resign My opinion of those resolutions will be found in the vote I gave—I have this evening visited your friend Col Carson & he desires me to say to you that we both concur in opinion that you will do yourself & friends injustice to think once of resighning, and that you hold on & continue to discharge your public duties with that independence of conduct & purpose—that has always characterized your course—He desires me further to say to you that he rec'd your letter today & that he is prevented from indisposition which confines him to his bed from replying to you now but that he will avail himself of the first opportunity so to do after he gets up

A vacancy is made in the Attorney Generals office by the resignation of Genl. Sanders[3] Gov. Iredell[4] & John R J Daniel[5] are candidates to fill the vacancy. The election will be made tomorrow—I fear Iredell will be beaten—Daniel will rally the parts pretty effectually Well may we cry *oh' pudor* oh' the degeneracy of the times when such man as Gov. Iredell must be sacrificed on the altar of party vengeance and our public offices filled by such men as J. R. J. D.—

Our legislature so far has enacted but little important business. We have been principally engaged in regulating the affairs of the Genl. Government & perhaps if we do not conclude to discuss the French claim & other important matters of national policy, we may give our questions of State policy a passing attention before long—I am happy to inform you, that a *bill* authorizing a call of convention to amend our State Constitution has passed our house & Sanguine hopes of its passage in in the Senate are entertained, but I think it quite doubtful—I

[3]Romulus M. Saunders.

[4]Ex-Governor James Iredell.

[5]John R. J. Daniel, a lawyer from Halifax County, was a member of the legislature from 1832 to 1834. In December of 1834 he was elected by the Jackson forces as attorney general of the state. *Biog. Dir. of Cong.*, 878.

have a request to make of you that you render some assistance to a Mr Vespasian Ellis of Accomack Va. Who is prosecuting some military claims for me—I have never seen Mr. Ellis but can take the liberty of recommending him as a Gentleman

He will be at Washington during the Session frequently He wishes some assistance in obtaining interest on claims. *commutation claims* I mean—If you think this worthy of a reply I would be glad to hear from you

Very respectfully yours
P. W. KITTRELL

[Addressed:]
Honl. Willie P. Mangum
Washington City
C D.

[Postmarked:]
P. W. Kittrell, P.M.
Sneedsboro, N. Ca.

WPM-LC

B. S. King[6] *to Willie P. Mangum*

RALEIGH 1st January 1835.

Honl. W. P. Mangum

Your kind favour in answer to my little hint has been recd. in due course of mail.

You have no doubt seen e're this, that the Resolutions alluding to your vote on the subject of the Deposits, has passed the Senate (as I Stated to you by a Majority of 5 votes.)[7] I refer you to the Register of Tuesday last, for their remarks and calculations on the Subject, and what would in all probability, be the result if the federal vote could be properly taken in the State. You will receive letters from your most distinguished friends in the State on the same subject. I have conversed with your friend Carson,[8] he is fully of the opinion that you should stand to your post, regardless of what has been done, He is now with me, is very Sick. Your letter to him was recd this morning, and he requested me to read it to him as a confident. I did so. He requested me to say to you, that, if possible he would get up

[6]See above, II, 238.
[7]The state senate vote was 33 to 28.
[8]Samuel P. Carson.

the scrapts of his speach together as well as he could, and write you after his return home, that a greater part was made from the spur of the moment and particularly applying them to some things which had dropted from others, at the time of delivery, and that therefore he could not make it out perfect. Mr. Branch has left the City for Halifax. I should be glad to here from you from time to time, on many subjects of importance which will come before. In great haste I have dropted these lines. Colo. Carson & Lady Joins me in our regards for you. And all say Stand to your Post as a faithful Sentinel of the peoples rights which I think is the language of fifty more that have expressed themselves in my presence.

Respectfully yours

Confidence. B. S. KING.

[Addressed:] Honl. W. P. Mangum
Washington City,
D. C.

WPM-LC

D. L. Swain to Willie P. Mangum

Executive Department
RALEIGH 2d January 1835.

Sir.

In compliance with the request [of the] General Assembly, I transmit to you the accomp[anying] Resolutions adopted by that body at its present Ses[sion].

I am Sir, Very Respectfully
Your Obedient Servant,
D. L. SWAIN.

To,
The Hon:
Willie P. Mangum

Enclosure

North Carolina Legislature's Resolutions of Instruction[9]

[27 Dec., 1834]

Resolved that the Legislature of a State, acting as the representative of the people of said State have a right to instruct their Senators in Congress; and a just vindication of the character of

[9]See above, II, 232, 240-244.

our political institutions requires that such instructions should be given whenever a Senator misrepresents the will of the State upon great questions of national policy or in times of public emergency.

Resolved that the Honorable Willie P. Mangum, one of the Senators from this State, in the Congress of the United States, be, and he is hereby instructed to vote for expunging from the records of the Senate of the United States, the resolution declaring that the President, in his late executive proceedings in relation to the public revenue had assumed upon himself authority and power not conferred by the Constitution and laws, but in derogation of both.

Resolved that his Excellency the Governor of this State be requested to transmit forthwith to the Honorable Willie P. Mangum, and to the Honorable Bedford Brown, one copy each of the foregoing resolutions.

Read three times and ratified)
in General Assembly December)
27th. 1834.)
Wm. J. Alexander S.H.C.
W. D. Moseley SS.

WPM-LC

Jno. B. Bobbitt[10] *to Willie P. Mangum*

LOUISBURG, N. C. 3rd. January 1835.

Dear Sir:

Fearing lest you may resign your seat upon receiving *orders* from the Throne, I have thot' proper to address you a line on my little affairs. when here, I think you promised to have an interview with the Land Agent (Illinois); pay him Taxes, and forward on receipts. This I hope you will find convenient to do.

Nunc canamus paulo majora. What will you do with the Instructions? In this village we are afraid you will, whilst under the influence of too high-minded independence, hand in your resignation.—To shew our unwillingness to such a determination on your part, a little band of us met in Caucus last evening at the Clerk & Master's Office, where it was unanimously agreed you ought not to resign.—

[10]A close friend of Mangum who taught Mangum's children.

Since it is evident that $10000 have been spent in discussing unlawful Instructions, and that a majority of our Senate represents a minority of the Federal population of the State, we are firmly of the Opinion, that if you will come out with your defence in the News papers, or in some several thousand hand bills, the people will sustain you thro' good & thro' evil report. We are unwilling for you to resign for another consideration: It appears that a certain Gentleman,[11] not a thousand miles from Raleigh, who has been brot' into notice by your putting business into his hands, is endeavoring to Step into your shoes. A certain Gentleman of this (Franklin) County, and two of Warren County are, also, in all probability, aspiring to the same post of honor.—

We would remark, in conclusion, that altho' you are far better acquainted with the path that lies before you, than we are, yet, we, in our zeal for your welfare, have thot' it not obtrusive to throw into the Scale our mite of friendship.—Any hint from you, touching your determination, (which we hope will be like that of Mr. Burgess of N. H.) will be thankfully recd. by

Yr. Frd &c.
JNO. B. BOBBITT

[Addressed:]

Hon. Willie P. Mangum — Louisburg N. C.
Washington City. — Jan 3rd 1835

WPM-LC

Sam P. Carson to Willie P. Mangum

RALEIGH 4th. Jany 1835

My Dear Sir

Yr. favor of the 29th ult was recd, a few days since. I fear I shall be unable to comply with yr. request as to the publication of my speech.[12] I would willingly do so if bad health & more business than I can possibly attend to did not constantly anoy me— My spirits are almost broken & its with difficulty I can keep up, resulting from the villanous dyspepcia which is the most miserable of all curses that flesh is heir to.

---

[11]When he went to the Senate, Mangum transferred much of his law practice to Will H. Haywood, Jr., who, before the fight over the Bank developed, was a close friend of Mangum.

[12]Mangum tried to get Carson to publish his speech against instruction.

When I get home & at ease if I can collect my wandering thoughts I may probably try & write out what I said. I shall however want the *excitement* which the Occasion produced to make my speech interesting

Now Sir with regard to yourself. Your friends from every quarter of the State say *stay where you are* regardless of the efforts of the miserable panders of power I rec^{d}. a letter this morning from My Brother Chas Carson dated at Salisbury. he requested me to write you & say that the Resolutions had been the subject of conversation from the time of their introduction & every intelligent man that he had seen (including Jackson men) deprecated them & also the idea of y^{r}. being at all influenced by their passage. He says *Stand* to y^{r}. *post* & do the *talking* & if *necessary* send for him & he will go & do the *fighting* for he is confident he says, that he can whip a Score of the *d - d collaer dogs*"

You know Charly & I give you his own language

My own opinion is that at the end of the session you should write an address to the citizens of N^{o}. C^{a}. Showing the manifest *ignorance* of the Legislature in instructing you to do that which was *impossible* to be done, The gross absurdity of "expunging a *record*" when *no record* is kept. *"Record"* is a *Judicial* & not a legislative term. *"Journal"* is the *constitutional* term used, & which by the constitution is *imperitively demanded* to be *kept*— then how can you violate y^{r}. Oath by voting to expunge part of the Journal already published & upon which the *"proceeding"* alluded to, had been entered. I bearly give this hint that you may improve upon it if you should write—

I am too feeble to write present me kindly to Calhoun Poindexter Preston Tyler & any other friend who thinks of me

I am truly y^{r}- Friend
Sam P. Carson

Honbl
W P Mangum)

[Addressed:]
Honb^{l} W. P. Mangum
U S Senate
Washington City
D C

WPM-LC

Will. A. Graham to Willie P. Mangum

RALEIGH Jan[y]. 6th 1834 [1835][13]

My Dear Sir.

I had the pleasure to receive your last letter several days since,[14] and am glad that you have determined, not to succumb to the party dictations here As far as I am able to collect the wishes of our friends in the Legislature, they desire at all events that you should retain your place untill after the August elections, when perhaps it will be indicated whether the State is irrecoverably lost. I have talked particularly on this subject with Major Beard[15] who heartily approves that course. After that, the conflict between personal comfort & ease, on the one hand & constitutional duty on the other, if the decision be adverse, will become more serious—Gov. Branch & Mr Craige[16] of Rowan, whom I consulted, two or three weeks ago, thought, that a resignation after the adjournment of the Legislature would be preferable,—The former however did not speak decisively, and the latter, I think, will not adhere to that opinion—The dominant party have been silent on the subject since the passage of the resolutions, and if not ashamed of them. They, that is some of the leaders at least, are so disconcerted by subsequent events that, I believe, they would be willing to depart in peace—You have no doubt observed in the papers that the office of Att[o]. Gen[l]. has been vacated in the Commons by a considerable majority, many of us, myself among the number voting against it—This produced a resignation, & the office has been filled by J. R. J. Daniel Esq—Rumour here says, that the chieftains were invited to a caucus, to make a nomination. This gentleman being one, called in a sprinkle of the "rank & file," and upon a ballott received 36 votes. W. H. H.[17] 13. Bragg[18] 3.— Thus the party was bound by its own Laws to his support. And altho' there has been a good deal of under talk as to his imcompetency, they voted for him in full strength. Resolutions declaratory of the

[13]This letter refers to men in the legislature who were not there in January, 1834. It should, therefore, have been dated 1835.

[14]See above, II, 260.

[15]John Beard, Jr.

[16]John Branch and Burton Craige.

[17]Will H. Haywood.

[18]John Bragg.

opinion of the Genl. assembly relative to the public domain,[19] passed the commons on yesterday by a vote of 82 to 39. They declare that any act of Congress giving the lands to the new states, or reducing the minimum price, would be improper & unjust—and that, as the public debt is paid, there should be a distribution of Lands or their proceeds among the states, according to their shares in expenditure for the Union, or at least in proportion to their Federal population—In the Senate to-day they were laid on the table—Shipp[20] has given notice, that he will call them up, every day untill the end of the Session—the majority in the commons is so triumphant, that it matters not much, what may be done in the other house—They maneuvred & drilled desperately but all to no purpose—On saturday there were divers motions to lay on the table—when these failed adjournments were moved to hold private meetings—which at a late hour succeeded—On Monday various amendments were offered, on which the veto message, was distinctly condemned as you will see by the papers, and although there were but. small majorities, against the amendments, & motions to lay on the table, & many dodgings out of the house to avoid these questions, when the vote on the resolutions as originally introduced was taken the result was as stated above—they were exceedingly relieved by hearing of the action of the Senate today—The convention Bill has become a Law[21]—The details I have not space to give you—By the bye, this is another reason why your determination should be sustained, as it is a Legislative admission, that the people have not been heretofore fairly (& truly) represented in the Legislature. I regret to hear of the distraction among the opposition at Washington. Tho' less so here, it is desperately in want of some distinct line of action, which no body seems to have the wisdom or the courage to point out

[19]In the session of 1832-1833, Clay passed through Congress a bill to distribute among the states according to population the proceeds from the sale of public lands. This was to continue for five years and the new states were to have an advantage of 12½ per cent. The North Carolina Congressmen disliked the clause which favored the new states. In his message to the state legislature Governor Swain recommended memorializing Congress to pass a law for distribution which would treat the old and new states equally. Such a resolution passed the House of Commons, but the East defeated it in the senate. After December, 1834, distribution became a political issue. The Whigs consistently supported it as a means of obtaining revenue for education and internal improvements. The Democrats held with Jackson that distribution would be unconstitutional. Pegg, "Whig Party in N. C.," 20-22.

[20]Bartlett Shipp.

[21]For more than two decades the western part of the state had worked for a revision of the state constitution. In 1833 in an extra legal referendum, the people in several counties voted 22,971 to 817 for a revision. Throughout 1834 agitation continued. As a result of the pressure the legislature voted 66 to 62 in the House of Commons and 31 to 30 in the senate to submit the question of "convention" or "no convention" to the people at the next election. In the ensuing election the popular vote was 27,550 for and 21,694 against a convention. The convention met June 4, 1835, with the Whigs in control. Several significant changes which gave the west more control were made. Pegg, "Whig Party in N. C.," 28-34.

—all admit that something must be done—but what: or how: is the desideratum—Without a more intrepid & efficient press, nothing, I am convinced, can be accomplished—Maj. Beard, has made overtures to purchase a part of the Star office, but failed—The session will last a few days longer, perhaps untill the end of the week. I have spoken to several gentlemen, of your desire to be distinctly informed of the state of opinion among your friends in the Legislature—and they have promised to write you—Gov. Branch obtained leave of absence, & left for Florida about ten days ago—Whether he has written you or not I don't know—he proposed to do so—The question has been somewhat mooted here, whether in the event of a vacancy, the Gov. can appoint without convening the council—I think Gov. Swain inclines to exercise the power alone—as it is derived under the Federal constitution which speaks only of "the Executive" of the state—I hope you will prevail on the other members of the senate who are threatened with proscription to stand firm, at least untill the end of the present session. and I think I can assure you that your Friends in this state will be true to the bitter end—

With sentiments of high regard
I am D^r. Sir
Your Friend & Servt.
WILL A. GRAHAM

Hon. W. P. Mangum

WPM-LC

R. H. Alexander to Willie P. Mangum

RALEIGH—Jany. 6th 1834. [1835][22]

My Dear Sir,

I wrote you a letter in the early part of the Session—which you were so kind as to answer.—I have since then shown your letters to Mr Graham and have thought—much upon—the matters about which you wrote—me— and other gentlemen connected with us—in opposition—to this most corrupt [a]dministration—and have come—to the most positive conclusion in connection with my other friends—that you ought not to resign—

[22]The date of this letter should be 1835.

We have crushed the Attorney General—and Haywood is below par—which is proved—by Jack Daniels of Halifax—getting in a caucus which they held 36 votes—for Att. Gen. when he got but 13—

He has prejudiced the East against him—by going for a Convention—and has not acquired the confidence of the West.

The party cannot get along with such leaders—they have but little standing with the great body of the people of this State.

The inevitable result of things—will make—Van Buren their Candidate—and it would seem—to any person—that it—would require Herculean exertion—to make—him popular enough to get the vote of this State.

The party will sink—in this attempt—they will be *pleased*—to take him as their candidate.

We shall adjourn in a few days—

Yours truly,
R. H. ALEXANDER.

[Addressed:]
Willie P. Mangum Esq.,
Member of the Senate,
Washington City.

WPM-LC

James D. Wood[23] *to Willie P. Mangum*

FARMVILLE PRINCE EDWARD VIRGINIA
7th. January 1835

Dear Sir

Presuming on a slight acquaintance some years ago, in Granville N. Carolina: I take the liberty to ask of you, if perfectly Convenient, to send me when printed, the pamphlet containing the report of the Senate Committee on the Bank of the United States with the accompanying documents, also the report and documents of the Senates Committee on the Post Office affairs: I should have applied to the representative from this district; but differing as I do with him I cannot bring myself to ask favors of him— these documents may be of service at the ap-

[23]A planter who lived at "Poplar Hill" near Farmville. He was a graduate and trustee of Hampden-Sidney College and the treasurer of the Board of the Union Theological Seminary. *Va. Magazine of History*, VI, 184, 291; VII, 38.

proaching elections—The Van Buren party are making death like struggles to defeat Mr. Leigh—but the truth is that in several of the Counties I might say many, where a Majority has instructed; since the meeting of the Legislature when the instructions were handed in, the members have handed them over to their friends and with but moderate exertions accompanied with a true statement of the case, majorities have been got for the other side? this County is One instance—I trust in God that every friend to his Country will be firm: I feel a perfect conviction the current is beginning to run the other way, and that our Spring Elections will be greatly changed in consequence of these celebrated infamous instructions—

Very Respy Sir
Remain Yr mst obt—
JAMES D. WOOD

Thro mistake I commenced
this letter on the wrong page
which please excuse
[Addressed:]
The Hon'ble
Wiley P. Mangum
U. S. Senate
Washington City

Mail)

WPM-LC

John H. K. Burgwyn[24] *to Willie P. Mangum*

NEWBERN Jany 7th 1835.

Honble. W. P. Mangum
Dear Sir.

I take the liberty of asking your aid & influence in the support of a bill reported I believe by the Military Committee in H of R for the relief of Mrs. C. E. Clitherall widow of late Doctr. G. C. Clitherall of U.S.A. the claim I believe is perfectly just & fair, & most of the facts set forth in the Memorial are known to myself personally, as I then resided at Wilmington & was often at his station at Fort Johnson—the Bill I understood was reported last Session & passed two readings—

[24]John H. K. Burgwyn, Nash's nephew, attended West Point from 1826 to 1830. Later he was killed in the Mexican War. Cullum, *Biog. Reg. of Officers of U. S. Milt. Acad.*, I, 461.

I perceive a very elaborate & masterly report, has been made to the Senate by the Committee appointed to examine into the affairs of the Bank, should the same be printed & it be convenient to you to forward me a copy, you would oblige me—it is to be hoped yet that some project will be adopted, which will give us either a continuance of that Institution, or something similar in its place. I do not see how the Commercial Interest of the Country can do without it to say nothing of the fiscal concerns of the Government—

Your friends here are very anxious to know how you will receive the Instructions sent you by our loggerheads at Raleigh—they very much hope you will not resign, & entertain no idea you will follow them they do not appear the sentiments of a majority of the State—besides the sentiment seems generally entertained, that a Senator elected for six years is bound unless prevented by physical incapability or domestic causes to remain to his post during that time & I certainly believe you would offend more, in resigning, & would only gratify & not propitiate, those who wish you to do so. We feel a little anxious as to our situation with France—as to War it seems out of the question. We have all to loose & can gain nothing, not even honour for with her immense force & already prepared, we must suffer terribly in the conflict—We have hardly the means of defence, much less of attack, at our late constructed fort at Beaufort, Fort Macon, we have not even a howitzer, or a ball, or a keg of powder.

Excuse my engrossing your time, so much more profitably occupied, but believe me with respect & esteem dear Sir

Your faithful obedient
Servant
J. BERGWYN

[Addressed:]
Honble.
W. P. Mangum.

WPM-LC

Wm. Albright[25] *to Willie P. Mangum*

SANDY GROVE N. C. 8th January 1835

My Dear
Sir You have no doubt ere this time Seen the Resolutions

[25]William Albright, 1791-1856, was from Orange County, although he spent a part of his boyhood in the eastern part of the state. He was a farmer and merchant in what is today Alamance County. A religious person, he organized the first temperance society in North Carolina. S. W. Stockard, *The History of Alamance*, Raleigh, 1900, p. 110.

passed by our Legislature. instructing you to do Certain things and matters that they know you nor any Other Man of Honorable feelings could do, you know Sir what was their intention, it was to put the party screws to you, they hope to Irritate your feelings by trying to make it appear that you MisRepresent the wishes of the people of North Carolina, & that you will then Resign your office & come home & give up the field But Sir I for one hope you will not condescend to gratify their wishes in that Respect, you was Constitutionally Elected for six years, and you are not accountable to any set of Political Demagogs you are only accountable to your God & to the honest yoeman of the Country, and I do believe they will Sustain you in the Course you are pursuing, I have mixt a goodeal with the common People in this vicinity & have heard many of them Express their selves & have not heard. one Complain of your Course, Except, those that are looking up [torn] party for promotion, on 2d— day of this insts [torn] was at Andrew Albrights Esq. in Orange [torn] found a letter on his Counte[torn] from Col. A [torn][26] Giving a history of the proceed[ings] of the legislature on those Resolutions, wherein he went to pronounce all opposed to them to be Federalists. & C. I Read the letter & Gave some Explanations to the people (and there were Many present) and they all seamed to be pleased with your Course & denounced the Cols— doctrine, I hope therefore you will not be Run off the field. indeed Sir I think you are in duty bound to your friends & to your Country, to Stand to your post, the country might Suffer much for want of your Services. I hope Sir you will not take this amis, I Give you this information in order that you may be prepared to act, I know it is hoped. by the party that you will Resign. If you have time to drop me a line I would like to have your opinion on this matter. Yours Respectfully

WM. ALBRIGHT

P. S. Please accept my thanks for the document you sent me from the post office Committee

W A

[Addressed:]
Hon. Wiley P. Mangum
Washington City
D. C.

[26]The manuscript is torn, but there is enough to indicate that the first letter of the man's name is "A." It was probably Joseph Allison, who was in the legislature from Orange County at this time. He was a strong Jackson man.

WPM-LC

Michael Holt to Willie P. Mangum

HOLTS STORE January 11th 1835

Dear Sir

Yours of the 19 ultimo is duly recd. and the contents before me, I am well pleased with your determination—Straight forward, *fearless*, and *unappalled*—This is the language of an american of the first order, I am doubly pleased sir with your course, altho our members from Orange in the Legislature have not treated you with the respect due you as a County man

It is about their speed in principals and they will have their day—Their time will end and I hope to see the day that we shall be represented by men of principal and not a partie—I want men to keep out of the Kitchen—A Majority of N. Carolina is with you and your course in Congress—Orange the largest county in the State and a large Majority of Orange is on your side—Squire Trolonger[27] says he voted for our present Members in the Legislature to make laws, and not to decide upon your course in Congress—we have at this time and for a week past a very severe cold spell of weather—I will conclude by saying that you have many warm friends in the upper end of Orange—

With great esteem yos

MICHl HOLT

Honble W. P. Mangum

[Addressed:]

Honble Wiley P. Mangum

Washington City

Member of Congress U. S.

[27]For many years John Trolinger was chairman of the board of education of Orange County until Alamance County was formed and then he was chairman of the board in that county. He helped build the High Falls Manufacturing Company, a textile mill, and a part of the North Carolina Railroad. S. W. Stockard, *The History of Alamance County*, 144-145.

Two letter seals. The one with the motto "AUDACES FORTUNA ADJUVAT" is in the possession of Mangum Weeks, Alexandria, Va., and the one with the motto "SPERO DUM SPIRO" is in the possession of Mangum Turner, Winston-Salem, N. C.

WPM-LC

James Somervell[28] *to Willie P. Mangum*

WARRENTON, N. C. Jany. 14, 1835.

Dear Sir,

I approve of Mr. Clay's Report[29] upon the Relations between France & The United States *in toto.* It would perhaps have been desirable, at the present juncture, if possible to have passed over Mr. Rives entirely—but I do not perceive how this could have been done—I think he has been passed over very lightly.

I am anxious to know your course in relation to your Instructions from the State Legislature. I am most anxious that you should be presented to the State of North Carolina, as what I told you some years ago you were without knowing it, a man of the people & for the people—of the State & for the State.

An old fashioned Republican myself, or what I consider as synonymous, a Nullificationist, I should feel at no loss as to my course were I in your situation. I should do as my State told me to do. I sincerely believe that upon this matter the Legislature has spoken the voice of the State. Nay more I believe that the State Legislature represents upon all similar occasions the sovereignty of The State. Otherwise in great emergencies That sovereignty would be entirely unrepresented. I would not desert my post as Mr. Rives did.

It is unnecesary for me to say to you that I approve of your vote upon the condemned Resolutions of the U. S. Senate, most cordially. But our State thinks differently & she has a right to her own way in the business. She is our Mother & our Ruler & we ought to obey her. Keep her Flag flying at the mast head & sink or swim with her—or leave her!!

For this liberty which is not taken with you in public or intended to inveigle you into a private correspondence, the obliga-

---

[28]James Somervell, of Warrenton, was a student at the state university in 1798 and from 1825 to 1827 a trustee of the Warrenton Female Academy. He operated a ferry across Roanoke River near Warrenton. Grant, *Alumni Hist. of U. N. C., 581; Coon* (ed.), *N. C. Schools and Academies*, 620, 624.

[29]In 1831-1832 William C. Rives made a treaty with France by which France agreed to pay 25,000,000 francs in reparations for spoliations which grew out of the Napoleonic wars. For three years after the treaty was ratified France made no payments. Jackson, therefore, asked Congres for the authority to make reprisals on French property. This made the French problem the most serious one of the 1834-1835 session. As chairman of the Senate Foreign Relations Committee, which included King, of Georgia, Sprague, Tallmadge, and Mangum, on January 6, 1835, Clay presented a conciliatory report agreeing with Jackson on the justice of his claim but insisting that all peaceful means should be used first. The report concluded by declaring it was inexpedient to grant the authority requested by Jackson. Neither party of the Senate wanted to push the issue, and so they agreed to the resolution with the added clause that it was " 'inexpedient at present.' " Van Deusen, *The Life of Henry Clay*, 290-292.

tions I feel under to your father for acts of kindness in my youth & a desire to see you ever above all calumny & misfortune are the apology

of most respectfully
Yours
JAMES SOMERVELL

Hon. W. P. Mangum
[Addressed:]
Washington D. C.

WPM-LC

Anne Royall[30] *to Willie P. Mangum*

WASHINGTON D. C. Jany 16th 1835

Hon W. P. Mangum
Respected Sir

When I had the pleasure to see you yesterday in the Capitol I was indeavoring to ascertain whether the committee had power to procure my papers or whether a motion must be made in Senate when the *assistant* clerk informed me a copy *only* & not the *original* papers could be procured upon application to the Secretary Woodberry to ascertain the fact he sent me the inclosed

Will you have the kindness sir to hand the paper to Hon J. Tyler & pray him to apply to the committee—for an order (Hon. G. Moor is chairman) or ask him—or do it yourself (if you will be so good) to make a motion to the Senate to have them forth coming—

My anxiety on this subject I dare not conceal from my friends is owing to no motive but my inability to get on with my paper till next session of Congress!!! even this moment I received a *third* letter of complaint from Newnan Geo where I have 8 subscribers complaining they have not had any of my papers Sins the 8th of November !!! though I have sent two files & by various routs* my friends will see what this is done for & this being the very time my paper is most wanting I hope they will make some arrangement that the paper shall go on it has been partly supported by Gentlemen in this place would you know them? but keep dark Gen[s] Jessup[31]—Gibson[32] Gratiott & many of the clerks

[30]See above, II, 126n.

[31]General Thomas S. Jesup, who was with Jackson in the First Seminole War. *D.A.B.*, X, 61-62.

[32]Probably Colonel George Gibson, who was with Jackson in the First Seminole War and who later became the Commissary General in Washington. Bassett (ed.), *Cor. of Jackson*, II, 381, 411, 445; III, 120; *Congressional Directory for the Third Session of the Twenty-seventh Congress of the United States of America*, Washington, 1942, 51.

who go with us that is for their country—Take care of them I can not say any thing positive of Gen[l] McC[33]

I have the honor to be your grateful & devoted friend

ANNE ROYALL

N B Can nothing be done this session to relieve us from the cruel oppression of the Post office Department?- What is Senator Ewing about please intice him to come out boldly I will sustain him with proof enough to to prostrait the whole possee—

Hon W. P. Mangum

---

*shall publish the letter [This is Anne Royall's notation]

WPM-LC

Alexander Greer[34] to Willie P. Mangum

WHITE HALL P. O. Jan[y]. 16th 1835

Honb[l], Willie P. Mangum.

Dr Sir

Excuse the freedom of addressing a few lines to you, by one of whom you have no personal knowledge. Nothing but an anxious desire to obtain information on subjects of vital importance to every free and indipendant minde to every bossom, in which the love of country prevails over a blinde devotion to men and party;—could have induced him who now addresses you, thus to intrude upon your honor, you will perhaps say, why not apply to your representative, Sir if myself and others in this section of our country, cannot claim an intrest in you as our representative permit me to say we are unrepresented, For though the Eleventh Congressional district of North Carolina has a representative in the other house, yet we canont acknowledge him as our representative, though bound by his acts, and as you must be well acquainted with the political character and course of the Hon[b]. W. H. C.[35]—you can easily appreciate the character of the information he feels himself boud to furnish his constituents with. We here from the public prints discover that there is mutch valuable information in the shape of committee reports. &.C which it seems from the action of Congress upon them are intended to be spread before the people for their information such as the report of the Senates committe on

---

[33]Possibly Maj. Gen. Alexander Macomb, commanding general of United States Army, *D. A. B.*, XII, 155-157.

[34]He was an active Whig from Mecklenburg County. In 1835-1836 he served on the State Whig Vigilance Committee. *Raleigh Register*, Dec. 22, 1835; Jan. 12, 1836.

[35]Henry W. Connor.

foreign relations or relations with France. Post office, - - United States Bank, Sales. of public lands, &c—&c—&c. and gener[ally] such information as will enable us rightley to appreciate the course of those who rule over us, and enable us to answer those who unreasonably require us, to bow the knee to the man or to a name and submit our necks to the collar. without knowing why. or wherefore. in fine any information which your superior understanding and experience will think calculated to promote the best interest of our beloved country.— —

Dr Sir you will please excuse any improperity in the foregoing either in matter or manner an earnest desire for information is the only excuse I can plead for thus troubling you, I have given you a few hints of what sort of political information we stand in need of here Dr Sir it is earnestly hoped by not a few in this section that you will not permit yourself to be driven from the post you so honourably occupy, by the mad folly of a parcel of man worshipers who lately figured at Raleigh. It is confidently believed the country will sustain you and your worthy coleagues who have thrown themselves into the breach to defend the constitution against a band of ruthless ruffins and deluded man worshipers, who like the daughters of the horse Leech, are ever crying give, give, and are never satisfyed or say they have enough.—

Should you be so indulgent as to remember your humble servant, below is my address.

You will please extend your charity an indulgence to the many imperfections of the foregoing scrall.

Believe me Dr Sir with mutch respect and

Esteem your Humb[l] servt—

ALEX[r]. GREER

Alexander Greer
White Hall P. O.
Mecklinburg
No. Ca.

Honb[l]. John Q. Adams Eulogy on Layfyette

[Addressed:]

Honb[l]. Willie P. Mangum
Washington City
District of Columbia

pr mail (

[Endorsed:] Answered 22 Jan 1835

WPM-LC

John Branch to Willie P. Mangum

ENFIELD Jany 18th 1835

My Dear Sir,

I received yours of the 8th Ins. a week ago and can assure you that I highly aprpeciate the kind feelings which dictated it. I forthwith set about to write out my speech[36] on the infamous resolutions adopted by our Legislature In truth I had been urged to do so by so many of my best friends that I felt it to be my duty to comply with their wishes. Before I commenced I was apprehensive that the public expectations would be greatly disappointed I however begin now to entertain a different opinion. You will pardon me for the *vanity* of this expression. I ought rather to have said that the facts and the internal evidence which they bear of their *incontrovertible* character, cannot fail to be interesting to those who are in search of truth. It will be found to contain some facts which are entirely new to the public and presented in a way that cannot fail to draw down upon me the bitterest denunciation of those *in power*. I think you will be satisfied My only regret is that I have no literary friend near to me to consult with My positions are taken with great caution and my facts cannot be disturbed. I fear that there will be too much of it, and yet I cant see how any part of it can be well omited. I wish Edward's speech[37] to precede it—to which it is an answer. He will I think not hazard the publication of his speech In a few days I will have it copied and sent either to Halifax Town or to Raleigh— It may be two or three weeks before it is presented to the public.

In relation to the next Presidential election, I scarcely know what to say—I have strong political objections to Judge White and yet personally I esteem him very highly I should of the two presented in your letter prefer Judge McLean. I believe that Judge White is strictly an honest and an honorable man—and that he would lose his h-[torn] sooner than he would do a *mean* act, but it does appear to be that his judgment and conscience has and does now condemn what his acts *seem* to approve I fear too that the *Kitchen cabinet* would find him kin[torn] d tolerant

[36]Branch's speech was published in the *Raleigh Register*, February 17, 1835, and the *Tarboro Free Press*, March 7, 1835.

[37]W. N. Edwards, a Jackson supporter, maintained that the right to instruct was inherent in representative government, that those with the authority to elect had the authority to instruct. His speech was published in the *Tarboro Free Press*, Feb. 28, 1835.

—to them. However we will wait for further developments and then determine—

Your friend
JNº BRANCH

[Addressed:]
Hon. Willie P. Mangum
Washington City

Enfield N. C.
20th Jany 1835

WPM-LC

Francis W. Pickens[38] *to Willie P. Mangum*

WASHINGTON
18th. Jany—1835

My Dear Sir

I take the liberty of respectfully suggesting to you the propriety of Judge White moving an amendment to the constitution, incorporating in substance this principle, Viz. that duties on imports shall in no instance (except in time of war and then to continue no longer than the termination of such war))exceed twenty per. cent. *ad valorem*—valuation to be made in refference to the ports whence imported. This amendment to take effect after the termination of the "compromise bill." This movement whether successful or not would place the Judge in a position to command support in *certain quarters* upon perhaps higher grounds than being the "least of evils."

Looking at things practically, I make this suggestion for the purest and most honourable purposes.

I fear, in any event, the fate of the republic is already fixed. Under the great increase that will annually take place in our importations, the revenue will be nearly the same that it has been hereterfore. The public debt being paid, will leave a large surplus to be disposed of. Twelve millions will be collected in New York alone. A new system will spring up out of this state of things, which will in effect be to save disbursements from the general appropriations, that so much more may be left to be distributed by a cabal amongsts deposit banks, and which will be to New York the most profitable investment. This system will furnish to her the basis of at least $36,000,000 of banking capital. The machinery that is to control the disposition of

[38]Pickens, of South Carolina, was in the House of Representatives from 1834 to 1843.

the revenues hereafter, will have the power to impregnate [?] at least $45,000,000 of capital annually. This will not only produce effects upon the banks that will receive the revenues, but will check and to some extent render other institutions dependent He who knows that, in modern times, banks are the springs from whence issue the fountains that vivify and refresh all the walks and grades of civalized society, will at once perceive the tremendous but secret power they exercise over the destinies of a commercial people. With a league of banking institutions connected from Portsmouth to New orleans, receiving somewhat systematic impulse from one common source, and all aided by and in concert with 40,000 office holders in the first degree and then 40,000 more again dependent upon them, making at least 80,000—with all this you are not to wander when I say, that I fear the fate of the confederacy is already fixed, for far at least as concerns receiving a ruler every four years. The Roman people in their degeneracy receive their emperors from the hands of a military band, and I fear we are to receive ours from a band of office holders and money-changers.

If however an *honest* enlightened and *firm* man can be placed in such an *independent* position as can command the *consistent* support of the honourable and patriotic, we can make a vigerous attempt to rescue the country, and if we fail we can at least preserve and sustain our *character,* and *principles.* I have thrown out then, brief views to you confidentially, and *without committting* myself until I see the *Future*—

Yours very truly & sincerely

F. W. PICKENS

WPM-LC

Burton Craige to Willie P. Mangum

SALISBURY Jan. 21st. 1835:

My Dear Sir:

I recd. yours at Raleigh enclosing one from Mr. Green,[39] and should have acknowledged it earlier but for the bustle, haste & confusion consequent upon an adjournment. Mr. Green may do some thing, nay, much in the way proposed, and any thing which I can do to further his designs, of course will be cheerfully done.

---

[39]See above, II, 255, 259.

But the formation of State-rights associations in the several counties, by whom papers disseminating corrupt doctrines should be taken, & circulated among our people would effect more, but in the absence of such societies Mr. Greens plan may do.

With regard to the properity or impropriety of your resigning, about which you wished to know the opinions of your friends, I will give you mine, & though with diffidence I will give them with the candour with which they were asked. I do not believe that you were instructed by the majority of the people of the State I believe that Swains. calculation is correct, but still you were instructed by a majority of the Legislature. Public opinion has in the Senate at least, sanctioned their right to give such instructions, and whatever opinions we may entertain, about it ourselves, when a legislature is not elected with a reference to some *cure,* to use a live phrase, I think the Senator is bound to respect that opinion, and to resign. But admitting that this view is wrong would it not be good policy for you to resign? Could you not effect more among the people *here* by resigning, & making up an issue next summer with the last Legislature, than by holding on?

I think you could. I think, if you were to resign, after the 4th. March, or so soon *before it,* that the Gov. & Council could not appoint a successor in time for this session of Congress, that Swain would not convene the council; that consequently the next Legislature would have to elect; and that *you* could by making up an issue next summer, change the character of the Legislature, & be re-elected by as large a majority, as were against you in the last Legislature.

These are my opinions candidly though hastily expressed, I give them with great defference to the opinions of others, who may differ with me.

My friend Dr. Ashbel Smith[40] of this place, who ranks second to no man in N. C. as a man of science & learning is anixous to be appointed one of the board of visitors to West Point. If the application meets with your approbation, I would esteem it a personal favor, if you would use your exertions to have him ap-

[40]A native of Connecticut and a graduate of Yale University, Dr. Ashbel Smith moved to Salisbury where he first taught and then practiced medicine. In the 1830's he became interested in politics and for a short time edited the *Western Carolinian.* In 1837 he moved to Texas, where he became an important citizen. There he held numerous state offices and contributed much to the diplomatic, educational, and medical development of that state. In 1848 he became a member of the Board of Visitors of the West Point institution. *D. A. B.*, XVII, 239.

pointed, Genl. Cook[41] of this county is also I understand, an aplicantion for the appointment. As between these *two*, as far as qualifications go, there is no comparison. Smith is a man of mind and learning; Cook is not—

I have the honour to be
Very respectfully,
Your friend & ob^t^. St.
BURTON CRAIGE

[Addressed:]
Hon. Willie P. Mangum
Washington
D. C.

Salisbury N C
Jany 22

WPM-LC

Sydney Smith[42] to Willie P. Mangum

CHAPEL HILL January 22nd, 1835

To the Honorable Willie P. Mangum
Dear Sir

Not having the pleasure of any acquaintance with you, you may suppose me very impudent in asking any request of you I hope that you will pardon me on my request I have to make of you, I desire if it should be agreeable to your inclination, for you to transmit me a copy of Mr Adams oration on the character of La Fayette. It was spoken of in the papers in very high terms I am exceedingly desirous of obtaining it, esteeming it as well worth the attention of every American, The oration was delivered by so distinguished a man and an a person who's name is so dear to every patriot, Desirous that you may succeed in defending the Constitution of the U States from the encroachments of a tyrant and that after you have retired from the confusion of political life you may live in the grateful hearts of your countrymen I remain your humble servant

SYDNEY SMITH.

[Addressed:]
Hon. Willie P. Mangum,
United States Senate,
Washington,
Mail) D. C.

---

[41]General James Cook died in 1846. *Carolina Watchman*, Sept. 4, 1846.

[42]A native of Orange County, Sydney Smth became a lawyer who was admitted to practice before the Supreme Court of the state in 1839. In 1844 he represented Orange County at the Whig Congressional District meeting. He served in the legislature from 1846 to 1847. *Hillsborough Recorder*, Jan. 7, 1840; March 14, 1844; *N. C. Manual*, 741.

WPM-LC

John H. Brownrigg to Willie P. Mangum

CHOWAN. Co N C. 24.th Jan 1835.

Hon. Willie P. Mangum,
Sir—

At a meeting of a portion of the citizens of Chowan Co N. C held in the Middle district on Saturday 24th Inst. on motion of Capt. Collen Bunch—Dr. John H. Brownrigg was called to the chair and John E. Spencer appointed Secretary.

The meeting being duly organized the following preamble and resolutions were submitted and adopted *Ne^{m} Con.*

Whereas—The General Assembly of the State of N Carolina at their Session of 1834 and 35. have taken it upon themselves to pass certain resolutions instructing Wylie P. Mangum Senator in Congress from this State, to vote for the expunging from the records of the Senate of the U States the resolution declaring "that the President in his late executive proceedings in relation to the public revenue had assumed upon himself authority and power not conferred by the laws and constitution, but in derogation of both" Be it therefore resolved. That we a portion of the citizens of Chowan Co. highly approve the course hitherto pursued by Senator Mangum, and do request him to pay no regard to the directions given by the late General Assembly of the State of N. Carolina relative to the aforementioned vote—

Resolved That we do highly disapprove of said proceedings on the part of the Assembly and do pledge ourselves not to support for any office whatever, any member of that body who lent his aid in the passage of the resolutions.

Resolved That a copy of the above resolutions be forwarded to Senators Mangum and Brown of N. C. expressing to the former our approval and to the latter our entire disapproval of their respective courses—

Resolved. That the above resolutions be Signed by the Chairman and Secretary and Sent to the Edenton Gazette and U. S. Telegraph for publication—

Resolved That the thanks of the meeting be tendered to the Chairman and Secretary for their Services on this occasion—

On motion the meeting adjourned—

Jn. E. Spencer, Sec. Jno. H. Brownrigg, Chr.

In compliance with the above Resolutions we do hereby transmit you a copy and would so far trespass upon your time as to request an acknowledgement of its safe arrival.

J. H. B.
J. E. S.

[Addressed:]
Hon. Wylie P. Mangum,
Washington City,
D. C.
[Postmarked:]
Hertford No Ca.
Jan 28th

WPM-LC

Paul C. Cameron[43] *to Willie P. Mangum*

[1835]
Saturday morn:

My dear sir/.

I am greatly disappointed, in not being able to attend a meeting of the people at Red Mountain to day—: and I am not a little distressed at the cause which prevents me—! I fear that we have a case of murder on our plantation—one of the slaves has received I think a death wound from his overseer—I have no idea that he can live an hour—.

Permit me to say that should I have attended the meeting, my object was to place you and Judge Ruffin before the people as delegates to Convention—.[44] If however you, think it imprudent to come before the people at this time—and will not consent that your name shall be given to the nomination; I can but hope that you will upon this occassion sustain the claims of our friend Judge Nash.— He is every way worthy of the confidence of the people of Orange—: You may make any use of my name as a committee man or any thing else you please

Excuse my hasty note.
Your friend
P. C. CAMERON

---

[43]He was the son of Duncan Cameron and, in his youth, a pupil of Mangum. See Ashe *Biog. Hist. of N. C.*, III, 48.

[44]Dr. James S. Smith and William Montgomery were the Orange County delegates to the Constitutional Convention of 1835.

WPM-LC

Henry W. Connor[45] *to John Long*[46]

WASHINGTON CITY 24th Jany 1835.

Dr Sir.

Yours of 15th Inst has been recd. and at your request I have with great pleasure, had your account with the P. O. Dept. settled—as you will see by the letter of O. B. Brown,[47] inclosing drafts to the amt. addressed & franked to you by me—I had hoped they would have sent your pay, in some more convenient form—They refuse to pay you from returning by Troys Store, as they did not order the Sircuit.—Be assured My Dr Sir, the difference existing between us in relation to our political views has not, for one moment, interfered, with my personal kind feelings.—they are the same, now that, they were, when we were, associated in public life & pulling together. True, I regret, this difference of opinion, and that we are not, now pulling in the same cause in politics—doubtless we both, believe we are acting, honestly & conscienciously.

We have nothing new here—that you have not seen the panic, gotten up, for the people last year,—has passed by without injury—& this year has taken hold of the politicians I mean in Congress—all has been silent not a word of ruin & distress.—It is rumoured that the Senate will reject Tawny tomorrow.—who is before them for the Supreme Ct. bench, they have beheaded one or two of less note, by way of begining

I will at all times be happy to hear from you.

In haste
Yours most respectfully
HENRY W CONNOR

[Addressed:]
John Long Esq.
Oak Hill
Long's Mills P. O.
Randolph Cty.
N. C.

[45]See above, I, 196n.
[46]Long was a National Republican before he became a Whig.
[47]A Jacksonian in the Post Office Department at Washington, D. C.

WPM-LC

J. S. Smith[48] *to Willie P. Mangum*

HILLSBOROUGH Jany 26th 1835

Dr Sir

Permit me to inquire of you whether you have thought of attending to the little remitance to New York which you promised me when I saw you last that you would make for me.—Not having heard from Lawrence & Keese on this subject I think it probable you have forgotten or neglected it—

I would beg leave respectfully to draw your attention to it as it is a matter of some importance to me. I have promised payt. in this way to that house and some considerable time has elapsed since & I fear that they will consider me as acting in bad faith towards them from the neglect to comply—You will very much oblige me by attending to it immediately—You will recollect that I requested you to remit two Hundred and I will either a draft to Faddis[49] for one Hundred or I will pay it here to your order.

I have nothing new here to communicate to you that can be new to you. The *Collor* men think you should resign—the inteligent part of the people think you should pay not respect to the instructions—1st because the opinion is that the majority of the people are on your side—Secondly because the legislature has no control over you in the matter—3ly Because the legislature requires of you to do that which you cannot do with[out] violating your oath. It is then the hope and wish of your friends that you will retain your place—

I should like to hear from you on the subject of the next Presidential Election—Who will be likely to be placed on the tick. as the whig candidate? Can the whole opposition be united on one candidate—I can vouch for Clay & Calhoun I think But will Mr. Webster come in to our Southern measures? We feel much interest on this subject and hope that a spirit of concession and compromise will characterize the great whig party—All selfish & sectional interest and views should in this case be sacrificed on the alter of public good—For myself I feel disposed to surrender all partialities and preferences on this occasion as I think the same spirit pervades our Ranks in this part of the Country generally—

[48]See above, I, 8n.

[49]Thomas J. Faddis. See above, I, 398n.

Col William Horner has lost his wife with the prevailing influenza. Your other friends I think so far as I know are all well—

I am Dr Sir
Respectfully yours &c.

Hon Willie P Mangum J. S. SMITH

[Addressed:]

Hon. Willie P. Mangum
U. S. Senate
Washington City.

WPM-LC

Stephen K. Sneed[50] *to Willie P. Mangum*

OXFORD January 28th AD 1835.

My old Friend

Since the tremendous storm has subsided, I have concluded to write you a short letter. I recd. your message by Revd C McIver[51] relative to your determination as to the course you intended to pursue. I was not surprised Sir I felt perfectly satisfied that you had more political integrity, than to submit to the dictation of such a miserable Jacksonian faction as the majority in our legislature. I have no doubt but what you will be sustained by the people of No C. The little Dutchman I think is done over here; there is joy in this section of country in regard to Judge Whites nomination.[52] I am sorry that I cant get my man, Clay, but am willing to submit, if we can beat the magician. I should be very glad to hear from you and that often; I am now much engaged in making arrangements for my removal to the far West. I have lately recd a letter from Walter,[53] he is doing good business for himself and me; I send this by David Laws who goes to New York for the purpose of getting employment in some mercantile establishment. I believe you are well acquainted with him; he is a young man of the most, perfectly, unexceptionable character I know of in the world. He is an excellent accountant, writes a good hand, strictly moral in his habits, good sense, and unusually attentive to his business; and withal a "Flat River boy." If you feel an entire willingness to do so; I would esteem it as a singular favor, if you would write to some of your friends and acquaintances in New York soliciting their influence in aiding him in his views. Should you write be so good as to forward your let-

---

[50]See above, I, 5n.

[51]See above, II, 44n.

[52]In December, 1834, the Tennessee legislature nominated Hugh Lawson White for President.

[53]Willie P. Mangum's youngest brother.

ters to him in N York immediately as he at present thinks it uncertain whether he will go through Washington City.

Report says, that Sandy Harris, of famous memory, intends opposing Genl Hawkins, tell the Gen[l] not to be alarmed, "all dangers is not death," he can beat the little *scoundrel even* in Granville. Your family was well the latter part of last week.

You friend Sincerely
STEP K SNEED

[Addressed:]
Hon[l]
Willie P Mangum
Washington City

WPM-LC

Thomas L. Clingman[54] to Willie P. Mangum

[HUNTSVILLE, N. C., 30 Jan., 1835]

Dear Sir

I was prevented from writing to you when in Raleigh by the shortness of my stay there. Remaining as I did but a single day, the time was wholly occupied in passing my examination for a Superior court license, and in collecting from the politicians of the place the news of the day. There were a number of lawyers attending court from different sections of the State, so that I could form a tolerably accurate idea of the feeling of the people on political topics. They seem to be very generally dissatisfied with the conduct of the last General Assembly; say that it is the most worthless that has ever met, and doubt alike the propriety of their instructions to you, and the right of the body to pass them. Almost every person that I have conversed with expressed the opinion that if proper exertions were made, and the subject fairly placed before the people, that a large majority of them would condemn the conduct of the legislature and sustain you.

This I believe is the feeling of the intelligent part of the community, but you know that the main point is to make the mass of the people acquainted with the facts and to get them excited on the subject. Your friends are rather too inactive; not because

[54]Born in Huntsville, near Asheville, North Carolina, in 1812, Thomas L. Clingman became a good friend of Mangum. Until the middle of the 1840's he was a Whig, but in 1849 he was elected as a Democratic Congressman. *D. A. B.*, IV, 220-221.

they are either lukewarm or dispirited, but because they lack a leader and are waiting for someone to begin the battle. They say that you are the person most interested in the result, and that you ought to set a good example by exerting yourself to the uttermost on your return. I have not seen a single individual who thought that you ought to resign or obey. On the contrary they all express the hope that you will stand firm. I believe that you will be stronger while you retain your position as a senator and make war upon those who have assailed you, than if you were to yield for any cause whatever. Should you on your return make a half dozen speeches at as many dinners in different parts of the State, I feel confident that you will be able to carry a majority with you. At our next court I shall endeavour to have the subject taken up.

With respect to the presidency; thoug[h] Gaston, Nash, and some other prominent m[en] are opposed to White, I think he wil[l] run well in this state. I did not kn[ow] until I entered the state that he [had] so many friends. If he can be well [supported] North Carolina will in the end, I think go for him without a division. Why [do] they not put him in the field? Please do me the favour to remember me [to] your Mess. particularly to the ladies, and [say] to them that though I am far from W[ashington] the recollections of its music and beauty [are] still green in my memory. Also [give] my respects to Gov. Poindexter and Mr. [torn] and tell them that they shall hear from me shortly. I should like to get a copy of Mr. Calhoun's report when it is made.

I have the honour to be
Your most obedient
T. L. CLINGMAN

Huntsville Jan. 30th. 1835.
The Hon. W. P. Mangum

P.S. As I came through Raleigh Gov. Swain and Mr. Graham were complaining of your silence to them.

T.L.C.

[Addressed:]
To the Hon.
W. P. Mangum
Washington City
D.C.

WPM-LC

John Martin[55] *to Lewis Williams*

WILKES COUNTY N Carolina 30th January 1835

Dear Sir' I have set down to drop you a line but I feel that I Can say little more to you than howdydoo, such is deranged state of our mails I know but little of passing events for the last two months I have seldom Received a Raleigh paper in less than two weeks and frequently longer after they are published and the washington still more eregular so that they are hardly worth a Reading— Our Members of assembly has been home nearly three weeks and I only Received the account of their Adjournment by the last mail, which was the only news of their proceedings during the session worth looking at if indeed that was, which I for one Very much doubt, they surely have accomplished less for the benefit of the State than I ever have known done at any session in my Recollection The Convention bill that they have passed I have so many objections to I had Rather they had not have passed it at all and I very much think that I shall Vote no Convention; during their session when their Ridiculus Resolution was before them instructing Judge Mangum I was urged by some of our friends to write to the Judge informing of him that it was the opinion of his friends in this part that he should pay no attention to the instructions of such an unprincipaled faction—as they were, which I should have done but for the Reason of my not being apprised of the fate of the resolutions until the Legislator had Risen, and I am heartily glad he had taken the course he has and has not given to the members of our present Legislator the optunity of geting two members in the U States Senate to miss Represent the people of N Carolina for I Cannot nor do not believe that a majority of the good people of this State will support the measures of this mad Administration if the question was farely brought before them. we have a small exebition of Jackson Vanbureanism in this part but I think it is a scarce article I know of two of Whites papers that is taken in this part of the County which I think may be taken as the test amongst newspaper Readers; I lack word to express my astonishment that any Considerable number of the members of Congress should incline for one moment to support

[55]He was a former member of the legislature from Wilkes County.

the President in his Runmad and Ruinous wish to get up a war with France for disguise it as he may his proposal is war and nothing else, who ever heard of a nation like us going to war to make money, when I saw the Recomendation in the Presidents Message I looked upon it as Idle Gasconade and the thought never entered my mind but that it would fall still born, for although I knew something about party discipline I never could believe that any man who had a free people to face would ever be led to support such a ruinous measure to gratify an old tyranical unprincipaled man, I hope yet better Councils will prevail for if we get into a war with france there is no man living Can tell where it will end, of one thing we are sure our Commerce will be swept from the face of the Ocean for all urope will prey upon us under French Commissions and instead of gaining five Millions when ever we get a peace which only God knows, when that will be, we should have a National debt of hundreds of Millions and I fear [the] last Vestage of our Libertys swept from under us, [torn] if Genl, Jackson Could live out the time we should [torn] him for our despot; but I am no Polititition, my mind for some years back has been occupied in Other Concerns but I hope the whigs will be able to stay the hand of the destroyer if not in the House of Representatives I have great Confidence in the Senate where the liberty of the people of this Country I hope Rests in Safety; I have Received several enclosures and two writen Communications from you, for which I now make my acknowledgements you should have heard from me sooner but I was Conscious that I Could not write any thing worth your trouble of reading; Genl, Duff Green is printing a work he Calls the Medical Register and Library, I Commenced takeing of it and the first numbers dwelt so much on theory I became dissatisfied and stoped it but before they stoped eight numbers Reched me and I was much better pleased with some of the latter numbers and from what I now learn it is the Cheapest and most Valuable work we Can get at the price if you will pay him ten dollars which is the price for a year I will Repay you when you Come home, I want him to send me all the back numbers beginning at No 9 and go on with the work until I wish it stoped; I will Conclude, myself and family are in tolerable health Our friends are also generally in moderate health we have something of an Influenza amongs us but I hope it will not be Very severe, I hope these will find you in good health give my Compliments to Judge Mangum & A. H. Shepherd till the latter Gentleman I have not seen any thing from him since he has been in Congress, I had almost forgotten to say howdydoo to my old friend Mr Graham[56] he has also forgoten me, Mr Clay honoured me with an enclosure last session of which I felt much gratifyed - - - -

I am Dear Sir yours with great esteem
JOHN MARTIN

The Honourable Lewis Williams
P S I have no Room to say much about President makeing, nor do I know much about it there is so many men spoken of I do not know who it is likely the whigs will settle down on but I think that there ought to be some understanding about it before you leave Washington I am willing to go for any good whig but will support any honest man that Can beat Van Burin, I want to hear from you on that subject—

J. M.

[Addressed:]
Washington City

WPM-LC

Resolutions of Fayetteville Public Meeting

[C 1835][57]

Whereas, in the present crisis of political affairs, every Freeman, is called upon to act. and whereas. the Executive Committee appointed at the late Meeting of the friends of James Seawall Esqr. hath called together this assemblage of the Free People of Fayetteville, to deliberate upon such measures, as may in their judgment, best promote the interests of this Borough and the general prosperity of the Country
Be it therefore Resolved

That the Freemen composing this Meeting cannot consent, by their influence, their example or their suffrages, to perpetuate the existance of the present party in power, neither can they

[56]James Graham.
[57]The contents of these resolutions would indicate that they were adopted in the winter or spring of 1835.

sanction any act or admit the policy of any measure, however pure the motive which produced it originating in violation of Law, and having a direct tendency to subvert the Constitution

Resolved,

That this Meeting cannot approve of the conduct of the Hon[l]. Bedford Brown one of our Senators in Congress because they have discovered that in his hands, the great interests of the country have been sacrificed to those of mere *party* consideration.

Resolved,

That we do heartily approve of the course of the Hon[l]. W P. Mangum, a Senator from this State, and that he is entitled to our confidence and support, that he has stood up the able defender of constitutional liberty manfully and boldly contending against the usurpation of power by the Executive, and resisting the principle that the will of one man, in this Republican Government shall be the supreme law of the land—

Resolved,

That our thanks are due, and are hereby tendered to the Hon[o]. Mess " Deberry, Barringer, W B. Shepard A. H. Shepperd Graham, William and Rencher, Representatives from this State, for the faithful discharge of their duty and for their bold and manful defence of the Constitution from Executive usurpation,

Resolved

That the policy pursued by James Seawell Esq[r] our Representative in the last Legislature, is highly approved by this Meeting, that his efforts though ineffectual, were well calculated to subserve the best interests of this Town; and that his devotedness to the cause of Internal Improvements together with his ardent and unremitting desire to promote the general prosperity of this place, points him out as the fittest character to represent us again

Resolved

That having confidence in the political opinions of Mr. Seawell, and beleiving that he will properly represent the views of this Meeting, and that he will give his hearty opposition to the high handed measures of the present Executive by endeavours, so far as he may have it in his power, to restore the Constitution, to its former purity—we will give him, our hearty support at the Polls .

A true copy from the Minutes
ISHAM BLAKE JR *Secretary*

WPM-LC

William A. Graham to Willie P. Mangum

HILLSBORO Feb. 4th 1835.

My dear Sir

My engagements at the Supreme Court after the adjournment of the Legislature prevented me from being much at home until within the last few days. Of course I have heard, but little of public affairs, and of the popular sentiment in regard to the Resolutions of instruction—A gentleman from the neighborhood of Mason Hall informs me, that our Senator[58] directed several letters to that office during the session, stating that it was expected, that you would & attempt to revolutionise this county upon your return, & urging them to be true to their party &c. You are doubtless apprised of the passage of the Convention Act—by our Legislature—It is believed that it will be sanctioned by the people—In speaking of delegates to be chosen from this county your name has been mentioned among others—If you have any desire of the kind, your presence here at March Court would be important—No one is yet announced, nor, so far as I know, *generally* spoken of—I have not, since my return, seen your brother, or any of your friends from the eastern section of the county—

When I left Raleigh Maj Beard had returned and was negogiating for one half of the Star office—I hope he may procure it—He would give some efficiency to the press at Raleigh, and might exercise a legitimate influence on public opinion. As I remarked to you in a former letter nothing of this kind can be hoped untill the papers at Raleigh acquire more spirit—

A gentleman from Edenton informed me, on yesterday, that a meeting had been held in Chowan, voting Resolutions, which di[sap]proved the proceedings of our Legislature—some account of which, will probably be sent you—The majority, if it exist here, is hardly so decided, as to induce us to propose such a meeting here—

You will pardon me for mentioning a matter of business, about which we conversed when I last saw you—Mr. Yarbor-

[58]William Montgomery.

ough[59] when he left this place handed me the bond and Writ against yourself & Mr. Cain in favour of Mr. Alston[60]—I wrote to Mr. Jas. J. Alston, in Tenn, who replies, that he desires the money as soon as practicable. If I recollect aright, you expected to be able to discharge the bond, at Christmas last—Mr. A. instructs me, in your absence to bring suit against Mr. Cain but I shall take no step in the matter untill your return, & hope you will find it convenient to take up the bond—

With much regard I remain,
Yours Friend and Servt.
WILL A. GRAHAM.

Hon W. P. Mangum)
(
Senate U. S.)

[Addressed:]
Hon. Willie P. Mangum
Senate of U.S.
Washington, D. C.

WPM-LC

Priestley H. Mangum to Willie P. Mangum

OXFORD N. C. Feb. 6th 1835—

Dear Sir.

I write you after an absence from home of two weeks—therefore I have it not in my power to inform you whether our families are well or not—

You have seen that we shall probably have a Convention of delegates, in the course of the year, to amend our State Constitution. Mr. Nash[61] has confered with me this week on the subject of Candidates from our County, and thinks that you and he could make a safer run against Montgomery & Allison,[62] who are understood to be candidates, than any other two persons in the County—And thinks it is desirable that you should have such an opportunity as the occasion of your being a candidate for the Convention would afford, to enlighten the people

[59]Probably Samuel Yarborough, Mangum's neighbor.
[60]See above, I, xxiv-xxv, 337-338, 370-371, 520.
[61]Frederick Nash.
[62]William Montgomery and Joseph Allison.

of Orange in regard to those principles of action in Congress, for which you have been arrained—

Your friends, I think, are disposed to afford you this opportunity, if you want it.—Some of the opposition, would *of course* prefer some other person than yourself. Mr. Ruffin[63] no doubt desires it, and has friends, who would be disposed to call him out in preference to you or Mr. Nash—But it is, understood that Ruffin is in favor of *retaining Borough representation*—And that would certainly ensure his defeat as Mr. Nash & I think.—Mr. Mebane[64] and Doct. Smith[65] would probably have wishes on the subject—But it is believed that you & Nash would stand a better chance of success—These things are not yet matured—but the people are beginning to look about on the subject—I am requested to ask you to write to Mr. Nash and to such other persons as you may think proper, on the subject of your being a candidate as above.—

It is understood among us, that you have determined not seriously to regard the *Instruction resolutions;* and your personal and political friends are all, so far as I know or have heard, well pleased with your determination. It is believed that those resolutions, were not, by any means, a fair or just expression of the will of the State.—I have a strong belief that N. C. will take up Judge White & with him beat Van Buren, provided his own people will heartily *shoulder* him.—

We are at a loss to account for your inattention to epistolary writing. None of us receive letters from you; and altho' that may be an argument in favour of *your impartiality,* yet it affords neither evidence of your friendship for us—or any sure guaranty for building up friendships in others.—

We have snow from 3 to 5 inches deep this week—& hard weather.—

Yrs respectivelly
P. H. MANGUM.

[Addressed:]
The Hon.
Willie P. Mangum,
(Of the Senate)
Mail. Washington City,
D. C.

[63]Chief Justice Thomas Ruffin.
[64]James Mebane.
[65]Dr. James S. Smith.

WPM-LC

William J. Bingham[66] *to Willie P. Mangum*[67]

[7 February, 1835]

A meeting of the citizens of Hillsborough was held on Friday the 30th instant, to adopt resolutions expressive of their feelings on occasion of the death of the late Rev. Dr. Caldwell, President of the University. The Hon. Frederick Nash was called to the chair. The object of the meeting being briefly explained by the Chairman, the following resolutions were offered by the Rev. William M. Green, prefaced by a very feeling and appropriate address, who was followed by Hugh Waddell, esq. in terms no less suited to the occasion.

Resolved, That this meeting has heard with unfeigned sorrow of the death of the Rev. Joseph Caldwell, D.D., the late venerable and much-loved President of our University.

Resolved, That in his death we deplore the loss of the Christian, the Philanthropist, the Scholar, and the Public Benefactor.

Resolved, That, as a tribute of respect to the memory of the deceased, the members of this meeting do wear crepe on their left arms for thirty days; and that the same be recommended to the alumni of University generally.

Resolved, That the "Executive Committee" of our University be, and they hereby are requested, if consistent with their views of propriety, to appoint one of the alumni of the University to deliver a eulogy on the character of the deceased, at Chapel Hill, on the afternoon of the day preceding the next Commencement.

Resolved, That a copy of these resolutions be sent to the afflicted widow of the deceased, to the officers of the University, to the Governor of the State as ex officio President of the Board of Trustees, and to the Hon. Duncan Cameron, President of the Executive Committee.

---

[66]William James Bingham, 1802-1866, the son of the founder of the Bingham School, graduated with highest honors at the University, where his father taught. The son studied law and then took over his father's preparatory school for boys. William James Bingham had the reputation of being stern and rigid in his discipline. Nevertheless, his pupils had great affection for him and his community was conscious of his numerous deeds of charity. His school in Orange County became one of the most famous preparatory schools in the South, and he was frequently referred to as "The Napoleon of schoolmasters." Ashe, *Biog. Hist. of N. C.*, VI, 69-73; A. D. Smith, *Western North Carolina: Historical and Biographical,* Charlotte, 1890, 150-152.

[67]The first part of this is a printed circular. The remainder is in Bingham's handwriting.

Resolved, That the Editors of the Hillsborough Recorder, Raleigh Register, Star, and Standard, be respectfully requested to publish the foreging resolutions.

The above resolutions were unanimously adopted.

W. J. BINGHAM, Secretary.

Hillsborough, January 31st, 1835.

[In handwriting of W. J. Bingham]

HILLSBORO, N. C. Feby 7th 1835.

Dear Sir.

I take the liberty of sending you a copy of the resolutions adopted by the citizens of this town on occasion of the death of Dr. Caldwell, not doubting your sympathy with us. What citisen of N. Carolina did not drop a tear over one of her best, most devoted & warm-hearted, tho' one of her adopted sons? You knew & felt & appreciated his worth.—The good man—the patriot is gone. [May] his mantle fall on the politicians of our State.

Allow me to congratulate you, Sir, as I have done myself & my country, that you did not suffer yourself to be 'instructed' out of the Senate. I trust you will never have occasion to regret yr decision, and that N. Carolina will continue to have one Senator at least, who will dare to raise his hand & his voice against executive misrule, so long as that misrule shall last.—Excuse this scrawl. A wounded finger almost disqualifies me for writing.

Very respectfully

Yr obedt sert

W. J. BINGHAM

[Addressed:]

Hon. Willie P. Mangum

Washington City

D.C.

WPM-LC

Henry Seawell[68] *to Willie P. Mangum*
(Confidential) *Strictly So*

RALEIGH 7th February 1835

My Dear Sir

I have been confined since Tuesday at home by a deep snow—This is Saturday night—This morning (I should have said I had been confined till to-day)—I went to town to pay off some bills & called at the Executive office—The Gov showed me your letter and asked my opinion of the matters stated I told him I had received a letter from you, but it contained no intimation of the character, which the letter to him did—That I dislike to be a volunteer but upon his pressing me to write to you what I expressed to him, I have ventured upon the task.

My opinion is (without a shadow of doubt as to its correctness) you owe it to your friends, to your self, & above all, to your Country, to stand firmly at the post which the intelligence and patriotism of N. C. has placed you—You were elected without any reference to parties. Your political notions were then known; your opinions of Federal & State powers made the best of qualifications, together with the ability to sustain them—and against adverse winds, tides, & every other current, but "Nags head"[69] which indeed for a season opposed you, you were elected for *Six* years a Senator of the United States. Those who supported you, (I speak of the majority) did so from a Sense of duty. They then believed your service needed in the Councils of the nation—*Some of them* have made personal sacrifices they can never regain, whilst it is true, others aided your cause, from interested motives, which no longer retain them on your side. If you resign before you come home & *consult your friends* it will be said by your enemies, *as has been said,* that certain men in Washington have advised it—and It will be made a theme of public discussion & will gather such strength, that you cannot over come it. I pretend to no political sagacity; but my experience, has given me confidence in every thing relating to the nature of man—I tell you in plain terms, the resignation of your situation as Senator, *at the close of the Session,* will deprive the country of all the usefulness it is in your power to afford. I think it is in your power to affect a grand revolu-

[68]See above, I, 10n.
[69]See above, I, 400.

tion on the State;! but it must be effected without its appearing to be matter of *design*—If I had you by my side by my own fire, I would say to you, "keep your own council, come home, let the people of Orange know you are tired of the present station that you would be willing to act in a public character nigher home, (*this done not by direct solicitation*) and I doubt not, that you would not only be elected, but carry with you whom you pleased; & I have as little doubt, revolutionize the Genl Assembly—but to do this, your knowledge of human nature will tell you, that you must first take the lead in something *relating to the State,* where no politics are concerned—this will give you a command, which you are to admirably calculated, to weild to advantage; & having secured the controul, your patritism will guarantee its proper aplication—my *head upon it,* you can be successfull by such a course—In your letter to me, you ask me what I think of Judge W?.[70] If I did not know him personally & therefore have some pretensions to julge of his *calibre.* I should have answered unhesitatingly. But the fact is, experience has shown us, that some thing beyond good intentions are required of a president—He like the physician who is attend the sick bed, should not only have a knowledge of the properties of medicine, but the remote & proximate causes of the disease—he shoud under stand the anatomy of the body, with all its functions, veins, and Arteries. can the most partial friend say this of Judge W in relation to the body politic of the U. States? The most that can be said of him is that he is honest & well meaning, possessed of respectable talents, but altogether without the rudiments of the *Statesman* who is to weild the destinies of the Union. The vessel of State, coud not be commanded by him. He must of necessity have a captain on whom he is to depend for every thing but the manual exertion of the crew: Again, to aid in the accomplishment of such a state of things seems to me worse than to do nothing—It is giving countenance & support, in favour of measures, which tho they may be better, as regards the comfort of the people, must nevertheless disclose to them the fact, that *qualification* was not in view when the selection was made, and whatever becomes odious in such an administration through its weakness or wickedness, must as in present administration, measureably be chargeable to those contributed to produce it.

[70]Hugh Lawson White.

I never shall forget a private conversation I once had with Mr J C C[71] on this very subject near the close of Mr Adam's administration. I urged to him the danger of selecting a man compelled to rely on his cabinet—and if he remembers my remarks, they were made in my room at Brown's Hotel, he will say, my prophesy has been fulfilled. The true rule is to persue principle; let the country see who it is that have brought upon it the evils continue to vote for qualified gifted men—never allow as admissable that any other should be supported, and tho such efforts may for a season fail under a combination of circumstances yet when evils are brought home & felt by the people, they well know by whom they have been deserved, & fly for refuge to those warned them of their danger, holding their former leaders in utter detestation; who fall like Lucifer never to hope again. Further—what has been the political course of the gentleman alluded to? has he *ever* forsaken the party in a Single vote? who is [he] to be surrounded by? [torn] of the [torn] stamp, as must be the case to save him from disgrace, even from them, can there be a hope that he is to strike out a lot of measures, different from what he has constantly mentioned & recommended? It seems to me there cannot, & that nothing can be gained by sustaining such a man. It may be that I am wholly mistaken in him—If so I am in error & hope I shall be pardoned, as I have no malice or ill will towards him—I hear some gentleman say he can get the vote of this State—I don't believe it—All the methodist will support the old P M—[72] they begin to preach of his piety already. I have answered the gentleman referred to me in the best manner I can—I have taken upon to offer an opinion upon a point not submitted to me, which I was induced to do at the request of one of your friends; I will not obtrude an opinion not call for by any person, that is, what is to be done for the best? I say if a qualified man can be selected on whom the whole opposition can be thrown, bring him out. If that cannot be done avoid going over to the enemy to support one in their camp less odious; but permit the prominent men in the opposition to offer—let the matter come to the house of representatives & try what can be done there those in the field now will hold on—nothing short of choaking can get them off—these animonisties during

[71]John C. Calhoun.

[72]He probably refers to Justice John McLean, who was Postmaster General from 1823 to 1829, and who had many followers in North Carolina.

the Contest, will be most warm against their own political opponents. They will *fall out* and worse cannot befall the country, and its friends saved the humiliating mortification of committing over him to avoid a heavier curse threatened by another—These are my views—they are the result of my best [torn] & dictates the best wishes of my [heart] for the good [of my] Country—Have you seen the *Register?* the article was written in haste, in bad taste published without correction, and to oblige you, It is badly printed without punctuation—& with very bad type—I shall write to you in a few days enclosing a notice which I wish you to fill up as to time & place for taking your deposition, which I wish you to send to Jesse Person to have it served—please retain a copy that the caption may correspond with the notice—I set off the 20 this month on the Wilmington riding. I must send you also a commission. but I *repeat do not resign.*

Your friend & Servant
HENRY SEAWELL

Honb W Mangum

WPM-LC

John Branch to Willie P. Mangum

ENFIELD February 8th 1835

My Dear Sir,

I have returned by this night's mail my speech, after a very careful examination of the proof sheets, forwarded to me by Lawrence and Lemay.

I have adopted every precaution to make it as effective as possible. It will be found to contain a mass of highly interesting facts, which ought to be extensively circulated not only in North Carolina but throughout the Union. It will appear in the next Star,[73] and will very soon be sent out in pamphlet form. I have order[d]. a thousand copies to be distributed at my expense When it reaches Washington, if you think it worthy of circulation, some means ought to be adopted to put it in the hands of every reading man in the country. The facts set forth are incontrovertible and most of them can be established by satisfactory evidence. If they produce no effect, I can only re-

[73]It also appeared in the *Tarboro Free Press*, March 7, 1835, and the *Raleigh Register*, February 17, 1835.

gret in silence that our countrymen are perversely and wilfully blind. I know no public man who has been more injured than Mr. Calhoun, and I think that he will feel it to be his duty, and interest, to contribute to the circulation. I felt a strong desire to have something more in behalf of Mr. Clay, but *upon that occasion* I deemed it *prudent* to be silent. I shall never be entirely satisfied with myself untill I have done ample justice to his eminent talents, and chivalrous patriotism. In truth My Dear Sir, he has a strong hold on my affections. When I denounced him in the Senate,[74] I was a stranger to his heart and hardly done justice to his head.

Present me in the most respectful and friendly terms to Governors Poindexter and Tyler and say to them that I will take the liberty, in a few days, to send to each of them, a copy of my speech. I never felt the want of their high order of talents more than when I delivered that speech. Truth is said to be mighty; and yet in this our day the natural order of things seems to be reversed—*truth is now powerless.*

Accept my cordial assurances of esteem

JN BRANCH

To Hon. Willie P. Mangum
Washington City

[Addressed:]
Hon. Willie P. Mangum
Washington City

WPM-LC

C. P. Mallett[75] *to Willie P. Mangum*

WASHINGTON 9th Feby, 1835

Dear Sir

I would be pleased that with my name. you add to your list that of. My. Father in law. William H Beatty who has been for many years. Chairman of the county court of Bladen his address is at. Beatty's bridge—where you might also address. James Kerr—at Gravelly Hill—John D. Beatty—John Cro-

[74]On March 30, 1826, in the debate on the Panama mission, Branch made a long speech in the Senate attacking the usurpation of power by Adams and Clay. He proposed resolutions in which he stated that by not consulting the Senate before planning to send delegates to the Panama Congress, Clay and Adams had acted unconstitutionally. Thomas H. Benton, *Abridgement of the Debates of Congress from 1789 to 1856*, VIII, 482-494.

[75]See above, I, 527.

martie Robert Murphy—at Elizabethtown, N. C. Dr. A. McDowell, and William Richardson I have heard a general complaint that the representative of that District sends nothing but *Extra Globes*—of which I have known. more than 400—in one office by one mail. I shall take the liberty to advise you. If I have anything which I believe would interest you—

I am very Respectfully

C. P. MALLETT.

P.S—was obliged to return without reaching Philadelphia—and shall proceed homewards this day—

[Addressed:]

Washington

WPM-LC

Mades[76] .... *to Willie P. Mangum*

CHAPEL HILL Feby. 14th 1835.

Respected Sir,

You will no doubt be astonished on the receipt of a letter from an entire Stranger, particularly when he introduces himself by asking favours, which You are under no obligations whatever, either from friendship, or even acquaintance, to grant.

But as I suppose it is the fortune of all publick characters, (to whom we look up for counsel) to be frequently troubled by communications from those with whom they have no personal acquaintance; and therefore must have their patience somewhat inured to such unprofitable trouble, I hope your astonishment will not be turned into disgust, when a Schoolboy of Your Old Alma Mater presumes to address You.

Hoping therefore that if You should be so much amersed in business when this comes to hand as not to be able to attend to my request, You will at least not treat it with contempt, I will proceed without further preamble to inform You who I am and my object in addressing You.

My name (vide infra) I am from Randolph Cty. N. C. and wish to obtain a situation in the Military School at West Point.

[76]The signature is torn off. The Mr. Mock referred to in this letter was William Mock who graduated at West Point in 1836. He served in the Florida war, 1836-1841. In 1841 he resigned his commission and moved to Missouri and in 1849 to California. Cullum, *Biog. Dir. of Officers of U. S. Milt. Acad.*, I, 655-656.

I came here last June and stood for admission into the Junior class but was rejected on Greek—I therefore Joined the Senior class on the Sciences and am now regular on all their Studies—I am measureably dependant on my own exertions for support, and have Just acquired sufficient knowledge to intoxicate the brain, and am anxious for an opportunity to sober myself again —Besides I feel inclined to a Military life—Mr Mock is now at W. P. from my District but will not Graduate until June 1836. I am now in my 18th year and should be very loath to wait untill he returns—I know nothing myself of the laws by which the distribution of cadets are governed, but have been informed that there are several vacancies in this State, and that by the application of our Senator for a situation it might be obtained—These things however are all perfectly known to You and the information I have received may be incorrect—But if there is a possibility of obtain [torn] to enter next June, and You will be so kind to [torn] case and obtain one for me, I shall be [torn] rejoiced, and my high obligations and grate[torn] You shall be commensurate with [torn]

I am Sir, with the highest respect
Your humble servant
MADES—[torn]

The Hon[ble]. Willie P. Mangum

P. S. Please Sir, write me whether my views [torn] and if so, what success etc.—
as I blotted my name before, that You may [torn]
I will sign it again

MA[torn]

[Addressed:]
Hon[ble]. Wilie P. Mangum
Member of the Senate
Washington City
D. C.

WPM-LC

Duncan Cameron to Willie P. Mangum

ORANGE N. C. Feby 15th. [1835]

My dear Sir,

I have had the pleasure to receive your esteemed favors of the 7th and 9th inst—with the enclosures accompanying them—for all which accept my thanks.

The account given by you of the State of things at Washington is not only gloomy but apalling—and yet I fear—much fear, that the picture you have drawn is not more highly coloured than required by truth—and warranted by facts.

The People must rise in their strength, and say to their *mad* rulers "quoasque tandem abutere notra patentia?"—[77]

Much—everything depends on the Senate—they only can hold the Bull-dog (as Mr. Jefferson *once* called him) in check—as he vetoes their legislative acts—let them veto all his appointments bro't out under the patronage of the Kitchen Cabinet—when he nominates a Gentleman of fair standing—& (such a case will but seldom occur) let him pass—he will soon get both sick and ashamed of his associates and retire.

I am much gratified to learn that Mr. McLean will resign.—You know how *very high,* that Gentleman once stood in my opinion and confidence—no one stood *higher* with me—and I have been grieved, that he has so long given the countenance of his character, and the aid of his talents to *such an administration*—I trust that he will cut himself loose from his present associates—that he will come out openly and place himself (as far as is now practicable for him to do so) "'rectus in curia," devote himself to his natural friends, and with them, save the Country from the misrule of a corrupt and unprincipled party.

I rejoice for my country that in this season of darkness and clamor it has in her councils, such men as Clay, Webster, Calhoun "cum multis aliis" of high talents—sound patriotism, and noble bearing—men who will not shun to disclose to the people, the *whole truth*—let them hold and persevere—their influence must, and will be felt—and tho' we may, and certainly shall suffer much—yet, I do not despair of their ultimate success in rescuing the Constitution and Laws from the Banditti, who are now trampling them under their feet.

What madness it is—to seek [torn] defeating the succession (V. B.) by any other Candidate than Mr. Clay—Will those opposed to V. B. insure his election by division among themselves? A sense of common danger should produce unity of action—but we shall, I fear, be defeated by disunion.

Write me frequently and fully—Your Letters at this interesting crisis will be highly acceptable—but you must expect noth-

[77]This is the opening sentence of Cicero's *First Oration Against Cataline.* It should read: "Quo usque tandem abutere, Catilina, patientia nostra?"

ing in return but my poor thanks. Remember me kindly to Messrs. Williams, Barringer & Graham—

My dear Sir,
Yrs. truly
DUN: CAMERON

[Addressed:]
The Honble.
Willie P. Mangum
U. States Senate
Washington City.

Stagville, N. C., Feby. 15.

WPM-LC

John Bell to Willie P. Mangum[78]

WASHINGTON CITY
Feby. 25th. 1835

Dr. Sir

During the last summer & fall I was furiously assailed by my policital opponents for creating a division in the Jackson ranks in the election of Speaker of the H. Rep. & I was particularly charged by the partizans of Col. Polk with having obtained a triumph over him, by an intrigue with the opposition, & by pledging myself to their interests & feelings upon various subjects.[79]

In many parts of Ten. where I was but slightly known these reports operated to the prejudice of my political reputation; and I now ask of you as an act of justice between me and my accusers, fully to state, to what extent the charges are true as regards myself, & how far the impression prevailed with the political party to which you belong, that Col. Polk was more identi-

---

[78]This letter has been previously published in the *Tennessee Historical Magazine,* III (1917), 197.

[79]On June 2, 1834, Andrew Stevenson resigned as Speaker of the House of Representatives. Already supporters of James K. Polk and John Bell were trying to get Jackson's endorsement of their candidates. The controversy which followed weakened the unity of the party. On the first ballot Polk received 42, Bell 30, and Richard H. Wilde 64. After a few ballots, Wilde's friends shifted to James M. Wayne, of Georgia. When he failed to get the necessary majority, many of his supporters turned to Bell. On the tenth ballot, as a result, Bell won. The Jackson-Van Buren men had supported Polk, but there is no indication that Jackson applied any pressure. Bell received a few Jackson votes which, with those of the Whigs, elected Bell. Polk's friends then began collecting evidence to show that Bell had gone over to the opposition. Duff Green proceeded to claim that Bell's election was a defeat for the administration. Polk's friends now tried to turn Jackson and the Democratic Party against Bell. Bell's friends replied that Polk's defeat was due to the fact that Polk had been too closely tied to the nullifiers. Polk denied this. As a result, Bell wrote Mangum as a leader of the state's rights party what position his party had taken in the election. Joseph H. Parks, *John Bell of Tennessee.* Baton Rouge, 1950,70-74.

fied in feeling & opinion with that party than myself, & to what extent this impression was created by Col. Polk, or his political friends

Your Obt. Sert.
JNO. BELL

Hon
Mr. Mangum
of U. S. Senate

WPM-LC

Louis McLane[80] *to William S. Archer*

WILMINGTON Feb. 25. 1835.

My dear Archer/

I hope you will pardon me for taking the liberty of asking you to send the inclosed to the P.O. it contains a $5 note for a year's subscription. If the "Sun"[81] possess much fire like that of the "Jefferson," its beams will soon become too scorching for our friend the V. P.—

I wish it had pushed a little further, the idea of Benton's succession after V. B. and assumed this as it doubtless is, the basis of their alliance—for this is a topic of which too much cannot be said; and it seems to me, that the fault of most of the opposition papers has been, that of not dwelling sufficiently upon a popular point, and of not keeping it constantly before the people. The danger of a succession should not be lost sight of, and besides the general odiousness of caucuses, their tendency to perpetuate the succession, in defiance of the People may be used with great effect to defeat the convention. I take it for granted that the means of dissuading Judge White's Jackson and repub-

[80]See above, I, 195n.
[81]The Washington *Sun* was established February 21, 1835, and ran until August, 1837. *Union List of Newspapers*, 91.

lican friends in every part of the Union from participating in the convention have not, or will not be overlooked. The party of Genl. Jackson, as such, is ab initio, in both his elections, opposed to the principle of succession, and to that of caucus or conventional nomination. These are the two great fundamental principles inscribed upon his banner when originally unfurled, and wherever it has floated. Besides, who ever heard of a convention, until the claims of every prominent man in the party had been put down and the right of succession finally settled upon one individual? But while the *caucus system,* throughout its metempsychosis, and in all its tendences, cannot be too decidedly reprobated, the *cabal* which has given it its present shape, which has controuled its formation, and is to overawe and direct its decision, should not escape exposure. No man ought to be P. of the U. S. who is not prepared to put down forcibly, & forever, that irresponsible influence, which has done so much mischief, which has corrupted the public man, and is daily engaged in pulling down and ostracising the best, and building up the worst. —What is the Jackson party? In its foundation it embraced the original friends of the General, and first among these, is Judge White—it has gradually enlarged, until, from his last election, it would appear to embrace a large portion of all the People, and almost every State in the Union. When, therefore, we talk of the harmony of the Jackson party we ought to mean that of the American family, and any one who gives a less scope to his aims upon this subject, is not only unpatriotic, but looks only to the harmony of the K. C. and the office holders & office seekers—the convention at Baltimore will give harmony to no other class than these. It is not enough to put forth Judge White's unpretending character—; it ought also to be remarked that all his actions and conduct, simple, open, honest, & republican, as they have been, have had not the slightest reference to office —never, perhaps, did he perform an act or give a vote with the remotest expectation of being a candidate to this high office. For how many years has his competitor been confessedly in the field waiting only, and somewhat impatiently, at one time, for the expiration of general Jackson's term, to put on the purple? Assuming all varieties of shapes, casting off old & making new friends—forming an alliance here with Benton—and all for the same end?

What means have you taken to extend the circulation of the 'Appeal'[82] and the 'Sun'? I have no doubt many subscribers may be had here. I am waiting anxiously for an answer to my last letter. Will you have time to run up & see us after the session? If you can't use the hints in this letter, you might give some intimations to Bell, or Foster or both that would ensure the object. Depend upon it if this affair of Judge White's be well pushed it will succeed. The convention may be defeated altogether, or if it meet, it will become as odious as the old caucus.

Let me hear from you without delay

L. MCLANE.

HON. MR. ARCHER.

WPM-LC

Robert H. Jones[83] *to Willie P. Mangum*

WARRENTON 25. Feb. 1835.

My dear Sir,

A month or more ago, I received your letter acknowledging the receipt of two from me—a long one at Boston in the last Autumn, and a shorter one since the meeting of Congress. I have no doubt but they were as you seem to intimate very welcome and very intelligent—The latter recommendation I am sure they eminently possessed. I say this, because I can hardly dispute anything with you—Except the superior claims of Mr. V. Buren to be General Jacksons successor in the Presidency—which you most un[reaso]nably dispute and question. But my purpose is no[t n]ow to dispute with you, but to thank you for Mr. Clays [repo]rt upon the relations of this Government with that of France—and to ask you to come this way on your way home from Washington—I promise you protection against the *ferocious* assaults of all outragious *Jackson Van Buren men.*

To speak in sincerity and truth to you, I am much pleased not to hear of your resignation, since the instructions to expunge

---

[82]The Washington *Appeal*, published by William A. Rind, Jr., was published from February 7 to April 18, 1835, when it was absorbed by the Washington *Sun*. It was a White paper. Bassett (ed.), *Cor. of Jackson*, V, 328n.

[83]See above, I, 36n; II, 186.

&.C. My old friend Pete Browne,[84] used to say to me, "Robbin, you are a strange man"—I believe I am so, and that my friend was accurate in his ideas of me. But if I were to suffer crucifixion to morrow, I cannot help thinking, that the electors have a right to offer instructions and advice to their representative, but I deny that he is bound to follow such advice, or in the event of disregarding it, to resign his seat or Commission. I know, that I am much more independent than you are—for if you ever agree with me in opinion, you would be "*sining to the verge of indiscretion,*" to say so. However this may be, I am of opinion that, I cou'd make a very sensible speech, founded upon this distruction [*sic*] novel as it may seem to you. I now say farther, by way of sustaining myself in your favourable opinion—that if the representative is bound to conform to instructions—i.e. to vote to expunge &.C, this is not a representative Government, but to all practical purposes a pure democracy. Hence I affirm, if you are steady and persevere in right measures, the time is not very distant when you will receive a pardon for your present and continuing contumacy. The resolutions therefore, lately adopted by the legislature of your native State will not be long remembered—*Telum imbecile,* [*sic*] *sine ictu.*

Yesterday a very numerous meeting of the people assembled at the Court House in this place—preparatory to the contemplated Democratic Convention—proposed to be held at Baltimore in the Course of this revolving year—Of course you know, I must make a speech—and a speech I did make I wish you had been here, and had said a word against Van [Bur]en—I wou'd have roasted you in a good humour but [with] great severity—But all this a part—I love those who differ with me in politics, more than I generally do those who agree with me—This is one of the odd traits in my composition—The truth is, that I am a strange sort of body, and one more proof of my being so, is, that I esteem you highly and wish you much happiness, and lasting prosperity.

[Addressed:] ROB. H. JONES

Hon.

Willie P. Mangum

Washington City.

[84]Battle says he was a "hardheaded, close fisted lawyer, a native of Scotland, who accumulated a fortune of $200,000." He was on a commission that recommended to the legislature in 1825 that a publc school system under local control and supported by local taxes be established in North Carolina. Coon (ed.), *Doc. Hist. of Educ. in N. C.*, I, 235, 267-276; Battle, *Hist. of U. N. C.*, I, 431-432.

WPM-LC

D. L. Swain to Willie P. Mangum

RALEIGH, 7, March, 1835.

My dear Sir,

I understand that arrangements are making to tender you a public dinner at Chapel Hill, and another at Wake Forest.—I write this note merely to say that I think the former invitation should be excused, simply because the students cannot with propriety enter into the drama of political strife, and that I am very anxious you should attend the latter—I shall make arrangements to meet you at the Forest, and entertain sanguin hopes, that by united efforts, we may render some services to the commonwealth.

Yours very sincerely,

D. L. SWAIN,

Honble W. P. Mangum,

[Addressed:]

[Hon]ble

Willie P. Mangum,

Red Mountain,

N. C.

WPM-LC

E. H. Eure[85] *and Others to Willie P. Mangum*

HALIFAX March 10th, 1835

Hon. W. P. Mangum

Dear Sir

We the undersigned being appointed a Committee by the Whig citizens of the town of Halifax & its vicinity, to wait on you and solicit the pleasure of your company to spend the evening with them at the Eagle Hotel in this town at Seven o'clock.

---

[85]He was a member of the vigilance committee appointed by the Raleigh caucus, December 22, 1835. In 1822 he served in the House of Commons as a representative of Halifax County. *Raleigh Register*, Jan. 12, 1836; *N. C. Manual*, 637.

Having understood that the present is the only opportunity, the[y] can flatter themselves of seeing you in their village in some time, and the great anxiety they have to acknowledge their high regard for your patriotic and distinguished public Services as their representative in the Senate, of the United States, particularily your Galant Stand against the late usurpation of the General Government

Hoping it will suit your convenience thus far to comply With the wishes we have the pleasure to subscribe ourselves

Yrs. Very Respt,

E. H. EURE MICHL. FERRALL
THOS M. CROWELL WM. L. LONG.

Ed. L. Pitman
R. J. Hawkins.

[Addressed:]

Hon. Willie P. Mangum
Present.

WPM-LC

John Branch to Willie P. Mangum

ENFIELD March 11th, '35.

My dear Sir,

I have been in the *dumps* all day in consequence of learning this morning that you and Mr. Calhoun were so near me the last night, and yet I was not permitted to greet you even Why were you so cruel as to pass on in such an uncerumonious manner. I would have given much to have had you with me, for a few hours.

On monday next I set out for Florida and shall not return untill the month of June, on tuesday night or wednesday morning next I will meet you in Raleigh at Guion's Hotel. Pray make it convenient to ride down. Your friends there I am sure would be much gratified to see you. It is important that we should understand one another as soon as practicable—*the enemy is in the field* I should have taken another road but for the expectation of seeing you in Raleigh. I have written you several letters since I heard from you. Can it be that my letters have been intercepted? I write you however by Genl hall[86] and have received no answer to that letter If any thing prevents your meeting me in Raleigh by all means let me hear from you, at Raleigh or Tallahasee.

Your friend
JN BRANCH.

[Addressed:]
Hon. Willie P. Mangum.
Orange County
Red Mountain.

WPM-LC

M. Ferrall[87] et als. to Willie P. Mangum

[HALIFAX, N. C., 12 March, 1835]

Hon. W. P. Mangum

The undersigned a committee, upon the part of the citizens of Halifax, are instructed to request of you a copy of your remarks in reply to Col. Long's complimentary toast—Also your sentiments on that occation

An early attention to this subject is respectfully requested

With sentiments of high regard

We remain Yr. Obt Servts—
M. FERRALL
W. L. LONG
R. J. HAWKINS
E. H. EURE
E. C. PITMAN
T. M. CROWELL

Halifax March 12 th 1835

[Addressed:]
Hon. Willie P. Mangum
Hillsboro
No Ca.

---

[86]Thomas H. Hall.

[87]In 1843 he was the secretary of a Halifax Whig meeting. See below, letter of M. Terrall to Mangum, June 5, 1843.

WPM-LC

Robert C. Bond[88] *to Willie P. Mangum*

[RALEIGH, N. C., 19 March, 1835]

My dear Sir

You have no doubt received the letter of the Committee of Arrangements requesting your remarks for publication—It is expected and I should like for you to come out on the Resolutions—Col. Long's remarks will lead with his toast—something about executive encroachments, &c.—you no doubt recollect. It is designed yours will follow—then a few of mine, & then the toasts &c. You no doubt recollect. It is designed yours will follow—then a few of mine, & then the toasts &c. I shall touch only delicately on your name for the Vice Presidency, simply naming you in connection with that office—as due to N. C. &c. To this you may reply or not as you think proper—

I can assure you however it takes like wildfire—and at our Whig Meeting at Court White & yourself will be nominated.

Yours with great respect.

ROBT. C. BOND.

[Addressed:]

Hon. Willie P. Mangum
Hillsboro
N. C.

[Postmarked:] Raleigh, Mar. 19.

WPM-LC

William B. Meares to Willie P. Mangum

WILMINGTON March 19th 1835

My Dr. Sir.

I recd yours of 22nd ult. from Washington a few days, since. I was in Charleston when it arrived, & only reached home three days since, or I would sooner have answered it.

On the subject of our political affairs, I feel as you do, & see that we are rapidly approaching a State of degradation from which I fear it will be long,—very long, before we recover. As to our own State, I have utterly despaired for some years; & latterly have completely given up the ship, & in all my arrange-

---

[88]Robert C. Bond, Mangum's friend, was a physician in Halifax. See below, 402, James Simmons to W. P. Mangum, Mar. 9, 1836.

ments, had an eye to another location, not for myself, but for my children. I would go myself but that I am unwilling to sacrafice the comforts around me, & exchange them, now that my energies are decreasing, for the roughness of a wilderness.

As to my going to Congress, it is *out of the question.* I could not consent under any circumstances. I believe I would prefer going in the front rank of a Waterloo battle, to entering again the Arena of Politics—I doubt whether I could be elected, but I should care nothing for defeat.—Possibly, I may possess more personal popularity than any other in the district, but there is so much of whole hog Jackson in it that I do not think I could succeed.—Strange too as it may seem, there are some *private personal* considerations which would render it disagreeable to me to oppose the present incumbent.[89]—I believe I am the only man he ever placed under obligations to him, by person disinterested services: and although in political opinions, we differ as far as is the East from the West, yet I could not entirely forget a favor confered.—

As to our friend Hill,[90] I think he could not be elected, but I think his chances would be as good as mine.—

In the next presidential contest, I am in favor of *any one* against Van Buren. I hope he may be defeated & I think he can be if the South & West unite on any one.—I do not like White, but he is by far the less evil.—

In any event, but little is to be hoped for in this quarter.—The battle of Ner Orleans will always carry the day.—

I shall at all times be glad to hear from you, & learn how the puppets move

Believe me with sincere regard & respt

Yrs. truly

WM. B. MEARES

[Addressed:]

The Hble.

Wiley P. Mangum

Red Mountain

Orange Cty,

No. Ca.

---

[89]James J. McKay.

[90]Possibly Frederick J. Hill.

WPM-LC

John Bell to Willie P. Mangum[91]

N. Y. Mar 19th. 1835

Dear Sir

I was somewhat disappointed in not receiving the statement you were good enough to promise me before you left Washington. I suppose your engagements would not allow you to make it out before you set out.

You will greatly oblige me by forwarding it to Nashville as soon as you may have leisure to make it out.

Let me know also, if you please, how things look in N. C. & what we can do to aid the cause of Judge White

Yours, truly
JNO: BELL

Hon W. P. Mangum

P. S. Here the war will be better sustained on the side of Judge White than I supposed.

WPM-LC

J. Dandridge[92] *to Willie P. Mangum*

SENATE CHAMBER March 22d. 1835

Dear Sir

I have presented the enclosed notes to Mr. Glynn.[93] He says that it is entirely out of his power to pay them or even a part, and that if coerced he shall be obliged to avail himself of the benefit of the insolvent law of the District, which has already done in other cases. Under these circumstances My opinion is that it would be useless to bring suit on them. Glynn says he will renew them if required, and pay them when he can, which course would be best.

Very respectfully your
Obt Sert.
J. DANDRIDGE

[91]See above, II, 314-315. This letter has been previously published in the *Tennessee Historical Magazine,* III, (1917) 197.

[92]I am unable to identify.

[93]Probably John Glenn, of Baltimore. See below, letter of Richard Smith to Mangum, March 30, 1836, and B. B. Smith to Mangum, May 27, 1836.

Please write me [illegible] you desire.
W.P.M.

Dear Sir

I will add, that the opinion of Mr. Dandridge the atto: is entitled to full respect. Hoping this may find you & yours well I am dear Sir with great respect

Yrs Mo truly
WILLIE P. MANGUM

22d. March 1835 I will take new notes
W.P.M.

[Addressed:] The Honble.
[Postmarked: Raleigh March 31]
Willie P. Mangum
Member of Congress
City Washington

WPM-LC

Robert G. Moore to Willie P. Mangum

SPECTATOR OFFICE, NEWBERN,
22d March, 1835,

Dear Sir,

Permit me to congratulate you on your return from the toils of publick duty, and on the warmth of the reception given you by your constituents, and to thank you for the publick Docments which you kindly forwarded to the "Spectator."—You will have seen that the venal presses have opened against you in full cry, for the noble course you pursued in relation to the expunging Resolutions. This was expected; but it was not believed that the defeat of the servile plot would have been so severely felt by the heartless party as it seems to be. The bitterness of their denunciations shows that they have been touched to the quick, and you must expect the lasting enmity of officeholders and office-seekers from this time forth. The approbation of your own heart, and of every partiot, will more than compensate for this.

I have long wished to address you a line or two on a private subject, and I shall take this opportunity of doing so.—About two years ago my Son entered the Military Academy at West Point;[94] through whose influence, or whether in the regular Sen-

[94]See above, I, 442, 455.

iority of application, I am unable to say. Differing entirely from the course and views of our immediate Representative, the *Hon.* Jesse Speight, I have often had occasion in the performance of my editorial duties, to handle him a little roughly, and have consequently been charged by him and his supporters with a want of *gratitude*. He and they say that my son was permitted to enter only thro' the influence of Mr. Speight, and they logically infer that I am bound, in return, to support one whose whole course is corrupt and disgraceful. This I could not do, even if my life were the price of my obstinacy.—But to my purpose.—About the time of my last application, Judge Gaston wrote to you on the subject, and you informed him in reply that in case a certain young g[entleman] to whom you had given a promise [torn] not renew his application, you [would] appoint my Son. As I have [not known] whether the application was renewed [torn] my Son is indebted to you for his [torn] admittance, I will thank you to [in]form me.—I cannot feel [torn] gratitide to Jesse Speight in any [torn] case, and I should be glad to have [torn] that I do not owe him even the a[torn]ment of a favour. I did not [torn]-mit my applications through him [torn] was urged to do so by several of his friends, and shown letters from him expressing surprise that I should doubt his willingness to serve me.—Excuse me for introducing this unimportant matter.

I have the hon^r^ to be & c

RT G. MOORE
Ed. "Spectator"

Judge Mangum.
[Addressed:]
Hon. W. P. Mangum
Hillsboro' N. C.
The postmaster at Hillsboro)
will please give this the)
proper direction)

WPM-LC

Beverly Daniel[95] *to Willie P. Mangum*

RALEIGH MARCH 26th 1835

My dear Sir

It has so happened and I cannot tell you how, that I have never had the pleasure of taking your hand since you were ap-

[95]See above, I, 98n.

pointed to your present seat in Congress—And allow me my Dr Sir to say if there ever was a time when to see you would afford me more gratification than another, *its now*—on this impression I am speaking not only my own sentiments but that of all your virtuous & intelligent friends of this neighbourhood—

My object at present is to solicit your attendance at our Superior Court on the next week—your friends are desirous of seeing you on reference to matters and things in general—but more particularly in regard to a public expression their approbation of your political course in the last session of Congress which they seem determined to get up shortly—when & where not yet settled—

In reference to this matter there is but one opinion among the Patriots of our neighbourhood and that is, as you have stood boldly & fearlessly forward to arrest the strides of despotism over our Constitution & laws, we would not be worthy of the protection of either if we did not give you countenance of approval.

I am with consideration of the
highest respect & regard
Yr ob Servant
BEV DANIEL

The Honorable
W. P. Mangum

[Addressed:] The Honorable
W. P. Mangum
Red Mountain
Orange
N. C.

WPM-LC

Duncan Cameron to Willie P. Mangum

RALEIGH March 26. 1835.

My dear sir,

Our mutual and esteemed friend Govr. Swain called on me to day, and shewed me your letter.—We had much conversation on some of the matters mentioned in it.—as well as in some of your other late letters to him.—

Our conversation resulted in his requesting that I would write, and urge you to come down to this place *next* week.—Your visit here, would not only be gratifying to your friends personally,—but would afford an opportunity of *free* and unreserved conversation on various important topics connected with the present, and probable future condition of the country.—I hope it will be alike convenient, and agreeable to you to be here, as proposed.—If your riding chair is out of repair—send for mine, which is at *home,* and at your service—

My dear sir
Yrs. truly
DU; CAMERON

[Addressed:]
The Honble
Willie P. Mangum
Red Mountain
Orange
Roxboro' mail. N. C.

Willie P. Mangum to Thomas D. Bennehan[96]

SUNDAY 29th. March 1835.

My dear Sir:

Some of our friends have strongly expressed the desire that I should attend Wake Superior Court this week.—I have my riding chair in the hands of a Mechanic at Oxford & had hoped to get it yesterday or today.—Having learned that I could not get it for several days, & having written to Raleigh that I was afoot & my attendance at Wake would depend upon the expedition of the workman; Judge Cameron did me the kindness to write me by the last mail, that *his* was at home & at my service. —

As I have been hoping to get mine, and am disappointed, I feel great difficulty in sending for Judge Cameron's on *Sunday.* —Yet as I desire to set out in the morning, I venture to write to you, requesting that you will do me the favor to furnish me with one, either of your own, or have Mr. Cameron's procured for me.—

[96]The original letter is in the Cameron Papers, University of North Carolina.

I write to you, because I learn, Mrs. Cameron has not yet gone to Raleigh, & I am extremely reluctant to call her attention to a matter of this sort on the sabbath.

I am dear Sir
Very truly Yrs
WILLIE P. MANGUM

[Addressed to:]
Thomas D. Bennehan esq.
Stagville
No Carolina
By orange

WPM-LC

David Lowrie Swain to Willie P. Mangum

RALEIGH 7 April 1835.

My dear Sir,

My servant John will set out for your residence in the morning, as the bearer of dispatches from a committee of our citizens to you.—Your reply will be anticipated through the same medium.

The subscription to the dinner goes on bravely, in despite of the exertions of our friend Genr. S.[97] to thwart it.—More than 100 names are at present on the list, and [the] number will be greatly increased.

I have a letter from [torn] A. of [Cha]rlotte to show you [when] you arrive.

Yours very truly,
D. L. SWAIN.

W. Jones[98] has exhibited some favorable symptoms since you left here;—avows his preference for Judge White, but expresses great apprehensions lest the dinner to you, which he considers impolitic, should drive the Jackson men to Van Burenism.—Your speech will of course, give tone to the proceedings of the day. great good temper, should I think, be a prominent characteristic.—On all matters of this kind however, you have no occasion to take lessons from me.

[Addressed:] Honble
Willie P. Mangum
Red Mountain

[97]Probably he refers to General Romulus M. Saunders, who was a strong Jackson supporter.
[98]He probably refers to Wesley Jones, the state senator from Wake County in 1828, 1829, 1833-1834, and 1850-1853. *N. C. Manual*, 830-831.

WPM-LC

Sally Mangum's Report Card

[8 April, 1835]

Report of the Hillsboro' Female Seminary
for the Month ending April 8th
1835.
For the Class, consisting of Five.
Miss Sally Alston Mangum.

Spelling	4	Arithmetic	1.
Reading	3.	Gen. Standing	2.
Writing	1.	Gen. Deportment	Very Good.

W. M. GREEN Superintendent

WPM-LC

Willie P. Mangum to..................................[99]

ORANGE. The 8th April 1835.

Gentlemen,

I have had the honor to recieve your communication of the 4th instant, on behalf of "a number of my personal and political friends," in the city & neighborhood of Raleigh; assuring me "of their continued Confidence & esteem; & inviting me to praticipate with them" of a public entertainment in that City on the 15th instant.—

I am sensible that I owe this distinguished mark of respect to my humble but zealous cooperation in maintaining the great cause of constitutional freedom to *which* you & those whom you represent are ardently attached. Were it an offering to me personally it would be as indelicate in me to accept as it would be unworthy of you to tender it.—I can easily conceive that this manifestation of kindness may have been quickened, by a generous sympathy with my——

WPM-LC

.... *to Willie P. Mangum*[100]

WASHINGTON 14th April 1835

Dear Sir

I expect to leave home about the 25th. for the south, and have been examining the map to see how near I can approach your

[99]Apparently this is the beginning of the draft of Mangum's reply to the Raleigh committee's invitation to a political rally. Either he did not complete the letter or the rest of it was misplaced. The manuscript is in Mangum's handwriting.

[100]The name of the writer of this letter is torn off. The writing looks like that of Benjamin Watkins Leigh. Leigh was invited to the Charlotte meeting but he did not attend.

residence. Mr. Bullock[101] tells me that the nearest point is Raleigh (28 miles) Mr. Fisher[102] told me when here that our friend would celebrate the declaration of Independence at Charlotte on 20th of May. and this will enable me to take Richmond Charlottesville, Lynchburg & Salisbury in my route with a certainty of seeing you at Charlotte.

Young Dunn gave his note payable on the 1st Inst. but has not yet paid it. I will urge him to do so before I go. And I regret to be under the necessity of saying that in consequence of the turn over in my office and the derangement of my business I am not able to remit the money I borrowed of you, but I will soon be able to do so.

The country is fast separating on White and Van Buren. The democratic portion of the Whig party in New Hampshire have hoisted the White flag.[103] The friends of McLean in Ohio have abandoned him and the Journal & Sentinel the Clay & McLean papers at Columbus have been consolidated and will go for White. It is now well understood that R. M. Johnson will be the Van Buren candidate for Vice President and that throws the contest upon ohio Indiana & Kentucky.—Under such circumstances we must look to Ohio for a candidate for Vice President. Genl. Harrison has great popularity in the N West, and his nomination would do much to conciliate the Clay party of the West.—It would I believe be more acceptable to Clay than almost any other man. I see that your name has been suggested and that Tyler's has also been thought of; but as Webster & Van Buren are both endeavoring to make this a question between the North & the South is it not important that we should look to non slave holding State for allies.

I hope to see you at, Charlotte. Do me the favor to write to me at Richmond under cover to the Editor of the Rich^{d}. Whig.

Yours sincerely

[Addressed:]

Hon Willie P. Mangum
Red Mountain P. O.
Orange Co.
N. Car.

---

[101]He possibly refers to Erasmus D. Bullock, a commission merchant from Mobile, who originally lived near Mangum and who frequently went to Washington and New York on business.

[102]Charles Fisher.

[103]The governor and congressmen from New Hampshire were all Jackson men. *Raleigh Register*, Mar. 24, 1835.

WPM-LC

D. C. Freeman[104] et als. to Willie P. Mangum

WASHINGTON No C April 16th 1835

Hon. Willie P. Mangum
Sir,

The undersigned having been appointed a committee, in behalf of your numerous friends here, take great pleasure in forwarding you the proceedings of one of the largest public meetings ever held in this county, containing resolutions, passed unanimously, approving your political course and inviting you to a public dinner in this town, at such time as may suit your convenience.

The resolutions, we assure you, express the feelings of a large majority of the free-men of this county, and the invitation is given not as a mere formality, but to give them an opportunity of becoming personally acquainted with you and to pledge to you their support so long as you continue the able champion of the rights of the States and the fearless denouncer of federal usurpation.

Your acceptance, therefore, will give great satisfaction to your numerous friends in this Section of the State and will especially gratify

Your obt Servants

D. C. FREEMAN	JNO. L. BONNER
JOSEPH BONNER	SAML R FOWLE
WILL. A. BLOUNT	JOSHA TAYLOE
EDW. STANLY	ALLEN GRIST
THOS. A. DEMILL	RICH. H. BONNER
JAMES ELLISON	D B PERRY
JOHN MYERS	SAML. MASTERS
HENRY A. ELLISON	BRYAN GRIMES
SAMUEL LATHAM	GEO. HOUSTON JR.
NATHL. I. OLIVER	J. O'K. WILLIAMS

[Addressed:]

Hon. Willie P. Mangum
Hillsboro,
North Carolina.

[104] He was in the legislature in 1831 representing Beaufort County. *N. C. Manual*, 497.

Enclosure

Resolutions of a Public Meeting in Beaufort County

MINUTES.

[April 1835]

At a very numerous and respectable meeting of the citizens of Beaufort county, held at the Court House in the town of Washington, for the purpose of adopting measures expressive of their approbation of the course of the Hon. Willie P. Mangum, in the Senate of the United States, Col. Richard H. Bonner was called to the chair and John Myers and Joseph Bonner appointed secretaries, T. W. Barrow Esq, having been called on by the chair, explained in a forcible manner the object of the meeting — Whereupon on motion, made and seconded, the following committees were appointed to prepare resolutions expressive of the Sense of the meeting, Viz, D. C. Freeman, Joshua Taylor, Edward Stanly James, Ellison, Samuel Masters, John Myers and T. W. Barrow Esqrs. After retiring a short time they reported the following resolutions, which, having been submitted, separately, were unanimously adopted.

Resolved that we have witnessed with the greatest alarm the usurpations of the present chief magistrate of the United States in his attempt to subvert the rights of the States; in his unlawful seizure of the public treasure; in his attempt to overawe and control a coordinate branch of the government and in his endeavouring to influence the right of suffrage by a general system of rewarding his partizans and proscribing those honestly differing with him in politics.

Resolved that the conduct of our Senator the Hon. Willie P. Mangum, in ably and fealessly opposing the corrupt course of the present administration, meets with our warmest approbation.

Resolved that we witnessed. with indignation, the attempt made by our Legislature, at its late session, to embarras his political course, and to drive from the national councils one of the few of *our* political men who dare be honest in this worst of times."

Resolved that a committee of twenty be appointed by the chair to express to the Hon. Willie P. Mangum an approval of his political course, in the Senate of the United States; and to request him to accept of a public dinner, in this town, at such time as may suit his convenience.

The following gentlemen were appointed a committee in accordance with the last resolutions Viz, William A. Blount, John Myers, Allen Grist, Samuel Latham, J. OK. Williams, Edward Stanly, Samuel Masters, George Houston, Joshua Tayloe, N. J. Oliver, Thomas A. Demill, Bryan Grimes, Joseph Bonner, James Ellison, John G. Bonner, Henry A. Ellison, Samuel R. Fowle, D. B. Perry, and D. C. Freeman.

On motion made and seconded the chairman was added to the Committee

On motion made and seconded the meeting adjourned.

RICHD. H. BONNER,[105] Chairman.

Joseph Bonner
John Myers.

Secretaries.

WPM-LC

William Davidson[106] et als. to Willie P. Mangum[107]

CHARLOTTE N. C
April 18, 1835

Dear Sir

The Citizens of Mecklenburg County having determined to celebrate the approaching anniversary of the Mecklenburg Declaration of Independence made at this place on the 20th May 1775.—We the Committee appointed for that purpose respectfully invite you to unite with us in the celebration of that event.

Respectfully Yours etc.

WILLIAM DAVIDSON)
WILLIAM J ALEXANDER) Com
WASHINGTON MORRISON) of
FRANKLIN. L. SMITH) Invitation

[Addressed:]

Honble Wilie P. Mangum,
Red Mountain,
Orange Co.,
No. Ca.

---

[105]Richard H. Bonner was a member of the legislature in 1831-1832 and the Constitutional Convention of 1835. *N. C. Manual,* 497, 867.

[106]See above, I, 361n.

[107]This letter is in the autograph of Franklin L. Smith. See the next letter.

WPM-LC

Franklin L. Smith[108] *to Willie P. Mangum*

CHARLOTTE April 19-. 1835

Dear Sir

By this days mail the committee have forwarded you an invitation to unite with them in the celebration of the 20- May. This has been done on the information of Mr Smith whom you saw in Raleigh and from whom we learned you had not received the former invitation sent to Hillsboro,

The Van Buren men after a notification to hold a meeting on the 20- Instant—after a postponement for reasons some of which you will find in a copy of their notification which I enclose[109] you and after much druming in the Jackson ranks—succeeded yesterday in holding a meeting at which about forty-five persons were present. In their resolutions you of course came in for a large share of their abuse—for having as they say disgraced the State &C? This meeting was got up—supported and carried through by Hutchison[110]—whom you know and who is among the two or three Jackson men in the County who even pretend to possess any intelligence—This morning's mail brought with it the appointment of this man as Superintendent of the Mint—what a commentary on the corruption of the government—Without competency—without intelligence and with but little influence, yet this man by adhering to the ranks of the party has obtained an appointment which three years ago his best friends would not have supposed it within the bounds of presumption, he could have received—Jefferson in some of his writings gives it as a saying of Hamiltons (which by the by I believe to be a slander) that men could only be governed by force or corruption—" Van Buren seems to have adopted the latter alternative and the success with which he has met makes me tremble for our country—Yet the people are honest and need nothing but to be enlightened to become as much opposed to the present corrupt system of those in power [torn] the name of Jackson has made them blind to its faults—We hope that you will be with us on the 20th. and if it is thought improper on that occasion to introduce political subjects we have given notice that a meeting

[108]See above, I, 349n.

[109]The enclosure was not found.

[110]James M. Hutchinson was a member of the legislature from Mecklenburg County in 1834-1837, and 1865-1867. *N. C. Manual,* 700-701.

will be held on the 21st. which will be largely attended and when you will have an opportunity of making such an impression on the public mind as the uprightness of your course and your abilities so well enable you

Your humble Servant

FRANKLIN L. SMITH

[Addressed:]

Honble Wilie P. Mangum
Red Mountain
Orange Co.
N. C.

WPM-LC

William C. Preston to Willie P. Mangum

COLUMBIA. [20 April, 1835]

My dear Sir

Do let me know how you are geting on personally & prolitically. I have heard nothing of you since we parted except that you feasted in Hallifax and feasted in Raleigh. Please tell me how affairs are geting on in the North State. Our paper here broke out against Judge White some time since with a most sudden and unexpected violence, without consultation or discretion. Both papers have changed editors since my return and will in future be more discreetly conducted. If they do not assist our friends they will at least refrain from attacking them, and I can now assure you with entire certainty that if your candidate can be sustained by the Southern States So. Carolina will be found in the Sister hood. There is to be sure great coldness on the subject in this state, but that you must indulge to us, & if in a moderate way we can be of service to you drop me a line & it shall be attended to. Many of the leading gentlemen of the State will be here at a meeting of the trustees early in June, when we shall be able to understand more fully than at present our respective views Suppose you call in upon us for a day or two at that time. What can we do for Genl. Green. Will you join us in becoming responsible for him each individual as far as $1000. with a security on his property.

This State may be said at present to take no interest in politics whatever, but things are in agitation which will produce some excitement by the winter. The Union party will in all probability rally as a party on Judge White, with the view of recovering themselves, by advocating for the first time a decent measure, and also of driving the more violent of the other party on *anti federation* ground *some* will be driven in that direction, but very few. They (the Union party) will find themselves in great difficulty. The President has agreed to visit them this summer & how will they receive him when they have declared for White. His visit may be intended in part for your benefit.

Calhoun is buried in the mountains. Hamilton is to be made President of a bank McDuffie is reviewing the militia with absorbing enthusiasm. The Mercury has come out for White on its own hook.

Mrs. Preston joins me in the kindest greetings.

I am Dr. Sir
Yr. obt. Sert.
WM. C. PRESTON.

20th April 1835.
Hon. Mr. Mangum.

WPM-LC

John D. Eccles[111] to Willie P. Mangum

FAYETTEVILLE N Ca April 24th 1835

To the Honorable)
W. P. Mangum) Sir

The undersigned Committee acting in pursuance of instructions from your friends in the County of Cumberland and Town of Fayetteville, who have approved your Political Course in the Senate of the United States, and are desirous of expressing Their approbation in a Public manner

Respectfully invite you to a dinner at this place at such time as will suit your convenience to attend the same

Yours Respectfully

JOHN D ECCLES	J. W. COCHRAN	JONES FULLER
CHAS T STEWART	E. L. WINSLOW	JOHN M HUSKE
BENJN ROBINSON	E. J. HALE	THOMAS SANDFORD
JOHN W WRIGHT	PARIS J TILLINGHAST	HENRY ELLIOTT
HU CAMPBELL	HON HENRY POTTOR	HENRY M TURNER
JAS. H. DICKSON	O P. STARK	PETER MCKELLER

[111]John D. Eccles was a member of the legislature in 1832. In 1832 he represented the state university as one of its attorneys. *N. C. Manual,* 577; Battle, *History of the U. N. C.,* I, 351.

[Addressed:]
To the Honbl. W. P. Mangum
Hillsborough
Orange County
No. Ca.
In Haste—

WPM-LC

Walter A. Mangum to Willie P. Mangum

TILLATOBY TALLAHATCHIE COUNTY MI:
April 25th 1835

Dear Sir,

I take up my pen once more to let you know that I have not forgotten you. I have written to you frequently since I have been here—but have not received the 1st mark from you. I am yet in great hopes that I shall draw a letter from you this Spring or Summer & say to me if you have any knowledge that our lands will be sold this next Fall. Is it possible to put Jackson & his kitchen Cabinet down, their corruption is more & more verified every day, and with a slack reign by the opposite party, there is no telling what course or extent they would take. Judge White, stands pretty fare to make a good run, in this Section or State. I see that your State legislature has taken a high step,[112] but it is hoped their mandate will not be noticed——

It is unnecessary for me to say much about my country as I expect that you have had a very correct description of it. I will say it is a *fine country*, it is a money country & will ever be so, as long as cotton will command ten cents per pound, our cotton is bringing at New Orleans at this time 23 cents per pound, a glorious harvest for the Mississippi planter — This Country would suit you up to the notch, You might give a loose to your heart & pocket & get rich—everybody is rising here, there is no pulling down one & building up an other—in this Country. I have made money since I have been here—& am doing better than I ever could have done in N. C. my land here I could sell for something like Eight thousand dollars—I have two plantation, one of them I have my negroes on & have planted 100 acres in cotton & should we not have a storm this summer or fall to through down the timber on it, I shall make between 75 to 100

---

[112]He refers to the resolutions of instruction.

bail wighing 500 lb the other plantation I have rented out for $6 pr acre, say 52 acres cleared land—I should like to hear particularly from you & Priestly what you are doing & how you are getting on—I often times think of you both with deep mortification, to think that you have so little enterprise—Priestly is less excusable for he has plenty of time to explore the West I learn that Old Mr. Cain[113] is dead—You will receive some property from the estate—if it consist of negroes is it possible that you will keep them in a starving world, I hope that your better Judgment will devise the most prudent step——

A heavy press of emigration to this country, land sells high—very common $10 per acre up to $50.

We are generally healthy in this country & have been so ever since I have been here—every thing is different from N. Carolina. You find the most learned & intelligent engaged exclusively on their farms &c. &c. &c. I am yours with regards

W. A. MANGUM.

N. B.

Give my respects to my Father & tell him should we live till this winter next, I will send him a present of 1 or 2 hundred dollars—*he maye rely on it*—tell him that I have one of the prettiest tracts of land that he ever saw perfectly level 10 & 15 feet soil lying in front of a high mountain with as good springs as I ever saw any where—I have very little wish to visit my native home I know its poor & barren—Old acquaintances are no more to be found there, but young & strange ones to supply their place & I am sure would be of no pleasure to me—I am perfectly satisfied with my home & my Country—

W. A. MANGUM

[Addressed:] To
The
Hon: Willie P. Mangum
Red Mountain P. Off
Orange County
North Carolina

La Grange
19 June

[113]William Cain, Sr., Mangum's father-in-law, died July 28, 1834. *Raleigh Register*, Aug. 12, 1834.

WPM-LC

John Beard, Jr. to Willie P. Mangum

SALISBURY April 27th 1835.

Dear Sir,

In a few days I shall start to the South West, and as I expect to pass thro' Knoxville I would be glad to see Judge White. It did not occur to me when I saw you; I must therefore ask of you the favor of a line of introduction to the Judge, enclosed to me, and directed to Knoxville. I am acquainted with his brother-in-law John Williams,[114] but when I was in that country a few years ago they were *not on speaking terms.*

With much regard
Your friend & Obt
JOHN BEARD JR.

[Addressed:]
Hon: W. P. Mangum
Red Mountain
Orange County
N. C.

WPM-LC

Charles Fisher to Willie P. Mangum

SALISBURY April 30th 1835

Dear Sir,

You doubtless have seen in some of the papers before this the call for a meeting of the people of Rowan on the 18th of May, and also that your attendance is wished for — Genl. Polk[115] promised the rest of the Comtee. to write you the letter which I presume he has done, but he is now absent from home & I can not ascertain to a certainty whether he has, or has not written, and therefore think it the safest plan to write you myself—If you have not recd. the letter from the General, I beg you to make the proper allowance for the failure, and to consider this as complying with our duty. It is generally expected that you will be here, and address the meeting—the meeting will be a large one,

---

[114]John Williams was born in Surry County, North Carolina, in 1778. He moved to Tennessee and held numerous offices including that of United States Senator from 1815 to 1823. *D. A. B.*, XX, 271-272.

[115]Thomas G. Polk, a graduate of the state university, was a member of the legislature in 1829-1832, and 1835-1837. Later he moved to Tennessee and eventually to Mississippi. *N. C. Manual,* 792; Grant, *Alumni Hist. of U. N. C.*, 498.

as we do not do things by halves here—The Governor will most probably be here—Under the expectation that you, and the Governor will each make an address, the rest of us will say nothing, or very little—

I fear V^{a}- is gone to the enemy.[116] If so, it will make our struggle the harder in N^{o}. Ca—

Let me know as soon as you conveniently can whether you will be here or not

Yours very respectfully
CHS. FISHER

[Addressed:]
The Hnbl
Wilie P. Mangum
Red Mountain P. O.
Orange County North Car.

WPM-LC

S. S. Southworth[117] *to Willie P. Mangum*

PROVIDENCE R. I. May 4. 1835

My Dr Sir/

Will you do me the favor to say, whether you do or do not consider any portion of my conduct in connexion with the Poindexter affair[118] unbecoming the conduct of a man of honor? In the past I acted, I was actuated by motives friendly to Gov. Poindexter and a devotion to truth. Partizan warfare has attempted to attach bad motives to my conduct, and I am mortified to add, what is due to truth, that the Governor has refused to give me assurance that he does not warrant the accusations of my foes.

---

[116]In the spring election for the Virginia House of Delegates the Jackson party won 72 and the opposition 62 seats. *Hillsborough Recorder,* May 29, 1835.

[117]In his *Memoirs,* IX, 265, 311, J. Q. Adams says: "Southworth is one of the representatives of the class of political writers for hire . . . He has been one of the most virulent lampooners of the whole tribe." At this time he edited a Providence newspaper. In 1842 he edited the New York *Gazette.* Louis H. Fox, *New York Newspapers, 1820-1850: A Bibliography,* in *The Papers of the Bibliographical Society of America,* Chicago, XXI (1928), 48.

[118]George Poindexter of Mississippi was thoroughly disliked by Jackson and Van Buren. In January, 1835, while Jackson was in the funeral procession of William R. Davis, a member of the House from South Carolina, Richard Lawrence attempted to assassinate the President just outside the rotunda of the Capitol. At the time of the seizure of Lawrence, Jackson expressed the opinion that the would-be assassin was a tool of Poindexter. Thereupon, Poindexter wrote to Jackson to ascertain if the reported statement was a correct quotation. His letter was returned without being opened. The *Globe* then took up the matter and got witnesses to prove Poindexter's implication. Poindexter requested an investigation of a Senate committee. The committee, which included Nathan Smith, King of Georgia, Wright, Tyler, and Mangum, unanimously exonerated Poindexter, even the Jackson men supporting his innocence. Wiltse, *Calhoun: Nullifier,* 244-246.

I proceed to Boston to-morrow, to take charge of a newspaper to be devoted to the political interests of Judge White; and if you will do me the favor to reply to this note, will you direct your letter to that city.

Very Respectfully your obt. Servt &C.
S. S. SOUTHWORTH

Hon. Willie Mangum
North Carolina

[Addressed:]
Hon. Willie Mangum, U.S.S.
Red Mountain
North Carolina

[Endorsed:]
Rec^{d}. & ans^{d}. 5th June 35.

WPM-LC

J. H. Brooks[119] *& Others to Willie P. Mangum*

W. F. INSTITUTE, May 5, 1835.

Mr. Mangum.

Sir, the members of the Euzelian Society, convinced as you know they must be, of your literary merit, are anxious to have your name enrolled among their honorary members, you will therefore do them a considerable favour by permitting them to inscribe it on their roll. Please answer us by mail as soon as practicable.

In behalf of the Society
Yours most respectfully,
J. H. BROOKS)
T. J. RAYNER &) Com.
E. BURNS.)

To the Hon. W. P. Mangum.
[Addressed:]
Hon. Willie P. Mangum
Red Mountain
Orange County
N C

---

[119]A student at Wake Forest College, Josiah Hawkins Brooks became a prominent Baptist minister in Virginia and in Chatham and Davidson counties of North Carolina. George W. Paschal, *History of Wake Forest College*, Wake Forest, 1935, I, 357, 617.

WPM-LC

V. M. Murphey[120] *to Willie P. Mangum*

HILLSBOROUGH 9th. May 1835.

Dear Sir.

Mr. Kirkland[121] is absent this morning. I took the liberty of opening your note as the bearer informed me that it contained an order. I have procured the best French Brandy in Town.

I send by your boy some letters and papers one letter you will find open. I suppose accidently done at your Brothers, as it was sent there & returned to the office—Annexed is a Bill of the articles.

With great regard
Your obt. Servt.
V. M MURPHY.

Honble W. P. Mangum
To Cain & Kirkland Dr.

To 3 Gallons French Brandy ——	30/-	$ 9.00
1. Jug " "		1.50
Hillsborough 9th May 1835.		10.50

[Addressed:]
Willie P. Mangum
Orange.

WPM-LC

George Washington Jones[122] *to Willie P. Mangum*

Near ENFIELD, HALIFAX N. C.
11th May 1835.

Dear Sir.—

I avail myself of this opportunity of writing you, thinking that you would be glad to hear from me.—

---

[120]Victor Moreau Murphey, 1805-1862, was the second son of Archibald D. Murphey. A graduate of the state university, he also studied law and medicine at the University of Pennsylvania. In 1835 he moved to Macon, Mississippi, from where he entered the state legislature and became clerk of the circuit court. In the Civil War he was surgeon for one of the Mississippi regiments. Hoyt (ed.), *Papers of Murphey*, I, 312n.

[121]See above, I, 139n.

[122]A graduate of the state university and a native of Mangum's neighborhood, George Washington Jones was, at the time of this letter, teaching school near Enfield. He became a lawyer, planter, and local Whig leader in Orange County. In 1844 he was the secretary of an Orange Whig meeting and in 1846 he was a delegate to the state Whig convention. Grant, *Alumni History of U. N. C.*, 328; *Hillsborough Recorder*, June 6, 1844; January 8, 1846.

You will see that I am in the vicinity of the little village called Enfield, amongst a parcel of real genuine Anti-Jackson-V. Buren men.

I am employed in teaching school & I have thirty-three *Students.* I was compelled to turn off some, as I have as many as I can manage. If I could have taken them, I believe I could have got fifty. My employers, (L. H. B. Whitaker,[123] Doct. Whitaker & others) guaranteed me three hundred dollars & board or I was to take the profits of the school if I chose. I shall realize upwards of $300, this year exclusive of all expenses. The family is wealthy & is able to give good prices for instruction I think therefore that I shall remain with them until I renounce the office of the birch & ferrule.

I presume you heard of my teaching school at Seth Jones's last year. Jones played off a trick with me which is in perfect keeping with his character. I went down to see him last May as I understood he wanted a Teacher—he told me that he wd. give me the rates of $100 per academical year for his own children, & that other gentlemen had written to him; who would send if he got a Teacher—As I was unacquainted with the man and as it was late in the year I concluded to accept his proposal, but to my astonishment I found out, when I commenced what he had said respecting the school was a tale of his own invention, however, as I did not have a dollar in the world; I thought I[wd]. remain until I could make a profitible engagement.—Accordingly I engaged myself to the above gentlemen—

When I went to settle my bill with Benton Utley the merchant with whom I traded at C. Hill, I found my account to be the sum of sixty nine dollars & twenty cents!!! which I found myself totally unable to pay. I took the acct which I have in my possession & told Utley I would pay it as soon as I could get it, *et res sic stat nunc*—

That debt has given me a great deal of uneasiness in as much as it was double the amount I expected to find it & as, I could not pay it. As I contracted it I feel bound by honor and justice to pay it. It has been a matter of no little surprise to myself that I could have been so infatuated as to contract a debt of such a magnitude. The only palliation I can give for it is that

[123]Later he was chairman of the board of directors of the Wilmington and Raleigh Railroad. Carey Whitaker, who was a physician of Halifax, was for several years in the state legislature. Grant, *Alumni Hist. of U. N. C.*, 660, 661; *Report of the Board of Internal Improvements of the Legislature of North Carolina at the session of 1850-1851*, Raleigh, 1850, Appendix C.

Match box, cigar case (Henry Clay's picture is on the back), ink stand, letter seal, and letter scale. The originals are in the possession of Mrs. John A. Livingstone, Raleigh, N. C.

youth have lapses and failings to lament from which none are exempt. I consider it the greatest folly I ever committed and it has taught me a lesson for the future—I have mentioned this circumstance thinking probably that you could suggest some way to get me out of the difficulty. My wages of course will not be due here until nearly the end of the year & I feel too great a delicacy in asking him for money before due, and them withal strangers—

I heard of your passing through Enfield on your way home from Washington on the next day and I regretted very much that I did not see you.—veri amici sunt tibi, hoc sectione

Yrs very respectfully
WASHINGTON JONES

P. S.
I am invited to a wedding on Wednesday the 13th ist., when I am to act in the capacity of *waiter* Revd. W. H. Wills[124] to Miss Ann Marih Whitaker daughter of Doctr. Carey Whitaker.—
G. W. J.

P. S. I was apprehensive that I should not have good health in this part of the country; but it is quite healthy & pleasant.
G. W. J.

[Addressed:]
Hon. Willie P. Mangum
Red Mountain
Orange Co.
N. C.

WPM-LC

Thomas A. Hague to Willie P. Mangum

[SALISBURY, 11 May, 1835]

Hon. W. P. Mangum
Sir

Supposing you will visit the Charlotte cellebration, & pass thro' Salisbury, I take the liberty of announcing to you that

[124]The Reverend W. H. Wills, the son of a merchant, was born in Tarboro in 1809. At twelve he left school and entered the store of a cousin for practical training in the mercantile business. When twenty-one he was licensed as a Methodist minister. For two years he was an itinerant preacher in Halifax and Granville counties. He returned for two years to the mercantile business. In 1837, because of an epidemic of smallpox and because of an invitation from relatives, he set out to explore the Lower South. Upon his return he wrote an article entitled, "A Southern Sulky Ride in 1837, from North Carolina to Alabama." After a few more years in the mercantile business he gave his full time to the ministry. He held many important positions in the Methodist Church. *Publications of the Southern History Association,* VI (1902), 471-472.

I am now the proprietor of "Old Point Comfort"—formerly occupied by W. H. Slaughter—

Just starting in Public life—I hope you will not deem me presumptious in the above annunciation. I feel solicitous to keep public attention directed to the establishment & can only say that if you think proper to partake of some of its *"comfort"* you will find the most sedulous care & unceasing attention, the greatest anxiety to please & studious endeavours to administer to your wants—it is the Stage house of the Boro' where the South Western & North Eastern line of stages dines—& I have the satisfaction to hope travellers are as well treated as at any other Stand—Should you think proper to honour me with a call I can only promise to do my best but not more.

I am Hon. Sir
Your Very Humble Servant
THOMAS A. HAGUE.

Salisbury N. C.
11 May 1835.
[Addressed:] To/
The Hon. Willie P. Mangum
Hillsboro'
No. Carolina.

WPM-LC

R. P. Letcher[125] *to Willie P. Mangum*

LANCASTER KY.,
22nd of May 1835.

My dear Sir

I have enclosed to you a letter to Govr. Branch, not reccolecting at present his Post Office, which I hope you will immediately transmit to him.

I can give you, no news from the west of a cheering character. I am living in the most perfect obscurity, soberly quietly (but I am sorry to say, not righteously,) see but little, & hear less, but from all I do see and hear, I would say, this state will go for Van Buren. The Jackson party are all for him, and the Clay party will not go for a Jackson man. Indeed some of them even

[125]Robert Perkins Letcher, a lawyer of Lancaster, Kentucky, was a member of Congress as a Clay supporter from 1823 to 1835. He was governor of his state in 1840-1844 and envoy to Mexico in 1849-1852. He was a close friend of Mangum. *Biog. Dir. of Cong.*, 1221; *D. A. B.*, XI, 193.

prefer Van Buren to White, but most of them, *curse* the whole concern, & will take no part between the aspirants. How is it in the North State? Oh! Virginia, Virginia, Virginia,—is a State worthy of all admiration!

Believing the country can possibly get along without my *valuable services,* I have determined to retire from all political strife. Whether I can be happy, *now* after living a *miserable life* of twelve years remains to be seen. I have some doubts on that point. A quiet, cozy, comfortable life, free from the mail, excitement & slander, may suit some men, very well, but I have doubts whether it suits my constitution.—so far, I have not had a fair experiment, because some of the News-papers, taking I suppose a compassion, upon me, are good enough to pour forth every week, almost, *Slander* in the greatest profusion. That together with the efforts, of some five or six accomplished, well trained liars and slanderers, have so far, kept me out of a state of torpidity. But should these fellows become so cruel & hearted as to deprive me of their kind attention, I can't say, what effect it will have.

Let me hear from you forthwith and repeatedly. I am happy to see the people of your state, don't mean to get rid of you, by *starving you out.* I should have liked very much to have been at one of your grand feast,[126] & heard some of your fine speeches. Stick to your post love the Lord, walk humbly, & obey the people, (not the miserable little petitte Larceny Demagogues) take care of their interest always, & you have nothing to fear.

Your sincere friend,

R. P. LETCHER

Hon

Willie P. Mangum.

WPM-LC

B. M. Edney[127] to Willie P. Mangum

LINCOLNTON May 26th 1835

Honl. Wiley P. Mangum

Dear Sir

The Committee of arrangement in accordance with the unanimous wishes of the Citizens, do most earnestly solicit your

[126]In the sprng of 1835 Mangum spoke at a great many political rallies in North Carolina, explaining his reasons for not resigning and building up an organization of the new Whig party.

[127]General B. M. Edney, a relatively young man at the time of this letter, became a perennial candidate in the 1840's for various state offices.

acceptance of an invitation, to attend a celebration in this village on the 4th July next

The Committee will consider themselves highly complimented with your presence & would gladly learn that you had responded to their invitation

Respectfully—B. M. Edney, CHAIRMAN

[Addressed:]

Honl. Wiley P. Mangum
Hillsborough
N. Ca.

WPM-LC

Rob. Williamson[128] *to Willie P. Mangum*

VERDANT VALE LINCOLN June 6th 1835

Hon. Wilie P. Mangum Esquire

Dear Sir

A celebration of the 4th of July next is agreed to be held at Lincolnton. I have been informed by some of the committee of Arrangement that letters of invitations were addressed to the honorable Bedford Brown, Connor, & yourself. In addition to this arrangement I have been requested by a number of the most respectable whigs of this country to address a line to you on the same subject, and to urge your attendance on that occasion. I do assure you it would afford me great pleasure as an individual to meet you in the day, & at the place appointed But believing as I do, that your presence & your public address will have a very salutary effect on the minds of many of the deluded people of this county my happiness shall be much increased. I sincerely believe Sir, that there is no section or portion of North Carolina where your presence is more needed than the County of Lincoln for the purpose of conteracting Majr. Connors undue & corrupting influence. Come, Sir, do not fail! The people anxiously look for you. Your political friends look for you and the cause of liberty & an unsetled community call loudly for your attendance. We must Fight—we must conquor—or die in the ditch.

Respectfully your sincere friend
ROB. WILLIAMSON

[Addressed:]

Hon. Willie P. Mangum
Hilsboro
No. Ca.

---

[128]Robert Williamson was a member of the legislature in 1818-1819, and 1821-1822. *N. C. Manual,* 684.

Willie P. Mangum to John Bell[129]

RED MOUNTAIN N. C. 15th June 1835.

My dear Sir

I have received your second note[130] requesting me to reply to the enquiries contained in a former one—"Whether I know or have any reason to believe, that you or any of your friends on your behalf made any, and if any, what advances to the State Rights party in the last Congress, to secure your election as Speaker of the Ho of Reps." and secondly "whether I know any reason to believe that you or they made any advances to any other party with a similar object, & to state my recollections of that election, if agreeable to me."

I can have no motive to withhold my entire recollections on this subject, & have to regret that a severe bilious attack from which I am just recovering has delayed a reply for some time.—First then, I have no knowledge, nor reason to believe, that you or your friends had any intercourse with the State Rights party *as such*—On the Contrary I have the strongest reason to believe that no such thing took place.—I know that several gentlemen of that party (your personal friends) were thoroughly for you.—But the mass of the party was not only opposed to your elevation, but had strong prejudices against you.—It is due to candour to say that I was one of the latter description.—The most of that party had *been compelled* to take position agt. the administration either partially or thoroughly.—They, or at least many of them, ascribed that necessity to the selfishness, the ambition & the intrigues of Mr. VanBuren.—While many of them deplored the seperation from the President, they regarded Mr. Van Burean with the deepest aversion & even abhorrence.—They could not have been induced to aid the views of any man who was known to stand in the relation of political friend to Mr. V.B.—

Those with whom I associated were regulated in their course as to the election of speaker mainly by this consideration & by the wishes of the Kitchen Cabinet which latter were of moment *only* as they were regarded as a fair exponent of Van Burenism.—That party then first turned their eyes upon Mr. Wilde of Ga; but in the event of his defeat, which was regarded very probable, they then looked to Mr. Polk of Tenn:—

[129]This letter has been previously published in the *Tennessee Historical Magazine*, III, 198-200. The ms in the Mangum Papers is a copy of the one Mangum sent Bell.

[130]See above, II, 324.

Many of us had been assured from a source speaking as if from full knowledge that we need entertain no hope of your co-operation in resisting Van Burenism.—That Tennessee had two parties, and that the only hope for cooperation in that respect rested upon the party with which Mr. Polk was identified; & that therefore, as between you & Mr. Polk, the obvious interest of the State Rights party was to support Mr. Polk & that reliance might be placed upon the friendly sympathies of that party; & their effective cooperation, if the course of events should render it safe & practicable.

Mr. Grundy well known as entertaining many opinions in Common with southern gentlemen & possessing the confidence of many of them, especially urged (which I am sure is in the recollection of many of them) that Mr. Polk was the only candidate from Tenn: upon whom reliance could be placed to resist Van Burenism & the Kitchen Cabinet.—

With these representations, & the impressions they were calculated to produce, the party *as such* determined to hold themselves together—to vote for Mr. Wilde as long as he had the least prospect of success, & when he should sink out of view, to move en masse, to the support of Mr. Polk.—

The lamented W. R. Davis[131] was by a sort of common consent charged with the duty of giving the "word" when the fire was to be poured in for Mr. Polk.

In the progress of the ballotting Mr. Wilde was reduced to a very small number—his prospects were regarded as utterly hopeless.—In this state of things the contest waxed warm & warmer between you & Mr. Polk.—Every one in the capitol seemed alive to the Contest & the result upon the announcing the result of a ballotting, the tidings instantly flew to the other end of the Capitol, & the sensation in the Senate seemed almost as strong as it was in the House.—

Upon one of the ballots you had risen & had drawn closer to Mr. P. The result was announced in the Senate Chamber to a groupe in the rear of the Vice President's chair. The Vice President was one of the groupe.—I witnessed the same at the distance of 15 or 20 feet. I heard nothing—My eye only gave me the information.—The Vice President seemed much depressed beyond his wont.—I instantly heard the same intelligence, & as instantly had a strong suspicion excited in my mind that we

[131]Congressman from South Carolina who died in January, 1835.

were imposed upon, or to use the language I then employed, that "we were cheated."—I hastened to the House and urged Mr. Davis in the most earnest & the strongest terms to "withhold his fire"—not to vote for Mr. Polk, or have it given, for that I had the strongest reason to believe that "we were all cheated".—

I never exchanged a word with Mr. Polk during the canvass on the subject of the election, that I remember until the instant after I spoke to Mr. Davis.—Mr. Polk was passing me hastily, stopt an instant & remarked that "if my State Rights friends intended to do him any good or to aid him, *then* was the time, then was the critical moment" or words substantially of that import, & passed on.

In reference to any advances made by you or your friends to *any party,* I have neither knowledge nor information.—In truth, I have no recollection of hearing any of your friends (out of the States Rights party) speak of it, except the Hon. Mr Peyton of Tenn; who called at our mess the day before the election, to see, as I understood, one of your friends Mr. Fulton[132] of Virginia,—I heard him converse at some length on the subject.—

I understood Mr Peyton to say that you were a Candidate upon administration grounds.—That you would continue to give a cordial support to the views of the admr.—but at the same time, in the event of your election, you would feel it your duty to award to all parties all their parliamentary rights.—That the only pledge or guaranty you would or could give, was to be found in your known principles, & your past public life.—

This is the first line I have written since my confinement by sickness.—It is written in great haste & in some pain.—I could be much more minute, but I trust I have substantially & satisfactorily replied to your interrogatories.—

I am dear Sir with great respect
Your obt. Sert
WILLIE P. MANGUM

The Hon John Bell Nashville

WPM-LC

John Bell to Willie P. Mangum[133]

NASHVILLE July 2nd 1835.

Dear Sir

I have recd. your letter of the 15th June accompanied by a statement which is entirely satisfactory, *except in one part,* in

[132]John H. Fulton.
[133]See above, II, 314-315, 324, 349-351.

which I am sure you made a mistake which your own recollection will enable you to correct. Your statement corresponds precisely with what you stated to me last winter except in this particular. The published statement of the ballots will shew that I am right. I allude to the *cause* of your *suspicion* that *you were cheated.* It was the *consternation* or *depression* you saw in Van Buren's countenance which alarmed you. Col. Polk was ahead of me until he had about 76 votes I think, & at that point I either came very near him or passed him. I have not the state of the ballot before me; but I am sure I am right in substance. It was at this point of time that you got alarmed & came down to the House. I have sent your letter back to you, that you may correct this mistake, if you shall find it one as I am sure you will. I have merely indicated by inserting some words the part of your statement which is erroneous. I hope you will, without delay, forward me a corrected statement.

I will write you soon on the state of our coun. I am now too much engaged.

Your friend & servant
JNO: BELL

Hon. W. P. Mangum
[Addressed:]
The honble.
Willie P. Mangum
Red Mountain
Orange Cty.
N. Carolina

WPM-LC

S. S. Southworth to Willie P. Mangum[134]

PROVIDENCE R. I. July 13. 1835

Sir

I have the honor to say to you, that your note of the 5 of June was yesterday received by me at Boston. The kind and flattering sentiments here expressed command my especial admiration, and elicit in my bosom feelings that never will be forgotten.—If Gov. Poindexter had done me justice, I should not have had any cause to regret that I had an agency in destroying the plot of 1835.—

[134]See above, II, 341-342.

Command me at any time, and at all times; let me be but placed in a situation that I can reciprocate your kindness, and the proudest aspirations of my heart will have been more than gratified. At Washington, I shall meet you in the winter, and if I can perform any service in your behalf command me. I could not say more in a volume, than that I am

My Dr Sir Your faithful & obt. Servt—
S. S. SOUTHWORTH

Hon. W. Mangum.
[Addressed:]
Hon. Willie P. Mangum
(United States Senate)
Red Mountain
N. C.

WPM-LC

Henry Seawell to Willie P. Mangum

RALEIGH 29th July 1835.

My Dear Sir

I wrote you several weeks[135] ago requesting you to name the time, & place, most convenient to you, for the taking of your deposition, & have waited with much anxiety for an answer. I fear my letter must have miscarried, or you have been called from home as the time would have allowed two mails, by this. Will you be good enough to write me immediately, that I may give notice—you know I have to be at Williamston the 4th Monday in next month. We have nothing with us of any moment to us or any body else. The result of the election in this County I think doubtful—my present belief is, that Hinton[136] will beat Whitaker[137]—tho a close poll. Billy Tribler [?] & Co., if beaten, deserve to be forgotten Those names as opponents are draged out, & use no exertions—whilst "e contra," every name & every thing else *fas aut nefas,* that will serve, is exerted, taken by the hand. Success to their opponents under such circumstances ought I should think, be something like annihilation to them. I fear that you & the Gov. are to go to Virginia to attend another feast political. I have heard of no other invitations. I wish you

[135]See above, II, 309.
[136]C. L. Hinton.
[137]Samuel Whitaker won.

good luck. *Fama, honor, mundus virtus, et crimine non deficiente* be your portion on earth—the line is somewhere in Horace.

Your friend,

HENRY SEAWELL.

Honbl. Willie P. Mangum.

[Addressed:]

Honbl. Willie P. Mangum,
Red Mountain,
Orange County.

WPM-LC

John Roberts[138] *to Willie P. Mangum*

ORANGE N. C. August 2 1835.

Dr Sir

I am solicitous for a little information respecting the land purchased by government of the Chickasaw Indian Nation. I wish to know the law relative to first settlers, & who yet have not purchased land but settle on public lands. Have they any superior claim, prior right, or privilege, above others in consequence of such settlement I have been told they have, am about to move there if the Lord will & wish to know before I go, and know no better a hand to apply to than yourself. And will you be so good as to inform me of any other regulations concerning it that you may think important for me to know, & you will confer a singular favor on your friend.

I can assure you if you do not love old Jackson better than I do you dont love him much. I greatly fear & did before he got in the seat which he now occupys that he will lay a foundation for the destruction of our independence. I am of opinion we are upon the borders of some awfull event.

I am Sir
Yours with great
Respect

JOHN ROBERTS.

Willie P. Mangum Sr.

[Addressed:] Willie P. Magum Senator
Orange
N. C.
Hillsborough.

[138]In 1840 he was a member of the Orange County Whig vigilance committee. *Hillsborough Recorder*, April 23, 1840.

[Endorsed:] Will Mr. Cane send this on as I know not the P. O. nearest Mr Mangum. John Roberts.
Address your answer to Cedar Grove, P. O.

WPM-LC

Isaac Croom[139] *to Willie P. Mangum*

Confidential

My dear Sir,

I send you this letter on behalf of the Committee & truly wish it may suit your convenience & inclination to visit us. We are a *true people* & our prospects for another year are *truly* flattering. I have been labouring for years against the "Slippery Elm, the wiley little dutchman & altho we send Van B commoners to the Assembly this year, the election has decided beyond all doubt that the County is for White—Our Senator Moseley[140] sails without *any* colours. He denies being for anybody & made publicly a *special* denial of being for Van B. We hold him a V. Burenite in disguise—He likes to be [on the] popular side as much as Jesse Speight & has [about] as much political independence & consistency—

Believe me very truly
Your fd & obt St
ISC. CROOM

P.S. If you receive this communication so as to answer it in ten days, address the envelope to myself at Beaufort, Carteret Co. if later, to Kinston, Lenoir Co

[Addressed:]
Hon.
Willie P. Mangum
Orange County
N. C.

ENCLOSURE

KINSTON, Augt. 18th 1835.

Dear Sir,

The Whigs of Lenoir County propose to give a public dinner at Kinston, on the 17th proximo to Jno. MacLeod Esqr.[141] of

---

[139]See above, II, 143n.

[140]William D. Moseley, state senator of Lenoir County from 1829 to 1837. *N. C. Manual*, 680.

[141]John McLeod of Johnson County served in the legislature in 1820-1821, 1823-1824, and 1832-1833. *N. C. Manual*, 669-670.

Johnston, as a token of the [pri]vate respect & public regard, for the ability & manly independence with which he advocated the cause of Constitutional liberty & unmasked Executive usurpation & misrule, in the late political struggle in this Congressional District—

The noble stand which you occupied, in the same great & sacred cause, in the Senate of the United States in one of the gloomiest periods of our Republic, demands our warmest admiration & praise—Our bosoms still throb with patriotic exultation when we reflect that in the hour of fearful need North Carolina had such a faithful & fearless champion to maintain the Cause of freedom & stand up in vindication of a violated & bleeding Constitution, utterly regardless of personal consequences.

We solemnly believe that if the monstrous claims to Executive power put forth in the name of President Jackson by the Candidate of Baltimore Humbug & the Pretorian Band of office holders & office hunters & designed to be enforced through the *popularity* of Genl. Jackson & the *unpopularity* of the Bank, shall be sanctioned by the people that Constitutional liberty will be at end in our Country—On behalf our Fellow Citizens we extend you a cordial welcome to our Festival & assure you that your presence will afford a high gratification to the participants.

With sentiments of the highets respect & considerations Your f[torn] & obt Serts

B COLEMAN
ISC. CROOM
JNO C WASHINGTON
JNO P DUNN
SNEAD B CARRAWAY COMMITTEE.
WM B KILPATRICK
SAML. C BELLAMY
WM. D. COBB
JACOB ELIOT.

WPM-LC

G. Greer & others to Willie P. Mangum

Dear Sir

HALLIFAX COURT HOUSE [VA.] August 27; 1835

Below you have a list of names who will attend a public Dinner given to B. W. Leigh Esqr at Raleigh or Hillsburro. I have not received an answer from Travis Epes Esqr of Nottoway. on the third monday in this month we had a verry large and full meeting at our Court house who took into their consideration the movements of the Fanaticks to the North great unanimity prevailed: our proceedings are published you will of Course see them. I think in Mecklenburg our prospects are improving: but here they are hopeless the Van Burenites here do not hesitate to charge the acts of Fanaticks to our account with a view to political effect: Halifax may considered as totally lost and in a hopeless condition.

Very respectfully
G. GREER.

William P. Goode	Edward R Chambers
Wiliam Townes	Charles P Greer
Thomas M Nelson	Philip Rainey
Benjamin Lewis	Nathaniel Alexander
John C Goode	Colo Canrad S Boyd
George N Kennon	Silas H. Harris
Colo Samuel Lockett	David Shelton

[Addressed:]
The Honorable Willie P. Mangum
Red Mountain
Mail. North Carolina

WPM-LC

Robert Latta to Willie P. Mangum

[4 Sept. 1835]

1835		Willie P Mangum Dr Robt Latta,	$ C
March	24—	1 Shear Sht /6 1 Shear mended & sht 1/ - -	15
April	9	1 old pair Shoes puton	15
	10	1 pair ol shoes puton - - - - - -	15
	13	irons to hold the trunk on Shear -	25
	18	1 Shear Sht /6 1 Shear Sht /6 - -	10
	22	nails made /6 1 band made 1/ -	15
		1 hoe eye mended - - - -	05
May	6	1 Shear Sht - - - - -	05
	15	1 Shoe made & boath puton - - -	20
		1 fals Coulter mended - - -	05
		1 Shear pointed - -	15
		1 Shear Sht & bar part laid -	15

June	18	1 Shear pointed & bar part laid -	20
		1 Shear pointed - - - - - - - - - - - -	15
		1 old pair Shoes puton - - - - - -	15
		3 matoc Sht - - - - - - - -	15
		1 hoxed the head putin & hoop -	50
		1 Cart wheal wedged - -	15
August	20	Chains mended - - - - -	10
		1 paid Shoes made & puton	25
Septem	4	1 Shear & screws made	1- 25
		Wood work for a too horse plow made	1- 00
		irons for moalboard & handle made	15
		1 Coulter Sht - - - - - -	05
		1 old Shoes puton - - - - - - - - - -	07½
		1 pair shoes made & puton -	25
		1 old Shoe puton -	07½
		2 Shears laid 3/ each - -	60
		1 moalboard made & puton -	25
		2 old shoes puton & 1 found -	20
		1 day and a peace of tying wheat -	75
			7 29 1

May	14—	1 Water pail made - -	- 75
		1 Churn the lid & dasher made and hoop and botom putin	- 25
		1 Water pail made - - -	75
July	9—	1 pail hoop with iron hoops - - -	25
			$ 2 00

1835		Robert Latta Dr W. P. Mangum	$ C
May	14—	15½ ℔ bacon - - - - -	
		10½ ℔ bacon - - - - - - -	
	20—	11 ℔ bacon - - - - -	
June	4	10¾ ℔ bacon - - - - -	
	7	50 herings - - - -	
	21—	9 ℔ bacon	
August	18—	10 ℔ bacon - - -	

WPM-LC

David Outlaw[142] *to Willie P. Mangum*

JACKSON 10th Sepr. 1835

My dear Sir,

I have the honor to enclose you an invitation to a public dinner to be given at this place, at such time as may suit your convenience. It is desirable that you should answer it as soon as possible, so that if you accept the Committee of invitation may have time to invite other gentlemen [whom] they wish to be present.

Permit me to urge you to accept the invitation if you can with any convenience. You may increase your own strength and that of the opposition by doing so. I take the liberty of mentioning the latter part of the week of the Superior Court, (say friday) which is the fifth monday after the 4th monday in this month.

Very Respecty.
Yours
DAV. OUTLAW.

Hon. W. P. Mangum.
[Addressed:]

To

Hon. Wilie P. Mangum
Hillsborough
No. Ca.

N°ampton Co H
Sept 11th

ENCLOSURE

[Septembe]r. 11th. 1835

Sir,

The undersigned, have been appointed by a large and respectable portion of the people of this Congressional District to invite you to a public dinner at this place, at such time as it may suit your convenience to designate.

In the performance of the duty assigned them, they trust that a few observations on the signs of the times, especially so far as they relate to the distinguished body of which you are a member, will be deemed neither mistimed nor inappropriate.

The pr [torn] f each Depart- of the govern [torn] constitutional vigour is [torn] eun the objects for which they [torn]ally instituted. By his great and [unexam]pled popularity, and his

[142] See above, II, 244.

immense pa[tro]nage, the President has succeeded in a great degree in rendering the House of Representatives, subservient to his wishes. The Senate has become therefore the principal practical barrier to Executive encroachment. Planting itself upon the battlements of the Constitution, it has boldly challenged all intruders whether open or insidious upon the provisions of that sacred instrument. It has said to the Executive "Thus far shalt thou go and no further."

As was to have been expected, this Course has exposed it to a warfare the most inveterate and deadly. No charge has been deemed too atrocious to be made, against no corruption to flagrant to be ascribed to men of whom Rome might have been proud in her palmiest days. An organized corps of pensioned presses, has exerted all its power to poison the public mind, by holding it up to public prejudice as an irresponsible aristocracy. A band of ambitious [office] holders and expectants have co [torn] fied it. Even the state Legisla[torn] suicidal blindness have, [torn] lent their aid to degrade that bra [torn] Federal Government, in which the Sovereign [power of] the Confederacy was directly represented.

Hitherto, the Senate has not quailed before the powerful opposition arrayed against it. Making its country's good and truth, the ends it aimed at, with unsurpassed eloquence ability and firmness it has maintained the great principles of Constitutional liberty; and calmly awaited the time when the sober judgment of the people would do ju[stice to its] motives.

When we say that the course of the U. States Senate in the trying emergencies in which it has been placed, has commanded our approbation we but feebly express our feelings. It has our highest admiration and gratitude. And we feel proud sir, that one of the representatives of our own State in that august body has mingled in the thickest of the fight not the least distinguished of those who were battling in the course of law and liberty against Executive supremacy; That with the courage and spirit of a freeman the representative of freemen, he has dared to call things by their proper names, to denounce the usurpation and the usurper,—the tyranny & the [tyrant].

It is to cheer you [in the] noble career which you have b[torn]-te you to renew the strife with [torn]ed zeal, that this testimonial of [torn] is offered. It springs from no spi[torn] latiion, but is the voluntary offering of [free] men who know

Walter Alvis Mangum, 1798-1868, youngest brother of Willie Person Mangum. (There is no available portrait of the other brother, Priestley H. Mangum.) From a daguerreotype in the possession of Miss Preston Weeks, Washington, D. C.

their rights and are determined at every hazard to maintain, to a public servant, whom the spirit of faction would degrade and proscribe—We pray you to accept, the assurance of the high consideration and respect, with which we are

Your Obt. Serts.

Committee of Invitation & correspondence.	Bartw. Moore Isaac Hall W. W. Cherry Robr. A. Ezell Dav: Outlaw,

---

WPM-LC

Willie P. Mangum to a Committee of Jackson

[Sept. 1835]

Gentlemen,

I have just received your letter of the 11th instant inviting me to a dinner at Jackson at such time as will suit my Convenience.—Altho much engaged I cannot forego the pleasure of meeting you.

There is not a spot upon this earth, that has more of my respect & affections than the rich & lovely valley of the Roanoke; & there reside many of my oldest & most valued friends. I have time only to say, that I promise myself much pleasure in meeting you & many of them.—I will mention Friday the 6th of November. And what is of infinitely more consequence, the stern & inflexible friends of *Liberty* & Law.—unseduced & unterrified—

I beg you to accept for yourselves & those whom you represent my thanks for this mark of consideration, & believe me to be Gentlemen

Yours friend & faithful servt

W. P. M

WPM-LC

Anne Royall[143] to Willie P. Mangum

WASHINGTON D. C. Octr 25th 1835

Hon W. P. Mangum

Sir

It gives me much pleasure to hear that you are mentioned as a candidate for the Vice Presidency to run on the *White*

[143] See above, II, 126n.

Ticket should the friends of Judge White so decide or rather the people, there is no doubt but you will be elected. May heaven speed you—You will have perceived I have not spared "the party" But in the little I have contributed to unmask Van Burenism I have been not only wholly unaided by advice, but means from the White party! True what I have done I have done for my country But I do think hard of the Tennesseeans particularly for though they were apprized from time to time of the cruel oppression inflicted upon me by the Post office yet I have not received *one cent* from that state since I had the pleasure of seeing you! & had it not been for the generosity of private friends in this city I should have wanted bread! The *Sun*[144] has fared better though it was well known to them, no one knew the secrets & corruption of the party from A to Z. better than I. & in fact I was the first to name Judge White to the Tennesse members of Congress, But to the point can not a few subscribers be obtained for me amongst your friends? a few would keep me afloat till congress meets Pray do not understand me to mean that you Sir should be personally known in the agency but as merely appealing to your goodness to name the subject to some friend! A word on the confirmation of Mr Kendall[145] if the senate confirms him rely upon it, it will be the worst act for the country they could do you see how they have served me thus Georgia went nearly the whole of my patronage & correspondence as regards that state is cut off A mos dare not prevent it he is a mere cover for the party which holds not only him But the President & vice President under their control of this I am certain! What is to be done? I assure you Sir If there be not a radical change in this department it will completely control the Presidential election Kendall's room is constantly filled with their agents & If congress has not the power within itself to cure this evil it is useless to hope for success—But I merely put you I mean the Senate upon their guard I can not think of a man suitable for Post Master Gen[l] the trust is an important one the Senate ought to attend to this the first thing—The Senate you will have foreseen is to be tormented the comeing session with the slave question may Heaven sustain them in the comeing

[144]Washington *Sun.*

[145]In May, 1935, Amos Kendall was appointed by Jackson to succeed Barry as Postmaster General. He was not confirmed until January 1836. Barry had been inefficient as Postmaster and had caused much complaint. Arthur M. Schlesinger, Jr., *The Age of Jackson*, Boston, 1945, 117.

storm—You see their is a probability of having Mr Clay in the field again! God bless you Sir

ANNE ROYALL

[Addressed:]

Hon W. P. Mangum
U.S.S.
Red Mountain
N. C.
(Orange Co)

WPM-LC

Robert G. McCutchen[146] to Willie P. Mangum[147]

CHAPEL HILL October 30th, 1835

Honoured Sir

A regulation of the Dialectic Society makes it the duty of its Members to elect some one among those that, have long since left us—to deliver an address before the Society, on the tuesday night preceeding commencement—The object of which, is, to encourage the Members in the performance of their various duties and thus aid in the accomplishment of the objects for which our Society was instituted—It is my duty in the name of the present acting Members to declare you their choice and to solicit your acceptance of the appointment for this next year

If you can turn aside from the occupations of busy life, and faithful service to a beloved Country, and spend a few leisure moments (if such be at your disposal) in directing, to the paths of virtue and wisdom, the feet of those that, and perhaps hereafter to have at their disposal the interests of the Country—be assured, Sir, the Dialectic Society will be highly gratified.

Yours
respectfully
ROBT. G. MCCUTCHEN

Hon. W. P. Mangum.
[Addressed:]

Hon. W. P. Mangum
Red Mountain P. O.
Orange County.

---

[146]A native of South Carolina, Robert George McCutchen, after graduating from the University of North Carolina in 1836, became a minister in his state. Grant, *Alumni Hist. of U. N. C.*, 386.

[147]Mangum was frequently invited by his literary society to deliver the commencement address. He usually declined.

WPM-LC

R. P. Letcher to Willie P. Mangum

LANCASTER KY
2^{d}. De^{r}. 1835

My dear Sir.

Will you be so obliging as to inform me, whether Govr. Branch thro' you rec^{d}. a letter from me after my return home last spring enclosing some papers.[148] I wrote you at the same, but got no answer from either of you. I excused *you* upon the ground that you had so much *eating* & *speaking* to do, that you had no time for writing. But I hope by this time, *your appetite is satisfied,* and therefore I shall expect a long letter, containing *all you know, all you believe, all you suspect, and all you guess.* Who will be the President? Let me know that first You know I told you *with very great modesty,* at least a thousand times that Clay was the man, who ought to be taken up by the opposition that he was much the strongest, & could *carry the day* with ease, if heartily supported by the South. I am not about to rebuke you, because I know your feelings were very much like my own upon that subject, but it is really a matter of great wonder and astonishment, that so many great men, distinguished for their good sense & prudence, all there together, for months, talking & reasoning, each anxious to beat the candidate of the party in power, should ultimately determine the best way to beat him, was to draw off the man of the greatest popularity, and of the best prospects for success, & divide their strength into three or four different parts, and each rally under their respective leaders. I was about to say, what nonsense, but I will not—I am no broken down *grumbling politician*—I hate all such characters. What I was about to say, is that the little memorandum, which you several times asked me to present, but which I forgot, is herewith enclosed—The credit upon it is I believe correct—Should it be so according to your notion, you can just hand Mr. Clay the small balance.

One other thing, get acquainted with Crittenden,[149] & I know you will like him *better if possible* than you ever did me. Remember me to Leigh in the most respectful & affectionate terms, and if you are not *cramed so full* that there is no room left in you, I

[148]See above, II, 346.
[149]John J. Crittenden, returned to the Senate in 1835. *D. A. B.*, IV, 546-549.

must ask the favor of you to drink a full glass of wine *good wine,* for me, with him

Truly your friend
R P LETCHER

WPM-LC

Willie P. Mangum to Charity A. Mangum

WASHINGTON CITY
Sunday 6th december 1835.

My dear Love,

I write to let you know that I got here safely last night at dark.—I was very sick for two days after I left home, but I am now much better—I slept well last night and my cold is sensibly abating—I am now at Dawson's—But it is uncertain whether I shall stay here.—I shall look out tomorrow.—I am here, as yet, entirely alone.—

Last night Judge Smith[150] of New Haven Connecticut, one of the Senator's died suddenly, sitting in his chair & his wife in the room. An affection of the heart, it is supposed.—

Give my love & a kiss for Father, to Sally, Patty & Mary— Tell little Mary, that she must be a good child; & tell Patty that Father expects her to learn well, & she must try hard.

Your affectionate husband
WILLIE P. MANGUM

[Addressed:]
Mrs. C. A. Mangum
Red Mountain
North Carolina

WPM-LC

Lotan G. Watson[151] to Willie P. Mangum

OXFORD Decr. 20th 1835

My dear Sir:

I have been induced to address you a line from having seen this evening a letter directed to you by Mr. Savage our editor in relation to an attack on you in the "Globe" & copied into the Warrenton Register, charging you with "anti-war speeches

---

[150]Nathan Smith.

[151]In 1826 Lotan G. Watson, of Granville, helped establish the *Greensborough Patriot.* Before that he taught school in the Oxford and Greensboro academies. *Check List of Newspapers in the Duke University Library,* IV, 543; Coon (ed.), *N. C. Schools and Academies,* 133, 170. In Volume I, 585, above, I mistakenly gave his name as Joseph S. Watson.

&c"[152] but which Mr. Savage declined sending as he felt delicatly on the subject not being acquainted with you. All that I know on the subject was that in 1812 & 13 you were at Judge Camerons a law student, & had not then taken a stand in life, but further I cou'd not say having paid very little attention to the passing events of the *time* I discover that the "Standard" the Globes ninth son is echoing the same, and concludes a paragraph in relation to yr. nomination by the "Examiner" for Governor as follows: "All we have to say is let him or any other blue light federal speechifier during the war try their luck before the republicans of N. C."[153] I do not know that it is a matter of importance to pay much attention to these matters, but I was desirous of knowing certainly whether or not it was a fact that you had made speeches of this kind. My impressions are that the war had terminated before you came before the people in a public capacity altho' there is a possibility that I might have been mistaken—Whether, however, the charges be true or false, you will always find persons in this region of Country who will see that you are not traduced.

With great respt. I am
truly yours.
LOTT G. WATSON.

[Addressed:]
Hon: Willie P. Mangum
U. S. Senate
Washington

WPM-LC

Willie P. Mangum to Charity A. Mangum

WASHINGTON
Senate Chamber 23rd. decr. 1835.
Wednesday.

My dear Love.

I am not yet quite well.—I have been a little feverish, & my cough has not quite departed.—The weather here has been cold and damp.—I recd. a letter yesterday from you, & was gratified to hear that you were all well.—Write at least once a week.

[152]All during his political career Mangum was accused of having been a Federalist while he was at the state university as a student. Mangum consistently denied the charge. The accusation grew out of a student disturbance on the campus during the War of 1812, in which Mangum probably expressed some Federalist ideas.

[153]The editorial is in the *N. C. Standard*, Dec. 15, 1835.

Fathers Kiss to Sally, Patty & Mary.—

I write to send a little tale "Rosamond Gray"—Read it to Sally, & get her to read it—& explain to her the dreadful consequences of disobeying her parents even in small things—God bless you My Love—

Your affectionate husband
W. P. MANGUM

[Addressed:]
Mrs. C. A. Mangum
Red Mountain
No. Carolina

WPM-LC

Robert Harris[154] *to Willie P. Mangum*

De. 23d 1835—

Judge Mangum

Sir—I verry soon concluded after I Saw you at Mr. Parrishes to let you have my Thrashing machine and deferred writing untill now concerning the matter that I might be able to ascertain whether or not I could furnish myself with another. I find it imposible for me to make it myself and I have tried every person that I know of that of whom Such a articl might be expected and they all tell me that to do it this Season is impossible with them, and to let you have mine *Judge* would be parting, with a convenience that I shall actually kneed myself. I would be Glad Sir—you must know to oblige you in that particular if I could do it concistently. I Saw Mr. James B. Johnson yesterday he told me that he was waiting on you and willing to Serve you Your friends are all well I Saw your Lady and family last thursday evining at Mr Parrishes at the wedding of James Lunsford's and Betsy's they were well and enjoyed themselves as well as could be expected in your absence

There is no news among us *Judge* that is worth relating. I suppose it woldnt be much out of place to tell you of a Sale scene at Ginny Taylor's ded. last tuesday yesterday was a week—Those contrary republicans and Devlish clan that you have around you when at home—the Boullings Dukes & Carringtons formed a sort of Jackson club and possessed themselves of His

154Robert Harris, a captain of the militia, had a mill and shop on Flat River near Mangum's home. *Hillsborough Recorder*, Sept. 10, 1834; March 20, 1835.

leading principle War & bloodshed They commenced their work upon our humble wagon maker but true whig Haywood Gooch and there was not a man on the ground but what was afraid to go to his relief but our noble spirited Col D C Parrish who rushed in at the risk of his own life and succeeded in rescuing him by taking the wolves on his own back—They had D[r] under their feet for ten minutes or more endeavouring to beat and stamp him to death and his cowardly friends Strong enough and a plenty of them was a fraid to interfere till at length Some disinterested persons insensed with Such out dacious conduct rushed in over powered them and Saved Parrish They are all returned all those that was concerned I am afraid they will not be rewarded thair for, their conduct they all ought to have been shot dead on the field and if I had been there armed I would have shot as long as powder would have burnt

Pork here is worth $7.50 and a rising Corn $2. Wheat $1. cotton $3.50

Yours
ROBT HARRIS

[Addressed:]
Hon. Willie P. Mangum
Washington City

WPM-LC

Richard D. Spaight to Willie P. Mangum

Raleigh December 31st 1835.

The Honorable
Willie P. Mangum

Sir.

In obedience to the request of the General Assembly of this State, I herewith transmit you a copy of the Resolutions, on the subject of the navigation of Core Sound.

I have the honor to be
Your obedt. Servant
RICHD. D. SPAIGHT.

[Addressed:]
To the Honble Willie P. Mangum
Senator in Congress
Washington City, D. C.

Enclosure

[31 Dec., 1835]

Resolution in aid of the navigation of Core Sound.[155]

Resolved, as the sense of the General Assembly of North Carolina, that it is expedient, that the Congress of the United States, should order and direct the Engineer in charge of the Dredge boat, now operating at Ocracoke, to remove the obstructions in Core Sound, between Beaufort and Pamlico Sound in this State, by means of said Dredge boat, whenever the same is not required by, and cannot operate upon the public works at Ocracoke.

Resolved further, as the sense of this General assembly aforesaid, that it is expedient, that the Congress of the United States, should make a sufficient appropriation in money, to clean out, and remove the said obstructions in Core Sound, so as to deepen the channel of the same, and to improve the navigation thereof.

Resolved that His Excellency the Governor be requested to transmit a copy of these resolutions, to each of our Senators and Representatives in Congress.

Read three times and ratified in General Assembly 19th Decr. 1835.

WILL H. HAYWOOD JR. *S.H.C.*
W. D. MOSELEY S.S.

I certify that the above is a true copy
Given under my hand 30th Decr. 1835.

W. HILL, Secretary.
Executive Office

1836

WPM-LC

George E. Badger to Willie P. Mangum

RALEIGH Jany. 2, 1836

Dear Sir.

The late Colonel Polk[1] never received his commutation pay nor bounty lands from the United States. In regard to the pay I am sure, in regard to the latter strongly believe the fact to be as I state it.—It is the purpose of his representations to apply

[155]These resolutions were published in the *N. C. Laws 1835-1836*, Resolutions, 122. See below, II, 371-373.

[1]Colonel William Polk died in 1834.

for what he was entitled to—and after a conference with Mrs. Polk I take the liberty at her request to write to you to ask your assistance in procuring some information on the subject— Sometime before his death the Colonel obtained a pension of 600 dolls under the act of Congress and I am under the impression that all the evidence necessary to entitle him to the Commutation pay, must have been filed in order to entitle him to the pension—but on this subject I am very ignorant & cannot here readily obtain accurate information. Will you have the goodness to ascertain if the requisite evidence be now on file in the proper office & if so will that evidence so filed be sufficient to support the intended application or must it be taken anew. If deficient what is requisite? Perhaps without personal trouble to yourself you may be able to ascertain from one of the officers and you will much oblige us by making the information as full & precise as possible acting upon the presumption that both in respect of the form and substance of the matter I am ignorant—

The inclosed letter[2] received by Mrs. Polk a few days ago will perhaps aid you. I need not say we have no notion of committing the claim to Mr. Duval. I have the pleasure of a personal acquaintance with Mr. Sylvester of the pension office and should you wish to call upon any one in that office, I believe he will not only take a satisfaction in doing what you desire, but also in obliging me—

Will you allow me now to ask your forgiveness for the trouble I am imposing on you? You will be at no loss to know the reason for the direction which I have given to my application.

I am very respectfully

Your Most obed. Sevt.

GEO: E. BADGER

Hon Mr. Mangum

Your early attention will much oblige us, as if proof is to be taken the witnesses are of course old & all may be hazarded by delay.

[2]The letter is not in the Mangum Papers.

WPM-LC

Zechonias Pigott[3] *& others to Willie Mangum*

BEAUFORT, N. C. Jan 10, 1836.

Sir.

During the last Session of our Legislature certain resolutions were adopted by that body, calling upon the Congress of the United States to aid in improving the navigation of Core Sound in the County of Carteret, copies of which no doubt have been forwarded to you by the Executive of this State.[4] In obedience to certain other resolutions of a public meeting of the Citizens of this County, holden in the town of Beaufort on this day, the undersigned as Chairman, and Secretarys of said meeting, were authorized to forward to each of the Senators and Representatives in Congress from this State, the following Statement of the condition and situation of Core Sound and the great necessity for improving the same. This Sound connects the Pamlico Sound with the important harbour of Beaufort which is decidedly one of the best harbours in the Southern States; and forms a part of the line of internal communication, which is now uninterrupted from Providence in Rhode Island to this port. Much however of the usefulness of this sound is impaired in consequence of the obstructions which exist therein.—Upon entering this sound from Pamlico, the first impediment is met with at Harbour Island Bar, which affords only a depth of Six feet water, but is easily susceptible of improvement and when made will remain so permanently, as it has a hard, solid bottom, and is not affected by the current—in fact the depth of water has undergone no change within the memory of the oldest inhabitant—passing on thence you enter two fathoms water untill you reach Drum Shoal, which possesses a muddy, or sticky bottom, and affords about Six feet water; this shoal will yield readily to the operations of a Dredge Boat, and when cleared out, which can be effected at an insignificant sum, will no doubt remain so without further improvement. After leaving this shoal the sound affords an uninterrupted navigation of from eight to nine feet water which will answer all of our purposes untill

[3]In 1831 Zechonias Pigott of Beaufort, Carteret County, was "chairman of the County Court, treasurer of public buildings, master of wrecks, and chairman of patrols." For these he received no compensation, but they reveal his influence in the county. Johnson, *Ante-Bellum N. C.*, 77.

[4]See above, II, 368-369.

you reach Piney Point shoals upon which there is an uniform depth of water of five feet only, and the extent of the shoal varies from a mile to one mile and a half in width; but such is the character of the bottom, and the little or no influence which the tides and currents have upon it that it is susceptible of verry easy improvement, and when improved will remain so it is verily believed in a permanent situation. Upon passing over this shoal you again enter eight feet water, untill you come to the last obstruction in the navigation of this sound viz Bell's Marsh shoal which is about two miles in width, and affords an average depth of five feet water. All these obstructions with the aid of a Dredge Boat, can be easily removed, and from the information which we have received from competent Sources, in a comparatively short time and for an insignificant sum, compaired with the importance of the improvement to the State and Country at large. The operations of the Dredge Boat at Ocracoke are necessarily suspended during the winter and stormy months, but it is confidently believed that the Boat could work upon the shoals in the Sound at all seasons of the year, and to a very great advantage, as it would be protected from the excessive inclemency of the weather and the influence of storms. At Harbour Island a Light Boat is to be stationed which is now nearly completed and will shortly assume her station. The undersigned need not mention to you that from the difficulties incident to the navigation of Ocracoke and Cape Look Out. this Sound if improved would become the thoroughfare for all our trade from Newbern and the North Counties to the West Indies and the South, and in time of War must be of infinite importance not only to our State but to the United States in general. The Harbour of Beaufort, is defended by a fortification of the second class and in time of war is the rendezvous and depot for our mercantile marine, privateers, and their prizes as it is of convenient access, and the inlet affords a depth of water of from twenty to twenty two & a half feet. The whole State of North Carolina is deeply interested in this improvement; and the undersigned trusts that this fact will be a sufficient apology for troubling you with this communication. We indulge the hope that you will contribute your aid towards obtaining the requisite appropriation and the Services of an Engineer, together with the use of the Ocracoke Dredge Boat, or such other means as will effect the contemplated improvement. Should Congress require a Survey and estimate previously to definite action upon the matter, we would suggest that the services of Lieut Swift[5] of the Engineer Corps might be obtained for this purpose. He is stationed near this place and has the controll of the public Boats attached to the Ocracoke Dredging operations, which are well adapted to the purpose of surveying or reconnoittering the Sound and are now unemployed. And we have no doubt he could obtain from the officers at Fort Macon such auxilliary aid as would enable him to proceed forthwith upon the work.

The Undersigned have the honor to be your
obedient Servants
ZECHONIAS PIGOTT Chm.
J HELLEN)
(Secys.
BENJ L. PERRY)

WPM-LC

Memucan Hunt[6] to Willie P. Mangum

RAIL ROAD RIDGE MADISON CO. MI. 12th Jany 1836

Honored Sir:

I am on the eve, in conjunction, with a young gentleman, late of N—Ca., of commenceing a compilation at large of the facts relating to the detection of Murrel's plot[7] for masacre and plunder throughout the slave holding States as discovered and procured by Mr. Virgil A. Stewart.[8] We feel a pride in having had the undertaking conferred upon us by Mr. Stewart and hope to do neither discredit to our Birth place or selves in its preparation. It will contain every thing that has transpired in this great valey of import tending to satisfy the Slave holders of the importance and rapidly progressing combination of one of the most helish and ingenious plans for their distruction that could have

[5]He refers to Joseph Gardner Swift. See above, I, 461.

[6]See above, II, 226.

[7]The John A. Murrell gang that operated on the Natchez Trace in the late 1820's and early 1830's. He was captured by Virgil A. Stewart in 1834.

[8]Virgil A. Stewart first published in 1835 under the pseudonym of A. Q. Walton *A History of the Detection, Conviction, Life and Designs of John A. Murel the great western land pirate . . . . To which is added a biographical sketch of Mr. Virgil A. Stewart.* Athens, Tenn., 1835. 75 pp. The next year, under the name of H. R. Howard, he published *The History of Virgil A. Stewart, his adventures in capturing and exposing the great western land pirate and his gang,* New York, 1836. 273 pp. Born in Jackson County, Georgia, he became a printer and manufacturer of cotton gins. By the time he was twenty he was a successful business man. In 1831 at the age of twenty-one he started for the Choctaw country and while helping a storekeeper with his business learned about the Murrell robberies. He then joined Murrell, learned of his former crimes, and arrested him.

been devised. The scenes at Livingston & Vicksburg will of course have a place. The confessions of Phelps who was shot at Vicksburg in the fall of '34, *etc.*

This Book, I have but little doubt, will have the most extensive circulation amongst all classes in the slave holding States of any production in letters that has preceded it We wish to take advantage of this, as we consider it, propitious oportunity to vindicate the existence of domestic slavery.[9] We believe with Gov. McDuffie that it is a blessing instead of a curse, that political is the only deploreable slavery and without domestic political slavery is inevitable, and that to be a patriot to vindicate our great principles of constitutional liberty is to advocate domestic slavery for always. I believe moreover most unqualifiedly that it the will of God that it should be so, and there is a superfluity of evidence in the scriptures to maintain the position.

Now my dear sir, comes the object of this communication, and it is, to ask your, and through you Mr. Calhoun's aid in the preparation of an appendix to Mr Stewart's Book on this subject. Be pleased to advise with Mr Calhoun on the subject and honor me with your opinions—would it not be well too, to recommend the education of our young people, (in the south) exclusively at home? Please procure and forward me Professor Dews[10] pamphlet on slavery it has been several years since I read it, but at that time I looked upon it as the ablest production of the kind I had ever seen.

Do me the honor to tender my respects to Mr Calhoun & Mr Leigh.

I have no news from home that you have not been advised of long since. I must congratulate you upon the adoption of the amendments to the constitution.[11] It will I have no doubt secure your re-election to the senate of the U. S. should you not be nominated and receive the appointment of Vice President, pardon me, I do assure you that there is no individual who it would give the Whig party in this State more pleasure to vote for, and in the other Southern states so far as I have been enabled to judge, than yourself.

[9]After Murrell was captured, rumors spread that one of his purposes was to start a slave insurrection in the Southwest. Several anti-slavery men who were captured in 1834-1835 confessed that they were members of the Murrell gang. In nearly every rumor of threatened insurrection in the years 1833-1836 efforts were made to connect Murrell or members of his gang with it. *D. A. B.*, XIII, 369-370.

[10]He refers to Thomas R. Dew, who, in 1832, published his famous essay on the Virginia debates on slavery.

[11]He refers to the significant changes in the state constitution in the convention of 1835 to give the western part of the state, where the Whigs were strongest, larger representation in the legislature.

I have been informed by my friend Colo. Eaton[12] of the Legislature of N. Ca. that in all probability I will receive the appointment of Elector on the White ticket in our district,[13] and to know that your name was to be associated on that ticket would greatly gratify me.

I am a candidate for the Legislature in Granville and when I left home had every reason to believe that our whole ticket would succeed in that county.

Mr. Walker[14] has been elected to the senate of the U. S. from this state for the next six years. Our defeat in this important election it is said was oweing to a division amongst ourselves. There is no doubt but that this State will vote for Judge White. Gov. Runnels[15] was of much greater personal popularity than Gov. Linch[16] and there was nothing to defeat Gov. Runnels but his Van Burenism and since the election he informs me that he was fourced into the position against his inclination.

Believe me, I am your friend sincerely

MEMUCAN HUNT

To

Honble W. P. Mangum
U. S. Senate

N. B. My Post Office is now at Canton, Madison Co.

[Addressed:]

Honbl. W. P. Mangum
U. S. Senate
Washington City
D. C.

Via New Orleans. Madisonville Mi
Jany 18th 1836

[12]He probably refers to Charles R. Eaton, who represented Granville County in the lower house of the legislature in 1835-1836. *N. C. Manual,* 623.

[13]Hunt did not give up his legal residence in North Carolina until 1837.

[14]Robert J. Walker.

[15]Hiram G. Runnels, who served as state auditor, from 1822 to 1830, was governor of Mississippi from 1833 to 1835. A Jackson supporter, he denounced Clay's resolution of censure of Jackson for removing the deposits. After being defeated for reelection by the demagogy of Franklin Plummer in 1835 he accepted the presidency of a state bank. Dunbar Rowland (ed.), *Encyclopedia of Mississippi History, Comprising Sketches of Counties, Towns, Events, Institutions and Persons,* 2 vols., Madison, Wisconsin, 1907, II, 580-585.

[16]Charles Lynch, a native of South Carolina, held nearly every Mississippi state office and shifted parties almost as frequently as he changed offices. An opponent of nullification and the Bank and a friend of public schools and internal improvements, he was considered a good candidate for governor in 1835, because he would gain many Jackson men and for opposite reasons the supporters of George Poindexter. In the campaign his opponents called him the " 'White, alias Van Buren, alias Jackson, alias Anti-Jackson, alias anything candidate'." He was elected by a majority of 426 and took his seat in 1836. After his term he became head of the Alabama and Mississippi Railroad and president of a bank. Dunbar Rowland, *Encyclopedia of Mississippi History,* II, 151-157.

WPM-LC

——————[17] *to Willie P. Mangum*

PETERSBURG Jany 13th 1836.

Hon[l]. Willie P. Mangum,

My dear Sir—

I do not often need the counsel of my political friends, in matters connected with my business: but on the present occasion, I must beg the favor of your kind suggestions—I am now anxious to engage in a small adventure to the West Indies in quest of Sugars—Do you think there is any danger in a trip to be commenced in a fortnight, & prosecuted with usual vigor? In other words, do you suppose that the French Affairs will be likely to interfere with it? Your means of information are so vastly superior to mine, that I thought it prudent, to ask for all *allowable* disclosures of your opinion upon the subject. Should you deem it improper at this time, to make such statements, you know full well, that no complaint would be uttered, or indignity felt [by] me. . . .

[Addressed:]

Hon[l]. Willie P. Mangum
U. S. Senate
Washington City.

WPM-LC

Jona. H. Haughton[18] *to Willie P. Mangum*

NEW YORK 13th Jany 1836

Hon[r]. Willie P. Mangum
Washington City

D[r] Sir

Allow me as a citizen of the State you have the honour to represent, to address you on a subject of much interest to her citizens & the citizens generally of the United States. I am the Senior Partner of two Commercial Houses, one in this city & one in Edenton N. C; the House in Edenton N C own Six vessels regularly trading between this City & that place & between

[17]The latter part of the letter, including the signature, is missing. I do not recognize the handwriting.

[18]A graduate of the University of North Carolina in the class of 1825, Jonathan H. Haughton was a successful Edenton merchant who represented his town in the House of Commons in 1833. Grant, *Alumni Hist. of U. N. C.*, 265; *N. C. Manual*, 556.

Edenton N. C & the West Indies. After having given you the above information, you will of course excuse me, when I ask you, in what manner your Hon°. Body will dispose of the all absorbing question, Will there be any War between this country & France? My only hope has been in the Senate of the United States & I ask to assure you, I should place *great reliance* on your opinions—Under a hope that your *Colleague* may be induced to go with you & the Hon° Senators from S°.C^a (which I fear he will not do)

I am Resp. Yr. Ob. St
JONA. H. HAUGHTON

Please refer to
Wm.B.Shepherd Esqr
Rep^r. of Edenton District
for my standing at Home—
[Addressed:]
Hon°. Willey P. Mangum
U. S. Senator
Washington City
D. C.

WPM-LC

Thos. J. Lemay[19] *to Willie P. Mangum*

RALEIGH Jany. 15th. 1836

Dear Sir,

In compliance with your request we send you a copy of the old Constitution of No Ca. and a copy of the amendments, adopted by the Convention which lately met in this city. By comparing the two your friend will be able to see what the Constitution now is.

We would be much indebted to you whenever your leisure will permit, for your views in relation to matters and things at Washington. Distant as we are from the scene, it is impossible to know always what course it would be most prudent to pursue, or how our movements might affect the interests of our party.

A copy of the Journal of the New York Legislature about the time of the war would be of great service—also any other authentic Documents which would enable us to lay before the people the double-dealing of Van Buren—

[19]Lemay was one of the editors of the Raleigh *Star*.

Any accessions also which you could make to the subscription list of the Star would be gratefully acknowledged. Without a considerable increase of its patronage the present arrangement must necessarily be temporary.

Very Resp[ly] THOS. J. LEMAY
Your Ob[t]. Ser[t] DAV: OUTLAW

We should like also the Journal of the New York Legislature for the year 1820—

[Addressed:]

Hon. W. P. Mangum
Washington City
D. C.

WPM-LC

P. H. Mangum to Willie P. Mangum

HILLSBORO' Jany 17th 1836.

Dear Sir,

I have expected to receive a letter from you before this time. You are waiting to be moved, I suppose, by one from me. The prospects here are so doubtful that I fain would close my eyes on the future, and say nothing of hope or expectation. The more I see & hear & reflect, the more I am confirmed in my views of the final results of our political fortunes in this state—which I communicated to you, by letter, one or two years ago, which I don't remember. The Whig cause, as it has been set up in North Carolina, can not ultimately be triumphant here—however correct the principles may be on which it is founded—& however pure in heart & sound in mind its advocates & however base, unprincipled & selfish its opponents. The honest portion of the republican party here are sacrificed & will continue to be vanquished—because of the fact that circumstances have forced them into a unity of sentiment on the questions which some two years ago divided parties & still divide them, with the classes & orders of society in N. C. that are & always will be obnoxious to popular odium at home. And between that portion of the republican party and those classes & orders of society, which I mean—there is no more sympathy of feeling or congeniality of sentiment in general, than is to be found among aliens in blood. What will be the consequence? If the whig cause should triumph here in the approaching presidential contest, there is no other state of things likely to arise, which would bring together in heart & hand the discordant materials [torn] Whigs *here* are composed—[torn] of the connexion *now* wo[torn] adhere,—so that the just inf [torn] counsels of the State of the best [torn] of the republican party will be paralyzed. This will be the case unless the Whig cause triumphs now, & the great body of our Citizens are caused understandingly to appreciate the motives & principles involved in the struggle of the present times. Ignorance may be enlightened—but prejudices cannot be seasoned down. Be this as it may.

I learned by Ellison[20] a few days ago that your family were well. We are usually well.

Nothing has transpired here but what you have heard thro' the medium of the papers.

Will you inform me of the currents at Washington, & the probabilities & prospects in the presidential election? What of a F. war

Yrs
P. H. MANGUM

[Addressed:]
The Hon:
Willie P. Mangum
(of the Senate)
Washington City,
MAIL D. C.

WPM-LC

James W. Bryan[21] to Willie P. Mangum

BEAUFORT
CARTERET CO. Jany 18. 1836.

Dear Sir;

I have not the honor of a personal acquaintance with you, but trust that my apology in addressing you, will be found in the nature, and character of the business, to which I shall call your attention.—At the last session of our Legislature, certain reso-

[20]Ellison G. Mangum.

[21]A graduate of the University in 1805, he studied and practiced law in Cartaret County. He was a member of the Constitutional Convention of 1835, the state senate in 1835, and for many years a trustee of the University. John H. Bryan was his brother. Grant, *Alumni Hist. of U. N. C.*, 81; Johnson, *Ante-Bellum, N. C.*, 505; *N. C. Manual*, 539.

lutions calling on Congress for aid to improve the navigation of Core Sound, in this county, passed that body. This thoroughfare is of great, & infinite importance to this Section of the State, as well as to the whole Eastern part of North Carolina. Accompanying my remarks in the Senate, is an estimate of the expense per month, (provided we can have the use of the Ocracoke Dredge boat which is now lying idle at Newbern), to which I would beg leave to refer you.—The Charleston Steam Navg. Company have already determined to run a line of boats thro, this Sound, as Soon as its navigation is improved.—Mr. Swift[22] an Engineer is now at Newbern & probably by proper exertion, he might be ordered to make a Survey, estimate &c in time for an appropriation by this Congress.—this can easily be done in any season of the year. Your attention to this matter, and active exertions in its behalf, will be gratefully remembered by my late constituents, and highly appreciated by

Your Obe^{t}. Ser^{t}.

JAMES W. BRYAN

P. S. Be pleased to mention the matter to Mr. Brown.—

[Addressed:]

To.

Hon Wilie P. Mangum

Senate

Washington City

WPM-LC

Weston R. Gales[23] to Willie P. Mangum

RALEIGH, Jan, 22 1836.

My dear Sir:

A day or two after the close of the late session, I had the pleasure to receive an interesting letter from you predicated on the supposition that that body was still in session. Just at the moment, a brother and sister of my wife, from Massachusetts, paid us a visit, and in consequence thereof, my time, not devoted to pressing business, has been fully occupied.

The White party here (which comprises every portion of the opposition to Van Buren) are sanguine of success, and are about adopting a train of measures to guarrantee it. I send you en-

[22]See above, II, 372-373.

[23]At this time he was editor of the *Raleigh Register*.

closed a notice for a meeting in this City, on the 30th inst. at which Gen. Dudley,[24] of Wilmington, will be nominated as our Candidate for Governor, and Gov Tyler will probably be named for the Vice-Presidency, seeing he has accepted the Maryland nomination. Whatever is done here, will be received as a *cue* throughout the State; so that if you can, from your more commanding position, aid us with wise counsel, there is yet time for it. Meares[25] was to have been our candidate, but it was found that the charge of federalism (what magic in a name) would be brought to bear against him to a degree that we did not like to hazard. Meares is my favorite, but *compromise* is the talisman which must ensure success. Dudley, it is thought, is not vulnerable at any point, having once been an ardent Jacksonite.

I also send you a Circular just issued by Haywood, in which there is an unfounded and ungenerous fling at you. As he visits Washington in a few days, ostensibly to negociate a loan *for* the State, but really to bargain with Van Buren for its vote, I think it right to apprize you of his having travelled out of the way to injure you, that you may treat him as he deserves.

There is but one opinion on our ranks as to your successor in office—and that is that you are to succeed yourself. I heard several whig members of our last Legislature say, they would not come again but for the pleasure of voting for you.

You will confer a great favor on me, if you will let me have the pleasure of hearing from you occasionally. Most of our friends in Congress, thinking probably that our communication with Gales & Seaton is frequent, do not even send us documents. Now the fact is, that I never received a *political* letter from either of them in my life. So that between two stools, I literally fall to the ground.

I am dear Sir,

Your faithful fd & Servt.

WESTON R. GALES.

P.S. The Special Message[26] is viewed here as the quintessence of indiscretion.

---

[24]He refers to Edward B. Dudley, who served as governor from 1836 to 1841.

[25]William B. Meares.

[26]On January 15, 1836, after being provoked at the failure of negotiations with France over the spoliation claims, Jackson sent Congress a special message in which he asked "for a nonimportation act, and for 'large and speedy appropriations' for the navy and for the coastal defenses." Wiltse, *Calhoun: Nullifier*, 250; Richardson (ed.), *Messages and Papers of the Presidents*, III, 1407-1412.

WPM-LC

Wm. M. McPheeters[27] *& Wm. J. Clark to Willie P. Mangum*

GREENSBOROUGH No. Ca. 23 January th 1836

Dear Sir

We hope that you will excuse the freedome we have taken in addressing you.—Feeling as we do, a deep interest in the affairs of the nation at this critical juncture—when our country has to contend not only with foreign, but what is still more to be dreaded domestic foes—when party spirit predominates—and the enchantment of a *name* guarrantees the sanction of any measures, whether calculated to elevate or debase the nation—Menaced as we are, by a foreign war, for which the country is by no means prepared—Any public documents, which you can make it convenient to forward us, will be most thankfully received, as we expect to remain in this place for the next six or eight months in the capacity of students and will, necessarily be deprived of facilities for informing ourselves on such subjects.

With the highest respect &c

We remain your

obedient servants

WM. M. MCPHEETERS

WM. J. CLARK.

To the Honourable

W. P. Mangum

Senator in Congress.

[Addressed:]

To the Honourable

W. P. Mangum

United States Senator

Washington

D. C.

[27]He was probably the son of the Reverend William McPheeters, one of Mangum's teachers. The son was born in 1816 and after graduating at the state university and practicing medicine for years, he became a professoı of medicine at the St. Louis Medical College. Grant, *Alumni Hist. of U. N. C.*, 403.

WPM-LC

Wm. Albright[28] *to Willie P. Mangum*

SANDY GROVE N. C. 30th. January 1836

My Dear Sir

I take pen in hand to write you a few lines to make enquiry in to a Certain matter that I am not quite Certain Can be come at, however I hope through you it can. The question is this, Will Judge White if Elected President Veto the Land Bill if passed by Congress. This is a question we his friends in this part of N. Carolina wish to be answered, We go for an Equal distribution of the proceeds of the Sales of the publick lands, and we are told by the Van Buranites that President Jackson will always Veto it, & that Judge White will also Veto it, & Mr. Van Buren of Course, they do not deny but he will do so, and for this cause the party in our last Legislature voted down the Land Resolutions.[29] Now we say if Judge White is that consistent Republican that we are told he is, he will not veto the Land Bill when passed by the immediate Representatives of the People, and we can Hardly believe that he will again vote against it. We do sincerely hope he will not vote against it this time, and we would be much Gratified to hear that he would not veto it if President, for it certainly is a stretch of discretionary power that a Republican ort not to use in so plain a case, where the People have so much interest in Stake, and also where it would Check Executive power & patronage, and Close that Great fountain of National corruption, that is likely to Ruin our fine Institutions. If you think it advisable I would like you would show this to the Judge, or mention it to him, in the most proper way, and then write to me, or if the Judge would be pleased to do so I, would like it, more hereafter.

Yours truly & Sincerely

WM. ALBRIGHT.

[Addressed:]

Hon. Willie P. Mangum
Washington City
D. C.

[28]See above, II, 278.
[29]See above, II, 54.

WPM-LC

Chs. Fisher to ——————

SALISBURY 2d February 1836

Dear Sir.

I arrived at home two days ago from Mississippi where I have spent the past four months. Among other things I was attending to the interest of certain Choctaws who have engaged me as their agent to do so. A friend on yesterday pointed out to me for the first time, the proceedings in the Senate on the 11th. January, or rather the remarks of several Senators on the presentation of a memorial by Judge Black[30]—Knowing as I do the origin of that memorial, I was utterly astonished to see what was said on the subject,—and above all to see the charge of *fraud* brought against these claims—So far as I am concerned the charge of *fraud* is one that I will not rest quiet under. and I now pledge you my honor to satisfy you & the whole Congress that the cases in which I am engaged are not only not *fraudulent*, but so palpably just, that they cannot be resisted. If there be any cases of fraud I have no connection with them, and will give the full use of my intimate knowledge of the nature of the claims, to detect them, & expose the authors. As to the memorial, I know the men who got it up, and their motives—they are the same characters who heretofore have been more, or less, engaged in combinations to cheat the government at the land Sales. Myself & others have defeated some of their calculations, & this is their revenge.

Mr Clays. correspondent on whom he seems so much to rely, presumes much on his credulity. What he says about the extent of the claim is not bearly exageration, but it is absolute absurdity.

In a few weeks the claim will be laid before Congress together with the papers to support it. Until then I ask you to form no opinion on it—I shall be a[t] Washington in the course of this

[30]On January 11, 1836, John Black, Senator from Mississippi, presented a memorial from the people of the northern part of Mississippi stating that a fraud was about to be practiced on the Indians. In the treaty of Dancing Rabbit Creek, the memorial stated, each Choctaw family head was given 640 acres and an additional amount for each child if he decided to remain as a citizen of Alabama or Mississippi. To obtain these acres, the Indian had to register within six months after the ratification of the treaty. Speculators approached those who failed to register their claims, even those who had moved to their new homes in the Indian Territory, and by small bribes got their signatures for claims to land which had already been bought by white settlers. Upon the reading of this memorial, Clay declared that he had heard that the fraud amounted to $10,000,000. It was referred to the Committee on Public Land Claims, which made its report May 22, 1836. *Register of Debates*, 24 Cong., 1 sess., 99-102, 1412.

month, but in the mean time, I wished to disabuse myself from any suspicion of fraud in connection with this claim so far as I am concerned. I will thank you merely to mention the contents of this letter to Mr Calhoun & any other of your intimate friends, as I would feel deeply distress[d] to have them suppose me to be connected with any fraudulent claim.

Yours with great regard
CHS. FISHER

WPM-LC

J. Eliot to Willie P. Mangum

TALLAHASSEE
2nd Feby 1836—

My. D. Sir,

In a moment of excitement I hasten to inform you of the real situation of affairs in this my adopted Country.

You, I no doubt, have long since heard of the hostilities & the many devastations committed by the Seminole *Indians.*[31] For the last four weeks an attempt has been made to raise an effective force to meet the exigencies of the country—but without effect—To meet the wants & requisition of our Governor a bill has been passed by the Council & sanctioned by the *Governor* authorizing the *governor* to raise by draft or volunteer 600 men. In this bill many objections occur which at first sight did not occur to many of the *Council men,* & that is, they did not foresee the event of imposing a $50 fine upon the yoemanry—The consequence has been—the fine paid—& no force to protect the Country—A second & more formidable objection is that our head officers are jealous of the Councils of each other—Nothing is done to relieve us of this state of affairs—We remain in "status quo" & this is likely to be our situation

To relieve us I must suggest the propriety of having General's Scott & Gaines[32] ordered to conduct & take in charge their affair

---

[31]Some Seminoles moved west as a result of the treaty of 1832, but others, for fear that they would lose their slaves if they moved, remained in Florida. These latter Indians were finally induced to agree to leave on January 8, 1836. Several incidents between the Indians and the army followed. Some chieftains also had personal quarrels. As a result, fighting broke out in January, 1836. General Clinch of the United States Army, aided by the militias of Georgia and Alabama, came to the whites' support as the second Seminole War began. Foreman, *Indian Removal,* 324-331.

[32]General Edmond P. Gaines took charge in the early part of 1836 and soon defeated the Indians, although some fighting continued for six more years. Foreman, *Indian Removal,* 331.

You may rely upon it the *man* has no confidence in the *conduct* of our commanding officers—"Truth is great & will prevail[">—I have no time to give you a true & correct history of our situation—it is deplorable—& this to satisfy the ambition of a few—farewell I am now called in caucus & must obey.

Yours J E ELIOT.

P.S. Show this to my Representatives friends & Senator Mangum —I do rely much upon their exertions—the fate of Major Dave & Companies should be borne in mind—

[Addressed:] Hon. W. P. Mangum
Washington
City,

[Postmarked:[
Tallahassee
Feb 2

WPM-LC

Thomas McGehee[33] *to Willie P. Mangum*

PERSON N CAROLINA 5th February 1836

Dear Sir,

Pardon me for troubling you with a letter of business when you have cause to be more than troubled with polotics. We have it in contemplation to erect a cotton factory at Milton and before I proceed further with the subject should like to know something more of the expence — will you please do me the favour to inquire of some of your acquaintances what would be the cost of 2000 spindls and all the fixtures necessary to set them to work—not including the water power for that I can calculate myself—I have no doubt but there are Gentlemen in congress owning such property and can give me usefull information will you please confur with them and give me there estimate p spindle

I believe I cannot refrain from saying something on polatics, Will Hr. Taney's nomination[34] be confirmed by the senate. Is Genl. Saunders an applicant for minister to Spain and if so will he get the appointment. I hope there is no prospect of a war with France—what think you of that matter—We have now to look to the sound discretion of the senate for there seems to be but little discretion elsewhere

---

[33]See above, I, 50n.

[34]Roger B. Taney was confirmed as Chief Justice on March 15, 1836.

Mr Leighs trials must be too great for common fortitude to bear for while he is honestly and faithfully fighting the battles of the southern people against the northern fenetics the Va assembly is relentlessly hunting him down[35]

When you obtain the desired information respecting spining of Cotton please inform me and any thing on the subject of politics would be acceptable to your Obedient servt

TH MCGEHEE

Hon. Wiley P. Mangum.

[Postmarked:]
Cuningham's Store N C
Feby 7th 1836

[Addressed:]
Hon. Wiley P. Mangum
Washington City.

WPM-LC

John Williams[36] to Willie P. Mangum

KNOXVILLE Feb: 6th 1836

Dear Sir

I understand the Legislature of Ky. has passed the bill chartering the Charleston and Cincinnati rail road— The several States having granted the necessary charters the only remaining obstacle to the completion of the road is the requisite funds —The Cherokee chiefs some weeks ago went on to Washington in order to sell their Country for five millions of dollars[37]—I met with Colo. Gideon Morgan[38] a few days since on his way to Washington whether he had been invited by the chiefs—He commanded the Cherokees during the late war & has married a Cherokee woman—These two circumstances give him great influence among the Indians—I conversed with Colo. Morgan on the propriety of the Cherokees taking two or three millions of the stock in the Charleston & Cincinnati rail road—He concured in the measure & will recommend that disposition of a part of the Cherokee funds provided he becomes satisfied that

[35]In February, 1836, the Virginia legislature passed resolutions instructing Tyler and Leigh to vote for Benton's motion to expunge from the Senate journal the censorship of Jackson for removing the deposits. When Governor Tazewell refused to transmit these resolutions to Tyler and Leigh, the presiding officers of the two branches of the legislature sent them. Tyler resigned within a few days, but Leigh waited until the meeting of the next legislature. McMaster, *History of the People of the U. S.*, VI, 312-13; *Ralegih Register*, Dec. 20, 1836; *N. C. Standard*, Mar. 10, 1836.

[36]Brother-in-law of Hugh Lawson White.

[37]On December 29, 1835, some of the Cherokee chiefs signed the New Echota Treaty.

[38]Colonel Gideon Morgan married an Indian woman and in 1817 became one of the leaders of the tribe. Bassett, (ed.), *Cor. of Jackson*, II, 300.

the road is to be made—As the Western part of your State is deeply interested in this great work I hope you will confer with Col° on the subject—A subscription by the Cherokees of two millions will insure the completion of the road—Has Mr. Adams gone over to the enemy?[39] I see he has quarreled with his friends —I take very little interest in the political *strife* going on in Tennessee at this time— I have been treated about equally bad by the leaders of both parties— And have only to wish them the success that attended the war among the Kilkenny cats— I presume the reinforcement in the Senate from Miss[i]. & Lou[a]. will enable the adm[on]. to carry their measures—I hope Congress will insist on the Presidents floging the Seminole Indians before he goes to war with France—The number of the Seminole Indians is greatly exaggerated—On the 10th of Feb: 1813. with about 250 volunteer troops I engaged the whole force of the Seminole Indians & routed them at the point of the bayonet— The highest estimate I could then make of their numbers was 750. including Indians & Negroes—Who will the opposition support for Prest. Without organization they will fall an easy prey to the enemy—

Respectfully your
Humble Servt.
JOHN WILLIAMS

Honb.
W. B. Mangum

[Addressed:]
The Honb.
W B Mangum
Senate U States
Washington City—

WPM-LC

John C. Taylor[40] to Willie P. Mangum

GRANVILLE Feby 7th. [1836]

Dear Sir.

The solicitations and general expectations of my friends place me under obligations to become a candidate for the senate of

[39]He probably refers to John Quincy Adams' support of Jackson's French policy. Adams felt that in this fight Jackson was doing what Adams himself did in the earlier Florida incident.

[40]John C. Taylor, of Granville County, was a member of the House of Commons in 1824-1825, 1827-1828, and state senate in 1836-1839. *N. C. Manual*, 622-623.

the next Legislature. Indeed I am already considered as standing in that relation to the county. I shall be opposed by the former incumbent Mr. Wyche.[41] I will take it as a particular favour if you will furnish me with a copy of the letter which was addressed to you by Mr. Wyche some short time after your first vote upon the act of the President in the removal of the deposits. There are several reasons which prompt me to make this request which it is unnecessary to repeat. But among others, it may be prudent in me to be furnished with the copy to rebut the imputations of an unfounded charge, as to my object in alluding to the letter during the last summer, before the people [of] Granville. I assure you that I will make no use of it to which you can take any exception. Mr. E. Bullock[42] of Washing-[ton] informed me while in Granville that the original letter was in his possession together with other paper[s] of yours. If you can do so with convenience I should [be] further obliged by your sending me a copy of M[r.] Clays report upon his land bill. I think our elections will be conducted with unusual spirit. The friends of Judge White have the prospect of a highly popular ticket for the house of commons. There is no doubt of our having an overwhelming majority in the county, altho' as you know it is next to impossible to decide an election in Granville wholly on partisan principles. I have however but little doubt of our success in the commons. The contest between Mr. Wyche and myself will be a very close one. I fear him only on account of that advantage to which he has uniformly been [torn] for his success in elections viz:
his local sit[uation] in the county.
Be pleased to send the entire
copy of the letter; and not to o-
mit the date.

Victory to the most industrious.

With gr. respect.

Yours &c. JNO. C. TAYLOR.

[Addressed:] Honble. Wiley P. Mangum
of the Senate of the U. States.
Washington.

---

[41]James Wyche. See above, I, 351n.
[42]Erasmus Bullock.

WPM-LC

William F. Gordon[43] *to*——————

ALBEMARLE, near Lindsays Store,
7th Feby 1836

My Dear Sir

Your letter dated the 28th Decr. last came to hand on yesterday only in consequence I suppose of its direction to Gordonsville post office—I consider the young Gentleman Mr. Mosly[44] who is Editor of the Va. Advocate at Charlottesville, to be of first rate talents as an Editor, he is well educated, writes well, is sprightly & solid too, of very high personal worth, & what is something in these times is *good game*.

We have made considerable efforts to retain him as Editor of our paper He has done & is doing great service to the White Cause here—We have induced him to print twice, instead of once a week. It requires an effort in this part of Virginia, to sustain ourselves against the powers of the Murphey[45]—if we lose him our cause will be in danger—I wish him every success. he is my personal friend. & I esteem him most highly—I cannot answer whether he will be willing to go to Washington—I shall probably see him in a few days, or weeks at most. When I will consult him—In any event, judge Whites friends ought to patronize his paper if it is well sustained *here,* I think we can carry Va. for him; our position is *central,* in the neighborhood of *R.* & *B,*[46] who have much power over the Jackson folk.—*both* of whom I fear will be for V. B. I have no doubt that he would be a good selection for your purpose, but his loss would weaken our cause *here*—Judge of these circumstances & let me hear from you again—If it is thought best by our friends at Washington, to remove him, I will do any thing, which my intimacy with Mr. Mosly can effect for the cause & to carry their wishes into execution—I regret that an accident should have so long delayed this answer as to induce a moments belief that I was unmindful of the Interests your letter involves—Wishing you victory over

[43]William F. Gordon was a member of Congress from the Albemarle district from 1830 to 1835. *Biog. Dir. of Cong.,* 1024.
[44]He refers to Alexander Moseley, who was at this time the editor of the Charlottesville paper.
[45]Unable to identify.
[46]Probably Rives and Blair.

the *New York Primmers* & a happy deliverance from the Greatest & Best

I am very truly your respectful &
obt. St
WM F GORDON

WPM-LC

Lewis Williams[47] *to Willie P. Mangum*

WASHINGTON Feb 9th 1836

Dr Sir.

I will thank you to let me have about 12 copies of Ewings Reports on Clays Land Bill[48]—I want one for each member of the Legislature in my district—We ought to circulate that Report far and wide in North Carolina, and indeed in all the old States.

Your obt Hble Servt.
LEWIS WILLIAMS

Hon. Wilie P. Mangum.
[Addressed:]
Hon. Wilie P. Mangum
Senate United States
Washington.

WPM-LC

J. D. Boyd[49] *to Willie P. Mangum*

CHARLOTTE N. C. Feb 10th. 1836

Dear Sir

I wish you to send me a copy of Mr *Wise.s Speech*[50] upon the Appropriation *Bill* I have read it in detached pieces I wish it

---

[47]See above, I, 134n.

[48]Thomas Ewing of the Senate Committee on Public Lands reported January 27, 1836, on what to do with the surplus. He included in his report Clay's earlier report on manufactures on April 16, 1832. In his report Ewing stated that the national debt having been paid off there was a surplus in the treasury, mainly because of public land sales. His committee reviewed the following possible steps to take: (1) reduce the custom duties. This, he stated, would cause too much of a controversy. Therefore, his committee opposed it. (2) Increase the appropriations for fortifications and the navy. Some, he continued, should be spent for this but not the entire surplus. (3) Reduce the price of public lands or turn the public lands back to the states. Clay's report which he included, he said, showed that this was unwise, for it would cause frauds. (4) Distribute the surplus revenue to the states. His committee, he added, favored this plan. "Report of the Committee on Public Lands on Senate Bill No. 40," *Senate Documents*, 24 Cong., 1 sess., 44 pp.

[49]J. D. Boyd operated a hotel in Charlotte in 1836. Later he moved to Charleston, where he also kept a hotel. See below J. D. Boyd to Mangum, Jan. 1, 1842.

[50]On January 12, 1836, Henry A. Wise, of Virginia, spoke in the House of Representatives against partial appropriation bills because they resulted in too large an expenditure for printing which would benefit Rives and Blair. *Register of Debates*, 24 Cong., 1 sess., 2173-2174.

entire whatever one may cost I will pay—an/ others making the same or equivalent developments I also want and a favour will be confered by Sending them to me—I do think and feel as Mr Wise did viz "I. sympathise with the *chair*" if the Hon. Speaker had any sensibilities left they must have been much excited, (tho Van Buren Sensibility is hard to find) in this country—

I would be glad to hear from you at any time—

Yours Resp
J D. BOYD

N.B. I see you had the Floor
and hope you pealed them[51]

[Addressed:]
Hon. W. P. Mangum
Washington
City
D. C.

WPM-LC

Rosewell Saltonstall[52] to Willie P. Mangum

NEWYORK Feby 10 1836

Honble W. C. Mangum
Revered Sir

I wrote you the day pr Mail to which refer you & pray your attention to me & my Discoveries of Moment to the World & to United States

Pray Deliver the inclosed & commune with Honble H Clay on my Discoveries now before the Senate my Soul adores Southern Members & Kentuckians where lays soled virtue to Constitution & Confederation of Thirteen.

Respectfully Yr Fidel
Humble Servant
ROSEWELL SALTONSTALL.

[Addressed:]
Hon. Wilie C. Mngum
U. S. Senator
Washington
D. C.

---

[51]On February 3, 1836, Mangum spoke against "tremendous expenditures" for defense against France. In the speech he included an attack on the postoffice corruption. *Register of Debates*, 24 Cong., 1 sess., 367-383.

[52]Unable to identify.

ENCLOSURE

WPM-LC

NEW YORK Feby 10th 1836

Honble H. Clay
My friend

I Discover with some pain a Man by name of E P Page Esqr with a Petition before Congress to obtain Florida Lands by his Discoveries which I conclude never will pass the Senate

This E P Page entitles himself the High Priest of Nature & has been months past preach^{g} in Tammany Hall in this City idolized by Regency & Mat V Buren administration

This Man High Priest if in Florida would raise more Rebellion that U. S. could stop

Three years ago E P Page gave me in this City his own Hand writing my Calculations were Right now he comes to supplant I Pray my Discovered Longitude may by Senators yourself &c meet immediate Reward

I have wrote the British Minister Mr Bankhead on this Subject do see him on this Subject I wish I was near a Knowledge of your Penetrating Eye trys to Console me My Discoveries in London is a Fortune for Three hundred Men I hold the Magic Square never Discovered in the age of Pythagoras to count either Vertical Horizontal or Diagonal make 7 or 28 & makes
7 X 3 21
8 X 3 24
9 X 3 27
is there any way for your Senators to have me Nominated Minister to St James Court

Your Cordial F^{d}

ROSEWELL SALTONSTALL

[Addressed:]
Honble Henry Clay
Senator
Foreign Committee
Washington City
pr D. C.
Honble. Mangum)
Senator)

WPM-LC

Wm. S. Ransom[53] *to Willie P. Mangum*

BIGBYVILLE, MAURY COUNTY, TENNESSEE,

Feb 10th. 36

Dear Sir

Here I am, in the verry vale of obscurity and pinioned down in one of its most secret nooks. I could no longer stand N. C. My native County I saw would never elevate me as long as I dared to act like a freeman, and rather than wear the trammels of a slave, or pine in neglect & eternal obscurity, I sought a more generous and hospitable clime. I left home in October and wondered about like the Hebrew of old, until my limited purse was exhausted, when I took up here with a school I would have set up for a Lawyer right off, but resolved not to get in debt, and I had tried strutting into practice too long to attempt to poke it off on these shrewd Western fellows. I am consequently now retired almost from the world, though in a densely populated Country, establishing a character for prudence, and making money to sustain me for a while at the Bar, until I can prove that I am possessed of *sterner stuff*. This is the native County of the Hon. J. K. Polk, but I donot know him nor do any of my few friends in Congress know that I am here which is one cause that prompts me to write to you that I may know how things are going on in Washington & occasionally get a paper or so franked. The people here are nearly all for White, I am told, notwithstanding Genl. Jackson's letters to Guywn & Nicholson.[54] These here are more independent than in the old States and I thought President Jackson knew Tennesseans better than to dictate to them. The Legislature of this State can't be managed

[53]A former editor of the Raleigh *Constitutionalist.*

[54]In the early months of 1835 it was evident that sentiment in Tennessee was turning against Jackson. Bell and White controlled the leading state newspapers. It was "rumored that Tennessee Democrats would not even send delegates to the administration-sponsored convention scheduled to meet in Baltimore." This news angered Jackson and so he wrote a letter to James Gwin, of Nashville, with the expectation that he would publish it asserting that he was always willing to abide the popular will. He then urged the people to send delegates to Baltimore. Later, on August 8, 1835, he wrote Gwin again denying that A. J. Donelson had abused the franking privilege of the President.

Because of the weakness of the Jackson newspapers, A. O. P. Nicholson had to take over and write editorials and letters to strengthen the cause. Parks, *Life of Bell,* 93-94, 126; Bassett (ed.), *Cor. of Jackson,* V, xxi, xxii.

easily while such men as Terry H. Cahol[55] compose it. Your friend E. Paschall[56] is down in the District also with a school—if the fellow will only keep sober he may rise If my cousin M. T. Hawkins makes a speech this session you must be certain to send it to me,—quid rides? I shall be extremely glad to hear from you, and that the aspirations of your best friends may be gratified—You live in their confidence and the possession of honours, health, and wealth is the prayer of

Truly yr Obt.
WM S RANSOM

P.S. Remember me to Bullock,[57] and tell him that if he should continue in Washington a few more years he may see me there on U. S. expense, there are some as poor chances in Congress as I am I think.

[Addressed:]

To The Honorable Willie P. Mangum
Washington City
D. C—

WPM-LC

P. H. Mangum to Willie P. Mangum

HILLSBORO' February 15th 1836.—

Dear Sir,

I wrote you some weeks ago but have not heard from you yet. Since the predominance of Van Burenism, I have not been favoured with any notices from Congress, as formerly; I suppose my Van Buren countrymen are of the opinion that none are of the people—as none are Democrats, but those of "the party" & therefore they are not under any obligation to enlighten the public mind without the pale of the 'Elite'.—I have just risen from the perusal of Mr. Calhoun's report on the subject of transmitting by mail "Incendiary publications."[58] That

[55]A Virginian who moved to Tennessee, Terry H. Cahol was in 1836 lieutenant-colonel of a Maury County regiment that helped defeat the Seminoles. J. C. Guild, *Old Times in Tennessee with Historical, Personal, and Political Scraps and Sketches*, Nashville, 1878, 122, 139.

[56]Edwin Paschall, who taught school in Granville County, North Carolina, before he moved to Tennessee, wrote a history of Tennessee for boys and girls. In his preface he insisted that too many school histories were fragmentary. He proposed, therefore, to present a continuous narrative. In a speech in the House of Commons of North Carolina, Robert Potter declared that "though his name [Paschall's] be like my own, unknown to fame, yet . . . I dare to call him immortal." Edwin Paschall, *Old Times; or, Tennessee History, for Tennessee Boys and Girls*, Nashville, 1869, 3-4; Coon (ed.), *N. C. Schools and Academies*, 134; Coon (ed.), *Doc. Hist. of Ed. in N. C.*, I, 326.

[57]Erasmus Bullock.

[58]Calhoun made his report on February 4, 1836. For a good account see Wiltse, *Calhoun: Nullifier*, 274-277.

man is at home on all constitutional questions—& gives to every thing he touches, the impress of unsurpassed, if not unequalled, greatness. But it is all in vain! Such coin will not [pass here.] His cause is such as to make [torn] droop his head, and the [torn] their countrymen. When our people, names have infinitely more potency, than substance, reason and argument.—I saw to-day, in the Globe of one of my neighbours, what purported to by a speech of yours on Benton's resolutions.[59] I suppose you never delivered such a speech—& if so, it may behoove you to give to the public, the *real speech*. Such scoundrels should not have it in their power to publish what suited their purpose, *with malice prepense,* to detract from an opponent—without my sending forth *a neutralizer.*—

We learn here that in the event that the Virginia resolutions pass—& probably they have already passed—that Tyler will resign.[60] If he does resign, how can the opposition in N. C., advocate his claims to the Vice-presidency? We are to have a meeting at our County Court, for the purpose of appointing delegates to meet delegates &c to nominate a Elector for this Electoral District—& to nominate an anti-V.B. candidate for Governor. It may be necessary to act on the subject of the Vice-presiden[cy torn]-nt to know from you, how [he stan]ds on the subject general[ly torn] in regard to the proposed instructions. —I don't like the selection.—I perceive that the Senate will be equally divided. What course do you design taking in that event? Mr. Graham informs me that he saw a letter from you to Mr. Outlaw, in which you spoke of resigning & taking a run in the Commons. What will be gained by that? to yourself or to principle?

Being weather-bound, I was not at Granville Court—& therefore have not seen your family. Some days ago a servant came up for Sally's trunk, as preparatory to going to Louisburg. The family were then well. I think Sal[ly] had better have returned

---

[59]On February 3, 1836, Mangum made a long speech attacking the administration for its corruption and for its defense program. This grew out of Benton's resolution to use the surplus revenue for defense purposes. The *Globe* carried a very short report of the speech, but the *Register of Debates* reported the entire speech. *Cong. Globe,* 24 Cong., 1 sess., Appendix, 72-73; *Register of Debates,* 24 Cong., 1 sess., 367-383. The full speech was also published in the *Raleigh Register,* April 5, 1836.

[60]On February 29, 1836, after he had received the Virginia legislature's resolutions of instructions, Tyler offered his resignation. He admitted the authority of the legislature to instruct him, but he felt it had acted unwisely in this case, for it would have been unconstitutional, he said, for him to have voted for the expunging resolutions, since the Senate was acting legally in keeping a journal of its actions. Leigh refused to resign until December 5, 1836. He explained in his letter that he was not resigning because of the legislature's instructions but because of private responsibilities. *Register of Debates,* 24 Cong., 1 sess., 635; *Raleigh Register,* March 22, Dec. 20, 1836; *N. C. Standard,* March 10, 1836.

to Hillsboro'—it would have pleased me better.—We have nothing important here. We are tolerably well. I have had the fortune to bury two negroes this winter,—Bob & Winny—and am on the buy without much mony. This is my fortune & no prospect of better.

Will you give some insight into the [torn] matters of Washington—either [torn] or the Cabinet.—

P. H. MANGUM.

[Addressed:]

The Hon: Willie P. Mangum
(*Of the Senate*)
Washington City
Mail. D. C.—

Hillsboro N C.
17th Feby 1836

WPM-LC

R. Macnamara[61] *to Willie P. Mangum*

ARMFIELD NEAR SALISBURY NO. CAROLINA

22nd February 1836.

Honble W. P. Mangum.—
Dear Sir.

It is with great reluctance I call upon my friends to do me a favour; but on the present occasion, I hope my peculiar situation will plead my apology.—

It has pleased the Almighty, to deprive me of my beloved Wife, in November 1834, leaving six Children to deplore her loss. My Oldest Son John Steele Macnamara, Seventeen years old, has been at English, and Latin Schools. I have a great wish that he should enter the Military Academy at West Point, as Cadet, for which I entertain no doubt he is qualified.

I hope you will find no difficulty in obtaining for my son a warrant from the War Department, so as to enable him to enter the Academy next Summer, as I understand, that North Carolina, has not supplied the Number of Cadets she is entitled to, under the regulations Established by Congress.

Perhaps you are not aware that my son, is the Grandson of the late Genl John Steele, of Salisbury who served with much

[61]Colonel Robert Macnamara, 1788-1843, married Eliza Steele, the daughter of General John Steele. Jethro Rumple, *A History of Rowan County, North Carolina, Containing Sketches of Prominent Families and Distinguished Men with An Appendix*, Salisbury, 1929, p. 190.

distinction during the Administration of Washington, and John Adams, Comptroler of the Treasury of the United States. I write by this days Mail to my friend and immediate representative, the Honble. A Rencher on this subject, with whom I request you will confer should you deem it proper, or necessary.—I have the honor to remain Dear Sir.

Your most Obt.
& Humbl Sert
R. MACNAMARA.

[Addressed:]
The Honble W. P. Mangum
Washington City.

WPM-LC

Hardy Bryan Croom[62] *to Willie P. Mangum*

TALLAHASSEE, FLORIDA February 22nd 1836

My dear Sir,

You will, no doubt, be somewhat surprised by a letter from the subscriber, your old acquaintance and friend, who has not for so long a time had the pleasure of meeting you, or communicating with you.

I have for some time watched with intense interest the struggle which the Senate has been making against the usurpations of our federal executive. God grant that it may avail to save from the general fate of past republics this deluded and almost besotted people! The day when the Senate yields will be an ominous one for this country! What will become of it if that disastrous spectacle should occur of

"*Our* Caesar with a Senate at his heels!"

I most heartily rejoice at the prospect of an accommodation of our difficulties with France. A war at this time with that nation would plunge this country from its present high prosperity into an abyss of suffering, and would throw it back in its rapid career at least half a century, and would terminate perhaps with the sway of a dictator firmly established!

I must now state, my dear Sir, that the immediate object of this letter is somewhat selfish, and at least personal to myself.

---

[62]Hardy Bryan Croom, of Lenoir County, North Carolina, graduated from the state university in 1817 and served in the state senate before he left for Florida for his health. Eventually, he moved to Alabama. Grant, *Alumni Hist. of U. N. C.*, 143.

A few years ago I was induced, by the State of my health, to remove my planting interest to this country, where I have spent the winters returning to North Carolina in the Spring in order to avoid the long protracted heats of summer in this climate—I have children in whose education I take a great interest, and for this and other reasons I think of settling myself and family either at Columbia or Charleston in South Carolina. One motive I have for the selection of these places is the admiration which I entertain of the people of that State, and especially its distinguished sons, Calhoun, Hayne, Preston McDuffee &C—I know it is in your power to give me the acquaintance and the favourable opinion of these gentlemen, and this is the object of my present letter.

At the same time it is proper for me to state that I have never given my assent to the *theory* of Nullification, although I am willing to allow that cases may arise in which I would be as willing as others to resort to the practice of that conservative or revolutionary doctrine whichever it be.

Differing somewhat on this point from these distinguished gentlemen my admiration of their characters and abilities is the more disinterested. I shall take it as the greatest favour if you can secure me their acquaintance. I expect to visit Charleston about the first of April on my return to North Carolina—If you can enclose a letter to Governor Hayne, directed to me at Charleston, to the *care* of *Peter Bacot,* Esq. I shall be much obliged—I should also be glad to hear from you by letter directed to me at "Rocky Comfort, Florida." Towards your colleague and my ancient friend Mr. Brown I entertained my former feelings of personal regard, though I differ from him throughout in his political course.

I remain very truly your friend and
humble Servant
H. B. CROOM.

To
The Hon.
W. P. Mangum.

P. S. It is in contemplation, I understand, to revive the "Southern Review," and if Mr. Legare[63] declines the editorship I would be willing to *assist* in that department, if I should be thought

[63]*The Southern Review,* which was edited by Hugh S. Legaré and Stephen Elliott from 1830 to 1832, was discontinued in the latter year. Legaré went to Europe and upon his return in 1836 there was talk of reviving it. William S. Hoole, *A Check List and Finding List of Charleston Periodicals, 1732-1864,* Durham, 1836, 29; *D. A. B.,* XI, 144-145.

worthy. Having organized a profitable estate here I should have some leisure for such pursuits—

[Addressed:]
The Hon.
Willie P. Mangum
Washington
D. C.

WPM-LC

Thomas G. Polk[64] *to Willie P. Mangum*

SALISBURY NO CAR

25th Feby - 36.

My Dear Sir

I [torn] spent some days [torn] the only doubtful [torn] Rowan—The Whigs, are active, vigilant and determined, to make a bold push to carry the county at the august elections—Many changes have taken place, & I do not despair of the county—At all events the majority will be so small on either side, as to weigh nothing in the general agregate.—For the purpose of aiding them, I will thank you to send me a few copies of Wise's speech, and *any others* which you may think, can be beneficially distributed in that county.

We s[torn] in the wh[torn] Govr. & the Legislature [torn] require & I learn from our friends in all parts of the State, that they are resolved to meet the coming crisis with the activity & the energy that behoves those, who are strugling to preserve what little of liberty is left us.—

In haste I am Dr Sir
Yours truly &
THO. G. POLK

[Addressed:]
To
Honl. W. P. (Mangum)
Wa(shington)
(D. C.)

---

[64]See above, II, 340n.

WPM-LC

Charles P. Green to Willie P. Mangum

BOYDTON VA March 1 1836

My Dear Sir

A friend of mine Edmund W Hening who is now the Editor of the Expositor[65] is interested as one of the heirs of his uncle John Banks deceased in a claim against the General Government which has been depending before Congress for a number of years, and remains as yet undecided. He informs me that the claim originated during the Revolutionary War for supplies of provisions clothing and for the use of ships furnished the Southern army under the comand of General Greene by his uncle John Banks The demand is in every point of view just and equitable. and supported by satisfactory testimony. He is desirous of knowing the exact condition in which it is placed at this time & what steps have been taken to secure its final adjustment Mr Hening informs me that Mr Thos Hord of Virginia at present in Washington who is the authorized agent to attend to the business—If your good office could be exerted in furnishing me with the information and forwarding his wishes I should esteem it as a personal favour confered upon me and Mr Hening himself will feel grateful for your attention. He suggest that you had better see Mr Hord who can give you some information about the matter. —It gives me pleasure to inform you that the little *paper* which I established in this place will for the future enlarged and conducted with the greatest ability, I can with confidence say that Mr Hening is in every respect equal to John. H. Pleasants as a writer. Owing to his limited pecuniary means he is prevented from taking charge of some paper that has a better location—to opperate upon the public mind. If this claim is substantiated I have no doubt but that he will establish a journal that will do great good in the South. We are geting fairly under way in this part of Virginia in opposition to Presidential dictation and from present appearances we are confident of success. It gives me the greatest pleasure to see in every paper that the people in the *Old* North State are rushing "to the rescue to the rescue" there has been meetings held in Wake, Chatham, Guilford, Rowan, Davidson, Cabarus, Wilkes, Burke, Halifax, and many others. I was glad to hear that you had declined runing for Governor for the

[65]*The Virginia Expositor and Southern Advocate,* which Green edited until the early part of 1836.

reason that you can do more good in your present station—every days experience convinces me that you adopted the right and only proper course in regard to "Expunging" that is to *remain* at your post and tell the *collar dogs* to go to H—. from every information you will no doubt be sustained in N C.—What will Leigh & Tyler do? What is Judge Whites prospect at present?

How does Genl. Duff get on? do not let him suffer. If we have to part from the Yankees as I fear that we will be compeled to do, he is better fitted to advance our cause than any other person I will thank you to give my respects to Calhoun, Preston, Pickins Hammond and all other Nullifiers say to Calhoun that ninety nine out of a hundred Whigs in this county together with nearly every student at Randolph Macon College[66] are of the *true* faith, this news you will rejoice to hear, as the *rising generation* will have to bring back the good old times of States Rights. If I did not know that you would not *criticise* on this my hasty *scroll* I would have taken more pains but as the mail is about to start and writing to a friend I have only to say good bye—

your friend
CHARLES PLUMMER GREEN.

[P.S.] Answer *this* as soon as convient
[Addressed:]
Hon Willie, P. Mangun
U. S. Senate
Washington
City.

WPM-LC

James Simmons[67] to Willie P. Mangum

HALIFAX NO C 9th March 1836

My Dear Sir.

Your esteemed favor of the 26th ultimo came to hand by a due course of mails; and candeur requires me to say that I felt particularly honoured by such an evidence of confidence from so distinguished a source and upon a subject of such vast importance. Doct [Robert C.] Bond kindly handed me your letter to him, by which I learn your views more fully than they were expressed to me.

---

[66]Randolph-Macon College was then located at Boydton.

[67]In March, 1835, James Simmons was vice president of the Halifax meeting which did honors to Mangum on his return from Washington. *Hillsborough Recorder,* April 3, 1835.

The Doct has probably written to you and several of your other friends have or will write you soon, should this however be the first letter which reaches you upon the subject from this section of the State, let me venture to predict that you will learn from all,—that the event to which you allude has thrown us into a state of confusion that is not to be envied even by John Q. Adams—We are now buisily consulting whether we had better continue our voige (being nearly half way) with a vessel somewhat leaky or return to port put her in the dry dock and take another.

I will abandon my intended metaphor and state to you a difficulty which appears to all with whom I have consulted upon the subject. Our friends have move almost unanimously & simultaneously upon the subject of the important approaching elections. The meetings have been preceeded by great pains to prepare the minds of the party to act with one accord, and, there was some difficulty in bringing on united action in consequence of (what some called) Mr Tylers Nullifying principles[68] (for them I should like him better were they stronger) In many counties great success has attended the efforts and in many instances there were enough present to make at least twenty Van Buren meetings. Those meetings have severally been addressed and preambles connected with resolutions (in all of which Mr Tyler has received a due portion of praise) have passed without division.

With many persons the majority, the powers and merits of great men are more highly valued before the person is seen (In my estimation Mr Calhoun Mr Leigh and————————are grand exceptions to that rule) Many of the people of our State have been induced to believe Mr. Tyler a very superior man to any in the United States except Judge White and you will allow they have excuse for so believing when you recollect that the active Whigs have been exerting themselves to make that impression ever since Maryland brought him forward We have a great number of very good men in our state who are not capable of investigating the claims of the different candidates, for themselves and consequently have to rely upon these more intelligent neighbours, who have but recently prepared them to take the Whig ticket and who would unwillingly undertake to substitute any other names for those which have now become familiar to the people.

[68]He refers to Tyler's acceptance of the right of instruction.

Virginia if not settled against us will have a stronger inducement to take our ticket. And as to the effect which Mr. Tylers course will have in our state in relation to our views of legislative instruction, we suppose it will not change a vote.

Mr. Calhoun remarked truly the other day that "we have not succeeded because we have not remained united."

Under these circumstances and innumerable others which will more readily suggest themselves to your mind, I most respectfully submit for your further reflection whether we had not better wait & see if Mr Tyler will not withdraw,[69] and if he does not, whether it would not be better to wait until the other counties have gone through with their meetings? otherwise posibly whilst we were countermarching in one county another would be marching forward and we might get our forces so scattered as to be unable to rally them or might at least suffer by *mutiny* or *desertion* It is also submitted, whether if there should be a move in this matter, it would not be better for it to originate in some other than Gov. Branches native county or even State I do Sir greatly fear the consequences of a retrogade movement, for not unfrequently an attempt to change the order of battle has given the enemy the victory

I will offer but one further reflection, which is whether our defeat is not almost certain, let who will be on our ticket for V. P—& consequently whether it is not more important that we should remain *in solid colum* & thereby hold a strong check upon the succeding administration, than to make any move by which a division may be produced in our ranks & we of course rendered still weaker. Virginia will sustain her brightest jewells Mr Leigh & Mr. Taswell and contribute her portion to the purity of the Senate & with a firm & patriotic Senate the Country is safe.

I hope my dear Sir although I have somewhat desented from your views, you will not attribute it to presumption, but if I am in gross error, believe it to be the result of extream anxiety for united action among the Whigs—which thank heaven are not of that india rubber quality like the opposite party which can be put into any shape by a little paragraph from a corrupt press

I cannot willingly conclude this communication without making known to you that the embarassed situation of my fathers

[69]There were many Whig meetings in North Carolina in the winter and spring of 1836 endorsng Hugh Lawson White for President and John Tyler for Vice President. There was considerable opposition to Van Buren. Nevertheless, the Jackson name enabled him to carry the state with a majority of 9,240 out of a total of 52,046. The Whigs did not organize their campaign effectively. Pegg, "Whig Party in N. C.," 150-154.

estate (he having died when I was only 12 years old) deprived me of all opportunity of education, which circumstance it is hoped will induce you to look indulgently upon my incoherent manner of conveying my ideas,—together with a want of grammatical arrangement & proper spelling—

Please present my respects in your own better way to Mr Leigh & Mr Calhoun, posibly the latter does not recollect one of the fiew who assembled around him in this place when the President has issued his proclamation against him. Belive me to be your devoted friend

JAS. SIMMONS.

In the course of business I have received the inclosed bills which are not current here & which I will thank you to exchange for me with the representatives. The Michigan note is thought to be a counterfeit which can be determined better in Washington than by me it being the only one I ever saw. I have intended writing to you for the purpose of giving some names to whom posibly you may send speeches documents &c. if you wish me to do so let me know and it shall be attended to

I am Dear Sir as before expressed
Your Devoted Friend
JAMES SIMMONS

[Addressed:]

Honble
Willie P. Mangum
City of Washington
D C.

WPM-LC

Samuel P. Ashe[70] *to Willie P. Mangum*

WESLEY HAYWOOD CO TEN.'
March 10. 1836.

Dear Sir

Hoping that tho' our acquaintance has been quite limited, yet as we are both native North-Carolinians and I believe in principle too, I trust I shall be excused for the liberty I now take in addressing you. Not having any other acquaintance in the Senate

[70]Son of John Baptista Ashe, of Revolutionary fame, Samuel P. Ashe after serving in the North Carolina legislature from 1823 to 1826 moved with his brothers-in-law, William B. Grove, John Hay, and Dr. John Rogers (a school teacher) to Tennessee. *N. C. Manual*, 577; Samuel C. Williams, *Beginnings of West Tennessee in the Lands of the Chickasaws, 1541-1841*, Johnson City, 1930, p. 118.

of whom I could, with more propriety ask the favour permit me to inform you that as the Heir (the Son) of John Baptista Ashe a Lt. Col. in the No Ca Line of the Continental army during the Revolutionary War I have lately thro my friend Col. Dunlap[71] of the House of Representatives from this State applied to Congress for my Fathers commutation pay, and he has lately written to me "that the proper Committee has reported in his favour as a Major, he having held only a Certificate & not Commission of promotion to the rank of Lt. Col., This Sir seems to me to be a strange and inconsistent conclusion, for all the affidavits accompanying the claim corroberate the B^r. Gen^ls, Certificate that he was a Lt. Col. several years before & at the conclusion of the War for if he was not a Lt. Col. he did not serve long enough to entitle him to pay at all but all the affidavits & Certificates shew that he did continue in the service "during the War," and Jones' defence of No Ca states the same, as well as other history. Indeed of this Sir there can be no doubt. However be this as it may, to the proper tribunal I submit, and if I can get what the House has agreed to I am satisfied, yet Col. Dunlap is fearful that in the Senate the *"Interest"* will be stricken out, this is an important item. My Father died when I was quite young and not untill a few years ago (about 3) did I know that there was any such pay due any one much less him as "Commutation pay" for had I known it I would have applied many years ago, because for the last 17 years I have been harass'd and almost ruined by having to pay Security debts: And now Sir as the last struggle for me is in the Senate, can I obtain the favour of you to do me justice there? this is all I ask. For if the claim is not a just one I don't want it, I believe it is & therefore I ask what the Law, contract & rights give me. Do examine my papers. And your exertions & influence in my behalf will be most gratefully remember'd.—I am so great an admirer of Judge White that I am almost ready to write to him it is a matter just now (as affording me relief from *security* debts) of so much consequence, and to Mr. Clay with whom I agree still more nearly in Politicks, But my humble situation in life forbids it and I must submit to their known sense of justice.

And now Sir can I venture to say to you—that as native No Carolinian I [am] proud to own you as a Brother Statesman, worthy the "old North State" unwarp'd by Executive patronage

[71]Colonel William C. Dunlap, a friend of James K. Polk.

or persecution, for tho' I am now a Tennesseean I never was a *"Jackson man,"* no not in the No Carolina Legislature of 1823, 24 & 25. But was one of those of the Crawford party. I am now a White man taking all things into consideration, tho' politically Clay is my favourite—a firm, honest, independent, uncomprising but courteous politician. His equal is not in the United States.—I need not tell you that White has a majority here, I do not believe that Genl Jackson was ever as popular certainly not now. I am persuaded there are not 50 Van Buren men in the Co & not but one *known* one in this neighbourhood.—Huntsman[72] is our Member, (tho' Crockett get our votes here) & as yet has gone straight, he is an independent man.

Hoping Sir that you will excuse my intrusion, assuring you it will not only be gratefully rememberd but most cheerfully reciprocated at any time I remain most respectfully

[Addressed:] Your Obt. Servt. &c

Hon. Willie P. Mangum SAM P. ASHE

U. S. Senate

Washington City D. C.

WPM-LC

John H. Crisp[73] to Willie P. Mangum

TRENTON TENNESSEE March 15 1836

Honl W P Mangum

Dr Sir

I understand that there will be a new District laid off in Mississippi for the federal court of the U. S. and consequently there will be an attorney on the part of the Government to be appointed my friend Joel H Dyer[74] is an applicant. Should he be nominated you will confer a favor by supporting his nomination with your vote and influence I ask this as an old No. Carolinian and number myself among your friends and Admirers Any attention you may give this will confer a favor on your friend

[Addressed:] JOHN H CRISP

Honl Wiley P Mangum

U. S. Senate

Washington City

---

[72]Adam Huntsman.

[73]He was the first doctor in Trenton. Samuel C. Williams, *Beginnings of West Tennessee,* 142.

[74]Born in North Carolina and reared in the Holston region of Tennessee, he was the son of one of Jackson's friends who fought well in the Creek, Seminole, and British wars. Samuel C. Williams, *Beginnings of West Tennessee,* 142.

WPM-LC

Willie P. Mangum to Charity A. Mangum

WASHINGTON CITY 15th, March 1836

My dear Love.

I have been sick for a week, confined to my room. Influenza is the complaint—I have been bled and have taken three doses of calomel—I am a good deal reduced, but am getting well again —I have attended the Senate to day—

I write merely to say, that I am tolerably well again, and hope to remain so.—I am getting very sick of this place, and very much desire to go home—I think of running home as soon as the weather gets better & the roads, unless we shall determine to adjourn in May, of which I have hopes—In that event, I shall not leave here before the end of the session.

I wrote to Mr Bobbett[75] this morning—Give our children a kiss for me, & believe as ever your most affectionate husband—

I do sincerely hope I may be able to live at home.—It would be better for my family as well as my own happiness—

God bless you My Love

W. P. MANGUM

[Addressed:]

Mrs. C. A. Mangum

Red Mountain

No. Carolina

WPM-LC

John B. Bobbitt[76] to Willie P. Mangum

LOUISBURG, N. C. 20th, March, 1836.

Dear Sir:

Yoursof the 15th inst. came to hand yesterday. It's contents I made known to your Daughter & Miss J. B. They were much pleased to hear from you, and of your partial recovery from your late sickness. They send their love and respects to you; and your Daughter bids me say she will write to you next week. With the Department of these young Girls my Lady is much

[75]John B. Bobbitt, of Louisburg, taught Mangum's daughters.

[76]A graduate of the state university in 1809, John B. Bobbitt became principal of the Franklin Academy in 1816. He had charge of the boys and Miss Harriet Partridge, of Massachusetts, had supervision of the girls. Later, they married and in 1820 temporarily gave up teaching. In 1832 they became joint principals of the academy. Edwin H. Davis, *Historical Sketches of Franklin County*, Raleigh, 1948, 42-45.

pleased. Sally is attending to music and some other (necessary) branches. Books & other things, which she may need, Mrs. B. and myself will furnish; and in all respects a paternal care, by your humble servt. shall be exercised. Her mildness and reserve, of which you are aware she is possessed, will necessarily secure to her an interest on our part for her wellfare.—On your return we calculate you will spend some time with us.—

Before concluding I must say to you, that two political meetings were recently held in our village: one of them espoused the cause of V. B. & R. M. J.[77] in glowing *colors*, as suitable persons to fill the Curule chairs: the other, the cause of White & Tyler.

We have read the letters of Gov. T.B.W.L. and J.T.[78] and are rejoiced to find you associated with such able expounders, not expungers, of the Constitution.—

Should you conclude to continue in the Councils of the nation, I am told your chance for success will be pretty certain: the cause of White, and that of V. B. will be made the Test.

Yrs. respectfully
JNO. B. BOBBITT.

Hon. W. P. Mangum
[Addressed:]
Hon. Willie P. Mangum
Washington City.

WPM-LC

Lewis Dishongh[79] to Willie P. Mangum

ONSLOW COUNTY N. CAROLINA March 23rd. 1836.

Mr. Wiley P. Mangum

My Dear Sir. It is now some 7 or 8 years since I had the honour to see you, and in fact I expect that you have entirely forgt that there is such a being in the world. I was borned and raised on Deep-creek in Orange County I saw you the first time that you declared yourself a candidate to represent the County in the General Assembly—you were elected and the next year—I think I am right—you came to my old Fathers where we were cutting of Wheat—and came to us in the field, and from thence you went to Hardy Hurdles where I saw you the next morning,

[77]Van Buren and Richard M. Johnson.

[78]Governor Littleton Tazewell, Benjamin Watkins Leigh, and John Tyler, of Virginia.

[79]A member of the state senate from Onslow County in 1831-1832, Lewis Dishongh was in 1836 a member of the state Whig Vigilance Committee for Onslow County. *N. C. Manual*, 734; *Raleigh Register*, Jan. 12, 1836.

as I had broken my sythe blade and had went there to have it mended. I was that year old enough to vote, and I did for yourself—old Lewis Dishhan as the people generally spell the name is my father—and you are pracably well acquainted with my older Brothers Reddick who is in the west and Nathaniel who is still in Orange County. I have been thus minute that you might posably recollect me—I never had any acquaintance with you—I left the county shortly after the time above aluded to—and have not been back only Transantly. In 1829 and 1830 I think it was I was elected from this county to reprasent the same in the Senate. In August 1833 and 1835 I opposed General McKay in the Wilmington District and it is likely with as much [illegible] to him and the friends of the Little Craut-eater as [could] [torn] have been done by any one else, for altho I am not a holehog Jackson man; yet I am a sworn enemy of the *Fox*.[80] Well Sir I have gone through my little introduction—I never came to the point—it is not to ask of you to procure a fat office for me—But to say to you what I think you should do—in this hour of difficulty. If you wish the State of N. Carolina to give the vote to White—you must send inteligents to the people. The post masters in this sexion are all for the *Fox*, the people read nothing hardly but what is taken from the *grate Globe*—your only way to counteract that is by the franking priviledge. Send large bundles to the *Whigs* at every post office with a request that They distribute them amongst those who will be shure to reade them. McKay is the most damned scoundle that the world can b[oast] of. He never sends [torn] but his own side. If you send any thing to the post offices they will not distribute to them.—Send them to the *Whigs*, known *Whigs*. There are five men in each County appointed by the Senteral Whig meeting—that will act for you and from them you could get any information that you might want. If all other names were with drawn—and the contest was between the *Fox* and *White* the Whigs would succeed, but you are the men to do the work.— Whilst Webster, Clay—Harrison or any one else is running the people will be jalous of intreague, be pleased to pardon me for bad

[80] Van Buren.

Writings spelling and above all the notions which I have intruded on you, but I am anxious to do right.

LEWIS DISHONGH.

[Addressed:]

Hon. Wiley P. Mangum
Washington City
District of Columbia.
Pr. Mail.

Onslow C House N C
March 26th

WPM-LC

John Scott[81] *to Willie P. Mangum*

HILLSBOROUGH, March 25th A.D. 1836

The Honble
Willie P. Mangum,
My Dear Sir.

Excuse me for troubling you with a few lines on the subject of the Orange elections for the General Assembly.

There is considerable excitement in this County upon two points, to wit, the Presidential election, and a division of the County.[82] The people West of Haw River are generally in favor of a division: whilst those who reside East of the River are generally opposed to it.

We are able to make out a White Ticket, for the commons which will undoubtedly be successful, to wit, Waddell & Graham[83] for the centre; one in the East end of the County say for instance Harrison Parker; and the other from New Hope, Cane Creek or the Hawfields.

But we are somewhat at a loss as to the Senate, Dr. Smith[84] is spoken of: I am inclined to the opinion that Allison[85] would beat him: Waddell is also spoken of: but it is somewhat doubtful whether he could be elected against Allison. Things will remain, as they are, until about our May County Court, when we must fill up the ticket.

---

[81]See above, I, 18n.
[82]The agitation for the division of the county continued until 1849 when Alamance was created from the western part of Orange. In 1844 when the people were permitted to vote on the division, 1,364 were for and 1,656 were against division. *Hillsborough Recorder*, Aug. 8, 1844.
[83]Hugh Waddell and William A. Graham.
[84]James S. Smith.
[85]Joseph Allison.

What I have to suggest, for your consideration, is this—If you should come to the conclusion, to resign your seat in the Senate of the United States, might you not so arrange it, as to take a seat in the Senate of our State Legislature next Session? This State will undoubtedly go for White as President & for Dudley for Governor. The next Legislature would re-elect you Senator to Congress.

In making this suggestion to you, perhaps I may take an unwarranted liberty, if so, ascribe it to my zeal in your behalf, rather than to any other cause.

No one knows, or shall know, the contents of this communication to you.

I remain Dear Sir
Your's sincerely.
JOHN SCOTT

[Addressed:]
The Honble.
Willie P. Mangum
Senate of U. S.
Washington City
District of Columbia.

WPM-LC

Richard Smith[86] *to Willie P. Mangum*

RALEIGH 30th.. March 1836

My Dear Sir.

I would have replyed to you sooner but expecting I might hear from Doctr. Montgomery first. but he has not written, and I delay no longer—. I had a Note on Mr. Glynn[87] that was burnt when you recollect my Store &c were all lost &. of course the Note. I have neglected to have it renewed last session I sent it to Genl. Barringer rather to late for him to attend to it and some weeks past I sent to Doctr. Montgomery in D. S. B: [*sic*] plan to try & get Mr. Glynn to renew it. after some time he was willing to give a note, but without seal. I wrote the Doctr. to take it if he would not sign a note under Seal observing that It would compel me to bring suit sooner than on a sealed note—

[86]Richard Smith was a well-to-do merchant in Raleigh. A Whig in politics, he served as a member of the Whig Central Committee, which was organized on December 22, 1835. *Raleigh Register*, Dec. 29, 1835. On July 19, 1841, he wrote Mangum that he was worth $100,000 to $150,000.

[87]See above, J. Dandridge to Mangum, March 22, 1835, and below, B. B. Smith to Mangum, May 27, 1836.

The Note was for \$195.55/100—I proposed for Doct^r. to compromise it if Glynn would pay only \$150 cash down and give him up the balance & all the Interest, which would amount to nearly as much as the principal. the Note being given & dated in April 1823. for a fair & bona fide transaction say for clothing &c out of my store.—. I had never pushed M^r. G upon it—and my long indulgence is certainly the strongest evidence of that fact. and as he was endeavouring to do something to be enabled to pay I continued to let him alone. until the present. & then applyed to him to renew the Note in place of the one lost. and to pay it if he possibly could.

I do not wish to use any coersive measures, unless you & Doct^r. M. think it necessary or advisable. He has the papers, and as he has them, I request the favor of you to see him when convenient & whatever you & he think best, I will be governed by your directions, or if you prefer it let me know, and I will direct you.—And as I do not know what Doct^r. M. has done since I last wrote him. You can know if you see him.—

I have written you upon this sheet. thinking you might find it necessary to refer to your & M^r. Dandridge[88] communications &c.—please to see Doct^r. M before you do any thing, to know what he has done. perhaps he bro^t. suit or threatened it.—I am like many others here, very desirous, for congress to make a distribution among the States of that portion of the revenue arising from the sale of the public lands.[89] I have read Mr Ewings able report. It is unanswerable. and if what he reports can be sustained, and I think it can, then the money, cannot legally be put to any other use. I see Pennsylvania has put in for hers. all the States should not only claim it, but demand it, as their right & property—And if refused, bring a suit—for each ones part, or all go together, as one case of a State would decide for all the others. This suit might be brought in the United States Court, at Washington, or likely you would know I only mention this, by way of bringing it to your mind, & to know whether you have ever thought of that, or of any other process. by which we would recover the portion belonging to our State being assured of \$1,000,000 now and about \$500,000 more yearly

[88]See above, J. Dandridge to Mangum, March 22, 1835.

[89]In December, 1835, Clay introduced in the Senate his second land bill providing for the distribution of 85 per cent of the proceeds from the sale of public lands to the states according to population. This distribution was to continue for five years. The Senate approved, but in May, 1836, the House tabled the bill. The Democrats then proposed a bill to distribute the surplus in the treasury among the states according to the number of representatives they had in Congress. This became law in June, 1836. Van Deusen, *Life of Clay*, 286-288.

—It would lessen our taxes very much build Rail Roads, Establish public Schools. &c &c. Will you please inform me the prospect of its passing—The Public debt being part of - - This Land money belongs now, to the States, and Congress in my humble opinion has nothing more to do with it—only like or in place of a trustee are bound to return it to the original owners, the States.—But O me! what is party a doing, and what is it that they will not do, why my dear Sir bring every thing into ruin, party, party wrong or if ever right no matter. It would seem that a mighty change ought to take place, when the people are so barefacedly gulled but so it is; a Spur for the Horse & whip for the fools back. I see verified throughout this country. I do despise any man to crawl at and cowardly submit to the party powers. I admire M^r. Wise's boldness he has told the truth in spite of all—. and so have you, continue to be firm & bold, you will yet come out the better by it, and in my Opinion, the time is not far distant. I think it possible yet that Vanburen will be defeated—I think the Abolition question will do for him. The present incubent is enough for a dose: Heaven forbid, us such another.

with much respect & esteem I remain
very respectfully yours &c.

RICHARD SMITH

WPM-LC

Warren Winslow[90] *to Willie P. Mangum*

FAYETTEVILLE March 31, 1836.

Hon. W. P. Mangum
Dear Sir.

Would you be kind enough to send me, if your leisure Serves, such papers or documents on the Subject of the *land Bill,* as may be necessary to make out a plain statement of the merits of the bill, & a short view of the Subject. We are anxious to prepare such a paper & give it an early & general circulation in this district. A rapid & effective organization of the White party is now going on, & I think we may flatter ourselves with a triumph in August, unless some untoward event should occur.

While writing permit me to mention a circumstance connected with the conveyance of the Mail on the great Northern Route, from this place, information about which should be in the pos-

[90]A graduate of the state university in 1827, he became president of the senate and acting governor in 1854-1855. Grant, *Alumni Hist. of U. N. C.,* 686.

session of some one at Washington. I do not see by the public prints that the matter has been known abroad. The Mail of the 2d. February from Fayetteville, containing also the Augusta Mail & the letters between here & Petersburgh has never arrived at [*sic*]. There was a considerable amount of money in checks & Bills & some few Bank Notes from this place, therein. None of the packages have ever come to hand. Mr. Kendall dispatched the Petersburgh Post Master to this place to look into the matter. He took an officer with him & went upon the line; they traced the mail as far as Blakely, where they ascertained, the Car had started on the day the Mail got there, an hour before its arrival. It was then thrown into an open Warehouse, & has never since been heard of. I believe it contained letters from South of this place as far as Augusta to Boston, northwardly. I had a check of $2,000 & $100 in Bank notes in the Bag. I only mention the matter, thinking the knowledge of fact may be useful to you. There must be some shameful neglect or inefficiency in the department, that Contractors are allowed to throw the great Northern Mail, about so carelessly.

With high respect
Dear Sir, Your friend & Servt.
W. WINSLOW.

[Addressed:]
Hon. W. P. Mangum
U. S. Senate
Washington City.

WPM-LC

John Hill Edwards[91] *to Willie P. Mangum*

[March, 1836]

Hon. Willie P. Mangum
Sir

A brief acquaintance with you & the cause in which we are both engaged in must be my apology for thus intruding upon you: I hope that you will hand the inclosed as it is directed *all* of the office seekers & holders are making use of the Franking privilege to disseminate their side of the Question and may not the friends of Judge White make use of the Franks to open the

[91]Unable to obtain any information about John Hill Edwards except that he married Margaret Peterson November 18, 1820. *Tyler's Quarterly Magazine*, VI, 182.

eyes of the People. If in an error I hope that you will pardon the liberty which I have taken by forwarding this on to you My Post office is Poplar Mount Greensville County Va. and if it be not too much trouble I should be glad that you would forward on to me your & Mr Leighs speeches against Expunging Yours with respect JOHN HILL EDWARDS
[Addressed:]
The Hon. Wilie P. Mangum
of the United States
Senate
Washington
City
D. C.

WPM-LC

Robert B. Gilliam[92] *to Willie P. Mangum*

OXFORD N. C. April 1st, 1836.

My dear Sir:

I received the very interesting letter which you did me the honor to address me sometime since, during the week of our Superior Court.—I intended to have replied to it, as soon as I returned from the lower courts, but when I reached home, I found a very near & much valued friend labouring under severe disease and I felt utterly unequal to the task of writing, whilst his case continued doubtful. The friend to whom I allude, Mr. Benjamin Kittrell,[93] died on Monday last, greatly lamented by a large circle of friends—His loss will be deeply felt not only in the social circle, but likewise in the political contest now approaching in the County.

When Mr. W^m^. Sneed left Oxford he was furnished with a list of names, for about two thirds of this County, and was requested to hand them to you.—That list you have no doubt received, and the residue will be forwarded during the ensuing week. A number of documents with your frank arrived in the mail last evening; but I have not yet had an opportunity of seeing their contents.—I would respectfully suggest that your speech on Benton's resolution[94] & Judge White's on the abolition

[92]An Oxford attorney whom Mangum depended on for political advice in his county.
[93]He was clerk of the Granville Court of Common Pleas and Quarter Session.
[94]See above, II, 392n, for reference to Mangum's speech against Benton's resolutions on defense.

question, ought to be freely distributed.—Every thing seems to be going on well in Granville.—We have found a full Whig ticket for the Senate & Commons, with a good prospect of carrying it through successfully. I view Mr. Wyche's defeat as almost certain, and I think the Commons ticket is on a still better footing. Mr. Eaton,[95] Mr. Fleming[96] & myself are the Whig candidates, and unless I am greatly deceived, they can't beat us.—Wherever I have been, the good cause is gaining,—and the best judges now think that N. Carolina will vote for White. In Franklin County the revolution is truly astonishing & is till progressing.—Col Ruffin[97] is the White candidate in the Senate, & will be elected, with a fair chance of carrying a part of the Commons ticket with him—The recent tidings from Orange & Wake are encouraging.—We have buckled on our armour in good earnest for the combat, and with a fair field, we shall give a good account of the enemy.—

I am gratified to perceive that your apprehensions in regard to the resignation of Mr Tyler have not been realized. I looked to Virginia with some concern, fearing a schism between the friends of Mr Leigh & Mr Tyler, but thus far, if any thing can be inferred from the press, all things go on smoothly—In this part of North Carolina (the rest I can't answer for) neither the resignation of one, nor the repeal of the other can cause us very serious embarrassment—The candidates for the Vice-Presidency are not much spoken of, nor their pretensions considered—They are regarded with but little interest, The absorbing topic, is the presidential election, and that alone will have much place in the minds of the people—The course taken by the Star, seems to meet the approbation of [torn] [fr]iends, whilst the suggestions of the Register [have] been coldly received. The Whig papers in the State have generally determined to support Mr Tyler, and the meetings of the people held since his resignation, seem to sustain them.—To abandon him *now,* I think, would cause us much difficulty.—

If Judge White speaks on the expunging resolutions, the speech ought to be extensively circulated—

---

[95]Charles R. Eaton.

[96]William Fleming.

[97]H. J. G. Ruffin, a physician from Franklin, was a member of the State Whig Vigilance Committee in 1836. *Raleigh Register,* Jan. 12, 1836.

If you can find time from more importance duties, it would afford me the highest satisfaction to hear from you.—

With the highest regards, I remain &c.

ROB. B. GILLIAM.

Hon. W. P. Mangum.
[Addressed:] Washington City.

WPM-LC

John Chavis[98] to Willie P. Mangum

April 4th. 1836

My dear Sir/

Notwithstanding I am looking anxiously for a letter from you by the next mail, yet my feelings compels me to write before it comes. The multiplicity of the petitions which appear to be presented to Congress praying that a Law may be passed for the abolition of slavery in the District of Columbia bears upon me with so much pain, that I cannot be silent any longer. All I expect to effect by writing is to let you know that I am radically and heartily opposed to the passing such a Law, a Law which would be fraught with so many mischievous and dangerous consequences. I am already of the opinion that Congress has no more right to pass such a Law than I have to go to your house & take Orange & bring him home & keep him as my servant. And I am astonished that the members of Congress act so much like a parcel of mullets nibling at baite upon fish hooks. Why dont they act like men who love their Country their wives & their Children, and come up boldly to the subject of those petitions & put their feet upon them & stamp them to the centre, of the earth, in such a manner, that all the powers on earth never could be able to raise them again—

It is clear to me, that the cession of the 12 miles square to the General Government does not give the smallest license to Congress to pass such a Law, and why? because the officers or managers of the Government saw it was not only absolutely necessary, to build a capitol & other houses for the different officers to live in & transact the business of the Government—but to lay off a part of the Land in Town lots, & sell them to purchasers that they might have citizens to maintain the members of Congress & other persons who might resort their for the purpose of trans-

[98]See above, I, 41n.

acting business. Then this being the case every purchaser has a complete & perfect right to put or place any kind of property on it he may think proper. Then as the Laws of the Country have made slaves the property of the holder equal to his cow or his horse and that he has a perfect right to dispose of them as he pleases. I ask what possible ground or pretext can there be for supposing, that Congress has a right to pass a Law for the abolition of slavery in the District of Columbia? It is clear to me that those petitioners might as well, and would do it with equal propriety ask Congress to pass a Law to sell the furniture out of the houses of the citizens as to pass a Law to take away their slaves from them. And suppose Congress was foolish enough to pass such a Law what would be the consequence? The Laws of the Land declare that no Legislative body shall pass a Law to take away the property of a man without making remuneration. And here I would ask has Congress the means at hand to remunerate the slave holders in the District of Columbia for the property here taken from them? They dare not put their hands into the National chest. that money is a sacred deposit & placed there for a very different purpose & therefore they dare not touch it. & what is to be done? What madness in those Petitioners—can any madness be equal to it unless it be that of a mans hastening himself by his folloy to eternal destruction! where if they would rightly consider it their efforts are paving the way to the destruction of the peace & happiness of the Country—

That slavery is a national evil no one doubts, but what is to be done? It exists & what can be done with it? All that can be done, is to make the best of a bad bargain. For I am clearly of the opinion that immediate emancipation would be to entail the greatest earthly curse upon my bretheren according to the flesh that could be conferred upon them especially in a Country like ours, I suppose if they knew I said this they would be ready to take my life, but as I wish them well I feel no disposition to see them any more miserable than they are—

I believe that there are a part of the abolitionists that have, and do, acting from pure motives, but I think they have zeal without knowledge, and are doing more mischief than they expect. There is I think, another part that are seeking for loaves and fishes & are an exceedingly dangerous set—And I believe that they are many & have their seats all over the United States, and I would advise the Americans that as long as slavery exists so long they ought to be on the alert & upon the watch Tower, for those abominable wretches I believe dont intend to give up the point Therefore to arrest their efforts as much as possible I would be glad that Congress would at once put to silence those petitioners; for the longer they stir them the stronger they will smell & their baneful scent I fear will spread throughout the United States & do much mischief—

Although I have ever been opposed to the election of Mr Van Buren, I never would suffer myself to believe he was an abolitionist until I saw his elaborate reply to Mr Ames & others,[99] and now I believe it to be an electioneering Trick from the beginning to the end & will in all probability, have its desired effect with many. & he is now standing behind the curtain, as a radical abolutionist looking on & laughing in his sleeves. Why dont he act like Judge White come boldly up to the subject & speak out like a man who loves his Country men women & children? No he is for the loaves & fishes I am the unshaken friend.

JOHN CHAVES

P.S. Pray dont fail to answer respecting the Rogers debt. I must conclude by observing that I am done, the pressure of this winter has put it out of my power to keep house after this year—but must depend solely & alone upon the bounty of my friends a painful consideration.

[Addressed:]

Hon. Willie P. Mangum Esqr
Washington City
Mail District of Columbia

Willie P. Mangum to Sally A. Mangum[100]

Washington City 7th April 1836

My dear daughter.

I received your letter sometime ago, and was very much pleased to learn that you were well.

[99]Van Buren voted for the bill to prevent the postmasters in slave states from delivering incendiary mail. In a reply to a letter he stated that Congress had no power to interfere with slavery in any state. He further stated that although Congress might have the authority, he felt that it was unwise to restrict slavery in the District of Columbia. McMaster, *History of the People of the U. S.*, VI, 364.

[100]The orignal is in the possession of Miss Preston Weeks, Washington, D. C.

I hope My dear, you continue well, and make it a point to attend to all your duties, in a way to give satisfaction to Mrs. Bobbitt.[101]—

It would be painful to me to hear, that you were disposed to be idle, or in any way inattentive to a full discharge of your duty.

I suppose that I shall never learn, that you are unkind to any one.—Nothing can be more disagreeable than a young girl with an ill temper.—It is much better to bear the unkindness of others, than to resent it.—Resentment and anger in a girl not only tend to make her hateful in the eyes of others, but they are wicked and sinful.—Some girls think it spirit & smartness, but in the eyes of good & sensible people, nothing is much more hateful. I hope My dear, you will be kind to all, obedient to your teacher, and attentive to your studies.—Let me say My dear, that I hope you will improve your hand writing as much as you can & be particular in your spelling.—To write & spell well is not a high merit; but to write badly & spell worse is a great defect. In a young lady it is as much observed, as would be a sore in a pretty face. If you do not learn while at school, you will never learn. Remember that your education is very backward.—Unless you try to learn you will grow up, if you live, a mere gawk; ignorant, and unfit to keep the company, with pleasure to yourself of intelligent & well informed people.—Ignorance in grown people is a great misfortune; and in those who had opportunity to be otherwise, it is a great sin.—

I had a letter from your dear Mother two days ago.—She and your dear little sisters were all well.—

I have been quite sick, but I am quite well now.—You will write to your Mother once a week, or at least once a fortnight.—And I shall expect to find no mistake in the spelling.—Write to me also My love.—

Be good & be industrious, and you will be a pleasure to your Mother & Father.—I hope the time may never come that I cannot say, as I now say, that

I am your affectionate Father

WILLIE P. MANGUM

[Addressed:]
Miss Sally A. Mangum
Louisburg
N°. Carolina

[101]Mrs. John B. Bobbitt was Sally's principal in the Franklin Academy.

WPM-LC

Outlaw & Lemay[102] *to Willie P. Mangum*

RALEIGH, April 8, 1836

Hon. W. P. Mangum
Dear Sir,

Yours of the 4th instant, was received yesterday. We have made our estimate of the additional expense of publishing twice a week agreeably to your request; and find that it cannot be done for less than $2,800 to $3,000. A temporary arrangement of that sort would more than double the expenses of the establishment. We deeply feel the importance of an enlarged sheet, or a semi-weekly publication. At present, although our paper is usually printed in the *smallest type,* we are unable to publish half the important matters which ought to be laid before the public. Our table is crowded with documents, which, to our great mortification, we are compelled to postpone from week to week, for the want of room; for many of which, we fear, we never shall be able to find space, with the present dimensions of our hebdomadal. We would therefore suggest that, if the amount required for publishing twice a week cannot be raised, the object may be, in part, accomplished, if we can be enabled to enlarge the paper. This may be done for about a thousand dollars, ($1000.)

We would thank you, or any of our friends in Congress, for an occasional communication on public matters,

Very respectfully, Yours
OUTLAW & LEMAY

[Addressed:]
Hon. Willie P. Mangum,
(Senate U. S.)
Washington City
D. C.

WPM-LC

Robert Ransom[103] *to Willie P. Mangum*

WARRENTON NO. C. 9th April 1836.

Honl Willie P Mangum.

Dr Sir I am not much of a reading man. But have just got through your good talk on Bentons Resolutions. And in the full-

[102]David Outlaw and Thomas Lemay were the editors of the Raleigh *Star*.
[103]He was the father of General Robert Ransom, of Civil War fame.

ness of my heart, cannot refrain from my full expressions of joy. All I can say is that *you* heel well, and put your gaffs. in every flutter do continue to flutter. Your cause is a good one, *lay on lay on*. How do they treat their wounds inflicted by that *tremendious* blow of *yours*. I shall be glad to hear from *at all times*, and particularly after another *sparr*. "Our cause is gaining every day[”]. As you say we *may* be defeated for a while. But success will ultimately come. Again I ask how do they treat their wounds. Can Van—the Tennessee Lawyer & Chapel Hill Expunger[104] make Salve and find wrapping bonds sufficient. Do let me hear from you & our Venerated *honest* Judge White. All the apology I shall offer for writing you is that you know I am *your friend*. With great respect.

ROBT. RANSOM.

[Addressed:]

Honl. Willie P. Mangum
Washington
City

Mail.

WPM-LC

Jesse Turner[105] to Willie P. Mangum

CRAWFORD C. H. A. Y.
April 16th 1836

Hon. W. P. Mangum
Dr. Sir,

[torn] years have passed away since I last saw you [but] the lapse of years, has not impaired the frie[ndship of] early youth nor cooled that ardent [torn] which I ever felt for your talents and [torn) great political struggles which [have dis] tracted the country for the last [torn]-ave occasionally differed but not[withstanding the] occasional differences in regard to men and [torn] time has never been within that period when it would not have been a source of the highest gratification to me to have seen you occupy the most exalted public station in the

---

[104]Thomas Hart Benton was expelled from the University of North Carolina. The Tennessee lawyer referred to here was probably James K. Polk.

[105]A graduate of the University of North Carolina and a student in law of A. D. Murphey, Jesse Turner moved from Alamance County to Alabama and then in 1834 to Arkansas. In 1840 he was elected president of the Young Men's Whig Convention of Arkansas. The next year he was appointed as a visitor to the National Military Academy. Later Fillmore made him Federal Attorney of the western district of Arkansas. Before his death in 1894, he served in the Arkansas secession convention and as judge of the state supreme court. S. W. Stockard, *The History of Alamance*, 156-162.

American Republic— and though it is the policy of the party now in the ascendancy to prostrate you and every other public man who dares to exercise the attributes of a freeman to disbelieve in the infalibility of Andrew Jackson, and that of his unprincipled appointee Martin Van Buren yet I cannot, I will not believe but that there yet remains virtue and intelligence enough among the American people to sustain finally that Spartan band (the United States Senate) who have hitherto upheld the Federal Constitution as it were upon their shoulders—its only protection against the assaults of the Executive and his myrmidons—If however we should be disapointed, and the power and patronage and popularity of Andrew Jackson should prove too strong for the virtue and intelligence of the people—You will have the heartfelt satisfaction of reflecting that you have discharged your public duty in a faithful, fearless and independent manner and have done all within the power of men to avert the evils which shall have come upon us but I pray to heaven for better days, and for you a prosperous and splendid political career. I hope that North Carolina our native State, first to declare herself free from British domination, will not be last in shaking off the tramels o[f Ja]ckson & Van Buren

My adopted [State] of Arkansas is probably on the threshhol[d of] admission into the Union as an independent State please further her cause to the utm[ost until] we succeed nothing can be more [torn] that the vote of Arkansas in the [torn] will be given to Hugh L. Wh[ite over] Martin Van Buren— I think I may safely hazard the assertion that White will get four fifths of the popular votes and though White is not my first or second choice I will cordially support him or any body else *(Tom Benton always excepted)* in preference to Van Buren our Delegate (A. H. Sevier)[106] may seek to make a different impression at Washington, as he no doubt will and we of Arkansas are willing that the ten[ant] of the *White house* should think that we are thorou[ghly] *Van Burenized* untill we get into the Union through their aid and co-operation we will

[106]Ambrose H. Sevier was a territorial representative of Arkansas from 1828 to 1836 and after its admission as a state 1836, he served as Senator from 1836 to 1848. *Biog. Dir. of Cong.*, 1509.

then let them know that they have been gulled and most wofully deceived.

With great respect I remain
Your friend & ob't Serv't
JESSE TURNER

P. S. excuse my course sheet of paper and write me on the receipt of this

J. Turner

WPM-LC

William R. Smith[107] *to Willie P. Mangum*

SCOTLAND NECK 18th April 1836.

Dear Sir—

I have several nephews & nieces in the State of Alabama who are the only heirs of the late Genl. Hogan[108] of N. C. who was a commanding General in the revolutionary war. There has been several inquiries made by speculators of the place of residence and their names which induces me to think there may be money or land coming to them for the services of their grand father.

My object in writing is to beg the favour of you to make the necessary inquiries and inform me by mail as soon as you can with convenience on the subject—If there is any thing coming to them from the United States will you be so good as to advise me how the heirs will have to proceed to get it.

I know of only two persons now alive that can prove them to be the heirs of the late Genl. Hogan if it should be necessary cant I take their depositions for the heirs as they are both very old & cant live much longer—If I can point out to me the way it must be done—I have wrote the heirs from the number of inquiries that have been made & that by men who it is known to have been buying up claims of this discription for some of them to come & make the necessary inquiries fearing my letter may

[107]A graduate of the state university, William R. Smith actively supported local schools. He and his son were trustees of the Vine Hill Academy in Halifax County in the 1830's. According to Battle, he was a "popular planter" of the Roanoke country. Battle, *Hist. of U. N. C.*, I, 791; Coon (ed.), *N. C. Schools and Academies*, 177.

[108]A native of Ireland, General James Hogan moved to Halifax County before the Revolution. After serving in 1776 as a delegate in the North Carolina Provincial Congress, he entered the army and fought in the battles of Bradywine and Germantown. In 1780 he was sent to Charleston, where he was taken prisoner. He died in 1781. In 1786 the state gave his son 1,200 acres of land in Tennessee and in 1790 Congress paid the son $5,250. After the son died in 1814 the son's widow and children moved to Tuscumbia, Alabama. Ashe, *Biog. Hist. of N. C.*, IV, 196-202.

miscary or they may neglect to come I should like to have more information on the subject before I write them again—

I am very respectfully
Yr. Obt. Servt.
WM R. SMITH senr.

[Addressed:]
Honble. Wilie P. Mangum
Washington City
D. C.

WPM-LC

A. P. Field[109] *to Willie P. Mangum*

(Confidential)

VANDALIA [ILL.] April 20th 1836.

Hon. W. P. Mangum
Dr Sir

I consider that there has been an entire want of Economy in the expenditure upon the national road in this State: and I am desirous of finding out as far as I can the real cause or ground work of Such duty on the part of the officers; Would it be too much for me to ask of you to make a call on the proper department to know the amount of money paid to the hands on said road—and the amount paid to the officers, and more particularly that section which includes this place, and also the names of persons employed on said road: at this place in Hawling or procuring rock for bridges. Lieut. Freeman who was here in the management of this part of the road—was a strong Van Buren and I am confident, that if you can procure the necessary information our cause will be much benefited I should also like to Know very much how much money the said Freeman has now in his hands and not accounted for. The reason Sir in my asking this of you is that I am now before the people as a cadidate for Congress: and in opposition to the Caucus nomination and If I can get these facts I shall expose the whole system to the people.

Yours with high
Esteem
A P FIELD

[Addressed:]
Hon. W. P. Mangum
Washington
City D. C.

Vandalia Ill
Apr 20

---

[109]A Whig candidate for Congress. He was defeated.

WPM-LC

William S. Ransom[110] *to Willie P. Mangum*

COLUMBIA TENNESSEE, April 20th. [1836]

My verry dear Sir

I received your prompt and friendly letter directed to me at Biglyville, with more than ordinary emotions of pleasure—In fact, Sir, I feel wholly unable to unfold even on paper, and after reflection how grateful I am for this additional proof afforded of your friendship for me, and the real interest you feel for my success through life—I can only say in return, that I wish yours may be as calm as you are virtuous, and as conspicuous as you are brilliant—Mine *shall* continue honorable and independent, if obscure.—

I read a part of your letter to some of our friends here and they were charmed with it I hope soon to get another touching on the movements of the Party—Soon we are to have a large meeting in this place, altogether political—Many subjects I presume will be opened for discussion and I intend to make my debut in the West with a Preamble and Resolutions—Not with a 4th Oration nor a charge to the Grand Jury—You will hear from me—Our cause is strong here, and like fame, "it gathers strength by going." Polk doubtless works the wires for his clan,—it is thought so by many, and he has a great many friends, but they are lessening daily—The Wise exposure and his manifest want of ability in the chair have greatly detracted from his former undeserved popularity—The Van Buren party are however making exertions worthy of a better cause, and boastingly affirm that Judge White will not get Tenn: *Credat Judeus* etc. for Polk's county will vote for him & here you know concentrated efforts will be made. I regretted to see Bynum[111] playing his old tricks in Congress. I had, but oh how vainly! hoped, that age, and promotion to a dignified position would have divested him of his splenetic and demagoguical practices—Poor Graham,[112] I pitty any man of fine feelings who has to deal with such a set as have waged their political warfare against him.

I see that the Editor of the Sun[113] proposes to sell a part of his establishment—I would like to get it and wrote to him a few

[110]See above, II, 394.

[111]Jesse Bynum was in the House of Representatives from 1833 to 1841.

[112]James Graham.

[113]He refers to the Washington *Sun*, which was established as a White paper February 21, 1835, and, except for the period May 18 to July 30, 1836, when it was suspended, ran until August, 1837. *Union List of Newspapers*, 91.

days to know his terms—I referred him to you, to Hawkins and to Bynum—though differing on general matters they surely will do me justice in a matter of this kind. I hope my dear Sir that you will give me an early response. I want you to write how the affairs of our Country progress, & some of your friends here want to hear from you—You have many a staunch one you know nothing of

I am in haste to leave town as it is nearly night & have to ride 10 miles, which is the best apology I can offer for this hasty and almost illegible scroll.

Most sincerely & devotedly your
friend
WM. S. RANSOM.

Direct to this place.

[Addressed:]

To
The Hon: Willie P. Mangum
Washington City
D. C.

WPM-LC

Willie P. Mangum to Charity A. Mangum

WASHINGTON CITY
Saturday 23rd. April 1836

My dear Love,

The Senate meets to day and I have just come in, a few minutes before the meeting.—

The weather here is extremely cold, and we have had very little spring.—It is the coldest & latest that I have ever seen.—There is scarcely a bud to be seen except a few on some of the earliest shrubs in sheltered & sunny spots in the gardens.

My health has continued good, and I am feeling extremely desirous of getting home.—I still think the session will draw to a close much earlier than usual.—I shall be rejoiced to get off from this place.—I feel extremely little interest in the progress of the public business here, so little goes according to my notions of right.—I very much hope, that My dear little Patty has got quite well. Kiss her & my little lady Mary.—The senate is just meeting. I hope to hear from you constantly—Your letters are very irregular. remember me often my love, & always think of me as

Your affectionate husband

WILLIE P. MANGUM

[Addressed:]

Mrs. C. A. Mangum
Red Mountain
No. Carolina

WPM-LC

John Barnett[114] *to Willie P. Mangum*

25th April 1836.—

Dear Sir

I have Consented to become a Candidate In the Senate[115] and neglect my own business, and endeavour to have a Whig Representation in whole or part from person [Person County] in the next Legislature and I must ask the favour of you to furnish me with: documents to prove Incontestably the amt of Surpulous money now In the pet Banks' and If posable let it be founded on Reports of Bank officers or Secataries or any one but Whig members of the Senate or house of Representatives; for If I can obtain documents that will prove Incontestably that the peoples money are used for the Benefit of a few favourite Banks for the Benefit of the Stockholders of Banks & the office holders If I do not Revolutionise Person and put In a white Representation I shall be greatly deceaved I argue the Case at this time and say we have 30 millions of Surpulous money now in the Treasury and they are still Continuing to enlarge It. that we are willing to Support our Country her wants If it takes all we can earn but a nuff is Sufficient and It is not Rite to draw any thing from us more than is necessary to supply the wants of the govermt—& If they do not love darkness Rather than lite Why do they oppose Mr. Wises Relution for the appointment of a Committy to Examine Into the Situation of the pet Banks. & assertain what Connection Mr. R. M. Whitney has with the Selection of the deposit

---

[114]See above, I, 110n.
[115]He was elected and served for one term in the state senate.

Banks.[116] If You can lay Your hands on any documents that will prove Mr. Vanburian has any leaning towards the Roman Catholicks, and If You Can furnish me with any thing that will go to prove that Mr. Taney is Connected with Roman Catholicks I. should be glad to get them In short I wish You to furnish me with any documents You Can get that will go to support our Cause We shall have 3 Whig Candidates in the feald and our motto is Victory or death and You Know I have always bean hard to kill in person I saw R Nichols[117] Esqr. a few days since he tells me he thinks there is no doubt of Orange Electing all White men Your strict attention to this matter is Respectfully Solicited

I am with due Respect.
JOHN BARNETT.

Honl W. P. Mangum.

N. B. Anything I can show to the person public in Print they will beleve. I want You to send me Mr. Bells Speech in pamphlet form that I may Show the Intregues and managemt of Vanburean men in the managemt of the Rascality and all other document that You Can think of that will aid our Cause

J BARNETT.

My object is to Show that the pet Banks is Responible to Governmt and for the Redemption of there own notes to the amt of 70 millions of dollars and there Capetal only amounts to 10 millions and then ask the people If they would be willing to Risk there own money in the Care of Such a Set of Insolvents that are Resposible for Such times as much as they are worth.

J BARNETT

[Addressed:]

Honl. Willie P. Mangum
Washington
City

---

[116]Although a former director of the United States Bank, Reuben M. Whitney helped formulate Jackson's plan for placing the deposits in state banks. He had a state bank of his own which he hoped would benefit from the new plan. In February, 1837, he was called before a House investigating committee, which Wise eventually succeeded in dominating. Claiming that he was afraid that he would be assassinated, Whitney first declined to testify. Forced to appear, he was drilled for about a week. In the course of the questioning, Henry A. Wise tried to make his life as unpleasant as possible. Later, Wise asserted that he had moved toward Whitney with the purpose of shooting him if Whitney had drawn a pistol. Whitney, sometimes called the "political scavenger" of the Jackson administration, also had to appear before a Congressional committee in 1833 when Biddle was being accused of unfair administration of his bank. E. I. McCormac, *James K. Polk: a Political Biography,* Berkeley, 1922, 31, 110-111; Bassett (ed.), *Cor. of Jackson,* V, 390-392, 452n; F. J. Turner, *The United States 1830-1850: The Nation and its Sections,* New York, 1935, 447; L. A. Gobright, *Recollections of Men and Things at Washington during the third of the Century,* Philadelphia, 1869, 14-15.

[117]Richardson Nicholls was a well-to-do man of Orange who was later asked to sign one of Mangum's notes. See below Mangum to W. A. Graham November 14, 1841.

WPM-LC

Wm. Cain[118] *to Willie P. Mangum*

HILLSBOROUGH 1 May 1836—

My dear friend

I have concluded to not to send William to the Episcopal school and no where else where boys are to be compelled to "inform on their fellow students for mischief or disorderly conduct,["] altho I think the notion founded on a false sense of honor yet if it prevails over the school; for a boy to disclose would be an indelible stain on him.

If you can select such a school as you are pleased with, I will send him to you, if you would be so good as to see him properly placed in school, for if you cant find such a school as you are pleased and satisfied with, I must beg the favor of you to procure a Teacher who is qualified to prepare boys for Cllege, upon the whole I dont know but the last course would be best and cheapest altho I prefer the former, an inducement to the private school is that Mrs. Cain dislikes, exceedingly for her children to be sent so far from her and particularly at this time, as her health is not good. I am waiting impatiently leave home, but cant do untill I can make some disposition of William or know how I can dispose of him—please let me hear from you as soon as convenient —I am very anxious to leave home with Mrs. Cain—

Your friend
WM- CAIN

[Addressed:]

The Honbl. Willie P. Mangum
of the United States Senate
Washington City
D. C.

WPM-LC

Collen W. Barnes[119] *to Willie P. Mangum*

NORTHAMPTON COUNTY N. C. May 2/1836.

Dr Sir I am Impeld by motives of Charity to call upon you to examine into a case which I hope will cost you but little trouble

[118]Mangum's brother-in-law who married Chief Justice Ruffin's youngest daughter, Mary. Their son William Cain referred to in the letter became a physician. Groves, *The Alstons and Allstons of North and South Carolina*, 424.

[119]Colin W. Barnes, a former member of the legislature, was appointed at the Raleigh caucus of the Whig party in December, 1835, to serve on the Whig Vigilance Committee for Northampton County. *Raleigh Register*, Jan. 12, 1836.

I know you are full of business and I am aware that your perplexities are great but I have no other person in Washington to whom I can apply with any degree of Propriety as our member[120] & myself is not upon very good terms & my relation & friend Mr Brown I expect has taken some offence at my opposition to him (all the effect of politicks) At least I do not feel willing to call upon either of the Gentlemen for a favour—I have an old neighbour who is poor & honest who was a revolutionary soldier who some time since made out his case and applyed for a pension which was Granted him & he obtained a certificate accordingly which he now holds he applyed to me some time since to prepare his papers and send to Fayetteville for his pension which I did. I wrote to Mr. John McRea who for many years has been in the habit of acting as attorney for the pensioners & sent his papers they were returned. & Mr. McRea writes me that Kedar Parker the Pensioner is suspended by order of J. L. Edwards for some cause unknown there. Mr. Parker has drawn money once or twice I am not certain which. According to his certificate he is Intitled to Twenty four dollars perannum, his certificate bears date the 2nd day of May 1833, you will be able to find it recorded in the pension office In Book E and Volume 6. page 51 by Nathaniel Rice Clerk. I make these statements in order that it may cost you as little trouble to examine Into the matter as Possible. You will do me the favour to examine into his Case and assertain for what Cause he is suspended, & let me know—perhaps he may be able to procure further evidence and get reinstated. If any man in the country is Intitled he certainly is—no doubts exists here as to his being intitled to a pension under the Act of Congress.

If you are in the habit of Franking any part of the proceedings of Congress I think It might be well to send a budget or budgets to Jackson. You have a number of warm friends here. & the cause which you are so manfully defending is gaining ground beyond calculation in this county I do not think that Vanburen can obtain one hundred votes in this County but in this I may be mistaken but I Cannot be mistaken much. We should like to see you among us again. We feel Great Anxiety for your reelection no man can be elected here who would not sustain you. I was a member of the Assembly when you were elected to the senate of the U. S. & you are aware of the difficulty we had to

[120] Jesse A. Bynum.

elect you. I was one of the Senate who nailed the flag until your presence were obtained. and I feel proud and ever shall that we succeeded; and as much as I can say in my feeble manner is Well done thou good and faithful servant you deserve well of your Country and man kind. If our Institutions are broken down your skirts will be clear

My dear Sir excuse my Imperfections. I have no Education & It is almost, As Great a burthen to me to write as could be placed upon me. I am in bad health and the weather very warm, but when I address you I cannot forbear in my feeble way to manifest to you my entire abbrobetion of your political course—Excuse my letter in every particular It is written in much haste & in much pain. And what I have said in regard to our member and the other senitor let It be confidential

Your friend &c
COLLEN W. BARNES.

[Addressed:]
Honourable Willie P. Mangum — Jackson N. C.
Washington City. — May 3rd

Mail.

WPM-LC

A Lazarus[121] *to Willie P. Mangum*

WILMINGTON N° Cª. May 1836.

Hon: Willie P Mangum
Sir

I take great pleasure in transmitting herewith, the memorial of the Citizens of Wilmington,[122] with a request that you will have the goodness to bring the subject before Congress—

I have the honor to be
very respectfully Sir
Yr Obt. Serᵗ. &c.
A LAZARUS
Chairman

[Addressed:]
Hon Willie P. Mangum
Washington City

[121]Aaron Lazarus was a wealthy merchant of Wilmington. Interested in internal improvements, he was a delegate to the Salisbury internal improvements convention of 1833 and a director of the Wilmington and Weldon Railroad. Upon his death in Petersburg in 1841 the *Hillsborough Recorder*, October 7, 1841, declared that he was "a public spirited and useful citizen, and a worthy man. He was extensively known." See also James Sprunt, *Chronicles of the Cape Fear River 1660-1916*, 150, 184, 190.

[122]This memorial was not found. In 1837 a memorial on dredging the harbor was included.

WPM-LC

John D. Amis[123] *to Willie P. Mangum*

CHOCTAW, May 13, 1836.

Hon. Sir

After expressing my earnest good wishes for your continued health, and tendering to you my warm approbation of the bold and patriotic stand, you have taken in the contest of "liberty against power," unequal as it is, whilst the latter are waging, not only a war upon the Treasury, but one of utter extermination upon every other institution of the country; I will beg of you the favor, (in some leisure moment of business) to present a petition which will be sent you, praying Congress for the establishment of a Post Office, at West Port Lowndes co. Miss—the little place is situated one mile south of Columbus, (the river intervening, and across which there is no bridge—If you could effect a *grant* for this small object, *Lowndes Co.* would be infinitely benefitted; that is, the western part of it. The petition is very respectfully, &c.—

I have but recently received, through the Nat. Intelligencer, your able and conclusive speech on Benton's Resolutions, and I do assure you, that the perusal of it, afforded me the greatest possible pleasure. To what end is it, that the Party in power intend to carry their abominable innovations, if not infractions of the Constitution, now that the "factious Senate" are out of the way—I fear, that the dangerous tendency of such measures as are now being perpetrated upon the established usages of Government, must inevitably lead to rupture and disaffection among the component parts of this Union and if not timely arrested, by compromise or legislative action, will end in anarchy and disunion. I take pleasure in suggesting my belief, that North Carolina, is awaking to the impending dangers, if not absolute bondage, of which she has been a chosen victim, and my reading information confirms the belief that "Dudley" will be elected, *whose* election will place beyond cavil the success of the White Ticket, in every political appointment. Be pleased, when convenient, to send me such political doctrines, as you may think

[123]The son of William Amis, of Northampton, John D. graduated from the state university and became a planter in his home county before he moved to Mississippi. His father gave him the famous race horse "Sir Archy" from whom John D. Amis made $7,600. Hervey, *Racing in America, I,* 198, 200, 201, 205, 206, 274.

calculated to instruct, (particularly those concerning the finances of the country), Speeches &c.

With devoted regard, I have
the honor to be, your
Obedient Servant
JNO. D. AMIS.

Direct to Columbus.
[Addressed:]
Hon. Wilie P. Mangum
U. S. Senate
Washington
D. C.
[Endorsed:]
Ansd 4 June 1836.
[Postmarked:]
Columbus, Mi.

WPM-LC

Paul C. Cameron to Willie P. Mangum

RALEIGH May 14th 1836

My Dear Sir/

Enclosed you have a check on the Bank of the Metropolis for the sum of two hundred and fifty dollars for the use of William Cain, at such school as you may place him—. I shall give William fifty dollars which will be a good-deal more than will be required to defray his expenses to Washington!

It had been my purpose, to accompany him to Washington, but I met with, Mr Devereux[124] this morning, who has promised to take him into his charge, as far as Norfolk, or Baltimore, at either of which places he will place him in the charge of some gentleman going to Washington, who will place him at your disposal.

I am Dear Sir your friend &
Most: obt: servt
PAUL. C. CAMERON.

[Addressed:]
The Hon W. P. Mangum, Raleigh
Washington
D. C.

[124]Thomas Devereaux. See above, I, 413n.

WPM-LC

Archibald Monk[125] *to Willie P. Mangum*

SAMPSON COUNTY N. CA. Coxes Store P. O

May 20th 1836

Hon. W. P. Mangum

Sir, I have not the Pleasure of a personal acquaintance with you—But I am one of Those who admire & respect your firm & patriotic Stand in the Cause of freedom & States rights & it is for that cause that I now address You. I am one of those who Sincerely believe that N. C. ought to have her Just right, & distributive Share of the proceeds of the Sale of the Public Domain[126]—& it is a question which will be considerably agitated at our next August Election—about the 25th of June Our Electioneering Campaign Commences—& I understand that our opponents—will Strive to Shew that, that Revenue will be needed in the Public Treasury that the appropriations of this Session will consume the Whole Surplus & funds now in the Deposite Banks—although I know this not to be a fact—Yet I wish for Some authority—to Deny the asertion—If you have any Documents — illustrative of the Subject — that is Official from the Treasury Department — please send me one — With respect yours &c

A. MONK.

[Addressed:]

Hon. Wilie P. Mangum
U. S. Senate
Washington
D. C.

Mail.
[Postmarked:]
Coxes Store N.C
20 May

[125]Archibald Monk was a member of the state legislature from 1829 to 1834. *N. C. Manual,* 802-803.

[126]Distribution remained a part of the Whig program in North Carolina in nearly every election.

WPM-LC

Willie P. Mangum to Charity A. Mangum

WASHINGTON CITY 22nd May 1836.
Sunday.

My dear love.

We are now within one day of the period fixed by the Senate for the adjournment of Congress, and no one can now better tell when we shall adjourn than he could have done a Month ago.— The weather is now very warm, and we shall have a great deal more of it, before we get off.—I do not think Congress will adjourn before sometime in July.—

William Cain Junr. arrived here last Thursday.—You I presume have heard, that he got into difficulty at Raleigh, and his Father has sent him to me, to select some school for him & place him in it.—I have not positively determined where I shall place him, but I think, it will be in the Catholic College in Baltimore— That is the best place I know of for a boy who is difficult to govern.—He will stay here perhaps, a week longer.—I have had a Cot set up in my chamber where he stays—He has grown a good deal, & seems very well disposed—

I am extremely anxious to leave here, & have never been more desirous to see you, my dear Love, & our children.—I have for a few days thought of little else.—

I am sick & tired of my daily attendance on Congress—The business is dull & uninteresting, and every thing is going wrong, and almost to ruin.—

I have not heard from Sally very lately, I suppose because I have not written.—

There is much excitement & stir here about Texas—I take but little interest in it—And I am utterly opposed to risking the peace of the Country for outlaws & adventurers.—There is no danger of it however, if the news be true that Houston has gained a victory over Santa Ana the Mexican President & general, & has taken him prisoner.—I believe but little of what I hear, as they have so many motives to misrepresent every thing.—

Kiss Patty & Mary for Father, & tell them that Father hopes to see them before long,

and believe me as ever your most
affectionate husband,
God bless you, My dear Love,
WILLIE P. MANGUM.

WPM-LC

Thomas McGehee to Willie P. Mangum

PERSON N. C. 22nd. May 1836

My Dear Sir,

I saw Mr. Paul Cameron a fiew days since who informed me that Mr. Cain had sent his son to a school near Washington City —I have no doubt it was from your recommendation and as I have a son that left the Raleigh school at the same time with Mr. Cains son and for the same cause—permit me to request the favour of you to inform me wheather that school is full whare situated by whom managed and what is the expence pr year for each student—I go upon the presumption that you *have* recommended it—I shall regret to have to lieve my native state for any part of the education of my sons for I think it important to educate boys in a community whare they expect to live and I have no idea myself of lieving old N. C. but if they do not alter the rule which my son violated and left the school at Raleigh I shall not return him but shall take away my other son

I hope that N. C. will be more erect this august than she has been I have no doubt but Person will git a Whig Senator and I *hope* will git a full whig representation please let me hear from you as early as convenient as I must take some demenial steps with my sons shortly and any thing from you relative to our publick matters will be interesting to your

Obedent Servt.

TH.. M'GEHEE

Hon. Wiley P. Mangum.

[Addressed:]

Hon. Wiley P. Mangum

Washington City

WPM-LC

William Cain to Willie P. Mangum

HILLSBOROUGH 25 May 1836—

My Dear Friend

I received your kind letter by yesterdays mail & and [*sic*] assure you we were all much pleased and are fully satisfied that you will do the best for William.

At whatever school you may place William, you will please ascertain as near as possible what sum it will take to support him. I mention this so that I may always be prepared in cases of that kind. I like if possible to be punctual or more than punctual in making remittances.

I have nothing new to inform you of, but that Mrs. Cain Thomas & myself will leave home today for the mountains and will be from home about three weeks and if Mrs. Cain's health is any improved we will take another trip after harvest: its our intention to be at home at or before the 20 June when I hope to have the pleasure of seeing you

All the children desire to be affectionately remembered to William and present to him a Mothers & a fathers love.

Yours Most gratefully
W*m*. CAIN.

[P. S.] The money sent by William or rather Mr. Cameron was Three Hundred Dollars, so your amount of it was all right. I presumed that amount would be fully sufficient for all purpose for the first half year. Mr. Cameron after he reached Raleigh declined going on in consequence of hearing of some of his black family being dangerously ill. Independant of three Hundred Dollars I gave Wm about 17 Dollars which I instructed William to give up, if it was required by the regulations of the school. I dont wish him to have more than you think it proper for him to have W. C.

[Addressed:] Washington City
D. C.
Hillsborough N. C.
25 May 1836.

WPM-LC

B. B. Smith[127] *to Willie P. Mangum*

RALEIGH 27th. May 1836

My dear Sir;

Your two favours of the 28th. March & 1st. April, came to hand, during my absence at New York, or, I should have written to you sooner, on the subject of the Glynn debt.—As I have already sustained a considerable loss by this man, I should dislike to be subjected to any farther loss, if it can be avoided—therefore, as you have been advised by an attorney, not to press the

[127]See above, II, 412. I have been unable to ascertain the connection between B. B. Smith and Richard Smith. They probably were brothers.

matter at present, I must beg of you, as by you suggested, to have the debt renewed.—

Your Course in regard to the Ramsay debt, is perfectly satisfactory, & I hope Mr. Storer may be as fortunate in collecting it; but in this, I am almost afraid to indulge expectation.—

Mr. Gales of Washington is now here on a visit & of him I made particular enquiry Concerning Glynn, & it is his opinion, that he might pay my claim, with perfect ease to himself, if he felt disposed to do so.—Mr. G. thinks him quite able to do so from his salary of $1,000 per Year; taking into view his small expenses, having no one to support out of that sum, but *himself & little son.*—not wishing myself, to put you to the least trouble or inconvenience farther, than I know it would afford you pleasure to serve an old friend, it occurred to me, that possibly if you could Yourself, spare the time to see Glynn, & in all probability, he might be induced at once to pay the money—But in this, of Course you will exercise Your own discretion.—If the money Can't be extracted either by persuasion or coersion why then I think he had better renew the debt by a *new note, & that with good Security, if it can be had,* & if not with, why then without it, if nothing better can be done.—

You may Rely upon it my dear Sir, that N°. Carolina, is safe for *Judge White*—

I see gentlemen daily from almost every quarter of the state, & they all Concur in the opinion that this state may be put down to Judge White by a majority of from 10 to 13,000 over Van Buren; & besides this, it is now generally conceded, that the *Whigs* will have a decided Majority in the Next Legislature.— In this County, we Confidently expect to return *4 Whigs*—So we go, & I trust in God, that we may Yet defeat the *Van Buren* faction all over W.— states. The People, I mean the Common people *(for the intelligent are already right)* are just beginning to wake up, & see things in their true light—They begin to find that Jackson is not that Demi God that they had supposed him to be; & I can assure you if you are not already sufficiently assured of the fact, from every sign in the political Heaven, it appears to me plain that the "Sceptre is about to depart from Judea."—

That God, in his infinite Wisdom, may Speedily grant it is my

Mahogany sideboard of Willie Person Mangum. (The mirror reflects a portrait of Mrs. Mangum's nephew, Ned Davis.) The original is in the possession of Mrs. John A. Livingstone, Raleigh, N. C.

most ardent prayer; & not, only mine, but the prayer of every true hearted patriot, in the land I verily believe,

& truly

Yr Ob— servant

B. B. SMITH

the Honble.

W. P. Mangum

Washington City.—

[Addressed:] To the Honble

Willie P. Mangum

Senate of the U States

Washington City

WPM-LC

Dennis Heartt[128] *to Willie P. Mangum*

HILLSBOROUGH, June 1, 1836.

Dear Sir,

Yours of the 27th was received yesterday, and according to your request I have consulted with Mr. Graham and Mr Waddell upon the matter suggested in it. They both concur in opinion that something of the kind would be useful. I have not received the pamphlet enclosed by you, but a few days ago I received a tract from Mr. Gales which I presume to be the same. It commenced with a comparison of the expressed opinions of Mr. White and Mr. Van Buren on the power of congress to abolish slavery in the district of Columbia, and ends with the letter of Mr Dudley. Mr. Graham appears to think that as a great portion if not all of this has already been before the public, that matter more useful might be prepared; which is also my opinion; but he will leave here in a day or two, and will be absent two or three weeks, and will therefore not himself have time. We shall probably print the tract as it is.

The matter relating to the Land bill, and the expenditures of *the party*, which you propose for the 2d. No. I think will be very useful in this county; particularly as two of the candidates have acted with *the party* in frustrating the action in our legislature relative to a division of the proceeds of the public lands. It is requested by your friends, therefore, that you will prepare the article.

---

30 [128]See above, I, 112n.

You will see by my last paper, that the candidates for this county are now all before the people; I presume you know them all. With the exception of Gen. Allison, none of our opponents are formidable, and we are therefore not without strong hopes of success. Good management, I think, will effect all we wish.

I have written this in great haste, but I believe you will be able to read it and understand my meaning.

Yours respectfully
DENNIS HEARTT.

[Addressed:]
Hon. Willie P. Mangum
M. C.
Washington City.

WPM-LC

William Roane[129] *to Willie P. Mangum*

FRANKLIN MACON COUNTY 5th June 1836

Honored Sir

Being completely crippled up with the Rheumatism for the last 2 or 3 years, I have taken but a small part in the politicks of the day although I cannot help observing & feeling an interest in what is going on. I am induced to write this letter by observing in the Fayetteville Observer a publication on the subject of the abolision Societies of Rhodeisland (said to be caused by a communication received from myself. I have no doubt of such a feeling existing not only in Rhodeisland but in the Northern & New England States generally—I am informed by a very respectable & intelligent Clergiman who has lately traveled through those States (he being a Southern man) that the subject of the manumission of our Slaves was introduced & discussed with him, wherever he went; that it is the every day chat, & talked of wherever you go amongst the common people & that it is contended that the general government has a right to abolish slavery—that Slavery being unjust & unchristian it is not important to inquire into constitutional powers, that it must be done *right or wrong*. He further thinks that if a candidate for office was to avow his opinions to be that "the Southern States should be let alone to manage slavery & their slaves as to them seems right, & protected in the enjoyment of that privilege that he could be rarely elected—

[129]See above, I, 376n.

Now Sir as to our own homes—Be assured Sir that some & not a few of our most influential & intelligent *Union Men* now declare "let the Federal Government once interfere so far in our domestic relations as to touch the subject of slavery and they from that moment are *States rights* men up to the *Hub,*"—nothing is more common than to hear such sentiments as this "*we in the South must meet in convention & declare off*"—Do our Northern Brethren wish a perpetuation of the Union? If they do they *must* mind their own business.—It is now becoming an every day chat: what are we to remain in the union for? Cannot we raise all the great staples of commerce as well as all the necessaries of life in the greatest abundance? Do our northern Brethren wish to continue to carry on our commerce as well as to fish, & manufacture for us & if they do why irritate our feelings by interfering with our domestic policy.—

I will declare to you Sir that I never have seen such a great change in 3 or 4 years as has occered in this district, when the doctrine of State rights was carried so far a few years ago in South Carolina we were almost to a man for the Genl. Government & against State rights as understood in S. C. now the doctrine is sp[r]eading fast that we must throw ourselves on our Sovereignty & that before long if the people of the nonslaveholding states do not mind their own affairs & let ours alone we must be off, & protect ourselves. It is now becoming a common discussion of what use is the Union to us. I should not have troubled you with this but to give warning of the march of Public Sentiment.

We here also often discuss the subject of the propriety of giving the executive more men or money as well as the necessity of clipping him of present absolute power over both.—

For my part I am a republican of the old school. I loath standing armies & Extensive navies. the Executive should not have the least controul over the treasure of the nation either mediately or immediately, his influence is almost irrisistible without we ought to guard against executive power whether he be a Washington or Madison, an Adams or Jackson—Van Buren or White, or anybody else. we here generally approve of your course & would wish to receive information from you on the above as well as any other subject.—

I will thank you to give my best respect to Mr. John Roane[130] of the house of R—

P.S. Some old fashioned Republicans not a few violent Party men as well as office holders & office seekers, and their retainers are for Van—but the great body of the people are opposed to the nominee[131] of the President although they were for him for President.—

Most respectfully Sir
Yours WM. ROANE

[Addressed:]
The Honorable
W. P. Mangum
Senator from N.C.
Washington City.

Mail.
[Postmarked:]
Franklin N C
7th June

WPM-LC

Thomas McGehee to Willie P. Mangum

PERSON N. CAROLINA 8th June 1836

My Dear Sir,

Your esteemed favour inclosing me a calendar of St. Mary's College[132] came duly to hand.

On the 15th inst. I shall attend the examination of the episcopal school at Raleigh and if they do not make such alterations in the government of there school as I think they ought I shall bring home my other son—in that event I think it probable that I had best place them in some preparitary school and from thence to Chapel Hill and thare graduate. I am gratified to see your opinion accord so well with my own in giving our sons a southern education and I have my fiers that it will become a matter of duty instead of a mere matter of opinion for to my mind abolition is a subject that many friends of the union should look upon as foreboding of something ill—I deeply lament they [*sic*] manner the subject has been treated in congress for I can

---

[130]John Roane was in the House of Representatives from Mecklenburg County, Virginia, in 1809-1815, 1827-1831, and 1835-1837. He died in 1838. *Biog. Dir. of Cong.*, 1466.

[131]In 1836 North Carolina voted for Van Buren over White by a majority of over 6,000.

[132]A well known Roman Catholic school in Baltimore. Chief Justice Thomas Ruffin and William Cain sent their sons there.

not see the propriety of the southrn people submitting to them the right of judging in so important a matter that is garanteed to us by the *constitution* an the *law*.

Should I determine after visiting Raleigh to send my son to you I will apprise you of it and beg that you will accept my grateful acknowledgement for your kind offer

Yours Truly
TH MCGEHEE.

Hon. Wiley P. Mangum.
[Addressed:]
Hon. Wiley P. Mangum
Washington City.
[Postmarked:]
Cunningham's Store N. C

WPM-LC

Maxwell Wilson[133] *to Willie P. Mangum*

EARLY GROVE [N. C.] 8th June 1836

Judge Mangum

Dr Sir after I had written to you & before you favours were recd we had our Batallion Musters, where our candidates for County representation made their appearance. I mean the Vanburen side of the Question, some few spoke among those that spoke was Mr. M. Hoke,[134] in his talk he gave his reasons for voting against Clingmans resolutions, and one of his reasons for his course he assignd that the plan of distributing the the surplus revenue was a lunge at Genl. Jacksons administration, that it was originated & brot. forward by Henry Clay with a view of Prostrating the administration, about this time a rain commenced that scattered the people, I was setting in the seat of the carryall in which he stood to be heard by his audience, when the rain stopd him & before the people had dispersed I contradicted the assertion the project had been agitated long before Mr, Clay reported his bill & that Mr Clays bill was only a response to the Presidents Message of 1829 & 30—this caused some inquiry, and shortly after your favour came to hand in-

[133]Unable to identify.

[134]Michael Hoke was a member of the legislature from Lincoln County from 1834 to 1841. In 1844 he ran on the Democratic ticket against W. A. Graham for governor. *N. C. Manual*, 685.

closing Judge Whites Speech on the subject, having heard his speech & reading Judge Whites I would say, nothing came in better season—& since the few who have seen Judge Whites speech I do think this County can be saved. I have never seen such a change in a few days—& I believe that it will be the salvation of our County to the White cause, although I had given it up as lost, but the news of many among our dutch farmers had a most powerful effect and I have thought if it is not too great a request I would ask you save our County, to the good cause, and to enable you I will give you a few more names, if you will send a few to Early Grove I will write a name in them & hand them out to Wilfongs Mills, send to P. M. J. Wilfong Solomon Duty Simeon & John Barger Harry W. Robinson, Danl. Whitner Sen & Junr—Abram Miller Elias Bost, George Smyer, Eli Star Jacob Lutes—to Willow Grove Andrew Shuford, Enos Sherrill—Reuben Hamilton, John & E. Bridges, Jonathan Bost, James Matthew & Andrew Wilson, Capt. M. Arney to Hokesville John Garnet, Jams Cowan, Frederick Hoke Will & Dad Hunsuker Dr. Nicholas Carpenter—Logan & Lou Isaac Lawrance—to Eves Capt Will Harman Archd. Panch Christopher Sigman John Smith Sen & Junr. Willm & George Aber—to Fishers Henry Clive, Willm Barry Dad Zettlemyer James Moore Snr, (Revd. Dan Moses, Jacob Hunsuker send three to Eves) a large section of Country have no officer if you would direct about half a dozen to Michael Link & neighbours to Wilfongs Mills—Lincolnton Robert Williamson Esqr & his Brother Thos. Williamson, John M Motz, Sen, Peter Stamey Danl. Lutes, Danl. Seagle Esqr. (Storekeeper) Major Hall Joseph Stamey—Col. Abr. Mauney David Crouse George Mauney Esqr. & more of your old friends about the village you no doubt yet recollect to Mull Grove to David McEllroy, Jacob Mull P. M. Robert Johnson James Ramsey Sen & Junr, Lawson Stamey Haylesville Dr. Wm. S. Harris who is a candidate on the White side of the Question he would distribute several to good purpose, the P.M. A. Hoyle & E Hoyle, Larken Stowe, a few to Wm J Wilson, & a few to Buffaloe Col Roberts would hand out, his Son Perry is also a candidate on the right side, to Forney a few to Bartlet Ship Esqr who would hand them out to good purpose to Doctor James Rudisill P. Master Huntersville a few—direct one to Dr. Hunter, William Scot—John D Rankin Thos Johnson, Dry Ponds one to John F Law, P.M. one to Jacob Link Isaac Law Alexander

Law Capt Jams Wilkerson, Andrew Dar Graham Farnan several to Gen. Graham

I will stop for the present fearful I am going too far, but the fact is there is nothing but one side of the question has been favoured with any information unless newspapers such as we afford ourselves, they are mostly taken by party dictation, I could have the speech reprinted at Lincolnton & distribute them but sir that does not come from the proper source, it is powerful to see with what attention any thing is recd when from our representatives we have had Benton over & over on that side but no person has noted our County on the White side of the question untill you have & you would laugh in the sleeve to see how every one is inquiring how does Judge Mangum know me I hope this will not be intrusion after the views I have given you

I am your verry humble servant

MAXWELL WILSON.

If I have given the same names at any off I did before, it is because I write from memory having no list.

[Addressed:]

The Honorable W. P. Mangum
Washington D. C.

[Postmarked:]
Early Grove
N. C. 11th June.

WPM-LC

A. J. Davie[135] *to Willie P. Mangum*

BALTIMORE 8 June 36.

Willie P. Mangum Esq.

Sir

I called twice to see you at the Hotel the first time you were out and the last time you had just rode off on your return

It may not be amiss for you to press on our Friends in New York that a convention be called on that subject in the Empire State to consider the propriety of divideing the surplus and I have no question much may be effected by a dextrous use of this question among the Sovereigns, if Van can be defeated at home there is no question he must go down and in my opinion if you could induce a belief even that his chances were doubtful, it

---

[135]Probably Allen J. Davie, the son of Willam R. Davie. He was a planter in Halifax County, North Carolina. Hoyt (ed.), *Papers of Murphey*, I, 327n.

would be fatal to his hopes, his troops are liable to fall off on the smallest excuse; and it would not be bad policy for the Whigs to create at least as much appearance of such an issue it would pay well politically

I shall start home in a few days and if you have any commissions there for me pray forward them

Offer my best wishes to my old Schoolmate Lee[136] tell him never despair, and we shall conquer—

Yours
truly
A. J. DAVIE

[Addressed:]
The Honl
W. P. Mangum
S. C.
Washington
City

WPM-LC

James Webb to Willie P. Mangum

HILLSBORO N. C. June 11, 1836

D Sir

Old Wm. Crabtree[137] who is a pensioner has lost his Certificate he is very poor and needy

What steps must be taken to get another Certificate to enable him to get his Pension

Please to inform me and I will take the necessary steps to Procure him the necessary

Your obedient
Sert.
JAMES WEBB

[Addressed:]
Honorable
W. P. Mangum
Washington
City.
[Postmarked:]
Hillsboro N. C.
12th June 1836.

---

[136]Probably Benjamin Watkins Leigh.

[137]See below, letter of Mangum to James Webb, June 16, 1836.

WPM-LC

P. H. Mangum to Willie P. Mangum

HILLSBORO' June 13th, 1836.—

Dear Sir,

You have understood that there are full Tickets before the people of Orange. The prospect of the success of the White Ticket is believed to be fair—& I think it very good, provided no impediment shall be thrown in its way by the local question of dividing our County. Every thing reasonable, just & fair on that score we are prepared to concede—but I much fear, that by reason of a despicably selfish policy of some, & indeed the most of our intelligent friends beyond H. River, near where the new C. House is expected to be located; they will attempt to avail themselves too confidently of the intensity of public feeling in the East touching higher & more momentous matters—& thereby jeopardize the triumph of correct principles in this election.—

I am requested to ask your assistance in procuring higher documentary evidence than news-papers are esteemed to be, of V. Buren's voting instructions to the New York Senator's in congress touching the admission of Missouri into the Union &c only on the condition of abolishing slavery &c.—[138]

The sound portion of our people, who have few means of informing themselves on topics of public concernment, entertain a general distrust of the integrity of our public prints—& I learn that the subject above adverted to, is capable of doing much provided the truth can be imparted in an unquestionable shape—Doct. Strudwick,[139] who sees a good deal of the Hawfield people, has pressed me to make this call on you.—

I have not heard very lately from your family. I presume they are well.—We have some sickness with our children. Our friend old Mr. Kirkland is ill, & I fear will not be better.—

Several of our friends have pressed me to say to you, that a resignation[140] by you would be deemed by them as a harbinger

[138]At the time of the Missouri Compromise, Van Buren joined in calling a public meeting at Albany to protest against the expansion of slavery. He did not appear at the meeting and he refused to be a member of the committee to send the resolutions to Washington. In January, 1820, he voted in the New York senate for resolutions instructing the Senators from New York in Washington " 'to oppose the admission, as a state in the Union, of any territory not comprised within the original boundary of the United States, without making the prohibition of slavery therein an indispensable condition of admission.' " Edward M. Shepard, *Martin Van Buren*, Boston, 1888, 62-63.

[139]Edmund Strudwick, 1802-1872, was a successful physician in Hillsboro. Ashe, *Biog. Hist. of N. C.*, X, MS. at Duke University.

[140]See above, I, xxxii-xxxiii.

of certain defeat by the White ticket in the State, for the next Assembly. I presume some have written you to that effect, as some have told me that they would do so.—

It will not do now-a-days to write secrets to or from Washington, it seems—as it is thought letters are broken, under a system of the most damnable [torn] ever established or tolerated in a free government. I therefore write as succintly as my purpose wi[ll] permit—nearly all your communications to D Heartt,[141]—two at least which he [received] had been opened—& one of them at least, he assured me, must have been opened on purpose.—

Yrs. respectfully
P. H. MANGUM

[Addressed:]
The Hon:
Willie P. Mangum
(of the Senate)
Washington City
Mail. D. C.

Willie P. Mangum to James Webb[142]

WASHINGTON CITY 13th. June 1836

Sir,

I have received your letter of the 10th instant in relation to the Post office & the Post Master at Hillsbor°.—I have shown it to Mr. Brown of the Senate, and enclosed it to the Department with the following endorsement, to wit—

"Senate Chamber
13th June 1836

"To the Hon: Post Master General
"Sir.

"I feel it my duty to enclose this letter to the Department—The veracity of the writer is unquestionable.—He is a gentleman of the highest standing as a man of business & for personal character.

"I have neither personal nor political inclinations in this matter.—I refer the matter to you from a sense of duty to a respectable constituent, & from a desire that actual grievance in

[141]Dennis Heartt.
[142]The original is in the James Webb Papers, University of North Carolina.

the Post office alluded to, may be corrected.—Being apprized of the complaints, I doubt not that the usual investigation will be had, & an appropriate remedy applied.

"Your obt servt.

WILLIE P. MANGUM" I have little expectation that you will be able to get a better postmaster than Mr Clancy,[143] especially if the citizens can manage to get him a good deputy.—

Clancy is honest, & that is a great matter—A change may give you one, to whom even greater objections may lie, than to Mr. Clancy.—That any man opposed to the adm. will be appointed is not to be expected; no, not even if every man in Hillsbor°. should request & urge it.—

No one feels more strongly than I do, the wretched condition of the public service, when things come to this pass.—What cannot be remedied, must be endured.—

Mr. Brown does not indicate any inclination to interpose in this matter, further than to request the Dept. to look to that office, & have an eye on the manner in which it may be conducted.—

With him & the representative is all power on this subject.— I need not say, that my opinions & wishes can form no motive for the action of the Department.

Your obedient
Sevt.
WILLIE P. MANGUM

[Addressed:] Doct. James Webb
Hillsborough No. Carolina

Free
Willie P. Mangum

WPM-LC

A. O'Grady[144] to Willie P. Mangum

DUPLIN COUNTY N. C. June 15th 1836.

Sir,

I have to acknowledge, at your hands, the receipt of Judge White's speech on the land bill; which is the *first* information I have received from a Member of Congress in a year or two.— No Sir, because I will not suffer Andrew Jackson to dictate to me for whom I shall vote for his successor, Gen. McKay, al-

---

[143]Thomas Clancy.

[144]Alexander O'Grady was a member of the House of Commons from Duplin County in 1832-1833. *N. C. Manual*, 595.

though we have a limited acquaintance, has entirely overlooked me.—The County of Duplin has always been almost unanimous for Gen: Jackson; but it is thought she would, at this time, go about one third for Judge White—and, if the good cause continues to gain ground as fast for the *next* few months, as it has for the *last* few, I do not think "the party" will get much to brag of.—Having understood that he who wishes to do a good days work should always begin *early,* I commenced about a year ago, and have procured about forty or fifty subscribers to the Star—I have *also* written four or five Communications on the subject, which although they were written in a plain farmer-like style, have not, perhaps, been *entirely* ineffectual. Any document, speech, or other paper you may think proper to forward, will be thankfully received by me, at Hallsville Post-Office, Duplin County, North Carolina.

Respectfully Yours
A. O. GRADY.

Hon: Willie P. Mangum.
[Addressed:]
Hon. Willie P. Mangum
City Washington
D. C.

WPM-LC

David J. Young[145] *to Willie P. Mangum*

YOUNG'S STORE 15th June. 1836

Dr. Sir

of all the Subjects connected with the Politics of the present time, I know of none so Little understood, or so Grossly misrepresented among us as the expence attending the collection of the Revenue of the United States. I have nothing (you know) to do in politics, but it is too bad for mens Interests to be compromitted by advantage taken of their Ignorance—and Still worse, when they would willingly go the right way If they knew it—there is (or ought to be) printed statements of all the Sallaries allowed by the Government to every officer employed in the collection of the revenue, if there be such I have never seen one, if there are any cerplus ones within your reach I would thank you to Enclose me one or two, the hopes of the Country So far

[145] A merchant in Granville County.

as I am Informed are with the friends of the "Land Bill" but the way things are done *there* of *late* days, Leaves more to fear than hope—

I am Respectfully Yr friend

Hon. W. P. Mangum DAVID J. YOUNG

[Addressed:]
Hon. Willie P. Mangum
Washington City, D. C.

[Postmarked:]
Oak Hill N. C.
17th June

Willie P. Mangum to James Webb[146]

WASHINGTON CITY 16th. June 1836

Dr Sir

I have just received your note of the 11th. inst. in relation to Mr. Crabtree's certificate.[147]—

I have forwarded it to the office, & hope to get a duplicate before leaving here, by guaranteeing its' non-delivery to Mr. C. until he shall comply with the usual requisitions of the office.— In that case, it will be forwarded to you, with the expectation that you will see that the usual affidavits shall be made, & forwarded, to the pension office.—In case that cannot be done, I will immediately transmit the requisite information.—

Your obt. Sevt.
W. P. MANGUM

[Addressed:] Doct. James Webb
Hillsbor°
No. Carolina

Free
Willie P. Mangum.

WPM-LC

W. Russell[148] *to Willie P. Mangum*

PORTSMOUTH N. H.
June 16th, 1836

Dear Sir

I arrived here some days since.—I am fully as well pleased with this nation as I expected to be. My cruising is from Cape

---

[146]The original is in the James Webb Papers, University of North Carolina.

[147]See above, letter of James Webb to Mangum, June 11, 1836.

[148]William Russell, of Granville County, was a student at the state university in 1824. He entered the navy but later returned to Granville from which county he was elected to the state legislature in 1842. *N. C. Manual*, 623; Callahan, *List of Officers of the U. S. Navy*, 478; Grant, *Alumni Hist. of U. N. C.*, 542.

Ann, Mass. to Portland, Maine. I have been much disappointed in the general appearance and improvement of the New-England States, I did not find every farm a garden spot, as I anticipated. The soil is hard and steril naturally, the country uneven hilly and very rocky. though there are some situations to the eye pleasantly situated and well fixed. I have discovered a great anti-Southern feeling existing throughout this region. in fact I believe my assertion will hold good, from what I have been able to learn—from Baltimore to Passamaquaddy. I have taken some pains to pulse the people in my travel—there are many who disguise this feeling as much as posible—in as much as they cant make five dollars by expressing their sentiments conscientiously & at the same time fully everywhere, the fact is certain—they have all made up their minds and stand ready to move against the admission of Texas into the Union—and I believe will seperate before they will submit to the admission, unless the continuance of slavery be prohibited, even if we in the South should desire it. I have not heard from No. Carolina since I saw you. You will oblige me if convenient by sending me Mr. Calhoun's speech on the deposit question[149]

I remain very Respectfully
and assuredly yours
W. RUSSELL

[Addressed:]
Hon. W. P. Mangum
U. S. Senate
Washington D. C.

WPM-LC

John A. Anderson[150] *to* ....

WINSTON 20th June 1836

Dear Sir,

I have no doubt eare this some of our friends from this County have advised you of the workings of the *Regency*—in this

---

[149]In 1835 the treasury had a surplus of $20,000,000 which later increased to $36,000,000. This came mainly from the sale of public lands. Clay and most of the Whigs proposed that the proceeds from the sale of public lands be distributed among these states. Afraid of the constitutionality of Clay's plan, Calhoun proposed a constitutional amendment to permit distribution. When his amendment died for want of support, he proposed the deposits bill. This bill provided for greater regulation of the federal deposits in state banks so that the President's control over the deposits would be weakened and so that speculation would be curbed. This was approved in the Senate February 27, 1835, but was defeated in the House. By May of 1836 Jackson had control of the Senate and, therefore, pushed the deposit bill with amendments through. The amendments provided for depositing the surplus with the states according to population. Although the deposits were to be considered loans to the states, no one expected them to be paid back. In this form the bill passed both houses and became law. Wiltse, *Calhoun: Nullifier*, 258, 266-267.

[150]See above, II, 116n.

County— You are aware no doubt that the Hertford Govermet officer, who has been absent in Washington 4 or 5 years, has returned amongst us. Claimed a residence dureing the whole time and have offerd his services, to represent us in the Commons, and in some instances I have been *informed* he has confidentially said that you must next winter be turned out of the Senate,—the parties heretofore, has been nearly divided in this County; the Whigs no doubt having a majority when properly consentrated, they often out manage us and by using *means*, not the most honerable, divide the party, and succeed over us. this they effected last year in the Senate, and effected their object by electing John Vann[151] by 3 votes,

The present campaign has openned; and prospects brighter than we ought to expect are daily developing, it self, and the regency at the present are in great Consternation. We are entitled to a member in each house—they first moved off with D E Sumner[152] in the Senate, and the Celebrated. old Isaac Carter[153] in the Commons—they soon discovered that Sumner could not get a desent support in the Senate against our candidate George W. Montgomery[154]— the officer before mentioned hurried to Arkansas—on business and returned in 4 or 5 weeks on his return new meetings & secret conclaves were held, Sumner was withdrawn, and D. O. Askew[155] at Pitch Landing was brought fourth—Wheeler[156] taking the place of old Carter, I presume better to manage your defeat this winter, and the former, to make inroads in our strong Grounds in the neighbourhood of P.L. & Jno Vann to manage and cary the old Jackson party in the neighbourhood of Murfreesboro — those arrangements were well planned and deeply arranged,—I saw Mr Rayner yesterday from Murfreesboro—and its vacinity, he assures me, that they have made a faction, that the most of the old Jackson party are de-

[151]John Vann represented Hertford County in the House of Commons in 1823-1824 and the senate in 1833-1834 and 1835-1836. *N. C. Manual,* 652-653.

[152]David E. Sumner was a student at the state university in 1809-1810 and a member of the state senate in 1821-1823. Grant, *Alumni Hist. of U. N. C.,* 602; *N. C. Manual,* 652.

[153]Major of the militia and sheriff of Hertford County, Isaac Carter, Jr., represented his county in the legislature in 1819-1820, 1822, 1824-1825, and 1830-1834. Winborne, *History of Hertford County,* 326; *N. C. Manual,* 652-653.

[154]George W. Montgomery represented Hertford County in the senate in 1834 and 1836. *N. C. Manual,* 653.

[155]David Outlaw Askew the brother of Dr. George O. Askew of Bertie County, was in the senate in 1827-1828. Later he moved to Mississippi and became a planter. Winborne, *History of Hertford,* 134; *N. C. Manual,* 652.

[156]John Hill Wheeler, the historian, was born in Hertford County in 1806. He held numerous political offices, including a seat in the House of Commons in 1827-1830, secretary to the board of commissioners to negotiate the French claims in 1831, superintendent of the U. S. mint at Charlotte in 1837, state treasurer in 1842, and minister to Nicaragua in 1854. He wrote numerous books, mainly history, about North Carolina. Ashe, *Biog. Hist. of N. C.,* 472-479; *D.A.B.,* XX, 50.

nouncing Van Buren, that their Strong Ground was so much split up, all the most influencial part had raised the *White* flag, and denounced, the Regency—others declaring they would not support a vannburen man, that he understood that the Leaders—of the regency had held a private meeting on Saturday last in Murfreesboro to consult and devise means, their determination was not positively known, but it was thought *(that the Officer would decline,* pleading *ill health and depart for Washington)* that a man near P. Landing (Jepha [?] Smith) would be sent out in the neighborhood to Pitch Landing—to take as much of our support thare as posable,—that Askew would be withdrawn, and their old champion, John Vann, would take his place, they have a beare hope that they will stick to him, if he offers—

I am this particular, thinking you would like to *here* of their workings in this quarter—*all will not do,* should they make an other change, it will only expose themselves, I can assure you we have two able hands in the field and every inch of Ground will be contended, and I am extremely sorry that the Washington Gentleman can not meet Mr R. before the people, when he would be called out and, asked for an explanation of his stewartship,

I think a few suitable dockuments from you for certain persons would aid our cause, such as you may think best to answer—the feelings of those new comers in our Ranks, your speech on (I think Bentons Resolution) Published in the Star has (whare it has reached) has been of assential service,—for which I have attached a List of names—& Places—

I understood yesterday that William Cherry[157] Esqr has become a candidate against Doct^r^ Mabane[158] in the Senate in Bertie —without a very great change we can do nothing thare,—North Ampton, is unanimous for us—Gates no chance, unless we get sufficient help from Chowan to put in a Senator—there will be no Vanburien members below Gates—

Very Respectfully

Your Ob^t^ Servant

JOHN A ANDERSON

[157]William Cherry was state senator from Bertie County in 1838-1839 and member of the lower house in 1844-1845. *N. C. Manual,* 503.

[158]Alexander W. Mebane, a major in the militia, served in the state legislature as a representative of Bertie County in 1829-1830 and 1833-1837. *N. C. Manual,* 503; Raleigh *Star,* Jan. 3, 1834.

William Campbell Preston, 1794-1860, for whom Mangum named his only son. From an oil portrait by G. P. A. Healy, painted in 1842. The original is in the possession of the National Museum, Washington, D. C.

to Murfreesborough
Thomas Griffith #
Silas Parker #
Allen Moore #
James Weston #
Alfred Darden Senr–
Samuel Moore –
Edward S. Jiggetts,
Thomas Downes –
William Scott #
Benjamin Porter #
David Gatling – #
Timothy Ridley
Jordan Gatling – #
Elisha D Britt #
Walter Myrick
Jethro Darden

Henry L. Williams
Asa Liverman #

To Pitch Landing –
John Downing – #
Isaac Taylor – #
John Winborne #
Harriss Vaughn #
Daniel Doughlie #

Winton
James Jordan #
William Jordan Sr.
Charles Powell, #
Wright Nichols – #
Michael E Newsom #
Benj^{a}. Wynns #
John Everitt #

most important

WPM-LC

Charles Fisher to Willie P. Mangum

SALISBURY 21st June 1836

Dr. Sir.

Since my return home I have seen nothing to make me change the conclusion to which we came at Washington, *namely* that we will carry the State for *White,* and elect *Dudley,* but that we have less prospect for the Legislature—If we gain certain large Counties, say, Orange, Wake, Mecklenburg, Lincolnton, we will have a large majority in the Legislature, if we loose them, we will be greatly in the minority. Now, a gain of 500 votes well distributed in all these counties would give the whole of them to us, including Surry & Stokes. We are getting the sperit up, and will do all we can, but I believe there is now more activity, and certainly more organization on the other side—I have been strongly pressed by our friends here, and elsewhere, to become a candidate for the Legislature, but after the most mature consideration I find that I cannot, without sacrificing too much, and violating engagements elsewhere. About the first of Septr. I shall leave home for the South.

The Bill for the relief of our Choctaw claimants,[159] has some provisions in it, that are unjust, and unreasonable—I allude to the *proviso* in the 6th Section, and the proviso in the 8th Section—I beg you to turn to the bill, and look at them—The nature of the case is simply this—These Choctaws claim under the treaty—they are either entitled to *all* that the Treaty promises, or to none of it—If their claim is not justly made, then cut them off altogether, give them nothing,—but if their claim is good,—then give them *all* that the Treaty stipulates—in a single word,—they are either entitled to *all* or to *nothing*—and Congress have no right to add to, or to take away from the contract—or in any manner to change it—In addition to this Congress ought now to pass such an act as will close this business, and save themselves further trouble—but this bill will not do this. If it pass in this shape, they must expect to hear again from the claimants. I beg you to give a little attention to this subject, and explain the points to some of our friends, whose engagements on other subjects may prevent them from giving any attention to it—

Nothing new among us.

Yours very sincerely

CHS. FISHER

WPM-LC

John Chavis to Willie P. Mangum

RALEIGH June 27th 1836—

My dear Sir/

I have long wish to write to you, but anxiously so, ever since May Wake Court, believing that you at all times take & feel a deep Interest in the promotion & Interest of Charles Hinton Esqr. I therefore wanted to give you as accurate history of the contest between Mr Hinton & Judge Seawell, as Candidates for Senate, in the next G. Assembly, as I could obtain—In becoming so, they were so much at points, and as angrily so, as any two men, perhaps you ever saw. Not long, or in a few days, after they had declared themselves. I met the Judge in the street & after shaking hands he asked me for the news of the day. & I answered him, that I was very sorry, that him & Mr Hinton was so much at variance. He said it was not of his seeking, & went on to give me a history of the case, too lengthy to relate, but in

[159]See above, II, 50n, 384n.

his usual & smooth manner, showing me not only the improper conduct of Mr Hinton. towards him, but his improper votes in the A-Sembly, among the prominent of which, was his vote for an assistant Clerk, for the Treasurer. Also that he not only voted against him, for Judge, but used all his influence to prevent him from being elected &C. I listened to him attentively, and at our parting, I repeated again that I was truly sorry that they were at variance & that in so great a degree— Shortly after, I sought an oppy. to converse with Mr. Hinton upon the subject, and I addressed him as I did Seawell, that I was very sorry that they were so at variance, he answered that it was not his seeking, why said I, that is what Seawell says & I wanted to know which of you is in fault. I heard *his tail* & I want to hear *yours,* & told him concisly what Seawell said, & he said he had said what was false, & that Seawell had wished him to do that which his honour forbid. He then told me, that when the great Bank question, was pending, that he went to the Judges house & told him that it was a subject too weighty for his abilities, & that he wished that he w^{d}. become a Candidate for the next G. A. . The Judge refused & said he had no Interest to serve & that he must continue. After this Judge Taylor dies, he then told him that if he w^{d}. decline he w^{d}. offer. He said he did know whether he could do so consistently with his duty & Interest, because it was then understood, that he w^{d}. be a Candidate, that if he declined it w^{d}. be thought that he declined to serve his Interest & not the people, & that it w^{d}. injure his views hereafter. The judge said he had not thought of that, & that it w^{d}. be best for him to continue. He said he told the judge however, that if he w^{d}. declare himself immediately he w^{d}. give place to him but if he delayed he could not. This he said was about three Months before the time they were to declare themselves. Thus the case stood for some time, too late for him to withdraw, when the Judge came to his house, & he said he knew his business, and told him what he said expected was his business, & they entered into a smart altercation & the Judge manifested a disposition to compel him to yield to him, & he told him that he could not consistent with his honour, & he said the Judge left him, evidently dissatisfied & the case remained so until about ten days before they were to declare themselves, when the Judge sent Mr. Alphred Jones[160] to him to insist upon his giving place to him, he said he told Mr Jones to tell the Judge

---

[160]See above, II, 140.

that he thought it very ingenerous in him to send one of their mutual friends, to make such a request at such a time & that he w^{d}. not do it. He said he had not spoken to the Judge from that time untill the day they declared themselves at the last May Court, when they had a smart dispute in which he told the Judge what he said was false,—Now you are to understand, that one of the Judges charges against Mr. Hinton was that he had promised to decline, which he says is false, only in the way I have above stated—When the Judge & myself were talking I told him that I understood that Mr. Hinton had given him the lie he said that want so, if he did he did not hear it, but Hinton says he did hear the word false and refered me to Henry Waren for proof——

After the Judge declared himself, he requested the printers not to publish it. And it was generally believed that his reason for that was that if he found that he could not be elected, that he w^{d}. decline; and he done so & I inclose you his circular[161] & you can lay your own construction upon it——

You are to know that when it was announced that the Judge had opposed Hinton, & what was believed to be his motives, & the manner he had treated Hinton in the outset. I never met with a more indignant prople than the Raleighans were & more determine to support Hinton. I dont believe the Judge w^{d}. have goten a Respectable vote in Raleigh.—

The general belief is that the Judge is fallen never to rise any more, & his circular appears to be read here with the utmost contempt, because it is firmly believed that he w^{d} not have declined if he had believed he would have been elected, for it is supposed that he can not believe that the appology he has made can possibly heal the wounds his incessant cries against Mr Hinton has made amongst the Hinton & Perry families. For all this I am sorry—I have given you the above statment for your private satisfaction & not for the house tops—

I had much to say to you both concerning our private Interest & of political subjects but the subject on which I have been writing has too nearly filled my sheet to enter upon those subjects, I can only state therefore that I am well & hope this may find you & yours well—The case of E Kimbraughs new trial has been ably argued; but the Judges have not decided. The disinterested Lawyers think he will not get a new trial—Please to write to

[161]The circular is not in the Mangum Papers.

me by male, & let me know of the welfare of your family. My best respects Mrs Mangum & tell her I had intent to come see her in next Month, but my Employers will not allow me any vacation———

I am your Ob^t. Hb. Servt—
JOHN CHAVES

P. S. Mr. Hinton says possitively that he voted for Seawell for Judge—

[Addressed:]

Hon. Willie P. Mangum Esqr
Orange

To be left at
Red Mountain post
office

WPM-LC

W. S. Ransom to Willie P. Mangum[162]

WARRENTON July 27th 1836

Dear Sir

In verry great haste I write to you to apprise that after two letters no response has been recd. from Turner [?] I am here at nothing—ready and most willing to do what my friends may think most advantageous to them—their cause—mine and to me I can purchase out the paper published here for $8.00—Here I have friends who will unite with you in placing me in any situation you mutually may agree on that I would accept—You know my sentiments—This verry little place today is the gayest in the State, aye, even in the U. S. of [this] size, come down soon—Here are my friends from the South Col. Alston, Mr Alston, Genl Parrish—Mr Macon[163] and several others—Do come and consult with them whether it be better for me to remain here or go to Florida where I am offered a good birth—Your presence down here would be advantageous to both of us, to our cause. You would be hailed here in a manner different from what you expect and come you must in ten days any how. If you consult your own interest, that of our State and my own you will not delay—Day after tomorrow is our election and a close one it will be. I am a great annoyance here to the party and they all wish me at the De'il but have to treat me respectfully—Genls John H. & M. T.

---

[162]See above, II, 394.

[163]He probably refers to Willis Alston, Thomas Alston, and Nathaniel Macon.

Hawkins had a great fight yesterday with Ths. H. Christmas[164] & others & were rather worsted—I will not say who was blameable *now,* because I did not see it.

Small as our party be in this Co. we are greatly in the way of the dominant one Somerell[165] & his sons go with us, so do the Halls & Plummers. Davison—Drake and others of note join and I swear it is thirty stronger now than when I came—Do Dear Sir come down soon—Your time will be—it shall be spent—more agreeably than it has been for years Shocco and Warrenton afford a large majority of friends to you—To express great feelings of gratitude to you I am convinced would be unpleasant—You know the sentiments of my bosom so receive them.

From Yr. Devoted

W. S. RANSOM

HON. W. P. MANGUM.

If you cannot come soon write—write soon—but come—Do come and you will see people from all parts of the State.

W. S R

[Addressed:]

Hon: Willie P. Mangum
Red Mountain P. O.
Orange County
Mail N. C.

WPM-LC

Jeremiah Pearsall[166] to Willie P. Mangum

DUPLIN 1. August 1836.

Hon. W. P. Mangum,

The Whig party in this County, generally approve your course, & during the present State of excitement, you have not been forgotten by them; In the Outset we were fearful we should have no part nor lot in the matter; but after consultation, we concluded that *E. D. Hill*[167] (who had some powerful friends on the other side, & who from personal considerations would support

---

[164]Thoms H. Christmas was a member of the North Carolina House of Representatives in 1852-1853. *N. C. Manual,* 838.

[165]He probably refers to James Somervell and his son, John B. Somervell, who were prominent in Warrenton life in this period. Grant, *Alumni Hist. of U. N. C.,* 581; Coon (ed.), *N. C. Schools and Academies,* 620, 624; *William and Mary Quarterly,* Ser. II, Vol. III, 161, 168, 267.

[166]Pearsall was a presidential elector for White in 1836.

[167]Edward D. Hill was a student at the University in 1831-1832. He failed in his campaign for the legislature. Grant, *Alumni Hist. of U. N. C.,* 281.

him) might succeed; and after he had identified his interest, with the Whig party (which party in the mean time was gaining strength) we required of him a distinct avowal of his sentiments touching the party,—We required him to say he would go with us throughout; first, for Dudley as Govr. then for the White electoral Ticket, & last (tho I assure you not least) for your re-election to the U. S. Senate. I think he will be elected, # [*sic*] *and in that event, some how or other you must pay some friendly attention to him, he is young & inexperienced; & tho he has promised us faithfully yet he has powerful friends of the V. B. Party.*—I hope he will do right# private & confidential.——

We are in the minority some, tho not discouraged; our ranks are gathering strength, and as we increase, we become bold; tho we have severe opposition, *every* inch of ground is disputed, & more general excitement than I have ever seen before, both sides *warmly* engaged——At our last Court I presented to the friends a few thoughts & suggested an address to the good people of the County; the proposition was readily agreed to, & the result, I herein enclose——We think it will have a good effect, & our object in circulating it now, is to operate on the August Elections "some may call it intriguing"——

Our party here is composed of Clever fellows generally, & who *must* exert influence in the community——

I have been one of the few who have dared to oppose the present Administration from its beginning, & tho I have had but few with me (in the last election *only eleven*) my personal popularity as yet, has not suffered; I believe Duplin would give me, as to a favorite son, and in the present contest, I find *many* are coming over to my side, & the best I dont think will be very bad—

The gentlemen who signs the enclosed circular,[168] are all clever, & mostly, influential, *some intelligent;* the first named, (lately become your warm friend,) is intelligent honest, fair, & of nice feelings—dont forget him, if you should have any important communication—

I conclude with the confident hope that the old State is about to shake off the yoke of bondage, & act as a sovereign people should—I have *just* rec^{d}. a Letter from Onslow, stating that David W. Sanders[169] would probably be elected in the Commoner

[168]The circular is not in the Mangum Papers.

[169]He was selected at the Whig caucus in Raleigh on December 22, 1835, to serve on the vigilance committee of Onslow County. *Raleigh Register,* Jan. 12, 1836.

from that County if so, one of the *very cleverest* fellows of the Whig party will be in the Commons from Onslow; *sure & true,*

For the success of our cause (yours included) I expect to be constantly engaged during the contest,

I greet you kindly & respectfully, & am your friend

and obedient Servant &C

JERE. PEARSALL

P.S. We thank you for your kindness, in sending to us valuable documents during the few months past— You may be surprised at this address; a few days together in Raleigh in 1823 produced a friendly feeling that has not declined, tho hav[nt]— seen you since—

J. P.

[Addressed:]

Honbl Willie P. Mangum
U. S. Senator from N. C.
Hilsboro
N. C.

WPM-LC

Jonathan McCarty[170] to Willie P. Mangum

CONNERSVILLE [INDIANA,] 17 August 1836.

Dear Sir

Since my return from Washington I have taken open ground for Harrison and he will get this state (Indiana) as certain as he lives let North Carolina Va & the South but do their duty and the Ned Rucker[171] men are beaten, I am anxious to hear from you & the prospects and probability of the result in your state. I hope Graham[172] is elected—the friends of sound principles have nothing to fear in the west Indiana Ohio & Kentucky will go for Harrison and I think Pennsylvania is also certain the elections in this State for members of the State legislature have resulted in the election of nearly two thirds of Harrison men. this is a fair test as the question was made with an eye to secure a Van Senator—but Hendricks[173] will be beaten the result is

[170]Jonathan McCarthy, 1795-1852, was a member of the House of Representatives from Indiana from 1831 to 1837, *Biog. Dir. of Cong.*, 1250.

[171]In the Baltimore Democratic Convention, which met in May, 1835, and nominated Van Buren for President, Tennessee had no official delegates. In order that Jackson's home state might not go unrepresented, the convention seated Edward Rucker, "a Tennessean who happened to be in Baltimore, and permitted him to cast the state's fifteen votes for Van Buren." After this, the convention was referred to as the "Ruckerized" convention. Parks, *Life of Bell,* 108.

[172]W. A. Graham was a candidate for the state house of representatives. James Graham was also a candidate for Congress in that year.

[173]William Hendricks, 1782-1850, served in the House of Representatives from 1816 to 1822 and in the Senate from 1825 to 1837. *Biog. Dir. of Cong.*, 1087-1088.

about as I told you it would be when I saw you last let me hear from you

Yours very respectfully
J. McCARTY

Hon W P Mangum
[Addressed:]
Hon. Wiley P. Mangum
Red Mountain Orrange Cty
North Carolina

[Postmarked:]
Connersville Ind.
Augt. 19th 1836.

WPM-LC

Memucan Hunt to Willie P. Mangum

OXFORD N. CA August 22nd 1836

My very dear Sir:

I herewith do myself the pleasure to forward to you a copy[174] of my address to the generous and brave in the U. S. Its perusal will give you a knowledge of my situation [*sic*] in and relation to the Texian Govt. I have but few acquaintances of political distinction in Philadelphia, New York & Boston. Will you be pleased to honor me with some letters of acquaintance to gentlemen in one, or all of these places, and enclose them to me at the city of New York? By so doing you will increase the many obligations which I am already under to you.

I set out for N- York to- morrow and fear that I shall not have the pleasure of seeing you before my departure from the U. States for Texas. You can my dear sir, to some extent, appreciate my gratification at the triumph of your principles in N- Ca, a circumstance the more happy from the kind personal feelings which you will pardon me for adverting to as perhaps it will be the last time I shall have the honor of testifying them to you.

I am dear sir, your
friend and servant
MEMUCAN HUNT

Honbl.
W. P. Mangum
N. Carolina
[Addressed:]
Honbl. W. P. Mangum
Red Mountain
N- Carolina

---

[174]This is not in the Mangum Papers.

WPM-LC

Invitation to the Fayetteville Barbecue[175]

FAYETTEVILLE, August 30, 1836.

SIR:

A BARBECU[E] [torn] will be given in the Vicinity of Fayetteville, on Thursday, the 8th S[ep]te[mber] [torn] the recent Triumph of the Republican Party of North Carolina, in [torn] [ED]WARD B. DUDLEY, of New Hanover County.

Your attenda[nce] [torn]-s, friendly to the elevation of HUGH L. WHITE to the Presidency.

[torn]-ee Shaw,	Christopher Munroe,
[Ben]jamin Robinson,	James H. Dickson,
[Al]exander D. McLean,	William Shaw,
[torn]ter McKellar,	Joseph Baker,
Paris J. Tillinghast,	William McMillan,
John Smith,	Thomas Sandford,
Henry Potter,	Roderick McRae,
John McKay,	Oliver P. Stark,
David Anderson,	William Nott,
Alexander Clark,	Duncan G. McRae,
Edward J. Hale,	John McLean,
Henry M. Turner,	John Winslow,
Edward L. Winslow,	John W. Huske,
John Murphy,	Jonathan Evans,
Geo. W. Hutton,	James Hart,

Committee of Invitation.

Hon W. P. Mangum

Sir,

The Whigs of Cumberland Would be glad to meet with you on the 8th Sept— to commemorate the victory achieved in the [el]ection of Govr. Dudley

The Committee

[Addressed:]

Hon W. P. Mangum
Hillsboro
N. C.

---

[175]This is a printed invitation. The letter at the bottom is in long hand.

WPM-LC

William Ashly to Robert Ashly

HICKMAN COUNTY KENTUCKY September
the 9th 1836——

Dear brother I once more am permitted through the mercy of God to Send you a few lines to inform you that I am yet in the land of the living and enjoying tolerible health at present I am living with Thomas Woods in Hickman County Kentucky and expect to stay with him Some time if I Should live except my mind alters he is a brother to Samuel Woods near Little river meeting house if you should see him you may tell him that Said Thomas and family ware well when this letter was wrote Brother James and family ware well a few days ago and is living in Weakly County Tennessee and doing as well as could be expected from his curcumstance he has got a piece of land on Obion river a[s] good as a crow would want to fly over he has had some bad luck in horses dying but still he gets along pretty well; I Seen brother Pettygrue and his wife a few weeks ago them and family ware well they are living in Carrel County him and his Son Robert they have bought land and Paid for it a I understand as for the news of the country crops of corn are a good as I ever seen any whare in my life there is a prospect of plenty in our land and generaly a good market for the Surpeless I think this the best place for an industrious man that I have ever seen I think you would do well to leave of ploughing them Stony hills and come here whare you can get something for your labour; it is a long & tiresome road to travel yet ware I in your place I would start & try to hold out untill I would get near the Mississippi river;

Please to remember me in love to all my Sisters & my dear mother if shee is alive I hope these lines will find you all in good health likewise give my love to all my old neighbours & friends in particular my old friends William Mangram[176] & the judge his son tell them I have not forgot their friendship to me and the may jovel hours we have spent together likewise William Yokeley & family I add no more but remain your loving and affectionate brother

WILLIAM ASHLY

Robert Ashly

N.B. you will Please to write to me as soon as convenient and

[176]He refers to William Person Mangum and his son, Willie Person Mangum.

dont neglect it; I long to hear from you all and know how you are & how you are doing and all the rest of my friends & acquaintance; I shall expect a letter from you in a reasonable time after you may have time to receive this if you should fail you will put me to a good deal of trouble in going to the post office for I shall be going or Sending to the office continualy when I think it is time for a letter to come

Brother James lives about ten miles from me Brother Pedegrue is about 60 or 70 miles

[Addressed:]

Robery Ashley

N. Carolina Orange County

Red Mountain

Willie P. Mangum to Sally A. Mangum[177]

ORANGE, Wednesday 14th Sept. 1836

My dear daughter

We have been looking for a letter from you for the last two or three weeks, but have received none. I hope my dear, you will write at least once in two weeks.—Your Mother is extremely anxious to hear from you.—We are all well, your Mother, your Sisters, myself and all.

I cannot now tell you when I can send for you. I will write to you again before long, & tell you. If I can make it at all convenient, I will bring you home a week before the end of next month. If my business shall make it inconvenient, you ought not to desire it.—

I hope my dear you endeavour to improve your time, and in all things, try to give satisfaction to Mrs. Bobbitt.—Your Mother & your Father would both be very much mortified, if they knew that you waste your time, & do not avail yourself of the opportunity of improving yourself, that you now enjoy. Patty & Mary both desire to see you very much & [torn]—

Write on *Wednesdays* & send by Raleigh & the letters will reach us Saturday mornings.—Mr. Bobbitt will have your letters put into the mail on Wednesday's.—Present my respects to Mrs.

---

[177]The original is in the possession of Miss Preston Weeks, Washington, D. C.

& Mr. Bobbitt.—Your Father & Mother send you their love & trust you will be a good girl.—

Your affectionate Father
WILLIE P. MANGUM

P.S.

I observed in your letters to your Mother, a great deal of bad spelling, which I was very sorry to see.—You said in both letters, that you wrote in a *great hurry.*—Now my dear, neither little girls nor young ladies should ever excuse negligent writing & bad spelling by saying they were in *a hurry.*—If they would spend but a little of the time that they waste before the looking glass & in idle talk, in writing carefully their letters they would not have to say *they were in a hurry.*—I hope my dear, you will never say so again, but always endeavour to perform every duty of that description, in the best way you can.—Your Father feels sure that to mention this to you for once, will have the proper effect, as he & your Mother both believe, that you will try to give them satisfaction as far as you can.—

They both hope & believe that you will endeavor to do your duty, & they have much pleasure in that reflection.

Your affectionate Father
WILLIE P. MANGUM

[Addressed:]
Miss Sally A. Mangum
Louisburg
Nº. Carolina

WPM-LC

Allen Rogers[178] *& Others to Willie P. Mangum*

WAKE COUNTY October 6th 1836

To the Hon. Willie P. Mangum
Sir

The undersigned having been appointed, a Committee, by a numerious assemblage of the Citizens of Wake County who after a Mutual interchange of opinions upon the future political prospect of our country & the Effects likely to be produced, by the recent, elections in this State, come, to the conclusion that the recent election for Governor, and members of the Legislature in this State evidence in a manner, not to admit, of

[178]See above, I, 270n.

a doubt, in the mind of the Most Skeptical of the complete triumph of Whig principals, and the certain rescue, at the approaching election for president and vice president, of the united states, of the Good old, North State from the aims, and support, of the arch Majician ablotionist and political intriger Martin Vanburan, & thereby the complete triumph of Republican principals have determined Publickly to manifest there Great gratification at, so Glorious, a victory, By a (Barbicue) and having since your elevation to a seat in the Senate, of the united States, after a Strict Scrutiny and examination of your conduct, & votes, therein found nothing to condemn, and much to approve and particularly. approving of your Strenious & able exertions to check Executive encroachments & usurpation upon the rights of the states & the people as Garrenteed, by that sacred, charter of our liberties the constitution of the united States and also approving of your Great and Manly course, & Efforts combined with those of many old, and long tried republicans in both houses of Congress, to restore the Good-old, republican doctrine of a Strict adherence to which all, the Granted powers, thereby confered, will be murged, in the General, Welfare & centered in the executive we do therefore in pursuance of instructions as said Committee. respectfully invite you, unite with us, in celebrating [torn] Glorious triumph, recently acheaved, by the Whigs in this State & to partake of a Barbicue, at the Store of Col. Allen Rogers Jr. on the 21st of october 1836

Yours. Respectfully
ALLEN ROGERS
THOMAS HICKS and others
Committee &c.

We shall be pleased, to Receave & acceptance as soon as convenient. directed, to Rogers store to Allen Rogers. P.M. our object, is to make it as publick as is possible. W.H.H. [William H. Haywood] refues to accept of an invitation, to meet with you But is desirous to Know what you said about him at Fishdam he says if the people at William Laws store in Wake—will give him a dinner he will accept of it, & reply to you, I wish you to prepare to Handle him at my house, with Gloves off he have made you the object of abuse for the Three last years, to explain the right of Instruction properly managed, will have a happy effect and it is important, for you, as you are charged, with disobeying the same your remarks were satisfactory to me at Fishdam, in bringing to the notice of the people that you had notified the party before you voted what course you should persu. I must conclude for the want of room yrs.

ALLEN ROGERS

[Addressed:]
Hon.
Willie P. Mangum
Red Mountain
Orange County
N. Carolina.

WPM-LC

Willie P. Mangum to Sally A. Mangum

RED MOUNTAIN 12th Octo. 1836.

My dear daughter.

Being at Col. Parkers, and the mail leaving this evening, I drop you a line, to let you know that we are all well except your Mother.—She has been very sick for four or five days, but is now up, and getting well.—I had hoped to see you this week, and should have been at Louisburg, but for your Mothers illness.—She has had violent cold.—

I shall come to see you probably in two or three weeks. If it shall not be convenient, I shall send for you in about a month.—

I hope my dear, you try to do all that you can to give satisfaction to Mrs. Bobbitt.—Your Mother desires me to send for you sooner, but I do not think I can conveniently do so.—

We hope to get a letter from you on Saturday.—Patty & Mary beg Father almost every day to send for Sister Sally.—

Present my respects to Mrs. & Mr. Bobbitt.

Be a good child & your Father & Mother will continue to love their dear daughter.

WILLIE P. MANGUM

[Addressed:]
To Miss Sally A. Mangum
Louisburg
No Carolina

WPM-LC

"Amicus" to ——————[179]

1 The noble President Jackson
Has run the Whigs to destruction
His message sent did satisfy
The Chambergs of France to comply
2 With the treaty to pay the money,
Now dont the whigs feel quite funny.
Condemn the message on all sides
Defended France, their country's hide;
3 Pity the men that cannot see,
What tories in heart, they can be,
They call themselves Whigs in heart,
They cant maintain it in one part.
4 Their conduct shows what they believe,
Doing all they can to decieve
They took the name that dont belong
To the party that's in the wrong.
5 They wish to dupe every man,
To vote against that Little Van
But says the Hero of the west
We should elect him for the best.
6 They tried they toil, but all in vain
To bring the Hero down to shame
A tree is known by the friut it brings
Just see how produce sells this spring.
7 Republicans must all unite
Then we will beat them out of sight
We think but little of their Clay
Van Buren will run on that day.
8 Webster will run, and so will White
But Van will beat them out of sight
Harrison will run, he wont do
Van Buren will beat all four too.
9 The four is made of "Fed" & tory
Unless I have been taught a story
Van Buren is the only man
That is a true republican.

[179] I do not recognize the handwriting.

10 What goes to show he is despised
By all the tories on that side.
The whigs in congress had the power
To aid us on at any hour.
11 Where have they lent their helping hand
But welcome France into our land
They saw our need, & our defense
They woud not vote a single pence
12 To save our nation from the French
That is the product of a whig
No more a whig than I a pig
Republican wishes to defend
13 Their Country from, all foreign fiend
The Glorious time is rolling round
For the whiggies, to run a ground
The contest will ere long, be
14 The whiggies done forevermore,
Where is the man, that cannot find
What Jackson, done for all mankind,
Tis not because they are so blind
15 They go because they are incline
To want Calhoun's dividing line
Thus let the tories go away
And follow their King & his sway
16 Then it will be a glorious time
To all the people left behind
A world of praise is justly due
To Old Jackson & Buren too.
So will I bring this to a close
For fear I might insult their four

A republican

These lines I send you, to amuse
Your thoughts upon my noble wit.

Amicus

WPM-LC

Will. A. Graham to Willie P. Mangum

HILLSBORO' Novr 4th 1836

My Dear Sir

I proceed to redeem my promise to write you, altho' I regret that I am aided by nothing but my own reflections on the subject we last conversed upon—Mr Outlaw[180] had been called to Bertie by the illness of his Father, & Genl Iredell[181] was absent on his circuit—I saw no one therefore at Raleigh with whom I could confer freely—I had thought of asking the opinion of Govr Swain on my return but I travelled in the stage which only stopped until the mail was opened at Chapel Hill—

My consideration of the matter however, impresses me more strongly with the belief, that you would act unwisely, to adopt the course you proposed on the day of the electoral election[182]—In the first place our information relative to the indisposition of a portion of the Whigs towards you, is not sufficiently certain, to be acted upon—It may turn out to be untrue— Or the few delinquents finding themselves a mere handful on reaching Raleigh may come in—But if unfortunately this should not be the case, your withdrawal would exert a pernicious influence on our cause. The timid in our own ranks, would look upon it, as the offspring of a conviction that Van Burenism was irresistible, and "The Party" would shout it, as the striking of our flag—I know how irksome to an ingenuous mind, is the idea of being bandied about, & used merely to effect the personal views of other men, but if there be really such among us, (I am persuaded they are but few) and they will not cooperate, I am clear that they should be made to take the responsibility of their course, before the public & their constituents—Some sacrifice of feeling must necessarily be encountered, but this should be met as you have already met the denunciations & slanders of the minions of power—Should you be nominated before the General Assembly, & fail to be elected, or should you decline after the meeting, it can only be said that you have held on, until all hope was lost—Would less be said, provided you decline now? Bear in mind my Dear Sir, that although there may be a few, who (from whatever motives) are unfavourable to your election these should not be allowed to controul your course or the destinies of our cause—the great body of our party (unless I am deceived) de-

---

[180]David Outlaw.

[181]James Iredell.

[182]By September, Mangum had decided to resign if the election went against the Whigs. In the election in August, Dudley, the Whig candidate for governor, won by a majority of 4,000, and the early returns for the legislature indicated another Whig victory. Mangum thereupon declared that he had been vindicated. When the final returns were in, however, it was seen that neither the Whigs nor Democrats had control of the two houses. Then two recently elected Whigs died. In the special elections for the two vacant seats, the Democrats won both places. Mangum, therefore, offered his resignation. Pegg, "Whig Party in N. C.," 102-103. See also above, I, xxxii-xxxiii.

sire your reelection—And they feel the obligations they owe to you, and would claim a reciprocity—I think they would take it ill, to see you voluntarily (as they might suppose) abandon their hopes—I yet retain the opinion, I expressed to you, that unless we shall succeed in electing you, our prospects are gone—If this however should be a mistake, possibly your not resigning, untill after the meeting of the assembly, might aid in the election of [another] Whig—I do not perceive in any event, that it [would] jeoperd our chances—Of this however you [are] more able than myself to judge—As to you [being] a burthen to the party, I do not believe it [would be as consid]ered generally; on the contrary, I verily believe [that] the generality fully appreciate their duties to you [but] do not esteem their triumph complete [until] you are reelected—But if any of [your] other friends should have been constrained to m[torn] to a condition of their own election, as Mr [torn] Person did—And you fail from that cause: however much it should be regretted, we must make the most of our situation, from the materials we have—although you might not be expected to aid personally in the election of another, still you would not be held blameless should you take any step which would lead to the election of a Van B. man, unless it might be to disappoint the personal hopes of some one, who had voluntarily created difficulties in our ranks—Whether your withdrawal now would prejudice the personal prospects any other Whig I am unable to say—I do not think it could in any point of view be beneficial to the cause itself—Mr Nash who is here concurs with me in saying you should not resign—In good or ill report I am Dr Sir Very truly Your Friend &c

Hon W. P. Mangum) WILL A. GRAHAM

[Addressed:]

Hon. Willie P. Mangum
Red Mountain
Orange
N. C.

WPM-LC

Thomas Patterson to Willie P. Mangum

CLEAR SPRING MD Novr. 8th 1836.

Dr. Sir.

For your use on 17th Novr. I inform you that Maryland Pennasy & Ohio have gone astonishly for Harrison—Ohio no doubt

10 or 12 thousand, Penna 12 to 15 thousd Maryd. more than 3000 majorities—a bet is just offered of 500 dolls in this town that Maryd has given 5000 majority for Harrison & refused, but I think this an extravagant calculation—You may rely on the general truth in this letter derived from all accounts verbal, written & printed in haste behind a bar in Clearspring I give you the news for use on 17th Inst.—You may depende on its general correctness so far as heard Yrs truly

THOS. PATTERSON
formerly Clerk in Congress Hall.

[Addressed:]
Hon. Wilie P. Mangum
Red Mountain
Orange County
North Carolina.

WPM-LC

John Chavis to Willie P. Mangum

Novr. 17th. 1836—

My dear Sir/

I write to let you know that I expect to move to Granville next fall, and in that case I shall not need your assistance in the case of Rogers & I thank God for it, as you have a better use for your money—

As to the flour I should be glad to get it, as that will not cost you much tho' it is at $10. pr barrel by the load yet there is a difference between giving a few bushels of wheat to make it when you can spare them, than to buy the wheat to make it—Please to have it sent to Mr James Lynns at J. Brasfields old place as early as possible for I need it extremely, and I shall not have the opp[y] of geting it from any other place—

I have not heard from any of the elections but Wake where we are beaten as I expected I have ever been fearful that the Whigs would not exert themselves as they ought to do. And I still have my fears that Van Buren will be elected. In a word I would not that you & Judge White should be beaten for a $1000 poor as I am. That you should be beaten by W. Haywood would be death to me—I suppose you have heard of the shameful affair of the Van Burenites sending out petitions to the people to instruct Gales to rise against you & to vote for W. Haywood for speaker. Thus you see the party go on regardless of all shame, determined carry their point at all hazards—

Pray dont fail to answer my letter respecting the charge of my going to Raleigh to raise information before you go to Congress, & to let me know upon a different piece of paper whether I am to get the flour or not—

Tell Mrs. Mangum I will come & see her in July if I can

I am your obt Hb[l] st—
JOHN CHAVES

[Addressed:]
Hon Willie P. Mangum Esqr
Orange

To be left at
Red Mountain P. O.
[Postmarked:]
Rogers Store, Dec. 2

WPM-LC

Samuel L. Southard[183] to Willie P. Mangum

TRENTON Nov 18: 1836

Dear Sir,

We have had an animated & severe struggle in New Jersey. The actual majority is not yet known—but sufficient returns have not yet come in to enable me to say to you with entire confidence that we have carried both our Congressional & Electoral tickets—by between 500 & 1000 votes. Van Buren has lost this State.

Respectfully &c
SAM[l] L. SOUTHARD—

Hon: W. Mangum.

[Addressed:]
Hon: W. Mangum
Red Mountain
Orange County
North Carolina—

---

[183]A native of New Jersey and graduate of the College of New Jersey, Samuel Lewis Southard became a teacher and then a lawyer. After holding several local and state offices, he was in turn head of the navy, war, and treasury departments from 1823 to 1829 and United States Senator in 1821-1823, and 1833-1842. He was also governor, state attorney general, and president *pro tempore* of the Senate. *Biog. Dir. of Cong.*, 1549-1550.

WPM-LC

Thos. J. Green[184] to Willie P. Mangum

COLUMBIA, TEXAS Nov. 19th 1836

My Dear Sir/

From my long and strong friendship to yourself, I cannot let this opportunity slip without writing. My strongest inducement for so doing, is, that I greatly desire to see your name among the foremost of my native land in advocating a great and glorious political measure about to be brought before your government, to wit The recognition of our Independence, and the annexation of Texas to the United States as a member of that Republic.

As a nation, we are at present in the full tide of successful government, as perfect in all its parts as the wisdom of our Constitution allows. The unparalleled success of our aims and the establishment of such a government, entitle us justly to claim political manhood. We have taught our enemies some truths of this kind, but their perverse and procrastinating policy may make them slow to acknowledge, and we appeal now to your Nation more just and most enlightened, with much confidence. I cannot be mistaken in believing the United States, will grant us what we so much desire; nor can I be mistaken in believing it the greatest political question which can occupy your government for many years to come; and rely upon it my dear Friend, there is much honour in store for him, who may be among the foremost in bringing it about. The richness, beauty, magnificence, geographical and geological of this country, is as far superior to the best portion of the United States, as the Duck River country to our own native counties. What then can possibly interrupt my assertion when we have a country here six times as large as North Carolina and six hundred times as rich? with Steamboats in 30 hours run of the great Orleans and Rail roads already pointing to her very centre.

I will not discuss this question now, but should you live to the ordinary age of an old man, you will see in Texas, a population six times as great as the largest States of your confederacy, with an export greater than that of the United States. The sorest reflection I have on earth is, that I cannot live to witness the political and individual grandeur of the next generation. I admit

[184]See above, I, 331n.

these wholesale assertions appear to be extravagant and ought not to be dealt to a Senator of your experience—my apology for so doing is that such men as yourself Calhoun, Webster, Clay & Preston are as unlearned of Texas, as I was before I came here, when my extravagant anticipations were as far below the reality as if they were opposites.

I hope you will give every assistance to Col. Wharton[185] our Minister to your government. Col. W. is my friend and connection whose intimate acquaintance you will prize.

Permit me in renewing an old acquaintance to hope you will write me soon. I am informed by the new government I will continue to occupy my former situation in the Army, which is Senior General in the line. Please give my respects to Mr Calhoun.

Your obt. hum. Servt and old friend
THOS. J. GREEN.

[Addressed:]
The Hon[ble]
Wiley P. Mangum
Washington
Per City
Col. Wharton)

Willie P. Mangum to Hugh Waddell and W. A. Graham[186]

RED MOUNTAIN 23rd. Nov. 1836.

Gentlemen.

I enclose to you my resignation of my seat in the Senate of the United States, which I beg you, to hand to the Speaker of the Senate immediately upon the receipt of it.—I enclose it to both of you, but one of you may be absent from Raleigh on its arrival.—

I have taken this step upon mature consideration, my inclination & judgment both assenting, & I shall be glad to know that our friends generally acquiesce in the propriety of the views, I have taken both of what is due to myself & those with whom I have acted.—However that may be, the step is taken; & I trust, it may result in advantage to the Country, as I am sure it will, in quiet to myself.—I shall not look back with any regrets.

[185]Colonel William H. Wharton, the Texan representative at Washington in 1836.
[186]The original is in the William A. Graham Papers, University of North Carolina.

I feel that I have done my duty, according to my sense of it. —But I shall look forward with Confidence, if not with exaltation, not doubting the ultimate eminence & glory that our common country is destined to whatever may be the trials & occasional humiliation which she & many of her patriotic sons, may from time to time, have to encounter.

Believe me Gentlemen,
Mo. truly & sincerely
Your friend & ob^t. Ser^t.
WILLIE P. MANGUM

[Addressed:] Hugh D. Waddell esq^r.
&
William A. Graham esq^r.
Raleigh
No. Carolina

[Endorsement:]
WILLIE P. MANGUM
Resigning seat in U.S.
Senate

WPM-LC

John C. Taylor[187] *to Willie P. Mangum*

Thursday 24th Nov: [1836].

Dear Sir,

I write in haste to satisfy that curiosity which you must feel in knowing the proceedings at Raleigh. In the first place Waddle was elected on monday upon the first vote for Speaker of the senate by a vote of 24 to 22. Arrington from Nash being absent but has since taken his seat. On the same day Haywood was elected speaker in the other house by a vote of 60 to 57, several of our party being absent, they are all however in their seats at present, except Mr. Muse[188] who probably will not appear at all. It seemed to be the opinion of our party in as large a meeting as could be assembled the evening before that we should make fight and the same principle or determination was expressed in reference to the election of Senator—with the qualification however that we stood on a comparison of strength a fair prospect of success. I think however that the prevailing

[187] See above, II, 388n.
[188] John B. Muse, of Pasquotank.

opinion now is that we shall not run; for the general belief is that the perquimons senator[189] is V. B. and in that event all agree that we should at once strike our flag. The party had a meeting in the Commons hall last night and it is pretty well known that there was so great a scism amongst them as to induce the necessity of another meeting. The persons in nomination before them it is said, and indeed I presume pretty well known—were Haywood and Strange[190] the latter of whom is upon the same authority said to have received much the larger number of votes—He it is believed by our side of the house will be their Nominee. Some of our friends indeed a great many of them encouraged the idea of taking up Mosely,[191] if we do not run, in opposition to their choice, and but one opinion prevails as to the practicability of electing him or of his acceptance.

The business of the legislature has of course been uninteresting thus far—but I have no time to enter upon this subject. I hope you will be with us in a few days; the question of senator so far as we are concerned will be settled in a day or two. I shall be very much disappointed if you have been unable to find the letter of Wyche; I think the views you expressed upon the subject of our general course in reference to the election of Senator, is more and more appreciated, altho' every man yet adopts them with the qualification in so many words, or condition that we stand no certain chance of success.

Sincerely Your friend &c
JNO C TAYLOR

[Addressed:]

Hon: W. P. Mangum
Red Mountain
Orange
County.

WPM-LC

Agreement Between Willie P. Mangum & Willie Stagg

[1 Dec., 1836]

Stagg is to live as overseer on the Plato place. Mangum is to find him Plato & another good hand, & Stagg is to work & super-

---

[189] Jesse Wilson.
[190] Will H. Haywood and Robert Strange. Strange was elected.
[191] W. D. Moseley, of Lenoir County.

intend, & also put his boys in the Crop, Mangum to find two work hands, & be at all expense, except supporting Staggs family, Stagg to do all the duties of a *faithful, diligent & attentive* overseer, both in the plantion & crop, as well as to faithful attention to Stock of all kinds—& to do every thing towards preparing for a succeeding crop. Mangum to give Stagg one fourth part of Corn, Fodder, Tobacco, Oats &c shucks, top fodder, & straw excepted, and one fifth part of the wheat—Stagg to have the Milk of a Cow, garden ground 300 lb. Pork, 4 Barrels of Corn, & 3 bushels of Wheat—Stagg binds himself to do the best he can, & in case of difference of opinion, to be governed by sd. Mangum—To keep the plantation in repair, & do everything else that a skilful owner, with the like force would do—
Witness our hands & seals this 1st Decr 1936

WILLIE P. MANGUM (Seal)
WILLIE STAGG (Seal)

Test
A. B. Mangum.[192]

N.B. had enough at that.

WPM-LC

William Cain, Jr., to Willie P. Mangum

St. Marys College
Baltimore Decr, 2d—1836

My dear Uncle

I have been expecting you for some days now but I saw in the Raleigh Register yesterday that you had resigned your office and I therefore suppose you will not be on to Washington City this winter. I have been thinking how I would enjoy myself in Christmas holydies at Washington for you promised me when I came here that I might go there and stay with you then but as it is I will have to spend it here going to church and I reckon it is better for me and I am very well satisfied to stay I like the college very well and much better than I thought I would when I first came and the fact is I would not leave upon any consideration I am very well contented there is a nother boy here from No Carolina about my size with whom associate and the time passes off very pleasantly and fast a day does not seem more than an hour I go to 3d Latin 4th Greek 2d Geography 2d Eng-

[192]One of Mangum's cousins in Orange County.

lish classes Father says I can either stay here to graduate or when I am prepared go to some other college I expect I will stay here for I always get behind hand by changing schools so often and I am very well contended here. Major Davie[193] was up here this evening to see me he came from Hillsborough some days ago he is as talkative as ever and as lively I believe if he were a hundred years old he would still be a young man that is in his ways I cannot write any more now give my love to Aunt Charity and the children. Please write soon.

Yours sincerely
WM CAIN

P.S. Please dont let any body read this W C

[Addressed:]

Hon. Willie P. Mangum
Red Mountain Post Office
Orange Cty.
N. C.

WPM-LC

J. J. Crittenden to Willie P. Mangum

Senate - Decr. 12th 1836

Dear Mangum,

It was with infinite regret that after my arrival here, I was informed of your resignation—It was no slight aggravation of this intelligence that it came upon me at the very moment I was expecting the pleasure of meeting you—

We are all full of regret, (that is, your political friends) and half angry with you for your resignation—We needed here the comfort & assistance of all our friends; & could illy part with you, nor do we perceive any necessity you were under to take the course you have done—You do not intend, I hope, to withdraw at such a time as this from the public service—Some of your friends here are already anticipating *active* service for you, and declaring that you must become a candidate for your Congressional District—I hope that it may so turn out, for however politics may go, (about which I will try to care as little as possible), I shall like to have the pleasure of your society.—

[193]Probably he refers to Allen J. Davie, the son of William R. Davie.

We are just witnessing the effects of Party predominance here in the election of Chairman of our Committees, in which we are at this moment engaged—Buchanan has beaten Clay, & Wright Webster, & King of Ala;, Davis &c &c &c—

This is laughable as well as melancholy, & I chuse for my own meditation the first mentioned quality as more congenial with my philosophy—

My object in writing you this scrawl is to open a correspondence with you—to find out where you are—what you are doing—what are going to do & all about you—

If you will no longer associate with us as a Senator, will you not visit us this Winter, and walk over your old battle fields—Veterans sometimes I expect, find more pleasure in this than they did in fighting their battles.

Yr. Friend &c.
J J CRITTENDEN

W. P. Mangum

[Addressed:]
W. P. Mangum Esqr
Red Mountain
North Carolina

Mail.
[Postmarked:]
City of
Washington Dec 12

WPM-LC

Thomas Sparrow[194] *& Others to Willie P. Mangum*

GREENSBORO' Cald. Inst. Dec. 13th
1836

To the Hon. W. P. Mangum
Sir,

In behalf of the Adelphian Society attached to this Institution,[195] we respectfully request that you would favour us by becoming an honorary member of our body; the object of

---

[194]Thomas Sparrow became a Presbyterian minister.

[195]In 1833 the Orange Presbytery resolved to build Caldwell Institute, named for David Caldwell. Rev. Alexander Wilson was elected principal. The legislature chartered the institution in 1836. James W. Albright, *Greensboro 1808-1904, Facts, Figures, Traditions and Reminiscences*, Greensboro, 1904, 19.

which being similar to that of other literary associations is too well known by you to require any comment on our part.

Respectfully your
Obedient Servants
THOS. SPARROW JR.)
(
WM. M MCPHEETERS) Committee.
(
SHELBY CURRIE)

N.B. An early answer is requested.
[Addressed:]
The Honor:
Wiley P. Mangum
Red Mountain
No. Ca.

WPM-LC

Jno. Shackford[196] *to Willie P. Mangum*

Senate Chamber Decr. 16th 1836

Hon. Willie P Mangum
Dear Sir,

It was with much regret I heard of your resignation, and much pain to see such men as Leigh, Clayton Tyler— yourself & others. leaving the councills of the nation: and many distinguished statesmen declining a reellection to the once— magnanamous and renowned Senate of the United States—My. Dear Sir, when the seamen quit the *helm*— 'where will the ship drive; can she be, ever safely, conducted into *Port*—

When in the West I communicated what was the state of the land beloning to Turner Bobbit; Then expecting to meet you here—disapointed in this—and fearing lest—you might not remember this matter— I take the liberty of annexing a copy of a letter from Moore Marten & Co- -
And to state, that as the time for redemption was open till March— I prefered recieving directions from you—before I placed the funds needed in the hands of the agents— I leave the business—untill your wishes shall be made known—with assurances it has been, and will continue a pleasure to serve

[196]Sergeant-at-arms and doorkeeper of the Senate.

you— No charge has thus far accrued— Should you wish me to do any thing further in the premisses—please advise me—

With great regard & respect—
Your Obedient Serv[t].
JNO, SHACKFORD

[Addressed:]
Hon– Willi P. Mangum
Red Mountain
North Carolina

ENCLOSURE

Moore Martin & CO–

Illinois Land Agency –

QUINCY – 19th – Sept – 1836

John Shackford—
D Sir.

We have yours of 9 inst Turner Bobbitts land S½ – 10. S–2 W[torn] was sold at tax sale 1835 & unless redeemed, will be lost in March next. To redeem & pay taxes—1835 & 1836—with our agency fees, will require between 29 & 30 dollars which cam be remitted in U- S Bank bills or a deposit to our credit with Mess- Meech & Dennis, St Louis & their receipt sent to us, we are now preparing our lists to pay taxes—& with the order [torn] practicable—

we are very Respy—
Yours etc
Signed — Moore Marten & Co

WPM-LC

John C. Taylor to Willie P. Mangum

RALEIGH 20th of Dec. [1836]

Dear Sir,

You will excuse me I know for so often reminding you of the "affair of the letter."[197] I should patiently have waited your own action on this subject, but that I am continually more & more

[197]See above, II, John C. Taylor to Mangum, Feb. 7, 1836.

convinced, that a matter, which from the strong conspicuousness of being in the right, I have hitherto given no heed to, may grow into a consequence if unattended to which may to some extent —to no little extent—be made to affect my popularity in Granville—. I sincerely hope that you may be able to lay your hand upon the letter itself—but if you should be satisfied of its being lost, even in that case you can very satisfactorily remove those, surmises, & suspicions, which by the influence, of a wily man, will not only be made to exist—but to strengthen, and increase with time.

An election for Senator of U. S. took place today; Judge Strange[198] was elected by a strictly party vote, with the exception of Mr. Boon[199] of Orange who voted for him.

I write in the Senate Chamber, during an evening Session where the confusion around me is so great as to make it necessary for me to conclude.

Respectfully & sincerely
Yours
JNO. C. TAYLOR.

[Addressed:]
Honble
Willie P. Mangum
Red Mountain
Orange Cty.

1837

WPM-LC

John Chavis to Willie P. Mangum

Feby 1st 1837—

My dear Sir

As Col Rogers[1] expects to be at your house on next Monday evening. I must once more request you to answer the letters I wrote you, respecting my being charged with my going to Raleigh to Teach the children of the free people of colour for the

[198]Judge Robert Strange. See above, I, 45n.
[199]John Boon. See above, I, 312n.
[1]Allen Rogers. See above, I, 270n.

purpose of raising information Your answer is to be founded upon letters I wrote to you when in Congress upon the abolition question[2]—

I expect to leave the neighbourhood the last of March, and I wish to be prepared to meet malicious reports. Col. Rogers can tell you all about the business—

I find that the Senate of the United States in Congriss has at last disgraced itself by expunging those resolutions.[3] I wonder if the party does suppose that they have taken the disgrace off of G. Jackson? and if they have, in their conception on whom do they suppose it rests? or do they suppose it has taken its flight and settled amongst the mountains in the Moon?—

I am a full blooded friend to the Charleston and Cincinnati Railroad, & to the proceedings of our late G. Assembly upon the subject.[4] Whether it is now completed or not they did a creditable act in granting a Banking privilege for that purpose What course of life do you intend to pursue? lay upon your back & kick up your heels, or do you intend to go to the Bar & take up Judge Nashes practice? it wont do for you to be idle. Your children must be educated, and if you still intend to pursue your plan of selling [setling?] at the right angles of two public roads[5] you must be exceedingly busy; but I hope by this time you ashamed of that plan & have given it up as a bad job—

I have been thinking about your opposing Montgomery.[6] What do you think of it? or do you think our government is too corrupt for you ever to attempt to go into Congress again, with a hope of producing a reformation? I would be glad that you would

---

[2]See above, II, 418-420. At intervals between 1808 and 1838, when Chavis died, he had a school in Raleigh for free Negroes. Joseph Gales attended the public examination of the school in 1830 and commended Chavis for his speech and work.

In the early years of statehood North Carolina was tolerant toward free Negroes. In 1826 a law was passed preventing the immigration of northern Negroes to the state. After that, sentiment gradually changed to be less tolerant of free Negroes. In 1835 free Negroes were deprived of the right to vote. By 1844 they were barred from the common schools. This change from tolerance to hostility had been brought about largely as aresult of the fear that the free Negroes would be used by the abolitionists. Johnson, *Ante-Bellum N. C.*, 610-612; Stephen B. Weeks, "History of Negro Suffrage in the South," *Pol. Sci. Qtr.*, IX (1894), 671-703.

[3]Shortly after Clay's resolution to censure Jackson for the removal of deposits passed in 1834, Benton introduced resolutions to expunge Clay's resolutions from the Senate journal. For nearly three years he kept up the fight until early in 1837 when the Democrats had control of the Senate. In January of that year by a vote of 24 to 19, thanks to the party whip, he succeeded. Wiltse, *Calhoun: Nullifier*, 235, 297-300.

[4]In 1836 the Louisville, Cincinnati, and Charleston Railroad was chartered by South Carolina. Later, the North Carolina legislature also granted a charter for the part that traversed that state. In 1836-1837 the North Carolina legislature was favorably disposed towards railroads. Nearly half of its part of the national surplus deposited among the states was set aside for internal improvements. Bank stock and railroad stock were subscribed to by the state. Charles S. Sydnor, *The Development of Southern Sectionalism 1819-1848*, Baton Rouge, 1948, 269; Pegg, "Whig Party in N. C.," 85-87.

[5]For some years Mangum considered moving to Hillsboro. Priestley encouraged his moving, but Chavis opposed it. See above, I, 44, 317-318.

[6]William Montgomery was up for reelection to the National House of Representatives.

give Col Rogers your definition of States rights, tho' he is a trifling numskull of a fellow, I know it would be pleasing to him; for if he is a trifling fellow he is capable of receiving instructions, & of communicating to others.—

Please to give my respects to Mrs Mangum & tell her if do go to Granville to live she may expect to see me at her house some time in July if I can get any cloaths fit to wear for I am naked at this time, & how I am to be cloathed I dont know—When you see my son Priestly you may tell him I have scratched his name off of book of friends

I am your Obt. Hbl St
JOHN CHAVIS.

[Addressed:]
Hon. Willie P. Mangum Esqr.
Red Mountain,
Col. Rogers. Orange.
[Endorsed:]
Rogers Store. 3 March.

WPM-LC

Robert Strange to Willie P. Mangum

Washington City Feby 8th. 1837,

Dear Sir

I received your favor of the 28th. Ult^{o}. in relation to the claim of the Messrs. Sneeds. I am obliged to you for the suggestions you make upon the subject; and will give them due consideration.

It will always afford me pleasure to hear from and shall be happy at all times to receive your views upon any matter about which you will take the trouble to write

The very day that Dr Sneed left here I had the subject of his claim referred and if it is now in the hands of Mr Crittenden a member of the Judiciary Committee who seems to be most favorably disposed towards the claimants. My own opinion is that the $11000 advanced to the contractor with the interest upon it, ought to be allowed as a matter of the strictest right between man and man: and upon the liberal system on which a government should act towards a citizen I think the property destroyed ought also to be allowed together with the delay prayed for. Upon reflection I will place your letter in the hands of Mr. Crittenden which will assist him much in the investigation.

We have been engaged today in counting the votes for President & Vice President and there being no election by the colleges as to the latter making a selection between the two highest candidates; these were as you know Johnson and Granger. Three senators to wit Judge White, Calhoun and Preston did not vote and of the rest Johnson received 33. votes and Granger 16.[7]

I have nothing worthy your attention except what you will see in the papers. As I have already said I shall always be gratified to hear from you and

am with high respect
Yours obt. servt.
RO. STRANGE

[Addressed:]
Honl.
Willie P. Mangum
near
Stagville P. O.
Orange County
N. Carolina

WPM-D

John C. Calhoun to Willie P. Mangum[8]

Washington
8th Feb. 1837.

My dear Sir,

I had intend to write you long since, but one of the most busy sessions I have ever witnessed has nearly suspended all my private correspondence till now, when I am on the eve of my departure.

The papers have kept you informed of the current of events here, and I shall limit my communication to what I believe to be the general result of the session, and the state of things at this time. In the main the former is not unsatisfactory. Most of the projects of the administration have been defeated, the land bills, the increase of the army, the erection of new arsenals and armory, new fortifications bill & & and [*sic*] the appropriations generally are far below those of last year, and will not, I think, exceed much those of the preceeding. We failed in carrying the

[7]Francis Granger, of New York.
[8]See above, II, 495.

deposite but under circumstances, looking to the future it is calculated to embarrass & wreck the administration.

The defeat of the administration in all the above measures was in the House. They have full control of the Senate, tho' I do not think the party adheres so closely together even there, as formerly. In the House they have lost much of their control, as the results of the session show.

As to the state of things at this time, I cannot doubt, that the administration is losing power, and is now in a minority in the Union.[9] The tone of the House is no weak evidence of this. It is perhaps the best test on that point. When an administration is going down, they first lose their control in the House; and hence on a change of party, the new administration is supported by the House, and opposed in the Senate. The change of language on the part of those in power is remarkable in relation to the two Houses. It is no longer the factus Senate. That epithet is now applied to the other House, while the Senate is regarded as the prop of power. This is not the only indication, that the administration is losing. The language of discontent is of late often heard in their ranks, and from those you would not expect, and a scism begins to show itself between those who would set up as the decent portion, and the Benton & Kindel party, which will be hard to close and difficult to control. Another source of discord is between the ins and outs of the party. Those in office are anxious to hold on, while those seeking office are equally anxious to have them turned out. So much for one side of the administration.

As to the opposition, as far as my knowledge extends, it stands firm. I know of no loss, and there is visibly a greater tendency of its various elements to come together, just as the basis of the national portion. wears out, and ours, which is the true opposition ground, strengthens. I have as you will have seen, taken a far more active part, than at preceding sessions; and this because I saw & felt our position was gaining strength, and that of our associates in the opposition was losing. At the next session, this will be more visible than ever. The materials of oppo-

[9] In the session which began in December, 1836, Jackson got through very few measures. Benton's effort to force the expunging resolutions through a hostile Senate impaired the unity of the Democrats. Rives, of Virginia, proposed that government obligations be paid in gold, silver, or the notes of specie-paying banks. Jackson was furious, but enough of his party supported the Whigs to put the measure through. The House also passed the bill, but Jackson gave it a pocket veto. This was indicative of his loss of control. Wiltse, *Calhoun: Nullifier,* 300-301.

sition will then be more abundant than ever, but they will all be such as belongs to us, and not the national branch

On the whole, there is no cause of dispair. Things are certainly improving. The only thing to be dreaded is that we may become tired of so long a struggle, and in consequence too many of our best and oldest men, of the most experience and influence with the country may yield to the current in dispair. This I would profoundly regret, and, I trust, that such will not be your feelings in particular. Remember, that we and ours on board, and must share the fate of the vessel, let who will be at the helm.

The House now is the field of action, and we greatly lack experienced and able men there. You must offer from your district, and come in. Let nothing dissuade you. We may make with proper efforts a thorough reform the next four years, and now is the time, or never. Never before could we have a victory worth having. One now would be permanent & glorious. Not only start yourself, but let a Mangum be started in every district in the state on our side, particularly in the Warren whether defeated or not. A meeting of young men would be desirable to give an impulse. Should you succeed which I do not doubt, if you will try, you must join Pickens & myself to mess together, with a portion of our families. Ann[10] is now at my elbow, and she request me to say to you, that she misses you much and would be glad to see you again in Congress. With your efforts our friends are sanguine, that the administration will be in a minority in the next House.

I enclose you three speeches (the only ones in pamphlet form) delivered this week. I leave this in the morning and you must be sure to write to me on receiving this. Direct to Pendleton South Carolina.

Yours truly

Hon. Mr. Mangum. J. C. CALHOUN.

WPM-LC

Robert Anderson[11] to Willie P. Mangum

WILLIAMSBORO, N. C. 4th March 1837.

Sir

We the undersigned as corresponding secretaries for the Committee formed to invite Hon. B. Peyton to accept of a publick

---

[10]Calhoun's daughter.

[11]Robert Anderson was a planter near Williamsboro in what was then Granville County. He was a trustee of the Williamsborough Female Academy. *Raleigh Register*, Dec. 30, 1834.

dinner[12] to be given him, in this place, and said invitation having been accepted, We respectfully invite you to honour us with your presence, on Saturday 18th March inst.

Your Obt. Servts.

ROBERT ANDERSON

M. NEAL

To the
Hon W. P. Mangum

[Addressed:]
Hon. W. P. Mangum
Orange County
N. C.

WPM-LC

Duff Green to Willie P. Mangum

WASHINGTON 6th March 1837

Dear Sir

I am making my arrangements to visit Texas, and may determine to locate myself permanently there. I feel that my family have claims upon me, which are paramount, and that on that theatre I may do as much or more service to the country as well as to them. In leaving Washington I cannot but feel the importance of looking to the future, and of bringing into the next Congress our ablest men, could I assume a position here—was I situated as you are I would labor day & night to overthrow the corrupt crew who have obtained possession of the Govt but I can do nothing Appeal after appeal has been made to the South, it will require some other pen, some one against whom there is less prejudice—The tongue of calumny has rendered me useless & I must take rest, that I may labor elsewhere. You can be elected and you owe it to yourself. You owe it to your country to come forward— We want you as a leader for the House— You in the House & Calhoun in the Senate the South may yet be saved.

---

[12]On returning from Congress to campaign for governor of Tennessee, Ballie Peyton stopped by Williamsboro for a public dinner on March 18, 1837. It was a large meeting at which there were the usual number of speeches and toasts. Anderson was on the arrangements committee. *Raleigh Register*, Apr. 11, 1837.

The last act of the old Tryant[13] was to slander our party, you owe it to us to meet his assertions as a representative of North Carolina. The questions before the country are eminently calculated to arouse the public indignation against the administration— The seizure of the public money, placing it in the banks in N. York to be used by Shavers, who lend it at *three* per cent per annum, the refusal of the Senate to distribute the surplus. The speculations in public lands. The refusal to permit an enquiry into the abuses of the Govt— The known extravagance— to say nothing of the slave question are topics so full of interest to the people that we must triumph if we act with becoming spirit.

Our young friend C. P. Green Esqr of Warren county tells me that he thinks of offering against Hawkins, He is unwilling to oppose Gilliam, but it is a question for consideration whether he cannot break into Hawkins' vote more in Warren, than any one else. they are of the same family—Green is bold, speaks well, is familiar with the facts and arguments and may do much good. I have advised him to see you and abide your advice.

Our friends in the West are sanguine and I am assured that there will be a general rally. Webster goes out of Congress. Clay surrenders and Calhoun will give Van a hard fight in a clear field, for such a crisis your place in Congress cannot be supplied by any one else. let me hear from you

Your friend

DUFF GREEN

[Addressed:]

Hon Willie P. Mangum

Red Mountain Orange Cty

Col Greene N. Carolina

[Added on the envelope by Charles P. Green:]

I expected to have gone on to see you before this time. I have some business at New York. On my return you may expect me at your house. I have in my possession, important documents to you which I will deliver in person. In great haste I am your friend

Baltimore M D CHAS P GREEN

March 15 1837

---

[13]On March 4, 1837, Jackson issued in pamphlet form his farewell address, which Taney had written after Jackson had given him the ideas. In this address Jackson appealed for unity against sectional conflicts, and he warned against monopolies and attempts to " 'adulterate the currency' with paper money." He also advised against speculation and other practices which would destroy the simple virtues of the people. The Whigs considered the address presumptuous of the "demagogic" leader. Turner, *United States, 1830-1850,* 451-452.

WPM-LC

Charles P. Green to Willie P. Mangum

NEW YORK
April 20th 1837

My Dear Sir

Inclosed you will find a package from Mr. Calhoun[14] which he gave me some time since in Washington as he expected that I would go on soon to North Carolina but having come on here where I have been compelled to remain up to this time disposing of a part of my interest in the "Texas rail road Navigation and Banking Company" The Charter was gra[n]ted to fifteen of us. I have sold out 300,000 dollars worth of my stock at a premium of 24,000 dollars. I send you by this mail one of the charters At the time I was in Washington I did not expect to go to Texas this summer, consequently had agreed to go to Warren and start opposition to *every Tory* in the county, but business that I cannot leave undone calls me away for a few months when I shall return and devote all my energy to assist our cause. It gives me pleasure to find you have so many friends in the North. You are aware of the necessity of a leader in the House of representatives—Wise, Peyton, Perkins [Pickens] and Thompson[15] are all too inexperienced you are the man and I cincerely hope you will become a candidate in your district. You can best know whether you will be elected or not. If Wm. H. Haywood is not a candidate I should suppose there would be no doubt of your election I regret that he did not go to Belgium I suppose he thought the pay not worthy of his labour I think so too. I have not time to say much about the pressure of the money markett. You have some little idea from the news paper. The Administration is going down very fast. If the Presidential election took place today Van could be beaten in this State. The only difficulty is in what manner to get *clear* of Clay and Webster. The South will go for Calhoun the great pressure there will be of great advantage to him, and as to Clay or Webster the South will not go it. I suggested to Calhoun the necessity of an immediate nomination he thought otherwise as it would embarrass his movements next Congress. You are the proper person to reconcile [torn] Clay. I do not re-

---

[14]Possibly he refers to Calhoun's letter to Mangum, February 8, 1837.

[15]He refers to Henry A. Wise, Ballie Peyton, Francis W. Pickens, and Waddy Thompson.

gard Webster. I have been very often to see your friend Noah[16] of the Star he is a Southern Man any suggestion from you to him will be thankfully received. My brother Genl. Thos. J. Green who is the agent for the Bank is here we leave tomorrow for North Carolina and thence to Texas. Genl. Green send his respects to you. I will be pleased to receive a letter from you as soon as you get this direct it to me at "Exchange Post office, N. Carolina." I regret that I have not time to go by your house—present my respects to your family though I have not the pleasure of an acquaintance.

I shall not make an excuse for this very hasty scroll as it is to a friend. Please to write soon. I am my dear Sir

Your Friend

CHARLES P. GREEN.

[Addressed:]

Hon. W. P. Mangum
"Red Mountain"
Orange County
N. Ca.

WPM-LC

Thomas D. Meares[17] to Willie P. Mangum

CHAPEL HILL April 23rd 1837

Dear Sir

Some time since I wrote you to notify you of your appointment of Assistant Manager of a ball to be given by the students at our annual commencement in June next. You will oblige us much by the permission to use your name; An immediate answer is requested. I have written to you twice before but directed my letters to Hillsboro' which I presume you have not received.—

Yours respectfully

THOS. D. MEARES.

[Addressed:]

Hon. Willie P. Mangum
Red Mountain.

---

[16]Mordecai M. Noah, former surveyor and collector of the port of New York, was a New York newspaper editor. He edited the New York *Enquirer* at the time of Jackson's election in 1828 and later took over the editorship of the New York *Star*. Bassett (ed.), *Cor. of Jackson*, III, 397; IV, 437, 438; V, 183, 481; *Union List of Newspapers*, 464, 476; *D.A.B.*, XIII, 534-535.

[17]A native of Brunswick County, Thomas D. Meares graduated from the University of North Carolina in 1839. As a student he was one of the declaimers of his literary society in 1837 and 1838 and chief marshal at his commencement in 1839. After graduation he married the daughter of Governor James Iredell and became a lawyer and planter in and near Wilmington. He served in the lower house of the legislature in 1856-1860 and in the state constitutional convention in 1861. Battle, *Hist. of U. N. C.*, I, 427, 433, 438-439, 447, 450-451, 456, 458-459, 482-483, 797; *Hillsborough Recorder*, Oct. 30, 1845; Grant, *Alumni Hist. of U. N. C.*, 422.

WPM-LC

Will. A. Graham to Willie P. Mangum

HILLSBORO May 25th 1837.

My Dear Sir

By the mail last night I received letters from Messrs W. R. Gales and C. L. Hinton, urging by all means, that we shall select a Whig Candidate for the Congressional Canvass from the County of Orange. They state that Mr Gales positively declines and are very anxious that either you, Waddell or myself should consent to offer, and to do so at once—As to myself I am not able to alter the opinion I expressed to you some time since—I have in the first place no wish to change my pursuits at present, and independently of that I am utterly unable to take the campaign preceding the election—without which I presume any candidate must be beaten—I deem it also my indispensable duty to obtain relief if practicable, from my present decrepitude, as soon as possible. No one who has not learned from experience, can truly estimate the privation under which I have laboured for twelve months past—and, I fear, the longer a remedy is delayed, the more doubtful will be its efficacy—My expectation is to leave here for New Bern on Sunday and go thence to the North—Waddell is absent at present having been sent for to Pittsboro on account of the illness of his mother, who I fear is no more by this time. Our hopes therefore, must rest mainly upon you.[18] I know well the scenes through which you have recently passed, and the hardship of any greater sacrifice of feeling but consider my Dear Sir that the condition of the country is at present one of great peril—that from your greater experience in public affairs than any other individual [in] the district, to say nothing of any other qualifications, it may be in your power materially to aid in restoring the suffering community to a state of comfort & ease—And though ungrateful heretofore the people of the district are still entitled to whatever of knowledge of our Institutions, & skill in Government you may possess, to avert the calamities which now overwhelm a large portion of the Union—I take the liberty merely to make these suggestions for your consideration, but with no purpose to influence the deci-

[18]In the spring of 1837 there was considerable pressure to get Mangum to run for Congress against William Montgomery, the supporter of Jackson. At a meeting of citizens of Orange County about the middle of June, he was nominated, but the editor of the *Hillsborough Recorder* declared that Mangum would not run because of "private affairs." A little later Graham was nominated. *Hillsborough Recorder*, June 23, 30, July 7, 1837.

sion to which your mind may come at last, after surveying the whole ground.—

Mr. Gales states that, tho' not at all so inclined, he believes that Maj. Hinton wd. consent to offer rather than that there should be no opposition—If you cannot consent yourself to serve, be good enough to confer with those gentlemen, as well other portions of the district as to a suitable candidate—

Going away myself I can do nothing, and were I to remain perhaps, I should be able to affect less.

With assurance true regard

Yours Very sincerely

WILL A. GRAHAM

Hon W. P. Mangum

P.S. Dr. Montgomery is here & a candidate.

[Addressed:]

Hon. Willie P. Mangum

Red Mountain

Orange

N.C.

[Endorsed on outside:]

Come up Friday if possible, I think Graham can be induced to come out, if he has proper advice—You, I understand have become mulish, otherwise I would not make this request.

A. M. KIRKLAND[19]

WPM-LC

Weston R. Gales to Willie P. Mangum

RALEIGH, June 1, 1837.

My dear Sir:

The die is cast! You must either consent to buckle your armor on in the cause of our bleeding Constitution, or Montgomery will, I fear, be re-elected. The Whigs of this county are true, and although many prejudices are entertained against you by some honest people, the necessary consequence of the *ex-parte* vilification with which you have been assailed by Haywood & Co. yet one good look at you and such a talk as you made at Hilslboro, would convert foes into friends. Until to-day, I thought Mont-

[19]Alexander M. Kirkland, a student at the University in 1823-1825, became a merchant in Hillsboro. He married Anna Cameron, daughter of William Cameron, in 1835. Later he moved to New York, where he died in 1843. Grant, *Alumni Hist. of U. N. C.*, 344; *Hillsborough Recorder*, July 9, 1834; February 27, 1835; May 11, 1843.

gomery could beat you in Wake, but I am satisfied, from representations which I have received, that you would beat him easily. I hear in all parts of the country of important changes, and have no doubt *vires acquirit eundo*. I promise if you will be a candidate, that I will take the field and attend the various musters, doing what I can. I should really regard your election from this District, as a greater triumph of sober reason over partizan bitterness, than almost the defeat of Van Buren himself.

Chas. P. Green passed through this City last week on his way to Texas. He was the bearer of a message to you from Mr. Wise, which he was anxious to deliver in *propria persons,* but was too much pressed for time to give you a call. It is this: That he and Peyton are too young to be leaders—that every movement by them is denounced as the intemperate workings of boyish impetuosity, and that you must come to the H. R. and be their star—their guide—their leader—in short, the Nestor of the Party.

This subject has occupied my thoughts much, and I should sooner have writen, but, to be candid, I was in hopes that Graham could be brought out. I preferred him, but on this ground only—*the certainty of success.* I knew he could muster more available capital than any man in the District, and I wanted to make assurance doubly sure by starting him. So far as an effect is to be produced, for future usefulness, no man in the three counties could present superior claims to yourself; and, next to Graham, and perhaps Waddell, your chances of success are equal. I now speak of Wake only. It may be, that in Orange and Person, you could command as good a vote as either of them. In Wake, I think you might calculate on 800 votes to Montgomery 700.

It is perhaps known to you, that my name has been mentioned, in connection with this canvass; but it would be madness in me, even if success were certain to suffer my name to be used. My pecuniary resources are not only extremely limited, but my business demands, and must receive my undivided attention. Nothing, I believe, could induce me to forego my determination on this head.

If you do not consent for your friends to use your name, I know no other chance but Major Hinton or Barnett.[20] Notwithstanding the defeat of the former so repeatedly for the Senate,

---

[20]Charles L. Hinton and John Barnett. See above, I, 110n.

I think he would comand an impo[rtant] vote in Wake, and would certainly receive many V. B. votes which I could not. He is wholly disinclined to the contest, but he is as true a Whig as ever fluttered, and will not, I think, like myself prove Dominico. Barnett's prospects you can judge better of than I can. He is a whole souled fellow and would take well with the more numerous portion of my constituency. But somebody we must have. As Nathan said unto David—"Thou art the man." Do write me, and let me say to the expectant public, that you are a candidate; and though some affect to think you down to ebb-tide, I am confident you will show them, that the Ocean at its ebb even, is still the mighty Ocean.

Yours very truly

WESTON R. GALES

[Addressed:]

Hon. Willie P. Mangum

Red Mountain

Orange Co.

N. C.

WPM-LC

Jno. M. Speed et als to Willie P. Mangum

WILLIAMSBURG June 9th 1837.

Virginia

To the Hon. W. P. Mangum

Dear Sir.

We have been appointed a committee on behalf of the students of William & Mary College to request, the pleasure of your company at a dinner to be given on the 4th of July—

In performing this agreeable duty, let us assure you, that we have held your political career in the highest estimation—Yes, Sir, we have seen you, with one of our most distinguished men, meet a common fate in the cause of freedom & the preservation of our Constitution. This is enough to endear you to us & to hope that you may be found among those whom we expect to have with us on that day—

We are Sir,

Your very resptf[1]—& obt Servants.

JNO M SPEED A C JONES

Committee

JOHN. J. JONES RO MEADE

WM. S PEACHY

[Addressed:]

To the

Hon. W. P. Mangum

Red Mountain

N. Carolina

If Judge M. should not be in
Hillsboro the P. M. will
please *forward* this letter
to him.

WPM-LC

W. S. Ransom to Willie P. Mangum

WARREN June 10th 1837.

Dear Sir

I certainly should have written to you before, and would have done so unquestionably, but immediately after my return with you from Washington I was called on by my relation and friend Mr. Willis Alston, of Georgia to go with him to settle an unpleasant affair with a gentleman by the name of Macrae who had challenged him while he and his family were at my mother's on a visit, under the circumstances, and ever ready too to assist my friends, personally, the only way in my power, I could not refuse, and had to be absent several months hunting about all over Georgia and Florida for an Englishman and Frenchman to fight—men, I assure you, I never saw nor heard of before I accepted their challenge for Alston. They did not meet however, to my great relief, and I returned home sound, after being upset twice in the stage. Since my return I have appointed a dozen times to visit you, but having charge of my Mother's plantation could never find it prudent and convenient to leave it—These Sir, really are my apologies, and I know will be sufficient. My crop, as we say down here, will be *laid bye* in a few weeks and then I intend to visit Orange with Dr. Brehon[21] and spend several days with you, agreeably to my last year's promise. I imagine, from my little experience that you are much happier in private than public life—It is retirement that fits a man for the latter, which is wearisome, unprofitable, and unthankful I believe that after a rapid and continued action of mind and body, however well we may seem to play our parts, we separate from the bustle and excitement of the crowd, seek the cool shades for a season and retire within our verry selves, that our souls become purer, our minds loftier and that our thoughts when we have occasion to express burst forth with renovated elasticity. I believe, Zimmerman says, it is through solitude that good writers inspire men to think, and that liberty of thinking, causes the progress and improvement of reasoning—That timidity never seeks solitude, men only love it who wish to throw off the shackles of a bigoted, ignorant or ungrateful world

Is there no chance to have Montgomery beaten? Graham ought to oppose him—We have dull times in this District—Maclin[22] and Hawkins[23] are of the same politics, the former is the smarter man and if no one comes out agreeing with me I shall vote for him. My cousin Thomas, though a fine fellow, is too indiscriminate in his approval of, yields too blind an approbation to, everything that emamates from the White house and is emblazoned in the Globe—I know that I never can be any thing here and nothing but duty to an aged mother and my love for her keeps me, but as long as I stay I intend to act independently alike regardless of being in or out of favour with the Lilliputian politicions and incorrigible demagogues that surround me.

I have lately read, verry attentively, the history of Jacobinism and was struck with the affinity between the Jacobins of France and the Baltimore Conventionists of America—If history indeed be philosophy, teaching by experience in the name of humanity lets show the people of our Country the experience of France. In Paris the Jacobin Club never was over 1800 yet by the energy intelligence and perseverence of its members in establishing af-

---

[21]James G. Brehon, the son of James Somervell, of Warrenton, had his name changed to that of Brehon in order that he might inherit the fortune of his uncle, James Gloster Brehon. After attending Warrenton Academy and the state university, the younger Brehon became a physician of wealth and good reputation. Lizzie Wilson Montgomery, *Sketches of Old Warrenton: North Carolina Traditions and Reminiscences of the Town and People who made it*, Raleigh, 1924, 116, 233, 234.

[22]Joseph J. Maclin was a Democratic member of the lower house of the legislature from Franklin County in 1833-1834 and 1836-1837. *N. C. Manual*, 609-610.

[23]Micajah T. Hawkins.

filiated ones all over France & by a constant correspondence they revolutionised the government and put every luxury owned by the nobles in the possession of the Sans Culottes except fish which they were too lazy to catch, or too excited—Think now of the Baltimore Convention[24]—How many men actually had an active agency in it? Not one in a hundred—Their proportion of free white males is not equal to the Jacobins, for they did claim every 20th man. You may see a comparison in the paper if I get time to draw it—

I recd. a letter from our friend C P Green a few days ago, he was on his way to Velasco in Texas to sell goods—His brother, Genl. T J Green, has made him rich and put him in business, he will return this summer—I expect you heard of J H Green's[25] death although it was not published, he died last summer—was worne down with the consumption—I will be sure to go to see you this summer in the mean time would be verry glad to receive a letter from you—Accept dear Sir, my hearty wishes for your health and prosperity and believe me ever and fondly your friend and

Obt

WM. SEYr. RANSOM

[Addressed:]

Hon. Willie P. Mangum
Red Banks
Orange County
N. C.

WPM-LC

C. L. Hinton to Willie P. Mangum

BEAVER DAM June 10th 1837.

My Dear Sir

Altho I have never taken a very active part in political matters and untill lately been very much disposed to have my thoughts entirely abstracted from the subject, I consider the present situation of the country as imperiously calling upon every individual to contribute his might be it little or much to her rescue.—We have been anxiously waiting for some move towards a suitable candidate for Congress from Orange. We *must*

[24]He refers to the Baltimore Convention of 1835 which nominated Van Buren for President.
[25]See above, I, 71n.

have opposition to Dr. Montgomery! We have been waiting with a hope that Orange would make a selection but hear nothing from her, I have mentioned your name to many of our friends, it would meet their entire approbation and I hope you will agree to take the field in *earnest.*—You know that great exertions has been made to render you unpopular in this county, and you would at first have greater difficulties to encounter than others, but there is evidently a great reaction going on and if you could as I believe might be easily done convince them that you have had injustice done you it would be ultimately to your advantage, our political friends would rather see you elected than any other man in the district and I doubt not but great exertions would be made for you. I hope it will meet your views if so dont delay, but come out at once, take your horse and go from house to house, for no man can do more when once aroused in that way than you can. You may calculate with certainty on the Whig vote of Wake and we would hope a considerable accession to our strength, let me hear from you on the subject. I expect to be at Chapel Hill next week where I should be gratified to see you, if not write me immediately.

With much respect
Yr friend
C L HINTON

[Addressed:]

Hon. Willie P. Mangum
Red Mountain P.O.
Orange County, N. C.

WPM-LC

John W. Graves[26] *to Willie P. Mangum*

SALEM N. C. 16th June 1837.

Hble. W. P. Mangum
Dear Sir.

I arrived here last evening and learned from Mr. Jacobson the Inspecter of the Salem female Academy[27] that he had already enged to take as many Girls as could be accommodated, and was very sorry that he could not take your Daughter at this time; but that the first vacancy should be reserved for her

[26]Probably John W. Graves, who was graduated from the University of North Carolina in 1814. Grant, *Alumni Hist. of U. N. C.*, 231.

[27]Charity A. Mangum, Mangum's wife, attended Salem Academy.

& that so soon as it occured he would give you notice; he thinks it quite probable a vacancy may occur in few weeks—I remained in Wake & Caswell so long that I am now so anxious to see my *better half & little ones*, that I set out for Georgia this morning, when I reach home and shall have received a letter from you, I will write you under more favorable circumstances & consiquently a longer letter, my Daughters desire to be affectionately remembered to your Daughters & family. And may Heavens best blessing rest upon you & yours both in time & eternity is the sincere prayer of your old school fellow & devoted friend

JNO. W. GRAVES.

[Addressed:]

Honble. W. P. Mangum
Red Mountain P. O.
Orange County.

[Postmarked:]
Salem N C
Jun 19

WPM-LC

Duff Green to Willie P. Mangum

WASHINGTON 17th June 1837

Dear Sir

I am gratified to learn from the papers that you are to be a candidate of Congress.[28] Of your election I will not permit myself to entertain a doubt.

I believe that you are the only man in the opposition who can be elected speaker and in these times that station is one of little less honor or responsibility than the Presidency. If it is in my power in any way to serve you let me know it. I will send you a prospectus for the Merchant & Reformer & also for the South Review with an authority to appoint agents to get subscribers the circulation of the paper may do a service.

You should let me hear from you.

Your friend
D GREEN

[28]He probably refers to the nomination of Mangum by a group of citizens of Orange County. Mangum did not run.

Mrs Green & Mrs Reed send their best regards to Mrs Mangum & hope to have the pleasure of seeing her this Session
[Addressed:]

Hon. Willie P. Mangum
Red Mountain P.O.
North Carolina.

WPM-LC

Mangum's Certificate of Appointment as Road Overseer[29]

August Term 1837.

Ordered.

That Willie P. Mangum be appointed Overseer of the road from the fork near the bridge over Flat River to Haywood Gooch's burnt blacksmith's shop.—and the following hands be taken off the roads in which they have heretofore worked, & put under said overseer on s^d. road to wit. John Moize's hands W. P. Mangum's home hands, Persons Berry, William Blalock, Joseph Lunsford. —Ordered that the Overseer put the road in good repair

J. TAYLOR *C C*

WPM-LC

Lot G. Watson[30] *to Willie P. Mangum*

OXFORD Sept. 15th 1837

My dear Sir:

Doctor Andrew H. Christian has it in contemplation in a short time to visit Mississippi and Alabama with a view to a settlement there

I presume you are acquainted with the Doctor, if you are not however particularly acquainted with him, I can take the liberty of saying that as a physician he deservedly ranks high, and is in manners, & conduct, a gentleman in the *full* sense of the term.—

Will you Sir be kind enough to furnish him with a few introductory letters to some distinguished men in the two States? It will be the means of affording him additional facilities in the prosecution of his object, & for which he will be thankful. Your

---

[29]This order is in Mangum's handwriting.
[30]See above, 365n.

compliance, will add one more to the many personal favors I have received from you—Please address to Dr. Christian Oxford.

Very respectfully
I am Sir, Y. obt Srvt
LOT G. WATSON

[Addressed:]
Hon: Willie P. Mangum
Red Mountain
N. Carolina.

WPM-LC

Henry W. Miller[31] *to Willie P. Mangum*

RALEIGH Sept: 24th 1837.

My Dear Sir,

I received from Mr Leonard Harbaugh of Washington City a note for ($215) two hundred & fifteen dollars against Erasmus D. Bullock esqr[32] as principal and you as security,—with instructions to apply to you for payment.—

I wish you would write me what disposition is to be made of it, by the first opportunity.—

Yours Respectfully
Your Obt: Svt:
HENRY W. MILLER

Hon: W. P. Mangum.

[Addressed:]
Hon: Willie P. Mangum.—
Red Mountain
N. C.—

The Post Master will please forward this to
Mr Mangum if he does not reside near Hillsboro'—

[31]A native of Virginia and a graduate of the University of North Carolina in 1834, Henry W. Miller became a Whig and a lawyer in Raleigh. On two occasions, 1843 and 1851, he ran for Congress but was defeated each time. Grant, *Alumni Hist. of U. N. C.*, 428.

[32]See above, II, 331n.

WPM-LC

Wm. C. Preston to Willie P. Mangum

WASHINGTON CITY
SENATE CHAMBER
[4 Oct. 1837]

My dear Sir,

Under any circumstances a letter from you could not fail to be a great treat, for you cannot so bury yourself that my anxieties do not reach your anxieties which were entirely from personal respect & attachment, but your letter has an additional interest from the incidents of my position at this moment.—You know how much Mr Calhoun & I, have been *alone* since you left us, and after all that we have done and suffered together, we are now separated[33]—or rather to speake with perfect truth he has left me—without warning. I therefore very much rejoice to see how exactly coincident your opinions are with my own—besides the advantage of having the authority of your concurrence—it is agreeable to find that I still have a valued old friend by my side—feeling and thinking with me,—Personally and politically therefore your letter is most welcome.—But how shall I express myself as to the compliment you and Mrs. Mangum have paid me—in the nameing of that boy?[34]—This high evidence of distinguished friendship gratifies me more than I can tell you—and with my affection for you and my destitution of boys—inspires me at once with a sort of paternal feeling towards the little fellow—and a ready evidence of the warm praises you bestow upon him.—May God Almighty raise him up as a successor and solace to you,—

Alas my Dear Sir—at the moment that I write Mr. Calhoun's hard wrung amendment has been passed 24 to 23[35]—Mr. Calhoun being the only member of the opposition voting for it. He concluded a speech more elementary and abstract than I have ever heard from him—against the whole banking system as being contrary to liberty—morals—intelectual development and

[33]When the panic of 1837 came, the Whigs blamed the plight of finances on Jackson's war on the Bank. They, therefore, advocated rechartering the Bank. Preston, of South Carolina, agreed with this Whig position, but Calhoun, because of his state's rights views, disagreed. Before this, Preston had not followed Calhoun in his method of fighting the petitions. As a result, the two men ceased to be political friends. Calhoun was soon to return to the Democratic party, and Preston was to remain in the Whig party. Wiltse, *Calhoun: Nullifier*, 347-348.

[34]Mangum named his only son, who was born July 13, 1837, William Preston Mangum, in honor of W. C. Preston.

[35]After the Van Buren forces introduced their Independent Treasury bill, Calhoun offered an amendment which indicated his acceptance of the Independent Treasury bill. On October 3, the amendment passed 24 to 23. Wiltse, *Calhoun: Nullifier*, 354-356.

republican equality—He declares the system has run out and that the only true currency is *inconvertible* but receivable gov^{t}-paper—Mr. C, has not been without such notions for many years—and considers this a favourable *financial* and *political* conjuncture to enforce his opinions The financial crisis he has I think overestimated for he seems to consider the whole country as animated against the banks with a deadly hostility.—but his political calculation has been much more mistaken and fatal.—His *mistake* has originated in part from his own saguine temper and in part from the miss statements of poor Duff Green—It consists in this—He considers Mr. Van Buren as actually defunct. — altogether past resuscitation — and that his party is without a head, and under the necessity of having one, — It was supposed that Mr. C could mount upon the vacant shoulders—Such notions I know have occurred to some of the more enthusiastic & less judicious friends of Mr. C, and their conversation has got out. Indeed many administration members from the South—especially from Georgia publickly speake of Mr. C. being their candidate after Mr. Van Buren,—What effect such vain delusions may have had on Mr. C. I cant guess—they may perhaps have added zeal to the assertion of his hard wrung principles and diminished his reluctance to quiet [quit] his old friends—It grieves me much to see him amidst his present associates, and to be compelled to stand in the attitude towards him which is enforced on me,—I rejoice however that we have passed thro the discussion without personal collision—But for Calhouns adhesion to it I should pronounce the whole scheme of hard money and subtreasuries to be the most monstrous compound of fraud & folly ever attempted to be palmed upon a people—and as for the political calculations of Mr. C's sychophants, for they are not friends, they have grievously circumvented themselves. Mr. Van Buren was not *entirely* dead, by this time he would have been so—but the accession of Mr. C. has kept him alive, and protracted his existence until I fear he will live long enough to kill my colleague—

You will have seen the tone of the Reformer towards our friends generally and towards me in particular,—not being willing to be killed off by hurt & inuendo—I made open war—abused Duff & [R. K.] Craille both and took the position of open enemy—A majority of the S^{o} Carolina delegation is with me,—

the state rights member from Georgia and all of your delegation except perhaps Mr Sawyer who doubts.

The only opposition man who has the slightest chance for the next Presidency is Mr. Clay—who is really a noble creature—His prospects however I regard as by no means flattering.—Webster and the hero of Tippecanoe are both in his way, and there is already a battery opened against him in the South,—Pickens denounced the Whig nationals on the floor of the house—and a systematic war is commenced upon them at home—having for its main object the inquiry of Mr Clay—The industry which will be used to this end will to say the least divide the southern opposition,—The most hopeful thing I see in the future is your going into the legislature. I do earnestly believe that by doing so you will put yourself at the head of the whole southern opposition, and perhaps controul the Legislatures—in which there will be a most vigorous contest.—I therefore entreat you to prosecute this notion, and let me add in all sincerity that you have no right to bury in obscurity the high endowments with which God has blessed you, for other purposes certainly than to grow corn & potatoes.

I leave here on saturday night next for home, altho congress does not adjourn for a week after—Monday night I shall be in Raleigh—Now you speake of a S°Western trip—meet me, and go on with me—but whether you do or not, come to my house in *Columbia*—come straight there—the stage driver will bring you to my door,—you can't come amiss—If we are not in just send the servt. for us—or rather just say to him, Judge Mangum—It would greatly delight both Mrs P. and myself if you could carry Mrs. Mangum that far. We will bring her back when we come to Congress. Please make me as favourably acquainted with Mrs M. as coloured truth will permit,—As for the boy—when he is six, I will give him a bible a horse—and a gun that he may learn to ride to shoot and to tell the truth — which the Scythians thought a sufficient education,—The Senate adjourns—adieu—

With the warmest friendship
& the highest respect
I am Yr obt svt—
WM C PRESTON

4th Octr 1837.
Judge Mangum

[Addressed:]
Honble
Willie P. Mangum
Red Mountain
Orange County
No Carolina—

WPM-LC

J. J. Crittenden to Willie P. Mangum

Senate Chamber, Octr; 11th, 1837

Confidential
Dear Mangum,

With more than common satisfaction I have received your letter of the 27th of September last—It relieves me from the apprehension which I had began to entertain, that you had forgotten me,—that happy at home, in the midst of your family, you had determined to exclude from your sanctuary all such profane things, as politics & politicians—

You are not more amased than we have been here at the course of Mr. Calhoun—To abandon friends, & to unite himself with Van Buren on such a subject, and at such a crisis, is indeed a mystery & a wonder—I can find no sufficient *reason* for his conduct.—What his *motives* are, I would not judge unkindly—I was attached to Mr C—& shall give him up with reluctance—I would banish from my mind, if I could, all doubt or suspicion, but in *confidence* & candour, I must say that it is my impression, his alienation from us is not confined to a particular subject—that he is gone from us—*gone over*—I wish I may be mistaken—But I have been chagrined at the *facility* with which he appeared to me to quit old friends, and the *amiable associations* so readily formed with *new ones*—But enough on this disagreeable topic—I chide myself for feelings & opinions about Mr C.,—which for the soul of me I can not altogether avoid—Mr C's course has produced more surprise than *effect*—He carries scarcely any body with him—He must himself, I think, be surprised that his high name has done so little—But limited as the effect has been, it has proved very embarrassing to us in the crisis in which we are placed.

Preston has acted with a noble independence in dissenting from Mr Calhoun, & has borne himself on the occasion in a manner worthy of all praise—The majority of the S. Carolina delegation in the other House are understood to concur with Preston & those that go with Calhoun are perhaps greatly influenced by generous feelings of personal friendship & devotion to him.

Your old friends here, almost to a man, concur in reprobating the sub-treasury system—I am pleased to know that you unite in this sentiment, and that scarcely any of Mr. C's friends in your State will go with him in this most strange & eccentric movement of his—

We are approaching, I think, a successful issue of our long political struggle—A vigorous & united effort for one year more must make us triumphant.—The people I verily believe are now with us—You must not be idle—You can place yourself on a high eminence by taking an active lead in your own State—I hope to hear that you have taken the field in due time, and are a candidate for your State legislature—From that position you can do much to serve your country & to elevate your high name & fame.

I expect to set out for Kenty: on the day after tomorrow.

Yr. Friend &c

J J CRITTENDEN

Hon Willie. P. Mangum.

WPM-LC

Henry Clay to Willie P. Mangum

ASHLAND 17th Nov. 1837.

My Dear Sir

I received your favor transmitting a N. Carolina News paper. I perused, with lively satisfaction, the article to which my attention was directed, and with still more the friendly sentiments expressed in your letter. I need not say that they are truly and cordially reciprocated.

I receive, almost daily, gratifying proofs of attachment and confidence from all quarters. Without regard to the practical consequences which they may or may not produce, I find in them abundant consolation for all political injuries which I have ever received.

I offer you cordial congratulations on the recent unprecedented triumph in N. York.[36] I now hope that I shall live to see the Goths expelled the Capitol, and honest faithful and competent men once more in the Administration of the Government. Who they may be, should be—with me, I say, most sincerely, it is,—a perfectly subordinate question.

Believe me ever faithfully
Your friend
H. CLAY

W. P. Mangum Esq.
[Addressed:]
Willie P. Mangum Esqr.
Red Mountain
North Carolina

WPM-LC

Hamilton C. Jones to Willie P. Mangum

SALISBURY 22nd Decmr. 1837

My Dear Sir

I received yours of 20th Inst and proceed without delay to give you my humble views on the suggestions made in your letter. I heartily agree with you that Mr. Clay is the only one under circumstances that the Whigs can expect to run with success I have already made my declaration in the Watchman to that effect See paper of Nov.: 25. I was hurried into it by an insinuation from the Carolinian that I was going to advocate a caucus to promote the election of Mr. Webster. Since I have hoisted the flag I have received the *all hail* of every prominent Whig I have met with I have received also letters from distinguished gentlemen in the West who have heretofore been opposed to him (as I have myself been) and they say I have done well to disabuse the party in the onset of the charge of favoring Mr. Webster I am rejoiced indeed to find a gentleman so experienced and for whose opinion I have so high a regard taking the same ground without concert. Mr. Webster can never get the full Whig vote of the South. His late declarations concerning Texas[37] (right enough pehaps in the

---

[36]In the election on November 6, 1837, for members of the New York legislature the Whigs won 101 seats and the Democrats 27. This meant a gain of 66 members for the Whigs. The New York *Journal of Commerce* estimated that the Whigs had gained 50,000 popular votes since 1836. *Hillsborough Recorder*, Nov. 20, 1837.

[37]In the Senate on May 9, 1836, Webster declared that the United States was under treaty obligations to maintain peace with Mexico. Again on October 12, 1837, he presented memorials of his people against the annexation of Texas. Fuess, *Daniel Webster*, II, 46-47; *Register of Debates*, 25 Cong., 1 sess., 533.

abstract) will of themselves like Banquos ghost stare him in the face and shake their gory or rather *sable* locks at him throughout the contest

I agree with you perfectly also as to the anger of conventions There is in fact no objection to them but we must avoid popular prejudice. Primary meetings of the People to appoint delegates say for Congressional districts is as far as we can safely go. We went that far against the caucus in 1822[38] and you know how successfully. A few leading notes from the most influential Whig presses will give the tone and all the rest is but to *swell it.* It is totally unnecessary for me to go more fully into this subject you have so perfectly anticipated me, not only in my conclusions but in the considerations that have led me to them. I think the Presses ought to come out *now* They should be cautiously plied on that subject for if one were to kick it might do great damage If Gales will respond to my former article I will again speak and go it as I ought Hale[39] will of course join in so will the Newbern Spectator the Wilmington paper, the Rutherford & Charlotte If the Star can be managed we can be heard and felt. If however Govr. Iredell is elected I fear the Star will be intractable. When the Press gets in full cry we will have little difficulty in getting up popular meetings and then huzza for old Rip if she does not have the honor of giving a President to the Union she will go very far towards forcing a candidate on the Party and as you say certainly the most efficient one

On the other topic to wit the most suitable candidate to be run for Governor I am more at a loss I am certain that neither of the individuals suggested by you would at all do except Owen and Branch. The former is a great favorite of mine but he is not *imposing* enough. The latter is my personal friend but I fear he has gone further towards the administration than merely supporting the sub Treasury: at least it is so reported here at any rate we can do better than take either. But that I think Governor Swains services essential to the prosperity of the university I would prefer him to any man in the State I think he is sick of that but we must hold him to it. Judge Settle[40] is a popular man and would do better than either of those suggested in your letter so would Tom Polk[41] but his purpose of running at

---

[38]For the fight in North Carolina over the caucus in 1822-1824 see Newsome, *Presidential Election of 1824 in North Carolina,* 40, 41, 63, 79-81.

[39]Editor of the *Fayetteville Observer.*

[40]Judge Thomas Settle. See above, I, 591n.

[41]See above, II, 340n.

some future time would perhaps put him aside All this is said at a hazard & said perhaps without much meaning for I do know a friend whom if I had permission to name would be more prominent than either. There are reason why I should not at this time at least. Perhaps I may again trouble you with some remarks on this subject

Very sincerely
Yours
H. C JONES

[Addressed:]
Honble. Willie P. Mangum
Red Mountain
Orange Co.
N. C.

1838

WPM-LC

David Clopton to Willie P. Mangum

RANDOLPH M. CAOLLEGE

Feby. 21st. 1838.

Hon. W. P. Mangum
Dear Sir

Having just learned that your place of residence was at Red Mountain I have thought it proper to address you another letter; since I do not suppose that you have received the two communications written previously to this, as they were directed to Hillsboro. It is with the greatest imaginable pleasure that I announce to you your election to deliver an address before the two literary Societies at this institution at our next annual commencement by the Franklin L. Society of which you are an honorary member. Be please to inform us immediately whether you will accept or not; as upon your declination we wish directly to take other measures to have that station filled. We hope that if it is possible you will do us the honor of an acceptance of the offer we have proffered to you.

Yours Most Obt.
DAVID CLOPTON
Corres. Secre. of F. L. S.

Hon. W. P. Mangum
[Addressed:]
To Hon. Wiley P. Mangum
Red Mountain
Orange Cty
N. Ca.

WPM-D

William C. Preston to Willie P. Mangum

WASHINGTON.
[28 *Mar.*, 1838]

My dear Sir.

T'were vain to send you a stated account of debtor & per contra which would shew you indebted to me a large ballance of letters. T'were vain for I know your habbits on this subject. I know you would not even liquidate the ballance by a *note,* but I have grown very anxious about that boy and must beg of you or Mrs. Mangum, to send me tidings of his growth and precocity —and fair promise—and the more so that my wife seems to think that it begins to be time for us to send for him and bring him home. Do you know that his name occurs in No. Carolina history? Both my Grandfathers were at Guilford as you will see in Lees Memoirs—Col. Campbell commanded a single corps, brought on the action at sun rise, and was the last at night fall to quit the ground. Col. William Preston commanded the Augusta troops. Thus you see the youngster has a sound Whig *ancestry.* I entreat you let me know how he is coming on, and yourself and Mrs. Mangum. Mrs. Preston joins in the most cordial greetings to her & to yourself.

Well you see we have given the Sub. treasury a black eye,—I could hardly bring the Whigs to vote for striking out the hard money—but I believe now they are all saitsfied of its propriety. It beat the *coallition* of Calhoun & the administratian.[1] It divided

---

[1]See above, Preston to Mangum, October 4, 1837.

their own ranks—and finally threw off Calhoun—who abused them like pick pockets.—Their leading people Buchanan, King, Wright secretly rejoice at this—but my colleague will not let them off so easily, he will make great efforts to rejoin & lead them. It would amuse you to see the strict intimacy between him & *Brown.* They walk behind the Presidents seat arm in arm. Brown steps forward, consults & then speakes, & when Mr. C. speakes *Brown* sends for him even proposes abusing his own party. While this last scene was going on I could not help thinking that if you had stept in you would have been as unwelcome as Banquos ghost at Mcbeths banquet—so we go—You saw Clays wanton and mad attack on the nullifiers.[2] Was it not scandalous—In truth he was hurried away by his pruriency for a joke—but it was poison in jest. Mr. Calhoun spares no exertion to bring his corps of nullifiers to the support of the administration that upon the junction he may assume the trunchion of command—I hope in God that you will all avoid the union in No Carolina. I think we have saved Georgia by Cuthberts motion,[3] and if No. Carolina stands firm I shall have firm hopes that the delusion will pass away from my own State—Judge White made a glorious speech—a wrapt spirit was upon him. He caught up the Senate and the galleries and bore us all along with him. The old man was inspired—and talking to him yesterday of his triumph I said I wish Mangum had been here to hear you. The tears streamed from his eyes. I have not been able to take much part as usual this winter in consequence of a crippled arm which has annoyed me greatly and yet continues to do so. Mrs. Preston's health is quite improved, and she yet promised to be a strong and hearty old lady. My daughter has not yet come on, but will be here with the first flowers. Tis but three days from your house here. Why not come over and take a week. It would

---

[2]On February 19, 1838, Clay denounced the Sub-Treasury bill when Silas Wright brought it up for discussion in the Senate. Among other things, he attacked Calhoun with much bitterness because this bill marked Calhoun's desertion of the Whig party. Despite Clay's four hour speech, the bill passed the Senate and was defeated in the House. But it provoked one of the bitterest debates in which Clay and Calhoun were arrayed against each other. Even Webster was drawn into it. Van Deusen, *Life of Clay,* 301-304.

[3]On March 21, after it was evident that the Sub-Treasury bill would go through the Senate, Alfred Cuthbert, a Senator from Georgia and a former Calhoun supporter, proposed to strike out Calhoun's amendment of the special session. (Calhoun's amendment separated the sub-treasury from the banks. He restricted the currency acceptable by the treasury to that issued by the government). Cuthbert's motion, despite Calhoun's opposition, passed. After the legal tender clause was removed, Calhoun refused to support the Sub-Treasury bill. It passed 27 to 25. Wiltse, *Calhoun: Nullifier,* 384-385.

give us a jubilee. Please kiss the urchin for me and believe me my very dear Sir

Your sincere friend
WM. C. PRESTON.

28th March, '38.
Mr. Mangum.
[Addressed:] Willie P. Mangum Esqr.
Red Mountain
Orange County
No. Carolina.

WPM-LC

Richard E. Sherril[4] *& Others to Willie P. Mangum*

DAVIDSONS COLLEGE April 6th 1838

Honoured Sir

We have the pleasure to inform you that you have been selected by a joint vote of the Literary Societies of this Institution to address them publickly, at the close of the present college session, on the 2nd August next. By complying with this request, you will highly gratify not only those who have made it, but also an extensive community. Permit us to assure you that there is an earnest solicitude, that you will thus favour us & our infant institution & in this way the cause of education itself. Trusting that you will favour us with an answer soon we subscribe ourselves

Sir with much respect
R E SHERRIL
R W MORRISON
JAS: KNOX
JOHN H LONG
Joint Committee

By order of the
Philanthropic & Umeriean
Societies.

To the Hon: W P Mangum
[Addressed:]
Hon. W. P. Mangum
Red Mountain N. C.
Care of Wm. A. Graham Esqr.

[4]A graduate of Davidson College in 1847, Richard Ellison Sherril became a Presbyterian minister who held pastorates in North Carolina, Mississippi, Tennessee, Kentucky, and Texas. Thomas W. Lingle, William J. Martin, and F. W. Hengweld (eds.), *Alumni Catalogue of Davidson College, Davidson, N. C., 1837-1924*, Charlotte, 1924, 45.

WPM-D

William C. Preston to Willie P. Mangum

WASHINGTON

[April 7, 1838]

Dear Mangum,

In addition to every other quality which can make a letter valuable yours possess in a very eminent degree that of novelty. —I have this moment received the immediate successor of one in September—but whatever there is to forgive in all this—is much more than compensated by that dear little Willie whose his black eyes I seem to see—and hope one of these days actually to see—Mrs. Preston who begs to be warmly commended to Mrs. Mangum & yourself instructs me to say that we cherish the hope with a sort of parental anxiety—one day to look upon the little fellow whom may God bless—As to our political condition here it is just this—*we* have the power to prevent evil and wicked measures. but not the power to do any positive act for the good of the Country.—Thus we can defeat the Subtreasury.—but we can do nothing in its stead not even keep Clays resolutions. which would allow the people a breathing spell until the fruits of the whig victories begin to be gathered.—and are not these victories glorious in the ancient dominion God grant that they may go on to your state.—and thus save the South from adopting the suicidal course suggested by Mr. Calhoun.—For of all the delusions that ever a sensible man bamboozled him self with the greatest is that the hard money project was a State rights measure and for the benefit of the South. Mr. Van Buren takes things with an admirable equanimity.—He does not seem to be disturbed or vexed—and thus does not add to his misfortunes by a fretted spirit—Your friend Clay is excited not to say elated by his position—Mr. Calhoun is in the midst of a great crisis—a tremendous war between corporations & incorporalities—in which the South is to sustain the great course of human liberty—joepardized by the contest—and if she does not join against the bank abbolitionism will prevail state rights will perish—the *south* will go to the dogs & *Clay* will be present.—to all of which Duff Green says amen and yonder crouching Cralle [R. K. Craille]—says bow-bow. As to my vice presidency—no more of that. "and thou lovest me"—Some kind jackanapes over here in Georgetown whose name even I dont know—set the thing agoing without rhyme or reason—No body gives him the slightest countenance and especially he gets none from me, who really am worried & displeased at this use of my name—It is an idle thing—without consequence—and I trust will be droped before it comes to a sufficient head to make it my duty publickly to interfere for its suppression which I will unhesitatingly do—if it were to be seriously spoken of.—Whom they will decide upon I have no idea They talk of you—Hayne—Tyler Southard [Nathaniel P.] Talmadge and others, but I think incline towards some gentleman from the middle States.

I rejoice to hear that you are going into the Legislature[5] where you will be able to serve the country more in the course of the next year than if you were here—We will all rally to you from every quarter of the South—and therefore I beg you to propose at an early day after the meeting of the Legislature—resolutions against the Subtreasury & hard money as anti Southern & anti State rights— If you succeed—I will make the fight upon them in S Carolina —

Can't you make us a flying visit—with Mrs Mangum & Preston. Tis but ten days—and it will rejoice us greatly.—

I am my Dear Sir
With respect & affection
Your friend etc

7th April 1838

WM C PRESTON

Judge Mangum

[On margin] Govr Davis & Southard send compliments to you—
The news from Mississississippi is Glorious

WPM-LC

William Montgomery to Robert Hall[6]

H. R. 20th April 1838.

Sir

Inquiry Has been Made of Me, Whether you and your Brother William had moved from Leeds Manor Fauquiere County, Virginia, Will you please answer, to Me. I do not know what the Inquiry is Made For. it is made By a Man in that Section.

---

[5]Mangum was defeated in his race for the legislature in 1838.

[6]See below letter of J. S. Barbour to Mangum on November 11, 1839.

We are Busily Ingagud in Hard Work, and are Doing, But Little. the Banks Have agreed to Resume payment on the First of January 1839. Judge Cameron passed through this Citty on His Return From the New York Bank Convention, the N. York Banks Resumes on or Before the 10th of May next, all the Banks will soon Have to pay, or surender. they never would Have stopped But For Nicholas Biddls Conduct. He produced the Suspension and Now Refuses to Resume until the Congress shall Be Compeled to Recharter a Bank of the United States. Yours Truly

W. MONTGOMERY.

[Addressed:]

Mr. Robert Hall
Redmountain
N. C.

[Endorsed:]

The first is I expect Lee the next is Monroe the next is Fauquier.

Willie P. Mangum to Sally A. Mangum[7]

Monday 30th. April 1838

My dear daughter.

Your Mother & I desired to write to you last week, but were prevented by accident.

We very much hope you are well, and doing well.—We are all tolerably well now.—Your Sister Patty has been in bad health, but is better now.—I did not think her well enough to leave home, & now it is so late, that I shall not carry her to school this session.—Your grand father is in very low health.

Such clothes as you need, request Mr. Bobbitt to get for you in Town.—I shall not now, probably see you before the end of the session.

At that time, I shall come down for you, and I hope to find that you have attended to your studies well, and that your deportment has been pleasing to Mrs. Bobbitt.

I do hope, My dear child, that you will not waste your time & spend it idly.—

Mary & William are well, and William is growing tolerably fast. Your Mother & the Children send their love to you.—Mr.

[7]The original is in the posession of Miss Preston Weeks, Washington, D. C.

Bobbitt will get anything you need.—I enclose $5. for your use which I hope, will answer you for little expenses.—Your Mother desires that you will write at least once a fortnight or oftener, to her.—

Present our respects to Mr & Mrs. Bobbitt. And remember that your Fa[ther] & Mother desire almost above every thing else, that their children may be good, & endeavour to prepare themselves to be useful & respectable.—

Your affectionate father

WILLIE P. MANGUM

[Addressed:]
Miss Sara A. Mangum
at Mr. Bobbitt's

[Return Address:]
Buffalo Hill
April 30
Louisburg
N°. Carolina

WPM-LC

Articles of Agreement of John Warren to Teach

[14 May, 1838]

North Carolina)
Orange County)

Articles of agreement made and concluded upon Between John Warren School teacher and we the Subscribers employers of the other part

witnesseth

That he the said John Warren promise to teach an English School in all its Various Branches that he is acquainted with for the term six or twelve months as may best suit both parties at a School house to Calld by the Name of Ebenezer That he the teacher John Warren further binds himself to keep a regular Day book of all the lost time of each Scholar an that of his own lost time he is bound to make up at the expiration of said term an time (And to be boarded amongst the Subscribers) And we the Subscribers employers of the other part promise to pay the said John Warren teacher at the Expiration of said term and time at the rate of five Dollars per year per Scholar that we the

Subscribers affixt to our respective names and further we promise to furnish every thing necessary and Convenient for the Accomodation of said School—

The Day and Date to be affixts when the School will open

The School will Commence May the 14th—1838

Anthony Dorothy	1	$ 5.
Elijah Teasley	1	5
J. J. Freland	1	5
John Barbee	¼	1.25
Rachel Bowlen	½	2.50
J McKisall	¼	1.25
Jos. G. Bacon	2	10
Andrews Murdock	1½	7.50
Catherine M. Jackson	½	2.50

WPM-LC

Robert B. Gilliam to Willie P. Mangum

OXFORD, May 16th 1838.

Dear Sir:

Mr Daniel A. Paschall, at the last term of Granville County Court, was appointed guardian of William Harris, in place of Dr. Bullock *removed.* Mr Paschall has understood that Dr. Bullock's land has been conveyed to you in trust to secure the payment of the debt due by him as the former guardian, and he is anxious to know what steps you propose to take in relation to the matter.—I know nothing myself of the situation of the business, but I presume Mr. P. has been correctly informed.—

Mr. Paschall desires that you will write to him, at this place, and he hopes you will make any suggestions that the nature of the business may seem to require.—

I am with high regard

ROB. B. GILLIAM

Hon. W. P. Mangum

N. B. I have never seen the Trust deed, nor do I know its contents—This note is indited at the instance of Mr. Paschall & upon the information given by him

R. B. G.

[Addressed:]

Hon. W. P. Mangum
Red Mountain
Orange County
N. C.

WPM-LC

William A. Graham[8] *to Willie P. Mangum*

RALEIGH May 24th 1838

Honl. Wiley P. Mangum
Dear Sir

Your kind letter was received one which does both your head and heart credit—Many has been the day that I have paced the floor of my prison house; and cast a longing lingering look out of my quarters; expecting to see you—hoping to see you—Since 18 years of age my associations have been with the first men of the nation. It is true I have been a sort of citizen of the world; spending about one half of my time for the last few years in the western part of N. Carolina. Strange things have occurred—Truth as Byron says, is stranger than fiction.—I am incarcerated here and treated as the vilest felon—For what! you emphatically ask. The pretext Sir is *debt*. But I thought I had thrown out in my letters to you dark shadows enough to shew where the substance lay.—No Sir—When I was brought here; it was intended "to put out the light and then put out the *light;*" What dark scheme is now concocting God only knows; But Sir I see this! and I know this! It is never intended that my voice shall be heard; beyond these prison walls—My case involves every thing that goes to the very root of the Liberty of this Country! It involves every thing holy and sacred in the rights & privileges of an American citizen—

I ask you to come and see me!—The request I make ivolves both my life—and what is much more sacred my *name* and fame—Strange that you should have taken up the idea that mine was a mere ordinary case! of *debt* from the urgent appeals I made to you!

Sir I appeal to you as a man—not as a lawyer!—I appeal to you as a christian! by every drop of warm and generous blood in your veins—by the love you have for our common country—as you wish Liberty to light the paths of your children through the world! I ask you as a man and a brother" to come & see me—I call upon you by that animal sympathy which, induces all of a kind, to run; to the relief of one who sends up a cry of helpless woe! to come and see me—I ask you by the prospects that

[8]This is not the political leader, William A. Graham. Later when Graham became a member of Congress he was chided about having been in jail. In a letter to his wife January 1, 1841, he refers to this case of a different William A. Graham. Graham Papers, University of North Carolina.

gild your vision in time—I ask you by your hopes of eternity—I ask you for god almighties sake to come and see me!

Your Friend
WM A GRAHAM—

[Addressed:]
Hon[l]. Wiley P. Mangum
Hillsboro
Orange County
N. Carolina

WPM-LC

Henry Clay to Willie P. Mangum

WASHN 31st. May 1838

My Dear Mangum

(Confidential)

I placed the letter which you did me the favor some time ago to address to me in the hands of Crittenden, as there were some parts of it on which you wished to hear from him. Judge my regret and surprize when he told me last night that he had not written to you! He is a good but a lazy fellow.

You will have seen that the Nat. Convention is fixed for Decr. 1839 at Harrisburg. I understand that the day was made so distant in conformity with the urgent desire of members from N. York, Vermont, Penna. and Ohio. I think that if you can overcome your repugnance to Conventions in N. Carolina that it would be desirable that you should be represented in it. The more general, fair and respectable the composition of the Convention may be the greater will be the influence of any recommendation that shall issue from it. And it is extremely important to prevent any cavelling, if there should exist any where a disposition to cavil, on the score of the Convention being partially constituted, and not being full representation of all the States.

I am happy to tell you that our Cause every where is making sure and certain progress: and that my *particular* cause could hardly be improved. In Penna. some weeks ago a bad spirit was manifested in an effort to hold up and adhere to Harrison, without reference to the agency of a N. Convention; but far from being seconded it has been generally rebuked, and I have no doubt will be abandoned, or rendered entirely impotent. A State Convention meets this day at Columbus in Ohio, and we are well assured here that it will pass a resolution to abide by the decision of the N. Convention. In Penna. a better state of things exists, and if Rinter[9] should be elected, we now believe that it will agree to the nominations which shall be made by the N. Convention.

Webster is not in a good state of feeling. He thinks that he is not sufficiently appreciated, and perhaps thinks correctly; but that cannot alter the case. He will be controlled by his friends, or will submit to the force of circumstances.

I have heard nothing lately from your State. What is the prospect there of the general cause; what your own? I have lately transmitted some documents to your county, at the instance of Mr. Waddell & Mr. Stanly. I presume the ridiculous charge against me of being an Abolitionist propagated by the Calhoun School, can deceive nobody. It is remarkable that whilst that charge is diseminated at the South, the Emancipator, the organ of the Abolitionists at the North, avows its preference for Mr. V. Buren, and its determination to oppose me, because the Slave interest will have in me a firm supporter.

The Administration party professes to believe that it will yet carry the subtreasury bill. We are not without fear, but we still think it must be defeated.

I pray you not to imitate my bad example of seeming neglect, and let me hear soon from you.

I remain always
Faithfuly Your friend
H. CLAY

W. P .Mangum Esq.

WPM-LC

John Trolinger & others to Willie P. Mangum

HILLSBOROUGH June 1st, 1838.

Dear Sir

It has become our duty, as the organ of the delegates assembled at Mr. George Fousts on the 19th May to [torn] the point through which they desire Orange County to be divided,[10] most

[9]Possibly Joseph Ritner, who was made treasurer of the mint at Philadelphia in 1841. *Raleigh Register*, April 20, 1841.

[10]See above, II, 411n.

respectfully to all. What will be your action, as one of our representatives in the next General Assembly in relation to said division?

An early answer to this enquiry will very much oblige

Your Humble Servants
JOHN TROLINGER)
SAML L. HOLT)
BRISCOE WARREN) COMMITTEE
JESSE GANT)
JOHN CHEEK)

Willie Mangum esqr.
[Addressed:]

Willie P. Mangum Esqr.
Orange.

WPM-LC

John B. Bobbitt to Willie P. Mangum

LOUISBURG, N. C. 12th. Augt. 1838.

Dear Sir:

Please say to your Lady, that her Letter, dated 1st Inst. to Sally was duly recd. And that she (Sally) will answer it soon. I inform you, that your Daughters are both well, and, as I am informed by their Preceptress, make good progress in their Studies. We have fourteen Boarders. Of this number, two are sick: one slightly; the other a little more seriously.—

This morning I was at our post Office, where I was met by Messrs Wood, Johnson, Thomas, and others of your political and personal friends, who informed me, in the language of Anger and Sorrow combined, of the result of the Election in Orange.[11] Upon receipt of this news I repaired home and related it to Mrs. B. who flew into a passion:—finally said "O tempora! O Mores!

As to myself, I now think, that Hope too has left Pandora's Box. It appears that the Purse is in the hands of the Enemy,

[11]Orange County voters voted for the Whig candidate for governor. They also voted for three Democrats and one Whig for the lower house of the legislature. Mangum was fifth in the race for the lower house. Mangum received 1,468 votes, and Sims, the successful candidate, received 1,474. Graham was the successful Whig candidate. *Raleigh Register*, Aug. 9, 1838.

and that hence he will be able, for many years to come, to hold the Sceptre. The present Incumbent will be easily reelected a Second term, and a third, if he choose.

Mr. Henry Allen, lately of Caswell, N. C. now of Mississippi, is here, and says he shall visit you in a short time. He has Law suits on hand.—

Upon receiving this, a line from you, touching your Wellfare, the Cause, if any apart from the one I have mentioned, of your defeat, &c. will be read with interest by your humble Servant

JNO. B. BOBBITT.

[Addressed:]

Willie P. Mangum Esqr.
Red Mountain
Orange County, N. C.

WPM-LC

Paul C. Cameron to Willie P. Mangum

ORANGE CO. FAIRNTOSH, August 23rd. 1838.

My Dear Sir

On yesterday, with other papers I received the Raleigh Register which I shall hand with this note to a boy of mine going to Person, with instructions to leave it at the House of H. Parker, with a request that he will forward it to you. You can hardly receive the Raleigh papers before friday night or saturday morn: and I am anxious to impart to you, the pleasing intelligence, that we shall have, a *Whig* Senate, House of Commons, and Governor! It will spread, like a prarie fire, over the Van Buren districts—& may it have the same cleansing and purifying effect! Come down and spend a day with us.—We will talk of our triumphs, defeats, and tho last, not least, our dismal crops.—My kinsman Mr Bennehan is now in Raleigh, but will be at Home tomorrow, and will be glad to see you—My best respects to Mrs Mangum: and say to William Cain I hope he is a close student.

Very truly your friend
& most: Obt: Servt
PAUL. C. CAMERON

[Addressed:]

Judge Mangum
Orange Co.

Willie P. Mangum to Alpheus Jones[12]

RED MOUNTAIN 10th Sept. 1838.

My dear Sir.

I am honored with your favor of the 18th. ult., informing me that I have "been chosen by the Dialectic Society to deliver the next Annual address before the two Literary Associations" of the University.

I feel profoundly sensible of the honor done me by this association & the more especially, as this is not the first occasion that I have been distinguished by the partiality of that ancient & honored Institution—The Dialectic Society. My anxiety has been great to comply with the request of the Society, and I have delayed this reply too long, perhaps, under a strong hope, that I might see my way clear to the discharge of this honorable duty, having a due regard to my indispensible engagement.—

Nothing could be more agreeable to my feelings, than to return to your peaceful shades to mingle in the duties & participate in the delights of purely literary occupations.—

To revel in the reminiscencies of those buoyant feelings & sunny thoughts (unrepressed & undimmed by the robust struggles of a stern & busy world) which lend an enduring charm to that delicious period of life, when in "sweet dalliance" we pluck the gay primrose & scarce feel the thorn.—

My probable engagements for the next spring & summer render it prudent, perhaps indispensible that I decline most respectfully, the honor you propose for me.—

I need scarcely say that it is with profound & anxious sensibility, I am constrained to decline this honorable distinction which will be enbalmed among my choicest & most interesting recollections.

The Dialectic Society is more endeared to my memory & more interesting to my affections than perhaps, even our venerable "Alma Mater."—I rejoice in its successes & hail its distinctions, with a warm cordiality, that may emulate in a feeble degree, the enthusiasm, that so honorably inspires the present generation of young men, who bear upon their shoulders the honors, the distinctions & the renown of that ancient & venerable Institution.—

[12]The original is in the Dialectic Society Papers, University of North Carolina. Alpheus Jones graduated at the University in 1839. After that, he became a planter in Wake County. Grant, *Alumni Hist. of U. N. C.*, 326.

Be pleased, My dear Sir, to present me in the best manner to the Society accompanied with my acknowledgements for the Honor intended me: & Accept for yourself

The assurance of my respect & esteem.

WILLIE P. MANGUM

[Addressed:]

Mr. Alpheus Jones
Pres. Dia: Society,
Chapel Hill

WPM-LC

Alpheus Jones to Willie P. Mangum

UNIVERSITY OF *N. C.*

15th Sep. 1838.

Dear Sir:

The object of this communication is to inform you, that you have been chosen, by the Dialectic Society, to deliver the next Annual Address before the two Literary Associations of this Institution, and earnestly request that you will accept of the appointment.

We anxiously hope that you will do us the honor to yield to our solicitations. You will lay us under an obligation, by so doing, which we can only hope to requite.

With sentiments of the greatest respect.

I am your's, truly,

ALPHEUS JONES, Pres.

P.S. The original, of which this is a duplicate, was directed to you, dated, 18th ult. But, from a fear that it has not reached you, I have been induced to write to you again.

WPM-LC

William S. Ransom to Willie P. Mangum

WARRENTON Set^{r}. 16th 1838.

My dear Sir

I will not in this [try to] touch on embarrassed and degenerate politi[cal] [aff]aires of our Country, nor fatigue you with [la]mentations about the discomfiture of friends; My object in writing is to obtain a letter from you to some distinguished friend in Alabama in favour of my nephew Seymour R. Duke who will start there in a week—Seymour is just Twenty years old and has been in a store for several years past is apt and attentive to business—writes and calculates well—is perfectly sober and of good moral habits in every respect and withal a good looking likely fellow of fine address—but he is poor, is young and has not an acquaintance in the South and I know that a letter from you to any distinguished gentleman in S. C. Geo. Alabama or Miss would greatly aid him in getting into business —I will vouch that he never disparages any character you may give him—he thinks Mobile will be the first place he aims to locate in—Write to Lewis or King or any gentleman of standing it will benefit him whether they get it or not

Write if you please as soon as you get this and enclose the letter to him or myself your compliance will be renewed evidence of your kindness to Dear Sir

Your friend sincere [torn]
WM. S. RANSOM.

P.S. If your answer cannot reach here by the 23rd. direct it to Seymour at Hillsboro, he would go by your house but will be in company inconvenient to leave—my kindest respects to your family—

WM. S. RANSOM.

[Addressed:]

To the Hon. Willie P. Mangum
Red Mountain
Orange Cty.
N. C.

Mail.

WPM-LC

John B. Bobbitt to Willie P. Mangum

LOUISBURG, N. C. 22nd. Sep.—38

Dear Sir:

After informing you there is no Sickness in our Village, I will say to you, that no new Flour has yet been brot' amongst us. It is in demand, and I think a Load might be disposed of on good terms;—At any rate I wou'd be willing to take some *Several* Barrels myself, and will venture to say, I *reckon* more might be sold. The market price, as none scarcely has yet been brot in, is not established. It woud, therefore, be proper for the Seller to *fix* his Terms. I will say, the price will not be under 8, and *probably* not over 10$.

This I have been prompted to write, from an intimation in a Letter from Mrs. M. to her Daughter S.

In conclusion: 'Cant you come down soon and stay with us two or three days? Your friends here wou'd be pleased to see you, and your Daughters wou'd be particularly glad to see you.

Yrs. &c—
J. B. BOBBITT

Hon. W. P. Mangum)
[Addressed:]
Hon. Willie P. Mangum
Red Mountain
Orange County, N. C.
Single

WPM-LC

Charles G. Nelms[13] *to Willie P. Mangum*

WADESBORO N.C. Oct 3d. 1838

Dear Sir

I had the pleasure of forming a limited acquaintance with you in Washigton during the winter of 1836, from that acquaintance, I take the liberty to write you this letter. The prospect is gloomy for a young Lawyer in this State, so much so that, I shall migrate to Mississippi, when I get there I will have to make references, I should be happy to include your name among the number, should it meet with your approbation you will please write me soon and oblige

Your Friend & Obt Servant
CHARLES G NELMS

[Addressed:]
Willie P. Mangum Esq.
Red Mountain
Hillsboro
N. C.

Mr. Cain will
please forward this soon

[13]A graduate of the state university, Charles G. Nelms moved to Holly Springs, Mississippi, where he became a lawyer and planter. He was killed in the battle of Shiloh in 1862. Grant, *Alumni Hist. of U. N. C.*, 453.

WPM-LC

John B. Bobbitt to Willie P. Mangum

LOUISBURG, N.C. 13th. Oct. 1838.

Dear Sir:

Yesterday about Sunset Atkinson arrived with nine Barrels of Flour, which I have stored away in my own Dairy. The price in Our Town is $9 pr. Bbl. and at this rate I can dispose of balance, say 4 or 5 bbls. (taking 4 or 5 for my part).

If the proceeds, or any part, you wish forwarded to you, let me hear from you.

With the bond of Mr. H. vs. Blue I hardly know what to do. He has no money, and no property but what is under a Trust. The best way, I think, is to use Soft words: it may be got, in this way, *perhaps,* in a few weeks: and this way I shall adopt first: afterwards proceed to rough measures.

Sally has not time to write, she therefore bids me say, she recd. the things sent, and with little Patsey sends respects & love to Ma' & Pa'—

We will get the Flannel and other things *necessary.*

Our schools will close 3rd day of December.—

All well—

Yrs. respectfully
JNO. B BOBBITT

[Addressed:]

Willie P. Mangum Esqr.
Red Mountain
Orange County, N.C.

Charity A. Mangum to Sally A. Mangum[14]

Monday Morning.

November. 1838

My Dear, Sally,

I Write you to let you know we are all well as usual, and desire to see you very much. Your Father left here yesterday for Hillsborough and from there it is likely he will go to Raleigh if so he may not get to louisburg as soon as you may expect him,

[14]The original is in the possession of Miss Preston Weeks, Washington, D. C.

if he should go to Raleigh he will return through louisburg. and if you have not warm dresses & desire Mrs Bobbitt to get each a dress and have it made you may have to come home in the stage with your Father if he should be detained in Raleigh longer than he expects. Give my Warmest Respects to

Mr and Mrs Bobbitt and accept my
love for yourself and sister

C A MANGUM

Sally A Mangum.,

[Addressed:]	[Return Address:]
Miss Sally A Mangum	Wilton N^c—
Louisburg, N C.	Nov. 20th..—

Willie P. Mangum to Thomas D. Bennehan[15]

FLAT RIVER 9th. Dec. 1838.

My dear Sir:

I beg you will accept my very especial thanks for your attention in sending me the Message of the President. By a very unforseen accident I received it yesterday; and almost clapped my hands with joy, to perceive that he is so bound down by his fanatic and ferocious crew, that he is obliged to stick to the Sub-Treasury plank & that in the ocean.

I trust, with you, that the whole set, will go down.—My faith in God's Providence will be confirmed rather more, by seeing the flagrantly guilty brought to punishment.—

I returned from Raleigh last Monday to Hillsboro by the stage, having spent a fortnight in that City, *"pro bono publico"* upon my own expense, which I could very little afford.—My object was to beat up the quarters of our derelict Senators.—

Resolutions have been introduced,[16] of which the papers give no account, & of which you probably, have not been informed, that must be *arsenic* to unfaithful public servants.

[15]The original is in the Cameron Papers, University of North Carolina.

[16]On December 4, 1838, Kenneth Rayner introduced in the state house of representatives these resolutions which Mangum helped draw up. The resolutions passed without appreciable change. They were sent to the two Democratic Senators, Brown and Strange, who insisted that the resolutions were not instructions and, therefore, not binding on them. They agreed that if the legislature would state that the resolutions were instructions they would resign. Brown and Strange were trying to force the Whigs to admit the right of instruction. The Whigs replied that the Senators understood the intent of the resolutions and if they were true to their principles they would resign. They did not resign until June, 1840. *Hillsborough Recorder*, Dec. 13, 1838; Pegg, "Whig Party in N. C.," 105-107.

They will be passed.—They condemn the expunging process as "an act of party servility calculated to *degrade* the character of the Senate of the United States—" I express the wish that the Senate will rescind it.—
They likewise condemn the Subtreasury in strong terms.—They condemn the pre-emption policy & the consequent waste of the public domain—& likewise require the *proceeds* of the sales of the public lands to be distributed according to the ratio of rep. in the Ho. of Reps.—They denounce the unexampled encrease of expenditures—and also the alarming increase of Ex: patronage.—Remember that our senators are committed on all these points.—

I hope, I believe, the senators will be driven out.—As to the successors, it would be comtenptible affectation to say, that I do not desire a *certificate* from the state, after suffering what I have—yet My Dear sir, I trust you will believe me, when I say, however important that point may be regarded by me, yet it is wholly subordinate.—

I intend to go to Raleigh again in a few days, say, perhaps a week.—

I shall pass your house & hope to see you—unless indeed you shall be in Raleigh, where I should be very glad to see you.

Very truly & sincerely
Yrs
W. P. MANGUM

[Addressed:]
Thomas D. Benneham esq.
Stagville
Orange
By Stanford

WPM-D

Kenneth Rayner to Willie P. Mangum

RALEIGH Dec. 31, 1838.

My dear Sir,

I have concluded to give you a synopsis of the "Signs of the times",—in this quarter,—supposing it will not be uninteresting to you.

You have seen that my resolutions[17] have passed both houses, —they have been sent on, and are now I suspect in Washington.

[17]Resolution of instruction.

It is rumoured here, in fact it is well understood on all hands, that Brown certainly will, and Strange probably, resign forthwith. All the knowing ones of the V. Buren party say that they *ought,* and as they think, will, resign their seats. A distinguished gentleman of this place remarked to a friend of mine yesterday, that he had it from the *very highest authority,* that Brown's resignation will be here as soon as it can reach him, after he receives a copy of the resolutions.—

The Whigs had a meeting last night, the first since you left here. I got up the meeting myself, and stated the objects of it as follows—first to discuss the propriety of some action on the part of the Whigs of the Legislature in regard to the next presidential election,—secondly, to have an understanding who should be run as the next Whig Candidate for governor—and third the obtaining and expression of an opinion as to who should be run for Senator in case there was a resignation before we adjourned, or whom we should recommed to the governor in case, the resignation was made to him after adjournment.

In regard to the first proposition I introduced resolutions, proposing that the Whigs should on some day this week assemble in Convention, and nominate Mr. Clay, subject to the decision of a national Convention—this proposition was sustained by Cherry, Waddell[18] & myself, and opposed by Graham, Gilliam[19] and others—as I expected, I soon discovered that a large majority was against me—all avowing their preference for Mr. Clay, but expressing fears that a nomination here, would operate to our injury—In other words, there was the same want of nerve and decision, the same shrinking from responsibility—which *you* witnessed on another occasion.—The resolutions were referred to a committee of 13 to report on them to an adjourned meeting to be held to night,—the committee met that night, and by a vote of 9 to 4, will report *against* the propriety of any action on the subject. Cherry, Dockery[20] Waddell & myself being the four in favor of action.—Strictly in character with N. C!—always afraid to move till other states have gone before, and then she brings up the rear.—I can not express to you the regret and mortification I feel, at seeing such timidity, or prudence, as they would say. The victory we have achieved, will be soon clouded by another defeat, for we never can maintain our position, while

[18]Will W. Cherry and Hugh Waddell.
[19]Robert Gilliam and William A. Graham.
[20]Alfred Dockery.

we are so fearful of responsibility. On the second proposition no action was had,—neither on the third—I shall tonight, propose to postpone, till the last of the week, our making any nomination for Senator, should a vacancy occur. I think on that matter, there will be a great want of unanimity among us. I fear some harsh feeling will be excited.—There are many gentlemen spoken of by their respective friends,—yourself, L. Williams, Mr. Gaston, Mr. Graham, Gov. Swain, Mr. Badger, & Jos. S. Jones,—and Wm. B. Shepherd.—Gaston's and Graham's claims will be strongly pressed.

Had you not better come down here, as soon as you receive this?—Some of us are determined to hold on to you, and not to surrender—the nominee will be selected in Caucus. I think you could be of great service to yourself, if you were on the spot. If your business is such that you *can not* come, why we will do the best we can for you, but I think it would be much better, for you to be here.—There is some doubt about their being a resignation before we adjourn, but still, a nomiation will be made, in accordance with the declared wish of Gov. Dudley, in case the appointment should devolve on him.—It is the opinion of many, that the senators will withhold their resignation till after the Legislature adjourns, but that one, or both will resign there seems to be no doubt entertained. Besides it is understood here, that the party intend to run [torn] as their next Candidate for Governor, and if so they will require of him a resignation that they may present him before the county as a martyr in the cause of democracy. The two houses have passed a resolution to adjourn on to day week the 7th of Jany—but the Whigs will prolong the time, if there is any probability of a resignation.

The V. Buren party have been in caucus two or three times during the last week. It is understood that one of the objects of their meeting was to consult on the propriety of nominating Calhoun as Vice. Pres. on the V. Buren ticket,—another object, no doubt, was to advise our Senators as to the course they should pursue.

Nothing done yet on I. Improvements We have the subject before one house in committee of the whole—I think it best you should come to Raleigh and if you do, come quickly.—With sincere respect,

K. RAYNER.

[Addressed:]

Hon. Wilie P. Mangum
Red Mountain
Orange County
N. Carolina.

INDEX

(Except for the chronological section under Mangum, Willie Person, all of the index is in alphabetical order.)

A

C

I

J

Mc

O

Q

R

T

U

Y